USED
BOOK

Sell USED
Buy USED

AT THE MSU
BOOK STORE

26ee

USED
PRICE

$ 8·96

355 — 4880

Nancy

A Managerial Introduction to Marketing

Second Edition

A MANAGERIAL INTRODUCTION TO MARKETING

THOMAS A. STAUDT

Director of Marketing, Chevrolet Motor Division
General Motors Corporation

DONALD A. TAYLOR

Chairman, Department of Marketing and Transportation Administration
Michigan State University

PRENTICE-HALL, INC., Englewood Cliffs, New Jersey

PRENTICE-HALL INTERNATIONAL, INC.
London

PRENTICE-HALL OF AUSTRALIA, PTY. LTD.
Sydney

PRENTICE-HALL OF CANADA, LTD.
Toronto

PRENTICE-HALL OF INDIA PRIVATE LIMITED
New Delhi

PRENTICE-HALL OF JAPAN, INC.
Tokyo

Current Printing (last digit):

10 9 8 7 6 5 4 3 2

Parts of Chapters 2 and 3 appeared previously
in Lazer and Kelley's *Managerial Marketing:
Perspectives and Viewpoints,* rev. ed.
(Homewood, Ill.: Richard D. Irwin,
Inc., 1962).

13–550145–8

Library of Congress Catalog Card Number:
71–113044

Preface

In the five years since the publication of the first edition a number of developments have taken place in the field of marketing. One notable development is the heightened interest in what might be termed macro-marketing or the role of marketing in the economy. Departing from the firm orientation of the first edition two new chapters have been added to provide an environmental perspective for the marketing decision maker. The book begins with a macro-marketing foundation through interpretation of the environmental framework within which the firm functions. The motivations underlying competitive behavior are examined as a means of exploring marketing as a philosophy of management, the marketing mix and the importance of rigorous analysis of consumer behavior. The chapter provides a statement of the competitive process and why marketing activities are such an important aspect of that process. A new last chapter examines the relationships between competition, marketing, and corporate and economic growth. This explanation provides a focus for evaluating the societal benefits derived from marketing action—the content of the interim chapters.

A new chapter has been added in the area of International Markets and blends into Part II, Foundations of Strategy—Interpreting Market Forces and Opportunities. The international market is viewed as another arena in which the firm may elect to operate and no attempt is made to treat the subject as a separate and distinct area. In Product Policy and Strategy, Part III, a chapter on New Product Development and Introduction has been added. The importance of this area to corporate vitality is highlighted, and the kind of analyses necessary for the go/no go decisions on new product candidates explored in detail.

Substantial revision has been made in many of the chapters with all relevant statistical data updated and the addition of examples wherever possible to clarify concepts presented in the first edition. In some instances the ordering of the chapters has been considerably changed to provide better continuity.

It is our belief that the changes made contribute to a broader understanding of marketing and at the same time have not detracted from the conceptual depth and logical presentation of the material in this first edition.

This book concerns the market affairs of the firm in a managerial setting. We conceive of the firm as a market entity, seeking to achieve its objectives of growth, survival, and profitability through meeting the requirements of effective competition.

Our objectives in writing the book are clear, its main thrusts follow certain professional convictions, and it is partially a response to the ferment that has taken place in education for business over the past 15 years. During this period, marketing education has been criticized in various quarters as lacking intellectual depth, conceptual structure, and the philosophical cohesion of other professional disciplines. The mandate that emerged from this academic soul-searching, and which represented a fairly unanimous agreement among curriculum planners as to what was needed, was to produce a businessman with the requisite competence and capacity to analyze a problem in its environment, to formulate the appropriate plans and strategies for meeting the situation effectively, and to take the necessary action to execute the plans as programmed.

There emerged in this context a recognition that business enterprise is continuously adjusting to the requirements of the market place. The market place represented by the needs and desires of customers expresses not only the basic characteristics of buyers within the market, but also the competitive forces at work. The management of marketing effort is increasingly seen to call upon the skill and ingenuity of businessmen in identifying the objectives of the enterprise, in developing appropriate strategies to obtain the objectives, and in mobilizing physical and human resources in a way which contributes to an optimum execution of the strategy selected. No one can deny that education has in the past produced many students satisfying such a mandate, but evidence was presented that this occurred in spite of the fact that instructional efforts and materials typically lacked this decision orientation.[1]

Let the nature of our mission then be evident from the beginning. We have intended to emphasize the following considerations:

ENTREPRENEURSHIP

The vitality, complexity, and challenge of entrepreneurship rarely seems to have been capitalized on in business education in general and marketing in particular. Marketing, however, has the best innate opportunity to capture the excitement of entrepreneurship among buiness students. For, as Peter Drucker has pointed out in identifying marketing and innovation as the only entrepreneurial functions, "Marketing is the distinguishing and unique function of a business. A business is set apart from all other human organizations by the fact that it markets a product or a service." [2]

In a closely similar, but not altogether synonymous way, we have emphasized competitive strategy with entrepreneurship.

COMPETITIVE STRATEGY

Marketing deals largely with the competitive strategy of the firm. The notions of competition pervade the discussion. Capitalizing on those assets of the firm which give it lasting competitive distinctiveness and differential advantage among rivals pervades the substantive content.

CONCEPTUAL STRUCTURE

Throughout, we emphasize the foundation of a conceptual structure. We allow description, technique, and even current practice to give way to a conceptual base. Always good pedagogy, this reliance on concepts seems virtually essential in view of the dynamic competitive future and the explosion of technology against which we now educate future managers.

---

[1] See, for instance, Frank C. Pierson and others, *The Education of American Businessmen* (New York: McGraw-Hill Book Co., 1959), Ch. 16.

[2] Peter F. Drucker, *The Practice of Management* (New York: Harper & Row, 1954), p. 37.

Management considerations are not something we add at the end or treat in a separate chapter, nor would we wish to be found guilty of mislabeling this book. Education in the managerial affairs of the firm with respect to its external environment is the *raison d'être* of this book. Subject matter areas included had to meet this test of relevance.

A WORKABLE COMPREHENSION OF THE COMPLEXITY AND INTELLECTUAL DEPTH OF THE SUBJECT

Marketing has not always attracted or challenged the keenest minds of business schools or the broader university student population. We believe it to be fully worthy of the best intellectual competence that can be brought to bear on the bewildering complex aspects of competition and competitive strategy. We have sought to convey this complexity while still seeking clarity of exposition and understanding. We have introduced conceptual and theoretical notions not normally associated with initial instruction in the field. We have done so, while relying on continued example and illustration to facilitate comprehension. Experience has shown that it is easy to underestimate students—to talk down to them. This is what makes for a dull subject and dull students. We genuinely believe the level of this book to be within the grasp of those receiving their first exposure to the field, and it is so intended.

AN INTEGRATED PHILOSOPHY OF THE ENTERPRISE

Too often in the past, students have been exposed to a "catalog-like" treatment of the many varied aspects of marketing. In these attempts to be comprehensive, so much has been covered that the student has lacked operational competence and mastery of either a coherent point of view or a body of knowledge. We hope an integrated philosophy is clearly perceivable here. One may contest its adequacy or validity, but he should not fail to miss it. Each part introduction reverts to the beginning and builds upon the structure. Each chapter is summarized in the broader context, and finally, the entire work is restated in a concise and succinct fashion in the last chapter. Some readers may prefer to read the last chapter first for this very reason. If this procedure is followed, you should recognize that this chapter is deliberately written in a slightly loftier tone than the others. This is done to stimulate the student to want to go further in his study of the field, and presumes that the first 32 chapters have established the necessary level of comprehension.

The 33 chapters are organized into seven parts, as follows:

Part 1, *Market Orientation and Managerial Enterprise,* elaborates the setting of the marketing problem, establishes a conceptual base for reviewing the functioning of the firm in its market affairs, and suggests an approach to a more efficient management of marketing effort.

Since the market place is the focal point of competitive action, Part 2, *Foundations of Strategy—Interpreting Market Forces and Opportunities,* will acquaint the reader with the complexity of forces at work in the market place, and the way they may be analyzed to aid in the development of competitive strategies. The product, as the principal means of market adjustment, is treated in Part 3, *Product Policy and Strategy.* The need to match product offerings with clearly identified market segments is examined. Part 4, *The Distribution Network and Mix,* describes the institutional alternatives available to the firm to link production with consumption. These external organizations must be molded into not merely an efficient logistical system to support market performance, but one which creates maximum impact at point of sale. Part 5, *Programming the Elements of Market Cultivation,* deals with the need to blend a number of activities into an effective communications and promotional system. Such activities as personal selling, advertising, and sales promotion are viewed partially as alternative means of market communication, and are designed to achieve a single purpose: effective demand cultivation. Part 6, *Organization and Control of Marketing Resources,* deals with the organizational designs necessary to implement selected strategies, and the tools used for control and evaluation. Part 7, *Summary and Conclusions,* explores the relationships between corporate, market, and economic growth and summarizes the entire content of the book through viewing the firm as a market entity.

It would be impossible to mention all the individuals who have made a significant contribution to this book. Special mention, however, should be made of our earlier mentors, particularly Professors Phelps, Davisson, and Griffin of the University of Michigan, and Professors Haring, Mee, and Edwards of Indiana University. Also, the early professional association with Wroe Alderson and Robert E. Sessions of the (then) Alderson and Sessions consulting organization is evident. In fact, the true influence of Professor Alderson may never be adequately measured, for he was the brilliant innovator of much of the theory and methodology that is current in marketing. In this book also is evidence of the fruitful association over the years with John P. Stevenson of Arthur D. Little, Inc.

We appreciate the assistance of several reviewers who offered helpful suggestions: Professors Robert J. Holloway of the University of Minnesota, and Eugene J. Kelley and Fred W. Kniffin of Pennsylvania State University. Professor William Knoke, Chairman of the Department of Marketing at the University of Iowa, afforded invaluable assistance in the writing of every chapter, offering countless perceptive suggestions for improvement of even the lesser details of the text. We also wish to express our thanks to Mr. Patrick Dunne for his help in the preparation of questions and answers for use in the companion teaching aids publication.

Most of all, the professional capital for this book comes from the by-now-quite-sizable number of senior executives of some of the nation's great enterprises, who in providing an almost unlimited variety of professional assignments, have made it possible to maintain a personal touch with the problems, meditations, and behavior of top management in its periods of competitive readjustment. Many of the examples and concepts throughout the book are direct evidence of these involvements. The professional enrichment of rigorous problem-solving is of enduring value to an educator.

Finally, we are grateful for the support of our colleagues at Michigan State University, whose advice and timely assistance made it possible to finish this venture. We express, also, gratitude to our wives and families, who, for the most part, were able to sustain a patient encouragement throughout.

While many have contributed to this book and it has been greatly improved by their contributions, we, however, take responsibility for any of its faults.

THOMAS A. STAUDT

DONALD A. TAYLOR

Contents

xi

PART TWO

Foundations of Strategy—Interpreting Market Forces and Opportunities 57

Customer Choice as an Orientation for Market Interpretation 59

5

What do we need to know about the market?   A classification of consumer choice problems.   Conditions that influence buyer choices.   Decisions in the market place.   A framework for market investigation.

Consumer Markets I: Quantitative Aspects 75

6

The historical method.   The survey method.   The buildup method.

Consumer Markets II: Behavioral Aspects 104

7

Psychological theories applied in studying purchase motivation. How are these approaches employed in marketing?   A purchase motivation study on automobiles.   Some practical considerations.

Analyzing Industrial Goods Markets 124

8

The market for industrial goods.   A classification of industrial goods.   Special characteristics of industrial goods and their markets.   Quantitative and qualitative approaches to market investigation.

International Markets 149

9

Why explicit treatment of international dimensions to marketing? Other factors.   Various forms of participating in international marketing.   Characteristics of markets outside the United States.

Stages of Market Development and Competitive Rivalry 166

10

Pioneering.   Market acceptance.   Turbulence.   Saturation. Obsolescence.

PART FIVE

Programming the Elements of Market Cultivation 377

A Managerial Introduction to Marketing

PART ONE

Market Orientation
and Managerial Enterprise

A basic premise of this book is that the enterprise must be viewed as a total operating system. Although business management today is a complex process, any single aspect of which requires extensive study, we believe that managerially it is important to perceive the firm as a totally functioning marketing entity. It is therefore necessary to place marketing in its proper managerial perspective in a competitive environment and in business enterprise.

The total concept of the firm can be appreciated if we understand the environmental field within which it functions. It is the myriad of independent decisions made by decision makers in the supplying firms and purchasing units that creates the environmental field and at the same time influences each and every decision. This complex of decisions is the substance of competition—the normal state in a free society. The need of the decision maker to continuously assess the future actions of purchasing units and supplying firms can only be appreciated if the system of competition is understood. Likewise, the need for creative, innovative management must be viewed against the background of an environmental field which may be characterized as a competition for differential advantage. Within such a competitive framework all firms are engaged in two basic functions—negotiation and power seeking.

At the level of the individual firm, to achieve a favorable position among its competitors, each firm engages in a number of contributory functions: research and development, personnel management and industrial relations, financial planning, purchasing, production, and marketing. Although all these are important, a more generalized description of the firm considers it as engaged in two interconnected basic functions, production and marketing. These functions are complementary, for unless goods are produced they are not available for consumption, and unless they are wanted for consumption there is no justification for their production. It is the market, however, that sanctions all the steps that precede consumption. The market holds veto power over the total enterprise. For this reason, a market

1

orientation is essential for the enterprise. More specifically, the competitive strategy and tactics of the firm should derive from market forces and opportunities. Once this concept is grasped *it is possible to think of the enterprise as an integrated production-marketing system that mobilizes all of its resources toward meeting the requirements of effective competition and the fulfillment of market potentialities.*

With market orientation as the basis for a philosophy of business management, it is possible to understand the managerial functions of marketing, the effective performance of which contribute to the achievement of the goals of the enterprise by enabling it to maintain a proper state of adjustment to its competitive environment. Managerial marketing functions, however, cannot be performed independently of each other or independently of the total operation of the firm. They must be integrated into the firm's very existence. This is achieved through what is known as programming, whereby plans are made to enable the enterprise to achieve its overall goals through purposeful or instrumental action in specific markets.

The purpose of Part 1 is to explore the competitive environment within which the firm functions, some aspects of business management, the role of marketing in the enterprise, the managerial marketing functions that must be performed, and the means for programming the firm's activities in such a way that goals are achieved.

Competition, Uncertainty, and Market Affairs

One of the more important managerial developments of the last twenty-five years is the recognition of the need for a market orientation by business firms. This is not to say that the processes of production are any less important, but only that a new focus is being emphasized in the conceptual structure guiding managers. This change in management perspective can be seen in the organizational structures of many firms today. Responsibility for a group of interrelated but hitherto isolated activities concerning market affairs has been concentrated organizationally in a systems focus. In the market place this change in orientation can be seen in the specificity with which business firms cater to minute groupings of consumers through a wide variety of products and through highly specialized media and places of purchase. The continuous development of new products is also evidence of the firms intent to cultivate intensively the great heterogeneity of demand that has developed.

So marked is the change in perspective that it has led to criticism of excesses from a variety of social scientists and to continued praise from others, who attribute to it much credit for the level of material progress that we have enjoyed. There is often sincere concern about the social consequences of actions by decision makers charged with the responsibility for managing the corporate affairs of the enterprise with "a socially responsible consciousness." The concern has its roots in an ill-formulated recognition of the environmental field in which these actions take place and in the search for a rationale of the market system as a whole.

This book is concerned with the way in which the firm conducts its market affairs and the way in which these actions contribute to the competitive posture, growth, and perpetuation of the enterprise. The decisions made by the millions of independent firms throughout the economy and the individual decisions made by the consuming public are responsible for the marketing environment at any given point in time, and it is crucial that we understand the forces that this environment creates. No decision maker functions solely in the narrow confines of the firm he represents; rather every decision is influenced by and influences the myriad decisions made by others. The single most important characteristic of this independent decision making by millions of participating units is the *uncertainty* it creates. Not only is uncertainty the constant adversary of the decision maker, it is our contention that uncertainty is the major factor responsible for the manner in which a firm conducts its market affairs, and also it is the principal element of an intensely competitive economic system. The market affairs of the firm are so closely related to the competitive state that exists that it is almost impossible to distinguish cause and effect—that is, to assess whether action in the market place is determined by or is a determinant of the level of competition.

The decision maker responsible for the market affairs of the firm should understand the competitive environment in which he must act. Only in this way can he assess the forces affecting the outcomes of his decisions and the need to exercise creativity in a continuous process of innovative and retaliatory actions. In this chapter we shall examine the relationship of competition, uncertainty, and the market affairs of the firm as a prelude to examining the policy, strategy, and operations of a competitive enterprise.

COMPETITION AS A PROCESS
OF ADJUSTMENT

The environment in which the firm functions has been characterized as competitive, free enterprise, and market oriented. These terms are frequently used, and much lip service is given to the desirability of the organizational forms and patterns of action they represent. Everyone has some notion of what these mean, but the intricacy of the mechanisms through which society fulfills its needs and desires is not generally conveyed by them. Too frequently *competition* signifies a haphazard, unorganized approach to the economic affairs of society, one in which something akin to a "law of the jungle" prevails. In reality, competition is an intricate, delicately balanced system through which society satisfies its needs and desires.

Many analyses have been made of the degree of competition existing in the economy. For the most part they have been concerned with the number of buyers and sellers, their size, and the relative concentrations of power held by them. These studies are concerned with the *structure* of competition. And although very useful for certain purposes they fail to provide an insight into the actions that firms engage in when they are competitive. One definition of competition is a rivalry between two or more for the patronage of another. This definition treats competition as a form of *behavior* rather than as the *structure* of the behaving units. Our concern is then with what the rivals do. It is these actions that constitute the market affairs of the firm and the intensity of competition which will exist.

The Need for Adjustment

Any society in which there is a division of labor must engage in a process of adjustment. So important, in fact, is the division of labor that some define marketing as "the set of activities that make possible (and in turn are made necessary by) the intricate division of labor that characterizes our economy." [1] Any society in which the work is broken down into minute parts requires some system "to guide the choices economic specialists make among alternative uses of their resources and to exchange among them the goods and services they produce." [2] To simplify the explanation let us think of society as made up of a large number of supplying firms and an even larger number of purchasing units. It is the responsibility of the supplying firms to deliver to the purchasing units that standard of living they wish to enjoy and have the capacity to command. In a number of ways the purchasing unit must adjust to the supplying firm. Rarely do we buy just exactly what we want. For us to be able to do so would require a production-to-order economy, with all of the diseconomies such a scheme would entail. Fortunately we ordinarily enjoy the shopping experience of seeking out those things that we, at the time, think will satisfy us most. Supplying firms do however make many adjustments to satisfy purchasing units. This is evident in the parade of new products made available each year and in the wide variety of any single item marketed at any given time. The actions each supplying firm engages in to make appropriate adjustments are the responsibility of its management, and the actions of all firms, the substance of *competition.*

What kind of system guides "the choices economic specialists make among alternative uses of their resources . . . to exchange among them the goods and services they produce"? One approach is that of the economist. In equilibrium analyses the economist has tried to describe the results of the adjustment actions taken by the supplying firms and the purchasing units. In Figure 1-1 a set of relationships between supplying firms and purchasing units is recognized. The relationships are expressed in flows quantified in both real and monetary terms. The quantities are based upon hypothesized relationships between prices and quantities, with psychological forces expressed in the utility and productivity curves assumed. Underlying the entire analysis is a system of conflict; conflict between firms as they vie for the purchasing units' patronage; conflict between supplying firms and purchasing units as they negotiate along the demand curves; and conflict between purchasing units as they bid for scarce resources in the market place. Equilibrium is simply that state which exists when the conflicts are resolved. It is a tight theoretical treatment of the way purchasing units and supplying firms adjust to each other. The major limitation to this description of adjustment is that it describes a result and fails to provide an insight into the actions taken to resolve the conflicts.

---

[1] Reavis Cox, *Distribution in a High-Level Economy* (Englewood Cliffs, N.J.: Prentice-Hall, Inc., 1965), p. 14.
[2] *Ibid.*, p. 14.

FIGURE 1-1
A Marginal Diagram of the Economy

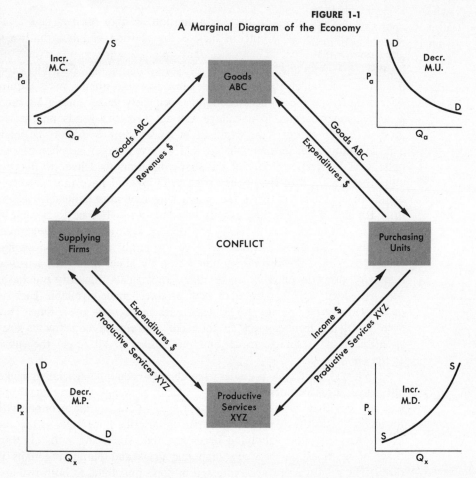

The Ecology of Competition

Another way of describing the way the participants adjust to each other is more behavioral, and it views competition as an ecological system. There are certain general advantages to using a systems approach to describe competition and particular advantages in comparing it with an ecological system.

A system is an aggregation or assemblage of things so combined, by man or nature, as to form an integral and complex whole. To analyze a system requires an identification of the parts in order to reveal their characteristics and the relationships existing between them. The systems approach is a way of examining a complex whole by studying the parts and their relationship to each other. When applied to socio-economic systems, the systems approach concentrates on the relationships between the participants, and postulates that all action is a result of the relationships between them. Any change in action is a result of a change in relationships caused by a change in the participants. A systems approach has two distinct advantages. First, a dynamic element is introduced as it is necessary to study the changes in relationships as the participants adjust to each other and create new relationships with each act. Second, the systems approach can be applied to any level of generalization. For example, the human body is a homeostatic system made up of a number of subsystems such as the circulatory, digestive, and nervous systems. A disturbance in any one of the subsystems will trigger a change in the functioning of the other subsystems and the system as a whole. The entire body may be studied as a system, also any one of the subsystems or, even more minutely, the organs in a subsystem may be studied as a system. We can examine the whole economy as a system or we can just as appropriately examine an industry, a company, or a division or department in a company.

An ecological system is a particularly appropriate way to describe our competitive system. An ecological system can be illustrated by a pond in a forest. The pond is composed of a number of participants such as fish life, insect life, and plant life. In a state of equilibrium the participants are in a perfect balance; with just the proper amount of each life form and all biological and zoological functions operating. If the conservation department adds fingerlings to the pond, a new set of relationships will exist between the life forms. Automatically the pond will start in motion a process of adjustment to restore equilibrium. When it has been restored, the composition of the life forms is different and the pond is structurally changed.

The competitive system behaves in similar fashion. We can visualize a set of purchasing units and supplying firms with a set of relationships between each and also between groups of supplying firms or industries and purchasing units. All the supplying firms are attempting to adjust to the needs and desires of the purchasing units by making a variety of offerings available in the market place. At any given time, the offerings are such that a given share of the market exists for each grouping of firms and for each firm within the grouping. Then a new firm may enter the market or an existing firm may change its offering. Immediately the system accommodates to the change, and a process of adjustment takes place which will redistribute the market shares and establish a new equilibrium. Then the new equilibrium may once again be disturbed by supplying firms attempting to recoup their lost position or perhaps to improve an already superior position. A disturbance can, however, have its roots in a change in the behavior of the purchasing units.

This is an ecological description of our competitive system. It is a closed system; it must be closed to function; however, it has the capacity to open up and admit new participants—new supplying firms, and purchasing units—or to eject old ones.[3] It has the capacity to adjust to any new set of relationships between the participants. The system is dynamic in nature, since any change results in a new equilibrium unsatisfactory to some participants. And as they attempt to improve their positions, new sets of adjustments are called for; the system is in a continual state of adjustment, therefore, to the many changes thrust upon it.

[3] For a more complete discussion of the paradox of openness and closure at the same time, see Wroe Alderson, *Marketing Behavior and Executive Action* (Homewood, Ill.: Richard D. Irwin, Inc., 1957), pp. 117–20.

COMPETITIVE UNCERTAINTY

So far we have not explained the reasons for change, which are an integral part of our competitive system. These motivational forces are found in the *uncertainty* present in the system. So central is the presence of uncertainty to the market affairs of the firm and so tremendous is its effect on the firm's competitive posture that a thorough understanding of uncertainty is essential. Uncertainty is present because of the division of labor and because we politically and economically uphold freedom of choice in both consumption and production. These characteristics of our society are highly prized, and it is not our purpose to examine their merits; however, it should be pointed out that alternative ideologies do not minimize uncertainty.

The uncertainty present is of three types: that related to time and space, that caused by the inability to aggregate purchasing unit preferences, and that resulting from freedom of choice in the producing sector.

Time and Space

Because we have a division of labor, that which is produced is generally for sale at a future time and in a market geographically distant. A farmer plants winter wheat in the fall for harvesting and sale in late summer. At the time of planting he has incurred much of the out-of-pocket cost, but he has no way of determining what price his wheat will command several months later. Even when the time of sale approaches information received on the radio midday crop report does not entirely remove the uncertainty of the best day on which to sell; prices are quoted in fractions of a cent, and they change frequently throughout the day. Uncertainty is perhaps even greater for the manufacturer of nonstandardized goods; there is no midday report on prices and the quantities moving at those prices. A Detroit toy manufacturer starts production in March on toys to be sold in June, for October delivery to businessmen in Los Angeles. The latter will sell to ultimate consumers in November and December. Any number of events over which the manufacturer has no control may influence its ability to dispose of the inventory at the predetermined time. Whenever production is for sale in a future period, costs must be incurred and the risk of recouping them, along with payments for the effort, is always present. There is no way of knowing that the output will be sold at the anticipated prices and time; yet the decision maker must make every effort to assess the probabilities of favorable outcomes before committing corporate resources.

Inability to Aggregate Purchasing Unit Preferences

Even if the uncertainty of time and space could be overcome by some presently unknown means of instantaneous communications, the inability to predetermine purchasing unit preferences would still remain as a source of uncertainty for the decision maker. As long as purchasing units are free to choose those products which most closely match their needs and desires, the information requirements of the decision maker are dispersed among all the individuals he is seeking to satisfy. And there is no known method of delving into the minds of the millions of purchasing units to determine precisely what they desire. In our high-level economy the desires of the consuming public are extremely meticulous; at times they appear almost whimsical. Purchasers today examine a wide range of products made available to them and select from among the many brands the one they think will most closely satisfy their own preferences.

There are those who would have us believe that business does have the means to determine precisely what the customer wants and the means to "manage" his wants in one direction or another.[4] It is true that to some extent the purchaser can be influenced if the offering happens to parallel his latent desires. But the number of business failures each year gives testimony to the inability to manipulate the consuming public. Granted, the causes of business failure are many, but the unacceptability of the product in the market place is surely a major one. Even giant corporations possessed of all the skills and abundant talent are not immune to the fickleness of the market place. Many a new offering, such as Ford Motor's Edsel, H. J. Heinz's concentrated tomato juice, and General Electric's appliance center panel, failed to develop sufficient customer acceptance to sustain production. (The financial commitments in these ventures varied in size, but all were sufficiently large to justify the most sophisticated research available.) These failures however should not be discouraging, but they should help instill respect for the risks connected with the uncertainty of consumer acceptance. To assess the probabilities of success, every effort must be made to analyze market desires as completely as possible. Managerially, the enterprise must tackle this problem with vigor, while at the same time recognizing that complete success in aggregating purchasing preferences is as yet unattainable.

Freedom of Choice in Production

The converse of freedom of choice in consumption is freedom of choice in production. The production structure compatible with a free society is one in which there is an absence of barriers to entry or exit, and freedom on the part of all participants to decide on what they will offer for consumption. It should be recognized that, in reality, in our economy various barriers to entry do exist. Some, such as the granting of public utility franchises, are consciously imposed by the government; others are imposed by the large-scale concentration of economic power by specific firms and the heavy investment requirements prior to market entry. The magnitude of these barriers vary, of course, and we attempt to disburse excessive concentrations of power through judicial processes. Notwithstanding limitations such as the above, however, there is relative freedom of entry and exit in our economy's production structure.

In entering a new product on the market, even though the decision maker in a single firm is able to make fairly accurate predictions about events related

[4] John K. Galbraith, *The New Industrial States* (Boston: Houghton Mifflin Company, 1967).

to time and space and purchasing unit preferences, he still must consider what retaliatory actions will be taken by other firms unfavorably influenced by his actions. The speed with which other firms follow successful moves makes the calculation of lead time and pay-out periods an extremely important part of the decision to introduce a new market offering. For example, recall the speed with which every major brewery followed Drewry's with a bottled draft beer, and how quickly Ford and Chrysler followed Chevrolet's introduction of the Corvair with their own compact cars. Because of this gains by the innovator must be swiftly realized if costs are to be recovered before competitors re-divide market shares in a less favorable way.

Since the knowledge of these actions is dispersed among the decision makers in all the individual supplying firms, it is impossible to eliminate this uncertainty and difficult to bring it within tolerable limits for managerial decision purposes.

UNCERTAINTY—
A PERMANENT FACTOR

The sources of the uncertainty we have been discussing have an enduring quality. Although many advances have been made in managerial tools in the last thirty years, such as the development of refined consumer research techniques, rapid information retrieval systems, computer simulations, and an improved body of decision-making theory, little has been accomplished in removing the sources of uncertainty. In 1945 the problem faced in a free society was stated as follows:

> If we possess all the relevant information, *if* we can start out from a given set of preferences and *if* we command complete knowledge of available means, the problem that remains is purely one of logic. . . . The peculiar character of the problem of a rational economic order is determined precisely by the fact that the knowledge of the circumstances of which we must make use never exists in concentrated or integrated form, but solely as the dispersed bits of incomplete and frequently contradictory knowledge which all the separate individuals possess.[5]

Again in 1965 the problem is presented:

> The exact number of agencies required by the country and their assortment by type, size, location, and the like could no doubt be worked out mathematically under two conditions:
> (1) If we had complete and detailed data concerning the choices consumers would make for themselves as to what goods and services the economy should produce. . . . The problem would be eased for the engineers, of course, if an all-powerful rationing board were to standardize choices for consumers. Whether the consumer would be better off is less certain . . .
> (2) If the standards of service to be met also were fixed and specified. . . . Here

---

[5] F. A. Hayek, "The Use of Knowledge in Society," *The American Economic Review,* XXXV, No. 4 (September 1945), 519.

again an administrative decision would simplify the mathematicians' problem, but we cannot arbitrarily assume that it would serve the consumer better.[6]

The increase in social and geographic mobility, the general affluence within the economy, the wide range of customer choices, and the great variety of competitive strategies by an increased number of firms have probably caused an increase in uncertainty over the past thirty years. Pervasive uncertainty, as a normal part of the competitive environment, has been established. For our purposes the more crucial issue relates to how the firm attempts to minimize uncertainty or reduce the risks stemming from it.

FUNCTIONS OF THE FIRM
IN THE COMPETITIVE SYSTEM

In a competitive environment in which the firm's success depends upon its ability to reduce risks through coping with uncertainty, two major functions related to market behavior are continuous. The first of these is *negotiation* and the second is *power seeking*.

Negotiation

In any system in which there is a division of labor, exchange is mandatory and is preceded by negotiation. In a very simple economy, negotiation can be seen in the haggling over price that goes on between the buyers and sellers in the market place. In our economy the act of negotiation is not so evident. Rarely do you have an opportunity to bargain with the salesperson in a retail store over the price you are willing to pay. There are cases, however, when you do, such as in the purchase of an automobile. When one businessman is buying from another, a fair amount of negotiation over price, terms, delivery dates, and service arrangements often takes place. In general, however, units purchasing for personal or household consumption do not negotiate in an overt manner.

Another kind of negotiation, however, does take place. It consists of a series of actions taken by a supplying firm to adjust whatever it is offering to more closely match the expectations of the purchasing unit. The firm is trying to ensure that it has the right product in the right place at the right time. If experience proves that it has failed, it will engage in another round of actions to more favorably influence the purchasing unit. Consider the number of ways a typical department store tries to negotiate with you as a customer. First, it tries to offer an assortment of merchandise which is complete and has depth in variety; then, it displays this merchandise in an attractive setting, hires and trains a competent sales staff, offers convenient parking, delivers merchandise to your home, lets you pay thirty days later, perhaps sends you trading stamps when you have paid, and at least once a week informs you in its advertising

[6] Reavis Cox, *Distribution in a High-Level Economy* (Englewood Cliffs, N.J.: Prentice-Hall, Inc., 1965), pp. 78–79.

of any special purchases it has made or special prices at which it will offer merchandise. The store is negotiating with you for your patronage. You, in turn, negotiate, and your ability to do so effectively depends upon your knowledge of alternative sources of supply and your ability to select that merchandise which most closely fits your needs and desires. Although bartering is not practiced in our economic system, ultimate consumers are exceptionally skillful in the way they negotiate with supplying firms. The amount of interstore and also intrastore shopping done for some products illustrates some consumers' negotiating capacity. Sometimes alternatives are limited, and this is a weakness of the system. Sometimes there are so many items to choose from that it is difficult to select. But what an advantage this condition is over the opposite state of affairs!

Power Seeking

Although the word *power* generally has an unfavorable connotation, it should be remembered that frequently it is a very good thing. When you are passing on a two-lane highway and an oncoming automobile appears, you might urgently need more power. Or consider having purchased a new automobile from a company that didn't have enough market power to stay in business. You are then confronted with far more difficult problems of servicing, parts replacement, warranty protection, and so on. There is also the kind of power that is struggled for in a negotiation. In any negotiation a certain amount of conflict exists, as each party is attempting to fare better than the other. Of course, no exchange takes place until each feels he is gaining. Throughout the negotiation each will seek power to more easily resolve the conflict in his favor.

What kind of power does the firm seek? It cannot exercise power over the purchasing unit—for the purchasing unit is sovereign! The purchaser selects from the array of offerings of a number of competing firms. It is the power of the purchasing unit to either accept or reject offerings which creates uncertainty. The power of any single supplying firm is weakened if the purchasing unit elects to patronize another firm. Consequently, the power sought is power over other firms which are making similar offers. The only way power can be achieved by a supplying firm is through establishing loyalty among purchasing units. When such loyalty is established, that firm is said to have found an ecological niche. This is a position of strength in that the loyalty is so strong that it is difficult for other firms to dislodge it. Rarely is this state enduring, for the very success of a single firm will trigger a series of actions by other firms attempting to recoup their lost position—or if they are particularly aggressive, to improve an already strong position.

Power is sought through product differentiation. Through differentiation, the supplying firm identifies its offering by giving it some distinction; it tries to create a preference among purchasing units that is sufficiently strong to withstand the negotiating efforts of other firms seeking the purchasing unit's patronage. The number of ways a firm may differentiate its offering is endless, and demands maximum creativity of those responsible for the market affairs of the firm. Most means can be easily copied, and as soon as they are, they no longer differentiate. Some of the more common forms of differentiation are (1) physical differentiation of the product; (2) psychological differentiation through communication; (3) differentiation in the purchase environment; (4) differentiation in after-purchase assurances of satisfaction in use; and (5) differentiation in price and terms of sale. To fully grasp the significance of differentiation, select any product, then three or four brand names in that product, and write down the various ways the suppliers try to give their offering distinction.

It is these differentiating activities, engaged in to reduce the risks of uncertainty, that create the system we call competition. Because the actions taken are designed to differentiate we call the competition a *competition for differential advantage*. Because these actions affect the relationships between firms and purchasing units, they constitute the competitive market affairs of the enterprise.

Through power-seeking activities, the firm seeks to reduce risks; still, it should cut in to that spectrum of market risk its resources lend themselves to. Profits are, in part, a payment for risk; so the firm should not always seek the lowest risk alternatives—not if growth of profitability is a powerful objective for the enterprise (which it is). Profits generally reflect the degree of risk entailed in any venture. With staple food products, for which demand does not fluctuate widely, profit rates on sales are generally low. In contrast, profit-sales ratios on many durable goods are relatively higher; such products suffer from wide fluctuations in sales volume because of consumers' abilities to postpone purchase.

Thus we are always concerned with the substance of the resources we can mobilize which make for market power. We are concerned with the differential advantage we can gain over rivals, which is hard to emulate and of enduring value. We seek to acquire and nurture a distinctive competence that is indeed the foundation of differential advantage and market power. This relatively complex underpinning to the notion of market orientation is important, and we shall explore and illuminate it throughout this book—in our discussion of product strategy, new product development, advertising, pricing, and all the other facets of competitive rivalry.

OTHER FUNCTIONS OF THE FIRM
IN THE COMPETITIVE SYSTEM

Although functions concerned with competition occupy the greatest part of the decision maker's time, all of a firm's actions related to the market are not competitive.[7] Some, for instance, are *cooperative*. Cooperation is frequent among agricultural producers: a number of farmers often pool their output of a standardized commodity and rely on a cooperative association to market it. We also see examples of industry-wide cooperation in advertising campaigns, conducted by trade associations, that are designed to increase demand for a class of product rather than for any single brand of the product. *Integration* is another form of noncompetitive action. This technique involves tying together

[7] See Cox, *Distribution in a High-Level Economy*, pp. 22–23.

different parts of the production and marketing process through outright ownership or on the basis of a contractual and administrative arrangement. The franchise agreements binding together the numerous Holiday Inns within the United States are representative of integration. Another departure from competitive action is the assumption by *government* of certain activities affecting relationships between buyers and sellers. Illustrative is the setting of rates in the public utilities industries, and also the production controls and market support programs in agriculture.

Conflict and the Commonwealth of the Market

A most difficult concept to accept is the way in which conflict and power seeking in the commonwealth of the market can contribute to the social well-being. This notion seems contrary to our desire for orderliness and tranquility. Yet we easily recognize the value of conflict and power seeking in other aspects of life and understand their relationship to persuasion in an open society. For instance, we value them in politics; our two-party system functions implicitly on persuasion and postulates conflicts of ideas and power-seeking behavior in the elective process. Our legal process is based on a jury's hearing the arguments between plaintiff and defendant, with justice being served and conflict resolved to the enhancement of the broader commonwealth.

The commonwealth of the market, although it has elements of intrinsic conflict and power seeking, has its roots in a free society. The moment individuals are free to engage in those activities they wish, the creative spirit of men will manifest itself. Some will be more creative than others or creative in different ways. In the economic sector, the creativity of individuals and firms results in a division of labor in which necessarily we would have more than we need of some things and not enough of others. Hence, so that each may participate in the output of the other, exchange is essential; this characterizes the commonwealth of the market. And as free individuals will have differing values, the exchange must be a bargaining process, in which values are equated. Each will bargain in such a way as to enhance the outcome in his own favor.

The value of such a system lies in its capacity to leave each free to engage in economic endeavors as he pleases, while enjoying the abundance derived from the commonwealth of the market. In an open society having freedom of production and consumption, conflict and power seeking could not be absent; if they were, exchange would be imposed and thereby justice would be restrained among all of us as "voters" or "jury" in the consumption function, with a corollary diminution in the underlying commonwealth of the market.

MARKET DECISION MAKING
IN A COMPETITIVE ENVIRONMENT

The decision maker must use every means possible to reduce the uncertainty he faces in the market place. This means a continuous monitoring of market trends to anticipate future events and sustained investigation of markets to more accurately assess purchasing unit preferences. Also, the retaliatory actions of competitors must be continuously anticipated. One of the more difficult problems today is to determine or identify the competitors for strategic purposes. For example, is a manufacturer of outboard motorboats competing solely against other makers of outboard motorboats or against producers of all types of power pleasure boats; makers of any kind of boat, including row boats, sailboats, and canoes; all businesses offering recreational services or products; and any enterprises offering any product or service used to occupy leisure time? Identification of the market in which power-seeking behavior is relevant, in this case, is crucial. Is the manufacturer in the outboard motorboat market, the power boat market, the boating market, the recreation market, or the leisure market? In reality, he functions, in part, in all of these markets.

Since competition is a dynamic process, the firm must be prepared to watch old decisions lose their effectiveness; it must be innovative enough to constantly renew its vitality. The speed with which successful offerings are neutralized by competing firms makes necessary a willingness to continually change market offerings if the firm is to be successful in capitalizing on market opportunity. There are complex competitive strategy issues related to instances in which a firm can appropriately provide market leadership; in contrast there are other occasions when it should follow the leadership of rival firms. In either case, there is little place for corporate nostalgia if the firm is to grow, survive, and perpetuate itself.

All actions taken by the firm should be predicated on a knowledge of how purchasing units will react to the total market offering and of what retaliation can be expected from rivals. Managements vary in their ability to cope with uncertainty, and it is this variation that results in a competitive environment made up of profits and losses and market leaders and market followers.

With this understanding of the environmental field in which the firm conducts its market affairs, we now examine the firm as a total system of action and the policies, strategies, and operations it engages in to maintain a good state of adjustment to its competitive environment.

Summary

The environment within which a business enterprise functions influences, and is influenced by, the myriad of choices made by independent decision makers in the millions of business enterprises making up our economy and those made by the many more millions of purchasing units. Those actions in which the particular firm participates constitute the competitive state which exists. Only through understanding the competitive environment can the decision maker assess the forces affecting the outcomes of his decisions and the need to exercise creativity in a continuous process of innovative and retaliatory actions.

Competition is a process in which purchasing units adjust to supplying firms and supplying firms adjust to purchasing units. This process of adjustment is an orderly, systematic process. One way to describe the system is by the equilibrium analysis of economics; in it, conflict between the participants is resolved through a balancing of supply and demand for goods and the factors of production. The major limitation of this approach is that it describes a result rather than the actions taken to arrive at the equilibrium state. Another way to view the process is as an ecological system. The systems approach is a way of studying a complex whole by studying the individual parts and their relationship to each other. An ecological system is one in which the relationships existing between various parts determine the actions taken individually, and the interaction continues until an equilibrium is achieved. An ecological system has the capacity to admit new parts or eject old ones, and it immediately sets in motion a set of actions to restore equilibrium once there has been a change in relationships. In an ecological approach to the competitive system, the participants are the supplying firms and the purchasing units. Each is adjusting to the other, and as the supplying firms strive to improve their position, new sets of adjustments are called for; the system is in a continuous readjustment process. The motivational forces stimulating departures from equilibrium are found in the *uncertainty* present in the system.

Uncertainty in the system has its roots in our inability to anticipate the behavior of purchasing units and our inability to forecast the retaliatory actions of other supplying firms. It is also related to the unpredictability of time and space factors. To reduce the risks inherent in uncertainty, supplying firms engage in two basic adaptive functions. The first is *negotiation;* the second is *power seeking*. The firm negotiates with purchasing units by adjusting its offering to more closely match purchasers' expectations. The firm seeks power over other firms by trying to establish a loyalty among purchasing units for its products rather than for those of rivals. Differentiation is sought through the following means: (1) physical differentiation of the product; (2) psychological differentiation through communication; (3) differentiation in the purchase environment; (4) differentiation in after-purchase assurances of satisfaction in use; and (5) differentiation in price and terms of sale. These differentiating activities that firms engage in to reduce the risks of uncertainty create the system of competition. Because they are differentiating actions, we call the competition a *competition for differential advantage.*

Decision making in an environmental field characterized as one of competition for differential advantage requires a continuous monitoring of market trends to anticipate future events and a sustained investigation of markets to assess purchasing unit preferences. It requires as well a recognition of the dynamic character of competition and a creative, innovative capacity to maintain the competitive posture of the enterprise.

Questions and Problems

1. Explain how competition is a process of adjustment.
2. In what way does the division of labor create a need for adjustment?
3. What are the limitations of the equilibrium analysis of economics as a means of describing the process of adjustment?
4. What is an ecological system? How can the ecological approach be used to describe our competitive economy?
5. Explain how the ecological system is open and closed at the same time.
6. How does uncertainty stimulate firms to act in the market place?
7. What are the sources of uncertainty in a free economy?
8. Select any product and state the uncertainties faced by the manufacturer of that product.

9. Why, do you think, is uncertainty still a problem with all our advanced technological and scientific breakthroughs?
10. How does freedom of choice in production create uncertainty?
11. How does the firm seek power?
12. Select any product and write down the ways the manufacturer of a single brand of that product seeks power.
13. What is competition for differential advantage?
14. What is the alternative to competition for differential advantage? Do you think it would be socially desirable?
15. Is it possible in a free society to have just a little bit of competition for differential advantage? Explain.

The Firm as a Total System of Competitive Action

2

Business management in the present American economy is a highly complex process which cannot be characterized easily in simple terms. Stated as succinctly as possible, however, business management involves the planning, organizing, and controlling of a combination of "inputs" to achieve a predetermined series of "outputs." This means that the administrative action of the firm is a goal-directed effort in which the objectives of the firm determine the way in which men, materials, machines, and money are combined in the form of operating systems. Although the objectives that influence the administrative behavior of the firm are extremely diverse, they share a common orientation. Most generally *a firm seeks to grow and to perpetuate itself, in addition to earning for its owners, managers, and employees an ever-improving return for effort.*

Business management is a complex process, but it is also a dynamic one. Faced with rigorous competition, accelerating technology, and a continuously changing operating environment, management must stand ready to make effective adjustments through time in its purposes, organization, policies, and systems. Above all, the firm must maintain vitality in the market place, where the focus of a private enterprise economy is sharpest.

FUNCTIONS OF A BUSINESS

A business firm is organized to produce and distribute something of economic value. In a free market economy, for any good or service to have value, it must have want-satisfying power called utility, and it must be scarce. A good which has utility but which is abundant, such as air, is a "free good" and hence has no market value. Once produced, goods must be made available via the exchange process, for the essential end of all production—both for the individual firm and for the economy as a whole—is consumption. Finance is a facilitative function basic to the whole business process. From a managerial point of view, however, *the firm is engaged in integrated production* (creation of utility) *to most profitably serve an area of market opportunity.*

Markets are the lifeblood of the business; they are its principal source of revenue. It is in meeting the needs and preferences of the buyers making up the market that the firm finds the economic justification for its existence. The realization of this viewpoint substantially sharpens the focus of the whole business process. It properly presents marketing as the cornerstone in a managerial philosophy with which to guide the actions of the firm. We have often seen firms characterized as machine-tool manufacturers, food processors, dressmakers, steel fabricators, or heating and air-conditioning assemblers. These characterizations are descriptively helpful, but they do not adequately convey the managerial orientation of the firm, for each emphasizes the principal employee activity. Actually, these activities are only preparatory to achieving the main goal of the firm, which is *profitably serving markets in which these products are consumed.*

PROFITS REFLECT THE
EFFECTIVE FUNCTIONING
OF THE FIRM AS A WHOLE

If the dominant goal of the enterprise is to serve profitably an area of market opportunity, then those assets and distinctive qualities of the firm which make for lasting competitive superiority must be fully capitalized on. In carving a niche for itself in the market, each firm must employ its resources in such a way as to develop a total "personality" for competitive purposes which gives it the greatest economic power and which rivals will find hardest to duplicate. In this mission, all resources of the firm are pertinent, including its research and development talents, engineering skills, production efficiency and know-how, and the effectiveness of its sales organization.

When one thinks of all the factors that can make for competitive superiority, it becomes obvious that the operation of the firm as a *whole* must be considered primary, rather than the functioning of any one of the parts. Moreover, in striving for profit maximization, management's problem is one of effective integration and combination of all the parts of the enterprise. In this sense, then, it cannot be said that marketing is more important than any other functional part of the firm, any more than it can be said that the carburetor is a more important part of a gasoline engine than the ignition system. The efficient functioning of the engine depends upon the optimum operation of each of the parts in a mutually dependent way. Translating this notion into management terms, we can think of the firm as consisting of a profit pipeline, into one end of which flows a series of inputs, ultimately being transformed into a series of outputs at the other end. In between, acting as successive valves or gates in the profit pipeline, are the principal functional phases of operations which account either directly or indirectly for this transformation. For profits, which are the energizing force within the business, to flow in an optimum way, all gates must be open. Close any one gate and the profit pipeline becomes clogged. Figure 2-1 is a pictorial illustration of the pipeline.

FIGURE 2-1
Business Functions in the Profit Pipeline

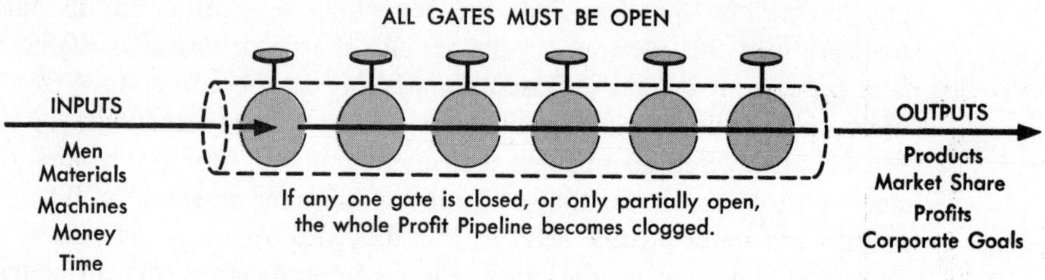

The operations of most industrial enterprises center around the six principal functional relationships shown as gates in the illustration. Each of these is strategic, and when performance in any one is inferior, the firm as a whole may be incapable of achieving its overall objectives. A few selected examples will serve to illustrate this point.

The crucial importance for many firms of the research and development area is evidenced by the fact that many companies estimate that a major proportion of their sales in the next ten years will come from products not now in production. American industry more and more is dependent upon technological development for its well-being. Product displacement, resulting from scientific research and engineering, is more rapid. The profitable length of life of many products is consequently much shorter than once was the case. For instance, in the electronics industry, three years is believed to be a long period of time for any firm to expect to have a preferred technological position with a product before competitors can offer new products with basic improvements. This means that firms are required to spend an increasing number of dollars for research and development, if only for defensive purposes. Successful opportunities to lag continuously in the pertinent technology of the industry are now more limited than ever.

Purchasing can play a very important role in the profit affairs of the firm, particularly where materials account for a large percentage of each sales dollar. For example, in papermaking, materials account for about 60 percent of the total costs. A paper mill had sales in the neighborhood of $15 million and profits from operations before taxes of $600,000. In that year, however, it was necessary to write down materials in valuation by over half a million dollars, leaving the firm barely above the break-even point for the business as a whole.

The total significance of the personnel management and industrial relations area is becoming better recognized. Human resources are perhaps the most significant resource of any firm, particularly over the longer period. The success of the firm, to a great extent, depends upon the quality of its people and their effective utilization. Indicative of this is the current widespread management interest in executive development programs, to provide able administrators to keep pace with industrial growth and decentralization, and provide a continuous supply of top management personnel. In the industrial relations area, consider the cost to Ford of its 1967 strike. Millions of dollars in profits were lost directly through the shutdown, and more millions indirectly before it could recapture its overall position in the market. To estimate accurately the total real cost of such a strike is almost impossible.

The importance to the firm of sound financial management is obvious. Capital budgeting and financial controls are a normal part of day-to-day operations in any soundly managed enterprise. Moreover, with the current rate of industrial expansion, long-range financial planning is increasingly essential if growth opportunities are not to be lost. It has been said that the end result sought for any business is financial, and all other activities are merely a means to the end. While such a position overstates the case and is oversimplified, none would deny the key influence to business welfare of good financial planning and control.

Production for many enterprises accounts for the bulk of personnel and the major expenditure of funds. In some industries, such as the manufacturing of fractional horsepower electric motors, the ability to match competitors' costs in automated line production is a prerequisite to any serious competition at all. That production is closely interdependent with marketing should also be noted at this point. Actually, one finds its meaning in the other. The major dichotomy between the two so often found in industry is neither sound nor practical, but this viewpoint will be expanded later on.

These examples and comments are intended to show that the operations of the firm as a whole rather than any of its operational parts must be considered as primary. The chief executive officer of the company cannot become pre-occupied with the overriding importance of any one functional area as compared with another. While some companies are primarily oriented in one particular way—such as soap companies being primarily merchandising organizations and scientific instrument companies being oriented to technical research and engineering—the point still holds: the operation of the firm should be looked at as a total system of action. Consequently, the gasoline engine analogy holds, and in this sense marketing is no more important than any other principal functional phase of company operations. But there is one overriding and all-powerful consideration with respect to the forces of the market place that provides the focus for management strategy.

MARKET VETO POWER
AND MANAGEMENT STRATEGY

While all individual actions taken in the functional areas can be considered as within management discretion, *it is the market which sanctions all the preceding steps prior to the making of a sale. This is to say that the market holds at least veto power over the entire system.* What is done in research and development, production design, production scheduling, quality control, inventory control, and the like must ultimately meet the test of the market place: Do buyers give their approval through allocating their own resources for the purchase of the product in sufficient quantities and at adequate prices? Since this veto power exists, and since the firm is organized for the purpose of profitably serving market opportunity, it follows that the strategy and tactics of the firm should be market oriented.

It is true that value added by manufacturing and distribution flows toward the market place rather than from it. However, the mere fact that succeeding steps in a system designed to move products from raw materials into finished form in the hands of ultimate buyers flow in this direction is no justification for planning and strategy to flow in the same direction. As noted earlier, the whole system of action should constitute goal-directed effort. The synthesis of this point of view is conceptually diagrammed in Figure 2-2.

The flow diagram, Figure 2-2, shows raw materials (or in whatever state purchased by the firm) entering the enterprise, and through design, equipment, human effort, and organizational systems and procedures being transformed into products destined for ultimate use. The managerially strategic and tactical action underlying the system as a whole is shown to be market oriented, or based on market requirements and specifications. Conviction in this fundamental notion is basic to any soundly managed, mature enterprise in a competitive free market economy. Value added to the product is of course shown to increase with each succeeding phase of operations within the system.

FIGURE 2-2
Integrated Production-Marketing System

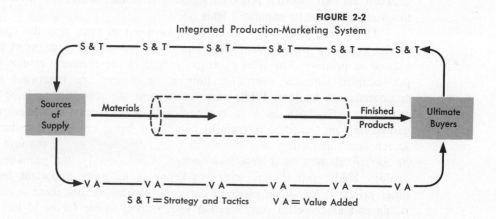

S & T = Strategy and Tactics   V A = Value Added

The philosophical objective of this whole system of action is maximum impact at the point of ultimate sale to precipitate purchase action within the boundary of optimum cost and revenue relationships. The qualification is important. Maximizing impact alone is not the objective. Reaching profit maximization is a prime target. This is achieved when impact is greatest, consistent with the total costs of developing that impact, and the revenues that would be forthcoming as a result of the purchase action that flows from it. Stated differently, this means *matching total effort with market opportunity.* The effort in terms of manpower and dollars should be only as much as the market justifies. Also, this effort must not only be of the right quantity, but of the right quality and character for greatest market influence. Operationally, this precise point is extremely difficult to determine, much less reach; but it is the model of what is wanted. To approach this model, an optimum combination of all cost centers wherever they exist is necessary (be they manufacturing or distributive), and the combination should be focused on market requirements. It is basically less time-consuming—and more profitable—for management to adjust its offering to the market environment, rather than to try to change the market environment to be responsive to what management prefers to supply. The old adage "You can have any color you want so long as it is black" may represent a happy state of affairs for a production executive, but it is as out of date as a sound business philosophy as the Model T Ford to which it was applied.

APPLICATION OF THE PHILOSOPHY

Two examples are offered to indicate how total effort can be successfully matched with market opportunity. One involves the addition of a new product to the line, and the other involves the revamping of an existing product line.

Adding a New Product Line

Shortly after the end of World War II, a major marketer of appliances analyzed the home freezer market. The firm had been considering expanding its product line; home freezers were a potential addition. The firm's analysis showed that this was a growing market still in its early stages of development. In interpreting purchasing and pricing data, a price break was discovered which seemed to contain the greatest promise for a substantial penetration of the market. Having analyzed competitive freezers and housewives' preferences, the firm selected a group of desired features that it believed would appeal to the widest segment of the market. Then the company drew up a set of specifications which could be given to development and engineering personnel to guide product design, sizes, product features, cost limitations, and essential components. In meeting product cost targets (derived from intended retail prices), for example, designers had in some cases to substitute new materials for traditional materials. Styling also was adjusted to make low-cost production possible. For instance, rather than using separate decorative trim in some places, ridges were stamped in the freezer cabinet itself and then painted. Manufacturing personnel had to lay out production systems to meet the target costs, which required line production and specialized tools. Management determined quantities and delivery schedules for factories which would permit (1) constant production schedules at a point of manufacturing efficiency, (2) purchase of materials in economic lots, and (3) low labor turnover. (If the labor force is relatively stable, it results in less scrap and fewer inferior pieces.)

This brief summary indicates the use of market targets at the retail level and how market requirements and preferences guide product design, choice of materials, manufacturing methods, and distributive costs in an integrated way in order to serve most profitably an area of market opportunity. Here we have an excellent example of an attempt to achieve maximum impact at the point of ultimate sale while keeping a prudent relationship between potential revenues and cost throughout the *entire* production-marketing system. (Shortly thereafter, this company became one of the largest producers of home freezers in the industry.)

Revamping an Old Product Line

The Emerson Electric Company undertook a basic program to improve its sales of electric fans. The program began with an analysis of Emerson's market position and the factors accounting for it. Sales had lagged behind the industry generally, and the firm's product line lacked certain new designs that had become good sellers. Also, existing fans in the line were poorly styled in comparison with competitors' newer designs. Finally, although Emerson's product was a premium quality line, its prices were no longer fully competitive, even with comparable quality offerings of rivals.

That portion of the market of greatest interest to Emerson was analyzed and target prices for it selected. In addition, consumer purchases were analyzed to determine the models and styles that were most wanted, as well as the product features and colors. These data were then appraised to provide design, engineering, and production personnel with relatively complete product specifications and cost limitations. Through redesign, changes in mechanical and electrical components, and adjustments in production layout, equipment, and inventory controls, an intensive effort was made to achieve target production costs.

The result: a substantially improved and broadened product line, geared to consumer tastes and price preferences, and produced at lower costs. An improved market position with better profits resulted almost immediately for Emerson Electric. Once again, market opportunity was capitalized on, market considerations provided the orientation for management strategy, an integrated action system was the focal point of the analysis, and cost centers were combined throughout the whole system in such a way as to provide greater retail impact within revenue boundary conditions.

WHAT IS MARKETING?

The definition of marketing has deliberately been avoided up to this point because of the necessity for placing the role and function of marketing in the perspective of a total system of action carried on within the firm. The Committee on Definitions of the American Marketing Association defines marketing as "those activities which direct the flow of goods and services from production to consumption." This definition, although widely accepted, places emphasis on the economic role of marketing and does not clearly portray the scope of executive responsibilities for marketing. From a managerial viewpoint, two specific notes of caution are urged in using the definition. First, those charged with marketing responsibilities within the firm dare not think of their job as *starting* with goods on the shipping platform. Secondly, and at the other end of the spectrum of responsibilities, executives cannot consider their job as *finished* when the cash register rings at the retail level or point of ultimate sale. Effective and creative marketing encompasses a broader area of activities at both ends of the scale.

Summary

On the basis of the above discussion, the following conclusions may be drawn:

1. Any business firm is engaged in integrated production (creation of utility) to most profitably serve market opportunity.
2. The functioning of the firm within the concept of a total system of action must be considered as primary, rather than the specific functioning of any one of the parts.
3. Marketing has priority of emphasis within the firm only by virtue of the fact that the market holds veto power over all the other activities carried on within the system.
4. Because of this market sanction, the underlying strategy and tactics of the firm as a whole should be market oriented. Activities carried on within the system as a whole should constitute goal-directed effort.
5. The objective for marketing, and indirectly for the firm as a whole, is thus one of achieving maximum impact at the point of ultimate sale to precipitate purchase action, within the boundary condition of an optimum cost and revenue relationship—which means matching total effort with market opportunity.
6. Necessarily within this system of thought, a tremendous premium is placed on accurately defining market requirements and understanding purchase behavior.
7. Cost centers over the system as a whole should be combined in an optimum way within the focus of market targets.
8. Finally, in its total mission, and particularly for purposes of reaching its longer-term objectives, management should capitalize on those qualities and resources within the firm, which give it a total personality that in some way or another makes for competitive superiority and lasting distinctiveness.

Questions and Problems

1. What is meant by *integrated production?*
2. What are the principal common goals toward which all enterprises tend to strive?
3. Why should the market itself provide a focal point for strategy formulation?
4. How would you define the term *management?*
5. Discuss the notion of goal-directed administrative action.
6. Think of all the different roles of profit in our economy. What is its managerial significance?
7. Defend the notion that marketing is no more important than any other major function in the successful management of an enterprise.

8. Defend the notion that marketing has a priority of emphasis for planning and strategy formulation.

9. Why is emphasis placed on developing competitive impact at the point of *ultimate* sale rather than the point of immediate purchase?

10. What is conveyed by the statement, "Markets are the lifeblood of the business"?

11. Why is it helpful to think of the firm as constituting one total system of action?

12. Indicate how the functions of research and development, and manufacturing and finance have a coequal status with marketing.

13. The notion "matching effort with opportunity" can be stated in another way. What would it be?

14. "Each major area of a business should always seek the lowest operating costs—that way, costs for the company as a whole will be lowest." Comment on the validity of this statement.

15. Take some time to think of all the different ways marketing might be defined. Write down one of your own definitions at this point in your reading. Refer back to it from time to time and make such modifications as seem appropriate, leading to a final statement at the end of the book.

Systems Design and the Managerial Functions of Marketing **3**

Conceptually, a business may be thought of as running efficiently when it is in a proper state of adjustment to its operating environment. For our purposes that means *staying in a proper state of adjustment to its market environment.* In order to accomplish this, good "sensing" devices are needed to provide continual surveillance of the market and of the changing character of its dimensions. Markets have extremely dynamic forces and qualities. Never static, they are constantly changing in their makeup, because of the behavior of forces underlying them. In response to these changes, marketing systems and the focus of marketing effort also must change. This implies that a marketing system must be a circular rather than a linear system, be "open circuit," and provide feedback to improve the functioning of the system in the next round of operations. These notions will now be explained to provide perspective for understanding the managerial functions of marketing, which will then be set forth.

These different systems may perhaps be best understood by comparing their nature with the operations of a furnace. The furnace example, which is presented in the next few pages, also will serve to show why a marketing system should not be linear.

THE LINEAR SYSTEM

Picture a hot-air coal furnace, fired by hand, that has a series of ducts leading to a number of floor registers throughout the house. When coal is burned, hot air rises and is distributed by the ducts, providing comfortable temperatures to the various rooms. After the fire dies down the rooms cool off, and the whole heating procedure must be repeated. This furnace works on a *linear system;* its components form a *line.*

It has a beginning and an end. The system itself has no way of responding to changes that affect it. The inputs (coal) cannot be adjusted to varying outputs (heat) by the system to accommodate different requirements in different parts of the house.

You can see that this isn't a very efficient system. First, it requires a highly skilled operator, one who knows just the right amount of coal to add for a desired increase in temperature, how much draft (air) will be needed, what the usual time lags are between "firing-up" and obtaining heat, how to bank the fire at night to conserve fuel, and how to handle any special idiosyncrasies of the furnace. But even with a skilled operator there are likely to be drafty rooms, uneven temperatures, and excessive fuel consumption.

By the same token, a marketing system that is merely an adjunct to a factory will prove inadequate also. The marketing system in this case would play a role similar to the ducts of the furnace, which simply carry heat to the rooms in the hope that occupants will find the temperature satisfactory. By analogy, the marketing system would merely carry to the market what the factory had produced with the expectation that all would be well. Now an extremely perceptive factory management with a keen intuitive sense of market characteristics and preferences might get along reasonably well for a period of time, much as a highly skilled furnace operator might with his furnace, but the same kinds of limitations are likely to exist. In both cases, necessary adjustments may occasionally be overlooked until it is too late for effective action. Our furnace operator may fail to notice the gradual drop in the temperature of the living room until it actually becomes chilly. When he rushes downstairs to shovel more coal into the furnace, he finds that the fire is out. Our factory operator could discover at the end of an apparently good first quarter an alarming pileup of finished goods inventories. In both cases, it could be too late for minor corrective changes.

THE CLOSED-CIRCUIT SYSTEM

A more efficient and more satisfactory heating system may be obtained by placing a thermostat in the living quarters and adding a stoker to the furnace. With these built-in devices, the furnace will function in a better state of adjustment to its environment. The desired temperature is selected by the homeowner. After the furnace has dispensed enough heat to reach this temperature, the thermostat is actuated; this transmits an electrical impulse to the furnace, shutting it off. The electrical circuit connecting the thermostat and furnace is a closed circuit; it provides a continuous, closed path for current flow (the thermostat opens and closes the electrical circuit).

Automatic temperature control in a closed-circuit system is called *feedback*. The action of the thermostat depends on the action of the furnace and, conversely, the action of the furnace depends on the action of the thermostat; each is both cause and effect of the behavior of the other. Each is both output and input—all the forces affecting the closed-circuit system are built into the system itself. Consequently, its operations are not subject to change from unexpected

29

Systems
Design
and the
Managerial
Functions
of Marketing

or random external forces over which it has no control—for example, an impending drastic drop in outside temperature because of a storm that has yet to arrive over the area. Likewise, it cannot raise the inside temperature a degree or two for psychological purposes because overcast, windy weather outside makes it seem colder in the house than it actually is.

The system we now have is reasonably satisfactory. It can, however, become still more effective. While it is possible to strike an average temperature for the house that partially suits the needs of varying quarters, a single temperature is not fully satisfactory. For example, activity quarters such as the kitchen or game room do not require as high a temperature as sitting areas such as the living room or study. Also, sleeping areas would be more comfortable with a third temperature. This demonstrates a basic consideration in programming marketing effort (almost an axiom): One expenditure of effort can seldom be all things to all people. Or more simply, one output cannot meet the precise needs of any single demand if the total demand for the output is actually made up of differentiated segments. To remedy this situation, several thermostats may be placed strategically throughout the house and the necessary modifications made in the heating plant, and now again, the furnace is capable of maintaining a better state of adjustment to the household environment it serves.

The marketing counterpart of our furnace at this point has several ramifications. First, "sensing devices" (such as the thermostat) are needed to insure that the overall market is reached and served with reasonable precision. The total market must be focused on initially, as it is the market that the system must satisfy. Next, feedback is important, so that adjustment in operations can take place on a continuing basis, as warranted by the market response to the firm's marketing activities. Finally, there must be an awareness of the various segments of the market and their accompanying variations if precise adjustment is to be achieved. Many firms have recognized this need. As it is impossible to be all things to all people with a single marketing effort, many methods are used to adjust to different segments of the market. A familiar one is the offering of "good, better, and best" product qualities in a single merchandise line.

THE OPEN-CIRCUIT SYSTEM

Returning now to our furnace, we might think that there is very little improvement yet to be made, since the system has progressed from a linear one to a closed-circuit one with feedback. But, to take account of external forces that influence its internal functioning, the system can be made *open-circuit*. For example, a rapid change in the outside weather will play a part in how well the furnace does its job because of the time lag between the moment when the furnace gets a signal to change operations (shut off or come on) and the effect of the signal to change the temperature of the rooms. If a severe cold front is moving into an area, the furnace will have no specialized mechanism to transmit information, so that an adjustment may be made in advance of the change in temperature. Not until the temperature of the rooms inside the house suddenly drops will the room thermostat actuate the furnace to provide more heat. But an outdoor thermostat can "sense" these changes and signal the furnace of radical temperature changes in advance so that time lags can be avoided. This system is called *open-circuit feedback* because the outside thermostat can actuate the furnace but the furnace cannot actuate the thermostat. The two units are no longer mutually cause and effect, as was the case with the inside thermostat and the furnace.

Now we have attained our prime goal, devising a nearly perfect system for keeping the furnace in an effective state of adjustment to its complete operating environment. The occupants will not be obliged to change or adapt their preferences for hot or cold rooms or their attitudes toward what constitutes a comfortable temperature in different rooms within the house. Nor are they forced to live with an inefficient system. The furnace adjusts to the family's needs regardless of whether the need for change comes from a change in desires of the inhabitants or from outside forces.

What, then, is the marketing analogy? "Outside" environmental forces over which the firm itself has no control are frequently crucial in maintaining an effective marketing effort. Technological change, creative invention, competitive forays of new institutions (discount houses, for instance), and the ever changing desires of the market all exert significant weight on the marketing system employed by the firm to meet corporate objectives. For this reason, a linear marketing system cannot be satisfactory; the system must have open-circuit feedback characteristics.

In summary, a marketing mechanism is needed which not only maintains a reasonable state of adjustment to the existing overall market environment (single thermostat in the house), but which also takes account of the varying needs of particular market segments (a thermostat in various quarters of the house), and which can anticipate impending outside events or forces which should be taken into account (outside thermostat). A marketing system must be of this sort because all the forces which influence the system cannot be "internalized"—that is, outside factors over which the firm has no control will inevitably influence the character of its marketing effort. Consequently, a circular-flow system is needed that can best be characterized as an open-circuit feedback system.

It is against the backdrop of this concept of circular flow that we now wish to consider the managerial functions of marketing. The managerial functions are distinct from the functions of the firm—negotiation and power seeking—in the competitive environment. The latter are adequate to describe the role of the firm in the total economy but too general to give operational direction to marketing activities within the firm. The managerial functions are believed to be philosophically in harmony with the essential systems requirements we have outlined. They provide, moreover, a basis for auditing, through functional analysis, the efficiency with which the marketing system is operating, which should be a prime requisite for classifying marketing functions.[1]

---

[1] Considerable debate has taken place over the years with regard to the functions of marketing. Although there is no common agreement as to what these functions are, perhaps the most widely accepted breakdown is the following: (A) Exchange functions: (1) Buying; (2) Selling—(B) Physical supply functions: (1) Transportation; (2) Storage

31

Systems
Design
and the
Managerial
Functions
of Marketing

THE MANAGERIAL FUNCTIONS
OF MARKETING

The following managerial functions of marketing are set forth with the view that they apply to any producing enterprise. It behooves management to exercise a high degree of planning, organization, and control so as to insure their effective performance. It should be recognized at the outset, however, that any given marketing activity might serve several of these functions simultaneously. For example, guarantees and warranties are used partly to match products with market requirements, partly to facilitate the transaction function, and partly as an instrument to insure satisfaction in use. These thoughts should be kept in mind as the following managerial functions of marketing are considered by the reader: [2]

1. Market delineation
2. Purchase motivation
3. Product adjustment
4. Physical distribution
5. Communications
6. Transaction
7. Post-transaction

Market Delineation

Every seller must ascertain in some way or other the potential buyers for his product. This is the first requisite for effective marketing performance.

The market may be delineated by as simple a device as hanging a sign out close to a farmhouse, FRESH EGGS 60¢ A DOZEN, which automatically tends to sort out the potential buyers from among the general population of passersby. At the other extreme, an elaborate market research program may be employed to carefully determine the potential buyers. Broadly understood, this function would include not only determining who the potential buyers are but also the other relevant quantitative factors that serve to delineate or define the market. For example: Where are the buyers located? When do they buy? How frequently do they purchase, and in what quantities? Truly effective performance of this function presumes a precise delineation of the market. The marketing affairs of the firm cannot be guided wisely on the basis of a generalized description of the market. It is not very helpful to an appliance sales executive to be told that the potential market for dishwashers consists of owners of all wired

---

—(C) Facilitating functions: (1) Finance; (2) Risk taking; (3) Standardization and grading; (4) Marketing information. This classification is useful when thinking in aggregate economic terms. It points up the fact that these functions cannot be eliminated from the total marketing process. But although these functions cannot be eliminated, they *can* be shifted back and forth among institutions—e.g., retailers such as supermarkets shift a part of the transportation function to consumers. This functional classification, however, has several limitations from a managerial marketing point of view.

[2] For an excellent discussion of another group of marketing functions, see Edward McGarry, "Some Functions of Marketing Reconsidered," in *Theory in Marketing,* Reavis Cox and Wroe Alderson, eds. (Homewood, Ill.: Richard D. Irwin, Inc., 1950), pp. 263–79.

homes with plumbing facilities. Nor could a motorcycle sales manager intelligently direct his marketing effort if the only definition of the market to guide him indicated that buyers were predominantly from the male population of the country sixteen years of age and over. A more precise delineation is needed which defines the market by such specific factors as age groups, income levels, educational backgrounds, marital status, geographic areas, urban or rural areas, and perhaps car ownership or nonownership.

In auditing the marketing effort of a firm, a first consideration is, thus: Does the firm know the markets for its products and their makeup with reasonable depth and precision? Such an audit also includes considerations of whether the market is large enough and of appropriate character to support profitable operations. A firm might know in detail the market for a given product, and it might be cultivating the market in an ideal way, but an adequate market may not exist to justify competing for available purchasers. Thinking of this function with respect to the introduction of a new product, a measure of market potential and the feasibility of market entry would be a first consideration.

On the basis of the above discussion, *the market delineation function can be defined as the determination of potential purchasers and their identifying characteristics.*

Purchase Motivation

In presenting a product or service for sale, every firm inherently does so with some major underlying assumptions with regard to purchase behavior. Whether these assumptions are consciously calculated, and tested with the aid of sophisticated psychological research techniques or merely by an inadvertent and perhaps unconsciously arrived-at conclusion, is immaterial. The universality of this function is evident. Some notion about what motivates buyers is inescapable. In the rudimentary marketing approach for selling eggs, cited earlier, the sign read FRESH EGGS 60¢ A DOZEN. Such factors as size, color, grade, packaging, and convenience, among others, are ignored. This sign implies that the two most influential factors that can be used for attracting buyers are freshness of product, and price. This may or may not be so, but it represents the position taken by our farmer-marketer. At the other extreme, pharmaceutical producers currently are spending large sums of money on motivation research to find out what factors underlie and influence the prescription habits of physicians, aside from the obvious therapeutic effects of one drug over another. In between these extremes, a number of examples could be used to illuminate the performance of this managerial function.

Such merchandising slogans as "99 and 44/100 percent pure—it floats," "Your taste can tell," and "It guards your breath," all represent some important decisions about what is best calculated to gain a favorable consumer response to the product. In a broader sense, any message that is transmitted to potential buyers necessarily contains information with motivational overtones. Inspection of advertising copy in any magazine quickly reveals the range and variety of appeals used for market cultivation purposes. Actually, even the mere announcement of a product for sale, with no apparent attempt at persuasion, still involves

33

Systems
Design
and the
Managerial
Functions
of Marketing

the performance of this function. In such a case, the marketer may have concluded that the motivational variables were so diverse that each potential buyer would be more effectively influenced when left to his own devices. One could argue perhaps that cost considerations in a case such as this preclude any verbalized attempt at motivation, and yet this position in itself is a motivation conclusion—namely, that cost is the predominant or sole motivational force.

Historically, marketing campaigns have been based predominantly on the perceptive judgment and keen insight of executives. More recently, research techniques have become available to measure more scientifically these motivational forces.

In auditing the marketing affairs of the firm, then, the second important functional consideration would be *whether the firm knows what the most significant forces are that underlie purchase behavior.* The purchase-motivation function, therefore, builds naturally upon market delineation. One would not have the means for understanding the forces that underlie purchase behavior without first knowing the potential buyers of the product. The relationship is thus a sequential one.

The second management function of marketing then is *the purchase motivation function which is the assessment of those direct and indirect factors which underlie, impinge upon, and influence purchase behavior.*

Product Adjustment

A business needs to stay in an effective state of adjustment to its market environment. In a major way, this means keeping the product line in harmony with market characteristics, preferences, and expenditure patterns. Few businesses can prosper through time with a static product line. Since markets are dynamic, product policy with respect to goods to be consumed in those markets must be dynamic. Reflecting this consideration, the product line should be periodically audited to see how well it is meeting its intended purposes.

Effective performance of this function depends to an important extent on how well the preceding two functions have been conducted. A product or product line is well adjusted only in the context of the specific market delineated for its acquisition and consumption and the motivational forces. So, again, the function is sequentially related to, and builds upon, those mentioned earlier. While this is true, it must be recognized that both markets and their motivational forces are characterized by change.

Chapter 6 will indicate how market change reflects fluctuating income levels, population growth, new-family formation, population mobility, and the like. Cultural and social forces influence consumption patterns, as does the changing nature of individual tastes and esthetic preferences. As a nation becomes more prosperous, people's wants become more specific in terms of their demand for products of precise characteristics, so that markets which were once quite homogeneous or uniform tend to become more segmented. This movement toward segmentation has had the effect of making a broader assortment of goods available to consumers to draw on in the market place for replenishing and extending their inventories of goods. As a result of all these factors, a given product line may be very much "in tune with the times" at one point, and poorly adapted to the market at another. Finally, the marketer finds his product-line problems complicated, in addition, by competitors' actions in technological innovation.

The product adjustment function is thus important managerially to insure that the marketing system is functioning effectively in the pursuit of corporate goals. Marketing executives must be continuously alert to opportunities in individual products to achieve a more entrenched market position. No amount of otherwise astute or skillful marketing can make up for a product (or product line) which is basically unacceptable to purchasers at the price that must be paid to acquire it.

This third function can thus be defined as including those activities which are engaged in to match the product with the market in which it is to be purchased and consumed.

Physical Distribution

Physical distribution concerns the actual movement of goods from points of production to points of consumption. This function thereby poses a problem of the economics of movement of goods through time and space. Once the market for a product is known, and the related motivational forces are understood, the product must be moved to the market in the most economic way, within the limitations imposed by these preceding considerations. The makeup of the market and its dispersion is an obvious factor in selecting channels for the physical movement of merchandise. The product itself is also clearly an important factor to consider in choosing its path of physical movement. Considerations of perishability, fragileness, bulk, weight, cost of handling, and potential damage through multiple handling are quite naturally pertinent. Not so obvious is the relevancy of the motivational function. This has a bearing on physical movement in that it relates to how, when, and why people want to buy goods. For example, if industrial buyers would accept 72 hours for delivery of parts, as compared with 24 hours, a strikingly different physical distribution system might result. Consequently, the means employed in making the product available must reflect these considerations. These circumstances account for the sequential position of this function within the classification.

While Chapter 16 will be devoted to physical distribution in substantially greater detail, several observations with respect to the performance of this function are appropriate here. First, the objective in performing this function is to integrate transportation, warehousing, and merchandising economics in an optimum way. Secondly, achieving this objective requires the best economic integration of production points, warehousing locations, and market areas. Third, within this framework, four basic decision areas call for careful planning. These areas are: (1) choice of the basic unit of shipment; (2) selection of the mode and method of transportation to the warehouse sites; (3) determination of production layouts and systems for storage and movement through the warehouse site; and (4) adoption of procedures and policies for transit outbound

35

Systems
Design
and the
Managerial
Functions
of Marketing

from the warehouse site. These are principal elements in designing an efficient physical distribution or supply channel.

The aspects of physical distribution are important managerial considerations because a very sizable part of total marketing cost is involved in this logistics function. So, in auditing the marketing affairs of the firm from a managerial perspective, "How efficient is the physical distribution of products?" would be a pertinent question for the analyst.

The physical distribution function is concerned with the actual movement of goods from points of production to points of consumption.

Communications

Unless communication occurs between the marketer and the potential buyer, no transaction can take place. A buyer must at least know of the availability of the product and its price. Sellers, on the other hand, are not merely interested in seeing that this minimum information reaches buyers. It is also important to supply pertinent information which leads to a favorable attitude toward the product and its sponsor, an overt purchasing decision, and satisfaction from the product when placed in use.[3]

Traditionally, marketers have been preoccupied with the individual problem areas of personal selling, advertising, publicity, and sales promotion as tools of demand cultivation. In a broader sense, while each of these has some individual status, they are all parts of a market-communications system. Viewing the problem in this way tends to open new vistas to thinking about informational requirements and the means of reciprocal transfer systems. From a managerial viewpoint, the principal question in selecting and coordinating the various demand cultivation components is really a communications problem—namely: How can consumers or buyers be most effectively reached in terms of the kinds and quantities of information that will have the most powerful influence in inducing them to act in a favorable way?

The communications function thus clearly draws upon functions previously enumerated. Any program for communicating with buyers would need to take into account all the data gathered in delineating the market, the motivational forces in the market, the way the product or product line had been adjusted to the market, and the channels used for physically distributing goods.

Communications is an inherent function in every marketing organization. Its principal purpose is demand cultivation, but it is not merely a bargaining instrument used in bringing buyer and seller together. Many other communications needs beyond this important one exist in a marketing system. From the layman's view, most of the activities called selling would be a part of the communications function.

[3] Communications is not the mere transmitting of messages containing information. There can be no communication until these messages are received and understood at the destination and a sense of psychological need is aroused. The essential requirements of an effective communications process are taken up in detail in Chapter 22, "Communications Theory and Marketing."

Marketing managers should periodically review how effectively the firm is communicating with potential buyers to assure that the most favorable action climate exists for serving company purposes. If gratifying sales are not forthcoming for the firm, one factor that could account for the difficulty might be the ineffectiveness of the nature, scope, and frequency of information reaching the market. Making a sales force more productive is often a matter of making communications more effective for impact purposes. The same could be said for other forms of demand-cultivation activities.

The communications function thus consists of the transmitting of information and messages between buyer and seller to the end that the most favorable action climate for the seller is created in the market place. It is anticipated that the results of the action will accrue to the mutual advantage of both buyer and seller as a basic premise underlying the exchange process. Managerially speaking, however, the purpose of communications is unmistakable—it is to precipitate in the market place action that serves the seller's purpose.

Transaction

The transaction function in marketing includes those activities which must be performed between the time a meeting of the minds occurs among the parties concerned and the actual transfer of ownership. It includes all processes necessary to place goods under the responsibility of those who are to use them, other than manufacturing to order, or transportation of goods. The principal domain of this function is the overt legal act of transferring title, and the facilitative activities necessary thereto. These facilitative activities are very important and often account for a sizable number of people in an organization. They include: order-handling systems, invoicing, billing, credit arrangements, determination of applicable discounts (if any), arrangements of time of delivery, effecting guarantees, and handling of any insurance policies applicable to the transfer of ownership. In the sale of industrial equipment other extensive services are often necessary before the buyer actually takes full custody of, and responsibility for, the goods. These include installation of the equipment, seeing that actual performance of the machine meets specifications, and training operators.

Let us look at an example of the transaction function in everyday life. A shopper entered a New York department store to find a Christmas gift for a friend. After reaching the housewares department, she selected a covered casserole dish in three minutes' time. At this point there was a meeting of the minds with regard to a market transaction. The preceding market functions had been effective in this instance—impact was sufficiently developed for purchase action favorable to the seller to take place. From the time the shopper announced her decision to the clerk until the transaction was completed and custody of the goods transferred, however, eighteen additional minutes were consumed.

Retailers, particularly, have devoted much time and effort to devising improved ways of carrying out the transaction function, but much work is yet to be done. When auditing a marketing system in order to appraise its overall effectiveness, careful consideration should be given to the efficiency of the

37

Systems
Design
and the
Managerial
Functions
of Marketing

mechanisms employed for facilitating the actual transaction and transferring custody of the goods. Systems for handling orders and service policies should come in for particular scrutiny. *The transaction function consists of those activities that must take place between the time agreement is reached by buyer and seller and the time of acceptance of custody of the product by the new owner.*

Post-transaction

A common viewpoint exists that, after custody of goods has been transferred, the marketing process has terminated. Managerially speaking, this is not a sound viewpoint. It implies that marketing systems are linear rather than circular. It does not contribute to achieving the continuing objective of management: an ever more entrenched market position and improved market share.[4]

Marketing responsibility does not stop with the ringing of the cash register at the retail level, at the point of ultimate sale, or even with actual delivery of goods. Management has a vital stake in seeing that goods give satisfactory performance in use. Unsatisfied customers can quickly destroy all that management has attempted to achieve in preceding marketing and production efforts. Carrying out guarantees and warranties on products, and maintaining repair parts and service facilities are obvious aspects of the post-transaction function. The adjustment departments and returned-goods privileges of retail stores also fall in this category. But marketing effort fully conceived should go beyond even this point. Marketers benefit from knowing who has purchased their goods, why, to what specific use they have been put, whether they are satisfactory, the limitations to their performance in use, and the features of the product which buyers like best.

The feedback of information should lead to a more precise delineation of the market, better understanding of the motivational elements in the market, improved adjustment of goods to market requirements, more effective communications—in short, more efficient performance of all the functions in the "next round of marketing effort" and in the continuous operations of the firm. Satisfied customers lead to new customers, and the circular flow keeps the firm in a better state of adjustment to the environment.

That effective use of the post-transaction function can result in good returns to the marketer can be seen in the following example. The owner of a new home visited a paint and wallpaper store in his community to select wallpaper and tools for repapering a bedroom. When he returned to the store several weeks later to buy paint for another project, the proprietor inquired about the success of the paperhanging. The customer said the paper looked fine, except that the seams had darkened where the rolls were butted together. No complaint was registered against the product, because the buyer assumed the fault lay in the way the paper had been hung—particularly in the way the edges had been rolled. Puzzled because he knew the paper should not darken that way, the proprietor offered to send an employee out to inspect the job. The employee

---

[4] See McGarry, in *Theory in Marketing,* eds. Cox and Alderson.

was unable to find anything wrong with the job itself, and finally, the proprietor himself visited the home (at his own suggestion). After a careful inspection, he concluded that the paper was at fault. The customer was allowed to select new paper of the same grade without charge, and an allowance was made to pay for the cost of hanging the paper. Result: that customer purchased all his other home decorating needs from that store, and he was so pleased that he told all his friends of his experience, and thus referred a number of new customers to the store. Sometime later, he received a note from the owner explaining that the problem had been traced to incorrect trimming of the paper, and steps had been taken to correct the situation.

As a consequence of concern for the post-transaction function, product adjustments were made, better understanding of application practices were developed, information modifications to future purchases were made on use of the material, and a more loyal customer following developed. The proprietor in this example knew that the marketing process was not necessarily completed with the ring of the cash register and the transfer of custody of the goods to the purchaser.

The post-transaction function, then, consists of the activities which assure satisfaction of the product in use, and the follow-through activities which provide feedback for more effective performance of marketing operations on a continuing basis.

Summary

For marketing purposes, the firm can be said to be operating efficiently when it is in a proper state of adjustment to its market environment. A marketing mechanism is needed which takes account of the varying needs of particular market segments, and one which can anticipate impending outside events or forces which should be taken into account. A marketing system must be of this sort, because all the forces which influence the system cannot be "internalized" —that is, outside factors over which the firm has no control will inevitably influence the character of its marketing effort. Consequently, a circular-flow system is needed that can best be characterized as an open-circuit feedback system. It is against this concept of circular flow that the managerial functions of marketing were considered. These functions are believed to be philosophically in harmony with the essential systems requirements outlined, and are useful for purposes of functional analysis of the operating efficiency of the firm. They are:

1. The market delineation function—the determination of potential purchasers and their identifying characteristics.
2. The purchase motivation function—the assessment of those direct and indirect factors which underlie, impinge upon, and influence purchase behavior.
3. The product adjustment function—those activities which are engaged in to match the product with the market in which it is to be purchased and consumed.
4. The physical distribution function—the actual movement of goods from points of production to points of consumption (optimum integration of transportation, warehousing, and merchandising economics).
5. The communications function—the transmitting of information and messages

39

Systems
Design
and the
Managerial
Functions
of Marketing

between buyer and seller to the end that the most desirable climate is created for action in the market place favorable to the seller.

6. The transaction function—those activities which must take place between the time a meeting of the minds is arrived at between the parties in a transaction and the actual acceptance of custody of the product by the new owner.

7. The post-transaction function—assuring the satisfaction of the product in use and the follow-through activities which provide feedback for more effective performance in the continuous functioning of the marketing system.

By proper planning and control of these inherent components of marketing action, managements can do much to insure the efficient functioning of their enterprises.

Questions and Problems

1. How would you conceptually define when a business is operating efficiently?
2. "A healthy firm is one that can effectively cope with its environment." What is meant by this statement? Do you agree with it?
3. "Effective business management is a continuous process of adaptive behavior." Elaborate on this statement, using your own terms.
4. Why can a business *system* never be fully a closed system?
5. Why does a business system need to have feedback? What are some of the elements of informational feedback needed?
6. "The marketing process ends with the ring of the cash register at the point of ultimate sale." Comment.
7. "It is impossible for a firm to be successful unless it knows its market intimately." Comment.
8. What specific items might be included in a thorough job of market delineation?
9. "If a marketer lacks appropriate resources for analyzing purchase motivations, he can simply ignore this problem and go on doing the best he can." Comment on this point of view.
10. List all the different ways you can think of in which market communication takes place.
11. "Selling is marketing." "Marketing is selling." Which? Both? Neither? Comment.
12. "If all advertising were eliminated, marketing costs would be substantially reduced." What factors, do you think, would bear on determining the validity of this statement? Base your answer only on what you have read to this point.
13. "Repair service is more a function of production than of marketing." Agree or disagree.
14. "Marketing begins before production and ends after production." Elaborate.
15. Which elements of marketing are controllable and which are not? What implications does this have with respect to the nature of the marketing system needed?

Programming Marketing Effort 4

Chapter 2 stated that the job of management is to plan, organize, and control a combination of inputs in order to achieve a predetermined series of outputs. It also stated that management action should be goal-directed; that the objectives of the firm should determine the way men, materials, machines, and money are combined into operating systems for effective market action that leads to the achievement of those objectives. This broad viewpoint provides the basis for programming marketing effort. With the additional conception of the managerial functions of marketing, discussed in Chapter 3, we may now turn our attention to planning an effective marketing program.

The marketing executive, as a manager, needs to develop a capacity to establish objectives and to use them in developing the marketing program. An important characteristic that distinguishes the professional manager of today from his less skillful predecessors is programming skill. The programming framework presented in this chapter should serve as a vehicle for understanding the principal variables that play a part in meeting competitive problems generally.

PROGRAMMING

Figure 4-1 is a conceptual diagram of the programming process. The programming process begins with the establishment of *objectives,* which are to be achieved through purposeful or instrumental action in specific markets. These markets must be carefully evaluated and analyzed to determine their nature and scope and the forces that influence market behavior. Then *market targets* must be selected and all effort must be directed toward achieving objectives through action in these markets. Depending upon the objectives and market targets selected, the manager must develop the correct combination of marketing activities to

40

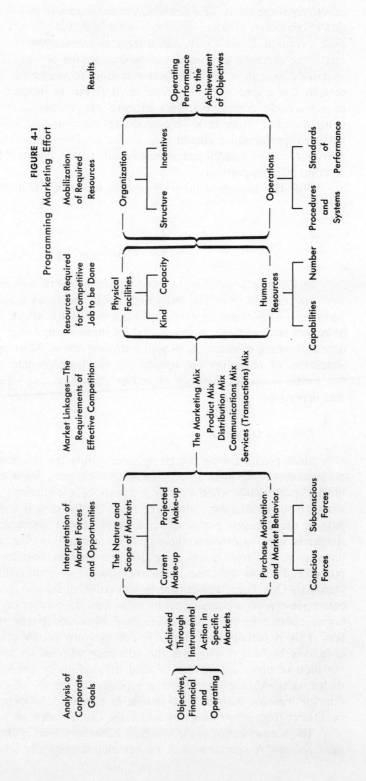

FIGURE 4-1
Programming Marketing Effort

effectively serve them. This combination is frequently called the *marketing mix,* and is composed of four subcombinations called a *product mix,* a *distribution mix,* a *communications mix,* and a *services (transactions) mix.* The marketing mix to be executed governs *the resources needed to meet the requirements of effective competition.* Facilities and personnel requirements are of primary concern in this respect. The *mobilization of resources,* through the establishment of a workable organization and effective operations, completes the programming process. When these programming elements are aligned and properly balanced, performance should lead to the achievement of corporate objectives previously established. Stated somewhat differently, it should lead to a matching of effort with opportunity.

With this glimpse of the total process, let us look at its components in more detail.

SETTING OBJECTIVES

In Chapter 2 we observed that at a reasonably high level of abstraction, any firm seeks to grow and perpetuate itself and to earn for its owners, managers, and employees an ever-improving return for effort. Highly generalized objectives such as these, however, are not sharp enough to give specific guidance or a clear sense of direction to administrative action. More specific and explicit statements of objectives are needed for the programming process. There are two broad categories in which objectives should be cast—namely, the financial and operational areas.

Financial Objectives

Since profits are the energizing force within the business, profit targets are a common starting point in programming. The word *profit* by itself is not very precise, particularly when various segments of a company's business are being analyzed for profitability. Moreover, since profitability is a major yardstick for judging management performance, it is of special significance that the profit standards used to evaluate the degree to which this objective is achieved be understood. Different profit standards are used in business for programming purposes. Perhaps the most important measure of profitability is *return on investment.* One large, rather widely diversified industrial goods manufacturing enterprise expects a potential return of at least 15 percent on its invested capital before committing its limited managerial resources to any new area of operation. This is perhaps the most relevant measure of the achievement of profit objectives because it measures the efficiency with which capital is utilized. A variation of this standard that is used in a relatively few cases is profits as a return on stockholders' equity. The grounds for the use of this standard is that a major business purpose is to maximize returns on stockholders' investments, as distinct from other forms of long-term capital, such as borrowings.

The second major profit standard frequently used is *the ratio of profits to sales volume.* A specialty-foods packer characteristically sets a profit target of

10 percent on sales volume. The significance of this standard is that it measures profitability related to volume of operations necessary to produce particular profit levels. In some cases, profit goals are stated in absolute amounts, often based on past years' results. One other measure used that should be mentioned is *earnings per share of stock outstanding*. When a company has paid an historic dividend over many years without interruption, such as in the case of one of the large utility companies, then programming may well start with the pool of revenue necessary to meet this requirement.

It should be noted that profitability targets can be established for various company divisions, product lines, classes of customers, or geographic areas. The true complexity of profit evaluation becomes apparent when this is done. For instance, suppose profit standards are applied to particular products for both programming purposes and evaluation of management performance. Cost-revenue analysis (of a simplified nature for illustrative purposes) for three products shows the following results: the sales of product A cover all direct costs incurred in conjunction with the production and marketing of the product and all fixed costs allocated to the product with some amount left over. From an accounting point of view, this is a clearly profitable product on a full-cost basis.

Product B's sales cover all direct costs and an additional increment for covering some, but not all, of fixed costs. For operations as a whole, it is more profitable to retain this product than to drop it (even though it shows an "accounting" loss) because it makes a contribution to overhead which would go on with or without the product. Product C's revenue does not even cover direct costs, and is therefore seemingly totally unprofitable even from an "out-of-pocket cost" point of view. Proper policy would seem to indicate that profitability would be maximized from concentrating effort on A, continuing B, and dropping C. Suppose, however, that the sales manager argues that he must continue product C because it is necessary to offer in order to sell some of the A product. If this argument is really valid, then C may be "actually" profitable, even though it shows a considerable "accounting" loss. That is, some of the costs associated with C are really incurred to sell A, and therefore perhaps some of C's costs actually should be borne by A. The point of the illustration is to show the complexity of profit and profit standards. Even more severe problems are encountered by management in attempting to accommodate both short- and long-run opportunities and evaluations.

While profitability goals are the most significant financial objectives, others of importance can be specified which have programming relevance. For instance, under certain circumstances, management may wish to conserve working capital, or, even more stringently, prevent a net outgo of cash. A packing company president, on assuming office, issued a statement relating to corporate expenditures, designed to conserve the cash position of the company. The previous president had depleted cash with a number of equipment purchases that had not yet been reflected in cost savings that more than offset the increased depreciation charges. So, on an interim basis, a key objective became to conserve cash, and this was reflected throughout the total programming of the firm.

Another example of a financial objective that could influence programming would be to raise the market value of stock. An electrical goods manufacturing company, in formulating its long-term product strategy, determined it needed to acquire a company as a means of diversifying its rather narrow consumer goods product lines. The president accepted this proposal, but wished to delay its implementation until the price of his stock could be raised so as to obtain a more desirable basis for acquiring a company by trading of stock. This meant that company programming would reflect short-term programs that would have the effect of raising the market price of the stock in the relatively near future.

Operating Objectives

Objectives other than those immediately and directly associated with profit are significant for programming purposes. (The examples given here are meant to be merely illustrative rather than definitive or exhaustive.) For instance, such an operating objective might be to achieve a particular balance between defense and commercial business.

An electronics company had 80 percent of its sales from governmental purchasers—mostly for defense—and only 20 percent in normal commercial markets. The president, believing the company lacked appropriate control over its own destiny because of the continuing potentiality of cancellation of government contracts, explicitly desired to more nearly equalize the proportions. In a somewhat similar way, the management of a photographic equipment company desired a better balance of business, from the high-priced equipment market and the lower-priced equipment market. Having previously been in professional-level equipment, the firm recognized its greater vulnerability to recessions because such purchases were more postponable in nature than tended to be true of lower-priced equipment.

A major appliance manufacturer desired a better balance between foreign and domestic sales. This firm was anxious to achieve a rather sharp rate of growth, and recognized that certain foreign markets were growing at a rate appreciably more rapid than U.S. markets. Accordingly, it established specific targets in terms of the balance it hoped to achieve in future years between the two major operating components, overseas and domestic.

Another kind of operating objective might be to broaden the customer base of the company. This objective was established in the case of an industrial chemicals company that received such an extremely heavy proportion of its sales from just five customers that the loss of any one of them would have had a serious effect on the business as a whole.

In certain instances a firm might have an explicit objective of maintaining a specific minimum rate of utilization of a key facility. An industrial-products company, with key technological interests in metallurgy, maintained a relatively high-cost steelmaking capacity of its own. It wished to operate these facilities as a hedge against steel strikes or a mobilization period in which steel might be in short supply, and also for its own research and development interests.

Careful programming was required, however, to maintain effective utilization of the facilities to keep costs within reasonable limits.

Objectives related to growth rates and industry position or leadership are often expressed in terms of share of market to be achieved.

To a casual observer some of these objectives may appear to go well beyond marketing considerations, and in some cases this is certainly true. However, all of them have market manifestations and provide initial considerations for programming of corporate effort, if in fact that effort is to be goal-directed. A final example illustrates this point.

To assure regular employment for the labor force could be another kind of operating objective. The president of one of the nation's largest paper mills indicated that one of his two key objectives was to be sure that each employee then working for the company would have a job ten years hence. Fulfillment of this objective required that the sales of the company's products be forecast that far ahead, and then that the level of labor utilization required for that volume of operations be forecast, with allowances for forseeable production automation. Any discrepancies from the size of the existing labor force would have to be made up from new products or new areas of operations.

This procedural point raises the question: How are the different objectives established? Defining objectives clearly is not always an easy task; often it requires considerable analysis of the problems and environment of the business. Certain objectives may be formulated primarily as management policy— earning a stated minimum return on the invested capital or maintaining regular employment for the labor force. Other objectives can be identified only after intensive study and evaluation of the firm's competitors and of the existing economic situation. Reasonable goals for programming are based on a thorough study of the business and the factors that affect it. Also, objectives, as well as the total programming process, must reflect a time perspective. As a matter of fact, *every* factor in the programming process has a time dimension. What may be suitable in the way of facilities, personnel, and organizational structure today, for example, may be poorly suited to corporate needs next month, or next year, or in longer-term periods as the operating variables change.

INTERPRETING MARKET FORCES
AND OPPORTUNITIES

Objectives can be achieved only through action in specific markets, and no matter how dispersed the activities of the firm are, and regardless of the number and variety of different markets, operating effort must ultimately be reduced to the level of specific markets. The sale of automobiles amounts to billions of dollars annually, yet they are largely sold one at a time to individual buyers. More particularly, there really is no such thing as the *electronics* market, or *paper* market, or *chemicals* market. Each of these markets has many, many separate components, and the marketer needs to understand the requirements of effective competition in the *specific* markets in which action will take place.

In analyzing specific markets for achieving objectives, the marketer should stress two tasks. First, he needs to understand the nature and scope of the market in question—primarily its quantitative features, from which he can measure the market potential. Thus the marketer must judge how long the current market situation is likely to exist, considering potential technological obsolescence as well as any other factors that could change the future character of the market. For his second task the marketer must analyze purchase motivation to determine those conscious and subconscious features which govern the behavior of customers. Manifest factors such as quality, service, and price require examination. At the same time, the more subtle influences that often lie below the threshold of consciousness (such as the degree of resistance to market change) should not be overlooked.

Market targets are an extension of the objectives that we discussed in the previous section, but they are considerably more specific than objectives. Targets indicate what must be accomplished so that the programmer's view of the future may be achieved through marketing action. Ordinarily, the first target to be set is sales volume; this is followed by other kinds of targets.

After a thorough analysis of the nature, scope, and motivation of the market, a publisher set up targets for the sale of technical books outside of colleges and universities. This sample list was taken from the publisher's more comprehensive list:

1. To gain management's support in purchasing books for corporate use.

2. To raise the status and serve the purposes of company librarians in order to receive their support in book merchandising.

3. To encourage company purchases by simplifying ordering procedures.

4. To identify executives with book purchases and thereby tie-in the use of books with job success.

5. To combat negative attitudes associated with the use of books, such as reading on the job being unproductive.

These targets, although only a sample of this marketer's comprehensive program, clearly show what is meant by selecting market targets. They serve as specific goals to which all effort is directed.

DEVELOPING THE MARKETING MIX

The several mixes that combine to form the marketing mix are the principal linkages between the firm and its markets. The *marketing mix* refers to the actual work that must be done to reach market targets and achieve corporate objectives. The desired action is broken down into elements by clearly distinguishing the separate phases of work. In the case of the publisher's targets, we must determine if the product line offered actually serves the specific market targets selected. If not, adjustments must be made in the line. The task of adjusting products to the specific market targets is known as *product strategy*. The actual product line which finally emerges is known as the *product mix*.

Once appropriate products are selected, provision must be made to link the highly specialized and geographically dispersed producers of goods with the demands of millions of consuming units. There has developed an elaborate organization of institutions—wholesalers and retailers—to help in the process of physically moving goods to the centers of demand, assembling unique assortments of goods to match the different segments of demand, and stimulating the exchange of commodities. Different combinations of these institutions are selected and organized into functioning units. The particular combination used is known as the *distribution mix*.

Communications is vital in bringing about the exchange of commodities in a free society. Without communications the consumer would not be aware that products are available. Furthermore, in a free society each firm competes for the consumer's favor through communicating with him in a persuasive way. Such activities as personal selling, advertising, sales promotion, dealer training, and so on must be organized into a unified force to help achieve market targets. The combination of means selected is known as the *communications mix*.

The presale and postsale services required to compete effectively in the specific markets must be analyzed. These services must be carefully geared to the particular product line, the specialized distribution channels or facilities being used, and the other activities required in personal selling. The proper *services mix* will help to cultivate demand and assure both proper product performance and customer satisfaction.

The specific marketing mix used is derived from the market targets considered earlier. It is now necessary to examine the resources necessary to execute the marketing mix.

RESOURCES

Physical Facilities and Human Resources

Physical facilities and human resources should be considered together because both provide the necessary means for the execution of the marketing mix. Human resources are the more important of the two, however, since frequently they cannot be purchased on the open market as can plants and equipment. The term *human resources* is used to describe the innate capacity, knowledge, experience, and skill which individuals and groups must have if they are to execute effectively the task required. Human resources are placed at this point in the programming sequence because if the firm is to be effective in the specific markets selected and achieve its objectives, the fundamental characteristics of individuals and groups must be determined by the tasks they are expected to accomplish. Thus, the programmer must consider two principal factors here: (1) the kinds of skills and capabilities required in the people who carry out the job to be done and (2) the number of people needed to do this work.

The term *physical facilities* is used in a broad sense to describe the equipment, supplies, and buildings needed to effectively compete in particular markets. The term covers all marketing facilities and may include the supporting production facilities required to produce the selected product mix. In general, physical facilities are designed to help individuals and groups either directly or indirectly perform their functions with economy and effectiveness. Occasionally, as is the case of an automated production line, it is necessary to think of the kinds of people needed for operating the facilities. Then we find that people are facilitative to the production equipment, rather than the other way around. The characteristics of facilities, however, are determined by the requirements of the functions they serve. As a result, the programmer should think first about the kinds of facilities needed and then about the capacity these facilities should have to meet market targets. These considerations will become clearer after you examine the detailed example of marketing programming, "The Case of the XYZ Paper Company."

MOBILIZATION OF RESOURCES

Organization

Organization determines how functions, facilities, and people are arranged, and their relationships to one another. We are principally concerned here with organization structure, which groups similar functions together, maintains proper balance between them, and integrates them in a way that makes for optimum cooperation and performance. Authority and responsibility in any organization should be delegated according to functional groupings. Good organization is important in developing a coordinated competitive effort. Without it, we have merely a number of individuals and groups functioning independently. Most units of today's large businesses are wholly or partially dependent on the broader systems requirements of which they are a part: think a bit about the jobs of the advertising, sales, and market research departments in a large corporation.

The organizational aspects of mobilizing resources is a matter of both structure and incentives. The proper structural design provides for proper coordination of activities, planning effectiveness, and clarity in decision and action centers, in dealing with the competitive affairs of the firm. Unlike other organizational parts in the business, marketing has both an internal and an external dimension, as is pointed out in Chapter 17, "Conflict, Cooperation, and Manufacturer-Dealer Systems." The organizational structure, however, should basically reflect the tasks required in markets and the basic approach to be used in reaching those markets. Organizational studies frequently start at the president's office and work down through the organization. The pattern urged here is that the analysis start with the market and work back and up. In other words, market affairs should be organized before factories, product development groups, and the like are organized. The organizational aspects of market affairs are treated in detail in Chapter 30, and are recognized here only as a vital aspect of programming.

If the firm has good people and good facilities, and both are well organized in a structural sense, it has most of the ingredients for effective job performance. Properly considered, however, only a *potentially* effective force exists. This potential energy must be released through proper incentives and channeled in productive ways through proper operational arrangements. Incentives are of special significance, for when broadly conceived and carefully implemented, they lead to a hard-hitting and aggressive organization, with high morale. Incentives include job opportunity, practices in job rotation and advancement, proper recognition for achievement, and numerous other variables as well as compensation. But here again these matters are sequential in programming. A sales compensation study or program should proceed only after the job to be done in markets is known, the specific tasks required of salesmen determined, the capabilities required of salesmen to perform those tasks evaluated, and the selection of salesmen geared to these needs. Then the incentives provided should (along with training and supervision) attract and hold such individuals and stimulate them to channel their efforts in the most productive ways.

An illustration of this viewpoint concerns the case of a producer of ethical drugs (prescription items) and proprietary (nonprescription) pharmaceuticals who invited four consulting organizations to submit proposals for a compensation-of-salesmen study. Three firms submitted cost estimates ranging from $20,-000 to $25,000 for the study. The fourth submitted an estimate of $90,000. When asked to defend the seemingly excessive bid, the fourth explained that the study required intimate knowledge of markets, purchase behavior, and the payoff to the company of having salesmen spend their time in alternative ways between different classes of customers. The firm further indicated that if these factors were already known, then the study could be completed within the equivalent cost estimates of the other three organizations. The fourth firm received approval of its proposal after management agreed to the need for the broader study.

Operations

Through the implementation of soundly formulated operating procedures and standards, the organization is made to function smoothly. Operations relate functions, facilities, personnel, and the organizational structure, transforming these components into action systems. To insure the effectiveness of operations, there must be procedures for completing specific projects, and standards against which to measure the results. Procedures for budgeting advertising appropriations, handling customers or sales inquiries, filling orders, and the like call for coordination among functions, facilities, and personnel.

Under ideal circumstances, each unit in an organization would know what standard its performance is measured against. Often this is not done, and although fair standards are sometimes difficult to determine, they are, nevertheless, important. Quotas for the sales force are a common form of standard, but standards should be extended into every aspect of operations—including such areas as warehousing, order filling, and credit extension. The proper use of job descriptions helps to facilitate the establishment of standards of performance. Also, it is important to note that if the basic job to be done changes, or operational procedures are adjusted, then standards must be modified accordingly. For instance, one of the telephone companies, in shifting to more of a market orientation with an objective of increasing the revenues from telephone service, developed a program for increasing the number of multiple phone installations in residences. It was believed that the installers were in an ideal position, on changing a number or the level of service from a two-party line to a private line, or in new installations, to persuade the housewife or home owner of the convenience of having several phones at different locations in the house. The installers' performance was evaluated, however, on the number of installations completed, and not on the sale of additional equipment. Until performance standards were changed to reflect the new job specifications for installers, the program was not very successful.

These factors complete the basic elements in the programming process. With careful analysis and with the proper planning, organization, administration, and control, the results should be that operating performance achieves the objectives originally established. Closure will have been completed so that the whole system of action will have become a goal-directed effort.

MANAGEMENT PROGRAMMING IN ACTION

Our discussion of management programming has been placed early in the book because it offers a practical conceptual structure for the development of well-planned marketing effort. It also provides a philosophy through which one may observe a wide variety of marketing systems in action. The following example is given in order to test the relevance of this programming structure in analyzing a basic adjustment made by management in competitive strategy.

The Case of the XYZ Paper Company

The XYZ Paper Company, a midwestern paper mill, had been known for many years as a leading producer of kraft papers used in making various kinds of bags, such as grocery and shopping bags. The mill was nonintegrated, meaning that the pulp- and paper-making were separate operations, not linked in one continuous process. Rival southern mills, having an important competitive advantage because of newer and faster equipment, lower taxes, cheaper labor, and greater efficiency because of integrated pulp-paper operations, had seriously infringed on XYZ's market position. A number of different changes were made by XYZ management in an attempt to regain sales. Colored papers were introduced, lighter-weight papers were developed, and a larger proportion of output was allocated to high-grade specialty papers. When the new kinds of papers failed to bring a substantial increase in sales, management finally concluded that a major new product would have to be added.

It had been observed that the use of plastic-coated papers, for which the company produced the base stock, had expanded considerably in both the industrial (for example, food packaging) and consumer (for example, paper picnic plates) areas. Statistics confirmed the accuracy of this observation: use of plastic-coated papers *had* increased tremendously in the most recent five-year period. Convinced that this was an attractive new area for expansion, the XYZ Company purchased the most modern coating equipment available. Recalling the advantage enjoyed by some southern mills because of their larger, faster equipment, XYZ purchased a high-speed coater which, at the time of installation, was one of the largest in the industry. Crews from the paper machines were trained to operate the coating machine—but they experienced considerable difficulty in getting it to perform properly. The sales force, at its annual sales meeting, was told about the installation of the new machine, and the technical research director described what grades of paper could be coated on the machine, and some of the important uses of the various grades. The sales manager delivered an inspired talk to the sales force on the growth potential of plastic papers; then he distributed price sheets. Shortly afterward, advertisements were run in the trade press, announcing the new operations, and the new program was put into effect.

Question: What do you think of the company's strategy up to this point? Was the expansion program soundly conceived? Can you spot any weaknesses in the approach taken by XYZ? Try to arrive at some tentative conclusions before reading further.

Sales response to XYZ's new program was poor. The coating machine was in use only about 10 hours a week, although fixed charges on the machine amounted to $25 per hour on a 24-hour-a-day, 5-day-a-week basis. There seemed to be two chief reasons for the disappointing results. First, the sales force had difficulty in selling the product. Potential buyers asked many technical questions that the salesmen were unable to answer. For example, one prospect wanted to know the temperature at which the plastic would be formed on the paper. To ease this problem of providing technical information, two men from the technical department were designated to help the salesmen on important or difficult calls. The second chief reason for disappointing results was that when orders were received, the coating machine operators had difficulty meeting the product specifications, which resulted in a high quantity of scrap and many delays in delivery. To combat the situation, the technical director of the company was asked to take charge of the equipment temporarily, and regular test runs were made at times when orders were not being filled, to augment the training of operating crews. Management felt that these changes would help the situation.

Question: How do you regard the program now? Have your earlier views been borne out? Do you see other mistakes made by the XYZ Company? What should the company have done when it discovered the two major difficulties in its program? Think about this before proceeding.

Although somewhat helpful, these changes did not materially improve the situation. Several months later two salesmen were hired to handle plastic-coated paper on a full-time basis in the principal markets, which centered around New York and Chicago. These important markets had not been adequately covered because the regular salesmen were kept busy with their usual accounts, and also, it seemed, because they were less enthusiastic about the coating phase of the business.

A short time later, management concluded that a reorganization of the coating operations was necessary. The company president decided to put a general manager in charge of all operations, to avoid divided responsibility and buck-passing. Since the technical director had been put in charge of coating production temporarily (replacing the general production manager), it meant that the same group was responsible for making the product and for judging whether it met quality standards. The sales manager criticized this arrangement, saying that quality control was one of his big problems in satisfying customers. He also criticized the company for failing to develop specific grades of coated papers for particular product applications. In response, the product development manager explained that the technical department was often unable to formulate the grades of paper the sales manager proposed. Even when the technicians were successful in using pilot equipment in the laboratory, he said, there were numerous delays before the product could actually be made on the high-speed coater.

The president thought the new general manager of coating operations should have a sales background, primarily since he considered the problem mostly one of marketing. Because no one in the organization appeared qualified, the assistant general sales manager from one of the larger plastic-coating firms was hired as general manager of coating operations. After working a few weeks for XYZ, the new manager asked to have a study made of specific markets within the general coated papers field, to determine which grades the company was best equipped to make and which were the most attractive from the standpoint of sales potential.

Question: Now do you begin to see more clearly some of the difficulties? How should management have approached this new area? Try to think through as complete an answer as possible before proceeding.

When the market study was completed, management realized that the company was in an unfavorable position to compete effectively in any of the markets that had originally appeared attractive. In the high-profit-margin specialty papers, XYZ was outclassed by the superior technical skill and specially designed equipment of the custom coaters. Specialty papers usually were produced in short runs which would negate the tremendous speed of the XYZ coater. Moreover, the downtime that would be needed between each run to ready the machine for the next job was economically unsound.

It was also discovered that the large tonnage grades which could be coated on the large machine could not use paper milled at XYZ. This meant that the basic paper stock had to be purchased on the outside, which completely canceled one of the company's original objectives in setting up the program—to place the paper mill on a better competitive footing. Ultimately, management concluded that the paper facilities and the coating facilities were basically incompatible. For that matter they were doubtful about XYZ's attempt to get into the coated-paper field. The coating operation was apparently destined to use only a very small amount of paper compared to the mill's capacity. Basically, the characteristics of the two businesses differed. Paper was sold to a relatively few large customers, who were in close liaison with the mill and who carried their own inventories. Coated paper, on the other hand, went to many small concerns, resulting in complicated ordering systems, extensive bookkeeping, and a major inventory to be carried by the XYZ Company.

Since business had materially improved in paper operations as the economy turned sharply upward, and since the coating machine had been operating only about one day per week, management decided to concentrate on the other phases of the business, and let the manager of coating operations do the best he could, recognizing that opportunity for profitable operation of this facility was extremely unlikely.

Question: What was wrong with the programming approach followed by the XYZ Company? What approach should have been taken?

We will concede that hindsight is better than foresight and that it is always easier to be critical than creative; nevertheless, it is obvious that many fundamental errors in programming were made by this company. Notice that for all practical purposes the programming began with the purchase of equipment. All that preceded this decision was the recognition that paper sales were declining because of southern competition and that the *generalized* coating field was growing. The initial error was inevitably compounded. In summary, let us look at some of the factors in this case.

1. Objectives were never clearly established. These would have been derived in part from a careful analysis of southern competition. This could have demonstrated what specific operational goals, for example, would have to be accomplished.

2. Only the *generalized* coating market was considered by XYZ, although marketing action inevitably takes place in *specific* markets.

3. Because it failed to identify the character of the market and the factors influencing purchase action, the XYZ Company was unable to establish market targets or to determine whether marketing effort would provide adequate opportunity for achieving management goals.

4. The necessary marketing mix was not adequately established and assigned; that is, what would salesmen be called upon to do? What would be required in the way of product development or technical activity? The proper moves for each area could only have been determined by knowing market characteristics.

5. Personnel were selected on the basis of their availability rather than on the basis of the skills needed to perform the necessary activities; that is, crews from the paper machines, and regular salesmen were assigned to the coating operation. Requisite qualities of human resources were woefully lacking in almost every segment of operations.

6. Machinery was selected without regard for the specific requirements to compete effectively in a particular phase of the coating markets. Rather, it was purchased because it was big and high-speed. The really relevant issues, related to the kind of facilities needed and their capacity, were not considered.

7. The organization structure failed to relate and integrate functions, facilities, and personnel. This is reflected in part by the subsequent changes that were made. Notice, for example, the difficulties encountered in selling; the regular paper salesmen were not organized and perhaps could never be organized to do a truly effective job.

8. Operating procedures were noticeably lacking. Product development, production, and order-handling difficulties are illustrative. Standards of performance were almost nonexistent.

On the basis of these observations, the general process of programming should now be clearer in terms of its usefulness for bringing about major changes in competitive strategy and adjustment.

APPLYING PROGRAMMING PRINCIPLES TO MARKETING PROBLEMS

The programming process should provide general insight into the nature of management problems and, in part at least, provide an underlying philosophy for understanding the prerequisite considerations for effective marketing action. As your study progresses to the various types of retailers, wholesalers, and other marketing institutions, ask yourself how their purposes must change with time, what functions they must perform to meet customer needs, what kinds of personnel are required if operating performance is to be satisfactory, and how facilities can be altered to effectively meet new competitors. This list of questions is not meant to be exhaustive, but only illustrative. Through creative questioning you can add to your fund of knowledge and increase your overall understanding.

Summary

The contemporary management process has been characterized by a goal-directed effort in which the total system of action is mobilized to accomplish the ends sought. Efficient management requires knowing how to combine a series of inputs in order to achieve a predetermined series of outputs. This is accomplished through the programming process.

The programming process is an approach to "management by objectives." It begins with the establishment of *objectives*. Specification of both financial and operating objectives is important. The objectives are achieved through purposeful action in *specific* markets. After complete analysis of potential markets, *market targets* must be selected. The next step is to determine the requirements of effective competition in terms of the *marketing mix* that must be provided to reach the targets selected. With the complete requirements analyzed, the necessary *resources* in the form of facilities and personnel must be provided. *Mobilization of resources* through the establishment of effective organization and operating procedures completes the programming process.

When programming is undertaken with sufficient planning and control, marketing performance should achieve the established objectives. Programming skill is essential to the successful marketing executive in today's complex business environment.

Questions and Problems

1. What is meant by programming?
2. Why is it necessary to know something about corporate goals before programming marketing effort?

3. How are objectives determined that effective marketing effort will seek to accomplish?
4. What, if any, is the relationship between objectives and standards of performance?
5. Give some indication of the complexity of profitability measurement.
6. What is the danger of overgeneralizing markets?
7. Make a list of as many different financial objectives as possible and indicate how they might influence the nature of marketing effort.
8. Give some illustrations of operating objectives and show the implications of these objectives for marketing.
9. What kind of analytical work and operating action might be required in meeting a corporate objective of assuring employment for the existing labor force for a period of ten years into the future?
10. What are the elements of the market linkage that serve to join the firm with its markets?
11. What is included in the term *marketing mix?*
12. In what ways are production facilities an important aspect of the firm's marketing affairs?
13. What is the purpose of organization?
14. Indicate how the element of time influences programming.
15. How is the programming structure proposed in this chapter consistent with the notion of "circular systems" indicated in Chapter 3?

Bibliography

Alderson, Wroe, *Marketing Behavior and Executive Action* (Homewood, Ill.: Richard D. Irwin, Inc., 1957).

———, *Dynamic Marketing Behavior* (Homewood, Ill.: Richard D. Irwin, Inc., 1965).

Bursk, Edward C., D. T. Clark, and R. W. Hidy, eds., *World of Business,* Vol. I (New York: Simon and Schuster, Inc., 1962).

———, and Dan H. Fenn, Jr., eds., *Planning the Future Strategy of Your Business* (New York: McGraw-Hill Book Company, 1956).

Cox, Reavis, *Distribution in a High-Level Economy* (Englewood Cliffs, N. J.: Prentice-Hall, Inc., 1965).

Dean, Joel, *Managerial Economics* (Englewood Cliffs, N.J.: Prentice-Hall, Inc., 1951), Chap. 1.

Drucker, Peter F., *Concept of the Corporation* (New York: The John Day Company, Inc., 1946).

———, *The Practice of Management,* "What Is a Business?" (New York: Harper & Row, Publishers, 1954), Chap. 5.

Ewing, David W., ed., *Effective Marketing Action* (New York: Harper & Row, Publishers, 1959).

———, ed., *Long-Range Planning for Management* (New York: Harper & Row, Publishers, 1958).

Galbraith, John K., *The New Industrial State* (Boston: Houghton Mifflin Company, 1967).

"Have Corporations a Higher Duty than Profits?" *Fortune,* LXII, No. 3 (August 1960), 108, 146–53.

Howard, John A., *Marketing Management: Analysis and Planning*, Part I (Homewood, Ill.: Richard D. Irwin, Inc., 1963).

Johnson, Richard A., Fremont E. Kast, and James E. Rosenzweig, *The Theory and Management of Systems* (New York: McGraw-Hill Book Company, 1963).

Lazer, William, and Eugene J. Kelley, eds., *Managerial Marketing: Perspectives and Viewpoints,* 3rd ed. (Homewood, Ill.: Richard D. Irwin, Inc., 1967).

LeBreton, Preston P., and Dale A. Henning, *Planning Theory* (Englewood Cliffs, N. J.: Prentice-Hall, Inc., 1961).

McGarry, Edward, "Some Functions of Marketing Reconsidered," in *Theory in Marketing,* R. Cox, and W. Alderson, eds. (Homewood, Ill.: Richard D. Irwin, Inc., 1950), pp. 263–79.

McKay, E. S., *Blueprint for an Effective Marketing Program,* Marketing Series No. 91 (New York: American Management Assn., 1954).

McKitterick, J. B., "What Is the Marketing Management Concept?", in *The Frontiers of Marketing Thought and Science* (New York: American Marketing Assn., 1957), pp. 71–82.

Thompson, Stewart, *How Companies Plan,* Research Study No. 54 (New York: American Management Assn., 1962), p. 202.

PART TWO

Foundations of Strategy— Interpreting Market Forces and Opportunities

We have seen in Part 1 that market knowledge is essential to the success of any business enterprise. The marketing system discussed in Chapter 2 pictures the customer as a focal point for planning and strategy formulation. The first two functions of marketing, "market delineation" and "purchase motivation," acquaint the marketer with the characteristics of the consumers the system is to serve. When the enterprise is functioning effectively, it maintains a proper state of adjustment to its operating environment; in fact, knowledge of that environment is the genesis of all sound marketing effort.

Now, in Part 2, the complexity of forces at work in the market place are introduced and a framework established for analyzing the nature of market opportunity. Characterization of markets logically rests on an understanding of consumer behavior—of the way in which consumers solve the numerous problems connected with the accumulation of goods and services in a free market economy. If we are able to understand the kinds of problems consumers face and the forces that influence their solutions, we will be able to characterize markets in a manner that will be most productive in planning and executing marketing effort.

Part 2 examines the maze of action and counteraction taking place in the market place and develops an approach to market investigation. Within this approach we explore the means used to delineate markets, both quantitatively and qualitatively. Although the treatment in this part is general, the kinds of influencing forces bearing on behavior in the purchase of industrial goods and in international markets are sufficiently different to require separate treatment.

In addition to the quantitative and qualitative aspects of consumer behavior, the competitive environment in which the product is sold influences the nature of the task required of the successful marketer. The competitive stages through which a product passes in its life cycle are therefore examined.

58

Foundations
of
Strategy—
Interpreting
Market
Forces and
Opportunities

Our description of the forces influencing market behavior is of necessity somewhat simplified. But the reader must not lose sight of the complexity of forces that interact in the consummation of any purchase. We do not attempt an exhaustive treatment of the subject; rather, we hope to open avenues of inquiry and stimulate more penetrating searches in this area. Both the quantitative and the qualitative aspects of markets are examined.

Customer Choice as an Orientation for Market Interpretation

5

A review of studies in market investigation would reveal thousands of studies by individual firms that are marketing specific products under specific conditions. There are significant variations in theoretical explanations of consumer behavior and in the techniques used for analyzing it.[1] Before specific quantitative and qualitative aspects of markets are considered, we must develop an orderly approach to market investigation.

In this chapter the question is first raised: What do we need to know about markets? To specify the information needed gives direction to the investigation. Since the answer to any question we might ask about the market is a result of actions consumers may take, we then examine the problems consumers face and the decisions they must make. The forces influencing consumers to make certain decisions in the market place are then explored, and the way in which these forces affect the decision is discussed. Finally, a diagram is offered to schematically outline the problems consumers face, the influencing forces at work, and an explanation of the way consumers make decisions in the market place.

WHAT DO WE NEED TO KNOW ABOUT THE MARKET?

If we had the good fortune to possess a magic wand which gave us the power to have any information we wished about the market, what would we ask for? At first the opportunity staggers the imagination, and any number of aspects of the market may come to mind. Yet there are only

[1] See Wroe Alderson, *Marketing Behavior and Executive Action* (Homewood, Ill.: Richard D. Irwin, Inc., 1957), p. 10, for a discussion of the variations in research.

60

Foundations
of
Strategy—
Interpreting
Market
Forces and
Opportunities

three basic questions, the answers to which would be invaluable in giving direction to our marketing effort. They are: (1) What will the market purchase? (2) How much will the market purchase? (3) Under what conditions will the market purchase?

What Will the Market Purchase?

To be successful in the market place, the seller must offer goods or services that are acceptable to the consumer. We are all familiar with the successes of Christian Dior in fashions, but relatively little publicity has been given to the failures. With each radical change by the pace setters in women's fashions, many designers "miss the boat" by bringing out creations to which consumers fail to respond.

The question "What will the market purchase?" is not limited to the introduction of new designs; it encompasses such things as making changes in the breadth of the line, bringing out new products to do old jobs, and trying variations on old products. In an interesting example, a young man detected a need when he watched his wife greasing a cake tin with a piece of wax paper smeared with butter. He devised a means of impregnating paper with vegetable oils to replace his wife's method, and began to seek a market. Is the market interested in such a product? Will it be accepted? A more striking example is provided by "the big three" of the American automobile industry, who deliberated until 1960 before entering the small-car market.

How Much Will the Market Purchase?

The answer to this question is not entirely unrelated to the preceding one. Certainly, the amount that will be purchased is dependent on consumers' reactions to the offering. Nevertheless, once a decision is made on what to offer, it is important that the seller have some notion, for a number of reasons, as to how much will be absorbed. First, predictions about the potential market size are necessary to decide whether or not to proceed. If the market is not large enough for profitable operations, a search for a more acceptable product must be undertaken. Second, if the market is large enough, the facilities required for production, or, in the case of retailers and wholesalers, the inventory needed, can be determined in relation to market size. Third, the quantity and allocation of marketing effort can likewise be determined.[2]

Under What Conditions Will the Market Purchase?

Products that are otherwise acceptable to the consumer may fail because they are not offered in the proper environment. The amount of effort the consumer is willing to expend before purchasing will influence the exposure neces-

---

[2] The importance of market size as it relates to the quantity, nature, and allocation of selling effort will be examined in Parts 4 and 5.

61

Customer
Choice as an
Orientation
For Market
Interpreta-
tion

sary for sale, and ultimately the kinds of outlets used to distribute the product. In buying household appliances and automobiles, consumers may desire the assurances of service and the availability of repair parts. With ethical pharmaceutical products, the reputation of the manufacturer may be a crucial determinant. These and other desires of consumers will influence the type of marketing effort necessary for success.

A complicating factor is found in the spatial and temporal dimensions of markets. Marketers generally do not deal with a single market but with a number of different markets, varying by geographic area and through time. Common to the key question we have asked is the matter of where the market will purchase certain products, in what quantities, and under what conditions. There may be slight variations in the product offered in order to find acceptance in different parts of the country. Brown eggs are far more popular along the Atlantic Seaboard than in the Midwest. The quantities that will be taken vary considerably from section to section of the country. In fact, market coverage may well be determined by the extent of market opportunity in different sections. Likewise, conditions of purchase will vary from section to section; in regions in which particular ethnic groups are predominant, the conditions of sale must be tailored to these groups.

Markets have a highly dynamic quality and relatively constant change is virtually certain. Because the desires of consumers are continually shifting, markets are in a constant state of flux, and last year's successful marketing program cannot necessarily be expected to produce equally satisfactory results this year.

Some changes in markets are caused by deep-rooted sociological changes; others may result from the action of competitors. In the first case we may ask why the market for men's summer hats has dwindled so sharply in recent years, or why the per capita consumption of meat dropped in the late 1930's and early 1940's. From a competitive standpoint, we can note the earlier experience of Lifebuoy soap, with its distinctive carbolic odor—a very successful product which has been displaced by the action of rival companies that were successful in conditioning the market in favor of different products. These shifts in customer preference are taking place constantly, and consequently the investigation and analysis of markets is an endless task.

A knowledge of consumer behavior is essential in determining the kind of marketing effort that can be expected to provide the proper adjustment to the external forces influencing the operating systems of the enterprise. How can answers to the three questions be obtained? Since markets are an aggregation of people, it is reasonable to turn for answers to those sciences which deal with the behavior of individuals or groups of individuals. But interesting as studies in the fields of sociology and psychology are,[3] they are of limited value to the marketer who is seeking to adjust his marketing efforts to the competitive en-

---

[3] For a discussion of the numerous studies available, see James Morgan, "A Review of Recent Research on Consumer Behavior," in *Consumer Behavior; Research on Consumer Reactions,* Lincoln H. Clark, ed. (New York: Harper & Row, Publishers, 1958), pp. 124–219.

62

Foundations
of
Strategy—
Interpreting
Market
Forces and
Opportunities

vironment. The marketer requires data that apply to the particular purchase action with which he is confronted and therefore must be highly selective in his investigation and analysis.

What kinds of problems do consumers face? What decisions must they make? Once the problems of consumers have been identified, findings from the behavioral sciences may be of value to an understanding of how consumers solve their problems in the market place. A classification of consumer choice problems will aid in developing an approach to market investigation.

A CLASSIFICATION
OF CONSUMER CHOICE PROBLEMS

The consumer in the market place is faced with a series of choices. The choices may be classified in different ways, but one simple classification is as follows:

1. Deciding how much to spend and how much to save.
2. Deciding which products and services to buy.
3. Deciding the specific sources from which to purchase.
4. Deciding the conditions of purchase.

Deciding How Much to Spend and How Much to Save
(The Spend-save Problem)

Through its productive activity, the economy in any given period of time generates a certain amount of income which is available for the purchase of the commodities and services produced. The proportion of that income which consumers elect to spend is important in three ways. First, the amount of current income consumers choose to spend, along with their access to credit and the condition of their savings and other assets, determines the quantity of goods and services they will purchase. Second, the amount of savings in any one period significantly affects the level of income out of which their future purchases will be made. Third, there is evidence that there are reasonably stable relationships between the amount of income earned and the amount consumers will spend on different kinds of products. Throughout this section we call this choice problem *the spend-save problem*.

Deciding Which Products and Services to Buy
(The Product-mix Problem)

How much of the income for any period will be spent on food, how much on housing, how much on recreation? The magnitude of the choice problem is tremendous. Consider the housewife with X dollars to spend for food. How much of the total will she spend on meat, on bread, on milk, on other items? Women's magazines frequently feature suggested household budgets for families in various income brackets. In real life, the household budget is more often a *result,* made out after the money has been spent, not a plan made out in ad-

63

Customer
Choice as an
Orientation
For Market
Interpreta-
tion

vance. Consumers appear to make haphazard independent decisions on each product. Nevertheless, consumers, when purchasing, do give consideration to those purchases that have been made before and those which are contemplated in the future. Obviously, more will be spent on food than on recreation, but how can the marketer of frozen orange juice get a larger portion of the total breakfast expenditure? This problem of determining the most advantageous assortment to offer the market is called *the product-mix problem.*

Deciding which products and services to buy is equally important to the businessman. The wholesaler and the retailer must make decisions on what assortments they will stock. Should the hardware retailer stock transistor radios? The bank owner and the manufacturer have similar choice problems. Should the manufacturer replace old machinery or add additional warehouse space in a given budget period? Although the businessman's decisions are dictated by supposedly more rational considerations, he too usually is confronted with a number of alternatives.

Deciding the Specific Sources from Which to Purchase (The Brand-choice Problem)

Since most consumer goods are identified by brands, this choice of sources is referred to as the *brand-choice.* Once the decision has been made to spend so much on food and a certain proportion of that on milk, which of several alternate brands of milk will be purchased? Or, if brands are not important in the purchase under consideration, which source of supply shall be patronized? For example, in buying coal, which of three dealers will receive the order?

Deciding the Conditions of Purchase

This choice problem is closely associated with the preceding one. The source of supply selected by an industrial buyer is often determined by the conditions under which he is able to purchase. Speed of delivery, quality of material, price, may all be determinants. Likewise, for a housewife purchasing milk, source of supply is frequently based on conditions of purchase. Milk may be delivered to the home, purchased in the nearby supermarket, at the neighborhood grocery store, or at the vending machine. In another product category, an automatic washer could be bought in a crate at the discount house in the next community, or from the local department store. In the first instance, the purchaser must provide transportation, undertake installation of the machine, and assume responsibility for repairs. In the second, the department store will deliver, install, and demonstrate the machine in the home, and often supply a year of free service along with the purchase.

Although we have discussed the choice problems in a set order, it would be a mistake to assume that they are independent of each other or that they always occur in the order given. The decision on how much to spend and how much to save may influence both the kinds of products that are purchased, the brand chosen, and the conditions of purchase. The thrifty family that saves a large proportion of its income may go without many luxuries, shop for high-

64

Foundations
of
Strategy—
Interpreting
Market
Forces and
Opportunities

quality merchandise at lower prices, and purchase goods with a minimum of costly service features. Conversely, the family that spends up to the limit of income, and beyond, may purchase a variety of luxury products and generally prefer to purchase in full service establishments at slightly higher prices. For many families the product-mix choice may come first and the spend-save decision is a result; however, there are limits to how far one may go.

CONDITIONS THAT INFLUENCE BUYER CHOICES

Now that we have seen the kinds of problems buyers face, we can ask, "How do they solve them?" Although marketers, economists, and psychologists have been attempting to identify the forces influencing buyer choices for many years, their findings are still inconclusive. Nevertheless, there is a classification of influencing forces which is helpful to the practicing marketer. Influencing forces may be divided into these three groups: [4]

1. Enabling conditions
2. Environmental conditions
3. Individual attitudes and opinions

This classification provides a convenient grouping for study purposes and is perhaps more indicative of the studies that have been done than of those that might be conducted. Further, it relates economic, sociological, and psychological studies to buyer choice problems.

Enabling Conditions

Income, assets, and access to credit are important in determining how much consumers will spend and how much they will save. Likewise, expectations of future income are determinative. Any decision to purchase a new home, for example, is directly influenced by the expected future income of the buyers. The general business atmosphere and its anticipated future are important factors in determining the level of purchases of many businessmen, primarily because suppositions concerning future profit expectations temper their current income position. A complete analysis of enabling conditions is usually imperative in any attempt to measure how much consumers will buy. To determine the quantity the market will purchase, we must first know how much purchasing power is available, and what conditions influence buyers to purchase one product over several others.

Environmental Conditions

Mobility, stage in the family life cycle, age, and social class all have a bearing on the products that consumers will purchase, and the quantities of

---

[4] The classification was originally developed by Prof. George Katona. See George Katona and Eva Mueller, "A Story of Purchase Decision," in *Consumer Behavior,* Vol. I, Lincoln H. Clark, ed. (New York: New York University Press, 1954), 30–36.

65

Customer
Choice as an
Orientation
For Market
Interpreta-
tion

each. To illustrate: A dishwasher manufacturer added a portable dishwasher to round out his line, and sales of this item far exceeded his expectations, particularly in one large upper-middle-income sector of an eastern city. Investigation revealed that most purchasers were junior executives who, in the course of their careers, purchased middle-priced housing on each assignment, knowing that they would most probably have to leave the community in about two years. Rather than purchase a standard dishwasher in each home, they preferred a portable one which could be taken with them.[5]

As important as mobility is the stage in the family life cycle. A life cycle encompasses a number of stages of development from life to death, and each stage is related to tastes and consumption behavior. Here are just a few examples of consumption based on stage in the life cycle: families with children five years old and under purchase chest rubs at a rate of 80 percent over that of the average family. Waffles are cooked most often by those in the 35 to 44 age bracket. First-born babies are fed an average of 50 percent more processed baby foods than are later-born babies of the same age.[6]

Individual Attitudes and Opinions

The range of attitudes and opinions that have been found to influence consumer choices is so wide as to almost defy classification. However, we do know that both conscious and subconscious factors influence consumer behavior. On the conscious level, attitudes toward color and design have proven to be of considerable influence in the purchase of automobiles—although the precise motivating forces that bind a consumer to a particular color or design are quite frequently not known to him. To illustrate the forces of subconscious behavior, let us look at the findings on consumers' attitudes toward prepared foods. Housewives' resistance to certain prepared foods was found to be based not on dislike for the products but rather on guilt complexes concerning their role of housewife and preparer of the family meals. The grandmother image was not easily discarded.[7]

In many cases it is not necessary that marketers understand *why* consumers hold certain opinions or attitudes toward various products. It is sufficient that the opinions and attitudes be known and market offerings be adjusted to them.

Two qualifications regarding influencing conditions are necessary. First, specific influencing conditions cannot be related to specific consumer choice problems. While enabling conditions affect decisions to spend and save, they also influence the mix of products purchased, brands selected, and conditions of purchase. Likewise, environmental conditions, such as social class, stage in

[5] See William H. Whyte, Jr., "The Consumer in the New Suburbia," in *Consumer Behavior,* Vol. I, Lincoln H. Clark, ed. (New York: New York University Press, 1954), 109.

[6] For a number of examples of the way stage in the family life cycle influenced purchase behavior see S. G. Barton, "The Life Cycle and Buying Patterns," in *Consumer Behavior,* Vol. II, Lincoln H. Clark, ed. (New York: New York University Press, 1955), 30–36.

[7] See Mason Haire, "Projective Techniques in Marketing Research," *Journal of Marketing,* XIV (April 1950), 649–56.

66

Foundations
of
Strategy—
Interpreting
Market
Forces and
Opportunities

the family life cycle, and ethnic background, have an effect on all consumer choices. According to a recent study:

> The higher the individual's class position, the more likely he is to express some savings aspirations. Conversely, the lower his class position, the more likely he is to mention spending only.[8]

Since the classification of social class, interestingly, does not rest upon income level, presumably some very high income units may fall in the lower social class.

The second qualification is that influencing conditions are not unrelated. Environmental conditions as well as attitudes and opinions have a pronounced effect on enabling conditions. Earning capacity and thrift, for example, are conditioned by past environment and by individual attitudes and opinions.

DECISIONS IN THE MARKET PLACE

With all the influencing forces at work, how does the consumer eventually make a decision? The precise answer to this question has long been sought, and perhaps we shall never know the explicit nature of the process. Without elaborating on the way in which particular influencing forces generate one kind of a decision over another, we are able to generalize on the nature of the decision-making process and thus identify those areas of inquiry which must be probed.

Historically, explanations of human behavior appear to rest upon a matching process: People behave in ways that are calculated to satisfy their needs. In the hedonistic tradition, individuals motivated by their search for happiness try to achieve the greatest happiness with the least effort. This *pleasure-pain approach* to human action is the very foundation of the *utility-disutility concept* of orthodox economics. But since this explanation is general and denies action not in search of happiness, the *means-end* or *problem-solving* concept has become more acceptable. This approach avoids placing a value judgment on the objective and states that all action is a result of the person's attempt to solve a problem and thereby achieve certain ends. Achievement of these ends utilizes certain means. Thus, a matching of means and ends has become a convenient way of describing the motivational forces behind human action.

When the means-ends process is used to describe consumer behavior, certain additional considerations must be examined. First, the process implies rational calculation on the part of the individual consumer. Second, how may the ends that consumers are seeking and the means they select to achieve these ends be characterized?

Rational Versus Nonrational Consumer Behavior

There are two broad classifications of theory with respect to the motivation of consumer purchases. One holds that the aspect of consumer behavior under study is in some sense irrational. Members of this school do not believe that

[8] See Pierre Martineau, "Social Classes and Spending Behavior," *Journal of Marketing,* XXIII, No. 2 (October 1958), 128.

67

Customer
Choice as an
Orientation
For Market
Interpreta-
tion

buying behavior can be adequately explained on the assumption that the buyer is acting on the basis of a clear conception of ends he is seeking and means which are appropriate to these ends. The opposing school believes in the essential rationality of consumer behavior in solving individual household problems in the purchase of goods.[9]

We shall use the term *nonrational* rather than *irrational* because the second term is often used to describe those acts which are not accepted by the group to which the individual belongs. According to this definition, all acts which are acceptable to the group are rational. But this simple division is not sufficient for marketing purposes. Our decision with respect to the rationale of consumer behavior is important. We shall now examine the question and consider *rational behavior to involve the process of matching means with ends.*

Any charge that consumers have acted in a nonrational way must be based on an outsider's judgment of what constitutes a rational action and what does not. Since the individual engaged in the action is the only one truly capable of rendering such a judgment, this charge is subjective and easily open to error. The charge "nonrational" frequently arises when sensory perception provides the basis for making a particular purchase. But it is quite possible to rationalize within the sensory aspects of personality. We cannot say that purchasing a pound of coffee because of its extremely pleasant odor is a nonrational act. Neither can we label nonrational an act in which certain subconscious forces have played a part. These subconscious forces may simply influence the nature of the conscious process that takes place before a purchase is made. If an irate wife calls her husband a miser for refusing to buy her a new winter coat, she may in fact be correct. But we cannot say that the husband's subconscious leanings toward thrift make his refusal a nonrational act. His refusal may be the result of a very rational process. For instance, he may reason that her old coat is still good and that, with some remodeling, it could very well serve her for another year. His tendency to thrift is a deeper need, forcing him to reason in a certain way.

Frequently the charge of nonrational behavior is based on a consumer's own admission that he has acted in a nonrational way. Obviously, a consumer may sometimes feel that he has made a mistake, but this can usually be explained in other ways. A desirable end last week may not be so next week. Take the case of a young lady who spends a week's salary on Monday for a new evening dress to wear to the dinner-dance on Saturday. The following Monday she may seriously question the appropriateness of her ends. It was therefore impossible for her to determine the proper means at the time of purchase. Uncertainty is present in all purchases, since consumers must match anticipated ends with alternative means available to them. The problem is magnified when we recognize that there is a difference between buying and consuming; the purchaser is usually buying for others in the household as well as for himself, and so he must anticipate their ends in addition to his own, and also the capacity of a number of means to satisfy them.[10]

[9] See "Cost and Profit Outlook," VII, No. 3, March 1954. Prepared by Alderson and Sessions Associates.

[10] For a more complete explanation, see Alderson, *Marketing Behavior and Executive Action,* pp. 165–66.

68

Foundations
of
Strategy—
Interpreting
Market
Forces and
Opportunities

While some purchases are clearly means to ends, many are made without any apparent deliberation. Katona suggests making a distinction between the types of problems consumers face in the market place—those that call for real decision making, and those that are handled on a habitual, routine basis.[11] The routine type of problem-solving behavior hardly suggests the presence of rational behavior. But this criticism is countered with the argument that rational insight, having once solved the problem, is no longer necessary after a habitual, routine behavior pattern has been established.

There may be other cases in which a given purchase does not contribute significantly to the purchaser's well-being. Then the person does not trouble himself to identify the appropriate means, but follows a trial-and-error procedure. For example, a person selecting a magazine at a railroad station newsstand may reason along two or three different lines. Instead of buying one magazine, he may choose two in the hope that one will suit him. If both prove unsatisfactory, he can buy another on the train or, as a last resort, look out the window if none of the magazines prove satisfactory. A casual observer would fail to detect any sign of rational behavior as he observed this action.

Many impulse purchases appear to be devoid of any rational process. Actually, impulse purchases may be the result of habitual, routine behavior of the type described above; they may take place on a trial-and-error basis, or a rational process may occur instantaneously at the time of purchase. Another type of impulse purchase is the result of a rational process which has taken place previously. Much Christmas-gift shopping would come in this last category.

To sum up, it seems that there is no clear-cut evidence that consumer behavior is nonrational. Claims made for such behavior can just as easily be used to provide evidence for rational behavior. It is unfortunate that the terms *rational* and *nonrational* are used. From a marketing point of view, it is important to recognize that consumers engage in some kind of *deliberate process* before purchasing. It matters little whether the deliberation is extensive, based on habit, governed by the senses, or influenced strongly by subconscious forces. The chief point is that a deliberate process is involved. Of course, some consumers have more capacity for matching means with ends, and the degree of deliberation for different kinds of products varies. However, once we know that such a process exists, the appropriate task is to identify the various elements in the process.

So far we have identified the kinds of problems that confront consumers in the market place. In solving these problems, the consumer strives toward certain ends and the selection of suitable means. How might these ends and means be characterized?

The Nature of Ends and Means

The decision to spend money or to save it, the allocation of expenditures to specific products, the brands purchased, and the conditions of purchase are

---

[11] George Katona, *Psychological Analysis of Economic Behavior* (New York: McGraw-Hill Book Company, 1951), p. 49.

69

Customer
Choice as an
Orientation
For Market
Interpreta-
tion

all made with some end in mind. How might we determine the ends consumers seek? In marketing circles the idea of "image" has been given considerable attention. As a result of influencing conditions, consumers have established *self-images* which express the ends they hope to achieve by making certain choices in the market place.

The Self-image

The concept of self-image is explained in the following quotation:

> Human beings characteristically act with self-awareness, exercise self-control, exhibit conscience and guilt, and in the great crises of life make decisions with reference to some imagery of what they are, what they have been, and what they hope to be.[12]

Marketers believe that by understanding the self-image they may obtain clues to the ends consumers are seeking. For example, conspicuous consumption may be interpreted as an attempt by the consumer to achieve a certain position in the community. This position is the consumer's image of himself at some point in time. More recently the notion of inconspicuous consumption has been popularized. Conspicuous consumption, in which the consumer purchases in a manner which sets him apart from the group, is explained by the consumer's desire to achieve an image which distinguishes him from the group. With inconspicuous consumption the image the consumer wishes to achieve and the position he wishes to occupy is one of the conservative, intelligent class. The fact that these two descriptions of the images people wish to achieve are at opposite extremes is not a contradiction. It does illustrate, however, that the images consumers have are in a constant state of change and are, in part, a result of the changing cultural environment.

Perhaps the self-image is never quite realized, representing only an *aspiration level* toward which the consumer directs all his efforts. We cannot overemphasize that the term *self-image* is only a convenient way of describing the ends consumers are seeking in the market place. We do not suggest that this concept explains *why* consumers have different images. What we must recognize is that people do possess different self-images, and that these images are extremely influential in determining the kinds of choices they make in the market place.

The Product-image

From a marketing point of view the products that are offered for sale constitute the means through which the self-image may be achieved. Products, brands, and conditions of purchase are viewed through the consumer's eyes as a means of achieving the self-image. In effect, a *product-image* is created in the mind of the consumer.

The product-image is determined by the same forces that shape the self-image. The reason for forming a product-image is to assess the product as a

---

[12] A. R. Lindesmith and A. L. Strauss, *Social Psychology,* rev. ed. (New York: Holt, Rinehart & Winston, Inc., 1956), p. 413.

70

Foundations
of
Strategy—
Interpreting
Market
Forces and
Opportunities

means for achieving the self-image. The tastes in furniture of two groups of people may well vary considerably. One group may prefer bright-patterned, massive furniture, extreme in design. The forces that shape the self-images in this group construct a compatible product-image for this type of furniture. The other group may be completely repelled by this type of furniture. It in no way contributes to an achievement of the self-image, and the product-image will reflect this.

It must be understood that a product as viewed by the consumer has many dimensions, and the product-image incorporates all of them. A product generally includes a particular brand; and consumers may have a favorable product-type-image, although a given brand-image does not satisfy their self-image. This is particularly true of gift merchandise. Sears Roebuck bath towels may generate a compatible product-image for most consumers for their own use, but Cannon towels are more likely to be bought as gifts.

Another dimension is the environment in which the product is offered for sale. Sterling silverware available only in leading high-quality jewelry and department stores may shape a product-image compatible with the self-image of most buyers. If the same product is available in a less fashionable environment, at cut prices, the product-image may change enough to be incompatible with their self-images.

From the foregoing discussion it is clear that the consumer sees a product as more than an object providing a certain objective utility. In his eyes it is a means to psychological as well as material ends. He looks beyond the immediate utility of the product, forms an image of the product, and intuitively if not consciously compares this image with his desired self-image. An automobile provides objective utility—transportation—but it is more than this; it is a means of achieving ends which are determined by the buyer's desired self-image. The reputation of the brand (the brand-image), the purchase environment, and even assurances in the use of the product, all contribute to the product-image—the psychological utility of the product or brand.

An explanation of the motivation underlying the matching of product-image and self-image is found in *self-enhancement*. Grubb and Grathwohl describe the process as follows: [13]

> In Figure 5-1 two types of self-enhancement are diagrammed. In this diagram individual A purchases symbol X. In doing so he is transferring the socially attributed meanings of symbol X to himself. The purchase and use of symbol X enhances his desired self-image. He also presents symbol X to audience B with which individual A wishes to identify. Individual A believes that audience B attributes certain meaning to symbol X and hopes that this meaning will be transferred to individual A by audience B, thus providing another source of self-enhancement.

Marketing effort is most powerful when the market offering is perceived as advancing the consumer toward his desired self-image. If the product-image

[13] Edward L. Grubb and Harrison L. Grathwohl, "Consumer Self-Concept, Symbolism and Market Behavior: A Theoretical Approach," *Journal of Marketing*, XXXI, No. 4, Part 1 (October 1967), 25.

71

Customer
Choice as an
Orientation
For Market
Interpreta-
tion

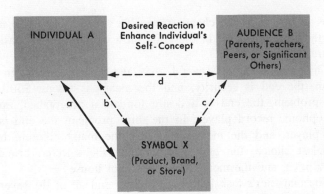

FIGURE 5-1
Relationship of the
Consumption of
Goods as Symbols
to the Self-Concept.

Source: Edward L. Grubb and Harrison L. Grathwohl,
"Consumer Self-Concept, Symbolism and Market Behavior: A
Theoretical Approach," Journal of Marketing, XXXI, No. 4, Part 1
(October 1967), 25.

is in conflict with the self-image, no action is likely to occur. Viewed in this
context, the seller is dealing with several different markets. Any useful grouping
of markets must reflect the differences in the self-images of those making up
the markets. Success can only be maximized if the offering creates a product-
image compatible with the self-images of the different segments of the market.
In all likelihood there will be no sale if the product-image is not compatible
with the self-image. A marketing manager aware of these psychological factors
will have a much better chance of directing his strategy toward satisfying the
consumer's self-image.

The Multiplicity of Ends and Means

Not only must the marketer consider that different segments of the market
have different self-images, but also that both the ends and the means are
different for each consumer choice problem. For example, consider the case
of a young couple deciding what to do with a $500 Christmas bonus. Their
first choice is to put the money in a savings account, since both have always
desired some financial reserve in case of an emergency. The dominant end here
is a desire for security, which may be related to a self-image of a responsible
citizen with the foresight to provide for emergencies. This choice—to save
money—may be in sharp conflict with another end, the couple's desire to
purchase a stereophonic record player to use at their house party on New
Year's Eve. This end is related to the self-image of a socially gifted hostess
known for successful parties.

But perhaps they can realize both ends. They could purchase a $300
record player and save $200. In shopping for the stereo, however, they learn that
only the lower-quality makes are available for $300, and that in tone these
cannot measure up to the better sets. After comparing many brands, the couple
prefers a $600 XYZ. This is unquestionably the best set. Having decided on
an XYZ, the search for a source of supply begins. The end in mind at this

72

Foundations
of
Strategy—
Interpreting
Market
Forces and
Opportunities

point is to buy from the cheapest possible source. They find a discount house where they can buy a set in the crate on a cash-and-carry basis for $480, and the purchase is made.

This case illustrates several ends and several means. In the first choice problem, the end is security, and the means is saving $500. In the second choice problem, the end is a desire for social acceptance, and the means is a stereophonic record player. In the third problem, the end is a stereophonic record player, and the means is one of the many different brands available. In the last choice, the end is purchasing the selected brand at the lowest possible price, and the means is the discount house.

The marketer's task is to cater to any and all of the several ends through providing market offerings in which the perceived images are compatible with the desired self-images.

This discussion should not leave the impression that marketing is an entirely passive process; that is, that marketers should restrict their efforts to seeking out consumers' self-images, adjust their products to them, and in this way insure success. If this were possible there would be little occasion for failure, but two circumstances prevent such a neat solution. First, at this time we do not have the means to precisely delineate the different self-images composing the market. We do recognize the presence of differences and undertake by various means to arrive at offerings that will hopefully precipitate purchase. Second, this solution assumes that marketing can do nothing about conditioning the consumer with respect to both the self-image he creates for himself and the product-image he envisions. Through time, and with the appropriate marketing effort, society can be conditioned to the point where various images and attitudes are restructured as related to market behavior.

Nor do we wish to imply that all consumer purchases are based upon matching self-image with product-image. Many products, such as light bulbs and spark plugs, are purchased solely for their functional value with little thought of the way in which they contribute to one's self-image. On the other hand, it is not these products that are troublesome to the marketer. However, we do believe that the matching of self-image with product-image does provide a conceptual framework for the study of consumer decision making in regard to a wide array of products offered in the market place.

A FRAMEWORK FOR
MARKET INVESTIGATION

From the foregoing we may conclude that the key element in market investigation is identifying the ends consumers have. Once self-images are pinpointed for each of the decisions consumers make in the market place, it is necessary to determine how consumers react to the different means by which they can gain the ends. A product-image will reflect the product, the brand, and the condition under which it may be purchased. If the product-image is perceived in such a way that purchase will allow the consumer to achieve his desired self-image, purchase is likely to follow. This behavioral pattern is shown in Figure 5-2.

73

Customer
Choice as an
Orientation
For Market
Interpreta-
tion

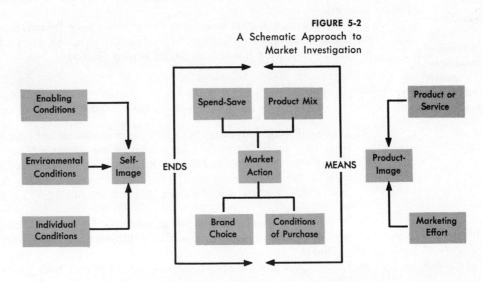

FIGURE 5-2
A Schematic Approach to
Market Investigation

To examine markets intelligently, then, it is necessary to examine the influencing conditions and determine how they affect consumer choice through shaping self-images and product-images.

Summary

Sound market planning requires answers to several questions: *What* will the market purchase? *How much* will the market purchase? *Under what conditions* will the market purchase? Since the answers to these questions are dependent upon consumer behavior in the market place, they can only be secured through an understanding of the way in which consumers act. Consumers are faced with four choice problems in the market place: (1) deciding how much to spend and how much to save (*the spend-save problem*); (2) deciding which products and services to buy (*the product-mix problem*); (3) deciding on the specific sources from which to purchase (*the brand-choice problem*); and (4) deciding on the conditions of purchase. Solutions to these market choice problems are determined by three sets of influencing forces: (1) enabling conditions, such as income, assets, and access to credit; (2) environmental conditions, such as age, mobility, social class, and stage in the family life cycle; and (3) individual attitudes and opinions.

These influencing forces are responsible for the development of ends consumers wish to achieve, ends which are expressed in the desired self-images consumers hold of themselves. As the consumer approaches the market place in a rational problem-solving setting, he perceives products as a means of achieving his ends. In effect, the product and the marketing effort related to it induce a perceived image of the market offering by the consumer. Theoretically, if the consumer feels there is a compatibility between this image and his desired self-image, purchase will take place. This is a matching process, since means and

74

Foundations
of
Strategy—
Interpreting
Market
Forces and
Opportunities

ends are matched through seeking compatibility between product-image and self-image.

Any approach to market investigation must center upon the influencing forces for different sectors of the market. Once these are identified, every effort must be made to provide a totally harmonious market offering.

Questions and Problems

1. In programming marketing effort, how can management use information on what, how much, and under what conditions the market will purchase?
2. Describe the nature and intensity of the problems consumers face in buying each of the following products: (a) a weekly magazine, (b) a new refrigerator, (c) a new suit of clothes, (d) a diamond ring, (e) a new automobile.
3. In what way does the difference in problems faced by the consumer in purchasing the products in Question 2 influence the marketing of these products?
4. Describe the product-mix problem of a local retailer with whom you are familiar.
5. Give examples of changes in consumer habits regarding the conditions under which they are willing to purchase. Have these changes in any way influenced marketing of the goods involved?
6. Why has it been so difficult to identify the conditions that influence consumer choice in the market place?
7. Name at least two products, the purchase of which would be influenced by stage in the family life cycle and social class of the consuming unit. Discuss the way in which these environmental conditions will influence purchase.
8. In attempting to understand consumer behavior for marketing purposes it has been said that "it is only necessary to work at immediate levels of causation." Explain this statement.
9. Think of several choices you have made in the market place in the last two days and label them as rational or nonrational.
10. What is the difference between a deliberative process and a nonrational process in making choices in the market place?
11. How does the ends-means approach aid in understanding the way in which consumers make decisions in the market place?
12. Select four brands of a single product and examine the advertising of each. Are there differences in the product-images the advertisers are trying to create? If differences are observed, characterize the desired self-image of the purchaser with which each might be compatible.
13. Explain in detail the role of consumer ends in investigating markets.
14. What are the basic purposes of analyzing and interpreting markets?
15. How is quantitative information used in the management of the firm? How is qualitative information used?

Consumer Markets I: Quantitative Aspects

The initial step in investigating markets is to delineate quantitatively the market under consideration. This is done for two reasons. First, to determine market feasibility, we need information on the size of the market, and whether it is large enough to permit profitable operations. Further, we need answers to such questions as: What production facilities are needed? What inventory levels are necessary? How many distributors and dealers are needed to reach the market? Second, quantitative identification of the market is necessary before qualitative investigations can be made. Until the market is determined quantitatively it is impossible to ascertain the type of marketing effort necessary to reach the previously ascertained volume. Such qualitative considerations as "product-image," price, and packaging and advertising appeals logically follow after quantitative market delineation has identified potential purchasers.

The overall task, then, is to obtain some idea of the quantities that may be sold, and to determine the identifying characteristics of the consuming units. In this chapter we will examine the methods employed in analyzing influencing conditions and their effect on the first two consumer choice problems, *the spend-save problem* and *the product-mix problem.*

Although there are many different types of market investigation, we shall limit our consideration to three: (1) the historical method, (2) the survey method, and (3) the buildup method. Since the historical method is used most frequently, we shall devote major attention to it.

THE HISTORICAL METHOD

The historical method relies on past events as a guide to future market behavior. The past events of particular interest to the marketer are those related to income—an

76

Foundations
of
Strategy—
Interpreting
Market
Forces and
Opportunities

enabling condition—and its influence on the spend-save and product-mix problems. The information used in historical studies is confined to already collected and published data, sometimes known as secondary data, and to internal company records. We shall examine the use and limitations of both types of data.

Analysis Using Secondary Data

The *Life Study of Consumer Expenditures* [1] provides the kind of information that is helpful in estimating the quantities of a product that will be purchased in a future period. In this study the purchases made by more than 10,000 households are related in detail to different characteristics of those households. The eight product categories analyzed are: (1) food, beverages, and tobacco; (2) clothing and accessories; (3) medical and personal care; (4) home operation and improvement; (5) home furnishings and equipment; (6) recreation and recreation equipment; (7) automotive; and (8) other goods and services. The seven household characteristics analyzed are: (1) household income; (2) age of household head; (3) occupation of household head; (4) education of household head; (5) stage of household in the life cycle; (6) geographic location; and (7) market location. In 1965 the National Industrial Conference Board published a report updating the original study done by *Life*.[2] This study used data collected by the Bureau of Labor Statistics in 1961 and 1962 and was once again sponsored by *Life*. At the date of writing this is perhaps the most recent and comprehensive study of consumer expenditures available.

How might this kind of data be used to characterize the total market opportunity for different products? The usual approach has been to analyze the influence of past enabling conditions. What has been the effect of different levels of income on the amounts households spend for various kinds of products? Figure 6-1 shows the level of spending at different levels of income, and Table 6-1 the allocation of expenditures to different product categories. From Table 6-1 we see that, with the exception of food, beverages, and tobacco, the proportion of expenditures allocated to different categories of products remains substantially the same in households of different income levels. Consequently, size of income does not seem to influence the allocation of spendable income; higher-income families merely consume more of the same categories of products consumed by lower-income groups. But although this is true for the broad product categories shown in Table 6-1, it may not be true for the different kinds of products within each of these categories.

For example, the higher income household, as might be expected, allocates a larger proportion of its recreation spending to sporting goods than does the lower income household. The practicing marketer cannot rely on broad statistical classification of products; rather, he must relate specific income groups to purchase of his particular product.

[1] *Life Study of Consumer Expenditures,* I (New York: Time, Inc., 1957), 12.
[2] Fabin Linden, ed., *Expenditure Patterns of the American Family* (New York: National Industrial Conference Board, 1965).

TABLE 6-1

Expenditures for Goods and Services
by Annual Household Income (in percentage)

Annual Household Income

	All House-holds	Under $2,000	$2,000–$2,999	$3,000–$3,999	$4,000–$4,999	$5,000–$6,999	$7,000–$9,999	$10,000 or More
Total	100%	100%	100%	100%	100%	100%	100%	100%
Food, beverages, and tobacco	29	36	33	30	29	28	26	24
Clothing and accessories	12	11	11	13	12	11	13	14
Medical and personal care	5	7	5	6	5	5	5	6
Home operation and improvement	19	17	20	18	19	19	18	18
Home furnishings and equipment	9	7	8	8	8	9	9	10
Recreation and recreation equipment	5	5	5	5	6	5	5	6
Automotive	14	11	13	15	14	16	15	15
Other goods and services	7	6	5	6	7	7	9	7

TABLE 6-2

Expenditures for Recreation and Recreation Equipment
by Annual Household Income (in percentage)

Annual Household Income

	All House-holds	Under $2,000	$2,000–$2,999	$3,000–$3,999	$4,000–$4,999	$5,000–$6,999	$7,000–$9,999	$10,000 or More
Recreation & Recreation Equipment—Total	100	100	100	100	100	100	100	100
Games, toys	9	5	8	9	12	9	9	9
Pet foods	3	3	2	3	3	4	3	3
Photographic equipment	5	1	4	5	4	5	8	6
Radios, TV sets, phonographs	20	22	28	28	19	18	14	12
Spectator fees	13	14	14	13	14	12	14	12
Sports goods, equipment	7	3	4	3	8	6	11	15
Other recreation and equipment	43	52	40	39	40	46	41	43

Courtesy of Time, Inc. Copyright 1957.

For estimating purposes, the relationship existing between income level and actual purchases made must be extended to include probable future income levels. Economic forecasts which include estimates of future income are con-

78

Foundations
of
Strategy—
Interpreting
Market
Forces and
Opportunities

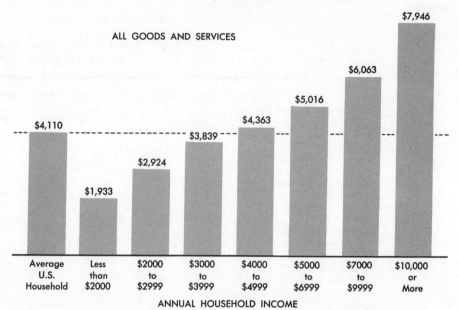

ALL GOODS AND SERVICES

ANNUAL HOUSEHOLD INCOME

ducted periodically by the government and by a number of private and quasi-public institutions.

Since detailed income data are gathered only once every ten years, at the time the census is taken, the marketer must be able to estimate income for the intervening years. There are several sources from which he can secure information on income levels in his particular marketing sector.[3]

Although estimates of income for the entire country are useful for the company covering national markets, estimated income for smaller geographic units is more useful to most companies, which do not operate in national markets. And even the national marketer must consider the variations in income in different sectors of the market, because these variations will undoubtedly influence the quantities of different products purchased in different regions.

The principles involved in the historical method are simple, but because the method must ordinarily be adapted to fit a specific situation, it is appropriate for us to look at it in more detail.

[3] The Bureau of the Census continually makes various sample surveys, estimates, and special studies, the results of which are published in many monthly, annual, or special reports. The marketer may become familiar with these by studying the Bureau's quarterly *Subject Guide*. In addition, there are many guides to marketing statistics, such as *Market Research Sources,* published by the Dept. of Commerce, and *Distribution Data Guide,* published monthly by the Office of Distribution, U.S. Dept. of Commerce.

Determining the Market for Photographic Equipment

Suppose that we are interested in the national market for photographic equipment. Working from broad general categories to the specific, we must deal with the recreation and recreation equipment category of spending. According to Table 6-1, 5 percent of the total expenditures were allocated to recreation and recreation equipment. Table 6-2, which is a finer breakdown of the category, shows that of the total spent on recreation and recreation equipment, 5 percent was spent on photographic equipment. Table 6-3 shows that of the total spent on photographic equipment, 2 percent was spent by families with incomes under $2,000, 8 percent by those in the $2,000–$2,999 range, and so on. When estimates of income are available, the various percentages may be applied to them, and total expenditures can be predicted.

Thus, the market is identified. A prediction can be made concerning the estimated quantity of photographic equipment the market will absorb, and concerning the distribution of that quantity to households of different income levels.

To further refine our analysis of the photographic equipment market, we can look at Tables 6-4 through 6-6, which show how environmental conditions such as educational level, occupation of the household head, and geographic location of the household influence buyer behavior.

Education of Household Head

In Table 6-4 we see that, of the total spent on photographic equipment, 13 percent was expended by households in which the head had finished grade school, whereas 29 percent was spent by households whose head had finished high school. You might wonder if the "finished high school" group is numerically larger, thus accounting for the difference. But since the data are based on 10,170,000 households in the "finished grade school" category and 10,860,000 in the "finished high school" category, we can only conclude that education has a definite bearing on the purchase of photographic equipment. The reason for the difference in consumption pattern is not of immediate concern to us.

Occupation of Household Head

Table 6-5 shows that of the total spent on photographic equipment, 21 percent is by households in which the head is in the "craftsman-foreman" group, and 16 percent in the "operative" group. Again, the size of the group does not explain the difference. There are 8,240,000 households in the craftsman-foreman group and 10,210,000 in the operative group. Although there are nearly 25 percent fewer people in the craftsman-foreman class, they purchased more than 50 percent more photographic equipment. Analyses similar to those in Tables 6-4 and 6-5 may be made on the basis of age of the household head and stage in the family life cycle, the results of which are summarized in Table 6-7.

There are a number of interrelationships among these different data. For instance, educational level is reflected in the occupational category, and both

80

Foundations
of
Strategy—
Interpreting
Market
Forces and
Opportunities

TABLE 6-3

Expenditures for Recreation and Recreation Equipment
by Annual Household Income (in percentage)

	All House- holds	Annual Household Income						
		Under $2,000	$2,000– $2,999	$3,000– $3,999	$4,000– $4,999	$5,000– $6,999	$7,000– $9,999	$10,000 or More
Percent of U.S. house-holds	100%	18	14	15	19	20	9	5
Recreation & Recreation Equipment— Total	100%	8	9	14	20	24	14	11
Games, toys	100%	4	8	14	26	23	14	11
Pet foods	100%	7	7	13	19	26	16	12
Photographic equipment	100%	2	8	14	17	22	24	13
Radios, TV sets, phonographs	100%	9	13	19	20	22	10	7
Spectator fees	100%	9	9	13	22	22	14	11
Sports goods, equipment	100%	3	5	6	22	20	22	22
Other recreation and equipment	100%	10	9	12	19	25	14	11

TABLE 6-4

Expenditures for Recreation and Recreation Equipment
by Education of Household Head (in percentage)

	All Households	Level of Education Attained by Household Head				
		Grade School or Less	Some Grade School	Finished Grade School	Attended High School	Finished High School
Percent of U.S. households	100%	19	21	18	22	20
Recreation & Recreation Equipment—Total	100%	13	16	18	25	28
Games, toys	100%	7	18	19	28	28
Pet foods	100%	13	17	17	27	26
Photographic equipment	100%	8	13	18	29	32
Radios, TV sets, phonographs	100%	16	18	19	23	24
Spectator fees	100%	13	19	18	23	27
Sport goods, equipment	100%	12	18	12	42	24
Other recreation & equipment	100%	13	15	18	23	31

Courtesy of Time, Inc. Copyright 1957.

education and occupation may be reflected in the income category. Nevertheless, markets must be delineated on a number of bases, some of which may overlap. It is true that income levels reflect educational levels, but the relationship between the two is not precise enough to use income level as the only way of describing the market. If we are to determine the best advertising appeals to influence potential buyers, it is more useful to describe the market in terms of both income and educational levels.

Geographic Location

Another important identifying characteristic is the location of various groups of buyers. It is important both from the point of view of the physical movement of goods and the kind of marketing effort to be employed in each of these markets. Variations will exist in the number of purchasers in different locations. Table 6-6 shows that of the total expenditures on photographic equipment, 28 percent was in the northeast region, 24 percent of this total in metropolitan markets and 4 percent in non-metropolitan markets. The southern regions account for 14 percent, of which 7 percent of this total is in metropolitan markets and 7 percent in non-metropolitan markets. It is much more costly to move products and to contact customers in non-metropolitan areas than in metropolitan areas. Likewise, the kind of effort needed to sell to nonmetropolitan markets is different from that needed in metropolitan markets. Cross-tabulation of the data in Table 6-6 with that in some of the other tables might yield information that would be significant for tailoring market effort to fit consumer needs in each of the different locations.

Conclusion

We may now ask: "What do we know about the market for photographic equipment?" The logic of the historical method—breaking down the market according to certain identifying characteristics—is apparent in Table 6-7. Notice that the data in Table 6-7 go beyond mere quantitative expression of the market and provide information on its more subjective characteristics. For example, there is a difference in the consumption of photographic equipment between households in which the head finished high school and those in which the head finished grade school. There is also a difference in the consumption of the same product between different occupational groups. These differences will influence the facilities needed to make goods available to the purchaser—the kinds of outlets that can most satisfactorily handle the product for different kinds of purchasers, the kinds of appeals made in all communications to the different types of buyers, and the organization and manpower requirement necessary to reach the market. The procedure provides reasonable quantitative delineation of the market, and much planning for marketing action can be based on it.

Analysis Using Internal Company Records

Internal company records can be used to delineate markets. The simplest method is to correlate past sales data with past income. Once a relationship is established, sales estimates may be derived from estimation of future income. More detailed information may be derived from an analysis of past sales by the type of customer, location, and other related factors. Records such as accounts receivable records, salesmen's orders, warranty cards returned, or delivery slips may also be used.

TABLE 6-5

Expenditures for Recreation and Recreation Equipment by Occupation of Household Head (in percentage)

	All Households	Occupation of Household Head							
		Professional, Semi-professional	Proprietor, Manager, Official	Clerical, Sales	Craftsman, Foreman	Operative	Service Worker	Farmer, Farm Laborer	Retired or Head Not Employed
Percent of U.S. households	100%	8	10	11	17	21	6	9	18
Recreation & Recreation Equipment—Total	100%	13	12	13	20	20	4	7	11
Games, toys	100%	14	11	13	18	27	3	6	8
Pet foods	100%	10	13	17	21	19	5	5	10
Photographic equipment	100%	13	17	16	21	16	3	5	9
Radios, TV sets, phonographs	100%	9	9	13	20	25	6	9	9
Spectator fees	100%	11	13	16	22	19	5	5	9
Sports goods, equipment	100%	38	8	9	22	13	2	3	5
Other recreation & equipment	100%	12	12	14	19	18	4	8	13

TABLE 6-6

Expenditures for Recreation and Recreation Equipment by Geographic Location (in percentage)

	All Households	Northeast Region		Geographic Location of Household Central Region		Southern Region		Western Region	
		Metro-politan Markets	Nonmetro. Areas	Metro-politan Markets	Nonmetro. Areas	Metro-politan Markets	Nonmetro. Areas	Metro-politan Markets	Nonmetro. Areas
Percent of U.S. households	100%	21	5	18	13	11	18	9	5
Recreation & Recreation Equipment—Total	100%	25	5	20	11	10	12	12	5
Games, toys	100%	30	5	19	10	10	10	12	4
Pet foods	100%	25	7	17	11	12	9	13	6
Photographic equipment	100%	24	4	24	10	7	7	18	6
Radios, TV sets, phonographs	100%	20	5	17	12	11	21	10	4
Spectator fees	100%	30	3	20	10	10	12	11	4
Sports goods, equipment	100%	27	5	28	9	7	7	13	4
Other recreation & equipment	100%	24	5	21	11	10	11	13	5

Courtesy of Time, Inc. Copyright 1957.

84

Foundations
of
Strategy—
Interpreting
Market
Forces and
Opportunities

TABLE 6-7

Market for Photographic Equipment. Based on
Buyer Characteristics (in percentage) *

Income	Total Market	Occupation of Household Head	Total Market
Under $2,000	2	Professional, semiprofessional	13
$2,000–$2,999	8	Proprietor, manager, official	17
$3,000–$3,999	14	Clerical, sales	16
$4,000–$4,999	17	Craftsman, foreman	21
$5,000–$6,999	22	Operative	16
$7,000–$9,999	24	Service worker	3
$10,000 and up	13	Farmer, farm laborers	5
		Retired, unemployed	9

Geographic Location	Total Market	Age	Total Market
Northeast region			
Metropolitan markets	24	Under 30 years	20
Nonmetro. area	4	30–39 years	28
Central region		40–49 years	23
Metropolitan markets	24	50–64 years	22
Nonmetro. area	10	65 years and up	7
Southern region			
Metropolitan markets	7		
Nonmetro. area	7		
Western region		Stage in Family Life Cycle	Total Market
Metropolitan markets	18		
Nonmetro. area	6		

Education of Household Head	Total Market	Stage in Family Life Cycle	Total Market
		No children and head under 40	13
		Younger children	47
		Older children only	16
Grade school or less	8	No children and head over 40	
Finished grade school	13	Married head	20
Attended high school	18	Single head	4
Finished high school	29		
Some college or up	32		

* Five percent of total annual household expenditures will be spent for recreation and recreation equipment; 5 percent of recreation and recreation equipment expenditures will be spent for photographic equipment.

Courtesy of Time, Inc. Copyright 1957.

For example, a manufacturer of farm tractors found through an analysis of past sales that his firm was selling an increasingly large number of units to nonfarm buyers for nonfarm purposes—to factories, mines, airports, and municipalities. By analyzing these nonfarm buyers more closely, management was able to classify them according to ten different types of business. Further analysis identified the number of buyers in each type of business according to geographic location.

The need for market delineation is not limited to large firms. It is equally important for the small firm, and its cost is not beyond the small firm's means. An example in the retail field will illustrate the case.

A suburban drugstore on the outskirts of a city of about 150,000 people has been in operation for nine months. Monthly sales volume is approximately $54,000. The owner has established a goal of a 30 percent increase in sales volume over the next two years. Two questions confront him: First, is the location such that he can expect a 30 percent increase? Second, what are the characteristics of potential customers of the store and how may they best be influenced? Some knowledge of the store's potential market is necessary to answer both of these questions. From records kept of prescription customers, the owner found that 70 percent of prescription sales were to people living within a three-block radius of the store. Working on the premise that prescription sales, the most profitable part of the business, are usually made to those customers who also buy the more frequently purchased drugstore items in the same location, he designated this three-block radius as his "primary trading area." Similar primary trading areas were identified for seven competitors. This left another section, designated a "secondary trading area," lying to the west of the store's location. Within the primary and secondary trading areas there are 2,200 households. From the *Standard Rate and Data Services,* the drugstore owner found the average expenditure by household per year in drugstores to be $139.34. Multiplying the $139.34 by 2,200 households suggests a potential market of $306,504, an estimated potential volume large enough to achieve the sales volume goal.

The answer to the druggist's second question, which concerned the identifying characteristics of consumers, was simplified because of the relatively small number of customers and the owner's constant contact with them. As he was personally acquainted with many people in the area, he began to identify formally the characteristics of the potential customers in the area and to tailor a marketing plan to influence them to trade at his store rather than at his competitors'.

Limitations of the Historical Method

The historical method is concerned with only two consumer choice problems: the spend-save problem, and the product-mix problem. We have made no analysis of influencing conditions but rather have examined the results. The data show how consumers have solved their problems under the influence of the enabling environmental and individual conditions of a given period of time. When data on how consumers spend and save, and how they allocate expenditures to different products, is analyzed, we know that these data reflect behavior in the past. When the data are used for prediction, we assume that the past pattern will be continued into the future. But although it is true that, for some classes of products, buyers cannot change their purchase patterns radically in a short period of time, it is also true that buying patterns for certain other products are extremely sensitive to changes in income.

In spite of this limitation in projecting historical relationships for prediction

86

Foundations
of
Strategy—
Interpreting
Market
Forces and
Opportunities

purposes, the historical approach is still widely used. However, many adjustments should be made in these historical projections, and the marketer using this method should be aware of the kinds of adjustments that might be made.

Other Considerations in Using the Historical Approach

Relating Income to Spending and Saving

For many years economists believed that there was a constant relationship between consumption and income. That is, that at any given level of income, consumers will spend a certain percentage—let us say, 94 percent of their income—and save the remaining 6 percent. As income rises or falls, spending will rise or fall proportionately, the proportion remaining unchanged. The rate of consumption accompanying income levels is known as the *consumption function.* Since income can only be disposed of in two ways, spending or saving, the complement of the consumption function is known as the *saving function.* Stability was inferred because the relationship between consumption and income and saving and income did not change over a long period of time. These functions were known as *stable functions.*

Closer analysis, however, indicated variations in the consumption function. When the time variable is introduced—that is, when shorter periods of time are observed—considerable variation is found. These differences were first observed by Duesenberry and are summarized in Figure 6-2.[4] As described by

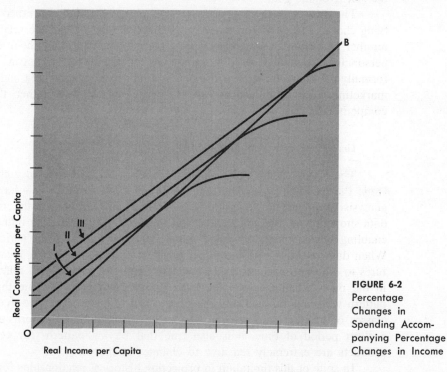

FIGURE 6-2
Percentage
Changes in
Spending Accom-
panying Percentage
Changes in Income

[4] James S. Duesenberry, *Income Saving and Theory of Consumer Behavior* (Cambridge: Harvard University Press, 1952), p. 114.

Duesenberry, the line *OB* is a long-run consumption function. Since it is a straight line, it indicates stability in the relationship between income and consumption. Curves I, II, and III are short-run functions accompanying cyclical fluctuations during the period studied. Since they are of different slope than the line *OB,* the percentage change in spending accompanied by a percentage change in income differs for each period. Also, as higher income levels are reached, there is a flattening out of the short-run curves of relationship and there is a change in the proportion used for consumption.

Another example of the way short-run income fluctuations affect consumption is shown in Figure 6-3. This figure shows the proportionate change in personal consumption expenditures accompanying proportionate changes in gross national product during the three short recessions that followed World War II. The differences observed in Figure 6-3 appear large because gross national product is used rather than personal disposable income.

The specific data relating to Figure 6-3 are as follows. During the early part of 1958 a reduction of approximately $23 billion in the gross national product (GNP) was accompanied by an approximately $6.5 billion decrease in consumption. In the 1953-54 and the 1948-49 recessions, consumption expenditures actually increased slightly in spite of a reduced GNP. During the recovery periods, the increases in consumption expenditures lagged considerably behind the increase in the GNP. During the very modest recession of 1961-62 the changes in consumption expenditures and GNP were negligible. Since 1962 the country has experienced the longest period of prosperity and growth in its history. Yet there are variations in the relationship between consumer expenditures and GNP. In 1965 a 7½ percent increase over 1964 was accompanied by a 5 percent increase in personal consumption expenditures.[5] Therefore, in the short run a change in income is not accompanied by a proportionate change in consumption. Consequently, historical distributions of expenditures do not necessarily follow the same pattern as income changes.

We should point out that a very small change in personal consumption expenditures, which may appear insignificant to the analyst examining consumption behavior over a wide span of time, possesses true significance to a businessman. Even a 1 percent change at present levels of disposable income represents a sizable change in the total market for a single product.

Consumption function analysis, rather than explaining a phenomenon, describes a result. When researchers recognized that, in the short run, the consumption function is not stable, they undertook additional research to determine the cause. A major criticism of past analysis was that it treated the disposal of earned income as a purely mechanical process. Actually, much spending is permissive, and is affected by the stage in the life cycle, age, occupation, and income level. To aid in analyses of the consumption function, income and consumption were classified by geographic area and by various personal characteristics of the consuming unit. That is, variations were sought for families at different income levels, in different stages of the life cycle, in different educational and occupational categories, and in different parts of the country. It was hoped that this kind of analysis might give an explanation of

[5] "National Income and Product in 1965," *Survey of Current Business* (January 1966), pp. 3–12.

Foundations
of
Strategy—
Interpreting
Market
Forces and
Opportunities

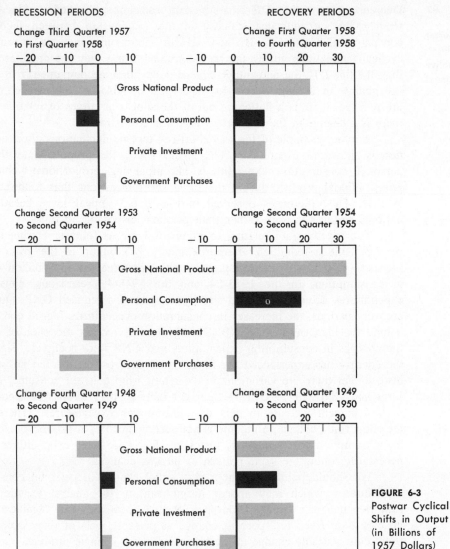

FIGURE 6-3
Postwar Cyclical
Shifts in Output
(in Billions of
1957 Dollars)

why consumption changes disproportionately to changes in income. Most available studies are what are known as *cross-section analyses;* that is, they describe consumer behavior for specific groups of customers, for specific classes of products, for a single year. Cross-section analyses, although useful, are inadequate because they fail to establish the relationship between consumption and income over a long enough period of time.

A very substantial amount of research will be needed in order for us to learn how different types of families dispose of their income over extended periods of time.

Despite the limitations of available studies, two categories of cross-section analysis are of special interest. Analysis of consumption of families of different income and at different stages in the life cycle for a single year may be used instead of time series of the same consuming units. They are adequate because income does not change instantaneously, but rather over a long period of time. Likewise, families move through a life cycle. If families at different income levels and stages of the life cycle behave differently as income groupings change and the composition of the family units change, the aggregate consumption function can be expected to change. Figure 6-4 illustrates the variation in

FIGURE 6-4

Average Annual Expenditures on Cars and Large Household
Items, by Income and Stage in the Life Cycle, 1947–50

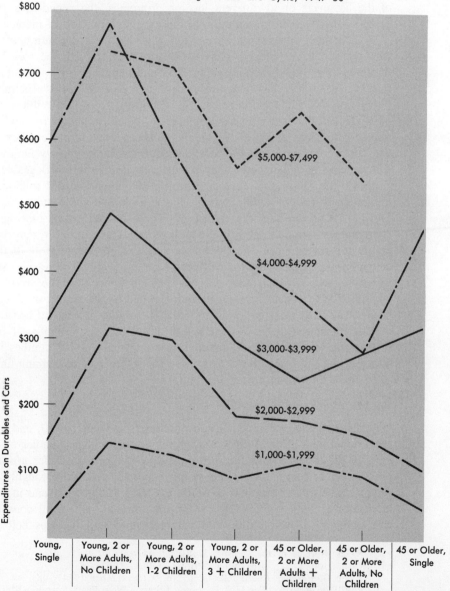

Source: John B. Lansing and James N. Morgan, "Consumer Finances Over the Life Cycle," in Consumer Behavior, *Lincoln H. Clark, ed. (New York University Press, 1955), p. 45. Reprinted by permission of New York University Press.*

90

Foundations
of
Strategy—
Interpreting
Market
Forces and
Opportunities

consumption patterns in consumer durables by consuming units in different income brackets and at different stages in the life cycle.

Population Shifts and Spending

The work of the demographer—the statistical study of populations—may have considerable bearing on analysis of the spend-save problem and the product-mix problem. Changes in population and the makeup of population, as well as changes in the rate of new family formations, can be tied into this kind of analysis. If there is an increase in the number of families in different stages of the life cycle or in different income groupings, the spend-save pattern will change as well as the distribution of the expended portion of income.

A number of changes have taken place in the composition of population over the last twenty years. The post-World War II birth rate reached a peak of about 4.3 million births a year in 1957 and remained on a plateau until 1960; it subsided sharply to about 3.6 million per year in 1966.[6] Estimates of the population in 1970 have been revised downward from 208 million to 203 million.[7] This downward revision is related to recent annual births and in no way reduces the large group of individuals entering the market as they move into the labor force. In fact, it can be expected that the rate of new family formation will increase as larger and larger groups move into the marriageable age class. In 1967, the number of persons reaching 18 jumped to 3.7 million, from 2.8 million in 1964. In 1968 there was a considerable percentage increase over 1967 in those reaching the age of 21. These people are of marriageable and, consequently, household formation age. Any fluctuation in the rate of new family formation automatically causes a nonproportionate shift in the number of consuming units in different stages of the life cycle. Today, for example, the group of families with young children is much larger than the group with older children. Ten years from now, the relative density of these two categories may be reversed. The point we want to make is that the number of consuming units in different stages of the life cycle is in a constant state of flux. If from cross-section analyses we observe different spending patterns for families in different stages of the life cycle, then a change in the number of consuming units in each stage could affect consumption habits.

Income Changes and Spending

Table 6-8 compares family income levels in 1950, 1960, and 1965. With the gradual upgrading of income in the United States, the number of consuming units in the lower end of the income scale has become smaller *absolutely,* and the number in every other category has expanded. In 1950, roughly three consuming units out of five had incomes less than $5,000 and one in five had an income of $7,000 or more. By 1965 approximately half of all consuming units had incomes of over $7,000 and only one-third had incomes below $5,000.[8]

---

[6] U.S. Bureau of the Census, *Statistical Abstract of the United States: 1967,* 88th ed. (Washington, D.C.: Government Printing Office, 1967), p. 6.

[7] *The Conference Board Record,* I, No. 9 (September 1964), 48.

[8] William Bowen, "The U.S. Economy Enters a New Era," *Fortune* (March 1967).

TABLE 6-8

Percentage and Numerical Distribution of Consuming Units
by Income Levels in Constant (1965) Dollars *

Family Personal Income	1950 Percentage of Distribution	1950 Number of Consumer Units (in Millions)	1960 Percentage of Distribution	1960 Number of Consumer Units (in Millions)	1965 Percentage of Distribution	1965 Number of Consumer Units (in Millions)
Under $3,000	30	14.6	20	11.3	17	10.2
$3,000–$4,999	30	14.6	19	10.7	16	9.6
$5,000–$6,999	20	9.7	22	12.4	18	10.8
$7,000–$9,999	13	6.3	21	11.8	24	14.4
$10,000 and over	7	3.4	18	10.2	25	15.0
Total	100	48.6	100	56.4	100	60.0

* Compiled from data available in William Bowen "The U.S. Economy Enters a New Era," *Fortune* (March 1967), and U.S. Bureau of the Census, *Statistical Abstract of the United States: 1966*. 87th ed. (Washington, D.C.: Government Printing Office, 1966).

By 1975 it is estimated that 50 percent of all consumer units will have an income of over $10,000, and they will command 70 percent of all personal income after taxes.[9]

Average income after taxes in current dollars increased by 83 percent from $4,216 per family in 1950 to $7,729 in 1965. In 1967 the $10,000-and-over group had an average income of $15,000.[10]

If different income groupings have different spending habits, then the movement to new income categories will affect the total consumption function and the products that are purchased.[11]

Shifts in population or changes in the number of consuming units in different income categories do not occur overnight. But we may be aware of these changes without fully realizing their significance from a business point of view.

Figure 6-5 shows a projection of population count by age groups for 1970. The greatest increase over the 1960 count is in the 20–24 age group. Absolutely the increase in this age group is about 6 million people. The increase is also impressive in the 15–19 age group and amounts to about 5 million people. The decline in the 30–39 age group will amount to about 2 million. These data are useful to the automobile industry when related to new and used car buying rates

[9] Lawrence A. Mayer, "The Diverse $10,000-and-over Masses," *Fortune* (December 1967).

[10] Mayer, "Diverse $10,000-and-over," p. 115.

[11] It was stated on p. 76 that the "allocation of income does not seem to be influenced by size of income, only that the higher-income families consume more of the same kinds of products as the lower-income families." Although this may be true in the aggregate, for specific products, considerable differences in allocation are present. Also, differing characteristics of the consuming unit have been shown to have considerable effect on the purchase of photographic equipment.

92

Foundations
of
Strategy—
Interpreting
Market
Forces and
Opportunities

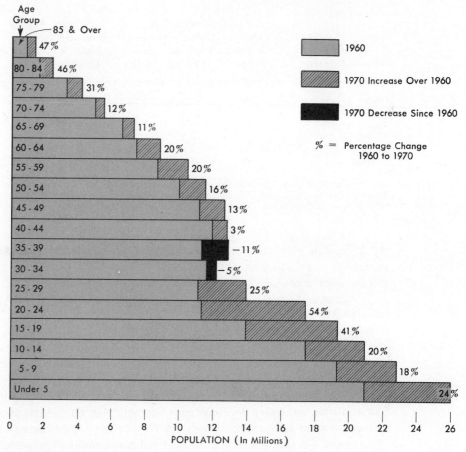

FIGURE 6-5

Population Count and Percentage Change
by Age Groups 1960 to 1970

Source: U.S. Bureau of Census Current Population Reports, Series P-25, Number 241, January 17, 1962, Series II Estimates, appearing in Dynamic Aspects of Consumer Behavior *(Ann Arbor: The Foundation for Research on Human Behavior, 1963), p. 12.*

by age groups. Figure 6-6 shows cause for optimism and also for concern. The industry can benefit from the large bulge in 20–24 year olds but the decline in the 30–39 age group may seriously affect new car sales, as this group has the largest new car buying rate. The two charts are interpreted as follows: [12]

[12] Robert Eggert, "The Changing Population and Its Impact on Durables Purchases," in *Dynamic Aspects of Consumer Behavior* (Ann Arbor: The Foundation for Research on Human Behavior, 1963), p. 7.

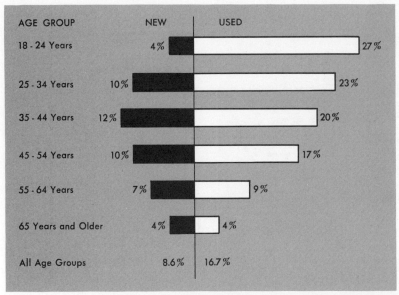

AGE GROUP	NEW	USED
18 - 24 Years	4%	27%
25 - 34 Years	10%	23%
35 - 44 Years	12%	20%
45 - 54 Years	10%	17%
55 - 64 Years	7%	9%
65 Years and Older	4%	4%
All Age Groups	8.6%	16.7%

FIGURE 6-6
New and Used
Car Buying Rates
by Age Groups

*Source: Survey Research Center, University of Michigan 1959–61 Average,
appearing in* Dynamic Aspects of Consumer Behavior *(Ann Arbor: The Foundation
for Research on Human Behavior, 1963), p. 14.*

Applied to expected changes in the population and assuming unchanged buying rates by age groups, the age group 35–39 will buy about 11 percent fewer new cars in 1970 than that age group bought in 1960. The share of new car sales going to this group will have declined from about 13 percent to about 10½ percent. The age group 20–24 will buy almost 60 percent more cars in 1970 than in 1960, and the share of all new cars that this group will have bought will have gone up from 7½ to 10½ percent.

Measuring Product Sensitivity to Income Changes

We have just examined the consumption function on the basis of time and buyer characteristics; we will now look at consumption on the basis of product characteristics. What types of consumer purchases exhibit the greatest variation as income changes? Figure 6-7 relates consumer purchases to income over a thirty-eight-year period. Notice that the relationship for total goods and services, with the exception of the war years, shows very little variation. The actual data vary from the trend line by approximately 1 percent. But the three groups of expenditures composing the total show considerably more variation. In the nondurable goods category the income coefficient is 0.7—that is, a 10 percent change in income is associated with a 7 percent change in consumption in the same direction. The income coefficient is 2.1 for durables and 0.5 for services.[13] The durable goods sector is the area in which fluctuations are the

[13] See Louis J. Paradiso and Mabel A. Smith, "Consumer Purchasing and Income Patterns," *Survey of Current Business,* XXXIX, No. 3 (March 1959), 23.

94

Foundations
of
Strategy—
Interpreting
Market
Forces and
Opportunities

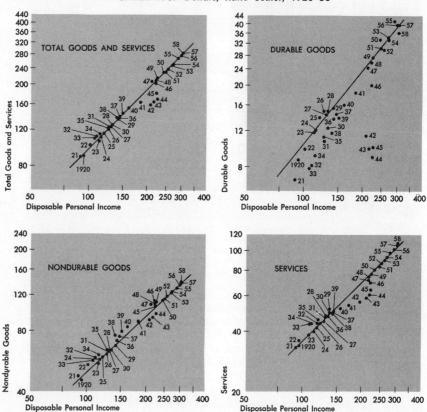

FIGURE 6-7

Consumer Purchases Related to Income in Constant Dollars
(Billion 1957 Dollars, Ratio Scale), 1920–58

greatest—a 10 percent change in income is associated with a 21 percent change in the consumption of durables.

This explanation has been given for the increased responsiveness of durable goods consumption to change in income:

> In the case of durable goods, the cyclical response has been sharp even in periods of relatively small business fluctuations. Such behavior results from the longer life of these goods and the flexibility of replacement and from the use of credit as an important element of financing. Consumers are more willing to increase installment debt when income is rising and are more reluctant to incur additional indebtedness when income declines and prospects appear less favorable. Lenders are likewise more agreeable to the process of debt creation in good times.[14]

[14] *Ibid.*

Although the greatest sensitivity to income change is found in durable goods, analysis of specific products reveals considerable variation between different time periods and between specific products and services. Studies conducted in 1959 examined the sensitivity of specific products in the durable and nondurable categories and services to income changes.[15] These studies showed considerable change in income sensitivity between the prewar and postwar

[15] See Louis J. Paradiso and Clement Winston, "Consumer Expenditure—Income Patterns." *Survey of Current Business* (September 1955); and Louis J. Paradiso and Mabel A. Smith, "Consumer Purchasing and Income Patterns."

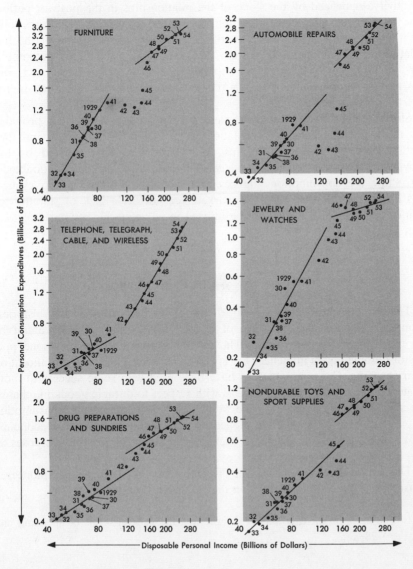

FIGURE 6-8
Examples of Shifts from the Prewar to the Postwar Relationship between Expenditures and Income

96

Foundations
of
Strategy—
Interpreting
Market
Forces and
Opportunities

periods. During the prewar years, most responsive to income change were new cars, radios, records, musical instruments, and jewelry and watches. Among the least sensitive were gasoline, magazines, tobacco, electricity, gas, hospitals, telephone and telegraph, and water. In contrast, during the postwar period the most sensitive categories were air transportation, radio and television repair, household utilities, telephone, telegraph, automobile insurance, and new cars. Among the least sensitive at this time were clothing of all kinds, books and maps, footwear, fuel and ice, and laundry services. Furthermore, when the postwar period is expanded to cover the years 1947–1958, marked changes in responsiveness are apparent. Over the longer period many items show an increased sensitivity. These changes are depicted graphically in Figure 6-8 for a select group of products. Furniture, and jewelry and watches exhibit a marked decrease in sensitivity, evidenced by the slope of the relationships in the postwar period. On the other hand, telephone, telegraph, cable, and wireless expenditures have become much more responsive, as is indicated by the steeper slope of the line of relationship in the postwar period. The remaining categories—automobile repairs, nondurable toys and sport supplies, and drug preparations and sundries—remain fairly stable, although the level of expenditure is much higher during the postwar period.

Since the coefficients were developed by correlation analysis, they probably reflect the long-run secular trend relationship in the postwar period, and they should be used with care. Since this period has been characterized by full employment, increasing incomes, and general prosperity, the data undoubtedly fail to show the consumption changes that would accompany sharp cyclical swings in income. Nevertheless, the marketer can detect a lack of stability for certain classes of goods, which can be utilized in adjusting his estimates of total market size.

THE SURVEY METHOD

The survey method has developed out of the recognition that historical relationships between the purchase of durable goods and income cannot be safely relied upon for forecasting. The ability of consumers to postpone purchases of durable goods influences the spend-save pattern and also the allocation of their spending. Consumer surveys have been used with some success to more accurately predict consumers' intentions with respect to durable goods purchases. These surveys permit more accurate predictions of the aggregate consumption function. Although originally developed for predicting the general economic outlook, such surveys should prove useful for business forecasting purposes as well.

The Survey Research Center at the University of Michigan has pioneered in consumer attitude studies based on the following propositions:

1. The basic problem is that of determining the general levels of spending and saving.

2. Consumer decisions to spend or save are dependent upon (1) the basic needs of individuals as represented by aspiration levels, status, security, and group conformity; (2) individual decision-making characteristics, such as problem-solving ability and information level; (3) constraints arising out of situational variables, such as income, family size, prices, and assets, as well as status roles and accepted patterns of activity; and (4) consumers' attitudes with respect to the expected outcomes from one pattern of action versus another.

3. Since previous research has demonstrated the dynamic character of consumer choice, any inquiry must focus on those influencing variables which change through time.

4. Since the basic needs of individuals as well as the decision-making characteristics of individuals are rather stable personality variables, they do not materially influence changes in consumer behavior.

5. Although the situational variable in part may change over time, it represents no serious problem, since the variable may be handled empirically with little difficulty.

6. The remaining variable, consumers' attitudes with respect to the expected outcome from one pattern of action versus another, is the area that may possibly explain the dynamic nature of consumer decisions with respect to how much to spend and how much to save.

7. It is known that much consumer spending is habitual and relies on expectations from similar courses of action taken in the past. On the other hand, much consumer action requires extensive deliberation, for example, in purchasing durable goods. Therefore, the significant changes in the spend-save pattern must be determined by changes in consumers' expectations concerning the outcome of different courses of action with respect to durable goods purchases.

8. Study of attitudes in relation to expectations will shed light on consumers' decisions to purchase durable goods or to save.

9. More specifically, the survey technique is used to measure, as frequently as possible, consumers' attitudes concerning expected outcomes from one course of action versus another. Changes in consumers' attitudes are then related to changes in the spend-save pattern of the group.[16]

The findings to date may be divided into two types. First, the level of saving versus spending seems to be directly related to consumers' past income and expected future income. Second, the purchase of durable goods is dependent upon past income and expected future income.

In general, the survey method, through assessing the consumers' outlook, attempts to judge the direction of change in spend-save decisions and attempts to relate consumers' outlook to changes in intention to purchase specific products. The survey method does not study the specific products. The survey method does

[16] For complete descriptions of the purpose and method see James Morgan, "A Review of Recent Research on Consumer Behavior," in *Consumer Behavior: Research on Consumer Reactions,* Lincoln H. Clark, ed. (New York: Harper & Row, Publishers, 1958), pp. 118–20. Also: George Katona, "The Predictive Value of Data on Consumer Attitudes," in *Consumer Behavior,* II, *The Life Cycle and Consumer Behavior,* Lincoln Clark, ed. (New York: New York University Press, 1955), 66–74. Also: George Katona, *Psychological Analysis of Economic Behavior* (New York: McGraw-Hill Book Company, 1951), Chap. 8. Also: Klein, Katona, Lansing, and Morgan, contributors to *Survey Methods of Economics* (New York: Columbia University Press, 1954).

98

Foundations
of
Strategy—
Interpreting
Market
Forces and
Opportunities

not study the specific forces generating a change in attitudes. It identifies these attitudes.

As a result of the work of the Survey Research Center it is generally accepted that the way in which people apprehend what they see, hear, and read, sometimes referred to as social cognition, has a short-run effect on attitudes and also influences consumer behavior. After many years of study, it is apparent that attitude change over longer periods has an important influence on consumer behavior. Professor George Katona has elaborated five aspects which have characterized consumer behavior in the past and probably will continue to do so in the future. They are as follows: [17]

Inflation and spending.—Because rising prices are resented and inflation is seen as being bad for oneself and the economy, inflation has a depressing effect on discretionary spending. The expectation of price increases means that more has to be spent on necessities and therefore less money can be spent on discretionary matters. Price stability is reassuring; uncertainty about paying the "right price" disappears, and planning ahead is facilitated.

Inflation and saving.—Inflation, however, is not a sure thing in the minds of most people, even though it creates uncertainty. Saving—the acquisition of reserve funds—remains as important as ever, and saving must be done in forms which are safe and convenient. Therefore inflation did not detract at all from the favorable attitudes toward saving accounts in savings and loan associations and banks.

Levels of aspiration—Gratification of needs does not mean saturation; instead it results in the raising of sights, provided people are optimistic and confident about the future. New wants arise when more pressing wants have been satisfied. Frustration, disappointment, or a pessimistic outlook make for feelings of saturation.

Provisions for retirement.—More widespread social security and private pension plan arrangements may be thought to destroy the felt need and the incentive to accumulate reserve funds. This notion is contradicted by recent findings, especially with middle and upper income people who are five to fifteen years away from retirement. For these people the goal of making adequate retirement provisions appears as something they are able to accomplish by supplementing the collective retirement arrangements by saving for retirement. The studies recently started indicate that interest in saving is more pronounced among those with whom expected retirement income is high compared to their current income than among those with whom it is low.

Saving and asset holdings.—The greater the wealth, the less will be saved—this thesis is supported by the notion about a decline in incentives to save and by the fact that spending is facilitated by asset holdings. Psychologically, it is correct that spending is one of the purposes of saving. On the other hand, levels of aspiration rise with accumulation of wealth. Also, those with larger assets have saved much in the past and have a habit of saving. Past studies have indicated that several rather than one motivational force prevails. Data from the 1960–1962 Survey of Consumer Finances panel, which enable us to study

[17] George Katona, "Long-range Changes in Consumer Attitudes," *Dynamic Aspects of Consumer Behavior* (Ann Arbor: The Foundation for Research on Human Behavior, 1963), pp. 100–101.

saving performance over 24 months, confirm past findings. People with large assets differ from people with small assets; both large saving and large dissaving is more frequent among the former than among the latter.

The above should not be interpreted to mean that there are no differences among different groups of consumers. There are differences in degree, but the above five aspects prevail in general.

THE BUILDUP METHOD

The task of market investigation becomes more complex when a firm attempts to appraise the market for new products. Yet it is even more important in this case to accurately judge the quantities that will be purchased. The large financial investment that precedes the introduction of a new product can be justified only if the market is sufficiently broad to generate profits for the firm. For new products, estimates of total demand have to be built up from analysis of particular uses, users, or individual market requirements. In some cases, total demand cannot be estimated accurately, but analysis proceeds until sufficient potential purchasers have been identified to reach a necessary threshold for commercially profitable operations in the new product field.

Consider the problems facing the producers of plastic resins. The potential uses of these resins had not been completely identified, and the size of the market was unknown. As another example, the manufacturers of television sets had very little to go on in the early days of TV. Here we had an entirely new product whose market opportunities depended upon how well and how quickly the behavior patterns of the public could be influenced.

Another illustration is the introduction of the compact car by American automobile manufacturers. In this case, market opportunity depended on whether or not the attitudes of the consuming public had or could be changed with respect to the traditional models and the small car. Was it possible through marketing effort to change these attitudes? Was the market large enough to warrant the investment necessary to bring out the small car?

Still another illustration may be found in one of the underdeveloped agricultural regions of the world. There may be enormous potential in central Africa, let us say, for agricultural machinery and fertilizer, but how quickly can the potential be developed? Consider the traditional patterns to be overcome, the educational job to be done. Can the necessary investment of time and funds be made while this educational task proceeds?

Businesses launching new products of these kinds risk a substantial amount of money in virtually unknown markets. Any information which can be obtained regarding the size of the market is of value to the decision maker.

Few industrial concerns are able to indulge in pure research. They must utilize the findings of pure research from other sources in creating useful, mar-

100

Foundations
of
Strategy—
Interpreting
Market
Forces and
Opportunities

ketable products. Therefore, in most instances, research programs aimed at new product development are based upon some hypothesis regarding the public's desire for or ability to use the new product. That is, there is usually some recognition of a market demand before the time, energy, and money are directed toward the development of a product to satisfy that demand. Frequently the finished product is a different sort of thing than originally intended. It may turn out that it will not serve the intended purposes but may conceivably serve other purposes. At this point, additional hypotheses are made concerning the product's usefulness. It is in the analysis of these hypotheses that a means is found for interpreting markets for such products. For example, the makers of automatic washing machines hypothesized that if the washing and drying mechanism could be combined into one unit, the space-saving characteristics of the product would open a market among residents of compact dwelling units. The increasing cost per square foot in residential construction puts space-saving devices at a premium. What other hypotheses might have been used? The reduction in production cost may enable a price differential over the separate washer and dryer and aid in displacing competitors. This, then assumes that the market for automatic laundry equipment would respond favorably to a price decline. Another would be the desire on the part of housewives to have a one-operation washday. All these hypotheses can be checked through market research to determine their validity. Space does not permit us to examine the specific techniques used for verifying the hypotheses, but once they are verified, the number of people that may be influenced by, let us say, the space-saving features of the product can be determined and projected for the entire marketing area. This approach is not as accurate as the previous approaches, yet where other methods cannot be used it is much better than nothing. The firm may never know accurately the total quantity that the market will absorb, but at least it is fairly certain the market will not reject the product to the point where the investment is lost.

Sometimes specific estimates concerning market behavior are not present, such as in the development of plastic resins. In such cases technical research must be done internally and through consultation with prospective users. Once users are identified, their characteristics are ascertained, and estimates are made of the possible quantities they might use. The task of interpreting the market for a product may be continuous, because new users seem to be continually appearing. The number of potential users in the early days of the plastic industry must have been at least great enough to warrant the investments necessary to begin production.

The following example from the Polychemicals Division of E. I. DuPont de Nemours and Company will serve to illustrate the kinds of data that may be secured by this approach.

A product development group explores a new product on a qualitative basis, finding out how it can be used. Simultaneously a market study group takes a cold, quantitative look—how much can be sold and where—actually as a check on product development's enthusiasm. If the product stands up to 50 tough sales questions, management may O.K. its commercialization, and salesmen fan out swiftly into the industries which it may supply. An elaborate sales-record-and-analysis mechanization charts the new product and all others by industries to keep things in balance.

This is the way it worked on the new polyethylene plastics: Polyethylene went first, naturally, into wire coatings and films; later into moulded articles, waxy, flexible, refrigerator dishes; beakers; squeeze bottles; and closures. But DuPont tossed it back to product development for future qualitative analysis, and discovered that its toughness and impermeability to grease and water imparted great strength to paper as a coating. In six to eight months Polychem's sales force saw 700 potential users and sold close to a hundred on using polyethylene for bag and wrapping papers. Thus a new market was born. Market study has more recently shown that polyethylene sales fall into four categories of use. About 60 percent of DuPont's volume was going into No. 1. Deliberately, then, DuPont is directing more of its product and effort into the neglected area for greater diversification. As more balance is achieved, production will expand.[18]

Summary

Quantitative estimates of market size are necessary for determining the magnitude of the marketing task and for undertaking more qualitative interpretations of market behavior. Three general methods are used for measuring the quantities that may be sold. The historical method relies on an analysis of the relationship between past income and consumption, and the allocation of consumption to various product categories. Such a method assumes stability with respect to the portion of income expended and the proportion saved, and stability in allocating the expended portion to different products. A demonstrated lack of stability makes necessary adjustments in market size estimates developed by the historical approach. Research in this area has shown that variations in consuming units create differences in the spend-save pattern and the product-mix purchased. Therefore, continuous analyses of the size of these different consuming groups is necessary. Of particular interest to marketers are those classifications of consumers based upon income size and stage in the family life cycle. Another area of analysis has revealed wide variations in the degree of responsiveness shown by buyers to certain classes of products when they undergo changes in income.

A second method, the survey approach, is used to inquire into the effect of attitudes held by consumers and their decision to purchase or not to purchase durable goods. Research in this area to date has revealed that consumers' evaluation of past experiences and expected future experiences with respect to their financial conditions is related to their decisions to purchase or refrain from purchasing durable goods. Therefore, an assessment of consumers' general

[18] See Lawrence P. Lessing, "The World of DuPont," *Fortune* (October 1950), p. 176.

102

Foundations
of
Strategy—
Interpreting
Market
Forces and
Opportunities

optimism or pessimism is needed to modify historical durable goods expenditure patterns.

A third approach, much less precise, is the buildup method. This method is used most in the case of new products introduction; it relies on market surveys to assess the validity of hypotheses concerning the use of the product. New products are generally developed with some specific use in mind. Quantitative estimates of consumer opinion as to the intended use may be used to build estimates of market size. Market analysis of this type is frequently done in conjunction with technical product research in which continuous studies are made to determine new uses which may be checked through field research in the proposed markets.

Regardless of the techniques used to get data to delineate the market, all methods have one point in common—they start with the buyer. In essence, the only way to ascertain possible future sales is to analyze possible buyers. The historical method, using either external data or internal sales records, is based on an analysis of past consumer behavior patterns. The survey method and the buildup method are more direct, and rely on actual contact with potential buyers. In all methods, ingenuity and imagination are required to devise ways and means to secure information about potential buyers.

Questions and Problems

1. Why are quantitative measurements of the market necessary for programming marketing effort? For other areas in the enterprise?
2. Describe the historical method of quantitatively measuring markets.
3. Select a particular type of product, then go to the library and collect all the information you can on that product from the *Life Study of Consumer Expenditures*. Develop a profile of the purchasers of that product.
4. In what ways can complete past sales records be useful in applying the historical method to quantitative investigation of the market?
5. What is the consumption function?
6. In what way is an analysis of the consumption function useful in analyzing the consumer's spend-save problem?
7. What is meant by cross-section analyses? How do they explain the instability in the consumption functions?
8. Why are changes in income and stage in family life cycle particularly influential in changing the consumption function?
9. Examine the data in Table 6-8. Speculate on the way in which these changes might affect the total purchases of cosmetics and beer.
10. Why are durable goods more responsive to income changes than nondurable goods?
11. How may income coefficients be used in making quantitative analyses of consumer markets?
12. Upon what propositions is the survey method based?

13. How might the buildup method be used to quantitatively measure the market for educational records encompassing a complete set of lectures on a given topic?
14. Why is sampling used in many quantitative market analyses?
15. What are the various kinds of factors that could reduce the reliability of quantitative market information?

Consumer Markets II: 7
Behavioral Aspects

Potential customers are identified through quantitative market investigation. But how can this potential demand be made effective and directed toward particular products and particular brands? What kinds of appeals must be made, what kind of purchase environment must be provided?

In Chapter 5 we saw that the amounts consumers spend, the products and brands they buy, and the conditions under which they buy are determined by several influencing conditions, conditions which create consumer self-images. These self-images reflect particular ends that must be satisfied by acceptable means. Marketing strategy deals with the creation of product images which are acceptable as means.

In Chapter 6 we saw that expenditures on some products were related to income, size of family, age of children, and similar objective consumer characteristics. Such objective findings—for instance, that more new cars are bought by people in the 35–44 year age group—help in formulating marketing strategy, but their value is limited.

For example, if in 1950 a marketing analyst had used objective data to estimate the 1960 demand for pleasure boats, his estimate would have fallen short. Why? Because objective factors don't tell the whole story. Other, subjective forces were at work between 1950 and 1960; and these forces, cultivated through carefully thought-out marketing strategy, were at least partly responsible for the expansion in demand.

To work out such a strategy, planners had to ask themselves *why* the consumer behaves as he does, rather than just *how* he behaves. How does the consumer see himself (self-image)? How does he see the product (product-image)? Does the product present the consumer an image compatible with his self-image? Answers to such questions provide insights into marketing opportunities not provided by studies of objective consumer characteristics.

Answers to these questions are particularly helpful in mapping selective marketing strategies. In the past the tendency had been to investigate markets as aggregates (that is, to identify the market for cosmetics as composed of so many women in different geographic locations). This procedure has led to uniform strategies, often oversimplified and incompatible with certain segments of the market. Markets are not homogeneous; it is quite possible for a single market to embody several self-images, each requiring a different product-image. A step in the right direction was the dissection of markets into groups of consumers with similar objective buyer characteristics. But analyses of the subjective factors—self-image, product-image, and so on— are necessary to achieve a closer correspondence between marketing effort and market opportunities. An excellent example is the youth market. Not so many years ago this market could be appealed to on the basis of youths' desires to imitate their elders. Children did not wish to be considered children, and most attempts to specialize product offerings to them met with failure. Today the reverse seems to be true. Youth has built an identity for itself. Products must be tailored, both physically and psychologically, to this group. If the product is too closely identified with the same product class used by the older generation, it is excluded from youths' schedule of wants. In fact, so enchanting is the identity created by youth that the older generation frequently tries, through its market behavior, to associate with the younger age class.

To achieve correspondence between marketing effort and marketing opportunities, market analysts have utilized some of the concepts of psychology. In this chapter we will discuss the psychological theories and research techniques used in studying purchase motivation. Then we will illustrate some of the ideas and techniques through a sample purchase motivation study. Finally, we will consider some of the practical problems encountered in studies of purchase motivation.

PSYCHOLOGICAL THEORIES APPLIED
IN STUDYING PURCHASE MOTIVATION

Psychologists disagree on which of their many theories offers the best approach to the study of consumer behavior; all have been used from time to time. Although there are many variations in psychological theories, they have been grouped into three basic schools. We shall discuss the approaches stemming from each.[1]

The Need-Satisfaction Approach

This is the approach of the laboratory or experimental psychologists who study the physiological needs of living organisms and observe how they establish behavior patterns to satisfy these needs. The subjects in such experiments are usually animals, but the need-satisfaction concept has been widely used in marketing literature. It has, for example, been applied in developing techniques

[1] The classification used is taken from Herta Herzog, "Behavioral Science Concepts for Analyzing the Consumer," in *Proceedings, of the Conference of Marketing Teachers from Far Western States, September 8–10, 1958,* Delbert J. Duncan, ed. (Berkeley: University of California), pp. 32–41.

106

Foundations
of
Strategy—
Interpreting
Market
Forces and
Opportunities

of salesmanship. In its application, the salesman is first trained to determine the prospect's needs. Once this is accomplished he adjusts his knowledge of the product, terms of sale, etc., to the specific needs of the prospect.

The Psychoanalytic Approach

This group of psychologists approach the problem from another theoretical structure. They believe that physiological needs cannot be completely satisfied within the bounds of society. Consequently, such needs create tensions within the individual and are repressed. Although they lurk in the subconscious, they still influence behavior.

Repressed needs may influence the conscious needs of the individual and the behavior he indulges in to satisfy these needs. An interesting example of the application of this theoretical structure is found in a study of businessmen's reluctance to use air travel for business purposes. After psychoanalytical techniques had been used to probe the subconscious of a small sample of businessmen it was concluded that their reluctance was a result of "posthumous guilt complexes." This means that subconsciously they were fearful, in event of a fatal accident, of what their wives would say about them afterward. Since this complex was so strong, it could not be removed and had to be compensated for.

One company's advertising appealed to the desire to get home from a business trip sooner so the businessman could have more time with his children. Most printed advertising copy showed pictures of young children running down the walk with outstretched arms to greet Daddy on Friday night instead of Saturday noon. This approach was used to compensate for the guilt complex, as it is believed anything to do with the love of children is one of the strongest appeals that can be made.[2]

The Gestalt Approach

The Gestalt psychologists employ a more inclusive approach to human behavior. Behavior is not explained by one set of forces only, as in the case of the psychoanalytic school, but rather by many forces. The word *Gestalt* means "configuration" or "pattern," and Gestalt theorists see human beings as acting in a goal-directed pattern. People identify their own needs and follow a conscious path toward satisfying them. The means-end or problem-solving approach discussed in Chapter 5 is a reflection of Gestalt psychology.

Gestalt psychology today views the individual as existing in a *life-space* (the atmosphere within which he lives and acts).[3] The goals he seeks and the means selected are not determined by physiological needs and inner personality variables only, but also by environment. This interaction between the person and his environment has caused social psychologists to place much emphasis

---

[2] Reported in Perrin Stryker's "Motivation Research," *Fortune* (June 1956), p. 226.
[3] Rensis Likert, at the 1954 Session of the Michigan Advertising Conference, in *Michigan Business Papers,* No. 30 (Ann Arbor, Mich.: University of Michigan Press, 1954), pp. 1–4.

on what is known as *reference group theory*. Some aspects of this theory have had considerable influence in marketing, and therefore we shall try to explain it.

Reference Group Theory

This theory suggests that behavior is influenced by the reference group, or audience B as it was called in Chapter 5, to which the individual belongs or aspires to belong. An explanation of reference groups is found in the following quotation:

> Descriptions of the manner in which individuals are influenced by group norms sometimes employ the term "reference group." This expression refers to the fact that people evaluate themselves and orient their behavior by reference both to (1) the groups in which they hold official membership, and (2) others to which they aspire or hope to belong in the future. A reference group is thus any group with which a person psychologically identifies himself or in relation to which he thinks of himself. It is implicit in this idea that his existing group memberships may be relatively meaningless to the person whose primary "ego anchorages" are established with reference to groups with which he is not formally or objectively linked. This type of anticipatory allegiance is especially noticeable in a mobile society in which the ambition to raise one's status is characteristically encouraged.
>
> Reference groups are thus said to establish the individual's organizing conceptions or frames of reference, for ordering his experiences, perceptions, and ideas of self.[4]

The stimulus of the reference group depends on the degree of psychological identification which the individual has with the group. Sometimes the identification is called *ego-involvement,* and, as suggested in the quotation, some reference groups may be ego involving and some may not. Let us use a simple example to explain this idea. If a plumber is walking down the street and the local attorney, with whom he has had an occasional business contact in the last six months, fails to speak to him, it is not likely he will engage in any behavior to gain recognition. In other words, the attorney does not represent a reference group with which the plumber is ego involved or one to which he aspires. On the other hand, if a plumber acquaintance from his own reference group fails to recognize him, he probably is ego involved and will engage in behavior calculated to gain recognition. A complicating factor is that the reference groups which are ego involving and those which are not are in a constant state of change. Let us suppose the same plumber to be strongly influenced by the family reference group. In an effort to improve the living standard of his family, he enters the contract plumbing business and is very successful. There is a possibility that the plumber now will shift his allegiances from his former occupational group to that of the attorney's reference group. Now he may engage in behavior designed to gain recognition by the attorney.

Family, occupational class, income grouping, and religious affiliation can all be reference groups. Let us single out the family as a reference group and

[4] A. R. Lindesmith and A. L. Strauss, *Social Psychology,* rev. ed. (New York: Holt, Rinehart & Winston, Inc., 1956), p. 241.

108

Foundations
of
Strategy—
Interpreting
Market
Forces and
Opportunities

speculate on its effect on behavior. Some families exert sufficient pressure on the head to control his social behavior, influence his occupational ambitions, and influence the very products upon which he is willing to spend his income. In other cases, the family has little influence on the head's social behavior; it may have little bearing on his ambition, and the products he buys may be in no way related to attempts to gain recognition within his household. In the first case, the family is an ego-involving reference group, and in the second, it is not. In the early days of television, much of the primary demand (demand for a product type rather than any one brand) was created by building social pressure against nonowners who failed to provide this medium for the enjoyment of their children. Overlooking the ethical consideration, this may be interpreted as an attempt to make the family an ego-involving reference group where it previously was not, with respect to using television as a means of enjoyment for the children.

In practice it is difficult to identify reference groups. For market predicting purposes the ego-involving reference groups must be identified beforehand; but unfortunately, when reference group theory is applied to market behavior, the only way to identify the influential group is to study past behavior, as well as the reference groups to which the individual belongs or aspires to belong. A cause-and-effect relationship is then made between the two sets of data. There is a serious limitation to this procedure. When one tries to identify influential reference groups *before* purchases are made, it is soon discovered that it is impossible to identify behavior.

Because of the above limitation, reference group theory in the form described above does not provide an approach which is widely used in marketing. However, an understanding of the theory is important, because a modification of it is used in market investigation. To avoid the problem of specifying an actual group, there has been a tendency to refer to *status roles* rather than reference groups.

The term *status role* seems to have no existence in the literature of social psychology. Yet it is used in marketing literature and apparently combines two ideas. The word *status* refers to position within a group. The idea assumes that every person has some position within the groups to which he belongs. For example, a mother has position within a family. Also, she is expected to engage in certain activities to fulfill that position. These activities are known as *roles*. In general, the activities necessary to fill a position are determined by the particular reference group in which the position exists.

It is important to understand that in filling a role no two people will engage in exactly the same activities, for two reasons. First, action is not solely determined by the expectations of the reference group, but also by personality traits and physiological needs. Since these may vary, considerable literature is available on the way in which a person fulfills a status position he occupies. Second, a person may aspire to another reference group and play a role which is more in keeping with the manner in which the status position is filled in that group. Even though the dynamic aspects of status role are recognized, there is a belief that people will generally perform in a given status position by playing a role which is dictated by the reference group within which the position exists.

From a marketing point of view, it is thought that if segments of the market can be identified in terms of individuals' perception of the *status roles* they engage in, it is possible to infer the reference groups to which they belong or aspire to belong and the kinds of market choices they will make to fulfill their status roles.

HOW ARE THESE APPROACHES EMPLOYED IN MARKETING?

We have examined three approaches used in understanding human motivation. All three provide a means to understanding the self-image, an indicator of consumer ends discussed in Chapter 5. The self-image is partly determined by ego-involving reference groups, which dictate status roles, which in turn are an expression of the person's self-image. The self-image is also partly determined by physiological needs, as well as by inner personality traits. The process is shown in the diagram below.

Do marketers have to use all three approaches to determine the ends of consumers? Probably not. It depends on how completely we wish to pursue the chain of causation—to what extent we must know the reasons that cause a group of consumers to have a particular self-image. In most cases it is enough to know that consumers have a particular self-image that causes them to behave in certain ways; it is not necessary to explore in detail the incentives, perceptions, and subconscious repressions which shape the self-image. The Gestalt approach is most useful to practitioners in the business sphere because the concept of status role as an indicator of the self-image includes the influences of the reference group, of physiological needs, and of inner personality traits. Therefore, by studying status roles, it is usually not necessary to use psychoanalytic techniques to probe deeper into the reasons *why* an individual acts in a certain way.

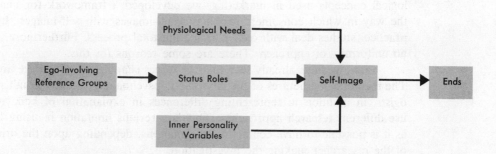

There are cases, however, when a deeper understanding of cause is important. For example, a study of the self-images of buyers of a particular brand of car indicated that they were different from the buyers of a competitive brand. Once this finding is known, it may be useful to probe into the reasons why buyers see themselves as different if marketing strategy is to be developed to win over buyers of competitive cars.

Although all these approaches have been used by social scientists, care must be exercised when their use is undertaken for marketing purposes. As a

110

Foundations
of
Strategy—
Interpreting
Market
Forces and
Opportunities

rule, the studies that have been conducted are not undertaken for improving the marketing of a specific product. One might think that groups of consumers with a given self-image could be appealed to by marketing a product in a certain way, but this kind of inference is particularly dangerous. People will not fit easily into classifications to which clear-cut self-images can be attributed.

A group of housewives, for example, might be assumed to imagine themselves as good homemakers, sympathetic mothers, and affectionate wives. This would make them the obvious market for brands of children's clothing, cookbooks, and home appliances appealing to these qualities. But even the least experienced of marketers would recognize that these same housewives also imagine themselves as *femmes fatales,* wishing to appear young and beautiful, and he would not fail to point some of his cosmetic advertisements in this direction. In short, the self-images of people are complex, sometimes even conflicting; many different ends must be satisfied. For this reason marketing analysts tend to believe that all investigation must be *action centered*—that is, directed toward finding out how a person will react to a particular product or brand.

Thus, our investigation becomes focused on individual reactions to specific products, and the object of the search is to determine consumers' self-images as they relate to a particular product. In this way we attempt through marketing effort to offer for sale products which will present a product-image compatible with the self-image.

Now that we have some idea of the way different psychological concepts are used in marketing, let us examine some of the techniques.

Research Techniques

Research into purchase motivation, as it is carried out in practice, may have a splintered appearance to the uninitiated. In our discussion of psychological concepts used in marketing, we developed a framework for analysis of the way in which consumers match product-images with self-images. In actual practice, studies deal with only parts of the total process. Furthermore, there is no uniformity of approach. There are some reasons for this.

First, we have already seen that the forces shaping the self-image are many. The theoretical structures of the laboratory, psychoanalytic, and Gestalt psychologists, in addition to representing differences in explanation of behavior, also use different research approaches. This is a serious limitation in using findings, as it is possible to have conflicting explanations, depending upon the orientation of the researcher making the investigation.

Second, it was suggested in Chapter 5 that, in the eyes of the consumer, a product is the sum total of its use value, its reputation, its environment in purchase, and its anticipated satisfaction in use. To examine every facet of this totality is just too costly. Research studies concentrate on single aspects of the totality, but rarely on all.

Regardless of the orientation of the researcher or the particular aspect of the total buying process investigated, there are only two ways to gather information about consumers. Behavior can be *observed,* or information can be *acquired* by questioning. When overt behavior is observed or straightforward factual questions are asked, we have what is called a *direct approach* to gathering information. Information can also be gathered by more subtle means, such as depth interviewing or the use of projective techniques in which indirect questions are asked. These methods are considered an *indirect approach*.

In both approaches, interpretation about motivation is inferential, since rarely are conclusions experimentally proved. Generally, purchase behavior is examined. Also, consumers are classified on the basis of objective characteristics or psychological variables determined by direct or indirect approaches. Behavior patterns are then matched with the objective characteristics or psychological characteristics, and cause-and-effect relationships are established by inference.

The difference between the direct approach and the indirect approach is in the type of questions asked of the consumer to elicit responses which help to identify the self-image or the product-image they envision. Since the purpose of this section is to point out broad approaches to the problem of purchase motivation, we shall not discuss the refinements in techniques used. This is a specialized area and requires specialized study. Let us now instead examine some types of studies that have been conducted.

One type of study has already been described in Chapter 6. There, purchase behavior was related to objective characteristics of consumers, such as age, occupation, educational level, stage in the life cycle, and income. This information is gathered through asking consumers simple factual questions.

When differences are observed in the purchase of a product by different groups, an inference is made about motivation. For example, Lazarsfeld found that, statistically, ". . . people of low income preferred sweet chocolates, fabrics with a rubbery touch, and strong-smelling flowers; upper-class consumers favored . . . bitter, dry tastes, irregular weaves, and less pungent fragrances." He inferred from this that "The lower income is starved for pleasant sense experiences or . . . the upper-income individual exhibits his sensual wealth by conspicuous non-consumption of strong stimuli." [5] Although a study may have statistical validity, the conclusion drawn depends on the orientation of the researcher.

There are certain advantages to such an approach. First, it pinpoints differences at an immediate level and uses inference as a substitute for deeper analysis along the line of causation. In other words, more refined techniques are not used to determine *why* a certain stage in the family cycle influences purchases in a particular way. Second, within limits, these studies can be carried out with already collected and published data. For example, the *Life Study of Consumer Expenditures* can be used, obviating the need for expensive collection procedures. Third, such studies may have statistical validity. That is, if sufficient data are available, statistical tests can be applied to determine the significance of the findings.

A variation is found in statistically relating purchase behavior to deeper personality traits rather than to objective consumer characteristics. Through psychological testing, personality traits are determined; and then differences in personality traits are matched against differences in purchase behavior, and

[5] Paul F. Lazarsfeld, "Some Aspects of Human Motivation in Relation to Distribution," in *Proceedings; Thirty-first Boston Conference on Distribution, October 19–20, 1959,* p. 61.

112

Foundations
of
Strategy—
Interpreting
Market
Forces and
Opportunities

inferences are drawn as to the reasons. Professor Lloyd Warner hypothesized that social status, interacting with personality components, creates "social classes" whose attitudes toward spending and saving differ and whose retail store loyalities and attitudes toward different products also differ. To test the hypothesis it was necessary to determine if a class system existed and if there were any class significances in the families' spending patterns, retail store loyalities, and taste in typical products.[6]

Consumers were divided into six different social groups which represent different personality, cultural value, and reference groups. Some of the contrasts between two of the groups follow.[7]

Middle-Class

1. Pointed to the future.
2. Viewpoint embraces a long expanse of time.
3. More urban identification.
4. Stresses rationality.
5. Has a well-structured sense of the universe.
6. Horizons vastly extended or not limited.
7. Greater sense of choice making.
8. Self-confident, willing to take risks.
9. Immaterial and abstract in his thinking.
10. Sees himself tied to national happenings.

Lower-Status

1. Pointed to the present and past.
2. Lives and thinks in a short expanse of time.
3. More rural in identification.
4. Essentially nonrational.
5. Vague and unclear structuring of the world.
6. Horizons sharply defined and limited.
7. Limited sense of choice making.
8. Very much concerned with security and insecurity.
9. Concrete and perceptive in his thinking.
10. World revolves around his family and body.

Behavior in each group was examined. One of the conclusions relating to the two classes just delineated is as follows:

Middle-Class people usually have a place in their aspirations for some form of saving. Thus saving is most often in the form of investment, where there is a risk, long-term involvement, and the possibility of higher return. . . . The aspirations of the Lower-Status are just as often for spending as they are for saving. This saving is usually a noninvestment saving where there is almost no risk, funds can be quickly converted to spendable cash, and returns are small.[8]

Other interesting differences between the groups are as follows: Upper-Lower Class consumers have many more household appliances than Lower-Lower Class. The inferential explanation of the finding is that "Upper-Lower

---

[6] See Pierre Martineau, "Social Classes and Spending Behavior," *Journal of Marketing,* XXIII, No. 2 (October 1958), 121–30.

[7] *Ibid.,* p. 129.

[8] Martineau, "Social Classes and Spending Behavior."

Class man sees his home as his castle . . . and he loads it down with hardware —solid heavy appliances—as his symbols of security. The Lower-Lower Class individual is far less interested in his castle, and is more likely to spend his income for flashy clothes or an automobile." [9]

Different social classes appear to choose department stores according to their social class. In shaping her store image, a shopper will consider the other customers in the store, the type of treatment received, familiarity with surroundings, and a number of other variables. The strictly economic characteristics of the store, such as price and quality, are important, but the shopper will not patronize a store willingly if the store does not fit her social class. A store wishing to cater to all segments of the market must take care not to unwittingly exclude some segments through poor social class identification. Likewise, the manufacturer must take care to place his goods in those outlets which have social class images compatible with the market he wishes to reach. This emphasizes the careful selection of outlets, which will be treated in a discussion of the distribution network in Part 4, Chapter 21.

Many marketers have failed to see the application of such findings to marketing strategy. The verification of the Warner hypothesis does provide a means of predicting buying behavior through social-class identification. Differences in behavior also indicate the appeals that may be made to different social groups.

Another group of studies seeks to determine precisely the process the consumer goes through when he buys. Early studies on the buying process focused on the frequency of purchase, the seasonal characteristics of purchase, the quantities and place of purchase. Mueller reports that in a study covering the buying process in television, refrigerators, stoves, and men's sport shirts, varying degrees of deliberation were used.[10] The degree of deliberation was determined by measuring five dimensions: (1) degree of circumspection, indicated by the length of the planning period and the number of alternative purchases considered; (2) the extent of information-seeking activity, indicated by the number of stores visited, the advertisements read, the advice looked for; (3) choosing with respect to prices, such as seeking information on good buys and examining different price ranges; (4) choosing with respect to brand, such as examining and getting information on several brands; and (5) the number of features considered, such as style, operating costs, service arrangements, and warranties. The influence of other factors, such as education, income, price, urgency, and unique opportunities to purchase, was also considered. Some of the findings are as follows:

1. Careful deliberation was practiced more frequently in the purchase of durable goods than in the purchase of men's sport shirts.

2. In the purchase of durable goods, there was wide variation in the extensiveness of deliberation before purchase, as indicated in Table 7-1.

3. Deliberation in the purchase of durables was less extensive when income was relatively high, when the price paid was relatively low, and when the education of the buyer was low (as indicated in Table 7-1).

[9] Martineau, "Social Classes and Spending Behavior."
[10] George Katona and Eva Mueller, "A Study of Purchase Decisions," in *Consumer Behavior*, Vol. I, Lincoln H. Clark, ed. (New York: New York University Press, 1954).

114

Foundations
of
Strategy—
Interpreting
Market
Forces and
Opportunities

TABLE 7-1

Summary: Relation Between Personal Characteristics and Degree
of Deliberation Shown by Durable Goods Buyers
(mean score on 21-point deliberation index *)

Education	
Grade school	7.7
High school	9.9
College	10.0
Income	
Less than $2,000	8.0
$2,000–$2,999	8.2
$3,000–$4,999	9.4
$5,000–$7,499	10.1
$7,500 and over	9.3
Occupation of head of family	
Unskilled workers	8.1
Farm operators	8.7
Professional and technical people	9.0
Skilled and semiskilled workers	9.4
Businessmen	9.5
Clerical and sales personnel	12.0
Age of head of family	
65 and over	7.5
55–64	8.5
45–54	8.9
35–44	9.5
21–34	10.2
Attitude toward shopping	
We prefer to make up our minds quickly	7.9
Depends	9.1
We like to shop around	10.0

* The mean score for all 360 durable goods buyers on the
combined scale ranging from 0 to 21 is 9.3. Means for subgroups
are based on varying numbers of cases, from 25 (professional people) to 198 (people who like to shop around).

*Source: George Katona and Eva Mueller, "A Study of Pur-
chase Decisions," in* Consumer Behavior, *Lincoln H. Clark, ed.
(New York: New York University Press, 1954), p. 65. Reprinted by
permission of New York University Press.*

4. Three other circumstances affected the degree of deliberation. When
a special opportunity to make a purchase, through friends, "sales," or a persuasive salesman occurred, deliberation was low. However, many buyers who
deliberate extensively purchase at sales. Under conditions of urgent need there
was an absence of careful deliberation. Also, when the buyer had had a previous
satisfactory experience with a similar article, there was limited deliberation.

In addition to the relationship of extent of deliberation to such factors as
education, income, age, occupation, and attitude toward shopping, other information concerning the way consumers deliberate, and under what circumstances,
was revealed. For instance, detailed information was developed concerning buyers'

information-seeking activities, the nature of their planning, the number of brands looked at, the number of stores visited, and the features considered. From a marketing point of view, four conclusions can be drawn:

1. The class of outlet must match the information-seeking desires of the customer.

2. The length of the planning period and the alternatives considered might indicate the kinds of communications which will have the greatest impact.

3. The number of stores visited gives a lead to the intensity of distribution needed.

4. The reliance placed on advertising as an information source indicates the relative role of advertising as well as the type of copy needed.

More recent studies have inquired into some aspects of the buying process. In one, the types and sources of information and the importance of out-of-store and in-store shopping in the purchase of small electrical appliances was studied.[11] It was concluded for this product category that a typical consumer does not go from store to store to gather information to compare products and prices. For the most part, out-of-store sources of information, such as mail-order catalogs, newspaper advertising, past experience with the brand or product, and discussions with friends or neighbors, were used.

In another study an attempt was made to test three hypotheses as follows: [12]

1. The consumer will shop more extensively where the cost of shopping is low.
2. The consumer will shop more extensively when she initially knows little about the product she is buying and the store that is selling it.
3. The consumer will shop more extensively when the value of the product is high.

In total, the number of interstore comparisons was low. But when related to the ease of making interstore comparisons and value of the product shopped for, there was a marked increase in interstore comparisons when the stores visited were in a downtown shopping district or large shopping center and when the item shopped for was of high value. The data did not confirm that consumers with little or no information will make many interstore comparisons.

What is the consumer looking for when he chooses a retail outlet? Two studies reported by Lazarsfeld are particularly interesting.[13] A study of how men buy ready-made suits revealed that shoppers are most interested in quality, with color, pattern, and appearance cited as other factors. But because the customer is usually inexperienced in judging quality, he wants first of all to find a supplier he can have confidence in. The retail store, which is usually the supplier, must therefore present an image of integrity and dependability. Its sales people must be able to instill confidence into the consumer.

Women's shoe-buying habits were also studied, and the investigators dis-

[11] John G. Udell, "Prepurchase Behavior of Buyers of Small Electrical Appliances," *Journal of Marketing*, XXX (October 1966), 50–52.

[12] Louis P. Bucklin, "Testing Propensities to Shop," *Journal of Marketing*, XXX No. 1 (January 1966), 20–27.

[13] Lazarsfeld, "Some Aspects of Human Motivation," p. 3.

116

Foundations
of
Strategy—
Interpreting
Market
Forces and
Opportunities

covered that, while an attractive display of styles was the best way to bring a woman into the store, a good fit and the handling of the fitting procedure would often determine whether or not she actually made a purchase. Women report they are uneasy when trying on shoes, and embarrassed at being in their stocking feet in the presence of salesmen. The personal manner of the salesman must minimize this discomfort, or a successful appeal to women's desire for style could be wasted.

Comparing women's attitudes in buying shoes with men's in buying suits, we see that the kind of store image which must be developed is entirely different in each case. The really important features the customer is seeking must be provided in the purchase environment in both cases, but the means of providing it differ. This kind of finding is important both to the retailer and to the manufacturer selecting outlets for his product.

Other studies deal with why consumers purchase a given product brand. Asked directly, a woman may give a hundred different reasons for buying a dress—some bearing on the purchase and some not. To get at the real reasons for purchase, one must find out what the person's true self-image is, and more subtle and indirect means must be used. For practical purposes, such studies focus on the product-image, which is interpreted as a reflection of the self-image. The favorableness or unfavorableness of the product-image reflects the degree of compatibility with the self-image. To get at these interpretations of product- and self-images, *projection* is a useful device. Projection is a technique in which the subject is presented with a stimulus that is incomplete in itself. The subject is asked to make sense out of it, and in so doing must project a part of himself into the situation.

Many variations of projection techniques are practiced.[14] In a *sentence completion test* a partial sentence is given to the respondent, who is asked to complete it. For example, the respondent may be asked to complete a sentence like "The trouble with color television is. . . ." *Word association* is another method. Here, a stimulus word is given to the respondent and he is asked to respond promptly to the word with the first thing that comes to mind. Sometimes the respondent is asked to record his reaction to a word along a scale representing polar extremes within a single connotation. For example, the word *mother* may be given and the respondent asked to check a scale with *good* at one end and *bad* at the other. This method has been used in testing advertising copy. *Cartoon tests* are also used. In a cartoon showing two figures, for example, one of the figures says something to stimulate a response from the other. The respondent is asked to fill in the speech balloon over the responding figure. Sometimes a form of *thematic apperception test* is used in which respondents are exposed to magazine illustrations or drawings and are asked to make up stories about them. Often respondents are asked to explain why they think someone else behaves in a certain way; they thereby project their own personalities into the explanation.

Previous studies on gasoline revealed that it was a very uninteresting product to most consumers. Most consumers considered all gasolines to be alike

[14] For a more complete description of projection as a technique, see Luck, Wales, and Taylor, *Marketing Research,* 3rd ed. (Englewood Cliffs, N.J.: Prentice-Hall, Inc., 1970), Chap. 19.

and the only important factors connected with buying were station convenience and service. Herzog reports on a study which used projection techniques to establish the product-images for gasoline.[15] In the study Herzog reports, however, there were three main product-images concerning gasoline: (1) gasoline was likened to other types of fuel such as electricity and gas, by a small percentage of people; (2) gasoline purchases were considered to be similar to purchases having to do with transportation, such as bus tickets and railroad fares, by another small percentage; and (3) more than half the respondents felt the purchase of gasoline similar to the purchase of other personal consumption items—things which keep the body fed, protected, and stimulated. The product-image in this case is viewed as an extension of the body. This view of the product could be catered to by product promotion in a number of ways.

Another example is a study on kippers (kippered herring). A large number of respondents reported that they did not use the product because they did not like its taste. Actually, most of them had never tasted the product. Using projective techniques, it was found that most people had "a mental image of barefoot dock workers, slopping around in these slimy fish in some far-away port."[16] With the knowledge just discussed, the communications mix can be designed to overcome, or at least compensate for, unfavorable images.

A PURCHASE MOTIVATION STUDY ON AUTOMOBILES [17]

Several years ago the National Broadcasting Company began a series of studies to determine the value of television as a medium for the promotion of heavy duty consumer goods. The automobile was selected for these studies. One aspect of the project was to gain an understanding of the buying process in the purchase of automobiles. A study was undertaken to determine the self-images of the buyers of cars in general and the self-images and the product-images found in the buyers of different brands and types of cars. More specifically, the study dealt with the differences existing between (1) buyers of different brands in the same price class; (2) buyers of different price classes; (3) potential buyers of the small American car and the standard American car; and (4) potential buyers of the small American car and the small foreign car. This illustration is used to show the kind of qualitative information necessary to match marketing effort with opportunity. It illustrates the way in which differences in self-images affect product choice and also the way in which differences in product-image require adjustments in product and marketing effort to accommodate these differences.

The study included a sample of the general public in addition to new buyers and old buyers. The following findings are based on a sample of 11,000 interviews distributed over the entire country.

Each new car buyer and each old buyer was asked to check from a list of

[15] Herzog, "Behavioral Science Concepts," pp. 34–35.
[16] Herzog, "Behavioral Science Concepts," p. 31.
[17] This illustration was taken from "Auto Motives, A Study in Customer Acceleration," sponsored by the National Broadcasting Co.

118

Foundations
of
Strategy—
Interpreting
Market
Forces and
Opportunities

personality traits those which he felt described himself. This information was used to develop self-images of buyers of different makes of automobiles. These self-images were then compared with the self-images of the general public regardless of make of car owned, and the results expressed in percent differences between the buyer of a specific make and the general public. That is, the number of buyers of a specific make declaring a certain trait were expressed as a percentage of total buyers. Likewise, the number of people in the general public declaring a specific trait were expressed as a percentage of the total. Differences between the percentage of total for buyers of car B and D and the percentage of total for the general public for each trait identified are shown in Table 7-2.

TABLE 7-2
Self-Image of the Buyer

| | Relative Difference Between Buyers and General Public | |
	Car B	Car D
Daring	+ 27%	− 40%
Unpredictable	+ 21	− 16
Impulsive	+ 11	− 15
Sociable	− 10	+ 14
Sentimental	− 8	+ 6
Ambitious	+ 21	+ 20
Thrifty	+ 16	+ 20

Courtesy of National Broadcasting Co.

Car B and car D are low-priced cars of different brands. In general, Table 7-2 shows that buyers of low-price car B thought they were more daring, unpredictable, and impulsive than the general public and less sociable and sentimental. The buyers of low-priced car D displayed the opposite characteristics. Both groups believed they were more ambitious and thrifty than the general public. Although the product-image for each of the two brands was not determined, we can infer that if purchase shows compatibility between the self-image and product-image, the latter must be considered different for each brand. From a marketing standpoint, it would be fruitful for manufacturers of both cars to analyze buyers more deeply to determine which characteristics of their cars appeal to which characteristics of their customers' self-image. Changes in the product in advertising appeals and in purchase environment may be necessary to tap the different segments of the market.

Table 7-3 shows a further refinement of the data in which self-images are related to price classes. Buyers of all three price classes consider themselves more efficient and adventurous than the general public. Many more buyers of high-priced cars believe themselves to be more efficient and adventurous than buyers of low- and medium-priced cars. All buyers consider themselves as less soft-hearted, sensitive, and shy than the general public, but more high-priced buyers than low- or medium-priced buyers profess an absence of these characteristics. With respect to thrift and practicality, buyers of low-priced cars consider themselves above average, medium-priced about average, and high-priced below average. The type of marketing effort needed to cultivate the market for differently priced cars must be tailored to these differences in self-image.

TABLE 7-3
Self-Image by Price Classes

	Relative Difference Between Buyers and General Public		
	Low-Price	*Medium-Price*	*High-Price*
Adventurous	+ 9%	+ 25%	+ 77%
Efficient	+ 13	+ 17	+ 29
Cautious	+ 9	+ 9	− 25
Soft-hearted	− 16	− 13	− 22
Sensitive	− 6	− 15	− 54
Shy	− 22	− 29	− 69
Thrifty	+ 14	− 1	− 32
Practical	+ 10	+ 2	− 25

Courtesy of National Broadcasting Co.

Since the small-car question was a crucial one in the automobile industry at this time, NBC also developed a profile of customers' product-images for small cars, both foreign and American-made, and for standard American-made cars. As shoppers were examining standard American-made cars in a showroom, they were shown a number of adjectives which might be used to describe a car and were asked to select those adjectives which best expressed their opinion of the particular car they were looking at. They were also asked to do the same thing for an illustration of a small American-made car. Car buyers, interviewed in the home, were shown a small-car illustration. To one-half of this group the car illustration was described as a new small American-made car, and to the other half a new small foreign car. The old buyers were also asked to select those adjectives which best expressed their opinion of the standard American car they had already purchased. The data shown in Figure 7-1 is limited to that given by the shoppers in the showroom and that given by the old buyers, to whom the illustration was identified as a new small American-made car.

Figure 7-1 shows the difference in the percentage of people applying particular adjectives to the standard American-made car and the percentage of respondents applying the same adjectives to the new small American-made car. For example, 64 percent more people thought the small American-made car was more economical than the standard. A glance at the chart indicates that the product-image of these two cars is quite different. These differences should be capitalized on in personal selling and advertising by emphasizing in each car the qualities most often attributed to it.

In comparing the small American-made car with the small foreign car the

120

Foundations
of
Strategy—
Interpreting
Market
Forces and
Opportunities

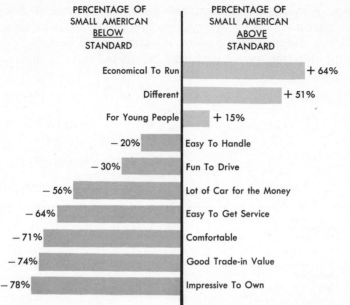

FIGURE 7-1
Image of American
Small Car Versus
Standard

data collected from old buyers were used. To one-half of this group the illustration was identified as a new small American-made car and to the other half a new small foreign car. The differences in the percentage of people applying an adjective to the new small American-made car illustration over the percentage of respondents applying the same adjective to the new small foreign car illustration are shown in Figure 7-2.

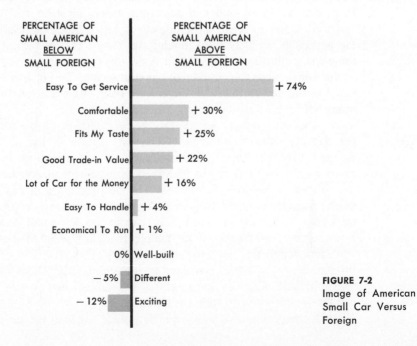

FIGURE 7-2
Image of American
Small Car Versus
Foreign

The small American-made car is felt to be superior to the foreign car in such characteristics as convenience in servicing, comfort, trade-in value, and "a lot of car for the money." The small foreign car is definitely considered more daring and exciting. Relating this information to the self-images of buyers of different makes shown in Tables 7-2 and 7-3, the small foreign car will appeal most likely to the high-priced buyers and the buyers of low-priced car B.

SOME PRACTICAL CONSIDERATIONS

You may wonder how success can ever be achieved without detailed analyses of the subjective characteristics of markets. Many companies know very little about what motivates consumers. They are unquestionably successful without this detailed knowledge. But the more precise a firm's knowledge of markets, and the deeper its understanding of purchase motivation, the greater the expectation that its marketing effort will be successful.

The real role of knowledge concerning purchase motivation is in designing programs which are competitively superior and contribute most effectively to the achievement of corporate objectives. If none of the rival firms is adjusting to the market's more subjective desires, competition will assume many other forms, but the ability of consumers to achieve their ends in the market place will be reduced.

Although the advantages of this kind of market investigation are many, there are limitations to its use in practice. Let us look at some of them.

Cost

Practically all of the studies described involve very costly collection and interpretation procedures. One researcher reports:

> Any competent motivation research report is primarily an interpretive (rather than statistical) analysis of the data in which the researcher draws conclusions and presents them in the report. This interpretation of the data usually requires many man hours of time of highly trained analysts. In analyzing our time sheets we find that professional time in hours on a study runs much higher than the clerical time and is only exceeded by the interviewer man hours.[18]

Most companies today are either unwilling or unable to incur the expense of this kind of research.

Timing

Regardless of cost, the value of motivation studies is rather short-lived. As influencing conditions change, so do self-images. Technological improve-

[18] Burleigh B. Gardner, "The ABC of Motivation Research," *Business Topics,* VII, No. 3, Summer 1959 (East Lansing: Michigan State University, p. 38). (Parentheses added.) Reprinted by permission of the publisher, the Bureau of Business and Economic Research, Division of Research, Graduate School of Business Administration, Michigan State University.

122

Foundations
of
Strategy—
Interpreting
Market
Forces and
Opportunities

ments and marketing innovations by competitors create changes in product-images. Consequently, studies must be conducted at frequent intervals to be reliable. In extremely competitive industries, moreover, there is frequently no time for a full-scale study of consumer behavior; in order to compete successfully the manufacturer must get new products on the market as quickly as possible. With many product types, a few months are all the head start that can be hoped for.

Personnel

There is a shortage of personnel trained to do motivation research. Much that passes for scientific inquiry is conducted by incompetent individuals using poorly designed research techniques. Businessmen must rely on the services of outside organizations to conduct this research. Even when competent analysts are used, the lack of knowledge by management about the theoretical orientation upon which much research rests and about the techniques used constitutes a barrier to acceptance by management.

Methodology

One of the greatest limitations of motivation research is the lack of useful techniques for analyzing consumer behavior. Techniques are still far from adequate for determining the nature of the buying process in detail. Moreover, as pointed out earlier, theories differ; and the different theoretical orientations can lead to different and sometimes conflicting interpretations of the same findings. Since the only source of information is the consumer himself, this research effort is trying to understand the most complex phenomenon in the universe—man.

Of necessity then, this section ends on a note of caution. Nevertheless, although the problems of determining purchase motivation are many, awareness of the subjective elements in consumer behavior is of fundamental—perhaps paramount—importance to the businessman. Moreover, although it may not always be possible to conduct elaborate, costly, and time-consuming studies, the competent manager, with his many years of experience in the market place, will often be able to deduce the possible effects of these subjective elements and make a shrewd guess at how the consumer will behave. This kind of thinking combined with the findings of quantitative market investigations will result in more effective marketing programs.

Finally, there are situations—for example, when the undertaking is such that rather large losses may be incurred if mistakes are made—in which the high absolute cost of an elaborate study may be relatively small.

Summary

In this chapter we have examined another aspect of market investigation, the qualitative aspect of buying behavior. The psychological orientation underlying the study of the consumer was considered in three parts: (1) the experimental approach of the laboratory psychologist, (2) the psychoanalytic approach of the clinical psychologist, and (3) the reference group approach of Gestalt psychology. All three are important to the development of research in the area of purchase motivation. For our purposes, Gestalt psychology seems to be the most useful for understanding consumer behavior. It represents a culmination of all of the approaches through the concept of goal-directed activity. The environmental field, the deeper personality traits, shaped both by physiological needs and repressed drives, interact to shape the consumer's desired self-image.

It was next shown how these theoretical explanations are applied in marketing. Several different research approaches were described. In practically all cases causation is supplied through inferential interpretation. A summary of the findings in a purchase-motivation study of automobile buying was described.

Some of the limitations of the use of research on consumer behavior were examined. But in spite of cost, timing, personnel, and technique limitations, it is important to understand the role of this aspect of market investigation. Every manager must consider the qualitative side of his market in designing the total marketing program. If the limitations prevent formal research, deductive analysis is better than nothing, and where the potential risk is great, the cost of formal research may be relatively low.

Questions and Problems

1. Why is the marketer interested in purchase motivation? Indicate the various areas of marketing that purchase motivation influences.
2. What is meant by reference group theory? How is this relevant to marketing?
3. Suggest at least five different reference groups to which a particular consumer might belong.
4. Why is Gestalt psychology particularly useful in analyzing market behavior?
5. "In practice, it is usually easy to identify the influential reference group to which a person belongs." Comment.
6. What is meant by the term *status role?*
7. Is it always necessary to know *why* a person buys as he does?
8. What is the marketing importance of consumers' self-images?
9. Indicate several of the research techniques which can be used in analyzing self-images.
10. What advantages do indirect methods have over direct methods in the study of purchase motivation?
11. Explain how different stages in the family life cycle can influence purchasing.
12. What are the names given to the various social classes? How are these classes determined? Do consumers tend to spend their money in the same way if they move into a new social class?
13. "Consumers, in their purchase patterns, intrinsically attempt to express a station-in-life." Do you agree? Elaborate on this statement.
14. "After enough motivation analysis, it should be relatively easy for the marketer to manipulate consumers to his own ends." Do you think this statement is valid?
15. What factors tend to limit the extent and usefulness of formal purchase-motivation analysis? What alternative approaches are open to the marketer working in this area?

Analysing Industrial Goods Markets

8

So far we have dealt with the objective and subjective characteristics of the markets for consumer goods—goods bought for personal or household consumption. But there must also be the plant, equipment, and materials to produce consumer goods and make them available for consumption. Those goods and services destined for use in producing other goods and services are called *industrial goods*.[1]

Industrial goods are used either directly in the production and distribution of other goods and services or indirectly to facilitate production and distribution. The market is called the industrial market and includes business, industry, and such institutions as banks, hotels, restaurants, advertising agencies, retailers, wholesalers, governmental agencies, schools, hospitals, and prisons.

The approaches to market investigation presented in Chapters 6 and 7 apply to the industrial market, but there are differences in the characteristics of buyers and sellers in the industrial market as well as differences in the forces influencing behavior. These differences have an effect on the way in which industrial goods are marketed; and as we examine the characteristics of the industrial market, we shall see the way in which they affect policies regarding price, channels of distribution, and communications.

In this chapter we shall describe the industrial market by explaining its complexity, the number and type of industrial buyers, and the size of the market. Industrial goods will then be classified and the characteristics of the market examined. Finally, other approaches to the investigation of industrial goods will be explored.

---

[1] R. S. Alexander and others, *Marketing Definitions* (Chicago: American Marketing Assn., 1960), p. 14.

THE MARKET FOR INDUSTRIAL GOODS

The Complexity of the Industrial Market

The industrial and commercial organization which makes possible the vast array of consumer goods is a highly specialized one. In the production sector there are a number of specialized plants which produce parts of the final finished consumer products. In the commercial sector there is a similar specialization. We find wholesalers buying from manufacturers and selling to distributors, and we observe purchases and sales between the many different types of facilitating agencies—banks, advertising agencies, hotels, restaurants.

Figure 8-1 shows the complexity of the industrial market. There are many specialized suppliers of materials in such categories as farm materials, minerals, utilities, durable and nondurable manufacturing, and imported materials. Purchases and sales between these specialized units are necessary to produce consumer goods, equipment, and construction (plants, commercial buildings, and residential houses). All of the equipment, much of the farm and imported materials, and much of the construction must find its way back to the material supplier specialists. There is also a large market among the materials suppliers; for example, the steel ingot plants must have instrument parts and the mineral suppliers must have shipping containers.

If we were to include those establishments responsible for the distribution or use of industrial goods as well as the facilitating establishments, such as banks and advertising agencies, we would have a picture of the buyers and sellers in the industrial market.

Buyers of Industrial Goods

Buyers of industrial goods can be grouped according to activity or "industry"—extractive industries (mining, lumbering, and fishing) and agriculture; manufacturing; distributive trades and services; and service industries such as transportation, communication, utilities, and government. The number of establishments in each of these categories is shown in Table 8-1.

Extractive Industries

Mining, lumbering, and fishing all require specialized equipment today. For example, the fishing industry needs such things as tackles, boats, radios, and cold-storage facilities. Both the mining and lumbering industries need extractive equipment and materials-handling equipment to move raw materials from their source to processing points.

Agriculture

Farmers buy seeds, fertilizers, farm machinery, and specialized structures such as barns and silos.

FIGURE 8-1
Major Commodity Flows

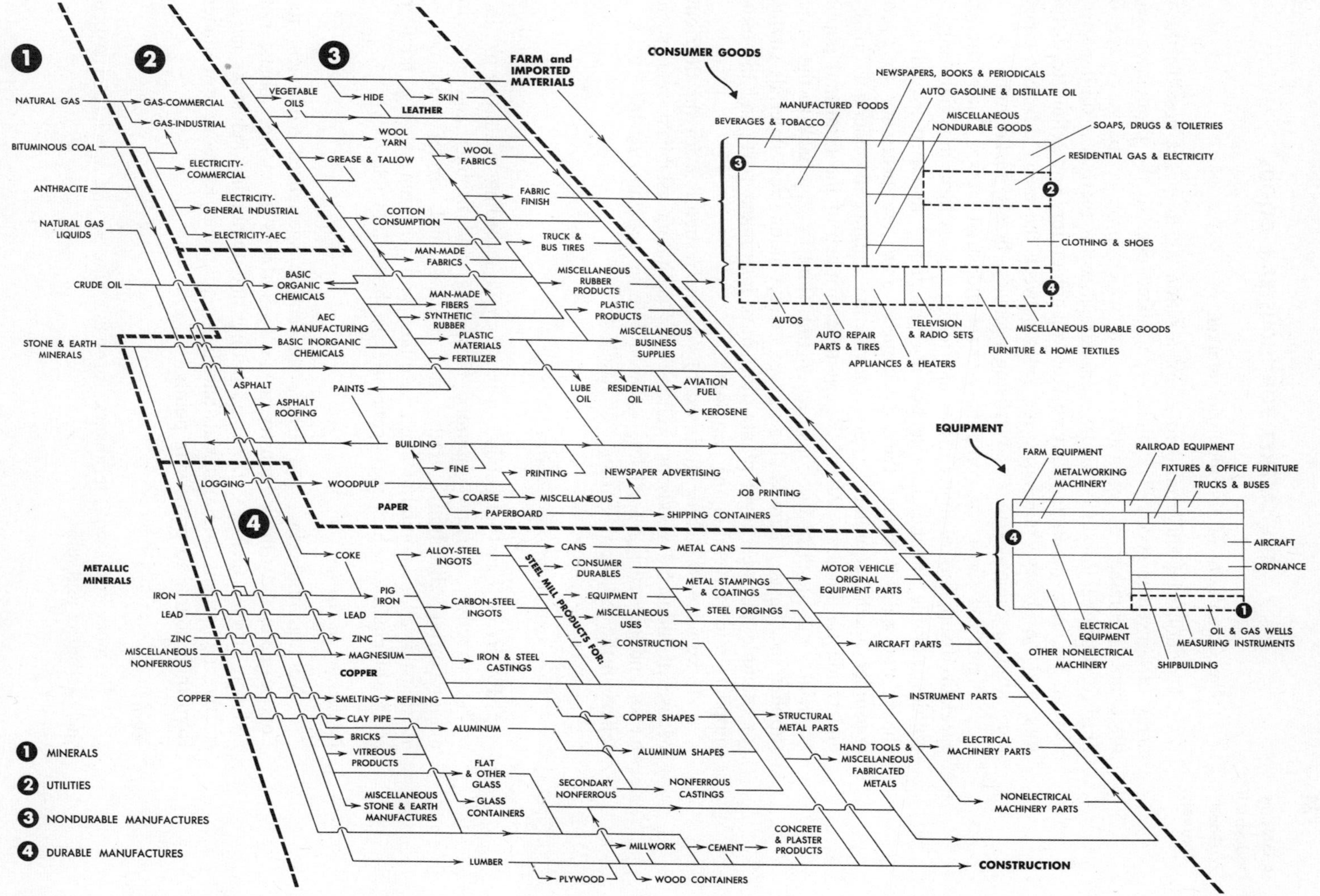

TABLE 8-1
Number of Industrial Goods Buyers
by Kind of Business

Extractive industries	
Mining	38,651
Lumbering	11,681
Fishing	23,249
Agriculture	3,158,000
Manufacturing	311,921
Distributive trades and services	
Retailers	1,707,931
Wholesalers	308,177
Service establishments	1,061,673
Transportation, communication, utilities	56,291
Government	93,526
Total	6,771,100

Source: Compiled from U.S. Bureau of the Census, Statistical Abstract of the United States: 1967, 88th ed. (Washington, D.C.: Government Printing Office, 1967.)

Manufacturing

As a market for its own goods, manufacturing is the most obvious user of goods and services destined for use in producing other goods and services. It is often mistakenly thought of as the only group of buyers of industrial goods, a misconception that ignores the very large market in the remainder of the economy.

Distributive Trades and Services

Retailers need stores, and equipment to operate them—display stands, cash registers, refrigeration units, meatcutting tools, etc. Wholesalers must have warehouses, office space and equipment, and materials-handling equipment such as conveyor systems and lift trucks. Service establishments such as beauty parlors need buildings and specialized equipment—hair dryers, furniture, and cosmetics. Hotels need buildings, furniture, kitchen equipment, and restaurant facilities. All are industrial goods as they are destined for use in producing services for consumers.

Transportation, Communication, and Utilities

Railroads, trucking companies, steamship companies, and airlines are an important market for many industrial goods producers. Telephone companies, television and radio broadcasting enterprises, and newspaper and magazine publishers require highly specialized equipment, such as telephone exchange equipment, radio and television transmission installations, and printing presses. Utilities use electric generators, transmission lines, and natural gas pipelines.

Government

Governmental agencies and quasi-governmental institutions, such as schools, hospitals, and penal institutions, buy large quantities of food, furniture

128

Foundations
of
Strategy—
Interpreting
Market
Forces and
Opportunities

of various kinds, teaching materials, and drugs. Military installations need buildings, food, and furniture, as well as military equipment such as trucks, tanks, rockets, guns, and clothing necessary to outfit the armed forces.

The Size of the Industrial Market

There is a mistaken conception that the market for industrial goods is smaller than the consumer goods market. From a marketing point of view the size of the industrial market is the total dollar value of all transactions between the various producers of industrial goods and services. This is so because marketing is involved in the consummation of these transactions. There are no reliable estimates of the total dollar value of all transactions in the industrial market, but a simple example will illustrate that the industrial market is larger than the consumer goods market.

Let us assume a very simple economy in which 100 units of product A are produced and consumed. The final price to consumers is $1 per unit, which covers all costs and the profit necessary to bring product A to the market. Consumer expenditures in this case are $100 (100 × $1). In our complex industrial structure, in which specialization plays an important role, let us say four specialized enterprises are necessary to bring this product to the consumer: the mine, the processor, the fabricator, and the manufacturer of product A. The processor purchases raw materials from the mine at 30 cents a unit. Thus, the mine has a market of $30 (100 × .30). The processor uses equipment and labor and sells the processed product to the fabricator at 50 cents a unit. His market is valued at $50. The fabricator takes the processed material and, using equipment and labor, fabricates it and sells it to the manufacturer of product A for 60 cents a unit, the market being valued at $60 (100 × .60). The total industrial market, then, is equal to $140 ($30 + $50 + $60), as against a total consumer market of $100.

From the example it can be seen that the number of transactions (and consequently the size of the industrial goods market) is dependent upon the degree of specialization in the economy.

A CLASSIFICATION
OF INDUSTRIAL GOODS

Industrial goods can be classified into (1) capital goods, (2) components and materials, and (3) supplies. While it is not always possible to neatly fit every product into one of the above categories, such a classification does provide a means for speaking in more specific and precise terms about the characteristics of the industrial goods market. Let us look at the differences among these different classes of goods.

Capital Goods

Capital goods include such goods as *plant and equipment,* which are used in the production and distribution of other goods but which do not become a part of the goods produced. The plant category includes factories, warehouses, retail stores, and wholesale structures. The equipment category includes all production machinery, materials-handling equipment, and furniture and fixtures, as well as transportation and communication equipment. These goods are used in manufacturing and distributing but are not a part of the product. Capital goods may be thought of from an accounting standpoint as those which are capitalized in accounting records and which are amortized over their economic life.

Table 8-2 shows the very substantial size of the capital goods market in 1966 and the shares going to different segments of the total market. An important item is the size of the nonmanufacturing and the utilities market. There is a tendency to think of the capital goods market as made up of manufacturers; yet this segment represents only 34.3 percent; nonmanufacturing constitutes 39.5 percent, and utilities 10.6 percent.

TABLE 8-2
Distribution of Capital Outlays, 1966

	Billions	*Percentage*
Manufacturing	27.0	34.3
Durable	14.0	17.7
Nondurable	13.0	16.6
Nonmanufacturing	31.1	39.5
Agriculture	5.9	7.6
Mining	1.5	1.9
Trades and services	12.7	16.1
Communication	5.6	7.1
Transportation	5.4	6.8
Utilities	8.4	10.6
Others	12.3	15.6
Total	$78.8	100.0%

Compiled from data in Statistical Abstract of the United States, 1967.

Components and Materials

Components and materials differ from capital goods in that they are a part of the total product the consumer purchases. *Components* are partially or wholly manufactured or processed goods. Tires, batteries, and spark plugs are components in the auto industry, as well as car frames, textiles, and engine blocks. *Materials* may be wholly or partially processed and include such goods as iron ore, copper, coal, lumber, and wheat. The distinction between components and materials is not always clear. In the baking industry, flour, processed from wheat, might be considered a component, but in fact it is considered a raw material.

130

Foundations
of
Strategy—
Interpreting
Market
Forces and
Opportunities

Supplies

Supplies include goods used to facilitate production and distribution processes. Like capital goods they do not generally become a part of the finished goods, but unlike capital goods they are used up in production, and from an accounting viewpoint are considered as an expense rather than a capital investment. This category includes such goods as industrial cleaning compounds, lubricating oils for equipment, and stationery supplies.

SPECIAL CHARACTERISTICS
OF INDUSTRIAL GOODS
AND THEIR MARKETS

Although there are many similarities between the marketing of industrial goods and consumer goods, the differences are sufficiently great to call for modification in marketing effort. At the root of these differences are special characteristics of the products, the market structure, the market demand, and the purchasing process.

The Product

Homogeneity of Product

A good many industrial products tend to have a high degree of similarity with the products of competing manufacturers: all fractional horsepower electrical motors, for example, are built to common NEMA (National Electrical Manufacturers Association) specifications and are therefore markedly similar. There are even fewer differences among competing materials—steel of a given technical grade is steel and likewise, all cement is cement, regardless of the source of supply. Skilled purchasing agents, interested in performance know this to be the case. This is contrary to the situation among many consumer goods, for example cigarettes—where competing brands which are substantially similar are made to appear very different through skillful packaging and heavy advertising. New product variations that prove to be advantageous tend to be quickly adopted by competitors. This results because of the characteristically high level of technical research and development expenditures among rival firms, and the fact that often slight changes in a product's design will obviate the danger of patent infringement and allow a competitor to adopt an improvement in his own product.

But ease and speed of copying do not mean that product improvements bring no competitive advantage, only that the advantage will be short lived and that new improvements must be constantly sought if a competitor wishes to maintain his market position.

Technical Considerations

Industrial goods are characteristically more complex than consumer goods. Also, since they are used in complex industrial processes, the marketing of them differs from consumer goods. Capital goods—electronic computers, textile machinery, automatic screw machines, turbines—are obviously complex; but so are some components and materials as well as some supplies. The sale of electric motors to original equipment manufacturers, such as tool manufacturers, is frequently on a specification basis. In marketing such goods, many more technical features of the product come into the negotiations. The sale of lubricating oils in the supply group is a highly technical job. There are as many as 300 different grades of lubricating oils, and much skill is needed to determine the proper grade for each machine and for the operation it is performing.

This complexity of form and application means that a close relationship between the buyer and seller is usually established to assure that the product meets the needs of the buyer. Technical assistance is needed at many points in the buyer-seller relationship. In many products, it is needed before the sale, particularly when the goods are not standardized but are made to consumer specifications. This is the case for most capital goods, such as electronic data processing systems, electric generators, stamping equipment, and large presses used in manufacturing. And many components require before-sale service— automobile carburetors, batteries, and electric motors, for example. Post-sale service is needed in the form of training operators for new equipment.

Personal representation over a rather long period of negotiation is usually necessary to work out the details of each sale. The skill required of the salesman in many cases calls for engineers or highly trained representatives to perform the selling job. The need for personal selling and the nature of the negotiation process make advertising and sales promotion less important in marketing many industrial goods. Advertising is usually placed in specialized trade journals, or direct mail advertising is used. Its major purpose is as a prospecting device for the personal salesmen. Sales promotion for the most part is confined to conventions and trade fairs.

To back up the sales that have been made, it is necessary to maintain adequate supplies of repair parts and to have the facility to expedite repairs if necessary. Unless repairs can be made rapidly, the breakdown cost to the buyer may be very high. Often the product may be so technical that skilled repairmen must be readily available. For example, elevator manufacturers must provide trained maintenance personnel wherever they make installations. Service on some industrial goods is so important that its adequacy is often the deciding factor in the buyer's choice from among several competing products.

The technical nature of industrial goods and the technical uses of them require that the distribution mix and communications mix be adjusted to the needs these technical considerations dictate.

High Average Value of Sale

Industrial goods usually have a high unit value. Or if the unit value is low, they are purchased in such large quantities that the average sale is high. It is common for capital goods to cost hundreds of thousands of dollars. The size of the average value of sale is important because it is the base which must absorb all sales costs. If the average value of a sale is high, the marketer can afford the high costs of skilled representation and the long periods of negotiation

132

Foundations
of
Strategy—
Interpreting
Market
Forces and
Opportunities

necessary to adjust the product to the customer's needs. If the average value of the sale is low, not as much can be spent in marketing to consummate the sale.

Infrequent Purchase

In comparison with consumer goods, the purchase of industrial goods is often infrequent. This is most true of capital goods, because they last longer and because replacement can be postponed. If the financial condition of the user is not sound, he usually can make his old equipment do until he is able to purchase new equipment.

There is a trend, however, among many forward-looking purchasers of plant and equipment to think of the economic life-span of capital goods rather than the physical life-span. Thus, they may have equipment with a physical life-span of ten years, but if technology after four years has produced more efficient cost-saving equipment, they will replace immediately. The economic life-span of the old equipment is four years. This has given special impetus to manufacturers of capital goods to seek technological improvements which shorten the economic life-span and step up the replacement cycle. Continuous appraisal of the product mix is an important aspect of this development.

Components, materials, and supplies are more frequently purchased than capital goods. However, in many cases once an acceptable supplier is found, purchases are on a contract basis and contact between buyer and seller is not as frequent as if original sales had to be closed each time a delivery was made.

The Market Structure

The word *structure* is used here to refer to the form of the market—the number and geographic location of buyers.

Limited Number of Buyers

The number of industrial goods buyers is much smaller than the number of consumers. In 1965 there were 60.2 million consuming units as compared to the 6.7 million industrial goods buyers shown in Table 8-1. For the individual producer of industrial goods the number of potential customers is further reduced by the specialization of the buyer. Whereas every consumer buys shoes, only textile manufacturers will buy textile machinery. Probably no producer of industrial goods will find customers in all segments (agriculture, manufacturing, etc.) of the market. If the individual industrial marketer sells mainly or exclusively to manufacturing enterprises, he meets another factor restricting the number of customers: the greatest buying power is concentrated in the hands of a few buyers because about 9 percent of the manufacturing firms account for about 80 percent of value added by manufacturing.

The number of buyers who must be contacted reduces the cost of personal selling. It is much less expensive to personally cultivate a few potential buyers than the large number that would have to be contacted in the consumer goods market. The number of buyers has implications for the kind of distribution mix selected.

Geographic Concentration of Buyers

The map shown in Figure 8-2 gives some idea of the geographic concentration of manufacturing. There is likewise geographic concentration in agriculture and the extractive industries. Geographic concentration is not characteristic of all industrial goods buyers. We find the distributive trades, service establishments, transportation, communication, and utility enterprises scattered all over the country. Nevertheless, there is more geographic concentration among industrial goods buyers than among ultimate consumers.

Whenever there is geographic concentration among the buyers of industrial goods the physical task of contacting the potential buyer is much easier and much less costly. Couple this characteristic with the limited number of buyers, and the physical task of contacting the market is much simpler than in the case of ultimate consumer buyers. Of course marketers of less specialized goods or of goods going to specialized but dispersed industries do not benefit from geographic concentration. Industrial cleaning compounds, for example, can be used by a variety of industrial goods buyers, and the market is almost as dispersed geographically as the market of the retailing industry.

Nevertheless, many marketers are confronted by geographically concentrated markets, and this fact is particularly influential in determining the directness of distribution and the means of solicitation used. When we examine the distribution and communication mixes in Parts 4 and 5, the influence of these characteristics will be more evident.

Market Demand

There are two characteristics of the demand for industrial goods that are different from the demand for consumer goods. They are (1) wide fluctuations in demand and (2) relative inelasticity of demand. Each of these characteristics should be understood in conjunction with the marketing of industrial goods.

Wide Fluctuations in Demand

The industrial goods market is for a number of reasons much more erratic than the consumer goods market. One reason for this irregularity in demand is that increases or decreases in consumer goods demand, on which the demand for industrial goods depends, cause much wider fluctuations in the demand for industrial goods. This is called the *acceleration principle* and can be illustrated by reference to our hypothetical example on page 138. Suppose that the demand for product A is cut 10 percent and only 90 units are demanded instead of 100. Total consumer demand is now valued at $90, or a cut of $10. The processor needs only $27 (90 × 30¢) of the raw material; the fabricator needs only $45 (90 × 50¢) of the processed raw material; and the manufacturer of product A needs only $54 (90 × 60¢) of the fabricated part. We have a $14 decrease in the demand for industrial goods along with the $10 decrease in the demand for consumer goods.

Although the absolute decrease is greater in the industrial goods market,

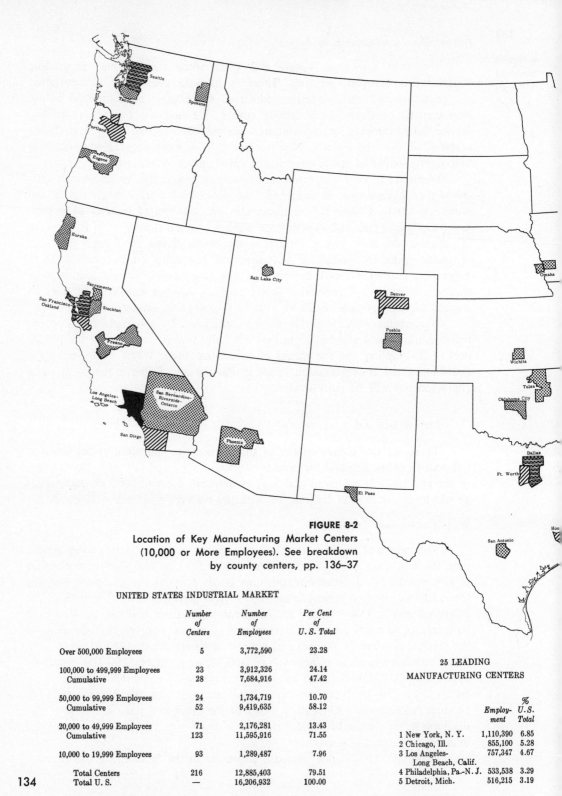

FIGURE 8-2

Location of Key Manufacturing Market Centers
(10,000 or More Employees). See breakdown
by county centers, pp. 136–37

UNITED STATES INDUSTRIAL MARKET

	Number of Centers	Number of Employees	Per Cent of U. S. Total
Over 500,000 Employees	5	3,772,590	23.28
100,000 to 499,999 Employees	23	3,912,326	24.14
Cumulative	28	7,684,916	47.42
50,000 to 99,999 Employees	24	1,734,719	10.70
Cumulative	52	9,419,635	58.12
20,000 to 49,999 Employees	71	2,176,281	13.43
Cumulative	123	11,595,916	71.55
10,000 to 19,999 Employees	93	1,289,487	7.96
Total Centers	216	12,885,403	79.51
Total U. S.	—	16,206,932	100.00

25 LEADING MANUFACTURING CENTERS

	Employment	% U. S. Total
1 New York, N. Y.	1,110,390	6.85
2 Chicago, Ill.	855,100	5.28
3 Los Angeles-Long Beach, Calif.	757,347	4.67
4 Philadelphia, Pa.-N. J.	533,538	3.29
5 Detroit, Mich.	516,215	3.19

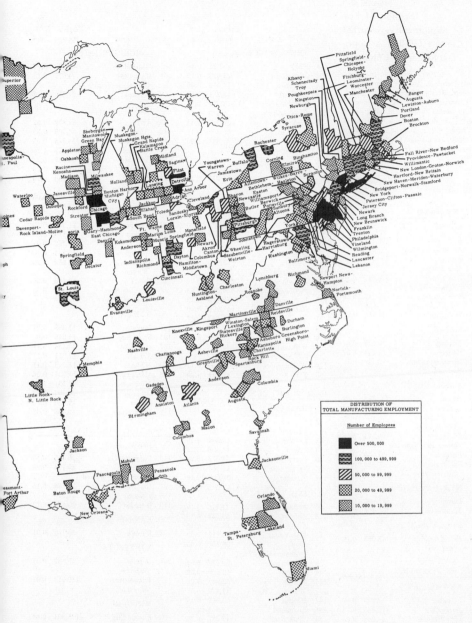

	Employ- ment	% U.S. Total		Employ- ment	% U.S. Total		Employ- ment	% U.S. Total
6 Boston, Mass.-N. H.	394,038	2.43	15 Paterson-Clifton- Passaic, N. J.	158,491	0.98	21 Jersey City, N. J.	119,965	0.74
7 Pittsburgh, Pa.	304,238	1.88				22 Providence-	113,055	0.70
8 Cleveland, Ohio	279,878	1.73	16 Cincinnati, Ohio	154,384	0.95	Pawtucket, R. I.		
9 St. Louis, Mo.-Ill.	253,829	1.57	17 Minneapolis-St. Paul,	146,913	0.91	23 Bridgeport-Norwalk-	106,193	0.66
10 Newark, N. J.	236,880	1.46	Minn.			Stamford, Conn.		
11 Baltimore, Md.	194,371	1.20	18 Hartford-	139,263	0.86	24 Gary-Hammond-	106,151	0.65
12 Milwaukee, Wis.	191,191	1.18	New Britain, Conn.			E. Chicago, Ind.		
13 San Francisco- Oakland, Calif.	183,748	1.13	19 Seattle, Wash.	125,115	0.77	25 Dallas, Texas	104,735	0.65
			20 New Haven-Meriden- Waterbury, Conn.	120,817	0.75			
14 Buffalo, N. Y.	170,978	1.05				Total	7,376,823	45.53

135

Foundations
of
Strategy—
Interpreting
Market
Forces and
Opportunities

FIGURE 8-2
Location of Key Manufacturing Market Centers (10,000 or More Employees).—Continued

In the tabulations below, metropolitan county centers (based primarily on Standard Metropolitan Statistical Areas) are indicated by *italic* type. Non-metropolitan county centers (including entire county) are designated by the name of the largest city in the county, based on the 1960 Population Census, and are indicated by roman (regular, non-italic) type.

Rank	Area	Employment	% U.S. Total
NEW ENGLAND			
CONNECTICUT			
23	*Bridgeport-Norwalk-Stamford*	106,193	0.66
18	*Hartford-New Britain*	139,263	0.86
20	*New Haven-Meriden-Waterbury*	120,817	0.75
94	*New London-Groton-Norwich*	25,742	0.16
189	Willimantic	11,414	0.07
MAINE			
208	Augusta	10,619	0.07
185	Bangor	11,754	0.07
150	*Lewiston-Auburn*	15,719	0.10
133	Portland	18,251	0.11
MASSACHUSETTS			
6	*Boston*	394,038	2.43
110	*Brockton*	21,517	0.13
39	*Fall River-New Bedford*	73,857	0.46
30	*Fitchburg-Leominster-Worcester*	99,594	0.61
106	*Pittsfield*	22,044	0.14
38	*Springfield-Chicopee-Holyoke*	73,910	0.46
NEW HAMPSHIRE			
186	Dover	11,600	0.07
82	*Manchester*	32,166	0.20
RHODE ISLAND			
22	*Providence-Pawtucket*	113,055	0.70
MIDDLE ATLANTIC			
NEW JERSEY			
123	Franklin	20,095	0.12
21	*Jersey City*	119,965	0.74
155	Long Branch	14,959	0.09
10	*Newark*	236,880	1.46
43	New Brunswick	65,646	0.41
15	*Paterson-Clifton-Passaic*	158,491	0.98
74	*Trenton*	36,163	0.22
135	Vineland	18,077	0.11
NEW YORK			
41	*Albany-Schenectady-Troy*	68,161	0.42
71	*Binghamton*	38,339	0.24
14	*Buffalo*	170,978	1.05
163	Corning	14,027	0.09

Rank	Area	Employment	% U.S. Total
NEW YORK (continued)			
144	Elmira	16,521	0.10
103	Jamestown	23,623	0.15
175	Kingston	12,912	0.08
145	Newburgh	16,284	0.10
1	*New York*	1,110,390	6.85
111	Poughkeepsie	21,446	0.13
27	*Rochester*	102,322	0.63
42	*Syracuse*	65,966	0.41
61	*Utica-Rome*	41,887	0.26
PENNSYLVANIA			
31	*Allentown-Bethlehem-Easton*	91,217	0.56
197	Altoona	11,254	0.07
214	Berwick	10,161	0.06
215	Butler	10,046	0.06
80	*Erie*	32,522	0.20
79	*Harrisburg*	33,893	0.21
102	*Johnstown*	24,020	0.15
59	*Lancaster*	42,900	0.26
167	Lebanon	13,340	0.08
183	Newcastle	11,881	0.07
4	*Philadelphia*	533,538	3.29
7	*Pittsburgh*	304,238	1.88
125	Pottsville	19,816	0.12
54	*Reading*	47,909	0.30
91	*Scranton*	27,833	0.17
120	Sharon	20,388	0.13
179	Sunbury	12,273	0.08
64	*Wilkes-Barre-Hazelton*	40,458	0.25
139	*Williamsport*	17,199	0.11
63	*York*	41,394	0.26
EAST NORTH CENTRAL			
ILLINOIS			
2	*Chicago*	855,100	5.28
196	*Danville*	11,267	0.07
162	*Decatur*	14,244	0.09
58	*Peoria*	43,608	0.27
68	*Rockford*	38,756	0.24
182	*Springfield*	11,943	0.07
146	Streator	16,028	0.10
INDIANA			
95	Anderson	24,796	0.15
118	Elkhart	20,537	0.13
93	*Evansville*	26,426	0.16
75	*Fort Wayne*	35,812	0.22
24	*Gary-Hammond-E. Chicago*	106,151	0.65
29	*Indianapolis*	99,758	0.62
164	Kokomo	13,800	0.09
174	Marion	12,949	0.08
187	Michigan City	11,470	0.07
147	*Muncie*	15,919	0.10
188	Richmond	11,454	0.07
65	*South Bend*	40,287	0.25
MICHIGAN			
194	*Adrian*	11,325	0.07
114	*Ann Arbor*	20,928	0.13
112	Battle Creek	21,133	0.13
108	Benton Harbor	21,954	0.14
5	*Detroit*	516,215	3.19
45	*Flint*	63,035	0.39
55	*Grand Rapids*	46,965	0.29
169	Holland	13,225	0.08
151	*Jackson*	15,502	0.10
96	*Kalamazoo*	24,792	0.15
88	*Lansing*	30,273	0.19

Rank	Area	Employment	% U.S. Total
MICHIGAN (continued)			
181	Midland	11,969	0.07
101	*Muskegon-Muskegon Heights*	24,077	0.15
98	*Saginaw*	24,699	0.15
OHIO			
35	*Akron*	84,858	0.52
49	*Canton*	56,390	0.35
16	*Cincinnati*	154,384	0.95
8	*Cleveland*	279,878	1.73
40	*Columbus*	69,617	0.43
28	*Dayton*	101,970	0.63
85	*Hamilton-Middletown*	31,286	0.19
166	*Lima*	13,496	0.08
90	*Lorain-Elyria*	28,641	0.18
113	Mansfield	21,032	0.13
209	Newark	10,519	0.06
205	Sandusky	10,782	0.07
148	Springfield	15,894	0.10
81	*Steubenville-Weirton*	32,286	0.20
47	*Toledo*	57,618	0.36
36	*Youngstown-Warren*	81,662	0.50
WISCONSIN			
191	Appleton	11,388	0.07
193	*Green Bay*	11,346	0.07
137	Janesville	17,384	0.11
136	Kenosha	17,911	0.11
132	Madison	18,513	0.11
216	Manitowoc	10,025	0.06
12	*Milwaukee*	191,191	1.18
122	Oshkosh	20,109	0.12
124	*Racine*	19,930	0.12
172	Sheboygan	12,988	0.08
WEST NORTH CENTRAL			
IOWA			
119	*Cedar Rapids*	20,455	0.13
66	*Davenport-Rock Island-Moline*	39,174	0.24
97	*Des Moines*	24,788	0.15
195	Dubuque	11,275	0.07
116	Waterloo	20,574	0.13
KANSAS			
53	*Wichita*	49,710	0.31
MINNESOTA			
204	*Duluth-Superior*	10,889	0.07
17	*Minneapolis-St. Paul*	146,913	0.91
MISSOURI			
26	*Kansas City*	103,801	0.64
211	*St. Joseph*	10,480	0.06
9	*St. Louis*	253,829	1.57
NEBRASKA			
78	*Omaha*	34,420	0.21
SOUTH ATLANTIC			
DELAWARE			
52	*Wilmington*	50,814	0.31
DISTRICT OF COLUMBIA			
72	*Washington*	37,608	0.23

Rank	Area	Employment	% U.S. Total
FLORIDA			
121	Jacksonville	20,308	0.13
176	Lakeland	12,882	0.08
69	Miami	38,592	0.24
161	Orlando	14,454	0.09
153	Pensacola	15,303	0.09
77	Tampa-St. Petersburg	34,805	0.21
GEORGIA			
33	Atlanta	87,821	0.54
109	Augusta	21,773	0.13
142	Columbus	16,739	0.10
199	Macon	12,331	0.07
156	Savannah	14,767	0.09
MARYLAND			
11	Baltimore	194,371	1.20
184	Hagerstown	11,360	0.07
NORTH CAROLINA			
180	Asheboro	12,210	0.08
168	Asheville	13,324	0.08
126	Burlington	19,782	0.12
99	Charlotte	24,500	0.15
178	Durham	12,388	0.08
92	Gastonia	27,151	0.17
56	Greensboro-High Point	45,023	0.28
128	Hickory	19,242	0.12
107	Kannapolis	21,994	0.14
152	Lexington	15,478	0.10
206	Reidsville	10,753	0.07
207	Statesville	10,708	0.07
73	Winston-Salem	36,191	0.22
SOUTH CAROLINA			
131	Anderson	18,529	0.11
198	Columbia	11,178	0.07
89	Greenville	30,098	0.19
173	Rock Hill	12,972	0.08
105	Spartanburg	22,576	0.14
VIRGINIA			
170	Danville	13,139	0.08
140	Lynchburg	16,852	0.10
158	Martinsville	14,723	0.09
141	Newport News-Hampton	16,789	0.10
160	Norfolk-Portsmouth	14,493	0.09
67	Richmond	38,883	0.24
165	Roanoke	13,784	0.09
WEST VIRGINIA			
104	Charleston	22,621	0.14
100	Huntington-Ashland	24,404	0.15
143	Wheeling	16,685	0.10
EAST SOUTH CENTRAL			
ALABAMA			
202	Anniston	11,006	0.07
44	Birmingham	64,482	0.40
177	Gadsden	12,576	0.08
138	Mobile	17,353	0.11
KENTUCKY			
34	Louisville	86,655	0.53
MISSISSIPPI			
213	Jackson	10,252	0.06
203	Pascagoula	10,939	0.07
TENNESSEE			
60	Chattanooga	42,460	0.26
129	Kingsport	18,814	0.12
76	Knoxville	35,278	0.22
62	Memphis	41,840	0.26
70	Nashville	38,450	0.24
WEST SOUTH CENTRAL			
ARKANSAS			
157	Little Rock-North Little Rock	14,759	0.09
LOUISIANA			
134	Baton Rouge	18,155	0.11
57	New Orleans	44,276	0.27
OKLAHOMA			
130	Oklahoma City	18,667	0.12
83	Tulsa	31,836	0.20
TEXAS			
84	Beaumont-Port Arthur	31,832	0.20
25	Dallas	104,735	0.65
190	El Paso	11,395	0.07
50	Fort Worth	54,740	0.34
210	Galveston-Texas City	10,496	0.06
32	Houston	90,796	0.56
117	San Antonio	20,548	0.13
MOUNTAIN			
ARIZONA			
86	Phoenix	30,473	0.19
COLORADO			
48	Denver	56,642	0.35
201	Pueblo	11,042	0.07
UTAH			
127	Salt Lake City	19,515	0.12
PACIFIC			
CALIFORNIA			
192	Eureka	11,375	0.07
200	Fresno	11,057	0.07
3	Los Angeles-Long Beach	757,347	4.67
115	Sacramento	20,584	0.13
87	San Bernardino-Riverside-Ontario	30,320	0.19
37	San Diego	76,497	0.47
13	San Francisco-Oakland	183,748	1.13
46	San Jose	61,305	0.38
212	Stockton	10,393	0.06
HAWAII			
154	Honolulu	14,973	0.09
OREGON			
149	Eugene	15,720	0.10
51	Portland	53,678	0.33
WASHINGTON			
19	Seattle	125,115	0.77
171	Spokane	13,061	0.08
159	Tacoma	14,552	0.09

the proportionate decrease is the same—10 percent, if no adjustments are made in inventory levels. Typically, however, retailers and distributors reduce their average inventories, which has an accelerating effect back through the distribution channels.[2] This situation is also intensified when we consider the role of capital goods in our economy, something overlooked in our simple example. Suppose the manufacturer of product A requires 10 machines, each of which will produce 10 units of product A. Also assume that all machines have the same physical life-span and that their age differences are such that one wears out each year and is normally replaced.

In the first year the demand for product A is 100 units; the manufacturer has 10 machines and one will wear out each year and will be replaced if

[2] The inventory "whiplash," or acceleration effect, is explained in Chapter 16, in the discussion of physical distribution management.

138

Foundations
of
Strategy—
Interpreting
Market
Forces and
Opportunities

necessary. The schedule below shows the demand for machines by the manufacturer of product A and the percentage of change in demand under different consumer demand conditions.

A small change in the demand for consumer goods caused a more than proportionate change in the demand for capital goods.

The acceleration effect on capital goods can be erratic, as one might expect. In our example we assumed a fixed ratio between the number of machines needed and output, but in reality there is usually some "slack." The manufacturer of product A might be able to absorb an increase in consumer demand in year 7 by putting on an extra shift and increasing capacity. No acceleration

Year	Consumer Demand Product A (Units)	Percentage of Change	Machines Needed (Units)	Industrial Demand for New Machines (Units)	Percentage of Change
1	100	0	10	1	0
2	100	0	10	1	0
3	110	+10	11	2	+100
4	130	+18.1	13	3	+ 50
5	130	0	13	1	− 66.6
6	100	−23	10	0	−100

effect would then take place. We also assumed the same physical life-span for each machine and an age distribution of machines in use that meant one machine would wear out each year. Neither of these assumptions is entirely accurate. The rapid rate of technological development has caused many buyers to think of the economic rather than physical life-span of their equipment, thus reducing the time at which capital goods are replaced. This then alters the age distribution of machines in use.

Some analysts of the capital goods market argue that the rapid rate of technological development in capital goods has caused a smoothing out of the fluctuations in demand.[3] This contention is supported by the data given in Table 8-3, in which during the period from 1955 to 1966, total outlays for plant and equipment were approximately 9-11 percent of gross national product. The term *dynamic stability* has been given to the characteristic.[4] Although the capital goods market has grown with the general economy, is it true that the fluctuations in demand have been smoothed out?

If we examine those periods in which there were recessions in the consumer goods field—1957–58 and 1961–62—we will conclude that there are still wide fluctuations. In Figure 8-3 the outlays for plant and equipment are compared with GNP less capital outlays. In the 1957–58 recession, the decrease in rate of growth in the economy from a 5.6 percent increase in 1957 to a 2.2 percent increase in 1958 was accompanied by a 14.9 percent decrease in capital

[3] See "Another Big Decade for Capital Goods," *Fortune* (December 1956), p. 101.
[4] *Ibid.*

TABLE 8-3

Distribution of Capital Outlays and GNP (1955–1966
(in billions of dollars)

Year	Non-Industrial [1]	Manufacturing and Mining	Utilities	Other [2]	Total	GNP	Percentage of GNP
1955	16.2	12.4	4.3	6.9	39.8	397.5	10.0
1956	17.8	16.1	4.9	6.3	45.1	419.2	10.7
1957	17.5	17.1	6.2	6.6	47.4	442.5	10.7
1958	16.4	12.4	6.1	5.4	40.3	444.2	9.0
1959	18.5	13.1	5.7	6.9	44.2	482.1	9.1
1960	18.6	15.5	5.7	7.4	47.2	504.4	9.4
1961	18.5	14.7	5.5	7.6	46.3	521.3	9.0
1962	19.8	15.8	5.5	10.6	51.7	560.3	9.2
1963	21.1	16.7	5.7	10.7	54.2	590.5	9.1
1964	23.4	19.8	6.2	11.3	60.7	631.7	9.6
1965	26.0	23.8	6.9	12.8	69.5	681.2	10.2
1966	29.6	28.5	8.4	12.3	78.8	739.6	10.6

[1] Includes agriculture, trade and services, communication, and transportation.
[2] Includes religious, educational, social and recreational institutions; hospitals; nonprofit organizations, and professional persons.
Compiled from Statistical Abstract of the United States, 1956–1966.

FIGURE 8-3

Comparison of Percentage of Change, GNP
Less Capital Outlays and Capital Outlays, 1955–1966

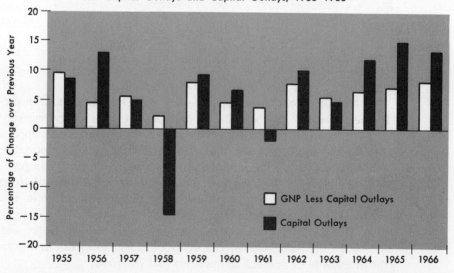

outlays in 1958. This amounted to a decline of 7.1 billion dollars in sales of capital goods. The very modest recession in 1961–62 also had repercussions. Although there was very little change in the rate of growth of the economy—4.4

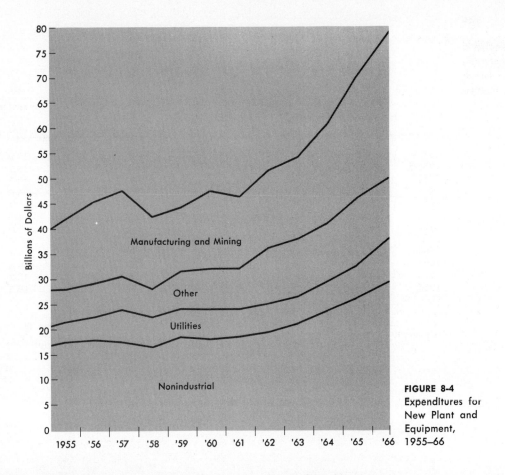

FIGURE 8-4
Expenditures for
New Plant and
Equipment,
1955–66

(Chart labels, top to bottom:) Billions of Dollars; Manufacturing and Mining; Other; Utilities; Nonindustrial. X-axis: 1955 '56 '57 '58 '59 '60 '61 '62 '63 '64 '65 '66.

percent over 1959 in 1960 and 3.9 percent over 1960 in 1961—capital outlays decreased 1.9 percent, or 900 million dollars, in 1961.

Not all sectors of the capital goods market are influenced in the same way. Figure 8-4 shows the behavior of different segments of the market from 1955 to 1966. In 1958 the nonindustrial part of the market, made up of agriculture, distributive trades and services, communication, and transportation, declined about $1.1 billion; utilities about $100 million; the "other" category about $1.2 billion. The largest decline was in manufacturing and mining, where expenditures dropped about $4.7 billion. In 1961 the dollar declines were spread almost evenly across all categories.

The market for components and materials also fluctuates widely. Figure 8-5 shows the percentage of change from month to month and year to year in the inventories of selected components and materials.

The fact that the demand for industrial goods fluctuates so widely has three implications for marketing. First, the buyer of industrial goods exercises extreme care before funds are committed for plant and equipment. The seller of industrial goods has the problem of adjusting supply to demand. Second, since the seller is faced with a fluctuating market, measurement of the market

FIGURE 8-5

Metalworking—Monthly Change Indices

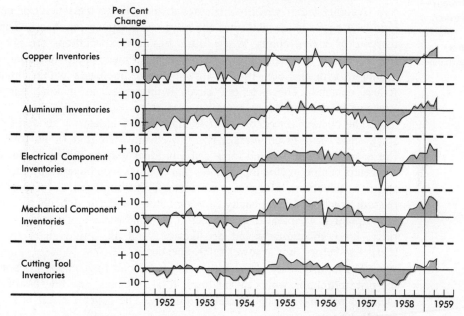

from year to year is even more important than in the consumer goods field. Because of the fluctuations, it is almost impossible to employ the historical approach so often used in the consumer goods field for predicting markets. Historical projections of past market behavior cannot be relied on. All indications are that the most important influencing force is the buyer's expectation of future business conditions. The survey and buildup approaches are more frequently used. Third, the wide fluctuations in demand have some influence on the elasticity of price demand. This characteristic of the market demand for industrial goods will be examined now in detail.

Inelasticity of Demand

The problems of adjusting supply to demand are aggravated by the fact that demand will not increase much with lower prices. In the consumer goods market, when demand falls off and inventories consequently pile up, price reduction is an effective competitive weapon. But in the industrial market a price reduction does not usually generate a proportionate increase in sales. This inelasticity of price demand is a result of the dependence of the demand for industrial goods on the demand for consumer goods. The buyer of industrial goods will hesitate in spite of price reductions if there is an anticipated drop in consumer demand.

It is sometimes argued that a reduced price on industrial goods would allow a reduced price on consumer goods, which generally will respond to price

142

Foundations
of
Strategy—
Interpreting
Market
Forces and
Opportunities

reductions. But since many components from different sources are used to produce a single consumer product, a slight change in the price of any one of them contributes so little to the total cost of the consumer product that the buyer of industrial goods is not influenced by the price change.

Another factor which contributes to the relative inelasticity of demand for industrial goods is the ability of the buyer to postpone purchases. This is so in the case of capital goods. When future business expectations are not favorable the buyer can generally postpone purchase of new plant and equipment and get along with the old. In the upswing, price increases within limits do not reduce demand. The potential buyer is interested in making ready for the expected increase in his own market demand.

The demand faced by a single marketer of industrial goods in competing for a share of a given market is more elastic than that of its total industry. For example, total demand for a given product may be cut back, but individual marketers competing for the demand that remains face buyers who are responsive to price reductions. However, two factors, the homogeneity of product in industrial goods and the paucity of competitors, make it difficult to use price as a competitive weapon. If a marketer of an industrial good were to lower his price, his competitors would do likewise; and all would share the available market as before, but at lower total revenues.

The homogeneity of product makes it difficult for competitors not to follow the price reduction which means lower total revenues; and fewness of marketers makes it possible for all to retaliate quickly. The general result is a uniformity among prices.

This tendency toward uniformity of prices is more true of capital goods and components than of materials. The materials market as a rule has many suppliers, and consequently there is a tendency for more price competition. However, the fact that many materials are sold on a contractual basis impedes price fluctuations, except at the time of contract renewal.

The Purchasing Process

Purchase on a Performance Basis

Industrial goods are bought to produce other goods or services that must be sold at a profit. For this reason, performance of industrial goods in the buyer's operation is the important consideration. Psychological factors play a minor role. Buyers of industrial goods must know what will best satisfy their performance requirements and be able to determine which products meet their requirements most fully. Frequently the purchasing enterprise must prepare specifications for producers of industrial goods. To be sure that expert knowledge is available, most companies have established an *organized purchasing unit,* composed of trained specialists who are aware of price trends, sources of supply, and new products, and who know their company's needs exactly. These buying specialists often use elaborate tests to compare the merits of competing products. The buyers of industrial goods many times have more technical knowledge than the salesmen selling them.

Emotional Appeals

Although the emphasis in purchase of industrial goods is on performance, emotional appeals should not be ruled out completely. Color and design of equipment are important. Such product attributes seem to have greater appeal when related to performance—for instance, to their effect on worker morale, fatigue, and productivity. But appeals to plant appearance or the desire to be technologically progressive are also effective.

The personalities of influential persons in the buying organizations may be appealed to. Individuals are concerned about their position in their company and are desirous of initiating or influencing the purchase of industrial goods which will demonstrate their value to the company. If new equipment, components, or materials result in cost savings, the individual initiating the change has an objective measure—savings in cost—to demonstrate his value.

Diffusion of Purchase Influence

Influences on buying are much more diffused than the specialized purchasing department might lead one to imagine. The department has final responsibility for the purchase; but unusual situations often arise, requiring the special knowledge of other departments. For example, the product and research department in a large company worked out a product modification that promised more sales but also required extensive changes in manufacturing equipment. To receive approval for the proposed changes in equipment, the changes had to be presented to an engineering program committee, whose task was to evaluate each change and its savings in cost. Next, a group from the plant studied every proposed change in equipment and made modifications in the proposals based on their knowledge of actual manufacturing conditions. Some of the questions involved in the evaluation by the plant group are shown in Figure 8-6. After the plant group had studied all changes, the proposal had to be approved by the plant manager, the division head, the executive vice-president and the vice-president for finance. Only after receiving their approval did the purchasing department initiate the purchase order.[5]

And each group that reviewed the proposal had to have knowledge of equipment available from competing producers. Marketers of industrial goods do not wait for the purchasing department to issue purchase orders, but seek to influence the decisions of each interested group by requesting the opportunity to demonstrate the superiority of their product. Frequently the decision-making groups request demonstrations from competing producers.

Although not all companies are as highly organized as this one, all are similar in that many people are influential in the purchase of industrial goods. This characteristic presents some unusual problems to the marketer. The salesman must know the decision-making process of the buying company and establish close relationships with important personnel. It is difficult to identify the influential personnel because they may vary depending on the type goods the company is contemplating purchasing. Even if the salesman is successful in

[5] *Tested Approaches to Capital Equipment Replacement,* American Management Association, Special Report No. 1 (New York, 1954), pp. 57–72.

FIGURE 8-6

New Equipment Questionnaire

New Equipment Questionnaire

1. Who is the requestor?
   (a) Department requiring equipment?
2. Why is this equipment required?
   (a) New installation?
   (b) Replacement equipment?
   (c) Change in process or manufacturing procedure?
   (d) Change in methods?
3. What is this equipment to be used for—what process?
4. How have we been manufacturing without the use of this equipment?
5. What other means or equipment are available in the plant, or purchasable for performing the required work?
6. What production capacity is required in the process concerned and what production capacity is available on present equipment? What is the productivity of this machine and what is required?
7. What are the comparative costs on the basis of material, labor and expense?
   (a) Present method?
   (b) Proposed method utilizing new equipment?
8. How will this equipment affect direct labor costs?
9. In what way will this equipment affect raw materials or processed materials?
10. What will be the effect on maintenance expenses as a result of the purchase of this equipment?
11. What maintenance problems does this equipment present?
12. Does this equipment afford a reduction in health or accident hazard in the operation of the equipment?
13. Describe how this equipment will affect the quality of the product.
14. Outline briefly the points discussed with the heads of those departments which are to be affected by either quality or quantity.
15. How has this equipment been demonstrated to run satisfactorily under mill conditions?
   (a) Can a satisfactory guarantee be attached to the purchase contract?
16. What consideration has been given to locating this equipment?
17. Has a market search been made of all the manufacturers of this equipment?
   (a) Who are the manufacturers?
   (b) Are the prices competitive?
   (c) What is the price of this equipment?
   (d) Are there any marked advantages or disadvantages to the various makes of this equipment?
   (e) Should the used-equipment market be considered?
18. Does this equipment include all necessary drives, motors, and auxiliary equipment?
19. When will this equipment be needed?
20. What delivery dates can be scheduled for this equipment?
21. What was the original value of the displaced equipment?
   (a) What is its present book value?
   (b) What is the bragg tab number?

NEW EQUIPMENT QUESTIONNAIRE
Thompsonville Plant

DATE ....

TO: Chairman of New Equipment Board

FROM: ....   SUPT.

ANSWER ALL QUESTIONS

1. This equipment is required as (check one):
   ☐ New installation
   ☐ Replacement equipment
   ☐ Change in methods
   ☐ Change in processing procedure
   ☐ Other—Explain ....

   ....

2. This equipment is to be used for ....

   ....

3. We have been manufacturing without this equipment by

   ....

4. This equipment will have an effect on present operations as indicated:

Good	No Change	Bad	Explain
☐	☐	☐	Production costs
☐	☐	☐	Quality
☐	☐	☐	Production capacity
☐	☐	☐	Maintenance problems
☐	☐	☐	Materials handling
☐	☐	☐	Safety hazards
☐	☐	☐	Other

5. I recommend the following make and model of equipment for investigation:

   MAKE ....

   MODEL ....

   SIGNED ....   SUPT.

Source: "The Competitive Demand System of Capital Budget Preparation," by Elliott I. Peterson. Reprinted by permission of the publisher from Special Report No. 1, Tested Approaches to Capital Equipment Replacement, pp. 62-63. Copyright 1954 by the American Management Association, Inc.

identifying the influential people, they are not always accessible to him, especially if they are high-ranking officers. Furthermore, even when the influential people are identified and accessible, many must be "sold." The number of people who must be convinced makes the sales task more difficult, since skeptics in the group may turn against the salesman's proposal those who had been favorably impressed. Only through developing an intimate knowledge of the purchasing procedures of each potential buyer and establishing a close personal relationship with influential personnel can these problems be overcome.

Reciprocity

Although currently most industrial buyers are predominantly influenced by performance, a few are strongly influenced by reciprocal arrangements—"You buy from me, and I'll buy from you." These reciprocal arrangements can include more than two buyer-sellers. For example, buyer A may refuse to buy from B unless B buys from C—the customer of A. Such an arrangement prevents buying according to performance and substitutes an altogether different basis for the choice of supplies. Reciprocity does not allow the purchasing department to always purchase the best value and restricts the market available to competitive marketers. In some cases there is no effective means of breaking these relationships. The marketer's only recourse is to maintain a relationship with the buyer until such time as the reciprocal relationship with a competitor shows signs of weakening. Although reciprocal relationships are not widespread, they are a situation with which some marketers of industrial goods must contend.

These then are the special characteristics of industrial goods and their markets. The analysis of any industrial good in terms of the product, the market structure, the demand for industrial goods, and the purchasing process will provide useful information when developing the marketing mix.

QUANTITATIVE AND QUALITATIVE APPROACHES TO MARKET INVESTIGATION

As mentioned previously, the wide fluctuations in demand for industrial goods makes it difficult to adjust supply to demand. Quantitative investigation in the industrial market is very important because the best way of preventing inventory buildups in the downswing is continuous and accurate forecasting of market opportunity.

A good way of qualitatively interpreting market demand is to analyze each customer's demand. In the industrial market the number of consuming units is usually much smaller than in the consumer market, and this procedure is often practicable. However, when the number of potential buyers is too great for this buildup procedure, the demand estimate may be obtained by much the same means as are used in the consumer goods market. That is, past buyers are classified according to objective characteristics, such as number of employees, kilowatt hours used, and size of payroll, and, in the case of retailers and wholesalers, square feet of selling space. These characteristics are related to past sales. For example, on the average, buyers with between 500 and 700 employees purchased

146

Foundations
of
Strategy—
Interpreting
Market
Forces and
Opportunities

300 units of product A last year. Next, all potential purchasers are identified and classified in the same way. The relationship between past sales and the objective characteristic found for actual buyers in the past is applied to all potential buyers, and a total market potential figure established.

The postponable characteristic of many industrial goods, particularly plant and equipment, make it very risky to build estimates of market opportunity by establishing relationships between purchases and objective characteristics of past customers and then applying these to all potential customers. The demand for capital goods depends on the potential buyer's estimate of future business conditions. Although capital goods purchases are planned many months and sometimes years in advance, many times unfavorable business expectations cause changes in purchase plans.

For the individual marketer of industrial goods, surveys which measure the potential buyers' attitude toward future business conditions are useful in measuring market opportunity. General studies of planned plant and equipment expenditures are made periodically by the Department of Commerce. If the individual marketer follows these with surveys of his potential customers' attitudes toward future business conditions, he can, by judgment, determine those plans that are likely to be implemented in the near future.

Qualitative analysis of industrial markets is relatively new, and investigation usually tries to find out the nature of the decision-making process in each company. Such information as (1) the way in which profits are projected on new equipment purchases, (2) identifying key personnel influencing decisions, and (3) purchasers' attitudes toward future business conditions is sought. Generally, this information is collected by the salesman, but it must be uniformly reported and summarized for analysis. New uses for the product is another area of continuous analysis for many industrial suppliers.

Although qualitative analysis in the industrial market is not extensive, the dollar size of the market and the complexity of selling in it seems to indicate that qualitative analysis will become an important activity in the future.

Summary

The industrial goods market deals in goods and services used, directly or indirectly, to produce other goods and services. Manufacturers are not the only buyers. Agriculture, the extractive industries, the distributive trades, service industries, and government and quasi-government institutions are all important parts of the industrial goods market.

Industrial goods may be divided into *capital goods, components* and *materials,* and *supplies.* Capital goods are those essential to efficient production and distribution, but not part of the final product. Components and materials are essential parts of the final product. Supplies do not enter the final product but facilitate the efficient operation of production and distribution and are used up in the process. Marketing of each of these classes of industrial goods calls for different market strategies.

Many similarities exist between industrial and consumer markets, but there are enough differences to influence marketing methods—differences in products, market structure, market demand, and the purchasing process. The most important industrial products characteristics are (1) homogeneity, (2) technical considerations, (3) high average value of sale, and (4) infrequent purchase. Although the industrial market exceeds the consumer market in total value, it contains far fewer buyers. Moreover, the specialization of most suppliers further reduces this number. A supplier specializing in textile machinery, for example, can sell only to textile manufacturers. Markets for suppliers of specialized products are geographically concentrated if the industries they serve are concentrated. The market demand differs from consumer goods demand in that it generally suffers from wide fluctuations in demand and from a relatively inelastic demand. The purchasing process differs in that the industrial buyer buys for performance primarily.

The need for first-rate performance gives rise to specialized purchasing departments in most companies and to diffused purchase influence. Nevertheless, buyers sometimes depart from rational purchase behavior and engage in reciprocal buying arrangements. These special characteristics of industrial demand and peculiarities of purchasing behavior influence sellers' choices of channels of distribution, their price policies, and their sales and promotional efforts.

Analyses of product, market structure, market demand, and the purchasing process are necessary to determine the requirements of effective competition. Market investigation is an important tool and may be more accurate in analyses of industrial markets than of consumer markets. Specialization of sellers as well as their small number and geographic concentration simplifies investigation, but interpretation of quantitative information is made more difficult by the ability of the buyer to postpone purchase of many industrial goods. Qualitative investigation is not yet much employed and concentrates on studying decision-making processes of buyers and identification of influential personnel.

Questions and Problems

1. Define industrial goods.
2. Differentiate between industrial goods sales and wholesale sales.
3. Contrast the bases for the classifications *consumer goods* and *industrial goods*.
4. Compare the size of the industrial market and the consumer market.
5. What are capital goods? What is included in this broad classification?
6. What is included in components and materials? From a marketing point of view, does it make a difference if some components or fabricated parts are identifiable in the end consumer product of which they are a part, while others are not? (Briggs & Stratton engines for power lawnmowers *versus* Tecumseh compressors for window air conditioners.) Elaborate and explain.
7. How are industrial markets different from consumer markets?
8. Explain why industrial goods have a wider fluctuation in demand than consumer goods. Is there a variation between the demand for capital goods and that for materials?
9. What are the marketing implications of this wider fluctuation in demand? Be comprehensive in your answer.

148

Foundations
of
Strategy—
Interpreting
Market
Forces and
Opportunities

10. Why is the demand for industrial goods relatively inelastic?
11. Why do prices tend to fluctuate less in industrial markets than in consumer markets?
12. What marketing implications, in terms of strategy for meeting downturns in business conditions, follow from a combination of relatively inelastic demand, relatively homogeneous products, and industrial purchasing against known future requirements?
13. What is meant by *reciprocity in industrial purchasing?* Do you think this practice is growing or abating?
14. What are the factors that cause quantitative and qualitative approaches to market investigation in industrial goods to be somewhat different from those in consumer goods?
15. "The basic philosophy of marketing and the approach to strategy formulation are the same for both industrial and consumer goods; yet the specific nature of marketing activity is quite different." Agree or disagree. Defend your position.

International Markets

Up to this point we have distinguished between consumer and industrial markets and recognized certain differences in the quantitative and behavioral characteristics of the two. But market opportunity has a way of transcending national boundaries, and marketers in the future can be expected collectively to be less provincial in their thinking and outlook. The change will come from increasing initiative on the part of business firms in pursuing overseas opportunities, as well as from competitive necessity. For this reason we wish to consciously interject at this juncture some of the dimensions of international markets and some of the ways in which these markets depart from usual practices in market interpretation and investigation.

The careful market analyst intently pursues the same mission in evaluating both domestic and international opportunities. That is, he seeks to evaluate all factors in the environment that are germane to the conduct of operations in particular markets to the end that profit potentialities can be projected, the magnitude of risk assessed, and the prospect of competitive success enhanced. The specific factors to be considered and the level of uncertainty will, of course, vary from case to case. The objectives, conceptual structure, principles of research design, and use of scientific method are in large measure universal. It is on these grounds that some writers omit any special treatment of markets in international or multinational environments. This chapter begins with a discussion of why international markets should be given consideration; then the meaning of foreign operations is explained. Next, emphasis is placed on the need for highly specific market feasibility studies in assessing overseas opportunities, and the chapter concludes by pointing out differences marketers can generally expect to experience in doing business outside the domestic market.

150

Foundations
of
Strategy—
Interpreting
Market
Forces and
Opportunities

WHY EXPLICIT TREATMENT
OF INTERNATIONAL DIMENSIONS
TO MARKETING?

The international dimensions of market opportunity will gain increasing attention from marketers primarily because of the growing significance of operations outside the domestic market. This "one world outlook" is in contrast to the tendency, prevailing in an earlier period, to place the entire burden for the conduct of operations outside the domestic market in an isolated international division of the parent company.[1] As overseas markets become more important and their managerial integration with domestic operations becomes more pronounced, one's knowledge and understanding of marketing dare not be rigidly anchored to existing domestic market arrangements.

World Market Orientation

We believe that students—and current managers, for that matter—should not have an excessively parochial view of market opportunity. We live in a shrinking world insofar as market proximity is concerned. Under the pressure of social, political, economic, and technological forces, world markets become more accessible day by day. Everywhere, what has been called "a revolution of rising expectations" goes on. These expectations can be fulfilled in large measure only through market mechanisms. Surely in the future the marketing manager, if he is not already doing so today, will ask himself such questions as: Where throughout the world markets are my best opportunities? Where can the most efficient production facilities be located—in the absence of any underlying predisposition toward the country of corporate origin? Where can we gain most advantageous access to technology, given the existence of cross-cultural talent pools and flows? Where can we tap least-cost sources of supply, given the technological potentialities of overcoming distance?

Profits and International Operations

A growing number of companies are doing business, on some basis, in foreign countries; and the relative importance of the overseas sector to profit performance and corporate growth is increasing for many companies. While the proportion of sales may be small, marginal increments to profitability may be great, particularly where firms are well above break-even levels in the domestic market and are using home market facilities for supplying foreign operations. The proportion of firms engaged in trade flows outside of domestic markets is expected to increase markedly in the future because of a number of factors, including: intense international trade promotional activity by government agencies at the federal, state, and local level; continuing trade negotiations to reduce tariff barriers and quota restrictions, taking place with various countries; private

---

[1] See *Organizational Structures of International Companies,* Study in Personnel Policy No. 198 (New York: National Industrial Conference Board, 1965), pp. 6–7.

sector programs in the Alliance for Progress and other collective efforts; the prospect of continuing large-scale military expenditures outside the United States, the prospect of increased East-West trade that would follow a further moderation in the cold war; and the sizable increase in companies jointly owned by American and foreign investors.

Market Expansion Outside the United States

In recent years the rate of economic growth has been appreciably more rapid in a number of other countries than in the United States. However, increases in gross national product on a per capita basis are as important as, or more important than, the aggregate rate of increase in GNP. For example, a 1 percent increase in gross national product per capita in the United States would have amounted to approximately $33 in 1965, whereas Portugal with an economic growth rate of 7.9 percent would have required a 10 percent increase in per capita gross national product to produce a dollar increase of approximately $39 per capita. Thus, while the rate of market expansion in other countries accessible to United States enterprises has been appreciably more rapid than in the home market, the American economy represents by far the most important market for a great variety of goods. This condition will continue because the absolute increase in per capita gross national product in the United States has exceeded that of all other countries—reflecting the much larger base from which the percentage increase of gross national product is calculated. There is little prospect that any nation can close the gap, since none has been able to sustain a growth rate above 8 percent for any length of time. The marketer, however, is principally concerned with market increases that can be capitalized on by his own market participation in a given product class. That is, if the particular firm could gain 40 percent of a per capita increase of $39 through market expansion overseas, owing to limited competition, and only 20 percent of a $70 per capita increase in the United States, the attractiveness of the overseas opportunity obviously would reflect the different levels of market participation contemplated.

Simple economic growth rates can be misleading in another way. On the basis of ownership of household goods per thousand persons, we in the United States are far above any other country in all product categories. As other countries reach a more advanced state of economic development and industrialization, however, virtually untapped markets will be opened up on a major scale for a number of product categories.

Development of Supranational Market Arrangements

The evolution of common markets constitutes an essentially new dimension in market opportunities implicitly reflecting the reduction in trade barriers, restrictionism, cartelization, and other competitive constraints. The great success of the European Common Market is likely to lead to its expansion by its accepting more countries as full members; already this success has inspired similar supranational market arrangements elsewhere. Other regional market integrations or common markets include the European Free Trade Association (Outer Seven),

152

Foundations
of
Strategy—
Interpreting
Market
Forces and
Opportunities

the Latin American Free Trade Association, the Central American Common Market, and the East European version of the Common Market (Comecon). The increasing rationalization of industry these organizations make possible, and the larger scale of operations that becomes feasible, should produce significantly more efficient enterprises—enterprise that will eventually become vigorous competitors of American companies in world markets. At the same time, the larger common markets will be more and more attractive to U.S. enterprises (in contrast to the many small markets that existed before market integration) and are likely to draw larger commitments of resources to them by U.S. firms.

Private Participation in the Economic Development Process

It is important to the national interest that American business become involved in the developmental process of the free world and, in particular, of the emerging nations. American enterprise might also further influence the direction of the Socialist states, in their moves toward a more market-focused management system as has already occurred in the Soviet Union and some Eastern European countries.[2]

John McKitterick of General Electric eloquently makes the case for the involvement of American enterprise in the developmental process: "If there is a single distinguishing economic characteristic that sets the twentieth century apart from all others gone before, the intensity and creative breadth of modern competition is surely it. The real question is how to use both competition and the diversified corporation to best meet the economic growth of the entire world. In an increasingly international trade structure it is the large and diversified corporation that truly has the dimensions to integrate production and markets in faraway places, to optimize costs, and to elevate competition to the world level.

"To take advantage of these diverse dimensions we must develop a generation of managers who can find ways not only to involve private enterprise in the development of other nations but in the creation of new jobs for the underdeveloped person." [3] The importance of this undertaking is magnified by the fact that in the next 40 years, if present trends continue, more people will be born than have been born since the beginning of man, and 85 percent of this population increase will come in the developing nations.[4]

The United States, a "Have-not" Nation

America, in the years ahead, will become increasingly a "have-not" nation; that is, it will be less self-sufficient and will need to rely more on other countries for raw materials. The gap between U.S. consumption and resources in zinc, magnesium, lead, copper, iron ore, wood fibers, and petroleum is widening. And

---

[2] See *New York Times,* June 7, 1965, "Marketing and the Cold War."
[3] John B. McKitterick, "New Markets and National Needs," *The General Electric Forum,* X, No. 2 (April–June 1967).
[4] *Ibid.*

although the development of synthetic and substitute materials is being intensified, we will nonetheless become more dependent on other nations for our own industrial well-being. This eventuality makes it imperative to have viable trade connections. Also, only through effective competition by American enterprises in world markets for other than raw materials can the proper relationship in our balance of payments be maintained.

OTHER FACTORS

Finally, in assessing market opportunities outside the domestic market, factors not directly related to the contemplated business venture assume major significance in judging profit potentials. In the United States, for example, the analyst might normally be expected to investigate differences between the states in tax laws and other legal matters related to doing business and also the prevailing climate in labor relations. But, he would have no cause to worry that a change of government might abrogate his constitutional rights or prevent him from taking currency out of the state to his headquarters location. Yet these considerations, which transcend the quantification of markets, and have become known as *extraproject factors,* are pivotal in assessing alternative opportunities between countries.[5]

For all of the above reasons, sensitivity to the international dimensions of market opportunity are increasingly germane to competitive effectiveness. Let us now look at the wide variety of involvements used in conducting business overseas.

VARIOUS FORMS OF
PARTICIPATING IN FOREIGN MARKETS

Foreign, as the term is generally used, means "related to or dealing with another nation." The means by which business may be conducted and markets cultivated when "dealing with another nation" are many and varied. The spectrum of organizational and operational involvement in international marketing runs all the way from the relatively simple licensing of patent rights for use in another country to (at the other extreme) a few truly international companies that do not hold a prime loyalty to any one country and are not concerned particularly with the expatriation of profits in a given currency.

Let us now examine briefly some of the principal means for engaging in international marketing.

Exporting

Exporting is perhaps the easiest and most common form of participation by American companies in foreign markets. It is also the least risky, for invest-

---

[5] See F. T. Haner, "Determining the Feasibility of Foreign Ventures," *Business Horizons,* IX, No. 3 (1966), 35–44.

154

Foundations
of
Strategy—
Interpreting
Market
Forces and
Opportunities

ments in the other country are not necessarily entailed, in export operations, nor must the company's own personnel be employed extensively. Instead of the company's sending its own personnel to conduct the sale and distribution of products in the importing country, commission agents can be engaged. Virtually all activities can be carried on from the domestic location and are largely concerned with securing proper licensing, insurance, and transportation and preparing the necessary trade documents. Because of the relatively limited risk and expenditure of funds involved, market feasibility studies for evaluating the availability of export profit opportunities can be minimal—in contrast to those which involve substantial investment commitments and physical facilities in potentially alien environments. Moreover, the increasing attractiveness of American products in many markets and the desire of established market representation agencies to handle these products make such export possibilities good for a wide range of both large and small U.S. companies. If sales in the foreign countries are made through wholesalers, the transactions normally take place in U.S. dollars, avoiding the more complicated aspects of fluctuations in exchange rates and currency conversion. On the other hand, the exporter loses a large measure of control over servicing and other factors connected with the sale of his product, as well as the product's market identity.

Franchising Arrangements

Franchising arrangements have many similarities to licensing arrangements, but the terms are not synonymous. Franchising is particularly relevant in the service industries, whereas licensing is more prominent in product-oriented enterprises. Holiday Inn's motel expansion in other countries is illustrative of franchising. It enables the company to control carefully the nature of operations and the specific elements in the market offers made to potential customers in the host country, while not requiring heavy investments. Revenue is increased from royalty payments made by host country franchise owners. Licensing agreements, on the other hand, characteristically provide great freedom for the licensee in how he will use the patent right he has secured. That is, the grantor makes no significant effort to control the nature of market cultivation strategies to be employed, leaving such matters to the discretion of the licensee.

Transnational Monolithic Companies

The transnational company is one which conducts operations across national boundaries and employs its own personnel in a number of countries and markets. It usually has sales offices in the countries in which it does business, but it may or may not have plants and warehouses. A variation to this pattern is companies having their own sales offices in major countries and using agents in minor markets. The approach is monolithic in that the same products and/or services are marketed in each country and generally the same approach to the market is followed; there is also a high degree of control from the home headquarters. This pattern was rather common as American businesses expanded overseas and exported their marketing methods and philosophies into other countries, while retaining control with their own personnel and operating their own facilities whenever the product was produced outside the United States. This pattern is still probably the most common one, but it is becoming less practical under rising pressures of nationalism and the need to adapt overseas operating entities more closely to host country environments.

Joint Ventures

The increase in joint ventures has been a response to the growing difficulty and risk in operating wholly owned subsidiaries in some countries. The joint venture constitutes a separate company owned by two or more companies, one of which represents host country investors. The joint venture permits the pooling of know-how existing between the two companies; tends to minimize adverse market acceptance that could derive from any anti-American feelings in the country; reduces the potential threat of expropriation of assets by hostile governments; promotes the prospect of adaptation of the enterprise to the cultural environment; and increases the likelihood that the enterprise will be geared, at least in part, to the national needs of the host country. The joint venture frequently reflects specialized contribution by the participating ownership groups. The host country enterprise would normally accept prime responsibility for establishing manufacturing processes and for production. The labor force thereby is largely made up of host country nationals. Characteristically, such complex matters as labor customs utilization, restrictions, legislation, and negotiation are better handled by nationals. Frequently, the American enterprise contributes the marketing competence and modern management processes. The companies joining in the venture frequently share in financial administration and in the conduct of the research and development function. The future will probably see a considerable expansion in this type of overseas involvement (closely akin to multinational companies) on the part of U.S. enterprises, as well as the development of the truly international company.

Multinational Companies

The multinational firm carries on its foreign operations in several countries through separate subsidiary companies, each managed on a relatively autonomous basis. The subsidiary companies may be wholly or partially owned or both. In that respect they may constitute a number of joint ventures, but not necessarily. The parent company acts more as a holding company with foreign as well as domestic investments. Each unit in a foreign country has a separate board of directors and its own president or managing director. While each unit functions under a high degree of decentralization and autonomy, some planning and control is normally exercised by the parent company. At a minimum the following functions tend to be centralized:

1. Determination of overall objectives—in terms of types of business to be carried on and markets to be served.
2. Allocation of financial resources—in the form of controlling investments and capital expenditures.

156

Foundations
of
Strategy—
Interpreting
Market
Forces and
Opportunities

3. Budgetary controls—reflecting anticipated results and expenditures.
4. Major executive staffing—selecting key personnel to head both major domestic and foreign components.[6]

In the multinational enterprise each unit establishes its own product line, determines its own channels of distribution, carries on separate advertising campaigns, follows its own pricing policy, and mobilizes its resources to meet its own objectives in the context of the competitive forces and total environment peculiar to that country. The parent company, however, seeks the eventual "expatriation" of profits to its own country and is basically oriented to its own currency and loyal to its own stockholders, who for the most part are citizens of the country of corporate origin. In these respects, it differs from the truly international company. Ford and General Motors are examples of multinational companies.

International Companies

The truly international company is virtually a world enterprise without tying loyalty to the interests of any one country. It does not function in terms of national sovereignty, and its own board of directors and stockholders are truly international in character. Its liquid assets are held in many currencies and in the negotiable instruments of numerous countries. Its long-term objective is not to expatriate profits into the country of headquarters location. From time to time it suffers disruption in its operation from the expropriation of some of its properties, but it seeks to remain aloof from political entanglements that reflect a highly partisan or nationalistic view. In contrast to the multinational company in which stability in local management is maintained through using nationals as chief executives, the managing directors of the international company are shifted from country to country. Its top board of directors is made up of individuals who have had experience as directors in several units functioning in different parts of the world. The international company maintains a degree of planning and control at headquarters similar to that of the multinational company, but it seeks an almost total rationalization of its worldwide operations, whereas in the multinational company, the several units operate more as individual total systems in their own country than as subsystems in a broader functioning complex. If the scale of operations of a multinational company should grow, its success would logically tend to lead it toward becoming an international company. Some examples of truly international companies are Lever Brothers, Royal Dutch Shell, and Phillips Electrical Company.

The concept of international marketing is thus seen to embrace a wide variety of "foreign involvements." Feasibility studies for assessing nondomestic market opportunities need to vary considerably in scope, detail, and precision, depending on the type of foreign involvement contemplated, because risks and investment requirements vary considerably. Of course, the value of information

---

[6] *Organization Structures of International Companies.*

is greater and the forecasting precision more critical in the riskier venture entailing larger-scale investment.

Market Feasibility Study

Feasibility studies for assessing profit opportunities in nondomestic markets need to be tailored to the objectives, the program contemplated, the country involved, and the particular situation facing the marketer. By way of illustration, a major tire company did not need a particularly elaborate feasibility study for deciding to bid at a carefully determined price on a large volume of truck and passenger car tires of given technical specifications, solicited by the government of one of the Eastern European Socialist states. The tire manufacturer, however, required an extremely thorough, elaborate, and detailed study in deciding whether to locate a manufacturing plant in the same Socialist state. As a matter of fact, domestic trade and public opinion were so strongly antagonistic that the manufacturer elected to withdraw, or at least delay, its announced plan for market entry. This illustration highlights the range of additional factors that must be considered in contemplating involvement in international markets in contrast to domestic markets.

As one analyst has pointed out, "The *pro forma* financial statements of a foreign business may indicate an extremely profitable venture, and yet it may be unattractive due to facts not directly related to operations. The complex question of what will happen to business profits in future years when they are earned in a distant country, taxed by a foreign government, divided with local partners, converted to dollars, and remitted across at least two borders requires a knack for understanding different cultures." [7] This statement is indicative of the extraproject factors that differentiate an international project from a domestic one. The extremes of extraproject considerations will vary from country to country, as environmental factors will differ from those in the United States. While a complete inventory of the special factors in feasibility studies for international marketing operations is beyond our scope, certain minimum areas of consideration need to be noted. At least the following broad extraproject factors should be investigated.

Political Environment

Political trends and the stability of government importantly affect the level of risk and the degree of market uncertainty relative to a venture contemplated in another country. Consideration should be given to: (1) whether the swings of government are toward more state ownership or freer functioning of the private sector of the economy; (2) the government's policy toward acquisition, mergers, or any special alignments with particular competitors; and (3) the country in question's relation with its neighbors and with the United States. In most countries, rather detailed governmental approval must be granted to foreign

---

[7] Haner, "Determining the Feasibility of Foreign Ventures," p. 36.

158

Foundations
of
Strategy—
Interpreting
Market
Forces and
Opportunities

enterprises wishing to enter a particular market sector, and the host government's attitude toward U.S. firms or domestic competitors is important.

Special Incentives

Closely related to the political situation is the government's atitude toward attracting outside investments. Market opportunities vary depending on the country's view of its own developmental problems and market needs. For example, a recent report of the Atlantic Council of the United States summarized market opportunities for American firms in Europe. It concluded that the Belgian government actively solicits U.S. investments which meet the need for more technical know-how, with especially favorable emphasis on electronics, precision optics, and chemicals. The Netherlands government favors highly automated new industries that make small demands on scarce labor. Italy values enterprises that bring new technology as well as investments in underdeveloped geographic areas, such as the southern part of the country. The French, despite some previous obstacles, want investments that introduce new technology, raise exports, reduce imports, and help develop certain regions.[8] Approval can, of course, be more readily obtained for market entry in these categories than in others. Special fiscal incentives may also be available for these types of investments.

Taxes

Taxes reflect the existence of special incentives as well as the restriction of outside enterprises in certain markets. The particular type of taxes levied on foreigners, their rate and historical pattern, are important considerations. Also relevant is the possibility of crediting local taxes against U.S. taxes, and vice versa, because American firms often ship component parts of final products into the U.S. market from overseas producing points. Taxes on conversion to foreign exchange are pertinent, given the American enterprise's objectives and policies of conducting its business in dollars and bringing home profits. Import and export tariff restrictions and quota must also be taken into account. In some cases these restrictions, which are used to control the volume of business done from foreign markets, can be more or less offset by the degree of national participation in the project.

Currency and Availability of Capital

Foreign exchange is largely handled in gold, dollars, or pounds; these latter currencies are known as reserve currencies. In converting local currencies to foreign exchange the degree of freedom is important. The value of currency in free markets, as well as official government rates, and the stability of both rates should be evaluated. Because of efforts to hold down dollar outflows for a better U.S. balance of payments, American businessmen are increasingly turning to overseas capital markets to finance their entry into and growth in international markets. Borrowings outside the U.S. have increased sharply, but typically at

[8] "Investment," *Time* (March 25, 1966).

considerably higher interest rates. The premiums stand to cut U.S. companies' foreign earnings, which in recent periods have been growing faster than domestic earnings.[9]

Social Environment and Customs

Besides the legal and economic barriers that confront an outside company doing business in international markets, the social constraints encountered are formidable. Knowledge of local customs, buying habits, work habits, and local conditions for doing business are vital in bringing about a profitable performance in foreign operations. The nation in question may have different customs affecting work and sales patterns that, while subtle, have a pronounced impact on management processes and results. For example, it is customary and acceptable in some countries to provide extra payments to certain trade officials in return for various amenities and privileges; these payments would be both illegal and directly counter to acceptable corporate morality in the U.S. Such practices will affect profits and may have an important effect on morale, company ethics, and employee attitude as well.

The overseas enterprise must be environmentally suitable to the host nation as well as to the firm's owner. To insure that the national interests are met, some countries impose restrictions on the employment of management and operating personnel that are noncitizens. Even without such restrictions, U.S. companies seeking to effect a good state of adjustment to the local environment extensively use foreign nationals in their operations. In Sears, Roebuck's Latin American operations for example, 99.3 percent of the employees are local nationals, including almost all store managers. Other devices are also used to integrate national and corporate interests. Sears buys 80 percent of its merchandise from 9,000 native manufacturers. This local purchasing program (which has been characterized as a private "Alliance for Progress") has helped the company become an integral part of each country.[10] Adherence to local customs in Sears' case is demonstrated by tool and paint merchandising. These product categories—virtual mainstays in Sears' U.S. stores—scarcely exist in Latin America because cheap labor and a middle-class aversion to manual work militate against any sizable do-it-yourself market.

The variety of extraproject factors that the marketer can encounter in individual countries will make for different situations in each and call for different adaptive techniques on a regional basis. However, certain general market differences that alter the nature of marketing effort from that characteristic in the United States can be anticipated by American enterprises doing business overseas. It is to these that the remaining part of the chapter is devoted.

CHARACTERISTICS OF MARKETS
OUTSIDE THE UNITED STATES

American marketers engaged in foreign operations can expect to run into a number of marked differences in markets which will influence the character

---

[9] "U.S. Investments," *Time* (October 1, 1965).
[10] "Sears Profitable Alianza," *Time* (March 4, 1966).

160

Foundations
of
Strategy—
Interpreting
Market
Forces and
Opportunities

of their efforts to achieve satisfactory commercial results. The differences could be almost endless, ranging from prevailing business philosophies to the minutiae of variations in life styles. While not exhaustive, the factors listed here cover a number of different areas, and they vary in degree among the developing and developed nations. The extremes of these factors will be found in the under-developed nations, but all appear in some measure in contrast to standards prevailing in the United States.

Literacy Rate and Education

The United States has the most educated population in the world and one of the highest literacy rates. While other advanced Western cultures exceed the U.S. literacy rate, in some of the underdeveloped countries this rate ranges from a high of about 98 percent down to a low of 5 or 6 percent. It is hard for the American marketer to comprehend the difficulty of doing business where only 10 percent of the people can read and write. His marketing communications often must put great reliance on pictures, diagrams, and simplicity of language in space advertising, billboards, packages, labeling, and other communications forms. The lower level of education also has distinct implications for the adoption of innovations and potential change in purchasing patterns.

We must also not overlook the substantial differentials, beyond the level of simple literacy, in groups in cultures other than our own. The better-educated tend to have an enhanced appreciation for sanitation, personal hygiene, and personal-use products, but this is not always independent of influences of custom and habit. According to one study, for instance, only one out of three Frenchman brushes his teeth and only one German out of five changes his shirt more often than once a week.[11]

Population and Life Span

The United States with only 6 percent of the world's population enjoys approximately 38 percent of the world's income.[12] The proportions can be expressed in reverse: while the U.S. has six times the income in proportion to its population, other countries have one-sixth of the income in proportion to the size of their population. Population density is not to be overlooked either. The United States has 52 people per square mile; Great Britain has 571; Japan, 672; Belgium, 789; the Netherlands, 922; Poland, 254; while the Soviet Union has only 26; Australia, 4; and Canada, 5.[13] The expected life span also varies substantially. In the United States it is roughly 70 years; whereas, in some of the Middle East countries it is as low as 34 years. Shorter life spans can affect stages in the life cycle and exert corollary influence on expenditure patterns. These population factors materially alter market demand over time and also the suitability of products for particular markets. For instance, they help to explain why

[11] Ernest Dictor, "The World Consumer," *Harvard Business Review* (July–August 1962), pp. 113–22.

[12] *Statistical Abstract of the United States: 1964*, pp. 906–7.

[13] *Statistical Abstract of the United States: 1965*.

the automobile market in most of the world has been oriented to small cars rather than to the larger cars characteristic of the U.S.

Promotional Media

The range of promotional media available in markets outside the United States is typically much smaller than it is here. The number of publications reaching all segments of the population, the existence and number of radio and TV stations, and the availability of facilitating organizations for such things as direct mail advertising result in the marketer's having many fewer alternative choices open to him as market cultivation media. For instance, most government-owned telephone companies abroad do not accept advertising, so there are no yellow pages.[14] And even where a particular promotional medium, such as TV advertising, may be available, it is likely to have a different structural form from that prevailing in the U.S. By way of illustration, Switzerland, which allowed its first TV commercial in 1965 was forced to ration time among 170 requesting firms. France limits television ads to ten minutes a night. Japanese TV time now is so valuable that sponsors are limited to fifteen seconds each or to "crawl-along slogans" that slither along the bottom of the tube while a program is in progress. Belgium, Holland, and the three Scandanavian countries allow no TV commercials at all. In Switzerland, TV ads are never shown on Sunday, and in Italy all the ads are run together in one eleven-minute TV advertising segment.[15]

Market Information and Data

Typically, outside the United States there is a distinct paucity of market data to guide the actions of firms in their cultivation of markets and in their evaluation of competitive performance. We are accustomed to the availability of a considerable quantity of market information from a variety of published sources and governmental agencies. In many countries, there are no publications comparable to our census volumes or the *Statistical Abstract of the United States*. Government agencies frequently do not have the requisite resources or skilled personnel for preparing these types of publications, nor do they recognize any special need for providing business firms with such useful information. When data are published, their reliability is hard to judge, and in some cases they may be quite misleading. The general scarceness of information makes measures of market potential, market share, and other elements of scientific marketing immeasurably more difficult.

Credit Availability

In a number of countries market expansion suffers from the lack of readily available credit. Consumer credit and installment buying were not very common

---

[14] In 1963 an international yellow pages publication was introduced covering 2,900 categories in 136 countries. It has apparently been a major success. See "Global Yellow Pages," *Time* (September 24, 1965).

[15] "Thriving on the Tube," *Time* (September 3, 1965).

162

Foundations
of
Strategy—
Interpreting
Market
Forces and
Opportunities

in the past; this significantly affected the potential market otherwise available for consumer durables. Trade credit in the business sector has also been quite limited, with custom favoring the use of cash transactions. Today in a number of countries (particularly the more developed nations), there is a trend toward more widespread use of consumer credit, but as yet lack of its availability is still a major limiting factor constraining marketers in the durable goods area.

Ownership of Consumption Equipment

In addition to the lack of credit, the lack of widespread ownership of equipment essential to other forms of consumption puts a constraint on market expansion in a number of product categories and market areas. For instance, in a recent year 948 radios were owned for each thousand persons in the United States against 123 per thousand in Italy. The ratios for washing machines, refrigerators, and ranges are equally or more dramatic. The scarcity of refrigerated storage space makes sale of economy size packages of perishable foodstuffs difficult; necessitates frequent trips to the market to replenish stocks; increases small orders and congestion in retail stores; and raises costs of distribution.

Income

Markets reflect the amount of money people have. The United States mass market reflects the high incomes earned by American workers. Table 9-1 shows the average hourly earnings of manufacturing employees in a variety of nations: [16]

TABLE 9-1
Average Hourly Earnings of Manufacturing
Employees in Dollars

1. United States	$2.65	10. Mexico	$ .56
2. Canada	1.96	11. Poland	.45
3. Sweden	1.51	12. Greece	.42
4. Great Britain	1.20	13. Peru	.41
5. Australia	1.10	14. Japan	.40
6. West Germany	1.04	15. Philippines	.21
7. Italy	.71	16. Colombia	.20
8. Israel	.63	17. Formosa	.13
9. Argentina	.58	18. South Korea	.08

Comparison will demonstrate the gap between American markets and those which prevail in other countries insofar as wage effects are concerned.

Buying Habits

All of the above factors plus custom and tradition work toward producing striking differences in buying habits in overseas markets. Buying habits should

[16] Source of data, U.S. Department of Labor as quoted in *Time* (February 18, 1966).

not be seen as a snapshot but more as a moving picture; that is, they are continually in a state of transition, elsewhere as well as here. Research has shown the kind of differences in buying habits that have affected the character of marketing institutions, marketing practices, and the nature of competition. Some of these differences may be seen from the following illustrations:

1. The European housewife, and her counterparts in other nations of the world, regards her daily shopping expedition as a customary social event and opportunity to intermingle and communicate with friends and shopkeepers. The market as an institution is thereby distinctly different from that common to this country, with its orientation to efficiency and customer problem solving.

2. Lack of income and ownership of consumption equipment such as refrigerators force consumers to buy in very small quantities. High unit prices reflecting high unit costs further support the daily shopping custom.

3. Consumers are slow to accept innovation in services while being more receptive to changes in products.[17] Bargaining over price between buyer and seller, for instance, has long been a market tradition and is still common; however, it is disappearing in Western Europe and declining elsewhere. Also, after a history of parsimonious shopping behavior, of cash-only purchases, or barter,[18] consumers are now buying on credit. Innovations in marketing services have been needed more than product innovations to accelerate market growth. But because customers have been slower to accept the former than the latter, most supplying firms have been product oriented, and competition has been quite sharply product focused. Considerable change from this historical orientation is now evident, and marketers in the future will need to be alert to market opportunities that a few years ago would have seemed strongly counter to established patterns of serving customers and to traditional buying habits.

Marketing Institutions

By and large, the rest of the world is characterized by small, highly specialized service retailers, and they seem to remain a vital part of the whole trade structure. This reflects years of custom and tradition, ingrained shopping habits, limited incomes, and, in some cases, legislation. For example in Italy, restrictive legislation has resulted in special shops for poultry, different shops for beef, and still others for veal. Licensing arrangements have been such that large-volume, one-stop shopping was curtailed even as the weakening of custom, rising income, and increasing automobile ownership might have encouraged it. In some countries self-service supermarkets have been making striking headway, but they are nevertheless clearly subordinate to the small specialized service establishments characterized by a larger number of employees per unit of output, higher gross margins, and lower stock turnover.

[17] George Fisk, *Marketing Systems* (New York: Harper & Row, Publishers, 1967), p. 751.
[18] "How the British React to Affluence," *Business Week* (January 19, 1963), p. 44.

164

Foundations
of
Strategy—
Interpreting
Market
Forces and
Opportunities

Business Philosophies

Essentially, American marketing development has been characterized by low prices, high volume, rapid stock turnover and narrow gross margins.[19] In contrast, a much different philosophy has operated in many other parts of the world, and only recently has been changing. The essential difference has been a preference for profit maximizing on a per unit basis, or (by indirection), a low-volume-high-profit philosophy. While this philosophy is moderating under the pressure of intensified competition resulting from a reduction of trade barriers, the lack of an expansionist policy continues to be reflected on a widespread basis. Even among the more progressive European firms, a conservative philosophy concerning marketing prevails at the present time. The Marketing Science Institute concluded after a study of fifty-two major European firms:

1. Most of the respondent firms were product oriented, making the customer do what suits the interest of the business enterprise.
2. Marketing tended to be a fragmented assortment of separate functions which lacked coordination and synthesis.
3. There was a striking lack of planning representing special efforts to meet anticipated changes in a firm's marketing opportunity or effort.
4. Product research was a technical question and seldom used as a competitive tool.
5. Only a few firms could see marketing research as a process involving the gathering of information for the purpose of planning, controlling, and evaluating marketing operations.
6. Interindustry and interfirm price and market agreements limited use of pricing and promotion as effective tools of competition.
7. Most firms preferred direct selling to the retailer or ultimate consumer.[20]

Summary

Markets outside the United States are of increasing significance to American marketers. Profits from international operations have been growing at a rate faster than those from domestic ones. In pursuing market opportunity, business firms are increasingly likely to have a more worldwide outlook, and the future manager's perspective should not be constrained by an excessively provincial focus nor anchored solely to the domestic culture. Risks, uncertainty, and profit relationships, however, can be sharply different in foreign operations from those in the home market, due largely to what has been termed extraproject factors. Foreign operations cover a variety of forms, ranging all the way from relatively simple exporting by a largely domestic enterprise, on the one hand, to the truly international company without special allegiance to any one country on the

---

[19] Writers estimate that Europe has two million existing retail outlets, but predict that, as American retailing methods are adopted and gross margins are reduced, the number will shrink markedly. See Ilmar Roosta "Retailing in the Era of the Common Markets," *Proceedings of the Retail Management Conference, British Institute of Management, February 19, 1963*, p. 8–9.

[20] Bertol Liander, *Marketing Development in the European Economic Community* (New York: McGraw-Hill Book Company, 1964), pp. 6–8.

other. Because risk and investment requirements vary so sharply, depending on the form of involvement in international markets, market feasibility studies must be tailored to the particular project and country contemplated. Nonetheless, general sensitivity to influencing political, cultural, legal, economic, and monetary factors is in order. In its overseas operations the American firm can be confronted with an almost infinite variety of special factors, but it can, in general, anticipate a number of common differences in outside markets, including lower literacy rates and education levels; shorter life spans and more rapid life cycles; restricted purchasing power; a paucity of market information; more limited promotional media; limited use of credit; smaller-scale marketing outlets; smaller unit transactions; more limited ownership of consumption equipment; sharply varying purchasing patterns; a different kind of focus for a concept of market efficiency; and a quite divergent business philosophy from that common in the domestic market. By varied means, the successful enterprise functioning in international markets must adapt to the environment of the host country and serve the interest of the host nation as well as that of its owners.

Questions and Problems

1. Identify the principal methods of international marketing. Discuss the characteristics of each method.
2. How will the economic development of other countries affect international market opportunities of U.S. companies?
3. What effects will the evolution of common markets have on American companies in world markets?
4. What is meant by the term *expropriation of assets?* What methods of international marketing are most likely to prevent this from happening?
5. How might international market opportunities affect corporate growth and profit performance?
6. What is meant by the "one-market view of both domestic and international opportunities"?
7. What is a market feasibility study? Illustrate its importance in international marketing.
8. What are the essential elements of any international market feasibility study?
9. Explain why market feasibility studies must be highly specific in assessing international business opportunities.
10. "Culture affects not only the absolute size of international markets but also the relative preferences for competitive products." Discuss.
11. In what ways do marketing methods usually differ between domestic and international firms?
12. What are the marketing implications of the differences in buying habits between domestic and international markets?
13. What are the distinguishing characteristics of international markets which produce the differences in buying habits in these markets?
14. How important is it for American businessmen to participate in international markets?
15. "The difference between domestic market characteristics and international market characteristics is one of degree." Comment.

Stages of Market Development and Competitive Rivalry

10

In the preceding chapters we have discussed the importance of market knowledge in the development of marketing effort.[1] In addition to the information acquired through quantitative analysis of the market and analysis of the purchase motivation characteristics of potential buyers, another consideration is important in interpreting market forces. The competitive environment in which the product is sold influences the potentialities of sale and the kind of marketing effort that must be used to capitalize on market opportunities.

Products pass through a cycle of perishable distinctiveness—that is, when a new product is introduced, it enjoys some unique advantage until it is copied by other producers.[2] As more firms produce a similar product, its distinctiveness begins to perish, and the initiator may lose some of his earlier competitive advantage.

There are rather well-defined stages through which a product normally passes. Five different stages can be discerned: *pioneering, market acceptance, turbulence, saturation,* and *obsolescence.*[3] Each stage represents a different competitive environment; consequently marketing effort must be adjusted to the new conditions.

Not all products pass through each of the five stages. Moreover, there may be a great difference between how well

[1] The conclusions drawn in this chapter constitute current generalizations from a variety of unpublished studies by one of the authors on behalf of the clients of Arthur D. Little, Inc., involving the investigation of a number of appliances and home-use goods as a part of product diversification assignments.

[2] See Joel Dean, *Managerial Economics* (Englewood Cliffs, N.J.: Prentice-Hall, Inc., 1951), p. 410.

[3] A quite similar classification, excluding the characteristics of each period, is used in Booz-Allen and Hamilton, *The Management of New Products* (Chicago, Ill.: Booz-Allen and Hamilton, Management Consultants).

167

Stages
of Market
Development
and Competi-
tive Rivalry

a product is accepted in the market and how long it stays in any one stage. Some products are fads; their sales rise quickly at first and then decline almost as rapidly. Others retain small but profitable market positions for many years, proving to have a rather small but durable niche in the market place. Although a wide variety of products have a tendency to go through the stages mentioned, these changes are more clearly discernible in consumer durable goods, such as washing machines, television sets, and refrigerators. For this reason, the discussion in this chapter is mainly concerned with such goods.

The variations in competitive environment in each stage are important from the point of view of market investigation. In this chapter we shall characterize the competitive environment in each stage by examining such factors as the size and character of the market, the competitive rivalry present, product changes, production and marketing costs, distribution outlets, and marketing effort. When certain characteristics are observed in an industry, the individual marketer can judge the current position of products in the various stages of market development and assess the future competitive environment more intelligently. In so doing, he can anticipate changes in marketing effort that may be called for to keep the firm in a proper state of adjustment to its changing competitive environment.

PIONEERING

This is the stage in which a new class of product is introduced. A new product, in this sense, is one which generally performs an old task in a new way, or does something which was not possible before. For example, the electric refrigerator was a new class of product in that it provided for the preservation of perishable food in an entirely new way. The television set provides a service which had not been provided before its introduction. The most important characteristics of the pioneering stage are: a slow sales rise, few direct competitors, frequent changes in the product, high production and marketing costs, high prices, and marketing effort directed at primary demand. Let us examine each of these characteristics.

Slow Sales Rise

In the pioneering stage, sales generally rise slowly. The marketer of a new product must break down potential buyers' habitual purchase patterns before they can be expected to respond to a new product. For example, the sewing machine was invented long before the time the Singer Sewing Machine Company provided the marketing talent to gain a place for the product in the market place.

The market for a new product is generally concentrated among those buyers having the greatest need for the product and enough purchasing power to fulfill this need. In addition to this group there is a second market group who might be induced to purchase. They, however, feel less need or desire for the product and generally have restricted purchasing power resulting from the need to purchase other things. A third group might be considered the indifferent group. The

168

Foundations
of
Strategy—
Interpreting
Market
Forces and
Opportunities

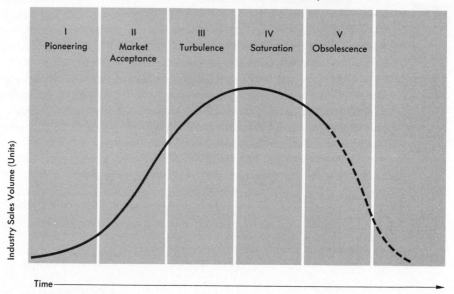

FIGURE 10-1
Stages of Market Development

people in this group see other ways of spending their money, which are just as satisfying.

In the pioneering stage, sales are usually restricted to the "core" group, which is generally made up of higher-income purchasers. Over a period of time, the product will "filter down" to lower-income groups as it proceeds through various stages of market development.

Few Direct Competitors

When a new product manufactured by one firm exclusively is introduced, it of course faces no direct competition from similar products, because no similar products exist. For example, the first electric refrigerator did not face direct competition during its earliest days on the market. But it did face *indirect* competition from the ubiquitous icebox. As long as the old cold-storage unit continued to preserve food reasonably well, many potential buyers of electric refrigerators preferred to spend their money on other things. The later makers of electric refrigerators competing with Frigidaire in the pioneering stage competed for the consumer's purchasing power, and in a sense were competing indirectly with all other products.

The number of direct competitors will increase if the product gains market acceptance, but in the pioneering stage the number will be smaller than in any other, except for obsolescence. Usually the number can be counted on no more than one hand.

169

Stages
of Market
Development
and Competi-
tive Rivalry

Frequent Product Changes

New products are usually not entirely free of technical imperfections which impair their performance. A soundly managed enterprise will make every effort to eliminate such difficulties as solutions are found for faulty performance which can prevent the product from gaining market acceptance. The firm usually will not wait for the introduction of a new model to correct these deficiencies, but will incorporate various minor improvements immediately. Even with elaborate quality control and testing devices, design and technical imperfections will often show up after a product is on the market. For this reason, frequent product modifications are not uncommon during the pioneering stage.

High Production Costs

Because of the great difficulty in forecasting demand for innovations, and the uncertainty of sales during this period, management is reluctant to make the heavy investments required in special equipment needed for efficient line-production methods. Management demands some assurance that sales will justify the expenditure. Job-shop methods using general-purpose tools are more flexible, and are therefore better suited to a period of uncertain sales and frequent changes in the product. When sales are more certain and the product perfected, the initially more costly but ultimately more efficient production-line methods are usually introduced.

High Prices

Because of frequent product changes, the production methods used, and the limited quantities produced, production costs are higher during the pioneering stage than in later periods. These high costs present difficult marketing problems. Pricing is one. It is difficult to decide, for example, whether initial prices should be based on pioneering production costs or on the lower production costs anticipated after sales have increased.

High production costs also complicate decisions on the amount of advertising to use or the reliance which should be placed on personal selling, a high-cost method of cultivating the market. During this period, expenditures made to cultivate the market should be high. Yet high production costs do not leave a sufficient margin for advertising and personal selling expenditures. If the price is set high enough to absorb these expenditures, it limits the market. If the price is set to cover anticipated future production costs and large expenditures made to develop a market for the product, then generally management must plan on operating at a loss during this period. The decision to operate at a loss in anticipation of future profit is not an easy one, especially when future sales are unpredictable. Characteristically, prices will be higher in this period than in those that follow. Prices will typically show a downward movement in the advanced stages of market development, which helps to make possible the development of the mass market. You may recall the decline in television prices following its pioneering period.

170

Foundations
of
Strategy—
Interpreting
Market
Forces and
Opportunities

High Marketing Costs

If management decides to make the necessary marketing expenditures to alter established buying patterns, marketing costs per unit of product sold will be higher during the pioneering period than in later periods. If marketing costs are held to a ratio to sales found in a more developed market, expenditures will probably be too small to gain market acceptance for the product. Traditional marketing cost-to-sales ratios must be set aside during the pioneering stage. This is another contributing factor to the higher prices that generally prevail during this stage, in contrast to later ones.

Primary Demand Marketing Effort

The marketer's first job is to win buyers' approval of the new product type; that is, to stimulate *primary demand,* in contrast to stimulating demand for the product of a specific manufacturer, which is known as *selective demand* cultivation. Although the product may have little direct competition in this stage, it does compete indirectly with the traditional products used to provide the service or perform the task.

For example, when the first automatic washing machine was introduced by the Bendix Corporation it competed with the older, manually controlled electric washers. Initial marketing effort stressed, therefore, the convenience of the automatic controls to the housewife. She didn't have to put her hands in hot water and she didn't have to handle the clothes for rinsing and wringing. But after World War II a number of directly competing automatic washers were introduced, and marketing effort then emphasized the advantages of the Bendix. Bendix Corporation, for example, stressed the superiority of the tumble-action cylinder design over the competitors' agitator-type design.

In summary, the small market, the fewness of competitors, the frequent product changes, the high production and marketing costs, and the need to direct marketing effort toward primary demand, all indicate why keen marketing judgment is called for in the pioneering stage. New-product marketing is as complex a competitive problem as any because of pervasive uncertainty, which is reflected in the high rate of failures in new-product introduction.

Characteristics of Pioneering

1. Sales rise slowly.
2. Competitors are few.
3. Sales to high-income groups (core markets).
4. Frequent product modifications.
5. Experimental production methods.
6. High production costs.
7. Product differentiation and limited lines.

171

Stages
of Market
Development
and Competi-
tive Rivalry

8. High marketing costs.

9. Limited distribution.

10. High prices.

11. Primary demand cultivation.

MARKET ACCEPTANCE

In the second stage of market development, widespread buyer approval is secured for the product. The following are the more important characteristics of this stage: market size increases rapidly, the number of direct competitors sharply increases, efficient production methods are established, the number of distribution outlets increases, and selective demand marketing effort begins.

Rapid Increase in Market Size

In the acceptance stage of market development, sales rise rapidly, and often at an increasing rate of increase. What is sometimes called a take-off point is reached, from which industry sales turn up sharply, signifying a growth market. The product, in this stage, begins a process of filtering down from the high-income or core buyers toward the mass market of middle- and lower-income purchasers. Although in the early period of the stage upper-income groups continue to dominate total purchases, the middle-income group begins to become important. The rapid rise in sales is made possible partly because of the conjunction of factors characterizing the period, which are discussed in more detail following: softening prices, the appearance of the first major product improvements, greater product reliability, and the increased competition.

Increase in Number of Direct Competitors

As the product becomes accepted in the market and a growth market seems assured, many more firms are likely to enter the market. As a result of the increase in the number of direct competitors, the first major product improvements (other than the modifications to perfect performance noted in the pioneering stages) are introduced. New producers often introduce refinements or innovations to make their own brands more attractive, and the pioneer firms are forced to follow with new models.

Continued increases in the number of competitors can be expected all the way through the period, with the total number likely to reach its highest level late in the period. Actually, the increase in the number of firms may even be characterized as an "explosion in the number of competitors." Larger firms in a hurry to enter the recognized growth market may do so by the acquisition of smaller firms; these acquisitions tend to be on extremely favorable terms to the seller (a high price-to-earnings ratio). In later stages, these same firms, under different competitive circumstances, may have difficulty in even finding a buyer for the enterprise at any price, and may even be forced into bankruptcy.

172

Foundations
of
Strategy—
Interpreting
Market
Forces and
Opportunities

Establishment of Production Methods

Changes in production methods take place. Continuing increases in sales and a more certain view of future sales encourage producers to shift from job-shop production methods to line or mass production. Risks are measurable enough to justify the large investment by management in single-purpose tools and fixtures for mass production. Decrease in production costs materialize both from the more efficient production methods and the increased scale of operations.

Price Adjustments

Prices in the acceptance stage of market development typically have a generally downward trend from previous levels, or *soften,* as the term is sometimes used. This occurs as the product begins to filter down through various income groups toward the mass market. Four factors tend to account for the lower prices which usually prevail. First, the greater volume of sales produces some economies of scale. Second, fewer product modifications, with accompanying costs of shutdowns and longer production times, are being made during production runs. Third, the adoption of more efficient mass production methods (line production) enhances scale economies. Fourth, the increase in the number of firms increases competition with both a theoretical and an actual tendency toward lower prevailing levels in the price structure. If this stage is reached during an inflationary spiral in the economy, the reduction may not be so apparent, but may still materialize on a relative basis in comparison with other goods.

Scramble for Distribution Outlets

With the increase in the number of producers, more distribution outlets appear, and there is a scramble for the acquisition of outlets by these producing enterprises. The newer competitors want the product exposure necessary to establish their brands, and older producers often wish to expand distribution to increase their market share. Not all manufacturers increase their outlets, however. Those who make a full line of products and have well-established distribution organizations often limit sales of a new product to their established outlets. The rapid rise in sales, giving a profitable volume for the industry as a whole, encourages many distribution outlets to carry several brands of the same product. Manufacturers' efforts to secure more distribution outlets make it easy for the outlets to acquire new brands. Dealers, therefore, tend to adopt what can be called a multiple-lines policy in contrast to simplified lines in both prior and following stages.

Stimulation of Selective Demand Cultivation

In the pioneering stage, marketing effort emphasized the cultivation of primary demand. Now, however, with market acceptance of the product class and the increase in direct competitors, manufacturers begin to emphasize the

173

Stages
of Market
Development
and Competi-
tive Rivalry

stimulation of selective demand. Instead of promoting features and benefits of the product class, they emphasize the advantages of their own brands in comparison with competitors' brands. This does not mean that all primary demand stimulation stops, however.

The differences observed between this stage and the pioneering stage indicate the kinds of changes that must take place. In summary, the increase in sales and competitors brings about changes in products and production methods with accompanying lower costs and lower prices. The distribution outlets must be expanded, and marketing effort shifts to selective demand stimulation. Moreover, profits for the industry as a whole tend to be healthy during this period.

Impact of an Economic Recession

A final characteristic is important with respect to products in the market acceptance stage. This is the period when the product is in the best position to resist the adverse effect of a significant downturn in the general economy—a recession or depression. It is possible, with proper modifications, for market expansion to continue during this period. Whereas a product caught in the pioneering period may be killed, those in saturation will tend to rise and fall with changes in the general level of business activity because of the postponable nature of such products, and a recession may hasten the departure from the market of those entering an obsolescence stage. Modifications necessary for surviving a recession in the market acceptance stage involve adjustments in product form, price reductions (usually directly related to product adjustment) to keep the product within the prevailing level of purchasing power, and the sustaining of promotional expenditures on the product. During the depression of the 1930's, for example, electric refrigerator sales continued to rise even though sales of other kinds of appliances sharply declined. But these sales gains were made only because the marketing adjustments we have discussed were made. Manufacturers introduced very simplified standard models without deluxe features. The standard models were sold at material price reductions, and relatively intensive promotional expenditures were maintained.[4]

Characteristics of Market Acceptance

1. Sales increase at increasing rate.

2. Explosion in number of competitors.

3. First major product improvements.

4. Line-production methods.

5. High-income groups dominate purchases, but middle-income groups become important.

6. Scramble for distribution outlets.

7. Dealers adopt multiple-lines policy.

8. Prices soften.

[4] Neil H. Borden, *Advertising in Our Economy* (Homewood, Ill.: Richard D. Irwin, Inc., 1945), p. 277.

174

Foundations
of
Strategy—
Interpreting
Market
Forces and
Opportunities

9. Profits healthy.
10. Selective demand cultivation.
11. Product capable of resisting a depression, with requisite:
    a. Product adjustments.
    b. Price adjustments.
    c. Promotion expenditures.

TURBULENCE

The stage known as the turbulence stage is so called because it represents a period of extreme competitive volatility. During this period competition is very intense, and there is a severe "shake-out" of marginal firms; only the most vigorous enterprises are capable of competing successfully. The most important characteristics of this stage are: the rate of market growth levels out, product policy changes, distribution outlets alter policies as a consequence of a profit squeeze, the number of competitors sharply decreases, and the general nature of marketing effort again shifts.

Leveling of Market Growth Rate

The first sign of a change in the stage of market development is usually seen in the volume of industry sales. Sales may continue to increase somewhat in this period, but the rate of increase typically declines. In this stage the product usually is sold to the mass market. That is, all income groups purchase, with the middle- and lower-income groups dominating. With this change in the type of buyer the motivating forces at work in purchasing change also. Price, for example, may be a much more important factor than it was in earlier stages. Likewise, changes in design of the product may be necessary to cater to the new groups of potential buyers.

Product and Service Adjustments

A number of changes take place during this period, the most important of which are: the introduction of annual models, with emphasis on styling; the handling of trade-ins; and the increased significance and complexity of product service and repair parts.

In the earlier stages, product modifications were made continuously, but now manufacturers introduce new models during each selling season. The introduction of annual models tends to be a response to the intense competition that prevails during this stage. Each manufacturer feels a more intense need to keep his product line up to date, hoping to achieve a competitive advantage through offering a distinctive product. After a time, model changes become more style and design oriented and somewhat less oriented to technical improvements, although the latter are still desired by manufacturers.

Although there may be a certain number of trade-ins in earlier periods, this period is the first in which trade-ins are frequent. The length of time the earlier

175

Stages
of Market
Development
and Competi-
tive Rivalry

products have been in service and the introduction of new models promotes an increased number of trade-ins. The proportion of total sales to previous owners of the product thus increases, and often exerts a downward pressure on prices. The effect of both price differences among competitive products and allowances made by dealers for older models is thus a twofold pressure toward a lower level of *effective* prices in the market.

Manufacturers not only introduce new models, but increasingly they tend to broaden their line of products to more effectively reach the differing segments of demand in the market.

As the product is in customer use for a longer period of time, the service and parts requirements increase. The broad-line policies of some manufacturers demand large quantities of parts, and the variety of brands handled by dealers results in parts inventories becoming increasingly more difficult to manage. Because of space requirements, labor costs, inventory carrying costs, and the added complexities of managing the greater varieties and numbers of parts, the cost of providing these services is likely to increase more than increases in revenues from them.

Dealer Margins and Profits Shrink

In this stage of market development, dealer gross margins and profits decline. The profit squeeze comes about because of pressures from both factors in the profit equation—cost and revenue. On the one hand, the effective price the dealer can obtain for the product declines. This reduction, as noted earlier, partly comes from the increasing price competition on new units and added price pressure from trade-in allowances. In addition, the introduction of annual models leads to carryovers of year-end inventories into the new model year. The sale of year-old models normally can be accomplished only with substantial price reductions, and in some cases at virtually liquidation levels. In these cases, distribution outlets are often caught in a position of being forced to reduce prices without any cost reductions. The result of all of these factors tends to be a reduction in the *effective* price level on a per unit basis over the entire selling season, and a consequent reduction in margin.

On the other hand, costs of doing business in the market have a tendency to increase as a result of the increased product services that must be provided and the increased inventories of spare parts that must be carried. The result of the two opposing forces is a cost-price-profit squeeze.

Brand Policy and Loyalty

To offset the pressure on profits, the distribution outlets try to reduce the amount of product service they provide and the number of parts they carry by reversing their earlier policies of carrying several competitive brands. Many will offer fewer brands, becoming more selective in how many manufacturers they will represent and how many products of any one manufacturer they will carry.

Partially as a consequence of dealer brand policy adjustments, institutional brand preferences among consumers strengthen during this period. When a

176

Foundations
of
Strategy—
Interpreting
Market
Forces and
Opportunities

consumer favors all or most of the products of a manufacturer's line (for example, General Electric appliances) over the lines of competing manufacturers, he is said to have an *institutional brand preference*. Thus, if he wants to buy a television set, General Electric has a preferred position because of this institutional loyalty.

In this period, institutional preference is strengthened because, as some smaller firms are forced from the market, the large manufacturers offer more assurance of good service and adequate supplies of spare parts. As dealers simplify lines it seems apparent that they will drop the products of smaller, specialized producers before they will drop those of manufacturers of complete lines of goods, such as General Electric. A consumer may, therefore, even ignore a relatively strong preference for a small manufacturer's product that is still available in the market, to gain assurance of future parts and service access, not knowing whether his preferred small manufacturer will survive. The strengthening of institutional brand preference, therefore, handicaps smaller firms while giving larger firms a competitive advantage.

Sharp Reduction in Number of Competitors

The increase in institutional brand preference, the need to provide product service and parts, the pressure to reduce prices during this stage, and the inability to get effective distribution of the product make it very difficult for the smaller firms to survive. Bigger firms with broad lines are in a much better position. Because of the breadth of their lines, they can induce distribution outlets to carry even those products that are not selling well. Many small firms go out of business during this period. The decline in the number of competitors is sudden rather than gradual. The position of the small firm thus shifts dramatically from one of strength during the acceptance stage to a struggle for survival during this stage. A small firm in the preceding stage may have been offered opportunities to sell out for forty to fifty times the amount of its annual earnings to a large firm anxious for rapid market entry during the acceptance stage; in the turbulence stage, it may have difficulty in making any reasonable sale of the business.

As this shake-out takes place, what might be called a "competition of desperation" emerges. In frantic attempts to survive, the smaller firms, rather than the dominant firms, tend to influence the basis upon which competition will be conducted. Price reductions and a bewildering assortment of promotional devices tend to accompany a "try anything" policy prior to imminent withdrawal, and the larger firms necessarily must formulate countering policies of their own.

Because this stage presents such a changed competitive environment, many changes in the character of marketing effort must occur. Only those firms that are willing and able to adjust to the new conditions can hope to survive.

Characteristics of Turbulence

1. Sales increase at decreasing rate.
2. Mass markets reached.
3. Annual model appears.
4. Product design oriented to style.

177

Stages
of Market
Development
and Competi-
tive Rivalry

5. Trade-ins appear.

6. Parts and service requirements increase.

7. Prices soften further.

8. Dealer margins and profits shrink.

9. Dealers simplify product lines.

10. Market segmentation increases.

11. Institutional brand loyalty strengthens.

12. Great shake-out in number of competitors.

13. Competition of desperation.

SATURATION

The most important characteristic of this stage is that replacement sales dominate the total volume of industry sales. That is, the majority of sales are to purchasers who have previously purchased the product type and are now purchasing a new one. The proportion of replacement sales to sales to first-time buyers of the product type varies from product to product. For example, over 99 percent of the wired homes in the U.S.A. have radios, and practically all sales are replacement sales, or sales to homes desiring an additional radio. On the other hand, only a small fraction of wired homes have a permanently installed automatic dishwasher.

Still, it might be conceivable that, at the moment, the automatic dishwasher market is near saturation. The motivating forces at work in the desire for an automatic dishwasher, and use limitations, as well as the limits on capacity to purchase, make it unlikely that 99 percent of all wired homes will own an automatic dishwasher in the foreseeable future. For this reason the maturity of the market is measured by the ratio of replacement sales to first-time purchases of the product type. While it is difficult to determine precisely when maturity is reached, a number of characteristics dominate this stage of development.

Changes in Market Characteristics

During this period sales tend to rise and fall with changes in basic economic factors. Industries may reach this stage with either increases or decreases in sales. Some product types, such as automobiles, remain in this stage for long periods of time, with generally upward sales trends. However, this can only be done with skillful management, because the dominance of replacement sales creates conditions altogether different from those experienced in the previous stages.

For example, sales during this period are very sensitive to changes in business conditions. You will recall from our discussion in Chapter 6 that ability to postpone purchase in the durable goods field makes such goods much more sensitive to changes in business conditions. Since the consumer already has one unit of the product, he may postpone purchasing a replacement if his purchasing power is restricted in any way. He may decide to get by with his old refrigerator, power lawn mower, air conditioner, or television set in order to be sure he can

178

Foundations
of
Strategy—
Interpreting
Market
Forces and
Opportunities

meet pressing financial demands. The strategies of product modification, price reduction, and intensive marketing used in the acceptance stage to effectively offset the impact of a recession are not nearly so reliable in this stage.

First-time purchasers in the market are few, and reflect basic economic factors. The actual number may depend on such factors as the rates of marriages, births, and new housing starts. Chapter 6 showed that some of these factors change relatively slowly. Offsetting this factor in some cases is the ability of the marketer to promote the idea that more than one unit should be purchased, such as is now reflected in TV, radios, and the "two-car family."

Frequency of Product Changes

Even during favorable business conditions, consumers have to be persuaded to replace old products. During these times they are more meticulous, or "choosey," in what they demand. As discussed in Chapter 7, the self-images that prevail in the market place are many and varied, and products must be adjusted if a satisfactory product-image is to be available. Since many consumers are quite content with their old products, an inducement to purchase requires the offering of a product which very closely satisfies the buyer's self-image. When a company offers many different varieties of the same product to cater to the many self-images in the market, it is said to be following a *segmentation strategy*. This stage is characterized not only by highly segmented markets, but also by a rather universal adoption of annual models to induce replacement purchase. This strategy is evident in such saturated markets as those for automobiles, television sets, refrigerators, and radios. Many different product varieties are produced, increasing the unit cost of production, unless engineering inventiveness is sufficient to keep costs low.

Necessity for Competitive Costs

It is more uncertain that a company can survive during this stage if its cost structure is not competitive. During pioneering and growth, firms with a somewhat higher cost structure could operate successfully because of the strength of the market. During the turbulent stage many of the higher-cost firms were weeded out, but now a comparable cost structure is almost a condition of any competition at all. Where fixed costs are a large part of total costs, such that significant economies of scale are present, there is inevitably a competition of the relatively few.

Changes in Distribution Outlets

With the need for a comparable cost structure also comes the need for distribution strength. Sales volume depends heavily on the strength of the distribution outlets handling a firm's products. During the pioneering and acceptance stages, manufacturers could obtain relatively good results in spite of a weak organization of distribution outlets. But in the mature period, having enough carefully selected, properly located, and sufficiently well trained distribution

179

Stages
of Market
Development
and Competi-
tive Rivalry

outlets becomes almost indispensable to successful competition. It is generally conceded that an important part of Chevrolet's leadership in the auto industry is due to the superior size and strength of its dealerships.

The system of distribution outlets used may be a manufacturer's most prized asset. Related to this strength is the proportion of business the manufacturer accounts for in the dealer's total sales volume. If the manufacturer represents a small fraction of the dealer's total sales, he cannot normally expect the vigorous support that is likely to be present when large proportions are involved. This factor again tends to benefit the larger, more broadly based company handling full lines, and is a limiting factor confronting the smaller more specialized producing enterprise. If then the product normally moves through exclusively franchised dealerships, such as is characteristic in automobiles, the number and size of the dealership organization is important. If the product moves through outlets shared by more than one manufacturer, the proportion of the dealer's business accounted for by the single manufacturer is of special importance during this period.

It becomes difficult to induce replacement sales, and since the market for first-time users may be small, some manufacturers may seek product exposure in as many different kinds of outlets as possible. A departure from using traditional types of distribution outlets, and experimentation with different kinds of channels, may be attempted for this purpose. Television sets, for example, are now sold in channels broadened considerably from traditional outlets such as appliance stores and department stores.

Logistics Complexity and Cost

During this stage the logistical aspects of marketing become especially complex and are often a high-cost component in marketing expenditures by manufacturers. This cost and complexity derives from the long period of product usage, the broad product lines directed toward highly segmented markets, the prevailing annual model practice, the large number of trade-ins, and the broadened distribution base of varied types of outlets. The logistics requirements for parts and products thereby become very sizable and costly, and the proper analysis of these requirements often holds significant potential economies for particular firms. In previous stages, the logistics aspect was not as significant in the total marketing effort. Not only is it a more substantial factor in this stage, but with the added necessity for competitive cost structures, its efficient management is virtually a paramount concern.

Stabilization of Number of Competitors and Erection of Entry Barriers

Market entry is now much more difficult than it was in the earlier stages. Established firms (now usually large) have already achieved the large sales volume and economies of scale that make low unit costs possible, whereas new entrants are not likely to achieve sufficient sales volume in a mature market to give them similar low costs. Other barriers are preferences for, and loyalties to, established brands; the difficulties in securing an efficient system of distribution

180

Foundations
of
Strategy—
Interpreting
Market
Forces and
Opportunities

outlets; the variety of products needed to provide a complete line; and the large initial investment required to match the production and marketing facilities of established firms. Consequently, few firms will enter a saturated or mature market.

The necessity for a reasonably competitive cost structure among rivals causes the departure of some firms from the industry during this stage, although it is marked by relative stability. The first two stages saw an increase in the number of firms, the third a rapid decline. Now for the first time, the number begins to stabilize. Few firms enter or leave the market.

The mature stage is a most difficult period in which to compete.

Characteristics of Saturation

1. Trade-ins dominate total market.
2. Sales rise and fall with basic economic forces.
3. Number of competitors stabilizes.
4. Markets highly segmented.
5. Annual model characteristic.
6. Competitive cost structure—a condition of survival.
7. Dealer strength critical.
8. Logistics complex and costly.
9. High entry barriers.

OBSOLESCENCE

In this period, innovations from competing industries make the product obsolete, and the market declines. There are many examples of products that have reached the obsolescence stage—for instance, horse-drawn carriages, Gramophones, coal stokers for household furnaces, and gaslights for indoor and outdoor lighting. As these products entered this stage, not all producers withdrew; some entered new business with different products, and some switched over to the innovations which had displaced their products.

An established product may also become obsolete as a result of change in consumers' purchase habits, attitudes, and values.

Market and Product Changes

There is an absolute drop in industry sales, and even more important, the decline will be gradual or abrupt, depending upon the speed with which the new substitute product goes through the earlier stages of market development. Generally, when obsolescence is caused by a change in consumers' habits, the change is more gradual.

When we discussed the pioneering stage we identified three groups of consumers on the basis of their need and desire for the product. During the obsolescence stage the decline begins among the third group—those who are somewhat indifferent. Successive erosions occur until only a small core of people who need and desire the product remain as customers. As these products gravitate back

181

Stages
of Market
Development
and Competi-
tive Rivalry

toward core markets, product lines tend to be greatly simplified from the very broad varieties that characterized earlier periods. Manufacturers rely more on product differentiation for capturing what little market remains than they do on broad product lines geared to different market segments.

Return to Cultivation of Primary Demand and Limited Market Exposure

Now again, as in the pioneering stage, the industry faces primarily indirect competition, although for a different reason, and marketing effort tends to return to the stimulation of primary demand in an effort to slow down the decline in the size of the market. However, companies have a tendency to spend less because of the decline in market opportunity. Industry-wide expenditures decline, and the expenditures of individual firms also decrease, partly because a smaller proportion of the sales dollar might be allocated to marketing and partly because even at the same allocation per sales dollar, lower sales mean lower expenditures.

The decline in marketing expenditures is accompanied by the use of more selective methods. In advertising, for example, narrower media are used, in contrast to the mass market media used in earlier stages. Major effort is directed toward the core market. Also, product exposure in the distribution network is not as important as previously, for the product tends to become a specialty good for the remaining core buyers, for which they can be expected to incur some inconvenience in purchasing. This tendency is a parallel movement, with the shift toward more selective promotional media and away from mass media.

Price Adjustments

Price also is used to preserve market position during this stage, and often follows a pattern of decline, then stabilization, and finally some upward movement. When a product moves into the obsolescence stage, producers attempt to maintain their sales by price concessions. Such price reductions are typically short-term defensive moves by which producers of the obsolete product hope to buy time to make the necessary technological changes in their product, to provide a more lasting solution to their problems.

Sometimes, however, price reductions are difficult to make. As sales decrease, per unit costs of production and marketing may increase, and a vicious circle may develop in which higher costs, if they result in higher prices, result in a further decline in sales. In the latter stages of obsolescence, however, demand may become more inelastic. This means that lowering prices becomes less effective in maintaining sales, or that firms could raise prices and pass on increases in cost to the consumer without sales decreasing. The best adjustment during this stage might call for either upward or downward price revisions, depending upon the consumers' reaction to the price change.

Decline in Number of Competitors

As total sales in the industry fall, the number of producers competing dwindles. It is possible that all firms might withdraw and the product no longer be

182

Foundations
of
Strategy—
Interpreting
Market
Forces and
Opportunities

produced regularly; but more commonly a sufficient market remains to enable a very small number of firms, or even only one, to profitably continue operations. There is a small demand even for such an obsolete product as gaslights, bought by those who value the charm and nostalgia associated with such lighting. For the surviving firms, profit opportunities can be quite attractive in the later phase of the period due to inelastic demand, few competitors, curtailments in market exposure that are possible, and the lack of need for broad product lines—assuming, of course, that sound management characterizes the enterprise. The surviving companies are often smaller specialized firms, because the limited market that exists is not attractive to the larger, more broadly based enterprises.

When this stage is reached, it is necessary for some companies to seek new products or make technological improvements in the old products, to slow down the continuous market decline. Unfortunately, many companies simply attempt to hold on by trying different marketing tactics until they are forced out of business.

Characteristics of Obsolescence

1. Sales declines permanent.
2. Number of firms declines.
3. Products gravitate back to core markets.
4. Product offerings narrow.
5. Prices soften, then stabilize, then increase.
6. Market exposure not as important.
7. Primary demand cultivation returns.
8. Profit opportunities can be good in late phase of stage.
9. Survivors tend to be specialists.

Summary

Every new product passes through a cycle of *perishable distinctiveness*. Beginning with its introduction and ending with its displacement, the product goes through rather well-defined stages of market development. Successive stages—pioneering, acceptance, turbulence, saturation, obsolescence—can be discerned, each with different competitive characteristics. The marketer, therefore, faces different problems in each stage, and must carefully adjust his strategy to meet each problem in turn.

We have seen how the stage of market development a product is in affects product strategy, pricing, type of demand stimulation, distribution outlets, services, production methods. Even firms acquiring companies or adding products to the line must ascertain their ability to compete effectively in the particular stage of market development which exists for the product or products. Firms are in a less risky position when the product line as a whole has items spread through the various stages rather than clustered in one area. Marketing effort, however, must be geared to the specific requirements of individual products and competitive conditions faced by each.

183

Stages
of Market
Development
and Competi-
tive Rivalry

Questions and Problems

1. Discuss the concept of *perishable distinctiveness* pertaining to products.
2. What are the various stages of market development that pertain to the product life cycle?
3. Do all products go through the cycle? Explain.
4. Do all products that pass through the cycle do so at the same speed? What would the influencing factors be?
5. What is meant by a product "filtering down through various income levels"? Can you test the validity of this concept from your own knowledge or experience?
6. Why do experimental, or job-shop, production methods tend to predominate during the pioneering stage of market development?
7. In which stage of development is the number of competitors likely to be the greatest? In which stage the fewest?
8. Trace what you would expect to be the pattern of breadth of manufacturers' product lines through the various stages of market development.
9. "Prices are likely to be at their very lowest level in the obsolescence stage." Expand on this statement, stating your agreement or disagreement with it.
10. At what stage is the great shake-out in the number of competing firms likely to come? Why? What kind of firms are these likely to be?
11. "Profits are likely to decline before market size declines." Can you provide any plausible reasoning to support this statement?
12. In what stage would you expect barriers to market entry for a new firm to be particularly difficult? Why?
13. "If the marketer has an unusually good marketing plan, it should be suitable for all stages of market development." Agree or disagree? Defend your answer.
14. "It is irrational for manufacturers and dealers to have limited product lines at one time, broader lines later, and then again narrow lines. Such variations only add to cost, and thereby limit profits." Comment.
15. What benefits can a marketing manager derive from being familiar with the various stages of market development?

Bibliography

Alexander, Ralph S., James S. Cross, and Ross M. Cunningham, *Industrial Marketing* (Homewood, Ill.: Richard D. Irwin, Inc., 1961).

Bliss, Perry, ed., *Marketing and the Behavioral Sciences* (Boston: Allyn & Bacon, Inc., 1963).

Britt, Steuart H., *The Spenders* (New York: McGraw-Hill Book Company, 1960).

————, *Consumer Behavior and the Behavioral Sciences* (New York: John Wiley & Sons, Inc., 1966).

Carson, David, *International Marketing: A Comparative Systems Approach* New York: John Wiley & Sons, Inc., 1967).

Clark, Lincoln H., ed., *Consumer Behavior: Research on Consumer Reactions* (New York: Harper & Row, Publishers, 1958).

184

Foundations
of
Strategy—
Interpreting
Market
Forces and
Opportunities

————, and N. N. Foote, eds., *Consumer Behavior: Household Decision Making,* Vol. IV (New York: New York University Press, 1961).

Dichter, Ernest, *The Strategy of Desire* (New York: Doubleday & Co., Inc., 1960).

Dynamic Aspects of Consumer Behavior (Ann Arbor: Foundation for Research on Human Behavior, 1963).

Ferber, Robert, and Hugh G. Wales, eds., *Motivation and Market Behavior* (Homewood, Ill.: Richard D. Irwin, Inc., 1958).

Frank, Ronald E., Alfred A. Kuehn, and William F. Massy, *Quantitative Techniques in Marketing Analysis: Text and Readings* (Homewood, Ill.: Richard D. Irwin, Inc., 1962).

Grubb, Edward L. and Harrison L. Grathwohl, "Consumer Self-Concept, Symbolism and Market Behavior: A Theoretical Approach," *Journal of Marketing,* XXXI, No. 4 (October 1967), 22–27.

Howard, John A., *Marketing: Executive and Buyer Behavior* (New York: Columbia University Press, 1963).

————, *Marketing Management: Analysis and Planning* (Homewood, Ill.: Richard D. Irwin, Inc., 1963).

Katona, George, *Psychological Analysis of Economic Behavior* (New York: McGraw-Hill Book Company, 1951).

————, *The Powerful Consumer* (New York: McGraw-Hill Book Company, 1960).

Life Study of Consumer Expenditures, Vol I (New York: Time, Inc., 1957).

Linden, Fabin, ed., *Expenditure Patterns of the American Family* (New York: National Industrial Conference Board, 1965).

Martineau, Pierre, "Social Classes and Spending Behavior," *Journal of Marketing,* XXIII (October 1958), 121–30.

Meyers, James H., and William H. Reynolds, *Consumer Behavior and Marketing Management* (Boston: Houghton Mifflin Company, 1967).

Newman, J. W., *Motivation Research and Marketing Management* (Boston: Harvard Business School, 1957).

Nicosia, Francesco M., *Consumer Decision Processes: Marketing and Advertising Implications* (Englewood Cliffs, N.J.: Prentice-Hall, Inc., 1966).

Outlook on Consumer Behavior (Ann Arbor: Foundation for Research on Human Behavior, 1964).

Shubik, Martin, *Strategy and Market Structure* (New York: John Wiley & Sons, Inc., 1959).

Warner, W. Lloyd, Marchia Meeker, and Kenneth Eells, *Social Class in America* (New York: Harper & Row, Publishers, 1960).

White, Robert N., "How To Use 'Product Life Cycle' in Marketing Decisions," *Business Management* (February 1962), pp. 74–76.

Woods, Walter A., "Psychological Dimensions of Consumer Decision," *Journal of Marketing,* XXV (January 1960), 15–19.

PART THREE

Product Policy and Strategy

The products offered by a firm should result from a deliberate plan to match the product line as closely as is profitable to the markets it wishes to cultivate. The plan for matching products and markets constitutes the firm's *product strategy*.

Planning of this sort is a natural consequence of what we observed in Parts 1 and 2 to be the firm's goals, and the behavior required to achieve them all. In Part 1 we observed that the main goal of the firm is to profitably serve markets in which products are *consumed*. The firm does this through offering buyers better "bundles" of utility (products) than its rivals. Because the market place is constantly changing, Part 2 followed naturally with an investigation of the forces that shape the diverse and changing wants of buyers. In spite of the many forces working on buyers, we found that it was possible to group them according to similar wants and needs, that is, to delineate markets. We saw also that changes in competitive conditions follow in some cases a fairly predictable pattern. Marketers can therefore arrive at general characterizations of markets according to the nature of the buying groups and according to the state of competition.

As it is now possible to characterize the kinds of markets available, the firm can choose from them and build or modify the product line to meet the demands of the markets selected. In short, the firm can begin to formulate a product strategy.

Determining the most profitable line of products to market is one of the most important and most complex management problems. This area of administrative action reflects factors both within and external to the firm itself. The total market offering includes such things as convenience of purchase, package attractiveness, brand image, services rendered, the reputation of the company, and other elements that are clearly supportive of, and integrated with, the product itself. Externally considered, the product is such a large proportion of the total market offering that it can be considered as the bridge which links the producing enterprise with the consuming market. As a consequence, the product line offered provides the principal component of competitive adjustment through which the firm aligns its corporate

185

resources with its market environment in an effort to achieve its goals.

Internal to the firm, the product line serves as the common element which binds together the diverse interests of all operating departments such as production, finance, marketing, purchasing, research and development, and personnel-management and industrial relations. The product line is the hub of the wheel around which the firm as a whole revolves.

In Part 3 we examine the alternatives available to the firm in establishing a basic product strategy. Although the firm must adjust its product line to its market environment, other considerations sometimes condition the firm to establish product lines which are oriented toward its manufacturing skills and facilities. As a result, different patterns of product diversity emerge. The reasons for and consequences of these patterns are examined. The need for continuous new-product introductions in a competitive environment requires screening of new-product ideas and careful analysis of the feasibility of new-product candidates. The procedures used in this phase of product strategy are explored. Regardless of the product line selected, it must be adjusted to the market. A number of means used to achieve product-market integration are discussed. Finally, the major factors to be considered when expansion of the product line is sought through diversifying or adding different product types to the line are analyzed.

Basic Patterns of Product Diversity 11

In this chapter we are concerned with the basic patterns of product diversity that a firm might employ in its overall strategy, and in the variations possible within these patterns. An understanding of these patterns helps to characterize the product lines of a particular company, is useful in defining corporate purpose, provides insight into areas where product additions might be made, and reveals some of the economic consequences of random product additions versus the economic benefits of carefully controlled additions. We will consider four principal patterns, based upon the production and marketing homogeneity or heterogeneity of the products, and then we will indicate how these four patterns can be accommodated either by a supply orientation within the firm or by an overall market rationale as the basis for determination of corporate purpose.

CONVERGENT PRODUCTION AND CONVERGENT MARKETING

The first basic pattern of product diversity is called convergent production and convergent marketing. The notion of "convergence" characterizes the way all products in the line utilize common production and marketing facilities. That is, raw materials and purchased parts "converge" on the same production facilities, and finished products "converge" on common marketing facilities. This arrangement is diagrammed in the following illustration.[1]

In this illustration, three different products utilize the same production facilities. They may require slightly different finishing operations, using varied supplementary equipment, but for the most part the same equipment, manufacturing methods, production skills, and labor force are used to pro-

[1] For what is believed to be the first exposition of this notion, see L. Lothrop, "What Our Firm Really Needs Is Something New," Part I, *Sales Management* (January 16, 1932), p. 82.

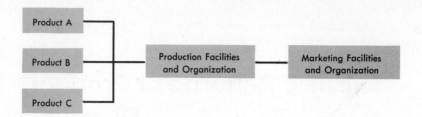

duce all three. Because the products are similar in market characteristics, a single marketing organization could sell all of them.

An office equipment manufacturer, producing such products as metal desks, chairs, tables, filing equipment, bookcases, and wastepaper baskets, is one good illustration of convergent production and marketing. Convergent production exists because each product is made from sheet metal and involves metal stamping, drawing, and finishing. Similarly, one marketing organization could distribute all the products, because they are destined for sale in a common market. This is a preferred pattern of diversity because it combines the least risk with the greatest chance for success as new products are added that retain this basic pattern.

All product expansion is hazardous. According to one study, 80 percent of the new products put on the market by 200 package goods producers failed.[2] Convergent production-marketing minimizes risks because, with the same production and marketing facilities, the firm can capitalize on its existing management capabilities, engineering talents, production skills, facilities, methods, knowledge of markets and market behavior, brand image, and position among dealers and distributors. In short, it can bring all of its competitive capacity to bear in marketing the new product.

Another advantage of this pattern of diversity is greater efficiency of operation throughout the firm. Economies of scale may be realized from the additional volume of business that usually accompanies product expansion. A broader base is provided over which to spread fixed costs, resulting in lower unit cost for the product. But a word of caution is in order. Expansion does not always bring economies of scale. A greater scale of operations provides the opportunity to adopt different methods which are appropriate to the larger volume of business. Without changes in methods, lower costs may not materialize. For example, product expansion may increase the volume of goods to be stored in warehouses. If the volume of goods moving through the warehouse doubles and this change is accompanied by twice as much inventory, twice as much space, twice as many order pickers, twice as much equipment, and twice as much clerical labor, there will be little or no cost reduction. In fact, cost might *increase* if proportionately more supervisors are required for the larger labor force and expanded operations. On the other hand, the greater scale of operations might make it possible to reduce costs by substituting electronic data processing equipment for hand tabulations in the control of inventories. The lower costs in this case would not have automatically accompanied the greater volume of business.

[2] "The Introduction of New Products," a survey made by Ross Federal Research Corp. for Peter Hilton, Inc.

The spreading of fixed costs over a larger volume of business constitutes the major element in economies of scale, but other elements are not to be overlooked. Materials may sometimes be purchased in more economical lots; more stable employment may be achieved, reducing the costs of laying off and recalling help. Also, waste circulation in advertising may be reduced. For instance, a baby foods producer advertising in *The Ladies' Home Journal* reaches many women whose children are past baby food age. This is waste circulation, since these mothers are not potential buyers. If the manufacturer were to add a line of junior foods, he would broaden the age range of potential users, and his advertising would apply to more of the magazine's readers. Waste circulation also exists when, for example, an American marketer's advertisements reach Canadian readers too far away from his distribution outlets to obtain his products.

Finally, the convergent production-marketing pattern is advantageous because it helps to strengthen even an established market position. For instance, a machine-tool manufacturer successfully added planers, vertical boring mills, and planer-type milling machines to an existing line of horizontal boring, drilling, and milling machines. In this case, the president of the company believed that the product additions would help to strengthen the company's already well-established position in the machine-tool industry.

Because the convergent production-marketing pattern permits continuous operations in closely related fields and is therefore the simplest and least risky of the four patterns, a thoughtful management would fully explore its possibilities before considering other patterns. Only when this pattern cannot achieve corporate objectives, should the manager explore other patterns.

CONVERGENT PRODUCTION AND DIVERGENT MARKETING

In this second pattern, all products utilize common production facilities but require separate marketing facilities and organization. The following diagram illustrates this pattern.

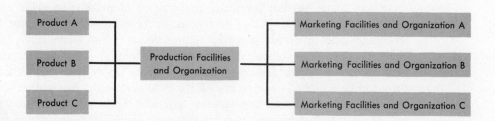

Here the products added can be manufactured with existing facilities, but because of different market factors cannot be marketed by a single marketing organization. The H. P. Smith Paper Company, for example, made meat-wrapping papers for packing companies. Then kitchen shelf paper, a product manufactured in much the same way as wrapping papers, was added to the line. The meat wraps were sold by the company's own sales force directly to the packers. The sales force was accustomed to dealing in the industrial market, where purchase factors are quite different than in consumer goods markets. But the new shelf papers, ultimately purchased by housewives, required distribution through department stores, variety stores, and supermarkets. Consequently, the industrial sales force was found to be unsuitable for dealing with these types of outlets, since it lacked a proper understanding of impulse purchasing, display space allocation, use of point of sale promotion materials, and other merchandising considerations in the mass distribution of consumer goods. These considerations led to the use of specialized marketing intermediaries for reaching the new markets to be cultivated for the shelf papers.

The product line of Kimberly-Clark at one time included printing papers, industrial wadding, building insulation, wallpaper, industrial wipers, facial tissue, and barbers' neck bands. All these products are made on basically similar primary machines, although various specialized pieces of secondary equipment are needed. Although production can thereby be characterized as essentially convergent, the marketing is essentially divergent. Under those conditions no single marketing facility and organization could cover such a broad span of different markets. The differences in business practice between printers, contractors, barber- and beauty-supply houses, and interior decorators make it unlikely that the requisite under-standing of user problems for effective marketing is within the competence and versatility of any particular sales force. This accounts for the divergence in marketing.

Now that the concept of *divergence* has been introduced, it should be recognized to be a relative term. That is, there are all degrees of convergence and divergence. Notice that in the previous case some specialized equipment was necessary in production. Thus, to a degree, there is an element of equipment divergence in this case. In another case, a manufacturer of hearing aids found his production skills adaptable to interoffice communications systems. This product expansion involved convergence of engineering, design, production skills, and quality control, but divergence in materials and equipment. A slightly greater divergence occurred in the case of a watch manufacturer who found his skills of production miniaturization adaptable to miniature scientific instruments. Here there was some, but not complete, convergence of production skills and tech-nology. There was a degree of divergence in these areas because some broader technology was involved (scientific control devices) and some new production skills (production in controlled atmospheric conditions). Thus we recognize con-vergence and divergence as relative terms, and the above examples indicate how there can be a limited convergence on the production side. For precise analytical purposes, one would need to assess the variations that would accompany product expansion in technology, engineering, materials, equipment, production methods, labor skills, and production controls. The term *convergent production* is used, however, when on balance there is a conjuncture of the major elements (equip-ment, methods, and skills) in the production process.

The same kind of limited convergence can exist on the marketing side, as illustrated by the appliance manufacturer who employs specialized salesmen in working with wholesalers in this one part of his overall product line. In addition, some specialized dealers are used that sell only laundry equipment. Some degree of divergence could take place in ultimate consumers, type of dealers or outlets, type of salesmen, methods of promotion, placement of advertising media, shipping methods, pricing policies, and technical information required in the selling process. The term *convergent marketing,* however, is used when on balance the variations are limited enough to permit a single marketing facility and organization to accommodate all product lines with reasonable efficiency.

The convergent production–convergent marketing pattern of product diversity is perhaps the most common of the four types, with convergent production and divergent marketing second in importance. Two conditions seem to foster the use of this second pattern after the first pattern has been fully developed. The first condition relates to high-fixed-costs industries and the second to the need to diversify market risk. High-overhead, decreasing-costs industries have high break-even points and suffer adverse profit consequences from unused plant capacity. Thus, where production costs are a large part of total costs, and fixed costs are a large proportion of production costs, management can be expected to exert every effort to maintain a high rate of plant utilization. This is done in order to achieve low total and unit costs and to take maximum advantage of the proportionately high profit opportunities above the break-even point after fixed charges have been recovered.

This cost structure creates a condition where management tends to be "machine oriented"—that is, more anxious to have product expansion that can utilize plant facilities than additions which fit nicely into the marketing organization. The high economic penalties of unused plant capacity in these kinds of industries (for example paper mills, where one machine may cost $25 million) lead frequently to a product diversity pattern of basically convergent production and divergent marketing. It is well to point out, however, that nothing may be gained in profitability if economies in production costs are offset by increases in marketing costs. Product expansion that provides somewhat lower manufacturing costs through convergent production may even adversely affect profits if the added profits require the establishment of an entirely new marketing organization that is more costly than the economies gained in production. As pointed out in Chapter 2, the firm must be primarily concerned with an optimum combination of cost centers throughout the entire system.

The second condition promoting this pattern of diversity is seasonal or cyclical fluctuations in sales, which firms try to offset and so reduce market risks. If all of a firm's products go to one market, its total sales will rise and fall as that market fluctuates. To avoid this condition necessarily means entering new markets —markets oftentimes different enough to bring about divergent marketing in product expansion. Not wishing to lose all convergence under these conditions, the firm often emerges into the second pattern of diversity—*convergent production and divergent marketing*. These conditions have occurred in the machine-tool industry, where extremely wide cyclical fluctuations in sales have been characteristic. Product expansion in this pattern has been attempted in order to make such firms less vulnerable to this type of market volatility. The Bryant Chucking Grinder Company, manufacturers of heavy internal grinding machines subject to extreme cyclical fluctuations, carefully evaluated the market for variable speed transmissions used in all types of plants that have moving conveyors. This was done to overcome cyclical fluctuations in sales. The specialized organizations needed to market very high priced machines and the market potential for technical machines such as internal grinders to a very small number of customers would not have been suitable for the marketing of transmissions to a broad market including all types of plants that have moving conveyors. Therefore, the second pattern, convergent production and divergent marketing, would characterize the product diversity of the company.

In all cases, when product diversity involves expansion into the pattern of convergent production and divergent marketing, managers must make sure that effective and profitable market cultivation is possible. The principal cause of new-product failure is the lack of a carefully planned and executed marketing program. An established market position is much harder to obtain than either new machinery and equipment or specialized production knowledge. The competitive advantage from product diversity, capitalizing on plant facilities and production skills, may turn out to be relatively short-lived, in contrast to a pattern that draws on the market strength of the firm as the source of its competitive position and differential advantage.

DIVERGENT PRODUCTION AND CONVERGENT MARKETING

This pattern utilizes a company's basic marketing structure and trades on its established market reputation, even though some products may require separate manufacturing facilities. It can be diagrammed this way:

The consumer appliance divisions of the larger appliance manufacturers, such as Philco-Ford and General Electric, are excellent examples of this pattern. They produce a full line of products—television sets, air-conditioners, and electric ranges, among others—requiring different production facilities. All these products are sold to a common market through a virtually common marketing organization. Depending on the product, there might be some variations among dealers (as for example TV and radio dealers handling only that part of the line, and some use of specialized salesmen for particular products from time to time), but on balance the marketing can be characterized as convergent. Another example would be building materials manufacturers, who make a wide range of different products and materials which are marketed through one sales and dealer organization.

Product diversity of this type is most feasible when the firm has a clearly dominant market position and market opportunities exist for other products of interrelated demand. A well-organized and well-established marketing structure and organization constitutes a particularly strong competitive weapon. Highly skilled sales personnel and a loyal dealer organization may be a company's most valuable assets, assets many competitors find difficult to duplicate. When a firm's line of products enjoys a dealer priority for marketing because of its great market acceptance, a major barrier to market entry by other firms exists. Consequently, product expansion that more fully meets dealer needs can help to strengthen the marketer against competitors' inroads.

Product diversity involving complementary lines using the same institutional brand promotes wider awareness of the brand name and stronger brand preference, and helps to establish a reputation of more far-reaching importance than is possible with one product line or a number of unrelated lines. Promotional effort on one product tends to benefit all. Also, a more sharply defined or clearer "corporate image" is likely to emerge in the market place under this pattern of diversity.

Centralized marketing activity often brings economies of scale. Costs of recruiting, selecting, and training a sales force and maintaining it in the field do not vary proportionally with sales volume. It may cost little more to have salesmen handle several products than to handle one—if the line is not too broad, time is available, and sales skills required are similar for all products. Economies in advertising may be possible through the elimination of waste circulation, combination promotions, joint displays, and greater use of institutional rather than individual item advertising. Other economies can occur in transportation, warehousing, and servicing—for example, through the pooling of shipments to obtain carload or truckload rates. Service and repair centers, once established, can usually handle greater volumes of servicing without proportional increases in costs.

This pattern emerges more commonly when the success of the enterprise is not so closely associated with utilization of high-fixed-cost capital equipment. Enterprise effectiveness may be oriented more to the market place, with proportionally less capital investment in equipment. Procter and Gamble, for instance, is largely a marketing-oriented rather than production-oriented enterprise. Its heavy expenditures reside in market cultivation effort, and it would be inclined to engage in product diversity that fits this pattern and uses its distribution organization, skills, and expenditures effectively. Procter and Gamble introduced "Puff," a facial tissue, through the same outlets it uses for its detergents and dentifrices. One might presume that the company's knowledge of mass marketing of low-priced, repetitively purchased "consumables" more than offset its lack of knowledge of paper making—which it purchased in the acquisition of a relatively small paper mill.

In the pattern we are discussing, as in any other, management must be concerned with the net effects of product diversity on the cost structure as a whole and on the firm's capacity to meet the requirements of effective competition throughout the whole production-marketing system. But there is a limit (again in both this and other patterns) as to how far diversity can be carried. Product lines may become too many and varied for effective assimilation by a single marketing organization. Once this point is reached and new organizational arrangements must be made, either by establishing several specialized sales forces by type of customer or by type of product, or by creating parallel organizations, costs may not be significantly greater in moving to an entirely new pattern of diversity.

DIVERGENT PRODUCTION AND DIVERGENT MARKETING

The last basic pattern of diversity involves separate facilities and organizations for both production and marketing. It can be diagrammed this way:

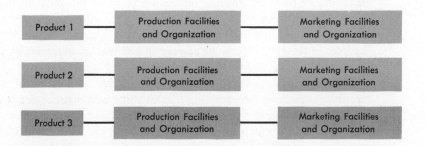

This pattern of diversity is akin to starting a series of new businesses. The products added are so different that they can neither be produced nor marketed through the same facilities. While this pattern has many limitations in comparison with the others, it is becoming increasingly common. Examples include the product expansion of Textron American, originally a woolen mill, into chain saws, outboard motors, and machine tools; a steamship company's entrance into the outdoor advertising business; and a food packer's entrance into the toy market.

Product diversity without any convergence should generally be avoided until opportunities to pursue those with some degree of convergence have been fully explored. All product expansion exposes management to a high rate of failure, but this pattern involves the greatest risk compared with the others, and is least likely to succeed. Most of the risks of starting new businesses are incurred, virtually no opportunities exist to utilize the existing skills and knowledge of the organization, and opportunities to take advantage of economies of scale in production and marketing are beyond this pattern. In short, each product line must stand alone on its own competitive merits without support from other areas of company operations. All the firm as a whole can transfer from one product to another are fiscal resources and general administrative skills.

Why, then, is this form of diversity so common? Technological advance, product innovations of research departments, and financially attractive opportunities for mergers or acquisitions perhaps account for most such moves. Technological advance, for instance, has moved a large segment of the aircraft industry into whole new corporate complexes and product diversity. Missiles, rockets, and other space vehicles have superseded manned military aircraft, and commercial aircraft production has resulted in large losses for the companies. With the large-scale research and development expenditures now taking place in many industries, scientists working on a particular problem may make discoveries in an entirely different area, discoveries that provide the basis for product innovations entirely outside existing company operations. The potential of the innovation may be such that management may undertake a whole new pattern of diversity in order to accommodate and capitalize on it. New patterns are likewise established simply because a financially attractive acquisition opportunity presents itself.

Finally, entirely new fields of endeavor have an alluring appeal for some executives. J. S. Knowlson, as president of the Stewart-Warner Corporation, expressed this attitude: "Willingness and eagerness of American businessmen to tackle the problems and reap the profits of new fields, after they have proved their abilities in the ones in which they started out, is as traditionally a characteristic as is their belief in free enterprise." [3]

In the event that this type of diversity is to be pursued, the divergent product expansion should establish a new strategic beachhead from which convergent product expansion can take place in the future. That is to say, the breakaway to completely divergent products should, by careful choice, provide further opportunities for convergent product expansion centering around the new area. This is preferable to a series of product moves, each of which would involve complete divergence.

In concluding the discussion of the various patterns of product diversity, we should recognize that each has its desirable features in the light of a particular company situation. Conversely, each may not be feasible because of company objectives, the nature of products, competitive factors, or the particular orientation of the firm. More specifically, the rate of corporate growth desired by management may preclude retaining a convergent production and convergent marketing pattern. Or, the nature of products may be such that closely related products have been fully exploited by a particular enterprise, and it must move from convergent marketing. Or, an enterprise may be facing such serious declines in sales in present markets and products that it must enter wholly new fields for survival. Finally, a firm may conceive of itself as essentially a financial entity pursuing profit opportunities wherever they may lead, the parent organization being more of a holding company than an operating enterprise. These illustrations should indicate that the basic pattern of product diversity to be followed is a strategic component that must be related to the individual firm. Our purpose is to think of the firm as a competitive and market entity and to arrive at a whole range of strategies that provide it with the best operating basis for survival and growth.

A BUSINESS RATIONALE

Having developed the basic patterns of diversity based upon the heterogeneity or homogeneity of its products in terms of production and marketing

---

[3] "Top Management Forum," *Industrial Marketing* (September 1953), p. 100.

components, let us now direct our attention to a rationale for the particular enterprise that might accommodate any or all of the patterns and serve to more sharply define corporate purpose.

The preceding discussion has been "product centered," yet products have a way of being displaced by competitively superior innovations. It is desirable, therefore, to seek a business rationale that accommodates "product patterns" and goes beyond them to provide a more enduring focus for the business behavior of the firm.

A Market Rationale

A market rationale tends to provide a more enduring focal point of competitive purpose than product definition alone. For instance, suppose a company characterizes itself as a producer of commercial refrigeration equipment. If the company directs all of its effort to this product orientation, it may at some point face a vanishing market, because it is conceivable that foods may be preserved without refrigeration.[4] Or a furnace manufacturer may find that temperature control may be maintained in the home by devices other than the current gas or oil furnaces, as for example either with heat-pumps or solar energy. If the business had been characterized as "home climate control," it might have a more enduring and relevant focus of competitive purpose. This is what is meant by the term *market province*—a statement of the end market application of corporate resources and effort that are relatively permanent in nature.

Other brief examples may be helpful before further pursuing the implications of market rationale. Our railroads might have considered themselves not as railroads, but as transportation companies, which could have facilitated entry into other media of transport meeting a broader spectrum of market needs as did the Canadian Pacific Railways. The American Telephone and Telegraph Company increasingly regards its business as "communications" rather than telephones. Oil companies see themselves as "energy companies." And a steam-shovel company recently characterized its business as "bulk materials handling," and expects to add a variety of expanded lines for industrial and construction use. In each of the above cases very heterogeneous production and marketing could be involved, but an integrating rationale for the business of the particular enterprise would exist.

There are fewer opportunities to provide this type of a rationale than there are for a more specifically product-focused base. The president of General Motors has stated that the many operations of the company essentially center around the use of motors and engines, and he has visualized this area as providing not permanent constraints but opportunities for the corporation. The industrial distributors known for years as "steel supply houses" are increasingly thinking of themselves as "metal supply houses" because of the greater importance of aluminium and the fact that it now competes directly with steel in many applications.

[4] For an excellent treatment of problems of this sort, see Theodore Levitt, "Marketing Myopia," *Harvard Business Review* (July–August 1960).

Some of the newer companies and industries have already shifted to the newer form of characterization. Some of the defense-related companies characterize their business as "aerospace" rather than rockets. These changes can have a profound effect both on product strategy and broader marketing strategy. The president of IBM's Data Processing Division recently stated:

> We are not only not in the computer business, we are not even in the data processing business. Our business is solving problems for management. We find a difficult analytical problem facing management, develop a solution, and then work out the system to be used in implementing our problem-solving. This orientation calls for a different kind of personnel, different training, different sales organization, and different product policy. We believe that the "software" (problem-solving skills, computer programs and service) are more important than the "hardware" (the machines).[5]

Let us now look in more detail at the way a given enterprise could be alternatively characterized and the implications it would have for patterns of product diversity.

The Gerber Products Company, whose well-known slogan is "Babies are our business—our only business," has long been a producer of baby foods. Perhaps the use of this slogan over the years is what produced the very strong image Gerber's enjoys among mothers. Researching the nature and depth of this image among mothers might show, however, that they unconsciously insert the word *food* in the slogan, thus: "Baby foods are our business—our only business." If the company then decided not to change this image, perhaps not wishing to "break faith" with mothers, the result would be a pattern of product diversity, almost the pure case of convergent production and convergent marketing. If, however, the image proved to be very much in line with the actual slogan, then this characterization of corporate purpose could provide an overall market rationale for what would be in reality a rather widely divergent pattern of product diversity. For instance, lines of baby toys, clothing, and furniture might be added. The company's pattern of product diversity would appear as follows:

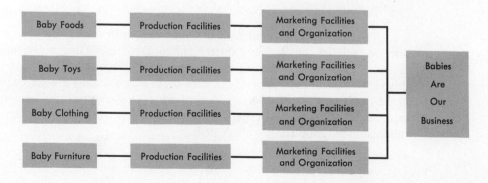

[5] A statement made before the Graduate Colloquy in Marketing and Transportation Administration, Michigan State University, East Lansing, October 1962, by Warren S. Hume, President, IBM Data Processing Div.

In these instances, very substantial operational heterogeneity would be involved among the product lines. Food, clothing, furniture, and toys have virtually no production similarity—either in research, design, materials, production methods, equipment, or skilled labor. Also, the marketing of each is actually very different from the others. Baby foods involve many stable items, whereas toys have significant fad characteristics, with virtually a whole new product line for each Christmas season. The types of retailers are very different, ranging from apparel stores to furniture stores, department stores, supermarkets, and a bewildering range of outlets for the distribution of toys. The competitive strategy would be to associate all products with the Gerber customer image among others. Such a market rationale could serve to integrate the various areas of corporate activity into a meaningful pattern accommodating divergent production and divergent marketing.

Let's look at another way in which the firm's view of itself might influence its pattern of diversity. Suppose Gerber's views itself only incidentally as in the "baby business" and essentially as a specialty-foods packer. This characterization would presuppose that the company's basic knowledge, skill, and organizational competence were centered in an unusual capacity for the successful movement of food products through supermarkets, backed by vigorous promotional effort at the store level among rivals seeking the same shelf space. Characterizing the firm this way could lead to the addition of specialty lines, for instance, geriatric and health foods. On this basis the business would look very different, as is shown following.

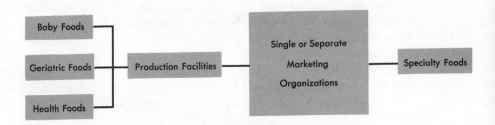

The diagram shows all products produced with essentially the same production facilities, but possibly distributed by three marketing organizations (or conceivably even one) through supermarkets and specialty food stores. Thus, this view of Gerber's "business" could result in a significantly greater convergence in the firm's patterns of diversity. A very different enterprise would emerge, with quite different patterns of product diversity, depending upon which market rationale was adopted.

A Supply Rationale

A supply rationale can likewise provide an integrating basis for the four patterns of diversity. This focus is more likely to prevail where the firm has a substantial proportion of its total investment in its source of supply. Some paper mills, for example, have many millions of dollars invested in timberlands, and might thereby see themselves essentially in the business of growing trees and using them commercially. They might, that is, pursue the marketing of all products that derive essentially from their timberlands base. Another way of characterizing such an enterprise would involve a shift in terminology, but change the nature of operations more significantly. The term *wood fiber utilization* would construe more of a technological orientation to business purpose, and this could be broadened still further by the term *fiber utilization,* which would allow for accom-

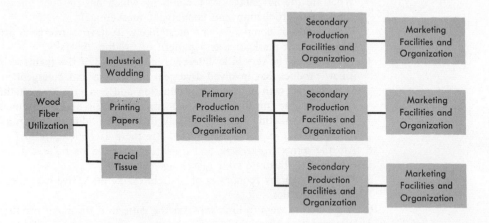

modation of the newer synthetic fibers. This latter characterization could lead to a strikingly different line of products. Finally, one might emphasize the production process more and characterize the firm as simply a member of an important segment of the chemical processing industry whose business was essentially tied to this process foundation. Using the wood fiber utilization notion, however, a somewhat more elaborate view of its pattern of product diversity could be shown as in the preceding diagram.

Summary

Product policy and strategy are important means of market adjustment and should be designed to efficiently integrate corporate objectives and resources—by means of products—with market forces in which these products are purchased and used. Four basic patterns of product diversity for an enterprise have been shown, based on the degree of homogeneity or convergence of products in production and marketing. Each of the patterns has been recognized as having its special benefits and limitations. A preference has been shown, however, for patterns that involve more convergence than divergence.

After basic patterns of diversity were developed, attention was directed to a rationale for the particular enterprise that might accommodate any or all of the patterns and serve to more sharply define corporate purpose as it would influence product policy and strategy. This poses a seemingly simple question, but one which is extremely complex, with major complications for product strategy: "In the light of the markets we now cultivate, what business are we really in?"

Questions and Problems

1. What are the basic patterns of product diversity as outlined in this chapter?
2. What is meant by convergence?
3. How would you characterize the product diversity of a company making a broad line of children's furniture?
4. What are the advantages to a company which has product lines involving convergent production and convergent marketing?
5. What kinds of companies are most likely to have convergent production and divergent marketing as a pattern of product diversity?
6. "There would be very little difference in the degree of risk incurred in adding a new product that involved divergent production and divergent marketing as compared with convergent production and convergent marketing, since the failure rate for all new-product introductions is high." Comment.
7. Why is a marketing advantage likely to be more "durable" than a production advantage of equal magnitude? Are there exceptions to this?
8. Are the terms *convergent* and *divergent* absolute or relative terms? Give examples to illustrate your reasoning.
9. What is meant by economies of scale in marketing? Give examples of these scale economies.
10. What factors seem to limit how far the pattern of divergent production and convergent marketing can be carried?
11. What factors, do you think, might account for the rather widespread current diversification into divergent production and marketing?
12. "No one pattern of diversity is clearly superior to any other—it depends upon the circumstances surrounding the particular firm." Comment.
13. How would you describe the term *market province?* Can you use it in a managerial context?
14. What is the advantage in characterizing a company's business as "bulk materials handling" instead of "steamshovels"?
15. Explain why product policy is an important means of market adjustment.

Product-Market Integration 12

In the preceding chapter we considered the basic patterns of product diversity and demonstrated that the product strategy of the firm should reflect an overall rationale. Now we turn our attention to the way in which products must match market forces and opportunities.

The marketer must determine the number of variations of any given product to be offered. This is sometimes known as *tactical product-line adjustment,* in contrast to the determination of the number of different products, which is called *strategic product-line adjustment.* This chapter will consider: the general concept of matching; the ways in which matching takes place; some of the difficulties faced by producing enterprises in these attempts; the necessity for varying strategies from time to time; and finally, means of reconciling opposing forces in supply and demand in achieving product-market integration.

THE CONCEPT OF MATCHING PRODUCTS WITH MARKET FORCES

The concept of matching products with market forces was discussed in Chapter 5, when we examined the need to create compatible product-images and self-images. At that time we suggested that ideally every firm should strive to develop a product-image compatible with the customer's self-image. However, consider the problem facing a manufacturer of women's shoes in deciding what kind of a product line to offer. Imagine the number of styles, the variety of materials, the assortment of colors, the number of sizes, and the prices necessary to fulfill the varied expectations of buyers. The number of individual items in the line would be infinite if the ideal of an exact match of product with customer preferences were to be achieved in every case. Unfortunately, there are economic penalties attached to excessive proliferation, resulting from the increased costs of production and marketing. Because of the heterogeneity of demand for most goods above the level of basic necessities, every enterprise has a

201

problem of determining the optimum number of variations of a product to offer. An enterprise has the option of offering only a single product, a large number of variations known as a *broad-line* or *full-line strategy,* or a small number of variations known as a *limited-line strategy.* The number of variations offered is sometimes called the *assortment.* The objective is to balance costs-revenue considerations throughout the overall system so as to arrive at an optimum product line from a profitability point of view. The broader the line, the more nearly it caters to the variations in desires in the market—but the higher the cost. The more limited the line, the less ideally it will match the market, but this may be compensated for by lower costs.

Since the ideal can rarely be achieved, we should like to add another dimension to the matching concept by developing a general characterization of any market as it appears to any firm.

Any market may be divided into three parts: (1) core, (2) fringe, and (3) zone of indifference. The core of the market for any product is the prime customer cluster, where the product ideally matches needs, desires, preferences, motivation, and purchasing power. In other words, the product-image for customers in the core is fully compatible with their self-images. As we move away from the cluster towards the fringe of the market, a less exact fit exists in any one of a number of purchase variables. The product-image for this group of customers is only partially compatible with the self-image. Finally, we reach a "zone of indifference," where no compatibility exists and it is almost by random chance alone that potential buyers will be attracted to the product.

The lesser degree of fit which exists outside of the market core must usually be compensated for by lower prices, which influence potential buyers to compromise exact preferences. The most usual expression of this compromise comes from the woman shopper who explains her purchase with the comment, "It wasn't *exactly* what I wanted, but it was such a good buy."

THE FUNDAMENTAL
MATCHING STRATEGIES

In seeking profitable product-market integration, two alternative strategies are possible, which have some degree of substitutability. The strategies vary primarily in the *degree* of product assortment, but in their extreme they constitute differences in the nature of the strategy.

A Limited-line Strategy Oriented to Product Differentiation

The marketer can attempt to cover a broad market with a single product or a very limited line, which he attempts to differentiate from the products of rivals both physically and also psychologically through promotion and advertising.[1] He recognizes some degree of heterogeneity of demand, but postulates essentially a single demand curve for the product type. Such variations in desires

---

[1] For the basic work in these two strategies, see Wendell R. Smith, "Product Differentiation and Market Segmentation as Alternative Marketing Strategies," *Journal of Marketing* (July 1956), pp. 3–8.

as exist are presumed to be capable of converging toward the product through large outlays for advertising and promotion, which tend to accompany such a strategy. This strategy assumes that consumer choices may be partially molded around any given point on the demand schedule. A term which describes this notion is *plasticity of demand*.[2] Both price and the large promotional and advertising outlays determine the quantity to be demanded. It, of course, also assumes the possibility of expanding demand or a shift in the entire demand curve to the right.

The results that can be expected from a limited-line strategy tend to be circumscribed by the ever-lessening degree of fit which by definition occurs as a larger market share is sought. Such market expansion is limited by the excessive and uneconomic outlays for persuasive propaganda that would be required to offset the inexact fit, by price concessions required to induce potential buyers to compromise their precise preferences, or by competitors' actions following essentially similar strategies which tend to cancel each other out. Usually a combination of all four factors sets an outer limit to the success of the single product or limited-line strategy.

A Broad-line Strategy Oriented to Market Segmentation

The broad-line strategy varies not only in degree from its previously mentioned counterpart but also in some rather basic postulates. The marketer following this strategy visualizes not just a single demand curve for the product type, but a series of demand curves, each having peculiar and distinct characteristics. He will rely on a more exact product fit with each of these essentially homogeneous segments for a deep penetration into each to achieve a sizable share of the total market rather than a broad but thin penetration over all of the segments. This strategy gives high priority to precise product planning and relies on the exactness of customer fit for effective product-market integration rather than relying heavily on promotional and advertising effectiveness.

This is not to say, however, that promotional expenses can be drastically curtailed as compared with the limited-line strategy, for the market must be informed and made aware of the significance of the variety in the assortment. But marketers following this strategy would appear to be less vulnerable to the promotional tactics of competitors (coupons, giveaways, audience ratings of TV shows, etc.) and to consumer indifference that can arise from advertising claims and counterclaims. The product rests on a more substantial foundation—a harmonious matching of product with customer preferences.

This strategy, however, tends to be limited ultimately in its effectiveness by the higher costs incurred through production diseconomies arising from excessive product assortments; by the magnitude of inventory problems and carrying costs; by the scope of the line that can be effectively assimilated by dealers because of space, promotional, and financial limitations; and ultimately by spurious product differences, which potential purchasers are either indifferent to or for which they are unwilling to pay the price premium which may be involved.

[2] Wroe Alderson, *Marketing Behavior and Executive Action* (Homewood, Ill.: Richard D. Irwin, Inc., 1957), p. 277.

One can conclude from consideration of these alternative strategies that the most effective product-market integration requires a precise measurement of the heterogeneity in the market and identification of the segments which derive from these differences. This is the only way by which intelligent cost-revenue expectations can be calculated. This consideration reemphasizes the importance of careful market investigation and analysis, treated earlier in Part 2 of the text.

WAYS BY WHICH PRODUCTS
ARE MATCHED WITH MARKETS

Three principal approaches exist for matching products with varying market segments. These segments can vary by the need for a different form of product; for varying quality and price levels; and by varying motivational forces.

Segmentation Based on Product Form

Perhaps the most common attempt to achieve effective product-market integration is to direct products of different physical characteristics to identifiable market segments which have different needs. For example, a best-selling major appliance at one time was the freezerless refrigrator, which was a manufacturer's response to the refrigerator needs of owners of home freezers. It is intresting to note, however, that this product was introduced as an unexpected by-product of a consumer preference study on freezer space in refrigerators. This study showed a conflict of opinion among potential purchasers, with the majority wanting more freezer space. A very small size group, however, preferred less freezer space than in existing models. Since the whole trend of design had been toward increasing freezer space, a more detailed analysis was conducted of those preferring less freezer space. The investigation indicated that these people were predominantly home freezer owners, hence the differing needs which could be capitalized on with the new model.

Many other examples of demand varying according to product form could be cited, but only a few are necessary: large refrigerators for families with several children, compared with smaller sizes for apartment dwellers; portable dishwashers for transient families, compared with custom installations in permanent residences; and a line of outboard motors that includes models for a trolling fisherman, for water skiing, and for the cruising yacht. While quality, price, and motivational factors may all be involved to some extent in these segmentation attempts, the dominant aspect of the matching process is the need for physical differences in products.

Segmentation Based on Quality and Price Differentials

Another frequently observed pattern of achieving product-market integration through a segmentation strategy is the making of adjustments for varying demands in price and quality. This historic method is observable from the earliest times. Quality levels, however, have market complexity that is not always clearly perceived when related to consumer use. "High quality" is usually taken to mean obvious superior physical quality as well as quality perceivable to consumers in the use of the product. We might think of professional carpenters' tools, refrigerators built to an extended thirteen-year quality base (a thirteen-year expected life-span) or only the finest overall quality of men's Oxford-cloth cotton shirts.

Below this superior quality level many other levels are possible, but in two different quality concepts. The first quality concept is to reduce actual quality, but maintain the level of user quality. For example, the shirt marketer might continue to use the finest quality material in the cuffs and collars of the shirt but reduce slightly the quality in the body of the shirt. Inasmuch as the cuffs and collars are the first to show wear in a shirt and in view of the fact that the tendency is to discard the shirt when such wear appears, the consumer quality in use would be the same as in the higher actual quality product.

Another example of "same consumer quality" but lower actual quality relates to the construction of waffle irons. Consumer testing agencies have compared the times required among various brands for the iron to reach baking temperature. When an iron takes an additional thirty seconds to reach baking temperature, economies in heating elements are possible, but this difference is hardly perceivable to consumers when all other factors of design and construction are the same.

A final illustration can be drawn from the canned foods area. Canned pineapple has become a favorite fruit for salads. The finest quality pineapple is without blemishes and of uniform shape. With such fruit it is possible to pack whole, round slices of perfect uniformity. The custom of housewives, however, is to cut the pineapple into cubes or pieces for many varieties of salad. Packers, removing minor blemishes and using fruit of slightly irregular shape, are able to pack diced pineapple of the highest grade, but from fruit which is not of sufficient "quality" to make uniformly perfect whole slices. The consumer, using the fruit for this purpose, however, is unable to perceive the difference.

These examples involve a change in the form of the product, which indicates that two or more kinds of segmentation can be combined in seeking effective product-market integration.

The second quality concept is to produce products with lower-quality levels of performance and physical criteria, directed to buyers whose needs, preferences, or purchasing power does not warrant the higher-quality product. The typical "do-it-yourself" fan does not want or require the quality levels in tools appropriate for a professional carpenter, because of both skill differences and intermittent use. This point seems obvious, but consider a slightly more complex situation. The best-quality home refrigerator might be built to a thirteen-year length of life quality base and sell at retail for $429.95. A similar model in size, features, and design might be built to a seven-year quality base and sell for $329.95. If one were to "use up" all of the "quality," the yearly depreciation cost on the "more expensive" model would be approximately $33 per year, whereas the "cheaper" product would require approximately $47 per year. But even so, the lower-priced model might appeal to young married couples whose purchasing power had to be spread over many items in furnishing a house or apartment, and whose needs therefore are better served by a lower-priced offering. The same low-priced refrigerator, however, might also appeal to consumers with much higher income and purchasing power. These buyers might not expect to keep the refrigerator long enough to "use up" the quality, either because of expected job mobility and the practice of sale and replacement on intercity moves, or because they forecast that many new features will appear in new models during the life-span of the purchased item which will bring about the trading-in of the old model on a new one after it suffers style obsolescence. Here again there is an overtone of "customer use" quality which has implications for product-market integration.

Segmentation Based on Psychological and Motivational Forces

The most difficult type of integration to achieve, based upon segmentation, is through matching products with psychological and motivational forces that are often hidden, perhaps even below the threshold of conscious awareness among purchasers. The difficulties here are many and the subtleties of the market place most pronounced. Yet these forces are often powerful and formidable. Rich rewards, nonetheless, are available to marketers who succeed in these integration attempts.

Consider the motivational forces in the already large and growing geriatrics market. The older portion of our population is increasing considerably more rapidly than the population as a whole. Attempts to market geriatric foods successfully on a broad scale have met with little general success. Products identified as such present an image to the older person that is displeasing. These people find unpleasant the subliminal suggestion that their teeth and digestive systems may not be as hearty as they once were. At least they do not like to announce this fact to others through the purchase of such foods in the market place and through conspicuous use. The image of a robust, virile, and active life is a more treasured self-image. Packers of baby foods find that a significant volume of their business comes from such older people who ostensibly may be "purchasing for the grandchildren." These purchases can take place without "conspicuous involvement of self-images" on the part of the buyer.

Another illustration of problems involved in this type of product-market integration can be drawn from products directed to the teen-age market. Here again is a rapidly expanding market that many merchandisers have isolated as an important segment of the overall market for their products. A feminine-hygiene product was directed to this market segment, identified in its brand name as a teen-age product, and introduced with very sizable promotional outlays. After a period of time the product was found to be not as successful as the merchandiser had expected. An important factor here was that teen-age girls' desired self-image was not one of an adolescent. More commonly, they preferred to think of themselves as attractive, desirable, mature young women of sophistication and poise. This self-image is not compatible with a personal product identified as teen-age.

Where purchasing patterns reflect different stations in life, product policy must be geared to these differences. Actually, a persuasive argument can be made for the theory that all consumer purchasing either directly or indirectly, consciously or subconsciously, reflects a person's preferred station in life, and his desired self-image.

Imagine the market for vacuum bottles, segmented wholly or partly on motivational forces.[3] The performance requirements for keeping liquids warm is approximately the same for the construction worker's lunch pail and the sporting gentleman's needs in attending a football game on a chilly November Saturday. The product images must be decidedly different if psychologically segmented demand components are to be effectively cultivated. The vacuum bottle for the lunch pail needs a "rugged, workmanlike, unpretentious, functional, 'he-man-like' " image. It would perhaps be black or of a plain color, with a cork stopper, and have an unpretentious metal or plastic drinking cup. The same performance requirement in the model for the typically well-equipped football fan cheering on his dear old Alma Mater would be implemented in quite a different way. It would be perhaps a colorful plaid, with a plastic cap or rubber closure, a gaily matched thermal drinking cup, and a color-keyed carrying case. Purchasers expressing different self-images in these two situations call for product-images that are quite different if the marketer's product strategy is to achieve good product-market integration on the basis of psychologically differentiated market segments.

Combination Approaches

The most fruitful solutions to effective product-market integration often employ a combination of approaches worked into a total product-line strategy. Various market segments that call for differences in product form, quality levels, price difference, and motivational orientation are identified and quantified. Product offerings which are designed to match these multiple variables in the overall product policy are then arranged.

An illustration of this may be drawn from the strategy employed by a large national brewery in attempting to increase its share of the beer market in the large metropolitan markets. The brewery marketed a well-known single brand, with very sizable promotional and advertising outlays directed at product differentiation, and sold the product in large volume at a premium price level. Ultimately, however, diminishing returns from promotional expenditures were perceivable, and more and more difficulty was encountered in increasing the share of the market obtainable by this brand. Detailed investigation and analysis indicated that the overall market had relatively distinct segments, some of which were dominated by "taste" preferences and some by price overtones.

Within the taste category two distinct "taste images" were perceivable. One large group preferred a "pale, light, and dry" beer. This group, however, could not distinguish such a beer, in blindfold tests, from other varieties. The convictions on the part of these customers, nevertheless, were so strong that they would not likely be persuaded to purchase any product promoted otherwise. Perceivable attitudes about light, healthful foods, low calories, subtle taste, and gracious living were likewise exhibited.

The second homogeneous group of important size preferred a "hale, hearty, and full-bodied" beer but, like the first group, could not tell this taste from others

---

[3] Vacuum bottles are often referred to as "thermos" bottles, although this is a brand name rather than a generic term.

in blindfold tests. This group also leaned toward the robust outdoor life, zestful humor, and more participative activity (fishing, hunting, etc.).

A third group was strongly price conscious, with cost transcending taste and with taste preference more undifferentiated. The strategy pattern for the brewer, then, to achieve a greater share of the overall beer market through better product-market integration, was first to introduce another product, different in physical form and promotional orientation, to more effectively cultivate the "pale, light, and dry" market. A second move was to acquire local breweries in order to offer a local, popular-priced product. This strategy replaced the dominant reliance on product differentiation in a single product with a plan to achieve better adjustment of products with markets through broader-line market segmentation based upon form, price, and motivational orientation.

PROBLEMS IN
PRODUCT-MARKET INTEGRATION

In the variety of attempts to achieve effective product-market integration, certain common and recurring problems appear in the product policies of many enterprises, and are worthy of being highlighted. While no attempt will be made to catalogue the myriad of difficulties encountered, five conceptually significant ones are singled out.

Product Lines That Are Both Too Broad and Too Narrow

That a product line could be both too broad and too narrow appears to be a contradiction. This occurs, however, where a marketer attempts to serve a number of distinctly identifiable markets with a broad assortment of products. The product line in such cases may be too broad, in the sense that the sales force cannot effectively spread its effort over so many different markets. That is, effort is diluted to the point where no market is cultivated sufficiently for a high degree of penetration because of the diffusion of effort and scattered offerings. At the same time, the product line may be too narrow in one or several of the various segments to effectively fulfill dealer and customer needs. This kind of situation can be seen in the photographic equipment field. A manufacturer might be offering 8-mm movie cameras to the low-priced mass amateur market, with distribution through drug stores, department stores, and jewelry stores, as well as photographic shops; expensive movie cameras, projectors, and still cameras to the professional-like top of the amateur market through photographic dealers; professional equipment direct to studios, institutions, and industrial users; and photocopy machines through business machines dealers. Such a product line might be too broad for effective selling by a given sales organization, and yet too limited in the offerings in any particular area to provide adequately for dealer needs and competitive requirements. For instance, the manufacturer may be competing against full-line producers in the higher-priced equipment. In such a case, a single or limited offering might not provide sufficient dealer sales to justify any great amount of promotional, display and selling effort on the part of the dealers.

These factors usually demand some pruning of the product line, as well as an expansion in other areas, to provide really effective product-market integration in the markets the marketer elects to serve. This situation is occurring more frequently with the trend toward diversification that has been evident in recent years.

Product Proliferation That Dilutes Economies of Mass Production

One of the most insidious dangers in attempting a high degree of segmentation with broad product lines is the dilution or even destruction of scale economies associated with mass production. This may tend to occur where an excessive preoccupation with customer-orientation exists. That is, an imbalance takes place in manufacturing and marketing costs. The most enlightened marketing concept, however, recognizes the need for an optimum integration of cost centers throughout the system as a whole. This point, you will recall, was emphasized in Chapter 2. Marketing people must thus share a large part of the responsibility for the evolution of product lines that ultimately defeat the major economic advantages related to mass or "line" production. The danger is an insidious one in that there is generally a much stronger compulsion to add products than to drop them.

Production inventiveness has been sorely tested to maintain high levels of efficiency in the face of broad product assortments and customer choices. It is true that scientific advances in production scheduling, routing, and control have made possible versatile manufacturing within cost limits previously unattainable. There is a point, however, beyond which versatility cannot be accommodated without cost increases. The American automobile industry provides a case in point. An assembly plant appears to be a showplace of mass production efficiency because of the scientific procedures in scheduling, routing, and control. But the industry makes options available in thousands of combinations to buyers in the purchase of a car. It is estimated that Chevrolet could produce at full production for more than a year and never make exactly the same car twice. Many of these customer decisions would appear to be more intelligently made by an automotive engineer—types of springs, brakes, axles, steering mechanism, carburetor, exhaust system, etc. Some choices appear to be a needless waste of decision making for both seller and buyer—an extreme case being the choice of thickness of foam rubber, in the seats, that has been available in the past. Some of the success of foreign makes, such as Volkswagen and Renault, in the American market may well be related to the simplicity of product lines and customer choices. Cost savings are possible that go well beyond mere manufacturing economies. Think of the complexity of order handling, accounting systems, pricing, materials purchasing, checking and verification of the finished product, billing, etc., that accompany the variety of customer choices offered in our automobile industry. The industry has come almost full circle, from the early custom building of each unit through the pioneering of mass production of a standard vehicle (the Model T) to today's custom building according to an individual order—either the dealer's or the ultimate consumer's.

This problem is common to a greater or lesser degree in the product policies of many firms. In attempts to achieve effective product-market integration, firms have permitted proliferation to go unchecked, a proliferation that in the end can prove to be a major obstacle in achieving the desired level of profitability.

The Trap of the Full-line Competitor

Evidence of recent years indicates that the full-line marketer on the whole has been more successful than his limited-line, more specialized rival. The result has been a trend toward so-called full-line product policies on the part of many manufacturers. The overall market strength, customer recognition, dealer priority, promotional impact, and customer franchise that can derive from the full-line policies of such firms as General Electric are very real facets of competitive advantage. When the strategy is used too much, however, it can engender an empty management slogan devoid of meaning. Herein lies the trap: each product addition is defended completely by the argument, "We must be a full-line house."

This argument becomes a defense for irresponsible product proliferation and obscures some very difficult measurement and conceptual problems. What is the precise definition of a *full-line policy?* Is it to be measured in absolute or relative terms? What meaning and significance are attached to the term by the trade? Is it possible to go beyond full-line in product assortments? Several firms observed to be strong advocates of the desirability of being a full-line competitor have been unable to define any standard for its achievement. The issues involved can be highlighted from product policy elements in appliance marketing. The industry has exhibited strong trends toward full-line competition, with many mergers, acquisitions, and expanded product lines.

To pinpoint the issue under consideration, however, reflect on product requirements in clock radios. First of all, is it necessary to produce radios to be considered a full-line appliance manufacturer? If so, is it then necessary to have a wide variety of various types and styles of radios? If so, is it necessary to have clock radios to be considered full-line? If so, must all of the following types be offered: 5-transistor single speaker set in six colors; 5-transistor dual speaker set in six colors; 5-transistor single speaker automatic shut-off and come-on in six colors; 5-transistor dual speaker automatic shut-off and come-on in six colors; 7-transistor, AM-FM band, single speaker in six colors—etc., etc., etc.? The tendency has been for this kind of evolution to take place under the presumed requirements and desirability of full-line competition. The number of models becomes so great, however, that it is unlikely that the market segments these products reach can be analyzed and quantified for meaningful revenue-cost calculations. Without such estimates it is impossible to arrive at an optimum assortment in product lines. Thus the relevant questions regarding assortment decisions are obscured by the presumed complete rationale of full-line competition.

Trading Up and Trading Down

One of the recurring problems of marketers attempting to stratify and segment markets by quality and price characteristics is the difficulty of marketing successfully products of both "high" and "low" quality in the same general class. When marketers known for marketing low-priced merchandise introduce products of higher price (and presumably higher quality), this is known as *trading up*. Conversely, marketers who introduce cheaper products than their original lines are regarded as *trading down*. Neither move is easy to assimilate without experiencing substantial imbalance between the sales of the two lines. The opposite effect tends to result, however, between trading up and trading down. When market segmentation is practiced that involves substantial trading down, a major risk is incurred in that the sales of the higher-priced line will be jeopardized. Sales increases gained by the new line are often at the expense of the older line. This result has occurred frequently in automobiles, major appliances, clothing, and jewelry, for example. The lower-priced Packard, for instance, enjoyed good market acceptance when introduced, but over a period of time the original price lines suffered continuous deterioration in market position. The sales success of newly introduced lower-priced lines can be accounted for partially by the tendency for the "quality image," market symbolism (prestige, status factors, and the like), and brand loyalty to be transferred or at least "slop over" from the old line to the new one. Product additions that do not add new business or succeed in holding old business that would otherwise be lost, but merely result in shifts of business from one product line to another, are generally unwelcome by management.

Several tactical approaches have been employed in trading down in an effort to minimize risks. Chances for success are likely to be greatest when at least several of the following conditions are present:

1. A distinctly different form accompanies the introduction of the new product and differentiates it from the older one.

2. Easily observable (for the purchaser) value differences exist between the higher- and lower-priced lines.

3. Different channels, in whole or in part, are used for the sale of the new lines.

4. Brand identification clearly differentiates the products.

5. Promotional orientation accompanying the sale of the new product is distinctly different from that of previous lines.

In order to avoid possibly jeopardizing the sale of the higher-priced lines, some companies have gone so far as to completely disassociate the new product from existing lines, using different enterprises entirely to handle the two products. When this is done there is little or no opportunity for the market strength of the original product and enterprise to be of assistance in gaining consumer acceptance for the new line. This procedure is therefore regarded as an unduly limiting factor by many managements, and an excessive price to pay for compensating for the market risks incurred.

Trading up involves the opposite problem, that is, the difficulty of gaining acceptance for the substantially higher priced new product line. There is difficulty in overcoming the market frictions of the lower-priced brand images and stereotyped corporate personality. The symbolism in markets and products is sufficiently strong to commonly cause marketers to fail in these attempts, even when new lines introduced have technological improvements. Numerous instances of this can be found in camera and watch markets, where low-priced-line marketers have been unable to penetrate the higher end of the market with any notable success. Successfully trading up to higher-priced brackets seems to require a number of intermediate moves of limited magnitude, so that over a period of time a new corporate personality emerges. Evolution seems more likely to succeed than revolution in these product-market integration attempts. Also, the conditions suggested for successful trading down are also relevant to tactical implementation of trading up. Finally, it should be noted that some marketers bring out new lines directed to substantially higher-priced markets, with the deliberate intention of providing a "prestige line" designed to help the sale of lower-priced products through association rather than for a calculated profitable penetration of the upper levels of the market.

Overextension of Product-images

A final subtlety in achieving good product-market integration is the problem of disturbing a successful product that has developed a strong niche in the market with attempts to make the product-image fit another segment. Rather than add new products as psychologically oriented market segments are identified, many marketers seek access to these segments through promotional reorientation of existing products. This is sometimes thought of as "freshening" products to keep them abreast of the times, particularly when some physical change in the product accompanies the change in promotion. The danger in this policy, however, is that the product-image will be blurred in the process to the point that its once firm foundation of customer preference in the historic segment will be lost. The results can be first, that little penetration of the new segment is achieved because the product has never been regarded as especially appropriate in the minds of buyers in the new segment, and at best is a substitute for other products psychologically more suitable; and secondly, the hold on the historic segment is weakened by the amalgamation of images to the point where competitors' inroads are facilitated.

For example, suppose we identify a psychological market spectrum that can be characterized at the extremes by two distinctly different purchaser profiles.[4] At one end we have a tradition-oriented group that can be characterized as the conservative, stable, older age, middle- and lower-income working class who accept life as it is and look for "old, reliable" products. At the other end we have the "modern" group, going places, doing things, seeking the exciting life; the sophisticated white-collar and upper-income working class, oriented to the new and the different. Suppose that a marketer has a product which has gained entrenched acceptance among the former group. He has in some ways an envied position, in that a new product has great difficulty in penetrating the "traditional" market —one cannot manufacture a brand-new heirloom; only time can confer this title and image to a product. Conversely, by definition *modern* is the latest thing, and new products find fewer obstacles when directed to this segment. Should the

---

[4] An actual case which cannot be cited for corporate security reasons, and is therefore disguised and somewhat generalized.

marketer attempt to "freshen" the promotion and product-image that have so successfully held the "traditional" market, he does so at the grave risk that he may be giving up one of his most powerful sources of competitive differential advantage.

As this situation has been portrayed, it would seem to call for product-line expansion rather than adaptation of the old line to suit the newly identified segment. One of the difficult problems of product strategy is the choice between these two alternatives under dynamic conditions and circumstances. This problem, in varying forms, is observable in many companies seeking effective product-market integration.

OPPORTUNITIES AND NEED
FOR CHANGING STRATEGIES
FROM TIME TO TIME

Because markets, technology, and competition are dynamic, the means employed to achieve effective product-market integration require adjustment from time to time. Flexibility that allows shifts in emphasis is desirable, and even basic changes in strategy may be called for. The marketer whose strategic and tactical patterns are always predictable has lost something of value in the area of "competitive gamesmanship." Shifts in the scope of the product line to a broader or narrower base are necessary in both countering competitors' actions and in positioning products more effectively in the spectrum of varying customer demands and competing product assortments.

The potentialities of varying product strategies through time can be demonstrated by the actions of one of the largest radio marketers some years ago. The marketing manager responsible analyzed the complex and seemingly confused market for table radios. Competitors' lines had proliferated, as had his own, and extremely broad offerings were available to fulfill almost any specific demand. Particular attention was paid in the analysis to volume of sales by price lines and the offerings available at these price breaks. A large peak in the purchase occurred at $49.95. A wide variety of 6- and 7-transistor radios were available at this price. In analyzing sales trends it was seen that a definite shift had occurred favoring large numbers of transistors, particularly the 8-transistor radio, the cheapest of which at that time was about $72.50. In a study of consumer preferences, the 8-transistor set appeared as a strongly preferred model by purchasers buying medium- and large-size table models. The marketing manager concluded after putting all parts of the analysis together that an 8-transistor radio that could sell for $49.95 would be extremely successful. Existing costs of manufacturing and marketing were such that this price target seemed impossible to achieve with existing models. The newly designed radio could meet cost requirements only with substantially more volume than any set then in the line had achieved. The marketing manager decided to withdraw all models within reasonable price limits on either side of the price and cluster all production on this single model.

The volume commitment given to manufacturing made possible specialized production methods and tools that increased economies of scale. The result of these actions was that this radio quickly became the largest-selling model by far in the entire industry. The demand converged on this price from both directions. Buyers who would normally have preferred to buy a radio in the $39-to-$45 brackets were traded up because of the very superior value they could receive for just a few dollars more. Buyers previously above this price level also converged on this price because the higher-priced goods did not represent nearly as good a value, and any minor preferences in product features in other sets were not important enough in the light of the higher prices.

Rather quickly the industry retaliated against this bold move to achieve a better competitive position, by adopting the same strategy. As this happened, the marketing manager made a second strategy shift. He took the same chassis as was on the $49.95 model, removed one or two features, put on a cheaper cabinet, and introduced the set at $44.95. He also added several features to the basic chassis, put it in a more expensive cabinet, and sold it for $54.95. This enabled him to "bracket" competition and make available more variety as competition had narrowed offerings to achieve cost economies to compete with the first move. The second move resulted in the holding of the improved market position gained with the first change.

This illustration is not intended as a marketing solution to all problems of strategic product-market integration. It is given to demonstrate the value and, at times, necessity of varying basic approaches or emphases. Also, it should make clear that one approach is not always better than another and there is not always one "best way." That is, a heavy emphasis on market segmentation and broad product lines is not always preferable to emphasis on product differentiation and single or narrow product lines, or vice versa.

RECONCILING DESIRABLE MARKET HETEROGENEITY WITH DESIRABLE PRODUCTION HOMOGENEITY

This chapter began by recognizing heterogeneity that characterizes demand, and that without economic penalties the model product line would provide an almost infinite assortment for consumer choice. A lesser degree of "product-fit" was recognized as purchaser clusters successively removed from the market core were encountered. As a product line moves further away from the core, a position would be reached where, in view of all factors of purchase influence, the given product would be unsuitable for potential buyers.

At this point, greater product variety is necessary if these potential buyers are to be made effective purchasers. Conversely, as this greater variety is incurred, cost penalties are incurred, particularly in manufacturing. While market requirements may provide strong incentives for diversity, modern production needs are best fulfilled through uniformity or similarity and convergence of products rather than divergence.

Herein lies one of the dilemmas of modern business. Management's responsibility is to reconcile these opposing forces in an optimum manner for the system as a whole. Two means of modifying or minimizing the conflict are of interest; each derives from the complex of forces affecting suitable product-market integration. The first we call the *principle of modular construction* and the second we call the *principle of postponement*.

The Principle of Modular Construction

In order to accommodate the heterogeneity that tends to pervade many markets but avoid excesses in manufacturing costs which could offset, from a profitability standpoint, the desirability of such accommodation, we recognize the principle of modular construction. This principle simply implies that whenever possible, accommodation takes place through variety of products based upon common components of construction. Product design would seek "modular uniformity" through utilizing basic "building blocks" in novel ways to achieve necessary variety in the product line. This would permit the maximum amount of convergence in manufacturing to conserve potential economies of scale in mass production. That is, variation in such product features as accessories, cabinetry, external design, color, size, shape, etc., often can be achieved without varying basic construction modules by various arrangement of minor construction modules.

A good example of the application of this principle is the radio manufacturer previously described, who used a common chassis for three different radio models, permitting a more precise adjustment of products with market and competitive forces.

The Principle of Postponement

The principle of postponement [5] states that in its final adjustment to customer specifications, any change in the form of a product should be delayed to the last possible moment. Alderson recognizes various points in the total production marketing system at which the type of upholstery wanted by a customer might be applied to a chair. His principle would delay this conversion to the last instant in the total process for the purpose of minimizing the basic assortment and inventories.

One of the best examples of the application of this principle is the color-metering machine found in retail paint stores. This machine mixes color concentrates with a neutral paint to give the exact shade of paint desired by the final customer, out of an extremely broad assortment. Another example of the application of this principle is Sun Oil Company's "custom-blending" of gasoline at the retail pump. Additives are added to the basic grade of gasoline at the pump in order to let the customer "dial" the octane rating most suited to his car. In these extreme examples, the final form of the product delivered to the customer is delayed to the last possible moment—simultaneous with consumer purchase. Economies in inventory and production costs to be achieved by this practice are obvious and substantial.

These two principles provide a means for reconciling conflicts in the de-

---

[5] Alderson, *Marketing Behavior and Executive Action,* pp. 423–27.

sirability of product diversity from a market point of view and the desirability of product uniformity from a manufacturing point of view. While their application is not always feasible, their intelligent use by management when practical is of benefit in accomplishing good product-market integration.

Summary

The marketer's objective is to balance cost-revenue considerations throughout the production-marketing system as a whole in arriving at an optimum product assortment. In seeking effective product-market integration, two alternative strategies are possible which have some degree of substitutability. These are the single product or limited-line strategy, oriented to product differentiation, and the extended- or broad-line strategy, oriented to market segmentation. Three principal approaches exist for matching products with varying market segments: segmentation can be based on the need for different product forms, or varying quality and price levels, or on psychological and motivational forces. The most fruitful solutions to effective product-market integration, however, often employ a combination of approaches in a total strategy.

In the variety of attempts used to achieve effective product-market integration, certain common and recurring problems in marketing enterprises are observable. The most pronounced of these are product lines that are simultaneously too broad and too narrow; product proliferation that dissipates economies of scale; excesses in product assortments attributable to importance of full-line competition; the imbalance of sales from trading up or trading down; and the weakening of product images in attempts to cover several market segments with a single product.

In view of the dynamics of the total competitive environment, variations in the strategy and tactics of product-market integration are an important part of "competitive gamesmanship." Finally, reconciling the apparent dilemma of opposing forces and needs in supply and demand, the principles of modular construction and postponement are relevant. Profitable product-market integration presumes precision in market measurement, cost analysis, careful planning, and competitive resourcefulness.

Questions and Problems

1. From a marketing point of view, what is the ideal product line, insofar as breadth of line is concerned?
2. Why isn't this ideal realized?
3. What is the objective in determining the number of variations to be offered within a product line?
4. What is meant by the "core" of the market?
5. Describe "a limited-line product strategy oriented to product differentiation."
6. Contrast the above with a "broad-line product strategy oriented to market segmentation."
7. What factors tend ultimately to limit the effectiveness of the product differentiation orientation; the market segmentation?

8. What are the principal ways by which products may be matched with varying market segments?

9. What is the difference between actual quality and consumer-use quality? Give examples to illustrate.

10. Pick an example of product assortments which, based upon psychological variables, seem to be matched with differing market segments.

11. What are the various procedures that can be used in minimizing the risks of "trading down"?

12. What is the so-called trap of the full-line competitor?

13. How is it that businesses sometimes find it useful to vary product-line strategies? Could you give an example of when this might seem appropriate?

14. Give several examples of the principle of postponement. For what reasons is this principle applied when practical?

15. Summarize the concept of product-market integration.

Programming Product Expansion Through Diversification

13

So far we have indicated that the composition of the product line ideally should (1) derive from an overall rationale for the business and (2) result in effective integration of products with market forces. We come now to a third basic viewpoint regarding the composition of the product mix— namely, that the pattern of diversity among lines should draw fully on corporate resources that are the most powerful source of competitive advantage. In short, the composition of the product mix *in its totality* should serve to blend market factors and enterprise resources into an integrated and unified pattern of competitive action.

This chapter draws attention to some aspects of the planning, analysis, and methods useful in programming product expansion that involve strategic diversification. The term *strategic diversification* is used to connote something more fundamental than increases in sizes, models, colors, or qualities of existing products. While changes of this type, strictly considered, involve "diversification," as pointed out in Chapter 12, they are regarded as "tactical" adjustments in the product line. Programming for strategic diversification involves programming for the addition of entirely different products than those already offered.[1]

While some firms have been notably successful in diversification, the experience of many others has not been particularly gratifying. The extremely high rate of new-product failure is evidence in itself that diversification requires more careful decision making than is usually anticipated. It also suggests that diversification may not be the most appropriate way to solve the problems that lead management to consider it as a course of action. This raises the question of when

[1] Much of the material presented in this chapter is drawn from Thomas A. Staudt, "Program for Product Diversification," *Harvard Business Review* (November–December 1954), pp. 121–31.

219

Programming
Product
Expansion
Through Di-
versification

a company should diversify. Conceptually, we can say, "When operations in present fields preclude the achievement of objectives as established by management." If opportunities in present markets are adequate for this achievement, more intensive cultivation of these opportunities is generally to be preferred to attempting similar achievement through diversification.

Much of the unsuccessful, ill-advised diversification of recent years might have been avoided if a careful analysis had been made of the problems which superficially seemed to warrant diversification. Symptoms of competitive problems, such as a declining market share, unused plant capacity, or shrinking profit margins, may in fact be early warning signals of the need for diversification. On the other hand, relief from such pressures may often be better achieved by more conservative means—as, for example, by greater efficiency in present operations, more productive deployment of current resources in present fields, more intensive market cultivation, or expansion of some present facility. The evidence of new-product mortality ought to caution thoughtful administrators to at least consider the appropriateness of alternative courses of action for achieving unfulfilled objectives before proceeding with diversification that may lead the enterprise into relatively unknown areas with greater risk. The burden of proof should be placed on diversification as the optimum solution to the particular problems requiring action. Moreover, diversification should not be considered as a short-term tactical adjustment, but rather as an effective weapon of longer-term strategy.

THE ROLE OF PLANNING

Many of the most successful diversification programs have been characterized by the selection of growth product fields closely related to principal corporate strengths and long-range company objectives and implemented in a way that produced good product-market integration. To achieve such results usually requires carefully formulated plans in advance of the search for new products. It is common, however, for managers to presume that nothing need be done before proceeding with the search for profitable new diversification opportunities. When this type of approach is taken to diversification, available products, companies, or new fields are brought to the attention of management, and each is examined individually for its suitability. The decision-making process takes place without the benefit of planning to provide guides for executive judgment. While this approach can be successful if carried far enough, it is not as likely to be productive as selective exploration of opportunities in light of the special character and problems of the particular enterprise. This procedure often saves time, money, and effort in locating diversification areas that match more closely the requirements and resources of the particular organization.

The following steps are regarded as constituting the basic elements of a planned program of product diversification:

1. A clear definition of objectives.
2. An analysis of the diversification situation in the light of present operations.

3. An audit of the tangible and intangible corporate resources to be capitalized on in diversification.

4. Establishment of specific criteria for new products in line with the three preceding points.

5. A comprehensive search for candidate products and areas and their evaluation against the criteria.

6. Choice of the means of market entry, that is, internal development, purchase of patent rights, merger, or company acquisition.

7. Careful implementation to insure good product-market integration.

8. Prudent organizational planning for integrating the added product or enterprise into the existing operations of the firm.

THE DEFINITION OF OBJECTIVES

A well-defined set of corporate objectives is a helpful starting point in any programming of the competitive affairs of the firm. This point was emphasized in Chapter 4. Objectives, however, must be cast in a way that is meaningful to diversification planning. A large electric-motor manufacturer insists, for example, that all new products should serve to increase sales of its basic line of fractional and small integral horsepower motors (in effect, products which incorporate its motors as components). But even this kind of objective, definite as it is, should express a fundamental need which will lead the company to want to increase sales by diversification, for example, to even out cyclical demand or to make up for obsolescence of existing products. The underlying motivation must be crystallized and made explicit if it is to have a constructive effect on product decisions. The following list of "reasons" for diversification indicates how broad the range of motives can be.

WHY COMPANIES DIVERSIFY

A. Survival

1. *To offset a declining or vanishing market*—A traditional example of this was Studebaker's move into the automobile field from its previous carriage manufacturing business.

2. *To compensate for technological obsolescence*—With the advance of technology, a producer of a part for battery sets found it necessary to manufacture electric radio sets in order to stay in business.

3. *To offset obsolete facilities*—Entering the industrial lubricants field was the response of a company engaged in filtering operations, when the methods of refining oil changed, making filtering plants obsolete.

4. *To offset declining profit margins*—Meat packers, for example, have made every effort to develop by-products in order to enhance profit margins.

5. *To offset an unfavorable geographic location brought about by changing economic factors*—Some northern nonintegrated [2] paper mills have found

---

[2] Here *nonintegrated* means that pulp making and papermaking are separate operations; in integrated mills they are one continuous process.

221

Programming
Product
Expansion
Through Di-
versification

it necessary to add specialty paper lines and convert their operations in order to meet the competition of southern integrated rivals.

B. Stability

1. *To eliminate or offset seasonal slumps*—A mechanical toy producer, motivated by a desire to offset a seasonal slump, began making electric fans.

2. *To offset cyclical fluctuations*—"The average machine-tool builder has over a period of years investigated and actually undertaken diversification projects, with the object of flattening out the peaks and valleys in the demand for regular machine-tool products," says the president of a large machine-tool company.

3. *To maintain employment of the labor force*—In 1943, when a substantial government parachute order was canceled with a request "to please stand by," one firm began the production of shower curtains, draperies, and negligees in order to maintain employment of 3,500 people.

4. *To provide balance between high-margin and low-margin products*—Housewares and soft goods have been added by supermarkets in part to achieve higher margins alongside low-margin food products.

5. *To provide balance between old and new products*—A food products manufacturer diversifies so that no product gets more than a third of company sales.

6. *To maintain market share*—A stove company, known for a low-price promotional line, purchased a company making a larger medium-price stove in order to capture a strategic share of the stove market.

7. *To maintain an assured source of supply*—Some companies have combined diversification with integration, aiming at independence from outside suppliers.

C. Productive Utilization of Resources

1. *To utilize waste or by-products*—A paper company added fiberboard to its line in order to make use of waste screenings and tailings.

2. *To maintain balance in verticle integration*—A canning company which had integrated backwards to manufacture cans for its own use decided to sell cans produced in excess of its requirements.

3. *To make use of basic raw material*—This is an important objective, for example, for rubber companies, who have become engaged in producing a wide variety of products from rubber.

4. *To utilize excess productive capacity*—In one instance the manufacturer of plastic light fixtures was able to convert idle equipment to the production of plastic dishes.

5. *To make use of product innovations from internal technical research*—The research department of a petroleum company developed a medicinal oil for its own use, then began to manufacture it commercially.

6. *To capitalize on distinctive know-how*—A company manufacturing hearing aids found its production skills adaptable to interoffice communication systems and subsequently diversified along these lines.

THE SITUATION ANALYSIS

Once objectives have been determined, they must be appraised against the specific circumstances surrounding the diversification problem by what can be called a *situation analysis*. The need for this procedure, and what it involves, can best be demonstrated by an illustration:

Company X decided it would be necessary to diversify to offset the serious inroads made by foreign competition and a declining demand. Preliminary analysis indicated that the market for the company's product was made up predominantly of young single men from the lower-income groups, without college education, and ranging in age from seventeen to twenty-three. As the company's growing idle productive capacity stemmed, in part, from a declining demand, one of the important objectives established for diversification was to utilize an increasing amount of excess productive capacity.

When the problem was studied in greater detail, it became evident that the decline in the market for the product resulted from the fact that the number of potential customers had diminished. This market shrinkage was primarily a natural consequence of the low birth rate in the economically depressed 1930's. Other contributing factors included the large number of men in the age group in military service (unavailable for consumption of the product) and an abnormally high marriage rate for the age group.

A forecast of sales for several years in advance showed that rather sizable sales increases could be expected as a larger number of potential customers became available from countering trends. Moreover, it was apparent that opportunities for additional sales were good as a result of slight but important modifications in the marketing program to counter foreign competitors. In view of this situation analysis, a substantially smaller percentage of productive capacity was committed to diversification than had initially been anticipated. The company was able to achieve its overall objectives with a limited diversification program tailored to the actual situation.

The principal purpose of the situation analysis, then, is to quantify objectives or make them more precise so that specific goals can be established for diversification—for example, to utilize a given percentage of plant capacity, to consume a given quantity of waste product, or to establish specific economic characteristics for product additions.

Alterations of present operations, which bring about improvement in the current general position of the enterprise, are a frequent by-product of such an analysis. Quite important, too, is the fact that a fuller understanding of the reasons for additions to the present line is brought about, so that the course of diversification can be followed more confidently; or, if diversification is shown to be unnecessary, expensive, wasteful action may be avoided as a result of this analysis.

THE RESOURCE AUDIT

Having carefully defined corporate objectives and having fully analyzed the operating situation or competitive environment surrounding the need for diversification, it is important to appraise in detail the tangible and intangible corporate assets or resources that can be capitalized on to greater advantage in entering new fields. The objective of the audit is to place the enterprise in the most favorable position to compete in the new field by most effectively using its resources and its distinctive competence. The principal diversification strengths (and limitations) of the several operating departments within the company—research, engineering, manufacturing, finance, and marketing—should be evaluated individually and collectively, and compared to competitors' resources in these areas.

The audit should begin with an analysis of tangible factors, including such things as financial strength, the nature of the manufacturing process, the type and quality of machinery and equipment used, the number and type of research personnel and facilities, the size and character of the marketing organization, and the nature and type of staff services available. These tangible resources are usually much easier to appraise than the intangible ones. Appraisal of intangible resources involves value judgments that are largely subjective and open to controversy. Oftentimes, however, the intangible strengths of the enterprise are the most important competitive strengths to be used for diversification. Important intangible considerations include the quality of engineering skills, the resourcefulness of technical research personnel, the flexibility or adaptability of management, the interests of management members, the recognizable attributes by which the firm is known in the trade, and any unusual know-how or competence which provides a longer-term distinctiveness and competitive superiority for the enterprise. Several cases serve to point up the importance of intangibles.

A large watch manufacturer chose for diversification a line of ladies' compacts, which initially appeared almost ideally suited to the company's operations. The firm was known for the quality of its product, had a well-recognized brand name, and was the most preferred line among jewelers. Ladies' compacts, however, proved to be out of character with the distinctive know-how of the company. The frequent and substantial markdowns which were traditional for this class of product, and the importance of style which called for frequent design changes, proved to be incompatible with the firm's traditional operations in which quite the opposite characteristics were present. On the other hand, the company's long experience in the manufacture of high-quality precision watches had provided almost unique competency in the field of miniaturization. Even though the company had no previous experience in the industrial market, later events indicated that an unusual opportunity for successful diversification existed in the field of miniaturized scientific precision instruments.

A second illustration involves a family-owned enterprise with a long history in the manufacture of a high-priced sports product. All members of top management had for many years been sporting enthusiasts. For more than a decade the company had considered diversification, but was reluctant to take a step in that direction except on the basis of absolute necessity. Under existing circumstances, additions to the product line would need a certain "glamour," on a par with its existing products, otherwise, they probably would not secure the necessary managerial interest and attention to assure a high probability of commercial success. Later events demonstrated this weakness. The company entered the industrial market with a product technically similar to, but not on a glamour par with its existing products, only to see the product fail.

A third (and perhaps extreme) example involves two companies that merged. On the basis of all tangible factors, the operations of each company seemed to complement the other. The principal members of the management of each company, however, came from quite different ethnic groups. Their prejudices proved to be so strong and their interests so dissimilar that after the merger, internal strife resulted in a serious weakening of the companies' operating effectiveness.

Diversification appears most likely to be successful when it capitalizes on the unique know-how or special qualities which provide the firm with its basic strength and effectiveness. Final judgment should weigh heavily the human capabilities available for moves into new fields.

PRODUCT CRITERIA

The fourth step in programming diversification involves establishing explicit criteria or specifications for products or product fields in accordance with findings from preceding analyses. Here, the purpose is to set forth in detail the characteristics of the ideal opportunity, which can then be useful in providing direction to the search for product candidates and in helping to evaluate them, once found.

The classifications of criteria can be established thus: (a) essential characteristics and (b) desirable characteristics. The essential characteristics derive from the primary strategic objectives which were established for diversification; these are the criteria which must be met if the diversification is to accomplish the ends which were originally intended. The desirable characteristics of the ideal addition result from the analysis of the particular situation faced by the company, and the resource audit of the major strengths of the company to be capitalized on in diversification.

For example, the actual criteria established for a manufacturer of internal-combustion engines equipment were as follows:

CHARACTERISTICS OF THE IDEAL DIVERSIFICATION OPPORTUNITY

Essential Characteristics

Must utilize existing excess production capacity.

Must require a minimum additional investment in production tools and equipment.

225

Programming
Product
Expansion
Through Di-
versification

Must involve a minimum incremental investment for sales and distribution.

Desirable Characteristics

Would be harmonious with the present well-known brand name.

Would be similar to the internal-combustion engine in purchase and performance requirements.

Would reach a broader market than now served.

Would support the sale of present products.

Would use the existing service organization.

Would complement rather than magnify the existing seasonal sales pattern.

Would involve medium-precision manufacturing.

Would involve high value added by manufacture.

Would provide a sound basis for further diversification.

Obviously, no individual product candidate could be expected to meet all the criteria established by management. Nevertheless, once relative importance has been attached to the individual characteristics, a meaningful basis exists for evaluating potential additions to the line.

SEARCH AND SELECTION

Experience indicates that a productive search for diversification opportunities has these four requisites:

1. Able personnel to conduct the search and appraise and screen candidate opportunities.

2. An economical basis for uncovering an adequate number of candidate products which appear to dovetail with diversification planning.

3. A rational basis for allocating expensive research in depth to the most worthy candidates.

4. Effective follow-up to insure decisive action.

Screening Process

In searching for candidate products which closely match the diversification criteria, a funneling process is involved which starts off with many new-product ideas and then narrows the field successively through (*a*) initial screening, (*b*) preliminary market audit, and (*c*) research in depth. Any number of sources can produce worthwhile new-product ideas—including a field survey of users, prospective purchasers, and distributors; an analysis of company sales experience; an analysis of competitive offerings; industrial designers; marketing and production executives, salesmen, and production workers.

The initial screening process is designed to eliminate product areas that do not compare favorably with the essential and desirable characteristics of the model product, solely on the basis of readily distinguishable factors. Thus, the products meeting the criteria for the engine equipment manufacturer previously set forth included: garden tractors, outboard motors, motor generator units, industrial trucks, materials-handling equipment, refrigeration machinery, air-conditioning equipment, engine accessories, compressed-air drilling equipment, industrial engines, measuring and dispensing pumps, and blowers and ventilation equipment.

The list of candidates surviving the primary screening can often be further narrowed by management judgment. A modest field investigation can usually provide the basis for quickly and convincingly discarding some products which at first appear to meet the desired criteria. For example, research was unnecessary to determine that a particular company with long experience in hand-blown table glassware was not capable of producing magnifying lenses, but a short, economical market audit was needed to reveal that the company was also poorly suited for the manufacture and sale of hand-blown laboratory-type glassware. This type of approach enables the analyst to use rational discrimination for allocating expensive research in depth to the more promising candidate products.

The final screening is characterized by thorough research of the limited number of products that have stood the test of preliminary research appraisal. A penetrating investigation includes an analysis of at least the following factors: industry growth and structure, competitive environment, important features and characteristics of existing products, potential technological obsolescence, characteristics of the market, purchase requirements and factors influencing the choice of suppliers, the effectiveness and costs of appropriate channels of distribution, methods and cost of demand cultivation, opportunity for market entry by a firm new to the field, competitive requirements for market entry, and the general suitability of the product field in the light of the specific criteria earlier established.

Throughout, of course, potential profit and return on investment must be the paramount consideration. Cost and profit analysis, together with the other research findings, should provide a reliable factual base for the judgment of executives who must make final decisions.

Entry Requirements

Before final decisions are made, a last consideration involves a comparison of corporate resources with the important entry requirements for any firm seeking to compete in the market in the proposed diversification field. In the following illustration, entry requirements are listed and a profile is shown of how well company resources dovetail with these entry requirements. Factors which register a poor fit or no fit should be viewed in terms of their availability and cost from outside the firm. Also, some assessment should be made of *how long* it would take to develop these resources from within the firm, should this be undertaken.

A merger or acquisition of an already competing enterprise might be the final outcome of this analysis if the entry outlook seemed favorable. This could come about if the firm did not possess an adequate assortment of resources and they appeared incapable of development from within, or if the time period

227

Programming
Product
Expansion
Through Di-
versification

would be prohibitively long. Also, purchase of a company might take place to gain access to patent rights or an already established and accepted product line which otherwise might involve inordinately long time lags of internal research, development engineering, and production. An alternative to both courses of action occasionally is the purchase of domestic manufacturing rights or licensing arrangements with foreign patent holders. In all cases, election of the most appropriate choice of market entry is a crucial aspect in diversification into new fields.

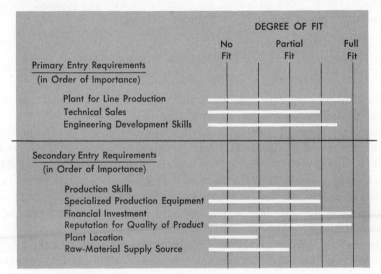

FIGURE 13-1
Entry Requirements
and Corporate
Market Resources

Implementation

The way basic decisions in diversification programming are implemented is, of course, also important to ultimate success. This involves two areas of particular significance which will be dealt with only briefly here. One covers the composition of the product line for entry into the new field to achieve good product-market integration. Since this topic was discussed in a previous chapter, it need not be repeated here. The other area covers provision for a good organizational arrangement for integrating the new activities into existing operations, a final point of managerial concern prior to launching the new venture. The general problem of organization is considered in Chapter 30. Three points, however, are particularly relevant here.

First, every new-product venture requires the attention of an executive personally committed to the achievement of successful results. Experience has shown that strong leadership is essential to insure the necessary enthusiasm, action, and control required in the early stages of operations.

Next, when such a "committed executive" is also responsible for an important part of existing operations, he may overemphasize the importance of the new products to the detriment of old ones. That is, in his desire to show an "accounting profit" on the new products, he may shift resources (selling time of the sales force, for example) to the profit disadvantage of old products. Both results are undesirable—namely, new products which suffer from the lack of administrative attention and enthusiasm, and new products which jeopardize the profitable sales of existing products because of administrative desire to succeed in the new field regardless of costs.

Finally, as a result of these factors, one of the newest methods for dealing with this problem is to use a team of new-products personnel to launch the products and be responsible for all phases of operations during the early stages of commercialization. When the new products are moved to the established organization, some of the personnel are transferred with the product in order to maintain continuity of leadership and administration.

COMBINING THE ELEMENTS
OF ANALYSIS

The following case demonstrates the application of elements of planned diversification outlined here.

The First Paper Company, a northern nonintegrated [3] mill, produced a variety of fine and coarse paper products. As was true with other similar northern mills, the company had suffered serious inroads from the competition of southern mills. Although a number of products were distributed through both fine- and coarse-paper merchants, the bulk of the sales were made to a relatively limited number of direct mill accounts which had been built up over a number of years through the personal efforts of company executives.

The mill's declining competitive position was abruptly magnified with the loss of one large and important customer, who accounted for approximately 25 percent of the gross sales of the company. In view of the critical condition of the mill, it was concluded by management that additional products were essential.

Several strategic objectives were established by management for new products. To improve the mill's position materially, they said, additions for the line should (a) be suitable for production on present equipment with no more than additions of accessory equipment; (b) be of a character precluding efficient production by southern mills; and (c) allow a minimum profit of $40 per machine hour.

The situation analysis indicated the characteristics of products that would be unsuitable for competitive southern mills, which enjoyed four principal advantages: (a) newer, bigger, faster equipment, (b) lower wage rates, (c) lower raw material costs, and (d) economies of operation from combining pulp and paper-mill operations. Hence, the new products of the First Paper Company should: have a high value added by the manufacturing process to offset or minimize the lower raw material costs and the cheaper labor of southern mills; require a type of pulp not readily accessible in the South; require relatively frequent, short production runs to offset or minimize the superior size and speed of southern equipment, which costs a great deal to shut down or leave idle; and

[3] See Footnote 2.

229

Programming
Product
Expansion
Through Di-
versification

also, if possible, be aimed at a market allowing a considerable potential sale within a relatively small radius of the company's plant, to take advantage of freight rate differentials (eliminating the expense of the long haul from southern mills).

When the resource audit was made, it revealed that the First Paper Company enjoyed a distinguished reputation in the trade as a quality mill, was known for its business integrity, and was particularly competent in the production of intricate grades of technical papers with close quality tolerances. This study also revealed a number of areas in the present marketing operations of the company that could be substantially improved. For example, inadequate market coverage existed and sales territories were of widely varying sizes. Some of these problems were amenable to short-term corrective action by management. Plans for diversification were then made which reflected the desired goals, the situation analysis, and the resource audit.

Next, a preliminary market audit was made of a wide range of market grades falling in the lightweight paper field. As a result, several particular grades were selected for comprehensive market appraisal. One of the products surviving the final screening and selected by management to be introduced to the market was a line of technical reproduction papers. The product dovetailed closely with the diversification plan and appeared to be an especially suitable competitive opportunity for these reasons:

1. The market for the product was growing at a rate appreciably more rapid than the field of lightweight papers as a whole.

2. A sufficient market potential existed for sales substantially in excess of the idle capacity on machines suitable for the production of this particular grade of paper.

3. The market was not dominated by the large, integrated pulp and paper mills; on the contrary, the smaller mills were capable of effective and aggressive competition. Buyers typically purchased in reasonably small lots, which precluded the long runs required by southern mills for efficient operations.

4. The product had a particularly high value added by manufacturing to minimize the raw material and labor advantages of southern rivals.

5. The number of potential customers provided a reasonably broad customer base to minimize the possibility of a large reduction in sales occurring through the loss of one account, as had happened in the past.

6. The majority of dominant buyers were located in close proximity to the mill, providing excellent opportunity for market penetration costs and the better service and quicker delivery that could be provided.

7. The product was particularly well suited to the technical knowledge and excellent quality characterizing the operations of the company. Precise manufacturing specifications had to be met in the new product.

8. The product was compatible with the present or contemplated production marketing facilities of the company. The grades to be offered were chosen after surveys of uses. Only modest operational changes were required prior to the introduction of the product. Finally, substantial evidence was available to indicate that adequate opportunity existed for market entry by a new firm.

The case described here indicates the feasibility of planned diversification as it applies to the solution of the peculiar problems of individual firms.

Summary

Diversification is a means of longer-term strategic corporate adjustment. Because all product diversification has substantial elements of risk, the burden of proof should be placed on diversification, in the light of more conservative alternative courses of action, as the optimum solution to the economic problems confronting management. If careful review indicates that diversification is essential, comprehensive planning and research are particularly important. The programming sequence involves a careful selection of objectives, an analysis of present operations and competitive environment, and a thorough audit of the tangible and intangible resources to be capitalized on in diversification.

These procedures provide the basis for selective exploration of product opportunities and simplify appraisal and decision making. Selective exploration proceeds through initial screening, preliminary market analysis, and research in depth.

In the past, failure to carefully assess the requirements of effective competition has been a major reason for misfortune in product diversification. Selection of the most appropriate means of market entry is therefore of special importance to policy makers; so also is careful organization planning for integrating the added product or enterprise into the existing operations of the firm.

Questions and Problems

1. How would you characterize the difference between strategic and tactical diversification?
2. Conceptually, when should a company diversify?
3. "Diversification is frequently an excellent defense against short-term competitive pressures." Comment.
4. What arguments can you give for supporting the role of careful planning in diversification?
5. What are the various steps in a program of carefully planned diversification?
6. Give examples of intangible assets that a company might possess that could be relevant to planning diversification.
7. What are some of the different sources for new-product ideas?
8. What are the various elements in a good search-and-screening process for diversification opportunities?
9. Indicate the various alternatives a company might follow in "choosing the means of market entry" in a diversification move.
10. What organizational dangers could you highlight in a new-product introduction?
11. What means might a company use if it wished, because of uncertainty of success, to limit its investment in a new-product or diversification move— from the production point of view? From the marketing point of view?
12. What is meant by the statement, "The burden of proof ought to be placed

231

Programming
Product
Expansion
Through Di-
versification

upon diversification as the optimum solution to competitive pressures that may superficially seem to call for diversification"?

13. "Not all diversification can or should be planned." Analyze this statement and give your opinion.

14. "Locating growth markets without intense competition is not enough for choosing areas of new-product introduction." Explain.

15. "Product policy is the hub around which the whole wheel of the firm revolves." Comment.

New-Product Development
and Introduction

14

In the previous chapter we examined diversification strategies by which firms make strategic moves into fields or areas of opportunity not previously served. Now we wish to present a rational process for new-product development and introduction, regardless of the degree to which the added product diverges from previous operations. First, we examine the prevailing competitive climate surrounding this process. Business firms are placing increasing reliance on new products for the achievement of their profit objective, and this is particularly true of high-growth companies. Evidence seems to be mounting, however, that the failure rate for new products is increasing, even with the adoption of more sophisticated management processes in their development and introduction. And a still more hostile environment for the launching of new products can be anticipated in the future. Economic penalities for new-product failures will increase at precisely the time that apparent prospects for their success are diminished and the need for new products is greatest.

Next, we make explicit certain premises concerning the conduct of new-product development and introduction as currently practiced by many business enterprises. These premises pertain largely to the careful husbanding of resources used in the development process and the desirable conjunction between technology and market affairs. Finally, a predominant part of the discussion is devoted to an elaboration of the new-product development process: the stages of corporate research, feasibility research, development, market testing, market introduction, and commercialization, including the phasing or sequencing of activities and actions germane to each stage.

PRODUCT ENVIRONMENT

In the American economy we have reached a stage in which economic growth in the future will largely come from the introduction of new products. Each ten years a significantly higher proportion of sales are coming from products that were not in production at the beginning of the period. This observation holds true for virtually all industries, but it is especially pronounced in the industries that account for a growing proportion of the gross national product.

Figure 14-1 shows the percentage of sales for the period 1959–63 represented by new products in a variety of industries. When all industries are aver-

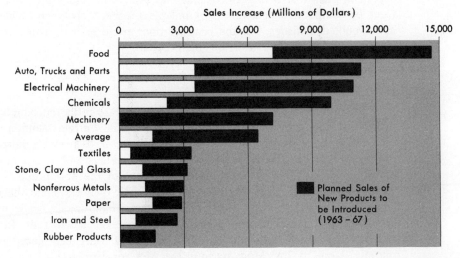

FIGURE 14-1
Planned Contribution of New Products to
Sales Growth, 1963–1967

Sales Increase (Millions of Dollars)

Source: Federal Trade Commission and McGraw-Hill as cited in Management of New Products, *Booz-Allen Hamilton, Inc., 1968, p. 5.*

aged, it has been estimated that 43 percent of gross sales in 1957 came from new products not available at the beginning of the ten-year period.[1] By 1966 it was estimated that this figure had reached 56 percent.[2] It is not unreasonable to assume that by 1975 more than two-thirds of industry sales will be accounted for by products not in production at the beginning of 1966. This reliance on new products for the achievement of corporate objectives is especially dramatic when related to high-growth companies. The Stanford Research Institute made a study of the 210 fastest growth companies over a ten-year period.[3] It revealed that only 15 percent had sustained previous growth rates. Forty percent grew moderately, 30 percent had stagnated, and the rest had disappeared either through acquisition by other companies or bankruptcy. Of special significance is the fact that more than 50 percent of the sales of high-growth companies came from new products while only 10 percent of the sales of low-growth companies

[1] "New Product Revolution," *Printers Ink* (October 31, 1968), pp. 21–27.
[2] *Ibid.*
[3] Quoted in "Key Factors in Corporate Growth," *Management Consultant*, No. 2 (1962), pp. 1–4.

came from this source. Of interest is the fact that the majority of high-growth companies achieved diversification by acquiring other companies in addition to internal developments. Finally, the current situation regarding the importance of new products is rather clearly revealed in a study of 742 companies, which covered the first six months of 1965.[4] Seventy and four-tenths percent of the companies anticipated adding new products during the period from January 1 to June 30, and these 522 firms expected to launch a total of 1,236 new products.

The evidence is mounting that future corporate as well as economic growth is dependent upon new-product development. Yet relatively little attention has been devoted to rationalizing the processes by which the corporation enters into this aspect of managerial activity. In an area so vital to continued corporate and economic growth it is imperative that improved skills emerge to deal with this facet of competitive behavior. Not only is the need strikingly evident in the above-quoted statistics, but the costs of poor performance further amplify the need for a concentrated effort on this problem.

Success with New Products Is Declining

Despite increasing effort, expenditures, and care in the introduction of new products, the odds for success seem to be declining. Earlier, mention was made of a 1954 study showing that 80 percent of the new products introduced by package goods manufacturers failed.[5] A 1957 analysis of the pharmaceutical industry indicated that probably only 8 percent of the new products launched would be best sellers, 10 percent would pay their own way, and the remaining 82 percent would fail.[6] By 1961 an American Management Association study concluded that 19 of 20 new products could be expected to fail.[7] In the same year, the industrial design firm of Lippincott and Margulies placed the failure rate at 23 out of 26.[8] More recently the McCann-Erickson advertising agency reported that of every 25 products test marketed only one succeeded.[9]

All of the above figures can be a bit misleading. It should be recognized that some firms, in contrast to the averages noted, have very enviable records of success in new-product introductions. Many times success or failure is a relative matter, difficult to measure precisely because of differences in accounting practices in treating new products and subject to varying conceptual interpretations. A more relevant measure of performance would seem to be the return on investment realized from new-product introduction expenditures rather than the success or failure of individual items. However, in spite of possible modifications in new-product failure rates, it is apparent that they are high and, if anything, have

[4] Press release, May 1965, Sales and Marketing Executives International, New York, N.Y.

[5] See Chapter 11, page 188.

[6] Thomas A. Staudt, "Determining and Evaluating the Promotional Mix," *Modern Medicine Topics,* XVIII, No. 7 (July 1957).

[7] Philip Marvin, "Why New Products Fail," in Thomas Berg, and Abe Shuchman, *Product Strategy and Management* (New York: Holt, Rinehart & Winston, Inc., 1963), p. 351.

[8] Burt Schorr, "Many New Products Fizzle Despite Careful Planning, Publicity," *Wall Street Journal,* April 5, 1961.

[9] *Ibid.*

been rising. There seems little reason to anticipate any sharp reversal of performance in this area. On the contrary, an even more hostile environment for new-product introduction can be expected in the future. The following factors will contribute to it.

By 1970 More Than Half the Population Will Be under Twenty-five Years of Age

Consumption patterns in the "youth market" are notoriously fickle. Purchase loyalty is continuously buffeted by more rapid and frequent shifts in taste than is characteristic in the older age groups. This factor increases materially the uncertainty connected with measures of market potential and profit opportunities for products directed toward this age group.

The More Rapid Pace of Market Change in General

More stability in expenditure patterns prevailed in previous periods, and trend analysis was more useful, with accompanying higher confidence levels. Recently, even in major expenditure items, such as automobiles, manufacturers have found it difficult to anticipate customer preferences for very far into the future. Product lines have been materially broadened, with an increasing number of items accounting for a smaller and smaller proportion of total production.

More Highly Segmented Markets

Markets in general have become more highly segmented than in earlier periods. This reflects in part the increasing levels of disposable income and also the discretionary spending power available to consumers which allows for the enjoyment of increasing precision in satisfying individual needs and preferences. Smaller clusters of demand are harder to estimate than larger ones, just as the outcome of a national election can be more reliably predicted than can be the myriad of voting publics being aggregated.

Research and Development Effort Expended Is Rapidly Neutralized by Competitive Response

Greater total research and development expenditures can be expected in the seventies alone than in all the previous periods in our history combined. This means that technological advantage at best is tenuous, and this aspect of differential competitive advantage can be expected to be short-lived. The implications for profit opportunities from new products seem clear; they are dramatized by recent experiences—General Electric's is illustrative: "We introduced the G.E. automatic toothbrush just two years ago. There are now fifty-two competitors. Our slicing knife, a product that we introduced approximately one year ago now competes with seven others, and at least that many more manufacturers are preparing to enter the market place." [10] The estimate of competitive entrance proved to be conservative.

More Rapid Movement through the Stages of Market Development

That television went through the various stages of the life cycle much more rapidly than radio is only suggestive of the future. Major changes in product

[10] Fred J. Borch, "Tomorrow's Customers," Speech made at Sales Executives Club of New York, September 15, 1964.

line and policy are called for in various stages of market development as was pointed out in a previous chapter. Consequently, a heavier burden and faster pace of creative obsolescence can be expected in time to come.

The Volume of New-product Development Required to Sustain Growth Rates

A well-known American high-growth company acquired a widespread reputation and achieved outstanding results for its new-product development. In fact, its sustained growth above the minimum target of 15 percent per year over a considerable period of time reflected an unusual degree of creative product innovation. As the company grew from a $100 million sale size toward upwards of one billion dollars in sales, it found it could not sustain previous records of performance in new-product introduction. Obviously, a great many more ongoing developmental projects had to be sustained simultaneously and problems of coordination, supervision, control, budgeting, management attention, personnel, and liaison increased. The result was a considerably greater number of failures, even with more sophisticated professional knowledge of test marketing, market simulation, sales forecasting, planning procedures, and other management processes associated with launching new products. At the same time, there was and is a need for a materially greater number of new-product launchings to sustain the target growth rate. This experience is likely to be repeated in other companies as they find themselves in similar circumstances.

Mature Companies Are Exhausting Opportunities in Closely Related Fields

As companies which have followed a relatively intensive product development program in the past age and mature, they tend to reach a point where they have exhausted obvious or especially attractive profit opportunities in closely related fields. Product development is then likely to proceed with increasing elements of divergence associated with it. Consequently, a lesser proportion of prevailing technical and management competence can be brought to bear on the new ventures; that is to say, the level of risk typically increases.

Industrial Firms Are Getting Further Removed from Intimate Contact with the Market

Many industrial goods enterprises have had an increasing propensity to enter the consumer goods field. A variety of reasons account for this propensity, including the desire to smooth out some of the extreme cyclical volatility that can be associated with industrial markets and the more attractive profit margins that are associated with success in many consumer goods fields. The distance created between personnel associated with the product development function and ultimate purchasers is often materially greater. This distance makes more complex the problem of knowing when the development effort has succeeded in producing "the right product." For example, a company with distinguished competence in adhesives worked closely with an aircraft manufacturer in an effort to make it possible to glue parts of the B-70 bomber together rather than to rivet them. Working closely together, the technical personnel of both companies established performance specifications for the new adhesive, given the design and flight characteristics of the aircraft. Thus, it was known with precision when the new product was developed that it would meet all market requirements. The same company, however, found itself in altogether different circumstances later, when it had to assess when the product was "right" in developing a new line of tape recorders for the consumer market.

For all these reasons then, we can anticipate a generally more hostile environment surrounding the new-product development function in the future.

Penalties for Failure

The penalties for failure are higher today because of several factors related to the larger-scale market entry now required to capitalize effectively on product innovation. We have just indicated General Electric's experience with carving knives and electric toothbrushes. The capacity of rivals to successfully readjust to successful new products with offerings of their own is one factor. It means that a larger-scale entry must be attempted initially if the firm is to gain maximum sales benefit during the period of fullest differential advantage. As Fred Borch says, "The honeymoon cycle of a new product is becoming shorter and shorter." This is in sharp contrast to the protected enclave the Gillette Company enjoyed for so many years with its safety razor blade, which made possible a more orderly and methodical buildup of both production and market development. The result of large-scale entry requirements is, of course, an increase in investments required to launch a new product. In many instances larger-scale production facilities account significantly for the increased investment requirements. Directly related to this consideration is the fact that efficient large-scale production facilities often require a large amount of single-purpose equipment and considerable automation. As a consequence, the production cost structure is tipped in the direction of a larger proportion of fixed costs in contrast to variable costs than would otherwise be the case. This means that the break-even point in launching the new product will be reached only with a larger sales volume, as is demonstrated in Figure 14-2. Notice that in the figure the profit angles above the break-even point and the loss angle below the break-even point are wider than if the product could have been launched with a higher proportion of direct costs in relation to fixed charges. The result is that losses are greater or profits are sharply below expectation if the product fails to achieve the anticipated volume. Moreover, if the product does not succeed and must be withdrawn from the market, the facilities do not readily lend themselves to the production of other products, assuming that a high degree of special-purpose tooling and equipment was involved. In a word then, the economic penalties for failure are higher.

PREMISES RELATING TO A RATIONALIZATION OF THE NEW-PRODUCT DEVELOPMENT AND INTRODUCTION PROCESS

Before discussing the various program stages, let us make explicit certain underlying premises relating to the proposed structure that are drawn from an observation of current corporate practice.

FIGURE 14-2

Breakeven Points at Different Levels of Fixed Cost

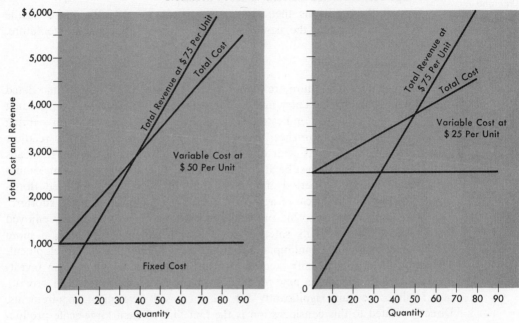

Too Many Rather Than Too Few Projects

A company can have difficulty in its research and development effort from having either too few or too many projects under way at any given time. The usual presumption is that companies experiencing severe shortcomings in the desired volume of new-product development simply have too few projects under way to produce the number that will survive all the stages in the product development process leading to successful commercialization. Indeed, there is a high attrition rate for new-product ideas and developmental projects. A very recent study shows that, in fifty-one companies, of every fifty-eight ideas only twelve passed initial screening. Some seven remained after a thorough investigation of their profit potential, three survived the formal development stage, two remained after test marketing, and only one is commercially successful. Thus, the presumption is that fifty-eight new ideas must be generated and seven developmental projects undertaken to produce one commercially successful new product. (This decay curve is shown in Figure 14-3.) Further, a new idea has been said to be a very precious thing, which should be nurtured, kept alive, and protected in the anticipation that one day it might well make a major contribution to the competitive well-being of the corporation.

Our observation of current practices in a number of major enterprises leads us to conclude that more companies are confronted with significant shortcomings in their new-product development because of grappling with too many ideas and

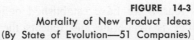

FIGURE 14-3
Mortality of New Product Ideas
(By State of Evolution—51 Companies)

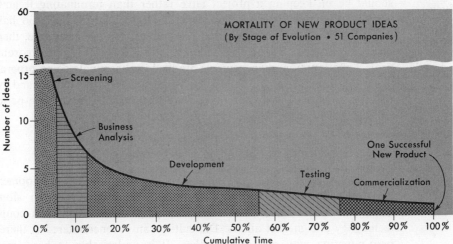

Source: Management of New Products, *Booz-Allen Hamilton, Inc., 1968, p. 9.*

developmental projects rather than too few. Indeed, the data noted above may well reflect this conclusion. Too many projects dilute the resources and effort that can be brought to bear on any one. The effort is often wasteful and inefficient because of the limited scale of activity in back of each and because an open project tends to attract charges to it even if only a small effort is being carried forward. Finally, too many projects tend to lead to a system that lacks decisiveness, lends itself to a haphazard rather than an orderly process, and often makes possible the carrying of ideas to other stages, thus bypassing appropriate terminal points. For these reasons, the structure we propose emphasizes a valuable corporate research stage prior to development; that is, killing off ideas and projects at the earliest possible time rather than consciously trying to keep them alive until it is believed that there has been a prudent husbanding of resources in conducting this function.

The Further Projects Go, the Harder They Are to Terminate

The longer a project is sustained in the development process and the greater the amount of expenditures that have been made, the more difficult the decision for management to terminate it. So frequently, the forlorn hope exists that just a little more time, money, or effort will produce the necessary breakthrough to success. This often is akin to "throwing good money after bad." There are many complex psychological factors that bear on an explanation of this phenomenon; they need not be dealt with here. Suffice it to say that the emotional involvements and attachments, the jeopardy of professional reputations, the prospect of irretrievable sunk costs, and the uncertainty that success may be just a little further down the road all lead to a decision climate which favors continuing the project. For this reason we have established definite kill points in the structure. The terminology is deliberate and reflects the conviction that the burden of proof should be on keeping a project alive rather than terminating it and killing it earlier rather than later. If the reader finds the terminology too harsh and is persuaded that the opposite line of reasoning is the preferred one, then the term *review point* can be substituted for *kill point*. In establishing rigorous tests for project continuation, managements are likely to terminate some programs which, if carried forward, might have been successful. On the other hand, we believe that the gains from early termination are likely over a reasonable period of time and number of cases, to outweigh the losses.

Conjunction of Market Affairs and Technology

The various stages and phases of the new-product development process are designed to bring technical research and market research along parallel tracks in a coordinated fashion in the hope that there can be a conjunction of technology and market affairs. Difficulties can be encountered if there is virtual preoccupation with one or the other. It is undesirable to have research and development personnel totally oriented to sitting back waiting for the marketing group to bring them a set of specifications for a new product in a defined area of market opportunity. In the first place, this method has limitations, as does any other single approach, to the uncovering of attractive growth opportunities. In the second place, it is hard to attract and hold talented technical research personnel if their freedom is so closely circumscribed and their areas for creative work so narrowly defined. If the morale of high-caliber technical personnel is to be sustained, they require an adequate measure of freedom to pursue avenues of inquiry that they themselves define as productive areas of exploration. Such freedom of inquiry might uncover unexpected but potentially valuable developments, perhaps considerably removed from the normal course of market affairs, which, however, the company might wish to exploit. But it is bad to have the technical effort of a company seemingly going off in all directions because of the absence of parameters around its work, which therefore bears little or no relationship to the company's present market concerns and competitive problems. Truly, having a conjunction of technology and market affairs is highly desirable. It is most likely to come about by deliberately designing parallel tracks of technical and market research into the various stages of the new-product development process.

We have emphasized the above three premises because we believe they may be responsible for much of the poor performance in the area of new-product development and introduction. The tendency to simultaneously pursue a number of projects is understandable in view of the low success rate observed in the past. On the other hand, it does dilute efforts and possibly is an explanatory variable of the low success rates. A reorientation to early termination rather than to the prevailing one of continued staging in hopes of a breakthrough would reduce the number of projects receiving significant effort at later stages in the process. The need to parallel track technical research and market research and coordinate their activities is as important as the other two premises for successful conduct of the entire process. Although more easily said than done, the need for organizational structures and management relations which permit this will contribute to higher levels of performance.

AN INTEGRATED CONCEPTION
OF THE NEW-PRODUCT DEVELOPMENT
AND INTRODUCTION PROCESS

Let us now turn our attention to the specific phases and stages of the new-product development and introduction process indicated in Figure 14-4. All of the items appearing on the chart will not be elaborated here for the following reasons:

First, some of the items listed require no elaboration, or little would be gained from expanding them beyond the level of detail shown. Second, some of the items have been discussed earlier and, while important, do not bear repeating here. For instance, the importance of establishing objectives has been emphasized previously on several occasions. Third, space simply precludes an elaboration of all of the points shown and, hence, the discussion is intended to be selective. You are urged to study the chart in some detail and become familiar with all the items included, as only the most important will be covered here along with those not sufficiently self-evident or complete.

Stage I—Corporate Research

The underlying philosophy of Stage I builds directly on that established earlier in the book. The emphasis is accordingly on goal-directed effort, with the careful setting of objectives and reasonable analysis of the prevailing competitive circumstances in which the firm finds itself. It is an attempt to build on the existing basis for differential advantage or competitive strengths of the enterprise. Perhaps the most important point is the definition of the company business, which has been treated previously but is deserving of some expansion here. Such a definition, if practical, provides a sense of direction for the company's technical efforts and tends to strengthen its overall posture in a problem-solving sense. The proper definition also helps to identify potential competitors and clarify the nature of the market offers (as distinct from solely products) that must be made if the company is to be competitively effective. Perhaps the meaning of this statement can be made clearer with an example. One of the largest chemical companies in Great Britain has a major division which principally holds ammonia-producing facilities. This division is the largest ammonia-producing enterprise in the country. If the division's business is defined as the ammonia business, then its competitors can be counted approximately on the fingers of one hand, and the market offers that must be made to meet the requirements of effective competition are reasonably straightforward and reflect the differential competitive advantage. However, by far the largest proportion of ammonia production goes into fertilizer, and the majority of the output is used in the division's own brand

FIGURE 14-4
The Flow of
New-Product Development and Introduction

Kill Point — PROJECT AUTHORIZATION

STAGE I
CORPORATE RESEARCH

1. Establishment of corporate objectives
2. Continuous surveillance of "marketing situation"
3. Analysis of corporate strengths and resources
4. Characterization of "the business of the corporation"
5. Specifications of criteria for new-product fields
6. Generation of "pool of product ideas"
7. Screening, selection and preliminary validation of new-product idea

Kill Point — FIRST MANAGEMENT REVIEW / DEVELOPMENT PROJECT AUTHORIZATION

STAGE II
FEASIBILITY RESEARCH

1. Experimental technical research
   a. Establishment of performance specifications
   b. Design studies of basic technical alternatives
   c. Feasibility of manufacturing
   d. Estimate of development time and costs
2. Market research
   a. Characteristics of market, its size and trends
   b. Nature of competition
   c. Specifications of product features to meet market requirements
   d. Strategy of product placement on form price–quality and psychological variables
3. Analysis and integration of findings
   a. Time
   b. Costs
   c. Manpower
   d. Commercial potentialities

Kill Point — COMPREHENSIVE MANAGEMENT REVIEW / COST – PRICE – VOLUME – PROFIT ANALYSIS

STAGE III
DEVELOPMENT

1. Technical development
   a. Leading to product prototype
   b. Laboratory and use testing
   c. Preliminary design finalization
2. Production costing and planning
   a. Materials
   b. Labor
   c. Equipment
   d. Space
3. Market forecasting
   a. Demand analysis
   b. Cost analysis
   c. Price analysis
4. Marketing mix plans
5. Break-even analysis

STAGE IV
MARKET TEST

Phase

1. Planning
   a. Selection of geographic area and accounts
   b. Complete schedules and budgets
   c. Establishment of standards to judge test performance
2. Experimental production for market test
3. Final production planning
4. Execution of market test
5. Analysis and review
   a. Product modifications
   b. Package modifications
   c. Marketing modifications
   d. Price modifications
   e. General performance of test against forecasts and standards
6. Final plans for launch with gudgets and fixing of responsibilities

FINAL MANAGEMENT REVIEW -- DECISION TO LAUNCH   Kill Point

STAGE V
MARKET INTRODUCTION

1. Buildup
   a. Production buildup
   b. Preliminary announcement to trade and sales force
   c. New-product program introduced to all sales personnel
   d. Training of salesmen, branches and dealers
   e. Distribution of product line to outlets
   f. Public showing and exhibits
   g. Distribution of promotional materials and advertising preprints
   h. Initial advertising and publicity
2. Launch
   a. First calls
   b. Filling of initial orders
   c. Field reports and information feedback
3. Follow-up and review
   a. Insure internal communication
   b. Prompt correction of "bugs"
   c. Measurement aginst controls

STAGE VI
COMMERCIALIZATION

Program absorbed by established organization and operating system as a going enterprise of fertilizer. If the division is characterized as being in the fertilizer business, then it has an altogether different set of competitors. More important, an indirect group of competitors which must be taken account of in market expansion attempts, emerges. For instance, if a farmer desires to raise the milk yield from his herd of cows, he can do it either by fertilizing the pasture lands, thereby providing better grazing for the cows, or he can do it through using feed supplements. Since both types of products are sold through common farm supply dealers, this has significant implications for the kind of market offers that must be made, including the type of sales personnel and their job definition. Finally, the division could conceive of itself as essentially in the business of increasing agricultural productivity through chemistry. In this event, its product line would quite likely require broadening to include chemically related agricultural inputs, such as fungicides, pesticides, and other chemical products that would be relevant to the business definition. This definition would again alter materially the competitors, both direct and indirect, the division would face. Agricultural equipment manufacturers, for example, have a similar mission of raising agricultural productivity. The point is that not only would the needs of the corporation be seen in quite different terms depending upon the definition of the business it is in, but, of particular relevance to our purposes here, it would have a major and direct bearing on the nature of the technical research effort to be undertaken by the division.

After some criteria have been set and parameters established for new-product exploration, a pool of product ideas needs to be generated. Hopefully, this is a continuing bank, systematically organized and categorized. Some may well lie dormant for a period until they can be formally reviewed and personnel are available to pursue them, possibly for later development at a more appropriate time. Ideas rejected once need not necessarily be totally discarded; they can be filed to await a more favorable market climate. For example, a cosmetic manufacturer rejected, on several occasions, the idea of an expensive line of men's toiletries but recently launched such a line on the presumption of a more hospitable social environment.

The high attrition rate of new-product ideas in this stage should not necessarily be viewed with alarm. At this point little money has been spent and rejection conserves scarce technical resources for clustered effort later. Criteria for project continuation will become increasingly rigorous in the later stages of development. It is desirable that only the most worthy ideas survive preliminary validation. Therefore, a majority of them should never reach the stage of formal development effort.

Those proposals that survive the first kill point should be moved directly to the stage of more formal feasibility research. The technical director should have sufficient authority to do this. Management review at this point would not be justified because too little information is available, and extensive executive time would be wasted on decision making that is more appropriate to a lower operating level in the organization. Furthermore, executive sponsorship of ideas at too early a stage can be undesirable because of emotional involvement that impairs objectivity and creates bias in the more critical decisions that eventually must be made. There is a time and place for deep executive involvement in the new-product development process, but it is at a later stage.

Stage II—Feasibility Research

Feasibility research is a stage often ignored or omitted in the structure. That is, once ideas have survived preliminary validation against the parameters of new-product exploration, they often jump directly into formal development. This bypassing can often be regrettable because more detailed analysis of their potential commercial worth may well show them as unworthy candidates for what can be relatively large-scale expenditures in the developmental stage.

The feasibility stage in most instances is not nearly as time-consuming as later stages. It is basically an attempt to reduce uncertainty to tolerable limits for decision-making purposes in a company's formal development effort. What is wanted is experimental technical research that considers basic technical alternatives, preliminary establishment of performance specifications, and an estimate of the developmental time and costs that can be anticipated if the company goes ahead with the program. Also when the concept of the product is sufficiently structured so that its commercial worth can be assessed within even wide latitudes of precision, then some orderly market investigation should be undertaken. Market niches the product is expected to occupy should be carefully considered, including the nature of the competition, both direct and indirect, it is expected to face. Size of the broader and narrower market and trends taking place in both should be evaluated. If, for instance, a radically new powerboat design was being considered for development, trends in the leisure market in general might be evaluated. The size, composition, and growth of the broad boating market; the particular makeup of the power boating sector; and its future must be considered. The most closely related indirect competition the design would face in the powerboat sector should receive particular emphasis. This is what is meant by analysis of the broader as well as narrower market the product would occupy. At this point also, the earliest aspects of competitive strategy should be considered as, for instance, the possible availability of and nature of operations of boating dealers.

At best these can be only rough estimates, as the basic design is not available, much less finalized, and little knowledge exists of costs, prices, and other specifics which lend themselves to increased precision of demand analysis. Nevertheless, the two areas of experimental technical research and market investigation should be put together in the form of the best estimate available of the time, costs, and manpower required should a formal development program be carried forward, along with the best available estimate of the commercial potentialities of such a venture. This material should then provide the basis for the first management involvement and review. Before specific developmental programs are launched, an important formal kill point must be passed. This gives management essential control of the bulk of its technical effort, serves vital means of information liaison planning, and provides additional insight into the potential competitive vitality of the enterprise in future periods.

Stage III—Development

The first phase of the development stage is a technical effort sufficient to lead to a product prototype. In the majority of cases this consumes most of the expenditures committed to this stage. The existence of the prototype makes possible a much higher degree of precision in planning and analysis, leading to a go/no-go decision or a decision to test the market prior to reaching a formal go/no-go decision.

With the existence of a product prototype further *laboratory testing* can be carried on and *use testing* undertaken. Use testing is important because products often perform differently in actual use than they do under laboratory conditions, where the operating variables can be closely controlled. These steps make it possible to arrive at a preliminary design finalization. The word *preliminary* is used because later customer preference studies or test marketing results might show the need for some design modification, which would be incorporated in the end product at the time of its formal launching.

With this degree of design certainty, production costing and planning can begin. This phase is essential in order that demand analysis can be sharpened from some estimates of product cost. Consequently, materials, labor, equipment, and space cost need to be considered, as well as the expected production rates and processes. Later, production planning will have to be carefully phased with market planning, and the foundation for that requirement can be provided through the information and analysis of the development stage.

With the existence of a particular configuration of product, a reasonable estimate of its costs under varying rates of output can now begin in addition to a vastly sharpened market analysis. The major objective here is to forecast the sales volume obtainable through various price alternatives and cost expenditures. Demand analysis for a new product is a notoriously difficult analytical assignment. In some cases the demand variables are so complicated that it is, for all practical purposes, impossible to estimate with any reasonable accuracy the total potential demand for the product. In this instance, the procedure may need to be reversed and a "threshold of profitability" research procedure used. This approach uses a "cost out" rather than "market back" orientation. That is, reasonable cost estimates are made for the production and marketing of the product. The price is then established on the basis of cost and a calculation made of the volume that would be required to "sustain satisfactory commercial operations." This volume is the threshold of profitability. The analytical market assignment then becomes one of attempting to analyze whether there appears to be sufficient pockets of demand to achieve this volume and where these pockets of demand are located. (The market may prove to be vastly larger in reality, but this could never have been estimated before the fact.) The analysis, however, is adequate to support the major decision, namely, a go/no-go choice if the product does not lend itself reasonably to test marketing. This situation is often the case with certain types of industrial equipment, but that issue will be considered in a discussion of test marketing.

Ideally, demand should be estimated for various proportions and total amounts of marketing-mix expenditures. These estimates then make it possible to calculate profitability on the basis of the varying sales volumes that would be achieved under several alternate marketing mixes, and the costs of production at these varying rates of output.

Stage IV—Test Marketing

The use of test marketing has increased greatly in recent years as a means of more precisely determining the potential success or failure of a new product prior to full-scale launching. The practice also enables marketers to anticipate the volume of sales expected in national distribution, with considerably higher confidence levels than in the absence of any prior testing in the real market on a localized basis. While the considerable advantages to be gained from test marketing account for its increasingly widespread use, we should recognize that marketers would prefer not to have to undergo test marketing operations and there are numerous situations in which its use would be inappropriate. The reasons marketers prefer to forgo test marketing are that it is expensive, time-consuming, competitively open, and can reduce the period in which the marketer enjoys the advantage of the absence of close substitutes for his product if it is an innovation. Competition openness means that the marketer has now made his intentions known to competitors, and they are free to gain whatever advantage they can from this advance knowledge.

What a Test Market Cannot Show

While test marketing makes possible more precise estimates of expected sales results of full-scale marketing and can be designed so as to identify limitations of the planned overall marketing program, it cannot answer all questions of interest to the marketer of a new product. It will not necessarily show whether the basic product concept is good in contrast to its implementation. That is, some products fail in test marketing because of style or design factors in the particular product configuration, but this does not necessarily mean that the basic product concept lacks market acceptance. If the product fails, then the test will not necessarily answer questions of why it failed. For instance, might different timing of the introduction have altered the outcome? If the test had run longer, could purchase patterns have been altered? What was the effect of tactical action by competitors? Was there inadequate knowledge and understanding on the part of consumers? Was extreme price resistance the major factor? And so forth. Conversely, if the test succeeds, the marketer does not necessarily understand why from a general analysis of test results.

Also, the test cannot show what will happen when competitive products that are close substitutes to the new product become available. That is, the product's capacity to resist competition generally remains unknown. Finally, tests do not of themselves indicate buildup in demand that can be expected over time because of the influence of unknown future environmental factors that cannot be built into the test at the time of its design.

Competitors' Reactions to Test Market Operations

A firm can respond to a competitor's test market operations in one of two ways: it may allow the test to proceed without interference, or it may engage in various tactics of its own in the hopes of scrambling the test results. If the competitor does the former, it may be that he is not alert to the existence of the test or its significance, or he may not be concerned about the impact his rival's program will have on his own market performance, or he may wish to monitor the test as closely as its sponsor in order to learn as much from it as possible. Competitive intelligence practice is such that the first possibility is extremely unlikely, whereas the latter is a growing competitive reaction to market testing by rival firms.

Rather than let the test proceed, the rival firm may engage in a variety of efforts to scramble the results and, indeed, may attempt to prevent the test from showing favorable results. The firm may elect to increase its own advertising expenditures, alter prices, engage in the use of coupons and other promotional devices, and generally intensify its own efforts to counter the potential success of the product in the test market.

When Not to Market Test

Market testing is not appropriate for all new-product situations. In fact, a number of factors can preclude its efficacy or desirability. One of the major decision rules related to proceeding with market testing or bypassing this stage and moving directly to the product introduction stage has to do with the relationship between decision costs and revenues. What costs will be "born" with the decision? That is, forgetting costs that have already been "sunk" and are therefore irretrievable, what new costs will be incurred with a decision to launch the product, and what revenues can be expected? On this basis, it may be "profitable" to proceed even though "all costs" will not necessarily be covered. For instance, it may be that sales would not be sufficient to recapture all development costs but would more than exceed the costs associated only with the production and sale of the product; hence the firm would be well advised to proceed, in some cases, to recover whatever "decision profit contributions" are possible. In the development of a new computerized machine tool, for example, the bulk of the total monies necessary for introducing the product may have been spread in technical research and development, with relatively small expenditures required afterward for sale of the product. In such a case, it may well be profitable to proceed even if only a few units could be sold on a to-order basis. In the development of a new detergent, on the other hand, relatively little money might have been spent in the development phases in contrast to the vast sums of money required for marketing preceding and following market introduction. In such a case, test marketing would seem highly desirable as a preliminary step to full-scale launching.

Another situation that militates against market testing (and is related to the above) occurs when the expenditures necessary for any level of customer purchase are a large proportion of total expenditures, regardless of the scale of operations. That means that there is an exceptionally high "start-up" cost. Which is why magazines and books do not lend themselves to test marketing. By the time one has assembled an editorial staff, produced the copy for the magazine, set the type and purchased the plates, the first unit of production would be the most expensive by far, and additional copies of the magazine would be slightly more than the cost of paper and ink—a relatively insignificant part of the total expenditure involved.

Another situation that, for all practical purposes, precludes test marketing is where the time period required to change purchasing habits, attitudes, and preferences would be too long for any reasonable pilot operation. For instance, a new powdered dairy product was programmed for a forty-eight-month break-even period. A three-month or six-month test would not be sufficient to alter taste preferences, and little could be gained from such a test. Indeed, the results might even be misleading because of the low initial response to the product. To run a test for a year or longer would merely give competitors a great advantage, and so alternatives to market testing are necessary. One of these is customer use testing through samples provided to respondents under controlled conditions of comparison with presently used products.

Other conditions that can militate against the feasibility of test marketing include the following: when the firm finds it essential to *match* a new product of a competitor, and a premium is placed on speed in bringing about a relative parity of product offerings; when the firm is so thoroughly convinced that its lower priced new product is superior to existing products that success seems assured; when competitive security seems vital in getting a maximum jump on rivals; and finally, when auxiliary installations or services would have to accompany the new product, such as in color telecasting.

Planning and Design of Test Market Operations

In conducting a market test there are a number of phases, the most important of which are the planning, the execution of the test, and the analysis and review of results. While none of the phases shown on the chart can be overlooked in an effectively designed test marketing program, our discussion will emphasize the selection of the test area, the establishment of standards by which to judge test performance, and the review procedures by which the significance of test results are considered in reaching a decision to proceed to full-scale market introduction.

SELECTING A TEST CITY: A number of factors must be considered in selecting a test city or cities for the pilot marketing program. Since marketers increasingly wish to test alternative elements of the market offer, such as variations in package design or prices for promotional campaigns, a few cities may need to be chosen. Several factors should be considered in making a selection. First, the city chosen should be representative of the broader market public. We will wish to project the results obtained in the test market to the national market and, consequently, the test market must be a statistically reliable microcosm of the broader market universe. Primarily, population characteristics should be similar; that is, age groups, levels of education, existence of ethnic populations, and income levels should coincide with the national market into which the product will be launched. Special factors may need to be considered for the particular product, such as car ownership, proportion of home ownership, and occupational clusters. Purchasing power and discretionary spending levels are usually particularly important. If the product is intended to reach a highly specialized market, then we might not want the test city to be representative of the national market, but to have a composition similar to the demand variables for that product.

Second, we should be cautious about selecting what might be called an "overworked" test city. Because the number of cities that are indeed representative of the national market are relatively limited, there is a tendency for some of them to reflect a test fatigue factor. Consumers in these cities may become conditioned in such a way that results of the test may not be valid for projections into national marketing. If, for example, follow-up interviewing of purchasers is an important part of the test, interview-weary consumers may either refuse to be interviewed again or may give answers that quickly terminate the interview. They may prefer to economize on time rather than tell their real feelings about the product. This fatigue factor may well become more important as the amount of test marketing of new products grows.

Third, the test city should have the same media alternatives available as are anticipated in the national promotional campaign. The full range of market cultivation media is important in that, if a different promotional mix is necessary in the test city in contrast to plans for the national market, the results achieved in the test may not be a valid indication of what can be anticipated with full-scale operations. If, for instance, television advertising is expected to be a major part of the expenditures for market cultivation, obviously the area selected would have to offer television time purchase in roughly the proportion anticipated in full-scale operations.

Fourth, the market selected for testing should be a relatively self-contained one, insulated in part at least from other markets, and without too much waste circulation in promotional media. That is, the test marketer would not like to pay for a lot of television coverage going into areas not included in his test operations. The proportion of coverage not related to his operations would constitute wasteful expenditures as could be the case with certain portions of newspaper advertising.

Fifth, the test city should be of an economical size. The area, on the one hand, should be small enough to be manageable and, on the other hand, large enough to be statistically reliable. Selecting one of the large metropolitan centers such as Chicago would constitute too big a job in getting the requisite distribution coverage, obtaining dealers' cooperation, having the necessary inventory backups, and the like for a test of relatively short duration. Moreover, the cost would be excessive for the purposes of the test market. Too small a city, on the other hand, would not have the full range of promotional media required, nor would it be large enough to give good reliability in projecting from the sample test geographic unit to the total market universe. Cities like Grand Rapids, Michigan; Hartford, Connecticut; and Columbus, Ohio, are representative of the size of cities most frequently chosen for test marketing.

Sixth, the city should be one in which the marketer can gain good cooperation from distributors, dealers, and retailers. He needs the cooperation of marketing institutions in setting up displays, giving the product proper shelf space or exposure, pricing it at the suggested level for the test, handling coupons which might be used in conjunction with introduction of the product, having sufficient inventories, and reordering promptly when those inventories are depleted. Such kinds of assistance help provide the basis for reaching a valid judgment as to whether the product will have market acceptance in national or regional distribution. Characteristically, marketers want full cooperation in the test in order to assure themselves that, if the product does not go well, it did not fail for lack of knowledge of its existence on the part of the purchasing public or for lack of the requisite promotional effort. On the other hand, there are occasions on which marketers are willing to have the product face significant obstacles on the assumption that if the product can succeed in the test under reasonably adverse circumstances, they can have high confidence that it will be successful in national distribution with full-scale support.

Seventh, the city chosen should have representative competitive conditions. That is, the kind of competition reflected in the test ought to be reasonably typical of what might be expected on the broader scale. Some markets are notoriously price markets, others have a preponderance of manufacturers' own wholesale branches in contrast to independent distributors, while others lack the variety of types of retail outlets such as discount stores, regional shopping centers, and the like. While no test city is a perfect replica of the national market, it should have a reasonable approximation of the basic competitive factors that are likely to exist on the broader scale.

ESTABLISHING STANDARDS TO JUDGE TEST PERFORMANCE: It is extremely important to the test marketer that he carefully predetermine the criteria to be used in judging the success or failure of the market test. All too often the expected rate of sales during the period of test is not sufficient as a measure of future success. Many other considerations are important. For example, which product is the new product displacing? What is the rate of repurchase of the product? Is the product reaching the intended market? Is it being used for the intended purpose or for other purposes not anticipated? Is the level of satisfaction provided by the product what the marketer anticipated? These considerations and others may be very critical in terms of the longer-term market position the product can be expected to enjoy. If, for example, the rate of first-time use was very high but the repurchase rate very low, the initial sales results could be quite misleading. In a product category which has "high flow" characteristics and relatively frequent replenishment, the test must run long enough to pick up the repurchase data. Moreover, distinctions need to be made between sales to retailers and sales to ultimate consumers. Gross sales results may be misleading because some of the manufacturer sales may be simply filling up the distribution pipeline rather than reflecting the rate of purchasing at the point of ultimate sales. An example of the perils in not having established adequate criteria for judging test performance can be observed in the test marketing of a personal-care product. The product was intended to be repurchased on approximately a monthly basis. Initial demand was considerably above sales projections. In interviewing buyers on their satisfaction with the product and intention to repurchase, an especially encouraging response was also obtained. The product was then hurried into national distribution, and six months after the point of introduction the sales level was substantially below that projected by the manufacturer. The product, however, was being used in a different way by the consumer from that intended by the marketer; it was being used only on special occasions rather than regularly. This helps to illustrate that care should be taken in predetermining all the relevant bases upon which the test performance will be judged.

ANALYSIS AND REVIEW OF TEST OPERATIONS: At the conclusion of the test, results should be analyzed to determine whether package, product, price, or marketing modifications are appropriate before launching the product into national distribution. In many instances, some variation of packaging or product will be tried in tests conducted simultaneously in several cities. As results come in, a complicated analytical problem is posed in determining the effect of the various approaches used. Did the variation in sales result from the difference in packages, for instance, or did it reflect better market coverage, better display, the absence of competitors' retaliation, or generally more favorable retail sales conditions in a particular market? In other words, in a direct comparison with results in other test cities, one cannot always ascribe a difference in sales to the effect of the distinctive marketing variable used in one market. One of the most successful cereal introductions reflected a rather significant package change resulting from experience in test markets. Several different packages were used in the test, and the one finally chosen for national distribution had a combination of the best features of those used in test marketing, on the basis of consumer preferences.

Reviewing the general performance of the test against sales forecasts and using the standards suggested above for judging performance should give the marketer the information needed for deciding whether to discontinue his plans for market introduction or to proceed with a full-scale launching of the product. It should be recognized that while the market test is being executed, final production planning is taking place. The last phase of the test market stage, therefore, reflects final plans for launch, with precise budgets and the fixing of responsibilities for market introduction. This is the point at which a final management review leads to a go/no-go decision.

Stage V—Market Introduction

The stage of market introduction characteristically has a buildup phase, a launch phase, and a follow-up and review phase. There must often be a significant time interval between the conclusion of market testing and market introduction in order that the proper buildup can be made in all markets preliminary to market introduction. The buildup has both the production and logistics component and a distribution and promotion component as well.

The production buildup may require time for the purchase of special production equipment, the laying out of production or assembly lines, the recruiting and training of some new employees, and the smoothing out of production operations after start up. This is, of course, preliminary to market introduction in order that the proper quantity of product can be in the distribution pipeline and in sufficient volume in all markets so that the initial demand generated by promotional expenditures can be capitalized on profitably by the marketer.

Simultaneously, there must be the proper introduction of the product to the company's own sales personnel, with sufficient training for them and assignment of responsibility. There must also be the training of dealers and distributors with respect to the program to be used in introducing the new product. A systems approach dictates that all elements in the total program be carefully coordinated and integrated. This includes, of course, distributor and retailer units as well as the manufacturer's own components.

The preparation of promotional materials, the purchase of space in magazines and newspapers and time on television, all require a buildup phase for market introduction in the promotional area. These efforts precede public showing of the product and the initial advertising and publicity. Characteristically, however, marketers like to have the benefit of some publicity prior to market introduction so that potential purchasers' interest can be stimulated and their anticipation heightened for the appearance of the product at the announced introductory date.

The days immediately following launch are some of the most critical and exciting of the whole new-product development and introduction process. All previous effort has led to the climax in these days, and the first returns from the field are watched with special care in hopes that the program is moving according to projection. But occasionally the burst of enthusiasm and a failure to pay attention to minute details during the introductory period have jeopardized market success. An official connected with the introduction of the Edsel expressed to one of the authors his belief that failure to assign each dealer a quota during the week of the car's introduction proved to be a regrettable error. Caught up in the tremendous mass of people viewing the car during the first few days, the retail salesmen became so engaged in discussion and demonstration that they failed to recognize the need for taking individuals aside for the purpose of writing orders, even if it meant that a number of people had to view the car by themselves.

Another illustration of this potential hazard relates to a now well-known pen. The method of filling it with ink was unique, and initial purchasers who failed to read the instructions carefully filled it improperly, with the consequence that it would not write very long without running dry. Quick reporting of customer complaints allowed the manufacturer to take immediate steps in the training of retail sales personnel to insure that subsequent purchasers did not experience the difficulty, and the problem was corrected before an adverse consumer image of the product had become widespread.

These examples illustrate the need for careful monitoring of initial results during the introductory period, along with the need for good internal communication and readiness on the part of the manufacturer to correct any "bugs," or product malfunctions, that show up in consumer purchase and use. Measurement against controls and performance standards is essential to the marketer's longer-term market well-being.

While the introductory approach suggested here reflects the value of having adequate inventories in the market place to capitalize on initial demand, it should be recognized that some marketers have successfully followed the practice of feeding a product onto the market relatively slowly and attempting to keep the supply just below the level of prevailing demand. This practice is used to create the impression that the product is enjoying heavy consumer demand; the underlying assumption is that what consumers find hard to buy may stimulate their interest to own, given widespread acceptance of the product.

A stage of commercialization is reached when the product is no longer subject to the special treatment extended to it during the introductory period, but rather is handled in a normal way within the established operating system as a part of the ongoing enterprise.

The Go/No-go Decision

The difficult task of killing projects at appropriate points in the process requires further elaboration. The first hurdle is in the corporate research stage, and there is little objective data to make the decision at this point. On the other hand, product ideas at this stage are many and varied. The decision must be made on the basis of how well the proposed product fits the overall objectives of the company. Is it appropriate for the business the company considers itself to be in? Does it provide a potential differential advantage for future competitive strength? In the feasibility research stage survival is a matter of having sufficient market opportunity to proceed. Estimates made are admittedly rough, but obvious potential failures should be evident. Once the development stage is reached, and product prototypes are developed and perfected, more precise measurements of market opportunity and production cost requirements can be made. At this stage the decision to move to test marketing is based upon a matching of potential costs and revenues. Test marketing is an attempt to try the proposed product under actual conditions of sale. It not only provides a basis for checking market opportunity estimates made at earlier stages but also an opportunity to measure volume possibilities under differing marketing treatments. If shortcomings in the market performance of the new product become evident and cannot be remedied, this may still be the point at which the product candidate is dropped. If it survives the standards established for the test, it will move on to market introduction and finally to full-scale commercialization.

Summary

Reliance on new products for the achievement of corporate growth and profit objectives is increasing. High-growth companies, particularly, seemingly place great emphasis on the development of new products, as well as on company acquisitions, as a part of their basic competitive strategy. Evidence seems to be mounting, however, that the failure rate for new products is increasing at a time when the economic penalties for failure are climbing higher. We can anticipate an even more hostile environment in the future for the launching of new products, owing, in part, to the relative increase in the youth market, the more rapid pace of market change in general, the phenomenon of more highly segmented markets, more rapid movement of products through stages of market development, the volume of new-product development now taking place, and because more mature companies will exhaust opportunities in closely related fields and move necessarily into markets in which their previous experience is not as relevant.

In attempting to rationalize the process of new-product development, it was noted that the effectiveness of a number of companies might be limited by their having too many developmental projects rather than too few, which dilutes effort. Also, the further a project is carried through the total developmental process, the more difficult it is to terminate, which places a premium on decisiveness in the early stages. There is a particular need for getting a closer conjunction of market affairs and technological development.

Six integrated stages in the total new-product development and introduction process were outlined beginning with the corporate research stage, which includes, among other things, a careful definition of the needs and resources within the company as it related to new products. In the feasibility research stage, an attempt is made, on a preliminary basis, to establish the technical and commercial feasibility of the product concept. The developmental stage follows, in which a product prototype is produced which makes possible sharpened cost revenue forecasts. A number of specific circumstances were explained to indicate that not all products should pass through the next stage of test marketing. Emphasis was given to the importance of decision costs and revenues and the potential value of higher-confidence levels in sales projections as a basis for deciding whether to test market or bypass this stage in favor of full-scale introduction. The planning, execution, and analysis phases of the test marketing stage were set forth, with particular attention given to the criteria for choosing the test market and for establishing standards by which to judge test performance. The last stage detailed was market introduction, with its accompanying buildup, launch, and follow-up phases. Emphasis here was given to the planning and monitoring requirements of introductory programs. Finally, the stage of commercialization for the new product would be reached when it was assimilated into the normal pattern of ongoing operations within the enterprise.

It was suggested that careful review be given each project before it passed to the succeeding stage and that top management attention be directed to the project neither too early nor too late in the total process. The view was expressed that the burden of proof ought to be placed on justification for moving the product to the next stage rather than on justification for the project's termination.

Questions and Problems

1. What are the stages of the new product development and introduction process?
2. What is the importance of a clear definition of the company business before beginning new product development?
3. What is the trend in the proportion of sales coming from new products? How has this trend been related to high growth companies and low growth companies?
4. Why are the penalties for new product failure becoming higher as larger scale market entry is required?
5. What are some advantages and disadvantages of test marketing a new product?
6. What factors must be considered in selecting a particular test market?
7. What environmental factors are likely to increase the already high new product failure rate?

8. Too many developmental projects may hinder a company's new product development program. Explain.
9. Test marketing is not appropriate for all new product situations. Discuss.
10. What is meant by feasibility research in new product development?
11. What is meant by "threshold of profitability" research? When is this procedure used in new product development analysis?
12. What actions might competitors take in response to test market operations?
13. Test marketing cannot answer all questions of interest to the marketer of a new product. Comment.
14. Discuss the significance of the coordination of market affairs and technology in new product development.
15. New product demand should be estimated for various proportions and total amounts of marketing mix expenditures. Explain.

Bibliography

Alexander, R. S., "The Death and Burial of 'Sick' Products," *Journal of Marketing,* XXVIII, No. 2 (April 1964), 1.

Ansoff, H. I., "Strategies for Diversification," *Harvard Business Review,* XXXV, No. 5 (September–October 1957), 113.

Berg, Thomas L., and Abe Shuchman, *Product Strategy and Management* (New York: Holt, Rinehart & Winston, Inc., 1963).

Conrad, Gordon R., "Unexplored Assets for Diversification," *Harvard Business Review,* XLI, No. 5 (September–October 1963), 67.

Corey, E. Raymond, "The Rise of Marketing in Product Planning," *Business Horizons* (Special Issue, February 1961), pp. 81–83.

D'Orsey, Hurst, "Criteria for Evaluating Existing Products and Product Lines," *Analyzing and Improving Market Performance,* Management Report No. 32 (New York: American Management Assn., 1959), p. 91.

Drucker, Peter F., "Care and Feeding of the Profitable Products," *Fortune,* LXIX, No. 3 (March 1964), 133.

Faison, Edmund W. J., "The Application of Research to Product Development," *Business Horizons* (Special Issue, February 1961), p. 37.

Green, Paul E., "Bayesian Statistics and Product Decisions," *Business Horizons,* V, No. 3 (Fall 1962), 101.

Greyser, Stephen A., "The Case of the Unproductive Products," *Harvard Business Review,* XLII, No. 4 (July-August 1964), 20.

Hardin, David K., "A New Approach to Test Marketing," *Journal of Marketing,* No. 4(October 1966), pp. 28–31.

Herrmann, C. C., "Managing New Products in a Changing Market," *Journal of Marketing* (January 1962).

Kotler, Philip, "Marketing Mix Decisions for New Products," *Journal of Marketing Research,* I, No. 1 (February 1964), 43.

Krespi, Irving, "The Application of Survey Research Methods to 'Model Line' Decisions," *Journal of Marketing Research,* I, No. 1 (February 1964), 30.

Levitt, Theodore, "Marketing Myopia," *Harvard Business Review* (July-August 1960), pp. 45–60.

Mandell, Melvin, "What's Ahead in Product Design?" *Management Review,* XLIX, No. 9 (September 1960), 35–37.

Marting, Elizabeth, ed., *New Products/New Profits: Experiences in New Product Planning,* No. 1 (New York: American Management Assn., 1964).

Marvin, Philip, "Developing a Balanced Product Portfolio," *Management Review,* XLVIII, No. 4 (April 1959), 20–26.

Mertes, John E., "Product Planning and Visual Design Policies," *Business Topics,* X, No. 3 (Summer 1962), 61.

O'Conner, Michael J., "Basic Patterns of New Product Strategy," *Marketing Precision and Executive Action* (New York: American Marketing Assn., 1962), pp. 387–96.

O'Meara, John T., Jr., "Selecting Profitable Products," *Harvard Business Review,* XXXIX, No. 1 (January-February 1961), 83–89.

Organizing for Product Development, Management Report No. 31 (New York: American Management Assn., 1959).

Parker, Donald D., and Richard A. Johnson, "Complexity of Distributing Products with Increasing Variety of Colors, Sizes, and Models," *Business Review,* XXIII, No. 3 (February 1964), 43.

Patton, Arch, "Top Management's Stake in a Product's Life-Cycle," *Management Review* (June 1959), pp. 3–26.

Pessemier, Edgar A., *New-Product Decisions: An Analytical Approach* (New York: McGraw-Hill Book Company, 1966).

"Product Planning: Key to Corporate Survival," *Management Review,* XLIX, No. 1 (January 1960), 31–34.

Smith, Dilman M. K., *How to Avoid Mistakes When Introducing New Products,* No. 3 (New York: Vantage Press, Inc., 1964).

Smith, Wendell R., "Product Differentiation and Market Segmentation as Alternative Marketing Strategies," *Journal of Marketing* (July 1956), pp. 3–8.

Staudt, Thomas A., "Program for Product Diversification," *Harvard Business Review* (November-December 1954).

Talley, Walter J., *The Profitable Product: Its Planning, Launching and Management* (Englewood Cliffs, N.J.: Prentice-Hall, Inc., 1965).

Tilles, Seymour, "How To Evaluate Corporate Strategy," *Harvard Business Review,* XLI, No. 4 (July-August 1963), 111.

Twedt, Warren Dik, "How Long Does It Take to Introduce New Products," *Journal of Marketing,* No. 1 (January 1965), pp. 71–72.

Wallance, Don, *Developing a Product Strategy,* Management Report No. 39 (New York: American Management Assn., 1959).

———, *Establishing a New Product Program,* Management Report No. 8 (New York: American Management Assn., 1958).

Wasson, Chester R., "What Is New about a New Product?" *Journal of Marketing,* XXV, No. 1 (July 1960), 56.

Weigand, Robert E., "How Extensive the Planning and Development Program," *Journal of Marketing,* XXVI, No. 3 (July 1962), 55.

PART FOUR

The Distribution Network
and Mix

In Part 3 we examined the way manufacturing enterprisers adjust to their operating environment through appropriate product strategies, strategies predicated on precise investigation of market forces and opportunities. Now we must provide a link between the highly specialized and geographically dispersed producers of goods and the demands of millions of purchasing units.

Without some form of organized system, the task of matching supply with demand would be excessively costly and time-consuming. Many tasks must be performed to match supply with demand. The first is the job of physically moving goods to the centers of demand. The second is the task of assembling, from the conglomeration of products supplied, distinctive assortments to match the different segments of demand. The third task is to stimulate exchange. An elaborate organization of institutions has developed to aid in the performance of these tasks. In total, these institutions provide a *distribution network* made up of retailers, wholesalers, and specialized agents.

The particular problems facing a single marketer will vary, and it is the job of the marketer to utilize those institutions which can most efficiently contribute to the achievement of corporate goals. The marketing manager must be familiar with the characteristics of the distribution network if proper combinations of institutions are to be selected and managed in an effective *distribution mix.*

To provide background information about the characteristics of the distribution network, this section examines in detail the problems involved in overcoming time and space through the network. Much of the section is devoted to the requirement of efficient goods flow through integrated market logistics as well as to the complex of conflict and harmony between participants in the network. The institutions in the distribution network, such as retailers, merchant wholesalers, and agents, are then described. The different institutions must be merged into a distribution mix to achieve the objectives of all participants. Finally, selection and management of the most efficient channels of distribution are explored.

Overcoming Time and Space Through the Distribution Network

15

Our treatment of marketing so far has been oriented toward the management of marketing activities within a business enterprise. It is now advisable to examine our economy in general and assess the problems which must be solved if goods are to be made available to buyers conveniently and at low cost. An understanding of the problems and their means of solution will give us greater insight into the ways in which individual enterprises may tailor their systems of managerial action to gain competitive advantage.

The use of specialization in our economy creates problems of time and space, which must be overcome if goods are to be made available when and where consumers want them. In fact, the task of overcoming time and space through efficient exchange mechanisms is so important that a number of specialized intermediaries have developed to deal with the problem. These institutions constitute a *distribution network* at the disposal of enterprises engaged in the distribution of goods and services.

THE IMPORTANCE OF EXCHANGE

Specialization and Exchange

The objective of economic activity is to maximize satisfaction from scarce means. This is best accomplished through specialization. The most primitive of societies resorts to specialization at its simplest to gain the greatest benefit from what little is available in the way of resources. The moment specialization exists, some members have more of those things in which they are specialized than they need and less of those things in which they are not. Exchange of the surpluses is essential in such a society, for it is the means by which individuals satisfy their economic wants.

261

In our society, goods are made available through a very complex industrial organization, in which specialization exists in a number of different ways. Enterprises in the extractive industries are, of course, specialized in the raw materials they are equipped to extract. For example, there are lumbering operations confined to timber for pulp, and others confined to hardwoods. Agriculture is specialized in dairying, grain products, beef cattle, truck gardening, etc. As we saw in Chapter 11, manufacturers often specialize in narrow product lines. When they do diversify, they usually try to relate their products to a common raw material base, a similar production process, a similar marketing operation, or some other conjunction of resources.

With a high degree of specialization among the producers of goods, one might well imagine that *exchange* would be an important function in our economy. In fact, so important is it that one economist states: "Indeed it is hardly too much to say that the study of exchange comprises nine-tenths of the economist's dominion." [1]

Value and Exchange

It is through the process of exchange that value is created in a specialized economy. Goods do not have intrinsic market value. Even finished goods stored in the warehouse have only potential value. It is true they are assigned a value in accounting records because it is anticipated that they will be exchanged in the near future, but they have no value until they are made available both physically and legally for use. Even then, value emerges only when they are made available to a buyer and an exchange actually takes place. The availability of the goods and the "wantingness" of the buyer determine the amount of value of the goods exchanged.

Another characteristic of exchange should be mentioned. The term *wantingness* in the preceding paragraph was deliberately used. Before an exchange takes place, both parties must feel that they will benefit from the transaction. There is no equality in the minds of the participants concerning the two items that are exchanged: the buyer must want the item he is buying more than he wants the money he must pay for it; the seller must want the money more than the item. The intensity of desire on the part of the participants is what determines the value. This characteristic of inequality is important to marketers, for the wantingness of the subject is stimulated by the different means of market cultivation discussed in Part 5.

In a highly specialized economy such as ours, in which money is used as a medium of exchange, we do not think of the seller as having varying intensities of desire for money. He is usually offering goods for exchange; this is his business. The desire he has for money determines the amount of goods he will make available for exchange. You will recall that this is known as *supply*. The wantingness of the buyer is also determined by how many such items he has, and his interpretation of the value of additional items. His willingness to give up money for additional items is known as *demand*.

[1] Kenneth E. Boulding, *Economic Analysis,* 3rd ed. (New York: Harper & Row, Publishers, 1955), p. 4.

263

Overcoming
Time and
Space
Through the
Distribution
Network

Study of the exchange process is concerned with the composition and nature of flows and their interaction. Economists are interested in the flow of goods to consumers and the flow of productive services to producers. At the monetary level, flows are analyzed in terms of income and expenditure within and between firms and families. In the aggregate, these flows represent supply and demand.

Important as this kind of analysis is, marketers are interested in another phase of exchange. Exchanges do not just happen. The heterogeneity of supply and demand creates barriers to exchange. These barriers must be removed if exchanges are to take place conveniently and at low cost. A part of the task of marketing is to remove these barriers and provide the means for efficient exchange. Let us examine the heterogeneity of supply and demand.

The Heterogeneity of Supply and Demand

The single most dominant characteristic of supply and demand in a specialized economy is heterogeneity. We can think of the supply segment as made up of a large number of geographically concentrated, specialized producers providing one large conglomeration of different types of goods. Table 8-1, on page 127, shows that approximately 4.8 million establishments (total industrial goods buyers less retailers and wholesalers) are responsible for the supply of all goods and services. Because they are specialized, each supplier produces in very large quantities. Supply is heterogeneous.

Demand is made up of the total of the individual demands of approximately 60.2 million households in the consumer market and about 6.8 million establishments in the industrial market. Each buying unit is searching for an assortment of goods which will satisfy its anticipated needs. The desire to acquire a unique assortment is not confined to the millions of households in the consumer market; it is equally a characteristic of the industrial goods buyer. The latter must assemble all the goods necessary to carry out the functions of the enterprise. We have already seen in Chapters 6, 7, and 8 how unique these assortments are for different segments of demand. Each assortment requires a much wider variety of products than any one producer can provide, and the quantities are usually much smaller than those offered by any single producer.[2] Demand is therefore also heterogeneous.

The Problem of Exchange

The difficulties in matching heterogeneous supply with heterogeneous demand constitute a barrier to efficient exchange. More specifically, three basic problems exist. The first problem results from the location of sources of supply and the centers of demand. Because the sources of supply are geographically concentrated and demand is comprised of millions of consuming units scattered over the entire world, there is the necessity for physical movement. The transport problem is aggravated by the fact that consuming units distant from producers

---

[2] There are exceptions to this, as in those cases where one manufacturer contracts to take the entire output of another manufacturer.

desire only small quantities of any single product, increasing costs of transportation. The second problem results from the kinds of assortments demanded. From the conglomeration of products produced, unique assortments of different products in different quantities than those in which they are normally supplied must be assembled to match the millions of individual segments of demand. The third problem is providing the necessary stimulation for exchange. Even though the other two problems are effectively handled, there is no assurance that exchange will take place. The buyer must feel he wants different items in his assortment more than he wants the money he has to give up to purchase them.

Unless some means were found to overcome these obstacles, consumers would have to spend endless hours searching out producers of items they wish to acquire. They would then have to physically move small quantities of these items to the locations where they are consumed. The inefficiency of searching for individual producers would reduce the variety of products consumers now enjoy. And producers would not be willing to offer a wide variety of products, as in all probability, consumers would be ignorant of their existence. A solution to the first two problems of exchange requires some means of reducing the number of contacts consumers must make with sources of supply to acquire their unique assortments and to minimize the distance over which small quantities of goods must be moved. The activity designed to solve these problems is known as *sorting*, and a complete understanding of this process is essential.[3]

THE PROCESS OF SORTING

Sorting is a process of *concentration* and *dispersion*. Concentration is needed to reduce the cost of physically moving small quantities of goods from the sources of supply to the centers of demand, and to create some semblance of homogeneity of supply in locations close to consumers. Dispersion is needed to create assortments of goods which approximate the assortments buyers demand, and to make goods conveniently available to them.

Let us imagine a distance scale, at one end of which are the 4.8 million producers of goods and services, and at the other end the 67.0 million consuming units. The first task is to concentrate like commodities at some point along the scale closer to the buyer. An example would be the centralization of agricultural products in the growing region. A large number of producers of wheat bring their supplies to the country elevator, where it is graded and stored until a sufficient quantity is accumulated to move it farther down the distance scale by means of economical shipments. In the case of wheat, it is moved to central markets closer to the buyer. This process of concentration is not limited to agricultural products. In the steel industry, producer installations are located in different parts of the country. The output of the different mills is shipped to warehouses closer to the buyers. The same is true of the processed food industry. Producing operations are usually located close to the agricultural regions which produce the base products. After processing, the finished goods are shipped in large quantities to warehouses farther down the distance scale.

[3] For a more complete discussion of sorting, see Wroe Alderson, *Marketing Behavior and Executive Action* (Homewood, Ill.: Richard D. Irwin, Inc., 1957), pp. 201–10.

265

Overcoming
Time and
Space
Through the
Distribution
Network

We now have homogeneous supplies in a number of different locations closer to the buyer. It would be a laborious and expensive task if buyers had to visit even these centers of homogeneous supply. It is now necessary to disperse these homogeneous supplies and concentrate assortments which approximate the assortments buyers desire farther down the distance scale. Goods which are associated in purchase and in use are shipped in large quantities from the concentrated supplies until an assortment of goods is located closer to the buyer. The distance from these supply centers to the buyer is still relatively great, and assortments in much smaller quantities are allocated to points located conveniently near the buyer. The assortments now assembled in any one location are not identical with those that buyers desire. However, the distance problem has been overcome, and the number of contacts that must be made is reduced. The buyer can now select from a relatively few assortments those items needed and, almost literally, carry them home.

The number of points at which goods are concentrated and dispersed in their movement from producer to buyer depends upon many things, including the weight of the product, location of supply, location of markets, competition, perishability, and a number of others. These will be discussed in Chapter 21.

In the sorting process we are dealing with a problem of transportation and storage. You will recall from economics that goods must, in addition to form utility, also have place and time utility before they accumulate value. That is, they cannot enter into exchange unless they are in the right place at the right time, or at least have the potentiality of being so. Since transportation and storage are costly, the way in which goods are concentrated and dispersed has an influence on the value these goods will command in exchange. Management of the physical movement task is discussed in detail in Chapter 16.

Although the broad problem of market cultivation will be discussed in Part 5, there is an element of market cultivation in the sorting process. First, exchanges are stimulated if goods are conveniently exposed to potential buyers. Exposure to purchase is very important for many types of goods and is dependent upon the particular sorting process used to move goods to the consumer. Second, the manner in which goods are offered is dependent in part upon the particular assortment in which they are offered. Let us consider the merchandise found in a hardware store as a specialized assortment. We can hardly conceive of a mattress within this setting as receiving any special stimulation. Likewise we can hardly conceive of a mattress kept in the storeroom of a furniture store as receiving any either. There is a qualitative aspect to the sorting process. Goods must not only be made conveniently available but must also be combined in the proper assortment and offered in a particular way before there is any stimulus to exchange.

THE NEED FOR
MARKETING INTERMEDIARIES

It has been shown that the process of sorting is essential to the efficient distribution of goods in a specialized economy. It matters little whether this job is carried out by producers themselves or whether it is done by other linking entities. Since specialization usually results in efficiency, it is natural that a number of intermediaries have developed to aid in the sorting process. These intermediaries tend to specialize geographically and in terms of the assortments they carry, thereby reducing transportation and storage costs. This is not to say that a single intermediary may not cover the entire country. However, if it does, it must internally specialize operations regionally, because to some degree all markets are local. The characteristics of different goods require different physical facilities, and the skills needed to stimulate their exchange are so variable that specialization in assortment offers many efficiencies.

The economic justification for the existence of marketing intermediaries can be demonstrated by three principles: (1) the principle of minimum total transactions,[4] (2) the principle of massed reserves, and (3) the principle of proximity.

The Principle of Minimum Total Transactions

In Figure 15-1 a simplified economy is represented in which there are four producers and eight buyers. The left-hand side of the figure shows that thirty-two transactions would be necessary for all buyers to acquire an assortment of goods. The right-hand side introduces an intermediary, and the number of transactions is cut to twelve. Transactions cost money, and anything that can be done to reduce them serves efficiency. Now let us examine the savings in transportation cost. On the left-hand side, goods are shipped to each of the buyers in very small quantities at a cost of $1 each for a total transportation cost of $32. On the

FIGURE 15-1
Principle of Minimum Total Transactions

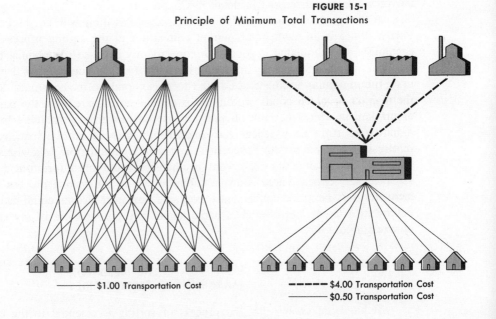

———— $1.00 Transportation Cost

- - - - $4.00 Transportation Cost
———— $0.50 Transportation Cost

[4] For a more complete discussion see Margaret Hall, *Distributive Trading* (London: Hutchinson's University Library, 1951), p. 80.

267

Overcoming
Time and
Space
Through the
Distribution
Network

right-hand side goods are shipped from the producer to the intermediary in large quantities, at a cost of $4 for each producer. They are delivered by the intermediary to the buyer in smaller quantities over a shorter distance at a cost of 50 cents each. The total transportation cost would be $16 ($4 × 4) + $4 (50 cents × 8), or $20, a saving of $12 in transportation cost. Furthermore, we have not mentioned the convenience to the customer through having goods readily available.

While it is possible that the number of intermediaries might increase to the point where the transaction cost would equal that of the thirty-two transactions necessary if no intermediary existed, this in practice is unlikely. Moreover, as the number of intermediaries increases, the savings in transportation costs may more than compensate for the increase in transaction costs. In determining the number of intermediaries, transportation costs should be balanced against transaction costs, and the most economical balance used.

The Principle of Massed Reserves

Storage, like transportation, is costly. Inventories must be held at each step in the concentration and dispersion of goods. Inventories exist at the producer level, at the accumulation level, at the assortment level, and in the household. Paradoxical as it may seem, the amount of goods in inventory when intermediaries are used is less than the amount that must be held when intermediaries are not used.[5] Throughout the sorting process, goods are located convenient to the final buyer; because goods are readily available, the stocks that households and firms must carry is greatly reduced. Since the final buying units are numerically much greater, the total quantity of goods in storage at any one time would be much greater in the absence of intermediaries.

The Principle of Proximity

Intermediaries are located closer to the buyer than are producers. In Parts 2 and 3 the importance of the manufacturers' adjusting products and strategies to market forces was shown. Intermediaries also contribute to this objective. Their proximity to the buyers makes possible more accurate investigation of buyers' desires. These establishments frequently are aware of forces in the market that producers, because of physical and institutional separation, would never observe. The intermediaries' interpretation of markets is reflected in the assortments they assemble and in the products they demand from producers. This does not mean that we can add intermediaries close to buyers at will. The costs involved in duplication in inventories would be prohibitive.[6] The fact does remain, however, that there are intermediaries close to buyers and, as such, they interpret buyers' desires and transmit them to producers through their purchases.

We have mentioned the fact that specialists have developed to reduce the

[5] Hall, *Distributive Trading,* p. 81.
[6] Bowersox, Smykay, and LaLonde, *Physical Distribution Management,* rev. ed. (New York: The Macmillan Company, 1968), Chap. 3.

barriers to exchange. It is now necessary to examine these intermediaries in more detail, as they constitute the broad *distribution network* from which the marketer can select a specific mix of outlets.

MARKETING INTERMEDIARIES CLASSIFIED

There are a large number of different types of specialized intermediaries.[7] Some classification of them is important as an aid in understanding the many different types and their operation.

While various intermediaries may perform services such as standardization and grading, as in the case of those middlemen handling fresh fruits and vegetables, or engage in minor processing, such as the roasting of coffee, these activities are incidental to facilitating exchange.[8] The broadest classification of middlemen distinguishes between those middlemen that purchase outright and actually take title to goods, and those that act in an agency capacity on behalf of clients. The former are called *merchant middlemen* and the latter *agents*. The classification by itself is too broad to be very useful; nevertheless, it is important, as the act of taking title to goods carries with it the risks of ownership.

Middlemen are classified in much more detail by the Bureau of the Census. Much data are published about different kinds of middlemen by this government agency. As these data are used extensively, it is important that we understand how the different classifications are used. They are used (1) in the interpretation of markets, (2) in the classification of middlemen for tax purposes, (3) in the administration of the Fair Labor Standards Act, and (4) in conjunction with a number of laws regulating commerce. Although court rulings deviate at times, the classifications used by the Bureau of the Census are almost uniformly accepted.

Merchant middlemen are of two types: retailers and wholesalers. *Retailers are middlemen primarily engaged in selling to ultimate consumers.* However, some manufacturers, such as Electrolux (vacuum cleaners), sell directly to ultimate consumers. For this reason, the Bureau of the Census has developed statistics on what is known as *retail* trade, which includes all establishments, whether they are middlemen or not, engaged in retailing. Retail trade is defined as including:

> All establishments engaged in selling merchandise for personal or household consumption and rendering services incident to the sale of such goods.[9]

These establishments are examined in detail in Chapter 18.

---

[7] The term *intermediary* is preferred by the authors because it signifies the concept of "linkage" of producers and consumers or industrial users, although the term *middleman* is more common. *Middleman* is the term used in government classifications and is used here in the classification discussion.

[8] *Standardization* involves the determination of specifications to which goods must conform. *Grading* is the act of checking goods for conformity to specifications. Generally, middlemen do not establish standards. Rather, they use trade or government standards and grade merchandise for conformity before offering it for sale.

[9] *Standard Industrial Classification Manual* (Washington, D.C.: Government Printing Office, 1957), p. 153.

269

Overcoming
Time and
Space
Through the
Distribution
Network

Merchant wholesalers are merchant middlemen primarily engaged in selling to retailers; to industrial, commercial, institutional or professional users; or to other wholesalers. Agents are engaged in the same kind of activity as wholesalers except that they do not take title to the goods in which they deal. Manufacturers engage in the same kind of activity as merchant wholesalers when they choose to own and operate manufacturers' sales branches with stocks. For this reason, the Bureau of Census has developed statistics on wholesale trade, which is defined as including:

> All establishments or places of business primarily engaged in selling merchandise to retailers; to industrial, commercial, institutional or professional users; or to other wholesalers; or acting as agents in buying merchandise for or selling merchandise to such persons or companies.[10]

The establishments engaged in wholesaling are examined in detail in Chapter 20.

Summary

Exchange is essential in a specialized economy. The heterogeneity of supply and demand constitute barriers to efficient exchange. These barriers may be considered problems of (1) physical movement, (2) matching assortments, and (3) stimulation. Sorting, the act of concentrating and dispersing goods as they move from producer to consumer, is a means of overcoming the barriers to efficient exchange. Specialization in the sorting process has resulted in the development of marketing intermediaries. Three principles—(1) the principle of minimum total transactions, (2) the principle of massed reserves, and (3) the principle of proximity—exemplify their role in the marketing of goods.

Middlemen, as the intermediaries are known, are classified as merchant middlemen or agents. The former take title to goods and must cope with the risk of ownership. Merchant middlemen are of two types: retailers and wholesalers. Retailers are merchant middlemen primarily engaged in selling to ultimate consumers. Wholesalers are merchant middlemen primarily engaged in selling to retailers; to industrial, commercial, institutional or professional users; or to other wholesalers. Agents are engaged in the same kind of activity as merchant wholesalers except that they act in an agency capacity. Retail trade and wholesale trade include all establishments, regardless of whether they are middlemen, engaged in wholesaling or retailing transactions.

Questions and Problems

1. What is the role of exchange in a developed country? In an underdeveloped one?
2. Would you anticipate that exchange will be of greater or lesser importance a decade hence? Why?
3. It has been said that the thing the affluent customer wants to save most is

[10] *Standard Industrial Classification Manual*, p. 147.

time. If this statement proves to be correct, what effect should this fact have upon marketing institutions?

4. In what way do transportation and storage create utility?

5. If air transportation continues to grow both absolutely and relatively, what effect, if any, will this have upon the function and role of storage?

6. What is the distinguishing difference between a wholesale and a retail transaction? To what extent can a wholesaler retail, and a retailer wholesale?

7. How can marketing intermediaries make for more efficient industrial purchasing? Can you diagram your concept?

8. Which do marketing intermediaries do: induce change in markets, or respond to change in markets? Defend your answer.

9. Are the functions performed by marketing institutions eliminated when those institutions disappear from the distribution structure?

10. Someone has said, "Sears, Roebuck has done more good in South America than the State Department." On what grounds might this be a plausible statement?

11. "Marketing institutions reconcile the heterogeneity of supply-and-demand forces." Comment.

12. What is meant by the process of sorting?

13. How does the principle of massed reserves influence distribution efficiency?

14. For legal purposes, why is it important to be able to differentiate between wholesale and retail establishments?

15. Comment on the notion that marketing intermediaries perform functions for hire on behalf of the manufacturer.

Physical Distribution: Integrated Market Logistics

16

The distribution network is designed to link producing enterprises with purchasing units in an optimum way. The network as a whole serves two primary purposes. One is generating demand. The other is overcoming the problems of time and space through efficient performance of the sorting function. This component we call physical distribution, or an integrated logistical support of markets. Physical distribution is defined by the National Council of Physical Distribution Management as: [1]

> A term employed in manufacturing and commerce to describe the broad range of activities concerned with efficient movement of finished products from the end of the production line to the consumer, and in some cases includes the movement of raw materials from the source of supply to the beginning of the production line. These activities include freight transportation, warehousing, material handling, protective packaging, inventory control, plant and warehouse site selection, order processing, market forecasting, and customer service.

In the context of the total systems approach of this book, physical distribution, if the firm is to be totally effective, must involve the flow of materials and finished goods.

So important is this activity that some have referred to it as the *other half of marketing,* and estimate that costs in this sector are approximately one-half of total marketing costs.[2]

[1] Definition of the National Council of Physical Distribution Management, Executive Offices, 307 N. Michigan Ave., Chicago, Ill.

[2] Paul D. Converse, "The Other Half of Marketing," *Proceedings of the Boston Conference on Distribution,* 1954, pp. 22–25.

THE ORGANIZING CONCEPT

Historically, organizational control over the logistical problems of the firm has been distributed among compartmented and sometimes isolated parts of the enterprise. Control has generally rested among more specialized groups and departments, each with a portion of the total responsibility for logistical elements that lead to the support of markets. The result has been that fragmentary action has been taken in favor of the immediate prime interests of each unit at the expense of adequate solutions to the overall logistical problems of the firm.

In the past, the purchasing department has tended to maximize purchase alternatives and control the factors which give stability to the landed purchase cost of materials, parts, and supplies. The traffic department normally has been concerned with minimizing the costs of intercity transport without reference to the total cost of distribution. The sales department has exercised its influence over shipments to customers for the purpose of rendering maximum service to accounts, and has determined the number and location of outlets to be served. The financial group has frequently directed its attention to minimizing accounts receivable, funds held in the form of inventories and interest and carrying charges. The production department has used its discretion in product scheduling, inventory levels, and economic lot size of production, so as to insure the fulfillment of its planned production rate and economize its manufacturing expenses. Under circumstances such as these, the prospect of discordant practices is increased and the likelihood of the most desirable solutions to the total logistical problem diminished. The purpose of physical distribution is to provide integrated planning, analysis, and control of the total logistical effort of the enterprise.

By virtue of the fact that the entire system exists to provide optimum logistical support of markets, and because market forces and opportunities are regarded as providing the focus for whole systems of business action, the physical distribution task is very important to the marketing organization.

One organizational arrangement that is becoming increasingly common is the placing of full responsibility for physical distribution on the marketing department. Such an organizational arrangement is shown in Figure 16-1. This choice is not always practical, in view of the institutional rigidities that develop in entrenched organizational arrangements within companies. The alternative exists of centralizing planning and analysis of firm logistics, while leaving operations and implementation to the respective departments. A second alternative, of course, is to centralize only some of the components of physical distribution— leaving production scheduling and inventory controls in existing department domiciles. A third alternative is to establish physical distribution as a staff and line function on a level with production, marketing, and finance. Such a unit would be responsible for transportation, warehousing, customer service, exchange channel, inventory control, material flow, order processing, packaging, and credit approval.

The degree to which all physical distribution can be effectively centralized

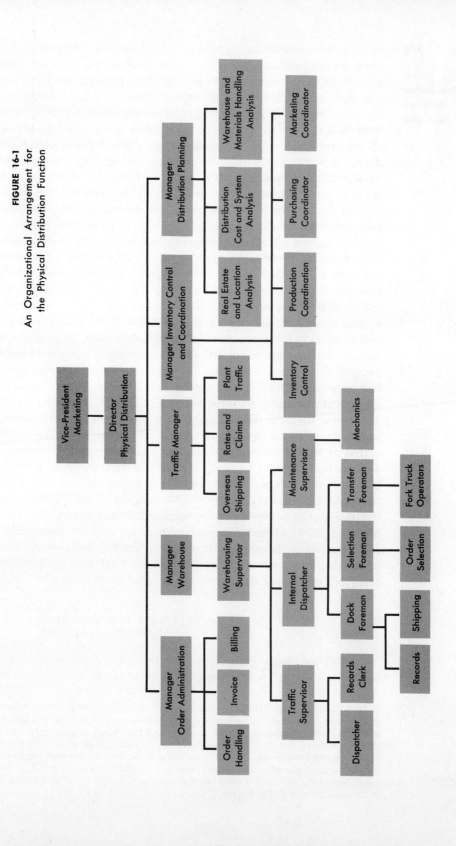

FIGURE 16-1
An Organizational Arrangement for
the Physical Distribution Function

in the larger multiproduct company, using any of the three alternatives, depends upon the operational similarities between products. That is, where materials, manufacturing processes, marketing channels, physical handling, and transportation services are closely related among various products, efficiency is enhanced, by increasing the degree of integration through centralized planning and operations. Where these similarities do not exist, it is unlikely that overall control for all physical distribution operations in one organizational unit is feasible. Thus, if one of a company's divisions produced steam engines, another baby foods, another wearing apparel, and a fourth printing papers, it seems apparent that no real benefits could derive from trying to centralize physical distribution activity. Each plant or division would concentrate on problems pertaining to its own materials, products, plants, marketing organization, and customers, and develop its own individual physical distribution policy and organization.

A second qualification has to do with the possibility of separating the logistics system into two parts—inbound plant materials, and outbound finished products. If an appliance manufacturer produces television sets, air-conditioners, and electric ranges in separate plants, it may be that parts, materials, and production systems are so varied that little benefit could be derived from centralized operations in purchased materials. On the other hand, all products might be sold through the same market outlets so that much would be gained through common physical distribution operations for finished products. Referring to the terminology of Chapter 11, firms characterized as having convergent production and convergent marketing are most susceptible to total centralization of the physical distribution function. Those having divergent production and divergent sales are least susceptible, as represented by the first example just given. Firms characterized as having divergent production and convergent marketing may best fit decentralized inbound logistics systems and centralized outbound physical distribution, while those having convergent production and divergent sales may choose an intermediate degree of fully integrated total logistics planning. These last two patterns—divergent production and convergent marketing, and convergent production and divergent marketing—may be susceptible to complete centralization of the physical distribution function on a totally integrated basis when fabrication-in-transit, storage-in-transit, and pool-car privileges are available from transport carriers and can be used to advantage.[3]

PRESSURES FOR IMPROVED LOGISTICS PLANNING

Although many companies have for years given serious attention to the logistics of market supply there have been some recent developments which

---

[3] Fabrication-in-transit privileges allow the shipper to transport partially fabricated products to production points where the manufacturing process is completed, and then transport finished products to the final destination, while paying only the long-haul rate, plus a small fee. Storage in transit is the same, except that goods are warehoused instead of undergoing fabrication. Pool cars are required where two or more shippers combine their shipments to a common destination and pay carload rates, rather than less-than-carload rates. Mixed car involves several commodities at different rates transported by one shipper at the carload rate at the highest C.L. (carload) commodity rate.

275

Physical
Distribution:
Integrated
Market
Logistics

have forced more concern in this area. These include increased product proliferation, more intense competition, and technological developments.[4]

Increased Product Proliferation

Not so many years ago differences in items in a product line were related more to product function than to nonutilitarian aspects. For example, a line of typewriters would include typewriters of different size, standard and portable, electric and manual, and typewriters with different size and style of type. Today they are made available in pastel shades to match any decor as are electrical appliances and even plumbing fixtures. The increase in variety means a lower volume of sales in each item, and this entails increased unit handling, inventory, and movement costs.

More Intense Competition

As more and more goods have been made available and unprecedented levels of affluence reached, the buying public has become much more meticulous in its buying behavior. Goods must be available when and where they are wanted and not at some future date. If the merchandising and promotion programs are to be effective, they must be backed up with adequate supplies and rapid deliveries. With such intense competition more and more firms have begun to view the logistical supply of markets as a natural extension of their total marketing effort and as a crucial area of competition.

Technological Developments

Partly as a result of the two pressures mentioned above, the costs of distribution began to rise during the late 1950's, creating a need for cost-reducing technology to cope with the problem. Developments in movement, such as more rapid transport, and combined land sea and air movement equipment, the introduction of sophisticated information processing equipment and the many new developments in materials-handling equipment, have made possible an integrated approach to the logistical support of markets.

DECISION AREAS
IN THE LOGISTICS SYSTEM [5]

A large number of decision areas are involved in an integrated logistics system. We shall discuss only the management aspects of the problems in these areas. We will be concerned basically with concepts rather than detailed analytical

[4] See John F. Magee, *Physical-Distribution Systems* (New York: McGraw-Hill Book Company, 1967), Chap. 1.

[5] In more detailed treatments of the subject the decision areas are classified as: (1) facility locations, (2) transportation capability, (3) inventory allocations, (4) communication networks, and (5) unitization. See D. Bowersox, E. Smykay, and B. LaLonde, *Physical Distribution Management,* rev. ed. (New York: The Macmillan Company, 1968), Chap. 5.

procedures. The detailed analytical methods employed in solving these problems involve a variety of technical fields, such as plant location and site selection, and require complex quantitative computations that are beyond our present scope of discussion.

The Market Place and Strategic Objectives

Determination of the qualities required of any system begins with a consideration of the purpose the system is intended to serve. This leads directly to a consideration of strategic objectives of the total marketing program and its logistics component. Logistical planning always takes place within the constraints imposed by the broader system of which it is a part. It is by nature supportive; it must meet a required *service level*.

The breadth and scope of the product line, as well as some measurement of market opportunity and motivational forces bearing on purchases, will have been determined. But the level of service the company wishes to provide its customers is a variable to be considered. Depending upon the number and location of customers, the frequency and size of purchase, and the willingness of intermediaries to hold inventories, the costs of a logistics system will vary considerably. Some general examples will help to clarify this point.

"It has been estimated, for example, that from 5 distribution points a company can reach 33 percent of the United States consumer market within a day; while from 25 warehouse locations, 80 percent can be reached in one day." [6] The options present under these circumstances are many: aim only at the 33 percent with one-day service; service the 33 percent in one day and the remainder in two or more days; incur the costs of 25 warehouses and try to reach the 80 percent with one-day service. There are many alternatives, and the best can only be determined on the basis of costs involved and the potential revenues these costs will generate.

"Judging from my own and associates' experience, approximately 80 percent more inventory is needed in a typical business to fill 95 percent of customers' orders out of stock than to fill only 80 percent." [7] The cost of 80 percent more inventory to handle 15 percent more of customers' orders out of stock must be judged against the potential revenues that 15 percent more customers provide.

Before a choice is made on the level of service to be provided, the costs of inventories to satisfy different service levels must be assessed. To deal effectively with the inventory problem, manufacturers need forecasts of sales, a study of inventory requirements and turnover, order-communication times, order-processing times, and transportation or delivery times. Only when these factors are reflected in good information and control systems can the inventory component of logistics planning be effectively handled.

The controls, moreover, must be made on an item basis rather than on an aggregate basis. That is, the controls must reflect the factors that account for cost differences. This is closely related to the volume of trade on particular

---

[6] John F. Magee, "The Logistics of Distribution," *Harvard Business Review*, XXXVIII, No. 4 (July–August 1960), p. 92.

[7] *Ibid.*, p. 92.

277

Physical
Distribution:
Integrated
Market
Logistics

products rather than to the aggregate volume of business. Table 16-1 shows that, in the typical case, a relatively few items account for a very substantial proportion of the total business. Notice that for industrial goods, 3 percent of the items account for 66 percent of total sales, and conversely, the bottom 74 percent of the items account for only 5 percent. In the past, management too often has been concerned with providing careful inventory controls on the very slow-moving items that tend to remain in stock for a considerable period of time. Yet these items are not the ones that account for the large proportion of logistical costs. The logistics concept, you will remember, is oriented to the more relevant dynamic flow of goods through time and space. Much the largest movement cost center is consequently restricted to a very few items that involve very high volume; these are the ones that should receive prime attention and precise control by management.

TABLE 16-1
Relationship of Inventory Items to
Sales (in percentage)

| Consumer Goods | | | | Industrial Goods | | | |
| Best-Selling Items | | Poorest-Selling Items | | Best-Selling Items | | Poorest-Selling Items | |
Items	Sales	Items	Sales	Items	Sales	Items	Sales
.3	22	50	14	1.7	50	74	5
14	50	29	5	3	66	50	1.2

Source: Robert G. Brown, "Estimating Aggregated Inventory Standards," Naval Research Logistics Quarterly, X, No. 1 (March 1963), 55–71.

The inventory problem is further complicated by reverberations throughout the pipeline whenever there is a change in the volume of customer purchases.[8] This effect is created partly by information lags and partly by changes required in the average inventory needed to support an altered volume of sales. This phenomenon is often referred to as "the whiplash effect." An illustration of this pattern is shown in Figure 16-2. The top curve shows fluctuations in monthly retail sales, with maximum swings of plus and minus 10 percent from average sales over the two-year period. In the same period, factory production varied from a high of 62 percent to a low of minus 100 percent from the monthly average.

The retailer in this example delivers the product three days after purchase by the customer and orders from the wholesaler after a one-week interval from time of delivery. He receives the goods two weeks after his order is placed. The effect of the time lag on retail inventory is shown in the second curve, where retail inventory can be seen to decline 7 percent when sales increase, but then level off. When sales go down 10 percent the retail inventory climbs 22 percent.

[8] For a more detailed discussion of this topic, see J. W. Forrester, *Industrial Dynamics* (Cambridge, Mass. and New York: The M.I.T. Press; John Wiley & Sons, Inc., 1961), p. 24.

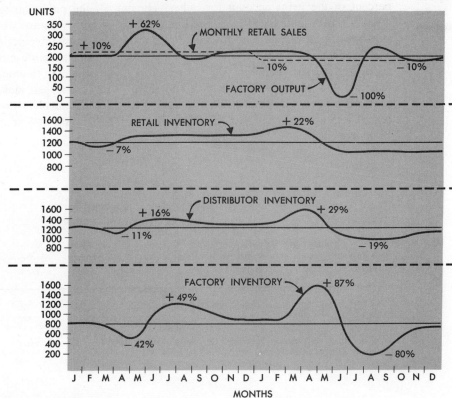

FIGURE 16-2
The Whiplash Effect: A Result of
Changes in Volume of Consumer Purchases

The distributor incurs even wider variations, ranging from 19 percent below average inventory to 29 percent above normal. The distributor's time lags result from his shipping the retailer's order ten days after its receipt, and his own receipt of replacement goods from manufacturers two and a half weeks after ordering them. The resulting inventory changes for the distributor are shown by the third curve.

The whiplash effect at the factory is still greater. The distributor's order is processed and shipped within a week, but because the order for stock is about three weeks away from the retail sale, the accumulation of time lags produces swings as wide as 87 percent above normal levels and reductions below the average of 80 percent in factory inventory. This variation is accompanied by and tends to produce the wide swings in factory output shown in the top curve. Notice particularly how wide the variations are in factory output, in direct contrast to relatively minor fluctuations in retail sales in corresponding time periods.

The curves in Figure 16-2 show inventory consequences of information lags in the distribution system. The inventory imbalances, changes in production

279

Physical
Distribution:
Integrated
Market
Logistics

rates, and numerous adjustments made in the total system because of this whiplash effect result in heavy cost penalties for the system as a whole. When information time lags are accompanied by changes in desired levels of inventory planned to maintain a relatively constant rate of stock turnover, the effect on the manufacturer from changes in retail sales is even more drastic.

Several variables, such as location and accessibility of potential customers, the amounts of each item in the line they purchase, and the inventories required to provide availability consistent with customers' desires, conjoin to determine the level of customer service to be provided by the system. Magee cites an example of the way these factors interrelate. "One analysis with which I am familiar showed that cutting the number of field distribution points from 50 to 25 would increase total transport costs 7 percent but cut inventories 20 percent and cut *total* physical distribution costs 8 percent (the latter representing roughly a 1 percent cut in the total cost of delivered product). This was accomplished at the cost of serving a few small markets—about 5 percent of the total—with second-day instead of first-day delivery." [9]

As in the above example the system employed is not always the least costly way of moving goods to points of purchase or consumption. The objective is to satisfy the broader marketing systems' needs in the least costly way. Determination of the physical movement costs to satisfy these service requirements may lead ultimately to the choice of an alternative customer service level in which revenues lost by lower service levels are more than offset by logistics economics.

Distribution Center Planning

Logistics systems frequently include a warehouse component to more efficiently serve dealer demand. The term *warehouse* conveys the thought of a repository for the more or less lengthy storage of goods; a static quality is associated with it; that is, "warehoused" goods are conceived of as being at rest at fixed point. The more modern term *distribution center* is used here in place of *warehouse,* because it conveys the dynamic aspect of the *flow* of goods. The concept of movement is intended, for the principal purpose of the distribution center is in fact to provide a more economical means of facilitating product flow via a transfer point that breaks bulk and improves the assembly of customized orders from various dealer destinations.

The efficiency to be gained by including distribution centers in the physical distribution system derives primarily from freight savings through consolidation of shipments, the time and expense that can be saved in customized order filling when inventories are close to the market, and by increases in sales effectiveness that accrue when stocks are close to the point of purchase.

The placement of a west coast distribution center by an east coast appliance manufacturer illustrates each of these factors in the use of a distribution center component in the logistics system. The demand for air-conditioners is greatly stimulated after five successive days of temperature above 90° F. As a result, demand is so erratic that dealers are reluctant to carry sizable inventories of the

[9] Magee, "Logistics of Distribution," p. 93.

product. The existing distribution arrangement required five or six days for dealer delivery after receipt of an order at the factory. Many sales were lost because of the unavailability of the product; demand was not just pushed back to a later period. By having a large inventory close to the market, marketing intermediaries could operate with smaller inventories, thereby reducing the total inventory that had to be held at any one time in the total logistics system. Also, they could capitalize on demand as it built up in the hot weather season. In addition, freight costs were reduced because of the long-haul *carload* shipments made possible by the establishment of the distribution center, in contrast to the *less-than-carload* orders previously shipped to individual distributors.

Physical distribution analysis therefore involves evaluating the feasibility of establishing a distribution center component. While the standard used in making the judgment involves the criteria of both cost and service, cost is the main consideration. Ideally the level of customer service has been determined and the problem is one of deciding on the number and location of distribution centers needed to provide that level of service at least cost. One of the major costs entailed is that of transportation—transportation from the points of production into the centers and transportation out of the centers to the points of consumption. Other costs include inventory holding costs, including obsolescence costs; interest charges; and costs associated with movement through the centers. Various elements will influence these factors and require complex computation. These elements are: the forecasted volume of movements through the center; the average order size; frequency of order; order variety; the number of shipping points from a given order; and the forecasted volume from various points. While the analytical effort that is necessary to make this judgment is technically complex, we can simplify the problem by analogy.[10] Just as a physical map of a geographic area shows the elevations, depressions, and contours of a land surface, a total-cost map or graphic portrayal of cost computations shows differences in the cost of physical distribution for different areas from different supply points. Distribution center locations would appear at the points which represent the deepest depressions on the total-cost map, or more simply the lowest point of each cost "basin." The limits of each cost basin would be similar to the ridge lines between river basins, which determine their respective drainage areas. The cost of serving a particular account located between two shipping points will be exactly the same at the cost ridge. A cost ridge is determined by a series of destination points at which the cost is equal for shipping from two or more locations. The various cost ridges circumscribe the areas to be served by the distribution centers in the cost basins and, thereby, indicate the number of centers needed to provide complete market coverage at least total cost, if complete cost data have been used in making the analysis.

Obviously the number of cost basins will depend upon the costs used in the computation. One of the major cost inputs is that of transportation in and out of the center. Consequently the transportation alternative selected will have a major influence on the least-cost combinations.

Choice of the transport alternative reflects a variety of factors. Each of the

[10] For a more detailed explanation, see Bowersox, Smykay and LaLonde, *Physical Distribution Management,* Chap. 11.

281

Physical
Distribution:
Integrated
Market
Logistics

major transport media has its own special qualities that make it especially suitable under particular circumstances. For example, air express dominates when a shipment involves a long distance, a high value-to-bulk ratio, and speed is an essential requirement; the railroads predominate in the movement of goods in which there is a long-haul, high weight and bulk-to-value ratio, without the need for speed. The objective, of course, is to choose the mode of transportation that matches transport services and costs with market requirements.

In this connection it must be recognized that shipping terms vary, and that the shipper's option of choosing the mode of transport depends upon price and terms of sale quotations. The two basic types of shipping terms are F.O.B. Origin and/or Mill, and F.O.B. Destination, with a number of variations from the basic types. F.O.B. (Free on Board) Mill places the responsibility of payment of freight charges on the buyer but allows him the option of routing or choice of carrier, while F.O.B. Destination shifts this responsibility and option to the seller. The initiation of damage claims and insurance protection follows in the same fashion. Both of the basic shipping arrangements can be modified by agreement. For instance, the seller can sell F.O.B. Mill, but allow freight to the buyer by deducting the cost of transportation from the invoice. This allows the buyer to select the carrier, route, and class of shipment, but he also has to pay the carrier and file any claims for damage in transit. On the other hand, the seller's transport costs can be kept the same, but he can control the choice of carrier, routing, and class of shipment by quoting his terms, "F.O.B. Shipping Point, transportation allowed and form of transportation to be selected by shipper."

The variation in shipping terms obviously affects the end delivered price of goods to the buyer, and thus influences the size of sales territory that can be served in competition with other sellers.

There are also cases where the seller, rather than using common carriers exclusively, will wish to own his own transport vehicles or delegate some or all of his outbound transportation to a contract carrier. Private carriers, a legal transport form, are limited to transporting goods for which they are the bona fide owners. They cannot transport goods for others on a fee basis. Consequently, the seller will own his own vehicles only when he can be sure of keeping the equipment fully utilized so as to maintain a low cost per ton-mile. Or, very specialized transport services may be required which entail the use of custom vehicles owned by the shipper.

Contract carriers provide service to one or a limited number of shippers. This factor makes possible a close personal relationship between the carrier and the shipper and means that the shipper's transport costs are entirely variable. This variable cost pattern contrasts with the substantial investment involved in vehicles when the seller acts as his own private carrier. Depending upon the type and size of the company, this can be an important element in the marketer's choice of the mode of transport. Many companies find it advantageous to use a mixture of private and common or contract transport devices.

If the feasibility of utilizing a distribution center location has been demonstrated, the selection of a specific site for the center is required. This is usually handled by a professionally competent real estate analyst. Property appraisals must be made, access to highways and railroad sidings evaluated, lease or purchase arrangements considered, the suitability of the land for construction purposes determined, zoning regulations reviewed, and a host of other detailed but important factors considered in the final decision for the specific site of the center.

After the site has been selected, the specific size, shape, and type of building to be constructed, and its layout must be determined. Here the overriding consideration is economy and ease of movement of goods, for the structure exists primarily to facilitate product flow. Consequently, the materials-handling engineer, layout designer, and architect must work closely together to provide the proper structure. Operating expenses reflect, in large measure, the nature of the structure and only secondarily the operating methods employed.

Finally we come to the design of the operating system to be used at the center, and the establishment of standards for measuring its performance. In attempts to reduce costs, increasing use has been made of automation by distribution centers. Inventory control is maintained with data processing equipment, pallet loads are assembled and moved by automatic transfer equipment, materials-handling devices are available for loading outbound vehicles, and of course motorized vehicles, conveyors, and such, are used for the internal transfer of goods. An efficiently designed distribution center, with proper layout, materials-handling equipment, electronic data processing equipment, and efficient operating procedures, has been known to handle an annual volume of $200 million worth of processed foods with as few as ten employees.

Order-filling Systems

A complete logistics program in support of a firm's market cultivation attempts includes the operations required in processing and filling customer orders. This is often most effectively accomplished when it includes a complete system, including the billing and invoicing associated with the sale of merchandise. Many firms, however, elect to separate the financial aspects of the order-handling function. Credit extension, determination of discounts, billing, and collection may be placed in the hands of the finance department. Since these activities are so intimately involved in the conduct of business with the customer and the movement of goods, a strong argument can be made for placing these operations in the physical distribution area under the general jurisdiction of the marketing organization.

INTEGRATED PHYSICAL
DISTRIBUTION ALTERNATIVES

The tendency to evaluate business operations in terms of profit rather than cost minimization has resulted in a more integrated approach to all phases of business activity. This is so because profits result from matching a series of cost inputs against revenues, which are a function of all costs. Cost minimization alone does not take adequate account of the effect of reduced costs on revenues, the other half of the profit equation. The cost minimization approach was in perfect harmony with the organizing concepts mentioned above. The profit

283

Physical
Distribution:
Integrated
Market
Logistics

approach requires the integration of all costs, as they all generate a revenue result. In the specific area of physical distribution, higher movement costs may be incurred if lower holding costs are the result. For example, air transport, a high-cost method of transportation, may increase revenues because of rapid availability and, at the same time reduce significantly storage costs at or near the place of purchase. With proper production scheduling, it may reduce inventory costs throughout the entire pipeline.

This is only one of the alternatives available. But transcending specific situations are more basic orientations to the kind of physical distribution system a firm may wish to develop. These are: (1) minimum total cost; (2) maximum service; (3) maximum profit; and (4) maximum competitive advantage.[11]

Minimum Total Cost

Such an approach places cost minimization ahead of customer service. That is, every effort is made to reduce costs without giving much attention to the effect of such a policy on revenues. Such a policy does recognize the integrated nature of physical distribution costs, and it attempts to find the least total cost for inventory, holding, and movement costs. Obviously no firm can carry such a policy to an extreme. However, there are situations in which more emphasis can be placed on cost minimization than on service levels. In very technical, high unit value industrial equipment, customized for individual purchasers, the physical distribution function may be minimal. The movement costs are the prime consideration. Delivery of Boeing 747 aircraft to ultimate purchasers would be done on a least-cost basis. In products such as food staples, in which there is little expansibility of demand and minimum differentiation by brand, the physical distribution components may be selected on a least-cost basis. We have already seen that a large proportion of total sales are accounted for by a small proportion of items in the line. Management may decide to handle the slower-moving items on a least-cost basis, without concern for the revenue results, and concentrate all of its efforts on that small proportion of items that are its primary products. Where there is a marked seasonal sales pattern, as in toys, the firm may follow a least-cost approach until close to Christmas, when it must assure delivery at almost any cost.

Maximum Service

This approach could be considered the polar extreme of minimum total cost. Sales could be held at very high levels while the company went into bankruptcy. Obviously maximum service is not possible, but the physical distribution system could be organized to emphasize this objective. Pharmaceutical houses generally follow such a policy and are proud of the fact that they can give twenty-four-hour service anywhere in the country on any item in their line. In fact, under emergency conditions, they will even do better. As was shown, a much larger inventory must

[11] These alternatives are discussed in more detail in Bowersox, Smykay, and LaLonde, *Physical Distribution Management,* Chap. 11.

be carried to give faster service to a very small proportion of customers. Those firms wishing to follow a maximum service policy will incur the costs of carrying that inventory. The potential revenues the additional customers will generate is a secondary consideration. There are circumstances under which this would be a very defensible policy. In high-fixed-cost industries the break-even point is much higher and there may be a very real need to generate sales even at the expense of high distribution costs. These industries are particularly vulnerable during recessions, when loss minimization may be the objective. Under these circumstances recovery of variable costs is the only constraint on making additional sales.

Maximum Competitive Advantage

Of course a maximum service policy also produces a competitive advantage, but there are some differences in implementation. On new-product introductions a company may incur losses for long periods of time before profits are made. During this period the product must achieve competitive entrenchment. Availability of merchandise at the consumer level is very important, and the company may be willing to incur higher costs on new products than on established products. Competitive position for any single company is not uniform for all products or in all geographic areas. In those areas where share of market is slipping, it may be necessary to depart from a least-cost approach if the firm wishes a predetermined share of the market. Variations in the physical distribution approach to take care of geographical variations in competitive position are very difficult to achieve. A large share of physical distribution costs may be fixed, such as warehousing costs and even transportation if the company owns its own movement facilities. Nevertheless, such differences in treatment of different markets may be necessary.

Maximum Profit

This differs from least total cost, since there is a consideration of revenues generated by the costs incurred. This approach is a theoretical ideal and approaches the "marginal cost equals marginal revenue" solution. That is, funds will be expended on physical distribution until the last dollar spent just equals a dollar in additional revenues. To spend less would be giving up the opportunity to earn more profit, and to spend more would incur losses. As yet this approach cannot be used. Although the logic of an integrated systems approach is well developed, research methodology has not advanced so far. It is recognized that there is an interaction between inventory costs, distribution center costs, movement costs, and sales revenues. Most studies optimize only one variable. That is, plant location and markets are fixed; transportation cost is optimized without regard for inventory costs. Or inventory costs are optimized without regard for movement costs. Perhaps in the future such an orientation will be possible. In spite of its operational limitations, it nevertheless is a sound theoretical foundation for guiding the planners of a physical distribution system.

285

Physical
Distribution:
Integrated
Market
Logistics

Summary

The distribution network is designed to link producing enterprises with purchasing units in an optimum way. The network serves the dual purposes of generating demand and providing a supportive supply function. The physical distribution portion of the network involves primarily the logistical support of markets. It is concerned with the optimum movement of goods through time and space to the end that the right assortments of goods will be in the right places at the right time. Logistics planning, being supportive by nature, must meet a required service level. This is why the physical distribution system employed is not always the least-cost way of moving goods to points of purchase and consumption. The objective is to serve the broader marketing systems needs in the least-cost way. Determination of total movement costs may, however, lead ultimately to a change in the service level that, through logistics economies, more than offsets lost revenues.

Historically, organizational control over the logistical operations of the firm has been fragmented and dispersed, with various segments of the responsibility borne by purchasing, production, traffic, warehousing, finance, and sales. More recent organizational arrangements favor placing physical distribution within marketing or as a separate managerial unit on an equal level with production, marketing, and finance. Three pressures—increased product proliferation, more intense competition, and technological developments—have contributed to more careful logistics planning. In the integrated logistical model, the individual components are conceived of as parts of a total system and susceptible to centralized planning, analysis, and control, and less frequently, actual operations.

Decisions concerning the form of physical distribution system to be used include strategic objectives related to the market place, including the level of customer service to be provided and the inventory requirements necessary to meet that level; the feasibility, location, design, and operation of physical distribution centers based upon the level of service decided upon; the choice of a transport alternative, as well as inventory costs and interest charges; and finally design for order-handling and filling procedures. Four alternatives in physical distribution planning are considered: (1) least total cost; (2) maximum service; (3) maximum competitive advantage; and (4) maximum profit.

Questions and Problems

1. List the parts of a manufacturing enterprise that have a participating role in a total logistics system.
2. What have been the deficiencies in the way these organizational arrangements have been traditionally handled in the past?
3. Should a physical distribution system be *designed to meet* a specific level of marketing service, or should the highly efficient physical distribution system *lead to and produce* a certain level of service? Comment and elaborate.
4. What are the various kinds of locational problems involved in choosing a total logistics system?
5. What is the "whiplash effect" in inventory fluctuations? What causes this?

6. Should a manufacturer be especially concerned to maintain extremely close control over his fast-moving items, or his slow-moving items that enjoy only very sporadic purchase? Why?

7. Indicate the kinds of situations in which you would expect air freight instead of rail freight to be the common mode of transport.

8. Under what kinds of price quotations does the seller pay the cost of shipping? Aside from the cost, why does it make a difference whether the buyer or the seller pays the freight?

9. What is the difference between the terms *common carrier* and *contract carrier?*

10. Under what conditions would private carriers most likely dominate transport volume?

11. Under what conditions might a maximum service orientation to physical distribution be followed by a company?

12. In your judgment, should all, some, or none of the following be part of physical distribution: order handling, billing, invoicing, and handling accounts receivable? Why?

13. If you were just developing a new logistics program for a manufacturing firm, would you have any preference between the terms *warehouse* and *distribution center?* What is the semantic difference?

14. If all components of a physical distribution system cannot be centralized organizationally, is there any alternative that can provide some of the same advantages?

15. Make a strong case for putting the entire physical distribution function under the direction of the marketing manager. Make a convincing case for not adopting this approach. Now take your own position in the matter.

Conflict, Cooperation, and Manufacturer-Dealer Systems

17

In the preceding chapter we examined the requirements for efficient physical flow of goods from production to consumption. The exchange flow, or the route of ownership transfer, may or may not parallel the physical flow. In the exchange flow our attention is directed to stimulating exchange. You will recall that in Chapter 2 the point was emphasized that the marketer's concern should be the development of impact at the point of ultimate sale. The producer-marketer, accordingly, must be concerned with the roles and effectiveness of firms in subordinate positions in the system, and not be preoccupied solely with his own role. He must insure that the total manufacturer-dealer system competes effectively with other systems. This is a departure from historical practice, in which each link in the system was regarded as having independent identity and ownership and, thereby, was basically responsible for the development and execution of its own programs of self-interest.

This chapter first considers the customer structure of a manufacturer-dealer system; then the inherent nature of such a system is analyzed. Next, the importance of the dependency level of the subordinate participants in the system is highlighted, and the means by which manufacturers establish responsiveness among dealers and maintain systems control is discussed.[1] Finally, there is an examination of legal questions involved in franchise agreements.

THE CUSTOMER STRUCTURE OF A MANUFACTURER-DEALER SYSTEM

Who is the manufacturer's customer? One way to answer this question is to trace the flow of orders through the

[1] The ideas of primary and subordinate roles and a complex of mutual expectations were developed by Professor Valentine P. Ridgeway, "Administration of Manufacturer-Dealer Systems," *Administrative Science Quarterly,* I, No. 4 (March 1957).

system. From this perspective, in a manufacturer-wholesaler-retailer-consumer distribution channel, the consumer is the retailer's customer, the retailer is the wholesaler's customer, and the wholesaler is the manufacturer's customer. This is so because a series of market transactions takes place in which there is a transfer of ownership at each stage of the distribution system. This approach has a further technical validity in that each of these participants is an independent legal business entity, rather than an agent acting in the place of his principal.

The wholesaler as a private business entrepreneur presumably cultivates his markets with his own resources in such a way as to best achieve his own goals. His functions traditionally include the development of retail outlets for products carried, and the "serving" of these accounts. His flow of orders, and the fact that the wholesaler is an independent legal entity, have caused manufacturers to regard the wholesaler as a customer, and to devote the bulk of their efforts to gaining a larger proportion of his business.

This orientation has tended to obscure the more fundamental point that the ultimate consumer or buyer is in reality *the* customer of all participants in the system. More recently it has been realized that unless the ultimate consumer purchases, it is only a matter of time until purchases at intermediate points cease and the middlemen "customers" of the manufacturer become dormant accounts. This realization has led to a philosophy which recognizes the ultimate consumer as *the sole customer* of the manufacturer, and the distributors and dealers as providers of a group of functions for hire. According to this view, the manufacturer's job is either to assist the distributors and dealers in performing their functions as effectively as possible, or to perform them himself, if he can do so more efficiently. While this is a rather extreme view, the trend is in this direction.

The reorientation of the nature of the manufacturer-dealer system has definite validity, but poses certain problems. These can be observed by analyzing the inherent characteristics of any manufacturer-dealer system.

CHARACTERISTICS OF MANUFACTURER-DEALER SYSTEMS

Primary and Subordinate Roles

In any dynamic system there is some classification of participants according to role. Based upon actions taken we can rank participants as performing *primary* or *subordinate* roles. In a manufacturer-dealer system the owner of a brand name generally plays a primary role. This is because the brand owner carries the most risk and stands to lose the most if the system malfunctions. As a result, the owning enterprise tends to be the focus of leadership, authority, and decision— in other words, plays the primary role. All other participants exercise subordinate roles.

The primary role is in most cases centered in the manufacturing enterprise. However, in merchandising its own brands, Sears Roebuck plays the primary role and factory suppliers, the secondary roles. A similar situation can exist with distributors' private brands at the wholesale level. In this case, both the manufacturer *and* the retailer play subordinate roles. In rather exceptional situ-

289

Conflict,
Cooperation,
and Manu-
facturer-
Dealer
Systems

ations, the brand name is owned by a manufacturer, but distribution enterprises play the primary role in the system. This could occur where a sales agent finances the manufacturer's output and dominates the distribution process to the extent that he can exercise great influence over the action in the system and, consequently, assume the primary role. In the usual situation, however, as the principal risk-holder, the manufacturer exercises the prerogatives and responsibilities of his primary position in the system.

A Complex of Mutual Expectations

In any manufacturer-dealer system there is a set of expectations from the system on the part of all participants. An understanding of these expectations makes it possible to more clearly perceive the nature of administrative actions which must be taken to sustain the system under vigorously competitive circumstances. Let us first consider the nature of the manufacturer's expectations.

While some variations in expectations result from differences in products, markets, and firms, manufacturers commonly expect the following supporting roles from their dealers: first, and usually most important, the manufacturer expects the dealer to provide continuously aggressive selling effort. This facet of the dealer's role is the manufacturer's principal concern. In fact, the bulk of the manufacturer's efforts with dealers is directed toward developing the highest possible level of performance in this area.

Second, the manufacturer expects dealers to conduct promotional programs from time to time to tie in with the manufacturer's own promotional effort. He expects the dealer to use merchandising aids, promotional materials, point-of-purchase displays, and cooperative advertising allowances in such a way as to effect a totally integrated promotional system.

Third, a manufacturer desires full-line coverage by the dealer. Manufacturers do not always market the full range of products through all dealers. In some instances, they provide particular classes of accounts with a special grouping of products. Whatever the grouping or line of products made available to the dealer, the manufacturer desires full coverage of the assortment. Opposed to this desire, dealers frequently promote only the best-selling products selected from a number of manufacturers. This practice, frequently referred to in the trade as "cherry picking a line," generally is condemned by the manufacturer, who feels that promotion of the entire line is essential to a balanced position in the market place.

Fourth, the manufacturer expects adequate product exposure supported by adequate inventory levels on the part of the dealer. In recent years, the tendency of numerous dealers to minimize their inventory holdings has caused much friction in manufacturer-dealer systems. In such cases, dealers carry only display models, and order merchandise only after a sale has been made from inventories further back in the channel. Some volume of business is bound to be lost from this practice; in certain product categories, the loss can be substantial. For example, demand for window air-conditioners reaches a peak after four or five successive days of temperatures over 90 degrees. When inventories are not immediately available at the retail level, the manufacturer permanently loses many sales.

Fifth, the manufacturer expects his dealers to practice responsible pricing. While difficult to define exactly, responsible pricing, in general, means maintaining a price level that is neither so high as to curtail the potential volume of business nor so low as to disrupt prices in the market to the degree that dealers can earn only minimum profits from the manufacturer's line. When a manufacturer's line is unprofitable to a significant number of dealers over any period of time, the manufacturer faces considerable difficulty in obtaining the kind of support needed from dealers.

Sixth, manufacturers expect adequate parts service to be provided by dealers when that is an important part of the sale of the product. Adequate parts service presents one of the more difficult problems manufacturers must solve. Here again, friction develops in the system when dealers fail to meet manufacturers' expectations.

Seventh, the manufacturer requires an adequate flow of market information from dealers in order to conduct his own business intelligently. Since in this type of system the manufacturer is physically removed from the ultimate customer, he needs access to information regarding what is happening at the point of ultimate sale. This information usually takes the form of sales reports, inventory levels, competitors' activities, price movements, and the like.

The dealer, on the other hand, has a number of expectations from the manufacturer, which tend to counterbalance those of the manufacturer and provide the basis for a mutuality of interest and a harmonious relationship. First, and usually most important, the dealer expects the manufacturer to provide an attractive, salable, and competitive line of products. That is, the dealer expects the manufacturer to maintain a line, usually through research and development, fully competitive with the lines handled by the dealer's rivals. Dealer grumblings and dissatisfactions are almost sure to occur when the product line is not competitive in terms of price, quality, features, or design.

Second, the dealer expects the manufacturer to develop a high level of consumer brand acceptance for his product. That is, he expects the manufacturer, through advertising and promotion, to create a favorable climate for dealer selling effort. The dealer believes that preselling is necessary if he is to compete effectively with dealers handling products that enjoy such preselling. In consumer goods particularly, this factor has become almost crucial in obtaining strong dealers. Strong dealers are almost in a position to elect the product line they wish to carry, and they strongly favor those that have customer acceptance.

Third, the dealer expects fair margins and equitable price treatment. Frictions develop from such pricing arrangements as a manufacturer's selling both through wholesalers to smaller dealers, and direct to large retail accounts. Prices may vary, depending upon the class of customer, and the dealer expects the manufacturer to maintain a price schedule that enables all dealers to compete effectively and profitably.

The fourth expectation relates to territorial trade protection. The dealer, in other words, presumes what he calls orderly distribution. Trade protection is expected when handling the product entails a considerable investment in inventory, spare parts, service facilities, and the like. The dealer expects the manu-

291

Conflict,
Cooperation,
and Manu-
facturer-
Dealer
Systems

facturer to respect the dealer's franchise and not give the line to a directly competing dealer.

Fifth, the dealer expects merchandising assistance in the form of dealer aids and promotion materials. He expects the tools needed to do an effective job; this he regards as a manufacturer's responsibility. Additionally, he expects prompt delivery, fair treatment on returns and allowances, regular calls from sales personnel, and, in general, businesslike servicing of his account.

Figure 17-1 shows a statement of policy concerning the expectations of both the manufacturer and distributors. You will notice that each of the expectations mentioned above is stated.

A System of Rewards and Penalties

Any manufacturer-dealer system operates essentially through a system of rewards and penalties. Rewards relate primarily to profits. The rewards for both the dealer and the manufacturer essentially reflect increased pofitability to both parties. Such profitability comes from coordinated and integrated action on the part of both parties. However, special incentives of a financial nature emerge for dealers from time to time in the form of special promotion of merchandise, movement of accumulated inventories, year-end closeout of lines, and so on.

Penalties involve foregoing profits, threats of disciplinary action, loss of the line, and, possibly, legal prosecution as, for example, under Fair Trade price violations by the dealer. Penalties relevant to the manufacturer involve emphasis by the dealer on other lines, inadequate inventories, inadequate promotion, or, finally, dropping of the line by the dealer.

A Structure of Authority

A manufacturer-dealer system involves a structure of authority which circumscribes the decision and action areas. The relationships among the participants in a system should be clearly defined by specifying the rights, privileges, and obligations of all parties. Definitions of this type frequently take the form of a written contract, but the main purpose of such explicit statement of relationships is to alleviate future misunderstandings. These contracts are known as *franchise agreements*. Some of the legal questions involved in them follow shortly, under "Franchise Agreements and the Law."

A Communication Structure

A particularly important feature of manufacturer-dealer systems is communications. Essentially, channels must be available for the orderly flow of information back and forth through the system. The system fails to work effectively when information is either overabundant or inadequate. That is, manufacturers can so bombard dealers with promotional aids, training materials, sales correspondence, and personal contact that the dealer is unable to absorb or use intelligently all the information provided. Consequently, he discards or ignores

FIGURE 17-1

A Complex of Mutual Expectations

A STATEMENT OF POLICY

INDUSTRIAL DIVISION

It is our firm belief that Black & Decker and its duly Authorized Distributors have fundamental obligations to each other.
We believe that mutually profitable operations depend upon mutual acceptance of those obligations as outlined.

WHAT DISTRIBUTORS CAN EXPECT FROM BLACK & DECKER

1. Selective Distribution:

Appointed on the basis of power tool potential in each marketing area.
Adequate to insure penetration of all markets for our products.
Selected in accordance with the terms of this "Statement of Policy."

2. Specialized Field Sales Assistance Through:

The largest, best-trained field sales organization in the industry.
Product and market training for Distributor's sales organization by means of effective sales meetings, power tool clinic sessions and joint sales calls in the field.
Availability of market potential information to assist Distributor's sales planning.
Assistance in the maintenance of a well balanced and current power tool and accessory inventory.

3. Healthy Profit Opportunities Through:

Equitable profit margins on power tools and accessories.
Assured inventory turnover.
Maintaining an orderly market.
Refusal to deal with Distributors who do not feel that the sales policies we suggest are based upon sound business judgment.

4. Aggressive Advertising and Sales Promotion Through:

The best known brand name in the industry.
The largest and best program of national advertising, direct mail assistance and display materials in the power tool field.

5. Leadership in Research and Development Through:

The broadest, most complete line in the industry.
Continued leadership in product performance, value, styling and innovation.

6. Leadership in Manufacturing From:

The largest, most modern plants in the industry.
Unparalleled quality control standards.
Thorough testing of all products before shipment.

7. Nation-wide Network of Factory-operated Service Facilities Which:

Offer prompt, expert repair service at reasonable cost.
Stock genuine Black & Decker replacement parts.

8. The Famous Black & Decker Guarantee Which:

Protects the purchaser against defective material or workmanship for the life of the product.

WHAT BLACK & DECKER EXPECTS FROM DISTRIBUTORS

1. Effective Sales Results Through:

An aggressive sales organization, knowledgeable in the application and selling of Black & Decker products.
Effective sales management focus on our line.
Adequate penetration of the potential market for our products in the Distributor's normal trading area.
Cooperation with Black & Decker's field sales personnel in developing sales programs, meetings and work schedules designed to build sales performance.

2. Vigorous Promotional Activity Through:

Imaginative advertising, direct mail activity, displays and catalog coverage of the Black & Decker line.

3. Protection of Black & Decker's Brand Name and Reputation By:

Following the sales policies recommended by the company.
Restricting sales to the Distributor's normal trading area.
Discouraging the sale of Black & Decker products through non-authorized sales organizations, so that the customer will receive maximum service after purchase.
Abstaining from marketing practices that, in any way, damage the reputation of the company or its products.

4. Maintenance of an Adequate Inventory By:

Stocking tools and accessories of a variety and quantity commensurate with markets served and the highest standards of customer service. ("Adequate Inventory" shall be a matter of agreement between each Distributor and the appropriate Black & Decker sales representative.)

5. Provision of Those Other Services and Functions Which Characterize a Good Distributor, Such As:

Extending credit to the user.
Following up customer inquiries.
Rendering prompt delivery from local stocks.
Making available prompt technical services to customers.
Keeping informed on market conditions.

With this STATEMENT OF POLICY, we reaffirm our belief in the economic soundness of the Distributor, our resolve continually to improve and diversify the products we offer and, through Distributor channels, to cultivate an ever-widening market for Black & Decker products.

THE BLACK & DECKER MANUFACTURING COMPANY

_____   _____
President   Chairman of the Board

293

Conflict,
Cooperation,
and Manu-
facturer-
Dealer
Systems

important as well as unimportant bits of information. Conversely, the dealer may fail to provide the manufacturer with information adequate to the performance of his primary role in the system.

Channels of communication must be known. In one particular situation, a dealer was found to have received information from seventeen different sources, including both manufacturer and wholesaler personnel.[2] Under such circumstances, the dealer hardly knew with whom to communicate when difficulties arose or when important available information should have been relayed to the manufacturer. Almost invariably, an inefficient and ineffective manufacturer-dealer system has an ineffective information flow.

When we consider the features of the manufacturer-dealer system, it is apparent that any manufacturer will seek and strongly desire a highly responsive dealer organization. Given this primary systems role, manufacturers have developed a great variety of programs to secure responsiveness and a measure of control over the system.

RESPONSIVENESS AND THE LEVEL OF DEPENDENCY IN THE SYSTEM

When we speak of responsive and nonresponsive areas of administration in the system, to what are we really referring? Visualize a manufacturer-dealer system as diagrammed in Figure 17-2. Here is shown the entire system: from the manufacturer's own marketing personnel, to the salesmen in the field, on to the distributor's (wholesaler's) management and sales personnel, continuing to dealer management and sales personnel, and finally to prospects and customers in the market place. We can regard the upper half of the figure as a responsive area of administration because the manufacturer has recruited, selected, trained, and compensated these people. Presuming this job has been done reasonably well, we can expect these line personnel to be highly responsive to programs formulated for field operation simply because they are the manufacturer's own employees and are paid by him.

An effective degree of control can be reasonably expected over field marketing operations up to that point in the total system. Beyond it, however, we encounter independent businessmen who are neither employed nor paid by the manufacturer, who generally carry other product lines, and who have other commitments and demands upon their time and resources. As a consequence, we cannot expect the same degree of responsiveness in this part of the system. The manufacturer's objective, however, is to have this part of the system respond as if it involved his own people. That is, he seeks the same degree of responsiveness and precision in implementing programs as if his own personnel extended throughout the system. Many devices are employed to bring this situation about, with the objective of making what otherwise would be a nonresponsive area of administration more like the responsive area. The manufacturer cannot command this condition; it is not a right, it must be earned. Much depends on the

[2] From *A Census of Appliance Retailing in the Saginaw* (Mich.) *Market,* conducted by the author for a major manufacturer, for private use.

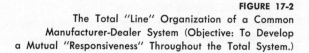

FIGURE 17-2
The Total "Line" Organization of a Common
Manufacturer-Dealer System (Objective: To Develop
a Mutual "Responsiveness" Throughout the Total System.)

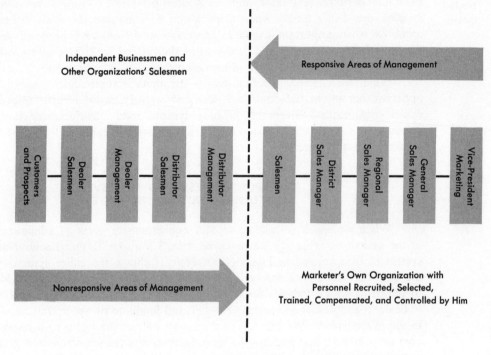

degree of dependence between the subordinate and primary participants in the system.

Dependency Level

The dealer has a high level of dependence on the primary participant when the bulk of the dealer's sales volume is derived from a particular manufacturer's line. That is, if the dealer derives 80 percent of his sales volume from one manufacturer, he depends heavily on that manufacturer for his income and, therefore, is likely to respond fully to the manufacturer's promotional and distribution programs. In effect, the dealer behaves as if he were one of the manufacturer's own employees. But if the dealer derives only 2 or 3 percent of his sales from the particular manufacturer's line, it is difficult to arouse him to the same level of responsiveness. He may legitimately conclude that, if he devotes his time and resources to a full implementation of the manufacturer's promotional program, the incremental revenue derived from that will be much less beneficial than the same amount of time allocated to another manufacturer's product line, which accounts for substantially greater sales volume.

295

Conflict,
Cooperation,
and Manu-
facturer-
Dealer
Systems

Suppose, for instance, that a particular dealer covers the full line of General Electric appliances and also carries a line of electric fans produced by a small electrical goods manufacturer. If the fan line accounts for only 2 to 3 percent of the dealer's total sales volume, it is difficult for him to justify implementing a promotional program of the fan manufacturer (even presuming it would be an effective stimulant to sales) when a more substantial gain in sales volume could be derived from devoting the same amount of effort to the more complete line promotion of General Electric (even if it was not as well conceived as the smaller manufacturer's plan). This illustrates a rather extreme case of a dependency level, but indicates the difficulties that might be expected in developing a highly responsive dealer organization.

On the other hand, visualize the level of dependency between the Coca-Cola Company and its franchised bottling plants. Since in many cases the bottling plants depend entirely upon Coca-Cola for their profits, we can expect them, even though they are independently owned businesses, to be fully responsive. Therefore, it is generally to the manufacturer's advantage to work toward increasing the dependency of those in subordinate roles in the system.

Let us now examine the specific ways in which manufacturers develop responsiveness and an effective measure of control over the system as a whole.

Means for Developing Dealer Responsiveness

A number of techniques are used by manufacturers to induce independent dealers to respond to the manufacturers' wishes. The means used vary, depending upon the product and its marketing requirements. Some of the more common methods may be classified as monetary, advertising, dealer sales training, inventory protection, and other operational aids.

Monetary

Monetary inducements are given in the form of discounts larger than those of competitive manufacturers. By making possible a large gross margin to the dealer, it is assumed that he will give special attention to the manufacturer's line. But there are certain limitations to the use of this means to gain responsiveness. First, if the product is faced with intense price competition, the dealer may not be able to benefit from the wider margin, as the selling price must be reduced to meet competition. The discount given must be adjusted to the resale of the dealer if it is to be effective. Second, the granting of larger discounts can be easily copied by competitors. If this is a useful device for securing dealer cooperation, it is almost a certainty that competitors will do likewise. Third, even though the product is not facing intense price competition, some dealers may use the discount to compete on a price basis. The wider the gross margin, the more opportunity there is to do this. This generally causes some dissatisfaction on the part of other dealers, thus weakening the entire system.

There are other monetary payments made to dealers; however, they are for the purpose of getting the dealer to engage in specific activities, rather than payments to use any way he pleases.

Advertising

Manufacturers selling through dealers try to get the dealers to coordinate advertising efforts with their own. Thus, an integrated advertising message is communicated to potential buyers with the possibility of greater impact than if each advertises in his own way. To achieve this integration the manufacturer must induce the dealer to advertise in a manner consistent with the manufacturer's program.

If the dealer is not prone to spend much on advertising, the manufacturer may enter into an agreement with him to share the cost. This is known as *vertical cooperation advertising* and is discussed in Chapter 24, "Advertising Management and Evaluation I." Sometimes the manufacturer pays for the total cost of advertising but advertises over the dealer's name in media serving the dealer's trading area. If the dealer does advertise, the manufacturer places large advertisements in media serving the dealer's area, and through cooperation with the media tries to get the dealers to place smaller advertisements, featuring similar copy, at the same time. The manufacturer's large advertisement increases the impact of the dealer's smaller advertisement.

Regardless of what means are used to induce the dealer to advertise, there is a need to provide him with advertising layouts, mats, and point-of-purchase display materials. Making this material available may be enough to stimulate the dealer to advertise; however, its primary purpose is to insure an integrated advertising campaign stressing a common appeal throughout the system.

One form of sales promotion is the use of demonstrators to aid in the sale of products at the dealer level. In the cosmetic industry demonstrators are used widely to aid dealers' customers in the selection of appropriate cosmetics and also to perform the sales task for the dealer. In the food industry, demonstrators are used to prepare foods and to "sample" customers in the dealer's outlet.

Dealer Sales Training

The manufacturer views the dealer's sales force as an extension of his own sales organization and strives for efficient representation of the product at the dealer level. Many manufacturers conduct training programs for dealer salesmen to insure that the product receives the proper kind of sales representation. Much of the training program emphasizes improving product knowledge and providing the dealer salesmen with information of the product's points of superiority over competitive products. It is hoped that by providing the salesman with more knowledge, his natural inclination will be to stress those products with which he is most familiar. If the dealer is an exclusive agency not handling competitive products, the dealer training is useful in aiding the dealer's salesmen to compete with the salesmen of dealers handling competitive products.

Personal selling is just one of many means used in communicating with potential customers. By exercising some control over the methods of sales representation at the dealer level, the manufacturer is able to integrate the entire communications plan.

Closely associated with dealer training is the use of sales contests for dealer salesmen, to provide an incentive for increased sales volume. Some of the more

297

Conflict,
Cooperation,
and Manu-
facturer-
Dealer
Systems

common objectives of sales contests are: (1) to get specific selling jobs done in the hope that they will increase sales volume, (2) to offset seasonal sales declines, and (3) to spread effort over the entire line. Monetary or merchandise awards are usually given, with a preference for merchandise awards. Merchandise awards are useful in bringing family pressure to bear on the salesman to strive for the award and are a constant inspiration to increase efforts. The major disadvantage in the use of sales contests is that they sometimes lead to undesirable selling practices. Control through personal supervision by the dealer is needed to prevent this from happening.

Inventory Protection

The maintenance of adequate stocks at the dealer level is of vital importance to the manufacturer. Dealers, because of limited funds, perishability of merchandise, or desire for rapid turnover and cost reduction, have a tendency to carry thinner stocks than are desirable from the manufacturer's point of view. The manufacturer wishes a sufficient assortment to protect against lost sales arising from the dealer's being out of stock when consumer demand is strong.

If a dealer is not financially strong, special terms of sale may be given to provide time to sell some of his merchandise before payment must be made. In product lines with a marked seasonal demand, such as toys, payment is often deferred until the selling season begins. If the product is perishable, the dealer may tend to minimize inventory unless he is permitted to return stock after a certain period of time. The returned-goods privilege is a practice in the chocolate candy industry. Dealers may also hesitate to carry adequate inventories if prices are not stable. To compensate for this reluctance to carry adequate inventories, some manufacturers give guarantees against price declines by making rebates on stock on hand when prices drop.

Other Operational Aids

Because the manufacturer's success is tied to the success of the dealer, the manufacturer strives to improve the dealer as an independent businessman. Some of the means used include providing the dealer with: architectural designs for buildings, dealership layout plans, aid in setting up more accurate accounting systems, and market research data on products and the dealer's trading area.

FRANCHISE AGREEMENTS
AND THE LAW

As we have seen, there are certain advantages both to the dealer and the manufacturer in operating together in a system. Since such a system involves independent legal entities, the responsibilities of the parties are often negotiated and given legal sanction through contractual *franchise agreements*.

Two provisions frequently found in franchise agreements have been the source of much litigation. They are: (1) cancellation without cause, and (2) the one-year franchise. Many dealers have taken legal action against manufacturers for damages suffered because of cancellation. After spending considerable sums to develop a market in an area, cancellation results in a substantial loss of investment. The use of the one-year franchise, with the manufacturer holding the option to renew, causes a similar uncertainty and a potential loss to the dealer.

In the past, dealers have not been able to collect damages under these agreements. The courts have held closely to the concept of freedom of contract. They have viewed the relationship as one of vendor-vendee, and recognized the right of each party to stipulate conditions, even "improvident" conditions. The dealer has not been able to claim damages for actions by the manufacturer specifically covered by the contract.

There is, however, a belief that a mutuality of obligation does not exist, and that the manufacturer exercises considerably more control than would be normal in a vendor-vendee relationship. This is particularly true in one-year franchises or those with "cancellation without cause" clauses. The "freedom of contract" concept is still very influential in manufacturer-dealer litigation, but there is evidence that the courts have been following a more limiting approach. In some cases the dealer has been able to collect damages; however, these have been special-fact situations. In the automobile industry an attempt was made to solve the problem of unjust cancellation through the passage of the Automobile Dealers Franchise Act in 1956. The Act gives the dealer the right to contest a cancellation in court if he feels the manufacturer has not acted in good faith. Most interpretations have been special-fact situations and it does not appear that the Act has materially changed the law in the area of cancellations.

A much more limiting factor in the writing of franchise agreements is found in antitrust legislation. An exclusive-dealing franchise agreement generally states that the dealer will refrain from handling competing lines and that the manufacturer, in consideration for his products' being stocked by the dealer, agrees not to sell to competing dealers in a prescribed territory.

Exclusive-dealing arrangements are not illegal per se. However, under Section 3 of the Clayton Act, and under the Federal Trade Commission Act, they may be illegal "where the effect . . . may be to substantially lessen competition or tend to create a monopoly in any line of commerce." A rule of reason has been applied in most cases. However, in 1949 the Supreme Court ruled against Standard Oil of California, stating that its exclusive supply contracts were in violation of the antitrust law. Standard Oil entered into exclusive supply contracts with 5,937 independent stations, or 16 percent of their retail outlets, in the West. Dealers agreed to purchase from Standard Oil all of their requirements of one or more products. The court held that the contracts restricted distribution to competitors, thereby substantially lessening competition, and tended towards the establishment of a monopoly. The legality of the contract has a relationship to the seller's size and share of market enjoyed. In 1959 the Supreme Court declared Sun Oil Company's exclusive dealing practices illegal. In this case the company had no written agreements prohibiting dealers from carrying competitive products or requiring exclusive handling of Sun's products. They did, however, enforce this through minimum quantity purchase requirements, refunds to dealers on a progressive percentage scale based upon quantity of products purchased, and right of cancellation unless minimum sales requirements were met. Restriction of dealers to only the products of the manufacturer may be illegal regardless of whether it is expressed or implicit.

299

Conflict,
Cooperation,
and Manu-
facturer-
Dealer
Systems

Territorial security provisions—or giving, as an exclusive privilege, to a single distributor the right to sell the product in a defined geographic area—are not illegal, per se. Most cases have been handled on a special-fact basis. However, in 1967, the Supreme Court did stipulate circumstances under which exclusive territorial arrangements are legal. Arnold Schwinn & Co. sold bicycles to dealers on the Schwinn-Plan, whereby Schwinn sold on consignment to Schwinn-Plan dealers. As Schwinn retained title and assumed all of the risks pertaining to ownership, the dealers were agents, and the restrictions imposed would be illegal only if they were "unreasonably restrictive of competition." [3]

Summary

The effectiveness of the channel of distribution depends not only on the channel decided upon, but also on the implementation of the decision. That is, the participating enterprises that make up the channel must be carefully chosen, and directed in such a way that the whole becomes a coordinated and integrated total system of action.

Within any manufacturer-dealer system there are present elements of both cooperation and conflict. Also, there are primary and subordinate roles played by participants. The primary role normally is performed by the brand owner; this tends to establish the focus of power, authority, and decision within the system. Also, the system functions on the basis of a complex of rewards and penalties, and on a set of mutual expectations. The manufacturer expects the dealer to: (1) provide continuously aggressive selling effort, (2) conduct promotional programs to tie in with the manufacturer's advertising efforts, (3) provide full-line coverage, (4) maintain adequate inventory levels, (5) practice responsible pricing, (6) provide adequate parts service, and (7) maintain an adequate flow of market information.

The dealer expects the manufacturer to: (1) provide an attractive, salable, and competitive line, (2) develop a high level of consumer brand acceptance for the line, (3) provide fair and equitable margins, (4) make possible some degree of territorial trade protection, and (5) provide merchandising assistance.

These expectations are not fulfilled unless the manufacturer in his primary role makes special efforts to gain responsiveness from the dealer. The means used include: (1) monetary inducements in the form of discounts, (2) advertising aids, (3) dealer sales training, (4) inventory protection, and (5) a number of other operational aids, such as store layout suggestions, aid in setting up accounting systems, and specific market information.

When the relationship between the manufacturer and the dealer is expressed in writing, the document is known as a franchise agreement. Franchise agreements involve many legal implications; legal counsel is desirable for both the manufacturer and the dealer involved.

Questions and Problems

1. Describe what is meant by the phrase *a manufacturer-dealer system*.
2. Explain how one whole manufacturer-dealer system can be in competition

[3] United States v. Arnold Schwinn & Co., et al., 87 S. Ct., 1847 (June 1967).

with another. Give examples. What are the implications of this notion for competition? For antitrust policy?

3. What accounts for the elements of both conflict and cooperation within the system?

4. What determines who performs the primary and who the subordinate roles within the system? Does the manufacturer always play the same role? Does the dealer? Explain. Is it always the same over time in a single system?

5. "Whoever controls the market dominates the system." Explain and elaborate.

6. What expectations do dealers have of the manufacturer component in the system?

7. What kinds of penalties may be incurred when these expectations are not fulfilled?

8. Is it realistic for a dealer to expect that a manufacturer will limit the intensity of competition *within* the dealer component of the system? Does your view hold in all cases over all categories of goods? To what kinds of cases is this expectation most likely to apply? Does the amount of dealer investment have anything to do with the matter?

9. What are the expectations manufacturers commonly hold with regard to the dealer component of the system?

10. What penalties can be invoked when these expectations go unfulfilled? Are there any special rewards?

11. What is conveyed by attempting to make the subordinate participant "a responsive area of administrative action"? Why is this a problem?

12. What is meant by the "dependency level" within the system? Give examples. What implications follow from a high or low dependency level?

13. What means might a manufacturer employ in increasing the responsiveness of subordinate members in the system?

14. Must these means involve economic incentives or pressures to be effective? Does this problem differ between the short run and the long run?

15. How would you judge when the total system is performing effectively? Are there any specific criteria you might apply in making this judgment?

Distribution Structure Alternatives I: Retailing

18

This chapter examines the quantitative aspects of retail trade, the different methods of retailing, and the different classes of retailers.

Our interest in retailing is threefold. First, retailing is an important segment of our economy. In 1963, the last year for which complete data are available, retail sales amounted to $244.2 billion, or approximately 61 percent of personal disposable income. About 10,000,000 people, or 13.6 percent of the civilian labor force, were engaged in retailing. Second, although our discussion so far has dealt primarily with manufacturers, retailers as business enterprises must perform the same kinds of managerial functions. The determination of objectives, interpretation of market forces and opportunities, and the selection of profitable product assortments are equally important to retailers. Third, retailers as institutions within the distribution network are combined with other middlemen to form the channels of distribution. Selection of the channels of distribution is predicated on a knowledge of the operating characteristics of the different classes of intermediaries available.

THE EXTENT OF RETAIL TRADE

In 1963, the last complete census of business showed that retail trade amounted to $244.2 billion, conducted by 1.708 million establishments.[1] Comparing these figures with 1958, we see that retail trade increased by $43.8 billion, or

[1] In 1963, 8,410,199 employees and 1,545,999 active proprietors were engaged in retail trade of $244.201 billion: U.S. Bureau of the Census, *U.S. Census of Business: 1963, Retail Trade, United States Summary* (Washington, D.C.: Government Printing Office, 1966). Estimate of personal disposable income for 1963 was $402.5 billion. Estimate of the civilian labor force 72,975,000: U.S. Bureau of the Census, *Statistical Abstract of the United States: 1965* (Washington, D.C.: Government Printing office, 1965).

21.9 percent. Adjusting for inflation, the *real* increase was $29.9 billion, or 15.0 percent.[2] This means that there was an increase of 15.0 percent in the volume of goods moved through the retail structure. Adjusted for population increases, the *net* increase in retail trade between 1958 and 1963 was 6.2 percent.[3] That is, consumer participation in retail trade increased 6.2 percent; the remainder of the 15.0 percent real increase is explained by population growth. To accommodate the real increase in retail sales, the number of establishments decreased from 1,794,744 in 1958 to 1,707,931 in 1963. The decrease noted is not evenly dispersed geographically or for retailers engaged in different kinds of business.

Retail Sales by Geographic Location

There are great regional differences in retail sales. Table 18-1 shows retail sales adjusted for inflation and population change and the number of retail establishments for 1958 and 1963 by geographic location. How can these data be used from a marketing standpoint? They may be the starting point in developing market potentials so important in determining the direction of marketing activity and in measuring performance.

Geographic differences in retail sales are largely a result of differences in population and purchasing power. Manufacturers of consumer goods may use these data in determining the geographic areas of greatest opportunity. For example, Table 18-1 shows that four divisions, South Atlantic, East South Central, Pacific, and Mountain, have had large increases in retail sales. One of them, the East South Central division, shows greater participation in retail sales by consumers than increases resulting from population growth. The real increases in retail sales in the Pacific and Mountain divisions has occurred more because of population growth. However, both the Mountain and Pacific divisions are high-quality markets in terms of purchasing power, with adjusted retail sales per capita of over $1,250 in each.

Changes in the number of retail establishments may indicate areas of under- or over-expansion in the retail structure. The four divisions with the greatest increase in retail sales had actual increases in the number of retail establishments, while the other five divisions experienced decreases. This may indicate that the retail structure has kept pace with both the growth in population and increased trade by increased efficiency. It might also indicate conditions of under- or over-expansion, but this can be determined only by examining each kind of business.

None of these suggestions could be accepted without rather detailed analysis. For example, it is necessary to look at absolute figures as well as relative figures. It may be that a high percentage growth does not indicate a real opportunity if the division started from a low base. The East South Central division has a real increase in retail sales of 18.6 percent, with 10.4 percent of this

---

[2] The data were deflated by applying the Retail Price Index published in the *Statistical Abstract of the United States: 1965* (Washington, D.C.: Government Printing Office, 1965). For the year 1958 this index was 100.7 and for 1963, 106.7 (1957–1959 = 100).

[3] The adjustment for population increase was made by calculating the percent increase in per capita sales. Per capita retail sales in 1958 were $1,142 and $1,213 in 1963.

TABLE 18-1

Real and Net Increases in Retail Sales and Retail Establishments by Geographic Divisions, 1958 and 1963

Geographic Division	Retail Sales (in Million Dollars)			Adjusted Retail Sales[a] (in Million Dollars)			Per Capita Adjusted[b] Retail Sales			Number of Establishments (in Thousands)		
	1958	1963	Percentage Change	1958	1963	Percentage Change	1958	1963	Percentage Change	1958	1963	Percentage Change
New England	12,452	15,088	21.2	12,365	14,137	14.3	$1,210	$1,292	6.8	112.7	102.7	−8.8
Middle Atlantic	40,390	46,948	16.2	40,107	43,990	9.7	1,196	1,233	3.1	372.4	336.7	−9.6
East North Central	42,177	50,611	19.9	41,882	47,423	13.3	1,177	1,273	8.2	355.5	333.7	−6.1
West North Central	18,207	21,054	15.6	18,080	19,728	9.1	1,206	1,259	4.4	174.0	158.3	−9.0
South Atlantic	25,493	32,365	26.9	25,315	30,326	19.8	1,011	1,092	8.0	237.3	239.2	0.8
East South Central	9,829	12,351	25.6	9,760	11,573	18.6	836	923	10.4	108.0	111.6	2.3
West South Central	17,670	20,991	18.8	17,546	19,669	12.1	1,070	1,094	2.2	174.5	162.2	−6.9
Mountain	7,924	10,147	28.1	7,869	9,508	20.8	1,213	1,266	4.4	66.9	69.2	3.6
Pacific	26,222	34,646	32.1	26,038	32,463	24.7	1,289	1,394	8.1	193.4	194.3	0.5
Total	200,365	244,202	21.9	198,962	228,817	15.0	1,142	1,213	6.2	1,794.7	1,707.9	−4.8

[a] See p. 302, footnote 2.
[b] See p. 302, footnote 3.

Source: U.S. Bureau of the Census, U.S. Census of Business: 1963, Retail Trade, U.S. Summary Vol. I, Part 1.

TABLE 18-2

Methods of Retailing, 1958 and 1963

Method of Retailing	Number of Establishments (in Thousands)				Retail Sales (in Thousands)			
	1958	Percentage	1963	Percentage	1958	Percentage	1963	Percentage
Mail-order houses	2,550	00.1	4,206	00.2	1,986,168	01.0	2,378,534	00.9
Vending machine operators	8,152	00.4	9,363	00.5	841,523	00.4	1,452,407	00.6
Direct (house-to-house selling)	63,977 *	03.5	66,223 *	3.3	2,573,622	01.3	2,372,703	00.9
Retail establishments	1,720,065	96.0	1,628,139	96.0	194,963,365	97.3	237,998,133	97.6
Total	1,794,744	100.0	1,707,931	100.0	200,364,678	100.0	244,201,777	100.0

* Many organizations engaged in house-to-house selling use "self-employed" canvassers. Each canvasser is counted as an establishment.

Compiled from: U.S. Bureau of the Census, U.S. Census of Business: 1963, Retail Trade, U.S. Summary Vol. I, Part 1.

increase accounted for by increased consumer participation in retail sales. A look at the absolute figures shows that this division in 1958 and 1963 had the lowest adjusted retail sales per capita of all divisions. Although the relative change is great, it does not possess the same magnitude of opportunity for many marketers as other areas. Review of these data simply pinpoints areas for further analysis.

Another important facet of the geographic location of retail sales relates to the variation of retail sales in the metropolitan centers from those of the rest of the country. The Bureau of the Census has established 217 standard metropolitan areas. These centers account for 69.5 percent of total retail sales. There has been a tendency for national manufacturers of consumer goods to be overly concerned with uniform national distribution of their products. A policy which concentrates marketing effort in the 217 metropolitan centers accounting for approximately 70 percent of all retail sales has much to commend it for certain marketers. The major increment of effort required to cater to the other 30 percent may not be profitable.

Retail Sales by Kind of Business

When differences between the rates of change taking place in both retail sales and retail establishments are analyzed by kind of business, further insights are gained concerning the way in which the retail structure is developing. Table 18-3 shows real increases in retail sales and establishments by kind of business. In certain product lines much of the sales increase was absorbed by existing establishments, with corresponding increases in sales per establishment, and in other lines by a growth in the number of establishments.

Most of the increases in retail sales were accomplished by increased efficiency. In the general merchandise, food, apparel, furniture, eating and drinking places and drug categories, gains of 28.9 percent, 9.4 per cent, 5.4 percent, 2.0 percent, 13.6 percent, and 17.7 percent, respectively, were achieved with decreases in the number of establishments. In every case there was an increase in sales per establishment. In the general merchandise category there was the greatest decrease in number of establishments—39.5 percent—and the largest increase in sales per establishment, 79.7 percent. The large increase in this business category would call for further investigation to determine if the field was underdeveloped.

In summary, analyses of retail trade change by geographic regions and by product lines may reveal substantial variations in market opportunities for expansion in outlets.

METHODS OF RETAILING

Retailing is the act of engaging in transactions in which the items are purchased for personal or household consumption. We normally think of retailing transactions as being performed by retailers; however, retailing is not confined just to retailers, who maintain establishments solely for this purpose. Table 18-2

TABLE 18-3

Real Increases in Retail Sales and Retail
Establishments by Kind of Business, 1958 and 1963

	RETAIL SALES (IN MILLION DOLLARS)			ADJUSTED RETAIL SALES[a] (IN MILLION DOLLARS)			NUMBER OF ESTABLISHMENTS (IN THOUSANDS)			ADJUSTED SALES PER ESTABLISHMENT (IN THOUSANDS)		
	1958	1963	Percentage Change	1958	1963	Percentage Change	1958	1963	Percentage Change	1958	1963	Percentage Change
Lumber, building materials, hardware, farm equipment dealers	$ 14,326	$ 14,606	2.0	$ 14,226	$ 13,686	−3.8	108.4	92.7	−15.9	131.2	147.6	12.5
General merchandise group	21,971	30,003	36.6	21,818	28,113	28.9	86.6	62.1	−39.5	251.9	452.7	79.7
Food stores	49,225	57,079	16.0	48,880	53,483	9.4	356.8	319.4	−11.7	137.0	167.4	22.2
Automotive dealers	31,905	45,376	42.2	31,682	42,517	34.2	93.9	98.5	4.6	337.4	431.6	27.9
Gasoline service stations	14,228	17,760	24.8	14,128	16,641	17.8	206.8	211.5	2.2	68.3	78.7	15.2
Apparel, accessory stores	12,569	14,040	11.7	12,481	13,155	5.4	119.3	116.2	−2.7	104.6	113.2	8.2
Furniture, home furnishings equipment stores	10,110	10,926	8.1	10,039	10,238	2.0	103.8	93.6	−10.8	96.7	109.3	13.0
Eating and drinking places	15,290	18,412	20.4	15,183	17,252	13.6	346.3	334.5	−3.5	43.8	51.6	17.8
Drugstores, proprietary stores	6,803	8,487	24.7	6,755	7,952	17.7	56.4	54.7	−3.1	119.8	145.4	21.4
Other retail stores	18,525	21,309	15.0	18,395	19,967	8.5	241.4	244.9	1.5	76.3	81.5	6.8
Nonstore retailers	5,413	6,204	14.6	5,375	5,813	8.1	75.0	79.8	6.0	71.7	72.8	1.5
Total	$200,365	$244,202	21.9	$198,962	$228,817	15.0	1,794.7	1,707.9	−4.8	110.9	134.0	20.8

a See p. 302, footnote 2.

Compiled from: U.S. Bureau of the Census, U.S. Census of Business: 1963, Retail Trade, United States Summary Vol. I, Part 1.

shows different methods of retailing, and indicates the imporance of each. Selling through retail stores is the most important, but the other methods warrant examination.

Mail-order Retailing

Mail-order houses are "establishments primarily engaged in distributing merchandise through the mail as a result of mail orders received." [4] They are classified as *general merchandise* houses, offering a variety of merchandise with wide assortments in each product class. The two most important examples of this type of establishment are Sears Roebuck and Montgomery Ward. In fact, excluding these two leading companies, the sales volume of mail-order houses is negligible. Forty-six companies, or approximately 1 percent of mail-order establishments, have sales of over $5 million annually and account for 54 percent of all mail-order sales.[5]

A number of *specialty* houses also exist. These concerns offer by mail narrow lines of products. Some of the more common lines handled are tobacco products, records, books, farm and garden supplies, novelties, and souvenirs. A third type comprises the manufacturers or producers who sell direct by mail. In the former category are manufacturers of men's and women's apparel and furniture. In the latter are agricultural producers, notably of citrus fruits, maple syrup, and cheese.

Characteristic of all mail-order houses is the need to spend large sums in direct-mail advertising or in the preparation and distribution of catalogs. The latter have become excessively costly for the larger mail-order houses. It is estimated that it costs from $2.50 to $3.00 to place a general merchandise catalog in a household. Other costs, however, are not as high as in the more traditional forms of retail establishments. Facilities are not as elaborate, and most transportation is paid for by the customer. Most mail-order warehouses are highly systematized, and low-cost labor can be used to perform routine services. Mail-order house operating costs are not comparable with other forms of retailing, since they generally include performance of the wholesale function as well.

As Table 18-2 shows, the number of establishments has increased approximately 65 percent between 1958 and 1963. The increase in mail-order retail sales was approximately 20 percent. The general merchandise houses have established catalog sales offices in practically all population centers, have established physical distribution centers to speed delivery, and have added the convenience of telephone order service. In spite of these cost-increasing additions, some houses, through expert merchandising, offer excellent merchandise at reduced prices. Specialty houses will probably continue to serve highly specialized segments of the market with unusual merchandise available through no other source.

[4] *U.S. Census of Business: 1963, Retail Trade, United States Summary,* Vol. I, Part 1, 1–8.

[5] *Ibid.,* pp. 2–46.

Vending Machines

Vending machine "operators" are "establishments primarily engaged in the sale of merchandise through coin-operated vending machines which generally are located on the premises of other businesses." [6] Although there has been an absolute change in the number of establishments and retail sales between 1958 and 1963, their proportion of total retail trade has not changed significantly. Establishments and retail sales amounted to approximately .5 percent of total establishments and sales in 1963, and .4 percent in 1958. Actually, the census data do not reflect the total magnitude of retail sales through vending machines. A large number of vending machines are operated in conjunction with the operations of manufacturing plants and wholesale establishments not included in retail trade. Also, the data do not include sales through vending machines owned by retailers included elsewhere in retail trade.

The use of vending machines for in-plant meals has experienced tremendous growth in the last few years. Thirty-two percent of all vended sales in 1964 took place in factories ($1,118,080,000).[7] Conservative estimates of retail sales are approximately $3.5 billion for 1964, a gain of 9 percent over 1963 and nearly double the 1954 volume.[8]

The gains made in the last few years have caused some to believe that vending machines will revolutionize marketing. But many observers believe that there are certain limitations to the use of vending machines. At first it was believed that they were limited to the sale of merchandise under one dollar, as the machines could not accept paper money. However, in 1959 dollar-bill changers were developed which check bills for authenticity, and make change. Vending machines were also once limited to handling nonperishable commodities, small in size and weight, with a high frequency of purchase and wide consumer acceptance. The perishability of the product is less of a limiting factor today. Technological developments in machine design have expanded their use to milk, ice cream, hot canned foods, frozen foods and juices, and pastry. In 1964 coffee was estimated to account for $268.9 million, ice cream $29.7 million, hot canned foods $28.6 million, and milk $81.9 million in vending sales.[9] There is evidence, however, that the product characteristics mentioned above, other than non-perishability, are still important in delineating the potential application of vending machines.

All in all, there is little prospect that vending machines will revolutionize marketing. Although the limitation in the use of bills has been overcome and some of the technological difficulties removed, the desire and need of customers for inspection of the merchandise and for personal selling in many product categories are definite limitations. Only items which have a mass market, wide con-

---

[6] *U.S. Census of Business: 1963, Retail Trade, United States Summary,* Vol. I, Part 1. Appendix, 10.

[7] *Vending in 1964,* National Automatic Merchandising Association, p. 3.

[8] *Ibid.,* pp. 1–2.

[9] *Ibid.,* p. 5.

sumer acceptance, low unit value, and high frequency of purchase will be successfully sold by machines.

Very few vending machine operators have costs below 38 percent; some costs run as high as 45 percent.[10] Unless a large volume can be maintained, costs are prohibitive. Sales will probably increase through extended applications in already acceptable products. The industry is currently experimenting with wider use of machines in supermarket parking lots and in apartment houses. This, along with the increase in in-plant food-vending installations, appears as the most profitable direction for vending machine expansion.

Direct (House-to-house) Selling

Direct (house-to-house) selling organizations are those "which solicit orders and distribute their products by house-to-house canvas."[11] Table 18-2 shows that, numerically, direct selling organizations are the most important type of nonstore retailer. Retail sales for this type of operation amounted to approximately 1 percent of all retail trade in 1963. The data on the number of establishments, however, are misleading. Many organizations use self-employed canvassers, and each canvasser is counted as an "establishment." In 1958 it was estimated that there were about 3,000 companies engaged in direct (house-to-house) selling.[12] A large proportion, 23.5 percent, of the $2.4 billion in sales, is accounted for by 0.4 percent of the organizations.[13] The remainder is accounted for by a large number of very small concerns.

We are all familiar with the many classes of products sold on a house-to-house basis. Some of the most famous direct selling companies are the Fuller Brush Company, Electrolux, Avon, Jewel Tea, and Stanley Home Products. However, a wide variety of other products are sold in this way. Storm doors and windows, water softeners, magazine subscriptions, nursery stock, cooking ware, and many food products are available on this basis. Direct selling organizations are not confined to manufacturers engaging in this form of retailing.

The success of direct selling depends on cost-revenue conditions. On the cost side, the absence of retail facilities is a large cost-reducing factor. On the other hand, motivation of the canvasser is thought to be an important element in the success of this type of operation. Monetary rewards are the main stimulus, with commissions averaging 40 percent, and supervision costing another 7 percent.[14] Although very little is spent for advertising or other forms of promotion, 47 percent is a very high sales-cost ratio. When delivery costs are added to this percentage along with the costs of recruiting, selecting, and training sales personnel, the total costs are very high. In fact, direct selling is the costliest form of retailing.

[10] *Vending in 1964,* National Automatic Merchandising Association, p. 5.

[11] *U.S. Census of Business: 1963, Retail Trade, U.S. Summary,* Vol. I, Part 1, Appendix, 10.

[12] See "Golden Doorbells," *Printers' Ink* (August 29, 1958), p. 55.

[13] *U.S. Census of Business: 1963, Retail Trade, U.S. Summary,* Vol. I, Part 1, 2–47.

[14] See Faye Henle's "Doorbell Pushers," *Barron's* (March 10, 1958), p. 5ff.

On the advantage side, direct selling provides the opportunity for perhaps the most aggressive form of retail market cultivation. The ability to demonstrate the product in the consumer's home, along with the added convenience of home buying and delivery, provides a real advantage. Exposure to sale does not depend on customers' visits to a retail store but on the number of calls made by the sales force. Fuller Brush Company representatives aim for ten calls an hour and fifty a day.[15]

Whether or not a favorable cost-revenue relationship can be established depends on the kinds of products offered. Because of the high cost, direct selling is limited to products with high gross margins; if products are of low unit value, a broad line is necessary over which to spread these costs. Over the years the Fuller Brush Company has added cosmetics to its line. Contrary to the belief of many consumers that elimination of middlemen results in lower prices, most goods sold on a house-to-house basis are more expensive than those moving through other kinds of retail establishments, although it is not possible to make price comparisons easily, as identical items usually are not offered in directly competing retail stores. House-to-house selling is generally limited to products that require demonstration or are purchased in this way purely for convenience. In the former case, success depends a great deal on the skill, ingenuity, and technique used in product demonstration. The "party plan," whereby the salesman arranges with a potential customer to give a party to which a number of friends are invited, is illustrative of a very successful method.

There are some definite limitations to direct selling, even when products appropriate to this method of distribution are offered. Maintaining a sales organization is a very real problem; annual turnover of salesmen among the sales force may run as high as 300 percent.[16] Oddly enough, direct selling organizations have their most difficult times during periods of prosperity. When the number of attractive job opportunities are great, the sales force is weakened. During periods of recession, it is much easier to maintain an efficient sales organization. Also, the aggressiveness that this form of retailing permits, seems to enable such organizations to fare better than other kinds of retailers during recessions.

Another limitation to direct selling is the enactment of "Green River Ordinances" by a number of municipalities. In 1933 Green River, Wyoming, enacted an ordinance which prohibited house-to-house solicitation except by permission or at the invitation of the householder. Since that time a number of other cities have enacted similar ordinances. This, of course, limits to some extent the markets in which direct selling organizations can operate.

Finally, direct selling in many ways has acquired a bad reputation. Over the years unscrupulous operators, selling low quality merchandise, have done much harm. A single unfavorable experience with this type of distribution makes the customer wary of even the most reputable organizations.

Direct (house-to-house) selling will continue to be an important type of retail operation. It provides a desired channel for aggressive selling. Frequently,

[15] "Golden Doorbells," pp. 55–56.
[16] Henle, "Doorbell Pushers."

it is the only course of action open to a manufacturer who is unable to gain distribution through the usual outlets. However, it is doubtful if direct selling will significantly increase its share of total retail trade.

CLASSES OF RETAILERS

Table 18-2 shows that retailing through retail establishments is the most important method of retailing, accounting for 97.6 percent of total trade in 1963. There are many different classes and types of retailers. Three broad classifications are based on: (1) product assortment offered, (2) ownership, and (3) sales volume size. Many different types of retailers exist within each of these classes.

Product Assortment Offered

Before proceeding to classify retailers on a product assortment basis, it is necessary to define more sharply two terms—*variety* and *assortment*. *Variety* refers to the range of products within a related merchandise line. That is, men's shoes, shirts, and suits make up a related merchandise line in men's clothing. *Variety* may also refer to a conglomeration of products with no natural association in use or purchase—furniture, food, and clothing, for example. *Assortment* refers to the range of choice in a specific product. For example, if men's shirts are offered in eight colors and seven sizes, a more extensive assortment is offered than if only one color and four sizes are made available. Using these two terms, we shall differentiate between different types of retailers.[17]

General Store

A general store is a nondepartmentalized store offering a wide variety of merchandise lines with no natural association and with limited assortments. That is, they offer foods, men's and women's clothing, hardware, and furniture. Each line has variety within it, but there is no association among the merchandise lines. The general store was one of the earliest types of retailers in the United States. With rather thin concentrations of population in earlier years, it was necessary to offer a wide range of merchandise to increase the average sale to each potential customer.

General stores are still found in rural areas or on the fringes of cities, but their numbers have been declining rapidly. Much of the decline may be accounted for by differences in definitions used by the different censuses. However, there has been a marked decrease in the number of such establishments. The growth of cities and improvements in transportation have been responsible for this decline. As population densities increase, it is possible to reduce the variety of goods offered and to specialize in those remaining.

Over the last few years, the tendency of supermarkets and drugstores to

---

[17] The use of *variety* and *assortment* to classify retailers has also been used by Professors Maynard and Beckman. See Harold H. Maynard, Theodore N. Beckman, and William R. Davidson, *Principles of Marketing*, 6th ed. (New York: The Ronald Press Company, 1957).

offer a wide variety of products with little or no natural association has caused many such stores to resemble general stores. The major difference is that supermarkets and drugstores still do the major share of their business in a single merchandise line. Also, there is considerable difference in managerial skill. The general store is traditionally owner-operated, with no departmental organization.

Limited-line Store

A limited-line store offers a wide variety in a single related merchandise line with extensive assortments. Food stores—combining meats, dairy, dry groceries, and produce—and men's and ladies' clothing stores and shoe stores are representative of this type. The growth of this type of retail outlet was dependent upon sufficient concentrations of population to support the narrower line. Today the limited-line store is the most important type of retailer in the United States. For the most part, limited-line stores rely on personalized service and superior locations for competitive advantage. Most are owner-operated, are not departmentalized, and, in general, do not have as high a level of managerial skill as some of the other types of establishments.

Of special importance in limited-line stores is the development of the *supermarket,* defined by the Super Market Institute as a "complete, departmentalized food store with a minimum sales volume of one million dollars a year and at least the grocery department fully self-service." [18] *Super Market Merchandising* defines a supermarket as "a departmentalized retail establishment having four basic departments—self-service grocery, meat, produce, and dairy—with total minimum sales of $500,000 yearly.[19]

Although most supermarkets are large, method of operation is the most distinguishing characteristic. Supermarkets usually handle groceries, meats, dairy, and produce on a self-service basis. Grocery departments often include as many as 5,000 different items. In the last 15 years bakery departments, health and beauty aids, housewares, beer, wine, and liquor have been added to the product mix.

In the early years of the supermarket industry, price was the major customer appeal. Reduced operating costs through self-service and high turnover were used to reduce gross margins. Unit profits were small but increased sales volume provided satisfactory absolute dollar profits and usually a high return on invested capital. As the success of this method of operation was demonstrated, more and more companies followed, until today a large proportion of food retailing is done through this kind of outlet. It is estimated that supermarkets comprise 4.5 percent of all food stores and do 46.4 percent of the food business.[20]

A very intense competition has developed among supermarkets, in the form of improved facilities and services, such as spacious, well-lighted, expen-

[18] Super Market Institute, *The Super Market Industry Speaks,* 1961, p. 3.
[19] "The True Look of the Super Market Industry, 1959," *Super Market Merchandising* (May 1960), p. 74.
[20] Estimates based on the assumption that food stores with sales of $1 million and over are supermarkets. See *U.S. Census of Business: 1963, Retail Trade, U.S. Summary,* Vol. I, Part 1, 2–6.

sively equipped outlets, with extensive parking facilities, and porter service, check cashing, and an increase in the number of shopping hours. All these competitive services have increased costs and minimized the opportunity to continue to operate solely on a price basis. Nevertheless, the supermarket industry has managed, through the addition of higher-margin nonfood lines and careful merchandising, to maintain its average markup and still offer the customer value in the essential food items. In 1960 the typical gross margin was 18.64 percent and typical operating expenses were 17.12 percent, with an average 1.52 percent net operating profit before taxes.[21]

A question that has frequently been raised is whether the supermarket industry will continue to acquire a larger share of the food retailing dollar. Some observers believe that there are two forces at work which may place the supermarket in a very precarious position in the near future. One observer has suggested that there may be a shopper revolt against self-service. When hidden costs of a trip to a modern supermarket are considered, it is doubtful that the price differential is substantially below the traditional service outlet of years ago.[22]

The lower net profit of the supermarket (for some of the largest companies it is barely 1.0 percent of sales) places this industry in a very vulnerable position should a new form of competition develop. Some department stores and large discount chains have entered the food field. Today the supermarket uses staple food items to build traffic, and maintains its margin through nonfoods. However, the newer competitors in foods use the entire supermarket complex as a traffic booster. The low net profits supermarkets make will not enable them to match price cut for price cut. The department store can often undersell the food outlet on most nonfood items.[23] In all probability the supermarket industry will find ways and means to adjust to changing conditions produced by competitors and the buying public.

Specialty Store

Specialty stores offer a limited variety within a single merchandise line with very extensive assortments. Shoe, shirt, hosiery, tie, and candy stores are representative. They select one major product and usually a few subsidiary products within a merchandise line. For example, a shoe store's major product is shoes, a product within the clothing line. Usually hosiery, handbags, etc., will also be handled. Such stores are most often found only in the denser shopping districts, as they must rely on extensive patronage to support the narrow line. Generally they have high-cost locations and rely more on advertising and other sales promotion means to increase volume than do limited-line stores. On the other hand, the narrow line does allow more specialized management.

---

[21] Super Market Institute, *Super Market Industry Speaks,* p. 11.

[22] Lecture given by Helen Conoyer, Dean, New York State College of Home Economics, cited in E. B. Weiss, *Planning Merchandising Strategy for 1961–1965* (New York: Doyle, Dane, Bernbach, Inc.). This publication is out of print and is no longer available from the publisher. Also, Colston E. Warne, "The High Cost of the Supermarket Revolution," *The Magazine of Economic Affairs* (November–December 1966), pp. 8–11.

[23] *Conoyer,* in Weiss, *Planning Merchandising Strategy,* pp. 37–38.

Departmental Specialty Store

A departmentalized store offers a wide variety within a single merchandise line, with extensive assortments. Men's and ladies' clothing stores in the larger cities are examples. They are organized on a departmental basis with a shoe department, dress department, fur department, etc. Departmentalized specialty stores are large organizations and, consequently, are able to take advantage of specialized management and buying power. They often establish excellent reputations and tend to be regarded as prestige stores for fashion merchandise.

Department Stores

Department stores offer a wide variety within related merchandise lines with no natural association, but are so departmentalized that each department resembles a limited line or specialty store. They differ from departmentalized specialty stores in that they are usually much larger and carry unrelated merchandise lines (such as home furnishings, clothing, jewelry, hardware, and foods). Because the practice of leased departments is common, all departments may not be under single ownership. Although leased departments are used in a number of different classes of retail establishments, they are primarily associated with department and departmentalized specialty stores.

Leased departments are generally found in such lines as shoes, food, furs, books, restaurants, beauty parlors, and optical goods. They are attractive to department store operators because they (1) allow the addition of new lines with minimum capital, (2) provide additional services for attracting patronage, (3) utilize excess selling space profitably, and (4) minimize the need for highly specialized management in such lines as optical goods, furs, and oriental carpets. The lessee benefits from the carry-over of prestige of the store to the leased department and also from the operating services of the store, such as credit, delivery, and promotion at a negotiated lease fee.

Size, along with breadth of variety and assortment, are the characteristics of the department store. The Bureau of the Census defines a department store as follows: [24]

> Establishments normally employing 25 or more people and engaged in selling some items in each of the following lines of merchandising:
>
> 1. Furniture, home furnishings, appliances, and radio and television sets.
>
> 2. A general line of apparel for the family.
>
> 3. Household linen and dry goods.
>
> An establishment with total annual sales of less than $5 million, in which sales in any one of these groupings is greater than 80 percent of total sales, is not classified as a department store.
>
> An establishment with total sales of $5 million or more is classified as a department store even if sales of one of the groups described above is more than 80 percent of total sales, provided that the combined sales of the other two groups total $500,000 or more.

[24] *U.S. Census of Business: 1963, Retail Trade, U.S. Summary,* Vol. I, Part 1, Appendix, 4.

In 1963 there were 4,251 department stores, or 0.25 percent of total retail establishments. Retail sales were $20.5 billion, over $4.8 million per establishment, representing 8.4 percent of total retail trade.[25] In 1958 they represented 0.17 percent of total retail establishments, and did 6.6 percent of the retail trade with an average sale per establishment of over $4 million.[26] Most stores in the department store field are large. Approximately 25 percent of the 4,251 establishments had sales of $5 million or over and accounted for 70 percent of total department store sales.[27]

The department store is a result of the development of large cities. Some of the best-known names in retailing—J.L. Hudson Company, Marshall Field and Company, Richs, and R.H. Macy and Company, for instance—are all located in large metropolitan centers, and are an integral part of these cities, perhaps even the hub of the downtown shopping district. This historical development in the downtown shopping district has created problems for them. They have large investments in land and facilities, which are taxed at high rates.[28] The disintegration of the downtown shopping district, caused by the movement to the suburbs and by overcrowded parking conditions, has made it very difficult for the department store to maintain its position on its home ground. In effect the department store has lost its accessibility to the customer. This is evidenced in the decreasing share of both retail sales and the department store's share of particular merchandise lines. An extensive study covering the period 1929 to 1953 concluded as follows: [29]

> Although department stores improved their competitive position in 31 lines, they still lost overall relative position, simply because they increased their share of the market largely in lines for which consumers are spending proportionately less. Conversely, lines in which department stores have been receiving a smaller or comparatively stationary share of the market are those for which consumer expenditures have been expanding.

Department stores have used many means to overcome this shortcoming in location, such as improved parking facilities, tie-in arrangements with public transportation companies, and extended night openings. The most significant means used, however, is the operation of *branch stores*.

The inaccessibility of downtown locations to suburban customers, and competitive inroads made by limited-line and departmentalized specialty stores in suburban locations, have caused department stores to follow their markets. Branch stores are located in shopping centers in the secondary shopping districts of large cities, or in summer and winter resorts. They are controlled by the parent

[25] *Ibid.,* pp. 1–6.
[26] *Ibid.,* pp. 1–6.
[27] *Ibid.,* pp. 2–20.
[28] For a more detailed discussion of this problem, see C. Virgil Martin, "The Department Stores and Downtown," *Proceedings of the Thirty-First Annual Boston Conference on Distribution,* October 19–20, 1959, p. 74.
[29] *Adaptive Behavior in Marketing,* ed., Robert D. Buzzell (Columbus, Ohio: Modern Art Publishing Co., for the American Marketing Association, 1957), pp. 206–29, as cited in Stanley C. Hollander, *Explorations in Retailing,* Bureau of Business and Economic Research, M.S.U. Business Studies, 1959 (East Lansing, Mich.: College of Business and Public Service, Michigan State University, 1959), p. 25.

store, and have little or no autonomy in management. Generally speaking, merchandise lines are adjusted to the needs of the suburban markets they serve and are not as broad as those found in the downtown stores.

Little data are available on the proportion of sales volume done by branch stores. In 1959 Carson Pirie Scott and Company of Chicago did 32 percent of its total dollar volume in branch locations.[30]

The movement to branch store operations was inevitable for the department store. In all likelihood this movement will continue as our cities expand.

Department stores have long had high operating costs. They offer a broad range of services, such as delivery, personal selling, liberal adjustment policies, and credit. They usually provide auditoriums used by community groups, and rest rooms, information bureaus, and children's playrooms. All these services, in addition to the other means used to improve the competitive position of the downtown store, result in high operating cost ratios.

In spite of the difficulties department stores have been experiencing in the past few years, they are a vital, dynamic element in retailing. Although they do not account for a large proportion of the total retail trade, they have led retailers in a number of important developments. One department store executive expresses this role as follows: [31]

> There is quite a contrast between the way a department store is viewed by the pseudoscientific analyst . . . and its own retail competitors. It has become a fad or fashion of the former to picture the department store as a frozen, inflexible, high cost and near obsolete form of distribution. On the other hand, every form of retail competition is (*a*) endeavoring to get a location near a department store to share in its security and (*b*) endeavoring to become more like a department store in operating techniques.

The advantages of convenience in shopping and specialization in operation have not been long lived. Credit, long a standby of the department store, has been adopted by many nonservice retailers. Specialization in product lines, along with wide price differentials, has declined in the last few years. Many specialty stores have broadened their lines and traded up facilities, and are offering more service. Still the department store should continue as a dominant force in retailing.

Discount Store

A variation in the department store is the emergence of a store known as a *discount store*. A discount store is defined as a "departmentalized retail establishment utilizing many self-service techniques to sell . . . general merchandise. It operates at uniquely low margins. It has a minimum annual volume of $500,000, and is at least 10,000 square feet in size." [32]

A study revealed that in 1965 (compared to 1964): (1) sales increased 22 percent, (2) the net number of stores increased to 3,216, from 2,951; (3) they

---

[30] Martin, "The Department Stores and Downtown," p. 73.

[31] B. Earl Puckett, "The Department Store—A Look Ahead," in *Proceedings of the Thirty-First Annual Boston Conference on Distribution,* October 19–20, 1959, p. 69.

[32] "The True Look at the Discount Industry," *The Discount Merchandiser* (June 1966), pp. 35–82.

accounted for 9.8 percent of general merchandise sales, (including food); (4) the average discount store had 63,539 square feet and an annual volume of $4,089,000; (5) there was a discount store for every 17,944 households in the nation; (6) women's wear had become the major factor in discounters' sales; and (7) food sales in discount stores represented 7.6 percent of total supermarket sales.[33]

Variety Stores

Variety stores offer a wide variety of low-priced goods with no natural association but with extensive assortments. The Bureau of the Census defines a variety store as follows: [34]

> Establishments primarily selling a variety of merchandise in the low and popular price ranges, such as stationery, gift items, women's accessories, toilet articles, light hardware, toys, housewares, confectionary. These establishments are frequently known as "5 and 10 cent" stores and "5 cents to a dollar" stores, although merchandise is usually sold outside these price ranges.

In 1958 there were 21,017 variety stores, representing 1.1 percent of total establishments and accounting for $3.6 billion, or 1.8 percent of total retail trade. By 1963 there were 22,378 such stores, representing 1.3 percent of total establishments. They did a sales volume of $4.5 billion, or 1.9 percent of total retail trade.[35] The familiar S. S. Kresge Company and F. W. Woolworth Company stores are representative of this group.

The variety stores are confronted with problems similar to those of the department stores in their downtown locations, and have also joined the movement to the suburbs. Another trend in this type of outlet is the tendency to trade up the price level of merchandise offered. Many have added such high-priced items as lawn mowers, outboard motors, and power tools. Some have experimented with credit policies. The term *junior department store* has been coined to describe those stores that have traded up their offerings. The "5 and 10 cent" store has long been characteristic of the American retailing scene, and will continue to be so.

Ownership

A retail store is classified as a single unit "if it is operated by a firm which operates only one establishment in a particular kind of business group," and as a multiunit "if it is one of two or more establishments in the same general kind of business operated by the same firm." [36] The former are generally referred to as *independent* and the latter as *chains*.

Table 18-4 shows that the American retail structure is predominantly independent. There has been a growth of chain stores in the general merchandise,

[33] *Ibid.*, "True Look at Discount Industry," pp. 35–82.
[34] *U.S. Census of Business: 1963, Retail Trade, U.S. Summary,* Vol. I, Part 1, Appendix, 4.
[35] *Ibid.*, pp. 1–6.
[36] *Op. cit.*, Vol. I, Part 1, Appendix.

TABLE 18-4

Single and Multi-Unit Retail Establishments
and Sales by Kind of Business, 1963

Kind of Business	Retail Establishments					Retail Sales (in Millions)				
	Total	Single Unit	%	Multi-Unit	%	Total	Single Unit	%	Multi-Unit	%
Lumber, building materials, hardware and farm equipment dealers	92,703	79,377	85.5	13,326	14.5	$ 14,606	$ 11,456	78.8	$ 3,150	21.2
General merchandise group	62,063	40,882	65.7	21,181	34.3	30,003	4,881	16.3	25,122	83.7
Food stores	319,433	278,364	87.1	41,069	12.9	57,079	26,197	45.6	30,882	54.4
Automotive dealers	98,514	89,375	89.4	9,139	10.6	45,376	41,540	91.1	3,837	8.9
Gasoline service stations	211,473	188,403	89.0	23,070	11.0	17,760	14,936	82.4	2,824	17.6
Apparel and accessory stores	116,223	83,130	71.5	33,093	28.5	14,040	7,255	51.8	6,785	48.2
Furniture, home furnishings and equipment stores	93,649	79,961	85.5	13,688	14.5	10,926	8,059	73.4	2,867	26.6
Eating and drinking places	334,482	311,792	93.4	22,690	6.6	18,412	15,545	83.3	2,868	16.7
Drug and proprietary stores	54,732	46,221	83.6	8,511	16.4	8,487	5,675	67.1	2,811	32.9
Other retail stores	244,868	215,798	88.1	29,070	11.9	21,309	16,006	75.1	5,303	24.9
Nonstore retailers	79,792	74,845	93.7	4,947	6.3	6,204	3,198	51.6	3,006	48.4
Total	1,707,931	1,488,148	87.1	219,783	12.9	244,202	154,746	63.4	89,455	36.6

Compiled from: U.S. Bureau of the Census, U.S. Census of Business, 1963, Retail Trade: Single and Multi-units, BC63-RS4.

food, and, in fact, most lines; but the independent store is the backbone of American retailing. Nevertheless, the growth that has been witnessed by the chains in many kinds of business has caused people to question the future of the independent store. For this reason, a closer look at the independent store will reveal some of its strengths and weaknesses. Then we shall examine the chain stores and some of the group activities of independents designed to counteract chain store competition.

Independent Stores

The independent store has certain strong points that it must capitalize on if it is to remain an important element in retailing. One observer lists these strong points as follows: (1) local ownership and management; (2) prestige as a leading business in the community; (3) ability to make decisions independently; (4) freedom from the pressures and politics of the head office; (5) flexibility that enables it to move quickly in response to current situations and circumstances; and (6) the power to administer with a thorough knowledge of its community and a more intimate knowledge of local consumer wants.[37] In general, the strong points of the independent store are closely allied to identification with the local community and market, and with flexibility of operation.

The weaknesses of the independent store are more impressive. The same author observes the following: [38] independent retailers prefer to ride on past reputations rather than adjust to changing competitive patterns. In some cases this is a result of the age of management. Many stores were originally opened by relatively young, enthusiastic, and aggressive owners. But as comfortable standards of living were achieved, the initiative for adjusting to every competitive shift was lacking and, under such circumstances, they lost their share of the market. In contrast with the chain stores, their management is *weakened* through conservatism. Sufficient capital has always been a limiting factor for the independent. The ability to compete on a credit basis, as well as the need to provide customer accessibility through expansion and modernization, requires large sums of money, which have not been easily available. And a relatively unnoticed shortcoming is found in the impact of estate taxes. It is almost impossible to pass on a going concern to the next generation, as studies show that, on the average, 25 percent of an independent store's assets must be applied to the payment of estate taxes. Consequently, there is little incentive for the coming generation to supply a fresh surge of interest and vigor, not to mention high-priced ability, to the management of family-held retail stores.

The foregoing remarks are not meant to suggest that the independent store is doomed. In fact, with the exception of the food field and general merchandise group, there has been only minor change in the proportion of sales done by independents in different kinds of business. Many techniques have been used to combat the competitive inroads of chain stores; these will be discussed immediately.

[37] J. Gordon Dakins, "The Future of the Independent Store," *Thirty-First Annual Boston Conference on Distribution,* October 19–20, 1959, pp. 75–76.
[38] *Ibid.,* p. 76.

Since the chain provides the severest competition to the independents, let us examine this form of retail organization.

Chain Stores

Although the outstanding feature of the corporate chain is perhaps the number of its units, this characteristic hardly explains its competitive strength. Much more important is its centralized management, with all of the advantages of specialization, buying power, risk distribution, and integration.

The corporate chain represents a polar extreme in terms of both centralized ownership and management. The term *corporate chain* is used to distinguish those organizations which own all outlets in the chain system from the cooperative or voluntary chains in which each outlet is independently owned and managed. The latter two types are discussed below. They exist in all the different types of retail establishments previously classified by assortments handled. Sears, Roebuck and Company and the J. C. Penney Company are department store chains; the F. W. Woolworth Company and the S. S. Kresge Company represent the variety store chain; the A & P and The Kroger Company are household names in the food field; and in the limited line and specialty store field, the many women's apparel chains, such as Lerner Shops, and the large shoe chains, such as Thom McAn, are representative. Some chains operate nationwide, whereas others are regional or local.

The advantage of chain retailing lies in its capacity to compete in price through achieving large volume at low operating costs. Volume is achieved through handling only fast-moving items, usually at a price differential backed with aggressive promotion. The large volume achieved is a function of: (1) buying policies, (2) operating practices and price appeal, and (3) aggressive promotion. We shall now examine each of these.

BUYING POLICIES: Some degree of centralization is found in the buying procedures of all corporate chains. If they are not centralized for the entire chain, they are centralized regionally. At least, very little independence of action is given to the store manager. In this way, specialized skills can be brought to bear on the buying problem. There is a tendency to handle only fast-moving items and to minimize costs of inventory at all levels.

OPERATING PRACTICES AND PRICE APPEAL: The ability to make a price appeal may be attributed to many things. The concentration of buying enables the chain to keep merchandise costs to a minimum. They can buy in such large quantities that favorable merchandise costs can be negotiated. There has been a tendency to attribute their ability to offer low prices to their bargaining power. In fact, much litigation has ensued over this issue.

Although some advantage in merchandise cost is achieved, three other factors are equally important. First, chain stores have adopted a policy of offering merchandise at a low unit markup. Second, many chain stores handle their own private-brand merchandise. In fact, many have integrated and own their own manufacturing facilities. They acquire a merchandise cost advantage in this way, thus it is impossible to make direct price comparisons with similar merchandise in other retail stores. Third, the chain stores have been very successful in reducing their operating cost ratios, which will be discussed shortly.

Before leaving this subject, it should be pointed out that in some merchandise lines, chain stores do handle high-priced merchandise. For example, the Florsheim shoe stores and Brooks Brothers clothing stores do not use price as a major competitive weapon.

PROMOTION: The chain stores have a definite advertising advantage. Where there are a number of units of a chain in a single community, the cost of advertising can be spread over all stores. The uniformity of operation and of merchandise handled makes a single advertisement effective for all stores. The proportion of total volume in the community done by the chain makes a larger advertising appropriation feasible, and the impact of chain advertising is usually greater than that of independents. The centralized management allows specialization in this area, and chain advertising is usually better conceived than independent advertising is. Likewise, in store promotion it is superior. The large number of outlets provides an excellent laboratory for experimentation and improvement in promotion methods.

Although many of these factors contribute to low operating costs, integrated wholesaling, and curtailment of services are of special importance.

INTEGRATED WHOLESALING: Many corporate chains have established their own distribution centers and purchase the bulk of their merchandise directly from the manufacturer. There is no particular advantage in circumventing the wholesale network unless the wholesale function can be performed more efficiently by the chain. In many cases, the corporate chains have been able to reduce the cost of movement of goods by careful location of warehouses near their stores. They also have been successful in achieving economies in the internal operation of warehouse facilities. Success has not been achieved in all cases, however, and appears to be dependent upon the size of the retail organization to be serviced, the breadth of the line handled, and the degree of centralization found in buying procedures. If considerable autonomy is given to store managers in the selection of merchandise to be handled, it is more difficult to operate the wholesaling phases of the business economically.

CURTAILMENT OF SERVICES: Many corporate chains have curtailed the number of services offered to the customer. Although this curtailment has been historical, it does not necessarily characterize all forms of corporate chain organization. For example, in the food field, it has been necessary to add a large number of services both to attract the marginal consumers not solely interested in price, and to compete with other chains that have used services as a competitive weapon. On the other hand, there is considerable difference between the services offered in a Sears, Roebuck and Company store and those in an independent department store such as the J. L. Hudson Company. The use of service curtailment as a means of achieving economy varies with the competitive conditions existing. If the public reacts adversely to curtailed services, or if competition is offering services, generally the corporate chain will fall in line.

In summary, all of the means mentioned are used to achieve high volume at low cost. The use of any particular means varies with economic conditions and competitive pressures.

Group Activities of Independents

Under pressure from corporate chain store competition, independents have replied in kind by forming retail cooperative chains. Likewise, wholesalers have formed voluntary group chains.

RETAILER COOPERATIVE CHAINS: The competition from corporate chains has caused many independent stores to adopt some of the practices of the corporate chain. Independent retailers attribute the success of corporate chains to their group buying and wholesaling activities. Some independents have tried to achieve the same economies without losing their independence. Cooperative organizations have been formed by a number of independent retailers for the purpose of operating their own wholesale establishments and pooling orders to gain lower merchandise costs. In some of the more successful retailer cooperative chains they have developed their own private brands, and have even achieved economies by uniformity of promotion.

The major purpose of the retailer cooperative chain is to achieve low cost of merchandise. They are usually organized on a stock-ownership basis, requiring a certain minimum holding for membership. The funds received from stock sales, plus initiation fees, provide the working capital for the wholesale organization. Merchandise is usually sold to the members at cost, plus the cost of operation of the whole sales organization. However, in some cases, a small profit is taken, which is later distributed in the form of dividends to the members.

VOLUNTARY CHAINS: In the case of the retailer cooperative chain, the initiative comes from the retailer. In the case of the voluntary chain, the initiative comes from the wholesaler. As more and more corporate chains have established their own wholesaling facilities, the independent wholesaler has lost business. Further, the competitive inroads made by corporate chains on the independent store have meant a reduction in the market for the independent wholesaler. Consequently, independent wholesalers have organized large groups of independent retailers into voluntary chains. The wholesaler, although recognizing the importance of low-cost merchandise to the corporate chain, has also paid considerable attention to the importance of skill in handling merchandise after its purchase.

Retailers enter into a contract with a wholesaler which specifies the activities the wholesaler will perform. The emphasis in the voluntary chain is not solely on group buying, but rather embraces an attempt to improve retail management of independent stores. Voluntary wholesalers usually provide help in such matters as establishing accounting systems and in-store promotion, planning group advertising, store layout, sales training, and a number of other managerial services, all designed to upgrade the management of the independent store. One of the best-known voluntary chains is the I.G.A., Independent Grocers Alliance of America. The stores cooperating in this voluntary chain, from all outward appearances, resemble a corporate chain.

Affiliation with a voluntary chain may be the answer for many independents facing chain store competition. There is evidence the voluntary chains are giving the corporate chains a competitive battle in the food field. In 1947 "affiliated independents account for 29 percent of all U.S. food sales, as compared with 38 percent for the chains and 33 percent for unaffiliated independents." [39] In 1964 it was estimated that "the affiliated independents have 49 percent of the business, the chains 41 percent and the unaffiliated independents 10 percent." [40]

Sales Volume Size

Although the American retail structure is dominated by some very large retail organizations, it is primarily composed of a large number of small retailers. Table 18-5 shows that in 1963, 1,089, 080 retail establishments, or approximately 71 percent of all retailers, had annual sales of less than $100,000. This 71 percent of retail establishments accounted for approximately 18 percent of all retail sales, totaling $232,043 billion.

The proportion of small stores versus large stores, by kind of business, varies. In all kinds of business the proportion of stores with an annual volume of under $100,000 is large.

To the marketer of consumer goods, the large number of retailers doing such a small amount of business means a substantial task in achieving maximum product exposure in all outlets available. There is a definite need to select outlets carefully and to be able to afford the cost of complete distribution if intensive coverage of the market is needed.

Another interesting fact about the size of retail establishments is that approximately 40 percent of retail establishments do a business of less than $30,000 a year in accounting for approximately 5 percent of the total of retail sales. Although net profit rates vary by kind of business, an average of 4 percent is liberal. On this basis, net profits for these retailers are $1,200 or less a year. This is accounted for partly by failure to record all costs. In many of these small establishments, family labor is used, and part of the family dwelling provides the premises for business. If all costs were recorded, the inefficiency of this sector of retailing would be even more apparent.

THE GEOGRAPHY OF RETAILING

Retail sales in the United States closely parallel the density of population. Approximately 70 percent of the population lives in urban centers (2,500 or more population). In 1963, $199 billion, or approximately 78 percent, of retail

---

[39] "The Best of Both Possible Worlds," *Forbes* (November 15, 1964), p. 47.
[40] *Ibid.*, p. 47.

TABLE 18-5

Retail Sales by Sales Size
and Kind of Business, 1963

	ANNUAL VOLUME								Total	
	UNDER $100,000				OVER $100,000					
Kind of Business	Number of Establishments	% of Total	Sales (Millions)	% of Total	Number of Establishments	% of Total	Sales (Millions)	% of Total	Number of Establishments	Retail Sales (Millions)
Lumber, building materials, hardware, farm equipment dealers	50,196	57.4	$ 2,143	15.2	37,303	42.6	$ 11,971	84.8	87,499	$ 14,114
General merchandise group stores	33,277	57.1	1,322	4.5	24,987	42.9	27,846	95.5	58,264	29,168
Food stores	204,427	70.1	7,582	14.0	84,646	29.9	46,640	86.0	289,073	54,222
Automotive dealers	38,591	43.4	1,499	3.4	51,060	56.6	42,200	96.6	89,651	43,699
Gasoline service stations	126,049	69.6	6,299	39.9	54,830	30.4	9,472	60.1	180,879	15,771
Apparel, accessory stores	73,639	67.3	3,178	23.4	35,753	32.7	10,369	76.6	109,392	13,547
Furniture, home furnishings, and equipment stores	57,374	66.1	2,126	20.3	29,458	33.9	8,356	79.7	86,832	10,481
Eating and drinking places	252,315	87.4	8,202	49.1	36,069	12.6	8,457	50.9	288,384	16,659
Drug stores, proprietary stores	24,330	46.6	1,348	16.6	27,733	53.4	6,802	83.4	52,063	8,149
Other retail stores	171,441	76.4	5,620	27.7	52,955	23.6	14,664	72.3	224,396	20,287
Non-store retailers	57,441	87.2	1,950	32.8	8,417	12.8	3,997	67.2	65,858	5,946
* Total	1,089,080	71.1	41,269	17.8	443,211	28.9	190,774	82.2	1,532,291	232,043

* Totals are less than in Table 18-4, as only those establishments in business the entire year are included in Table 18-5.
Compiled from: U.S. Bureau of the Census, U.S. Census of Business, 1963, Retail Trade: Sales Size, BC63-RS2.

trade took place in these urban centers. The Bureau of the Budget has established Standard Metropolitan Statistical Areas (SMSA), each of which contains the cities and surrounding counties that constitute a metropolitan area. In 1963 there were 219 such areas. The distribution of retail sales by SMSA's and city size is shown in Table 18-6.[41]

TABLE 18-6
U.S. Retail Trade by City Size, 1963

City Size	Total (in Billions)	SMSA[a] (in Billions)	Remainder (in Billions)
500,000 or more	$ 43	$ 43	$ —
250,000–499,999	18	18	—
100,000–249,999	21	21	—
50,000–99,999	23	23	—
25,000–49,999	24	12	12
10,000–24,999	30	14	16
2,500–9,999	31	11	20
Remainder of U.S.	54	28	26
	$244	$170	$ 74

[a] Based on 219 SMSA's as of 1963.

Source: U.S. Bureau of the Census, U.S. Census of Business: 1963, Retail Trade—United States Summary, cited in William Applebaum, "Consumption and the Geography of Retail Distribution in the United States," Business Topics, XV (Summer 1967), p. 28.

The specific location of retailing activity varies from city to city but the growth of the shopping center is a universal phenomenon meriting mention. As the cities have expanded through the development of large suburban communities on their fringes, it was only natural that new retailing facilities would develop to serve these new population concentrations. The planned shopping center emerged as the central hub of retailing in the suburban community. In the larger shopping centers, branches of the downtown department stores and national chains are the magnet, whereas in smaller centers the supermarket is the retail unit which attracts the smaller specialty and limited-line stores. In Table 18-7 the number of shopping centers by gross leasable area, number of stores, estimated annual sales, number of car spaces, and car spaces per 1000 square feet of gross leasable area are shown. As it is anticipated that the movement to the suburbs will continue, it can be expected that there will be a growth in shopping center development. One authority suggests that new centers will be built close to the new superhighways between smaller cities, providing a retail mecca for two or more smaller cities.[42]

[41] For a more detailed discussion, see William Applebaum, "Consumption and the Geography of Retail Distribution in the United States," Business Topics, XV (Summer 1967), pp. 25–41.
[42] Ibid., p. 29.

TABLE 18-7

U.S. Shopping Centers, January 1965

Size Center (In Square Feet GLA)	Number of Centers	Number of Stores (in Thousands)	Estimated Annual Sales (in Billions)	Number of Car Spaces (in Millions)	Car Spaces/ 1,000 Sq. Ft. GLA [a]
Less than 100,000	4,925	63	$14	2.1	8.3
101,000–200,000	2,066	49	17	2.5	8.3
201,000–400,000	698	25	10	1.5	8.1
401,000–800,000	316	15	9	1.2	6.6
Over 800,000	73	6	4	.5	5.4
Total	8,076	158	54	7.8	7.7

[a] GLA: Gross leasable area.

Source: Chain Store Age *(Executive Edition), May, 1966, p. E22, cited in William Apple-baum,* "Consumption and the Geography of Retail Distribution in the United States," *MSU Business Topics, XV (Summer 1967), p. 28.*

Summary

The retail structure in the United States is made up of 1,707,931 establishments doing $244,201,777,000 in retail sales. Between 1958 and 1963, after adjustments for inflation, there was an increase of 15.0 percent in the volume of goods moved through the retail structures. After adjusting for population increases, there was a 6.2 percent increase in consumer participation in retail trade. The real increase of 15.0 percent was accompanied by a 4.8 percent decrease in number of establishments.

Retailing may be conducted through retail stores, mail-order houses, vending machines, or direct (house-to-house) selling. Retailing through retail stores is by far the most important, accounting for 96.0 percent of retail establishments and 97.6 percent of retail trade in 1963. The remainder of total retail trade is divided among the other types of retailing, with direct selling the most important.

Retailers may be classified on the basis of product assortments offered—specifically as *general stores, limited-line stores, specialty stores, departmentalized specialty stores, department stores, discount stores* and *variety stores.* All are important in the retail structure; but the limited-line stores far outnumber the other classes. Since there are differences in the cost structures and modes of operation of these different classes of stores, familiarity with them is essential if they are to be used in the distribution channel.

Retailers in the United States are primarily independent, but a trend in retailing has developed toward multiple ownership. The multiunit retailers, through more efficient operation, were successful in competing with the independent stores. In 1963, they did approximately 36 percent of total retail trade. The *corporate chains,* a form of multi-unit organization, were most effective in competing with the independents. In retaliation, *voluntary chains* and *retailer cooperative chains* developed. The voluntary chains have been much more important than retailer cooperative chains.

Although the retail structure is dominated by a few very large retailers, it is primarily made up of a large number of quite small stores. Approximately 71 percent of all stores do under $100,000 in business a year and account for approximately 18 percent of total retail sales. At the lower end of the sales-size scale, approximately 40 percent do less than $30,000 a year, and account for approximately 5 percent of total retail sales.

Retail sales in the United States closely parallel the density of population. In 1963, 70 percent of the population lived in urban centers and about $199 billion, or 78 percent, of retail sales were transacted in these centers.

Questions and Problems

1. How do you account for the fact that between 1958 and 1963 there was a 15 percent increase in flow of goods through retail stores but a 4.8 percent decrease in number of retailers?

2. How do you account for the great differences in retail sales in the different geographical regions of the United States?

3. What conditions must be present to have effective retail demand?

4. What methods of selling at retail are open to the marketing manager? Which of these accounts for the largest sales, and why?

5. How do you account for the decline in department store sales as a percentage of total retail sales at a time when more and more department stores are opening suburban branches?

6. Discuss the reason why chain organizations tend to integrate wholesaling with retailing when such action runs counter to the advantages of specialization.

7. In what important respects does the retailer cooperative chain differ from the wholesaler-sponsored voluntary chain?

8. Describe the historical evolution of the mail-order house as a retailing institution. What factors do you think account for its growth pattern? What do you expect its future to be?

9. What factors might be presumed to account for the growth of automatic vending machines? What are some of the limiting factors to accelerated growth for this type of retail trade?

10. Although house-to-house selling is one of the most direct forms of marketing, it is also one of the most expensive. How do you account for this?

11. What is the difference between variety and assortment in retail product offerings?

12. How would you differentiate between a limited-line store and a specialty store?

13. What advantages does a small independent store have to capitalize on in competing with large corporate chains?

14. Corporate chains have shown a remarkably stable share of retail trade over a period of thirty years. Why?

15. From the point of view of proportion of retail trade, which types of retail establishments would you expect to be more important in the future, and which less important? Why?

Conglomerate Market Competition

19

The term *conglomerate market competition* refers to competition among different types of dealers and distributors selling the same commodity. Over a relatively long period of years there has been a trend for market outlets to "scramble" merchandise lines—that is, to diversify product assortments by adding different types of merchandise.

Scrambled merchandising gained momentum well before World War II but was accelerated strongly in the postwar years and currently shows no signs of abating. Drugstores at one time handled only pharmaceuticals but then added fountains, drug sundries, and notions, and now carry cosmetics, toiletries, magazines, watches, jewelry, portable appliances, housewares, cameras, home shop tools, and many other items. Tire stores at first added only the closely related lines of batteries and automobile accessories but now handle appliances, sporting goods, toys and games, bicycles, outdoor furniture, and housewares. Food stores added meats to their staple, dry groceries and eventually took on baked goods, drugs, toiletries, magazines, alcoholic beverages, flowers, and housewares. Some now stock clothing, portable appliances, portable electric tools, china, silverware, binoculars, and hardware items.

These few examples are only illustrative, for this trend toward product proliferation has taken place in virtually every line of trade, to the point where we are now experiencing what can be called "conglomerate market competition." That is, there is a wide variety of different types of market outlets competing in selling the same commodities. In this chapter, we will first examine the causes of this accelerating trend, and then we will consider some of the effects it is having on marketing practices. Emphasis in the latter discussion will be placed on assessing the consequences of this facet of market competition on manufacturing enterprises.

THE CAUSES OF CONGLOMERATE
MARKET COMPETITION

Many factors account for the increasing tendency towards scrambled merchandise lines. Some of these forces, having existed for many years, are basic and pervasive.[1] Others are more current in nature, deriving from dynamics in market forces and attempts by both producing and distributing enterprises to deal effectively with altered conditions. It is the combination of the two forces that is giving the trend its current momentum and propelling markets toward an even more bewildering conglomeration of merchandise lines.

The Large Pool of Common Costs in Market Outlets

Perhaps the most basic force that has led to continuous attempts to expand product assortment is the large pool of common costs in distributive outlets. The vast majority of all costs incurred among retail establishments, for instance, are for the benefit of all merchandise handled, with only a small minority of costs traceable directly to any particular product. Not only is there a large pool of common costs, but the bulk of these common costs are of the fixed, rather than variable, variety. Specifically, the bulk of costs does not vary directly with unit sales volume over short and intermediate ranges of volume increases and contractions.

To demonstrate the impact that this pool of common costs has on product assortment, let us take the case of a jeweler in a downtown location of average size, who restricts his merchandise to jewelry items. In common with all merchants, he would like to find a way of increasing his profits without substantially increasing his costs. As he contemplates the various ways to do this, he cannot help but consider some variation in product assortment: he speculates over the feasibility of adding a limited line of luggage.

As the jeweler surveys the store's layout, he notices that by moving a few counters, he could free one corner for the display of a limited line of luggage. He recalls that a nearby luggage dealer is selling a rather attractive men's two-suiter for $39.95, and learns that, with the trade discount, he can purchase a similar piece for $24.00. As he thinks about adding this merchandise, he recognizes that he will have very little additional cost in the sale of the luggage item. That is, he will incur no additional rent for space, will need no additional heat, light, or power, and will experience no additional depreciation of equipment and fixtures, and no additional costs in his credit department. Additional wages for sales personnel would not have to be taken into account, since the sales clerks are already being paid a salary and have considerable idle selling time. In short, the jeweler fails to see where any significant increases in expenses will be incurred from the sale of luggage.

The thought occurs to the jeweler that he could sell a men's two-suiter,

[1] For an excellent discussion of this subject, see Richard M. Alt, "Competition Among Types of Retailers in Selling the Same Commodities," *Journal of Marketing*, XIV, No. 3 (October 1949), 441.

equivalent to the luggage dealer's $39.95 item, for $31.95, providing a substantial inducement to customers to buy from him because of the price differential of 20 percent, while still obtaining a gross margin of 25 percent on his retail selling price, or 33 percent on his cost of merchandise. This would contribute an incremental profit of approximately $8 on every item sold. He reasons that, at the end of the year, the profitability of the store will be $8 greater for every piece of luggage sold. This seems to be a powerful inducement to add the merchandise, and he elects to do so.

The luggage dealer down the street finds it difficult to match his new competitor's prices because, since luggage is the only merchandise he handles, all his costs must be reflected in his luggage prices. Since the jeweler's luggage constitutes a superior consumer value, his luggage volume begins to expand rapidly. Now he decides he will clear more floor space and add another sales employee. Also, because demand is great enough, he decides he could purchase in larger quantities at more advantageous prices by visiting the New York wholesale market. He begins a somewhat more aggressive advertising program to support the rather rapid increase in his luggage business. By this time, however, the sale of luggage has generated additional costs—and these must be covered from sales revenue.

So we see that there is a point beyond which the merchant cannot go in pursuing this particular business philosophy profitably. In fact, some merchants would argue that the jeweler misinterpreted his cost structure from the very beginning by failing to expect every item to bear its proportional share of operating expenses. While there is a controversy over the wisdom of varied markups of merchandise, it is nonetheless apparent that the existence of this large pool of common costs has led many merchants to expand their product assortments. Countermeasures taken by the affected merchants, who expand their own product assortments, have contributed significantly to the scrambled and conglomerate merchandise lines we observe today. Competition among various dealers in selling the same commodity has thereby been significantly intensified.

Changing Consumer Shopping Habits

Changing consumer shopping habits have had a pronounced effect on the increase in product assortments. The most significant trend in consumer shopping habits influencing product assortments has been the shift toward self-service. As other retail establishments have recognized that some of their merchandise lines are amenable to supermarket-like merchandising techniques, opportunities have arisen for broadening the product assortment traditionally handled by those establishments. Drugstores, for example, have found that many of their items can be handled on a self-service basis. Once this fact was established, it was then possible to broaden merchandise assortments without substantially increasing labor costs. Some additional display and shelf space could be installed without having to hire more help to handle the selection of newly stocked items.

The whole idea of open stock, together with freedom for the customer to deliberate for any desired period of time over his choice of purchases, was accelerated during World War II, when labor was in such short supply that it was impossible for many retailing establishments to continue doing business in the traditional full-service manner. Department stores, for example, found that it was necessary to put some items of men's furnishings on a self-service basis. Men's sweaters, for instance, which commonly had been kept in glass display cases, and shown only on request by sales clerks, had to be put on open counters and "islands" for easy inspection and selection by customers. To the surprise of many merchants, customers *preferred* to shop this way—to examine and contemplate the purchase of goods—and impulse purchases increased.

This new shopping pattern was particularly well suited to some departments, such as toys and games, but not so well suited to others, such as fashion apparel. The point is that as establishments such as department stores, drugstores, variety stores, tire, battery, and accessory stores, and surplus and supply outlets, among other institutions, learned of the attractiveness of self-service, many new possibilities were opened for the expansion of merchandise lines into nontraditional areas. Self-service has accentuated scrambled merchandise lines among a variety of types of dealers.

Interconnectedness of Demand

One of the early motives for broadening product assortments was to capitalize on the interconnectedness of demand for closely related items. Gasoline stations, for example, added cleaners and polish, repair parts and accessories, batteries and tires. Men's clothing stores added shoes and men's furnishings. More recently, women's shoe stores added handbags and millinery, to provide matched ensembles.

While the existence of interconnected demand has made attractive openings for some merchants, it has provided barriers for others. For instance, the men's clothing store could with relative ease clear space for a limited line of men's shoes, recognizing that the buyer of a new suit often purchases a complete outfit, including shoes. On the other hand, it is difficult for the shoe store to retaliate by going in the other direction. The purchase of a new pair of shoes does not usually precipitate the purchase of a new suit of clothes. Also, the relative investment and amount of skill required for the shoe merchant to add men's clothing is substantially greater than the other way around. Shoe stores have found it difficult to broaden product assortments beyond hosiery, shoe polishes, handbags, handkerchiefs, neckties, and millinery.

There is also a perplexing psychological dimension to consumer associations of demand. Customers of supermarkets, for instance, seem perfectly willing to purchase automobile waxes and polishes along with floor waxes and polishes, but gasoline stations have never been able to sell floor waxes and polishes successfully alongside automobile waxes and polishes. Where a natural interconnectedness of demand exists, however, it seems almost certain that merchants will attempt to capitalize on the opportunity for successful expansion of product assortments. But movements in this direction have tended to weaken the position of the traditional limited-line store in competition with its multiline rival.

Desire to Increase Traffic Flow in Low-traffic Establishments

Both high- and low-traffic establishments exist in the retail structure. Food supermarkets and drugstores exemplify the high-traffic establishment. A relatively large number of buyers patronize these establishments each day, and quite a few are in the store at any given time. Furniture and appliance stores exemplify the low-traffic establishment. They normally have relatively few customers each day, and few in the store at any given time. Their overall volume of business does depend to some extent on the level of exposure to customer traffic. Consequently, some low-traffic establishments have added higher-volume merchandise lines (hardware) with appealing prices, in hope of attracting a higher-traffic count. By featuring such merchandise, an appliance store, for instance, hopes that the attractiveness of the major appliances and the abilities of a skilled sales force will succeed in converting a profitable proportion of the bargain hunters into purchasers of the major merchandise line. On the assumption that you cannot sell merchandise before attracting potential buyers to the establishment, merchants dealing in these categories of goods have attempted to stimulate the traffic count by this device, which of course intensifies competition throughout the market on the *added* category of goods.

Introduction of New Products

When a new product with substantial innovation is introduced, there is always a scramble among outlets to handle it. Over a period of time the product, if successful, may settle toward better-established and more orderly distribution. This progression can be observed, for instance, in the case of frozen foods. When frozen foods were first introduced, there was an attempt by many types of retail outlets, both old and new, to profitably exploit the new category of goods. Frozen-locker plants, home-delivery route salesmen, department stores, drug stores, delicatessens, ice cream dealers, and dairies, in addition to the traditional food store outlets, all were involved in distribution of the new type of product. The pattern of distribution which existed in the early days of frozen foods has now narrowed to a more limited number of outlet types. As the rate of new-product introduction continues to accelerate, it can be expected to contribute to the additional scrambling of merchandise lines among different types of dealers as they persist in their attempts to find new profit centers for their enterprises.

Improvement of Old Products

The improvement of old products has been as important a factor as the introduction of new products in contributing to the scrambling of merchandise. Some products when first introduced are of such a technical nature that they require specialized distribution agencies. Frequently, however, they are simplified to the point where it becomes feasible to sell them through nonspecialized outlets.

One of the early examples of this situation was the introduction of pneumatic tires for automobiles. This product required the specialized equipment and facilities of a tire dealer. Product performance was such that frequent repairs were required, and the item did not lend itself to mass distribution. As a consequence, the tire dealer sold virtually all the tires marketed. But when manufacturers improved the product and simplified servicing requirements, product characteristics permitted distribution through such outlets as gas stations, department stores, auto accessory stores, mail-order houses, and such new outlets as surplus and supply outlets, military post exchange stores, and discount houses. The rubber manufacturers, when testifying in a Federal Trade Commission hearing on monopolistic practices in the industry, used this evolution as a major argument in explaining why the tire dealers' share of the market had diminished so much in recent years.[2]

More current examples of the effect of product improvement on conglomerate market competition would be window air-conditioners, and television sets. Initially, window air-conditioners required installation by a licensed plumber, and consequently, had limited distribution. Today the window air-conditioner is an easy-to-handle, plug-in appliance with easy adaptation to any window opening; a much broader group of outlets are capable of handling the product and do. The same holds true for television. The complicated installation requirements of the early sets no longer exist, and there has therefore been a substantial broadening of the distribution base to discount stores, mail-order houses, furniture stores, tire stores, hardware stores, and even drugstores and supermarkets.

Emergence of New Types of Outlets

Because the market structure is in a constant state of flux, new types of outlets emerge periodically. Perhaps the most significant in recent years has been the discount house. The discount house began as a catalog establishment, with very limited space and without sales personnel, and obtained items on order from wholesaling establishments for delivery to customers. As it succeeded and developed, it expanded its base of operations, so that today it is handling a broad line of immediately available merchandise, and is offering additional service.

Initially, in attempts to protect established dealers, manufacturers refrained from selling to this type of establishment. But as the volume of business grew rapidly in the discount houses, manufacturers had to review their distribution practices: the new outlets were in some cases selling substantially greater volumes of merchandise than were the traditional dealers. In time, more and more manufacturers chose to provide the discount houses with merchandise, believing that these outlets would otherwise somehow secure it anyway from various obscure sources.

The discount house, however, is not the only new type of outlet. Others are cooperatives, initiated by labor unions and governmental employees; war

---

[2] Thomas A. Staudt, "Quantity Limits and Public Policy," in *Marketing: Current Problems and Theories* (Bloomington: Indiana University School of Business, 1952), p. 72.

surplus and supply outlets; trading-stamp houses; and home-party merchandising plans (discussed in Chapter 18). Obviously, as new types of dealers emerge, intertype competition intensifies with a conglomerate effect.

Consumer Credit

Many manufacturers have found it desirable to expand distribution through outlets with established credit customers and flexible credit availability. Cameras, for instance, were at one time marketed almost entirely through camera stores dealing primarily on a cash basis. Department stores and jewelry stores became important outlets because they made credit available and already had credit customers. Manufacturers presumed that sales volume would increase if installment credit was readily available, as well as desired outlets that could provide this service. Some furniture stores added limited lines of appliances, such as refrigerators and stoves, as a convenience to established customers who already had installment credit with the store. The purchaser of a refrigerator, for example, could easily be accommodated by simply lengthening the number of payments required by a customer from a previous credit purchase. Recently, credit has been made available in some previously "cash only" establishments, such as the J. C. Penney Company, and this has made it possible to extend merchandise lines into higher price categories.

Manufacturers' Diversification Practices

Manufacturers' product diversification programs have sometimes involved the trading-up and trading-down of merchandise lines (see Chapter 12). When this happens, the manufacturer may attempt to move the newly added lines through market outlets distinct from those handling the traditional items of merchandise. When Bell and Howell, for example, added low-priced movie cameras to its traditional line of relatively high-priced camera equipment, it chose to distribute the new items through such outlets as drugstores. Manufacturers sometimes desire different outlets for different quality merchandise, so as to avoid damaging the existing volume of business done through traditional outlets. In the goods where trading-up and trading-down has been common (cameras, watches, radios, sporting goods) interdealer competition has been increased from the larger number of different types of dealers engaged in selling the same general class of commodity.

Manufacturers' Service Policy

In recent times, manufacturers have come to accept more responsibility than formerly for the performance of marketing activities connected with the ultimate sale of their products. One of the most troublesome areas, particularly relevant to consumers' durable goods, has involved product service.

The appliance manufacturer, for instance, must make sure that adequate servicing and parts facilities are available if he is to remain in a strong competitive position. To make product guarantees effective at the consumer level, he must back them with easily accessible service establishments. An illustration of the way the acceptance of this responsibility has led to scrambled merchandising is the decision of RCA to establish its own service branches throughout the country for various products including television sets. One of the earlier reasons for allowing only established radio and television dealers to handle its equipment was the essentiality of service and repair facilities that only these outlets could provide. With the RCA service branch readily available to all local customers, it became feasible for a variety of outlets to handle the product. Dealers without repair service merely explained to the customer that if he had any difficulty with the set, the RCA factory service branch would handle the matter and honor the manufacturer's guarantee. Such arrangements provided by the manufacturer have increased the number of outlets competent to handle the merchandise by adding those specializing in the selling function and without repair facilities.

Production Automation

The manner in which production automation has contributed to conglomerate market competition has been obscured by the emphasis on its manufacturing and labor implications. Automation has been one of the strongest of the current forces leading to accelerated scrambled merchandising. This pressure comes about because automation changes the character of the manufacturer's cost structure, creating a strong incentive for increased sales volume.

This incentive derives from two factors. First, automation increases the fixed-costs proportion of total costs, with an accompanying reduction in direct labor costs. That is, machinery is substituted for manpower; in a fully automated factory, there would be almost no labor cost. The result of heavy fixed charges is that: (1) the break-even point is increased, (2) the volume of sales that must be realized to maintain existing profits is increased, and (3) the volume required to maintain the same profit as a return on investments is a still higher figure. In cases such as this, profit leverage increases. That is, a modest increase or decrease has much more effect on profitability than it had prior to automation (the profit or loss angle is much wider). The second factor is that although a plant can be automated to the same level of capacity as before, almost inevitably the plant's capacity is increased through automation. This only serves to intensify the problems of the altered cost structure. The result of the combination of the two forces is a driving incentive for sales volume. As the marketer assesses opportunities to bring about increased volume, he cannot help but contemplate the potentialities of distribution through outlets additional to those being utilized.

The pronounced trend toward production automation in recent years has exerted a strong force for increases in sales volume because of the critical profit consequences of volume increments. This force has manifested itself in the seeking of additional outlets beyond traditional ones for the sale of the product, and the consequent further scrambling of retail merchandise lines and conglomerate market competition.

THE EFFECTS OF CONGLOMERATE
MARKET COMPETITION

Given more intensified scrambled merchandising, what can be anticipated in the way of effects on marketing practices? The effects are likely to be: (1) reverberations in price competition and (2) altered marketing policies on the part of manufacturers and dealers.

Price Competition

As the number of competitive enterprises of different types selling the same commodities increases, it will have a mixed effect on price competition and the retail price structure. In view of the fact that outlets of different types have different cost structures, we can expect price variations to be observable in the market offerings of the various outlets. This will intensify the pressures on the less efficient outlets. However, a second price reverberation may materialize. As the less efficient outlet finds its market position jeopardized because of vigorous price competition, it may rely more on nonprice competition. That is, it will compete more on the basis of service, quality selling, credit extension, and repair and maintenance effectiveness. Thus, there will be pressures on the price structure, with more aggressive pricing taking place in some quarters and emphasis on service in others. On balance, one cannot anticipate price competition to abate significantly in the foreseeable future.

Further Decline in the Market Share of Single-line Stores

An increase in the degree of scrambled merchandising can only result in the further decline of the market share of single-line stores and limited-merchandise outlets. Stated another way, multiple line and general merchandise outlets can be expected to improve their market share at the expense of their single-line rivals. Jewelry stores most likely will sell a smaller proportion of jewelry, shoe stores will sell a smaller proportion of shoes, and luggage dealers will sell proportionately less luggage, with some highly specialized types of single-line stores, such as bicycle shops, virtually fighting for their existence. This decline has been taking place over a period of time in several lines of trade, and unless a substantial change in consumer shopping habits and attitudes toward nonprice competition or service establishments takes place, it can be expected to continue.

Battle of Brands

Because of the conglomerate nature of competition, the battle of brands has intensified. One device that market outlets can be expected to employ in order to gain a monopolistic position is the further development of private-label lines. Because private-brand merchandise is not generally available, the distributor and/or dealer who can create a preference for his own brand of merchandise is in an advantageous defensive position for interagency competition. We have already seen the major chain stores develop private-label business to a substantial degree; this probably will spread to many lines of merchandise where little private-brand business exists. The prospect of a decline in the number of brands in many lines of trade is not promising. The opposite is far more likely.

Responsibility of the Manufacturer for Demand Creation

The result of the effect of scrambled merchandising on private labels will be that manufacturers will exercise an increasing responsibility for the creation of demand for their established, nationally known products. This will be done to protect market shares in this conglomerate competitive structure—manufacturers will be reluctant to entrust their promotional effectiveness to dealers and distributors.

Many market outlets are caught in ambiguous market competition, to the point where their margins are inadequate to sustain promotional efforts. Manufacturers can be expected to rely on "pull"-type promotion, in which advertising, merchandising, and sales promotion are geared to the ultimate purchase level so as to draw the product through the various levels of distribution into consumption. This is in contrast to the "push"-type of promotion, in which the manufacturer expects each successive stage of the distributive network to forcefully promote the product to the next level, thereby finally winning a reasonable share of the market at the ultimate purchase level. This is one reason why we can expect aggregate advertising expenditures, running at an annual rate of 17 billion in 1966, to increase significantly.

Increased Emphasis on a Total System's Concept of Distribution

Directly related to the demand, creation effect will be an increased emphasis on the part of manufacturers to embrace a total system's concept of distribution. That is, the manufacturer will regard his total marketing system as being in competition with his rival manufacturer's total marketing system, and also the total systems of distributive rivals who have integrated backward to manufacturing. The manufacturer thus will seek to control all variables that make for effective marketing, and make every effort to integrate as carefully as possible all operations throughout the system, to the mutual advantage of the participants and his own enterprise.

Increased Pressure for Restrictive Legislation

As some manufacturers and dealers find it increasingly difficult to hold their share of the market in the face of intensified conglomerate market competition, they can be expected to turn to the government for help through restrictive legislation. We have already seen demands for restablishing the Fair Trade Laws, Unfair Practices Acts, and local ordinances covering door-to-door selling; requests for licensing the number of distributive establishments; pressure for more vigorous enforcement of the Robinson-Patman Act; and increased trade association activities to develop more uniform cost control and marketing practices. While all of these pressures are certain to increase, it is doubtful if they will be effective, because it is difficult to legislate against the inherent economic advantages one type of market outlet has over another. Stated differently: It is hard to legislate against the dynamics of the market place in a free enterprise society.

Summary

One of the major elements of our dynamic market structure is the increasing intensity of conglomerate market competition, competition among different types of outlets selling the same commodity. Scrambled merchandising has undergone a long evolution, but has increased at an accelerated rate in the postwar period and shows no signs of abating in the immediate future. Some of the factors that account for this market condition derive from long-standing characteristics of distributive outlets; others are of more recent origin. Among the more influential factors are the large pool of common costs in distributive outlets; changing consumer shopping habits, particularly the preference for self-service; inter-connectedness of demand among closely associated items; and the desire of low-traffic-count establishments to increase in-store buyer population. The introduction of new products and improvement of old ones, the emergence of new types of distributive outlets, manufacturers' diversification policies and service policies, and finally the strong shift to production automation in recent years are causes of more recent origin.

The effects of conglomerate competition have been felt for quite a few years. We can anticipate further reverberations in the price structure; a continued decline in the market share of single-line stores, in favor of their multiline rivals; a more aggressive battle of brands, with market outlets attempting to gain monopolistic position through private labels; and manufacturers seeking to protect their own brand position, thus incurring the added burdens of demand creation. Finally, the pressures for restrictive legislation are likely to be with us for some time to come.

Questions and Problems

1. Explain the term *large pool of common costs,* and the implications of its application.
2. What has been the effect upon the product assortments at retail of the shift toward self-service?
3. What is meant by the term *interconnected demand?* Are there any barriers to the effective use of interconnected demand by retailers? Explain.
4. What barriers and risks, if any, exist to adding high-traffic items to low-traffic stores?
5. In view of the early success of the discount house in the sale of appliances, what motivated this institution to change its product line and assortment?
6. What kinds of buyers do you think prefer self-service? Do you think this preference will change in the future?
7. Explain the marketing effects of production automation as it has affected distribution channels.

8. "Under conditions of extremely conglomerate retail market competition there would be no place for the wholesaler." Do you agree? Why?

9. Manufacturers' service and guarantee policies have had a pronounced effect on the retail distribution structure. How?

10. Why have some limited-line stores, such as shoe stores, found it difficult to retaliate with counterdiversification strategies to meet the impact of scrambled merchandising?

11. What defenses does a small-scale retailer have against continuing pressure from scrambled merchandising?

12. Has the consumer benefited from increasingly conglomerate retail competition? How? What are the disadvantages?

13. What aspects of conglomerate market competition would lead in the direction of generally upward price levels? Which ones would tend toward lower price levels?

14. Is there any relationship between the great wave of new products and the level of distribution costs? Is conglomerate market competition in any way connected with this relationship?

15. Is regulation to protect competitors against the forces of conglomerate market competition likely to be effective? Which direction could such legislation or regulation take?

Distribution Structure Alternatives II: Wholesaling

20

Just as a thorough understanding of the retail structure is essential to the marketing manager, so is a thorough knowledge of the wholesale structure. In 1963 wholesale trade amounted to $358.4 billion, substantially more than retail trade. This sales volume was achieved by 308,177 establishments.[1] Although the number of wholesaling institutions is considerably less than the number of retailing institutions, they are important intermediaries in the distribution network linking production and consumption.

This chapter examines the extent of wholesale trade geographically and by kind of business. Since wholesale trade is conducted by different types of establishments engaged in varied activities, the different types are described.

THE EXTENT OF WHOLESALE TRADE

In Chapter 15 wholesale trade was defined as including "all establishments or places of business primarily engaged in selling merchandise to retailers; to industrial, commercial, institutional or professional users; or to other wholesalers; or acting as agents in buying merchandise for or selling merchandise to such persons or companies."

Between 1958 and 1963 wholesale trade increased from $285.7 billion to $358.4 billion, or 25.4 percent. Adjusting the 1958 and 1963 sales to the 1957-1959 price base, the increase amounts to 25.5 percent. The increase in the number of establishments was from 287,043 in 1958 to 308,177 in 1963 or 7.4 percent.[2]

---

[1] *U.S. Bureau of the Census, U. S. Census of Business: 1963, Wholesale Trade—Summary Statistics,* Vol. IV, Part 1 (Washington, D.C.: Government Printing Office, 1966).

[2] *U.S. Census of Business: 1963, Wholesale Trade—Summary Statistics*, Vol. IV, Part 1. The 1958 and 1963 data were deflated by applying the wholesale price index of 100.4 for 1958 and 100.3 for 1963 (1957 — 1959 = 100). See *Statistical Abstract of the United States: 1965,* Eighty-Sixth ed. (Washington, D.C.: Government Printing Office, 1965).

Wholesale Trade by Geographic Location

The location of wholesaling establishments is not totally dependent upon the presence of population, as it is in the case of most retail stores. A wholesale establishment may exist in one area, with sales being made to distant points. Wholesale establishments are located in relation to the source of goods handled, the location of customers, and the transportation facilities necessary to move goods from the source of supply to the wholesaler and from the wholesaling establishment to the centers of consumption. On the other hand, there is some relationship between population densities and the location of wholesaling establishments. To the extent wholesalers locate close to sources of supply, the presence of a large number of manufacturers is accompanied by a concentration of population.

The entire eastern half of the country has a high density of wholesaling establishments, with the greatest concentration along the Atlantic seaboard. This is due to proximity of sources of supply, both domestic and foreign, and to points of consumption. In the western half of the country, with the exception of parts of the west coast, the points of consumption are much more dispersed, and manufacturing is less prevalent. The number of wholesaling establishments therefore is not nearly so great.

Wholesaling establishments are significantly concentrated in the large metropolitan cities. Such cities as New York, Boston, Philadelphia, Pittsburgh, Chicago, Detroit, St. Louis, Denver, Seattle, San Francisco, and Los Angeles are the important wholesaling centers.

Wholesale Trade by Kind of Business

There is considerable change in wholesale trade over a period of time by different kinds of business. In Table 20-1 a comparison of sales and establishments between 1958 and 1963 is made by kind of business. All categories, except tobacco–tobacco products, had significant gains in adjusted sales volume. Six categories—dry goods, apparel; groceries and related products; farm products—raw materials; scrap, waste materials; tobacco, tobacco products; and beer, wine, distilled alcoholic beverages—had decreases in the number of establishments.

TYPES OF WHOLESALING ESTABLISHMENTS

There are many types of wholesaling establishments, performing different activities for those who elect to use their services. This section deals with a description of the wholesale structure by type of operation. In Table 20-2 the sales and number of establishments of different types of wholesalers is shown for the years 1958, and 1963.

There has been little change in the proportion of total wholesale trade by different types of wholesaling establishments. The only gain has been in the

TABLE 20-1

Wholesale Sales and Establishments
by Kind of Business, 1958 and 1963

Kind of Business	WHOLESALE SALES (BILLIONS)		ADJUSTED WHOLESALE SALES[a] (BILLIONS)			WHOLESALE ESTABLISHMENTS		
	1958	1963	1958	1963	Percentage of Change	1958	1963	Percentage of Change
Motor vehicles, automotive equipment	23.5	36.6	23.4	36.5	56.0	23,139	28,895	24.9
Drugs, chemicals, allied products	16.6	20.8	16.6	20.7	24.7	10,305	11,438	11.0
Dry goods, apparel	13.6	17.5	13.5	17.4	28.9	12,045	11,756	-2.4
Groceries and related products	49.2	58.9	49.0	58.7	19.8	42,812	41,890	-2.2
Farm products—raw materials	28.6	34.8	28.5	34.7	21.8	17,314	16,214	-6.4
Electrical goods	16.5	22.0	16.4	21.9	33.5	13,273	16,211	22.1
Hardware, plumbing, heating equipment	7.9	9.4	7.9	9.4	19.0	11,516	12,814	11.3
Machinery, equipment, supplies	25.8	33.4	25.7	33.3	29.6	41,772	48,501	16.1
Metals, minerals (except petroleum and scrap)	22.1	26.6	22.0	26.5	20.5	7,471	8,475	13.4
Petroleum	20.3	21.5	20.2	21.4	5.9	30,520	30,873	1.2
Scrap, waste materials	3.1	3.7	3.1	3.7	19.4	9,661	8,288	-14.2
Tobacco, tobacco products	5.5	5.4	5.5	5.4	-1.8	2,963	2,824	-4.7
Beer, wine, distilled alcoholic beverages	8.7	10.7	8.7	10.7	23.0	7,861	7,598	-3.3
Paper, paper products (except wallpaper)	6.7	9.8	6.7	9.8	46.3	6,533	8,812	33.7
Furniture, home furnishings	4.8	6.6	4.8	6.6	37.5	6,976	8,119	16.4
Lumber, construction materials	10.6	13.8	10.6	13.8	30.2	11,721	14,139	20.6
Miscellaneous products	22.2	26.9	22.0	26.8	21.3	31,161	31,330	0.5
Total	285.7	358.4	284.6	357.3	25.5	287,043	308,177	7.4

a Wholesale sales are deflated to base period (1957–1959 = 100.0) by applying the wholesale price index of 100.4 for 1958 and 100.3 for 1963.

Compiled from U.S. Bureau of the Census, U.S. Census of Business: 1963, Wholesale Trade—Summary Statistics, Vol. IV, Part 1.

Table 20-2

Wholesale Trade by Type of Operation,
1963 and 1958

	SALES			ESTABLISHMENTS		
	Billions	*Percentage of Total*		*Number*	*Percentage of Total*	
	1963	*1963*	*1958*	*1963*	*1963*	*1958*
Merchant wholesalers	$157.4	43.9	42.7	208,997	67.8	66.3
Full-service wholesalers	156.4	43.6	41.0	203,672	66.1	62.8
Limited-function wholesalers	1.0	0.3	1.7	5,825	1.7	3.5
Manufacturers' sales branches and sales offices	116.4	32.8	30.7	28,884	9.4	8.8
Manufacturers' sales branches (with stocks)	54.8	15.6	14.6	16,408	5.3	5.3
Manufacturers' sales offices (without stocks)	61.6	17.2	16.1	12,476	4.1	3.5
Petroleum bulk plants	21.5	6.4	7.2	30,873	10.0	10.7
Agent intermediaries	53.3	14.1	16.2	25,313	8.2	9.3
Merchandise brokers	13.9	3.8	3.5	5,083	1.6	1.5
Commission merchants	9.5	2.7	4.1	3,416	1.1	2.4
Selling agents	8.3	2.3	2.4	2,574	0.8	0.7
Manufacturers' agents	10.9	3.0	3.4	11,189	3.6	3.5
Purchasing agents and resident buyers	1.2	0.2	0.4	220	0.1	0.1
Auction companies	5.1	1.4	1.6	1,894	0.6	0.6
Import and export agents	4.3	0.7	0.8	937	0.4	0.5
Assemblers of farm products	9.8	2.8	3.2	14,110	4.6	4.9
Total	$358.4	100.0	100.0	308,177	100.0	100.0

Source: U.S. Bureau of the Census, Census of Business: 1963, Wholesale Trade: United States Summary: *BC63-WA1.*

manufacturers' branches and sales offices category and probably reflects a tendency toward circumvention of wholesale merchants by manufacturers. This tendency is discussed in detail in Chapter 21. There are six different types of wholesalers; within each type exists a large number of variations in methods of operation.

Industrial Distributors

The industrial distributor is the industrial goods counterpart of the wholesaler in the consumer goods field. Industrial distributors are frequently overlooked in discussions of wholesaling, but familiarity with this type of wholesaling is essential in planning distribution mixes for industrial goods. Industrial distributors do the largest sales volume in iron and steel products and machinery, equipment, and supplies. In the latter two categories, they made sales amounting to $16.1 billion in 1963.

The industrial distributor frequently carries adequate stocks of repair parts, is located close to the customers he serves, and, because of the way in which industrial buyers purchase, needs a highly trained sales force. He rarely handles

343

the very expensive, technical, custom-built capital-equipment items but is very active in the distribution of less expensive industrial equipment and supplies. This type of establishment provides excellent distribution for the manufacturer of narrow lines of industrial goods, because he can give the kind of selling effort needed at lower cost than if the manufacturer were to try to sell direct to the many smaller industrial buyers.

Wholesale Merchants

Merchant wholesalers—who we said buy goods outright rather than act as agents—are by far the largest group. In 1963 they accounted for about 44 percent of all wholesale trade. Their main contribution to efficient distribution comes from their ability to supply goods rapidly and at low cost. To make goods readily available, full-service merchant wholesalers maintain stocks of merchandise close to the buyer. Their economic advantage is achieved through spreading the cost of moving goods to the point of consumption over a large number of items produced by hundreds and sometimes thousands of manufacturers. Drug wholesalers, for example, handle up to 30,000 different items yet daily can supply the corner druggist with his needed assortment.

The service wholesaler offers a full range of services to the manufacturer whose product he handles and to the buyer who uses him as a source of supply. He aids in the transportation and storage activities necessary in the movement of goods from points of production to points of consumption. He anticipates buyers' needs, searches out sources of supply, accumulates matching assortments, and performs a selling task for the suppliers whose goods he handles. He often extends credit to the buyer, as well as other forms of assistance, such as personnel training, display materials, store layouts, and the development of inventory control methods.

Table 20-3 shows merchant wholesalers by sales size and operating expenses for 1963. The small-size merchant wholesaler, in terms of number of units, is most important, but the largest share of the business is done by a relatively few large establishments. Table 20-3 shows that 11.0 percent of the establishments (annual sales volume of over $2 million), account for 54.2 percent of total sales of merchant wholesalers.

Operating expenses of a merchant wholesaler vary considerably by kind of business. For example, operating expenses as a percentage of sales of merchant wholesalers handling different kinds of goods in the $2,000,000-to-$4,999,000 sales volume range are as follows: [3]

New automotive parts	18.5%
Drugs, drug proprietaries, and sundries	13.1
Dry goods, piece goods, notions	11.4
General line grocery	7.7
General purpose industrial machinery	18.7
Tobacco and tobacco products	5.5

[3] U.S. Bureau of the Census, *U.S. Census of Business: 1963, Wholesale Trade, Sales Size and Employment Size,* BC63-WA2.

TABLE 20-3

Merchant Wholesalers by Sales Size
and Operating Expenses, 1963

Establishments Operated Entire Year With Annual Sales of:	ESTABLISHMENTS		SALES		OPERATING EXPENSES
	Number	Percentage of Total	Billions	Percentage of Total	Percentage
$20,000,000 and over	478	.2	23.3	14.8	4.3
$15,000,000–$19,999,000	273	.1	4.7	3.0	8.0
$10,000,000–$14,999,000	622	.3	7.5	4.7	9.2
$5,000,000–$9,999,000	2,654	1.3	18.0	11.4	10.4
$2,000,000–$4,999,000	10,213	4.9	30.8	19.6	12.8
$1,000,000–$1,999,000	17,616	8.4	24.6	15.6	15.5
$500,000–$999,000	28,612	13.7	20.2	12.8	18.1
$300,000–$499,000	26,640	12.7	10.3	6.6	20.4
$200,000–$299,000	23,561	11.3	5.8	3.7	21.6
$100,000–$199,000	38,545	18.4	5.6	3.5	23.0
Less than $100,000	51,563	24.7	2.7	1.7	25.1
Establishments not operated entire year:	8,220	3.9	4.0	2.5	15.8
Total	208,997	100.0	157.5	100.0	

Compiled from *U.S. Bureau of the Census,* U.S. Census of Business: 1963, Wholesale Trade, Sales Size and Employment Size, *BC63-WS2.*

Differences in the cost of performing wholesaling operations for different classes of goods result from: (1) the types of facilities necessary, (2) the rate of turnover of goods handled, (3) the market in which the goods are sold, and (4) the range of products and services offered. Much more expensive facilities are needed for food products, particularly perishables, than for wearing apparel. On the other hand, many food products are staples and turnover is high, with only limited stock kept at any one time. In contrast, the jewelry business, which experiences marked seasonal demand and a need to carry a large number of slow-moving items, incurs a much higher operating expense. The area covered also has a bearing on the cost of operation. When the establishment is located in a rather thinly populated area or where distances between markets are great (such as in the West), costs are naturally higher than in the more concentrated areas of the Atlantic seaboard.

Merchant wholesalers are classified as general merchandise, general line, and specialty wholesalers.

General Merchandise Wholesalers

These wholesalers carry a wide variety of merchandise in a number of unrelated lines, such as furniture, dry goods, hardware, and groceries. They are the wholesaling counterpart of the retail general store. They flourished when the general store was important, and like the general store, they have declined in importance.

General Line Wholesaler

This type of wholesaler carries a wide variety of merchandise in a single merchandise line, such as a complete line of dry groceries. The most predominant of the full-service merchant wholesalers, he services primarily the limited-line stores.

Specialty Wholesalers

These establishments specialize in a few items in a single line. In the grocery line, a specialty wholesaler may deal only in tea and coffee; in the drug field, he may handle only sundries and patent medicines; in the home furnishings field, only small housewares.

The advantages of specialization, such as well-trained sales people and up-to-date merchandise, are accompanied by a relatively high cost of operation. The narrow line of merchandise makes the cost of soliciting sales high, and unless the buyer purchases in very large quantities, cost of operation far exceeds that of the general line wholesaler.

Merchant wholesalers are also classified on the basis of services rendered as full-service or limited-function wholesalers. Wide variations in the cost of operation are also accounted for by the wide range of services offered. Limited-function wholesalers are divided into cash-and-carry wholesalers, wagon-truck distributors, drop shippers, and mail-order wholesalers. In 1963 the limited-function merchant wholesalers numbered 5,825, and did $1.0 billion in sales volume. A closer look at the activities of these merchant wholesalers follows.

Cash-and-carry Wholesalers

These wholesalers developed to meet the competition of the chain retailers; they perform their own wholesaling operations, as a means of reducing the cost of merchandise to independent retailers. Their operation was limited to concentrated markets in which it was feasible for the customer to provide transportation. Today cash-and-carry establishments are primarily branches of full-service merchant wholesalers.

Wagon-truck Distributors

This category includes "establishments primarily engaged in selling their merchandise from trucks or other vehicles, combining the functions of salesmen with those of delivery men and carrying a limited assortment of well-known, fast-moving items." [4] Wagon-truck distributors are used when time is important, such as in selling perishables, and where a large number of small buyers require frequent contact. They are common in such lines as cookies and confectionaries, and in automotive supplies sold to garages and service stations. Although this type of wholesaler should provide aggressive selling effort, this is not always the case. Personnel often are not well trained, and many operate with limited capital.

---

[4] U.S. Census of Business: 1963, Wholesale Trade—Summary Statistics, Vol. IV, Part 1, Appendix, 16.

Costs are high because of the narrow line and the small size of purchase. To operate profitably, these distributors require a reasonable variety in the line and a very dense market.

Drop Shippers

This type of wholesaler is usually found in products which are bulky and of low unit value. The main product lines in which drop shippers operate are coal, lumber, and construction materials. Drop shippers do not take physical possession of goods, but upon receipt of an order, direct the producer to ship directly to the buyer's location, thus saving the cost of handling the merchandise with change in ownership. The producer bills the drop shipper and the drop shipper bills his customer. Because the drop shipper purchases from many sources, his costs are likely to be less than those incurred when each producer sells directly to the buyer. The overhead selling costs are spread over a much larger volume. For instance, each producer would have the cost of extending credit on a relatively small scale, but the drop shipper can better afford this cost because of the buyer's purchase of several items from a single source—the drop shipper.

Mail-order Wholesalers

As the name implies, this wholesaler receives all orders from buyers by mail. No sales force is used to call upon the trade; rather, selling expenses are concentrated in the production and distribution of catalogs. Mail-order wholesalers are more important than is generally believed; they are quite prevalent in food wholesaling. Much of the business done by retailer cooperatives and voluntary chain wholesale establishments is by mail.

Manufacturers' Sales Branches and Sales Offices

These establishments differ from merchant wholesalers in that they are owned by manufacturers or mining companies and maintained apart from producing plants primarily for selling or marketing their products at wholesale. . . . Sales branches or sales offices located at plant or administrative offices are included where separate records are available and could be reported separately . . . data are shown separately for sales branches and for sales offices. They differ in that sales offices normally do not carry stocks of merchandise for delivery to consumers.

Sales as recorded for sales branches include direct deliveries from plants on orders from the branches as well as deliveries from branch stocks. Sales as shown for sales offices generally represent the value of orders written or booked by employers at the offices, including salesmen working out of the office.[5]

The inclusion of manufacturers' sales branches and sales offices in wholesale trade is an attempt to record the wholesaling activities of manufacturers. Table 20-2 shows that, as a proportion of total wholesale trade, sales by this group have remained fairly stable. Since 1958 the number of establishments has increased by several thousand.

The share of sales made by sales branches has remained stable, while there has been a slight increase in the share made by sales offices. Manufacturers' sales

---

[5] *U.S. Census of Business: 1963, Wholesale Trade.*

branches (with stock) generally operate in a manner similar to that of a merchant wholesaler. Manufacturers' sales branches (with stock) generally operate in a manner similar to that of a merchant wholesaler. Manufacturers' sales offices (without stock) are not concerned with the physical handling and movement of goods. They are simply offices, located in the field, from which the sales force works. In this respect, they have a type of operation rather similar to that of drop shippers.

Manufacturers' sales branches are often distribution centers for direct sales to other wholesalers, retailers, or manufacturers. In this sense the manufacturer has elected to circumvent the independent wholesaler completely. The reasons for complete integration of wholesaling by manufacturers, and some of the conditions which make it economically feasible, are discussed in detail in Chapter 21.

Petroleum Bulk Plants

These are establishments engaged in the receiving, storing, and marketing of gasoline, kerosene, distillate and residual fuel oils, liquified petroleum gases, and other bulk petroleum products. They are included as a separate group because of the distinctiveness in facilities necessary to handle these products. Bulk petroleum products are usually moved from the refineries to the independent bulk terminal plants, which, in turn, redistribute to retailers of such products or directly to industrial and agricultural producers.

Agent Intermediaries

Agent intermediaries (sometimes called *functional middlemen*) are an important type of wholesaling establishment. They are called agents because they do not own the goods distributed but rather perform services on a commission basis on behalf of principals. They are engaged primarily in selling or buying. Agent intermediaries accounted for $53.3 billion, or 14.1 percent, of wholesale trade in 1963, and represented 8.2 percent of all wholesaling establishments. Between 1958 and 1963 there was a decline in their share of wholesale trade, as well as a decrease in the number of establishments.

There are several types of agent intermediaries. The most important are commission merchants, merchandise brokers, selling agents, and manufacturers' agents. It is important that the major distinction between them be understood, for that reason, the aforementioned four types of agents will now be briefly described.

Brokers

Merchandise brokers facilitate the buying or selling of merchandise on a commission basis. They do not take physical possession of goods. Their main activity is bringing buyer and seller together; they usually operate on a non-continuing contractual basis and may represent either buyers or sellers. Generally the broker is limited in determining the conditions of sale, such as price and terms, and needs confirmation from the principal before the sale is closed. Brokers are perhaps used most frequently in the distribution of products which have seasonal production and do not require regular year-round sales solicitation. They are also used by small manufacturers selling in broad markets, and provide an inexpensive means of performing the selling task for the small producer with limited financial resources. They are familiar with market conditions and can offer their services to the manufacturer at a relatively low fee. Since their major activity is to bring buyer and seller together, overhead is low. In groceries and food specialties, in which they are most important, they operate on an average commission fee of 2.8 percent.[6] They also represent large growers of agricultural produce in the central markets. Table 20-2 shows that in 1963, 5,083 establishments did $13.9 billion in sales.

Commission Merchants

These agents primarily represent sellers on a noncontinuing contractual basis. They differ from brokers in that they take physical possession of merchandise and must provide warehousing facilities. They generally have more freedom in negotiating terms of sale, and they do not need confirmation from the principal. They seek the best terms possible, negotiate the sale, deliver the merchandise, extend credit, make collection, and deduct commissions before remitting to the principal. They are used primarily in marketing livestock and farm products. They are used in a very limited way in manufactured goods, primarily in dry goods. In 1963, 3,416 commission merchants did approximately $9.5 billion in sales. In 1963 they operated on an average commission of 2.7 percent of sales.[7]

Selling Agents

Selling agents are engaged primarily in the marketing of manufactured goods such as dry goods, groceries and foods, and furniture and house furnishings. They generally provide all of the selling activities necessary for a company and handle the entire output of their principals. In some fields, such as textiles and canned goods, they may represent a number of companies. They maintain a continuing contractual relationship with principals and have considerable latitude in determining conditions of sale. They sometimes finance production for their clients, and are not restricted to any particular geographic region.

Selling agents offer the smaller manufacturer a complete sales organization at relatively low cost and, consequently, are used in those industries where production is seasonal or where the individual manufacturers are small, with limited financial resources and widely scattered markets. For such companies to maintain their own sales organization is either prohibitively costly because of the seasonal nature of production, or impossible because of limited financial resources. In 1963, average commissions for selling agents were 3.9 percent of sales.[8] Table 20-2 shows that in 1963, 2,574 selling agents sold $8.3 billion worth of goods.

Manufacturers' Agents

Manufacturers' agents act as independent salesmen for the firms they represent. The major differences between the manufacturers' agent and the

[6] *U.S. Census of Business: 1963, Wholesale Trade,* Vol. IV, Part 2, Chap. 9, Table 11.
[7] *Ibid.*
[8] *Ibid.*

selling agent are four: (1) Much more control is exercised over the manufacturers' agent by the principal. Agents generally do not have as much freedom to vary prices or conditions of sale. (2) The manufacturers' agent does not handle the entire output of the principal; rather, he handles a part of the output in a limited, exclusive territory. (3) The manufacturers' agent represents a number of manufacturers of related but noncompeting merchandise, whereas the broker may handle the output of several directly competing producers. (4) Agents simply act as salesmen and generally are not involved in any financing of the principal's production.

Manufacturers' agents are frequently used in thinly populated markets, in which solicitation costs are high if sales are limited to products of a single manufacturer. By representing many manufacturers, the agent's costs are spread over a wider variety of goods and a much higher sales volume. Agents are also used by manufacturers of narrow lines in order to reduce the cost of selling. Because the relationship is a continuous one, manufacturers' agents may give excellent service, and can be induced to provide an aggressive, hard-hitting, personal selling effort for the client. They are used in both consumers' and industrial manufactured goods. In the consumer goods field they handle such items as groceries, dry goods, and clothing.

Table 20-2 shows that in 1963, 11,189 manufacturers' agents handled $10.9 billion in wholesale trade. Average commissions were 6.0 percent of sales.[9]

Assemblers of Farm Products

Agricultural production is such that the sorting process is difficult and expensive. The units of production are generally small and located some distance from the centers of consumption. Furthermore, buyers wish to purchase in large quantities. Assemblers operate in local markets in the producing regions. They usually purchase directly from the farmer and assemble sufficient quantities to economically ship produce to the central market.

Summary

The wholesale structure in the United States is made up of 308,177 establishments doing $358.4 billion in sales. Between 1958 and 1963 there was a 25.5 percent increase in sales after adjustment for inflation, and a 7.4 percent increase in number of establishments. There are changes in sales and number of establishments in different kinds of business. The number of establishments has not adjusted to changes in sales volume in those kinds of business categories which have experienced a decline in sales or remained stable over the period. In fact, in most cases the number of establishments has increased.

Wholesaling establishments are concentrated on the Atlantic seaboard and parts of the Pacific coast. Wholesaling establishments are ordinarily divided into five types: (1) merchant wholesalers, (2) manufacturers' sales branches and sales offices, (3) petroleum bulk plants, (4) agent intermediaries, and (5) assemblers of farm products. The merchant wholesalers are the most important type

[9] *Ibid.*

of wholesaling establishment. The cost of operation of merchant wholesalers varies because of: (1) the types of facilities necessary, (2) the market in which goods are sold, and (3) the range of products and services offered, and (4) the rate of turnover of goods handled. Merchant wholesalers are classified (on the basis of the range of products handled) as general merchandise, general line, and specialty wholesalers. They are also classified as full-service or limited-function wholesalers. Among the limited-function wholesalers are cash-and-carry wholesalers, wagon-truck distributors, drop shippers, and mail-order wholesalers.

Manufacturers' sales branches (with stock) and sales offices (without stock) represent those wholesaling establishments owned and operated by manufacturers. They may function as distribution centers from which sales are made to other independent wholesale merchants, or they may perform all of the activities of a full-service merchant wholesaler and sell directly to retailers or industrial buyers.

Petroleum bulk plants are a special kind of wholesaling establishment distinguished from the others because of the specialized facilities needed to handle bulk petroleum products.

Agent intermediaries differ from merchant wholesalers in that they do not take title of goods. The most important agent intermediaries are classified as: (1) merchandise brokers, (2) commission merchants, (3) selling agents, and (4) manufacturers' agents. They are used primarily by smaller manufacturers with seasonal production or with limited financial resources and narrow lines.

Assemblers of farm products are a type of wholesaling establishment instrumental in sorting agricultural goods.

Questions and Problems

1. Since retail prices are generally higher than wholesale prices, how do you account for the fact that wholesale sales are larger than retail sales?
2. What is *the* distinguishing characteristic that differentiates the agent from the merchant wholesaler?
3. What specific functions are performed by the drop shipper?
4. How do you account for the difference in product line sold by the drop-shipper and the mail-order wholesaler?
5. Why has the cash-and-carry wholesaler failed to achieve the same degree of market penetration that its retail counterpart, the supermarket, has achieved?
6. In view of the relatively high cost of operation of the specialty wholesaler, how does this institution continue to exist?
7. Under what conditions would a marketing manager employ the services of a selling agent?
8. In general, what advantages are to be gained by a manufacturer in using his own sales branches as compared with using service wholesalers?
9. Does the sale of industrial goods always involve a wholesale transaction? Why?
10. Differentiate between the terms *wholesaler, wholesale establishment,* and *wholesale transaction.*
11. After analyzing the data presented in this chapter, indicate the most significant trends in the wholesale structure.

12. Do you believe that changes in the wholesale structure precipitate changes in the retail structure, or vice versa?

13. Compare the operating costs and/or commissions of sales offices, drop shippers, and manufacturers' agents. What conclusions do you draw?

14. "Modern markets and the changing character of manufacturers are such that the traditional wholesaler will soon be extinct in the distribution structure." Agree or disagree? Defend your answer.

15. If needed functions can be performed more cheaply by an independent wholesaler than the manufacturer himself can perform them, the manufacturer should incorporate the wholesaler in his channel of distribution. Agree or disagree? Why?

Channel Decisions and Management

21

In Chapter 15 we examined the relationship of specialization to exchange, and the barriers to exchange resulting from the heterogeneity of supply and demand. In succeeding chapters the requirements of efficient goods flow through a system of physical distribution, some of the areas of conflict and resolution between manufacturers and middlemen, and the characteristics of retailers and wholesalers in the distribution network were explored. We now must integrate the producer, physical distribution components, and middlemen into a channel of distribution which produces maximum impact at the point of ultimate sale. Not only is the channel instrumental in physical flow of goods, but it is also the vehicle through which much marketing effort is channeled to buyers.

The purpose of this chapter is to define a channel of distribution, to determine the criteria for the selection of channels, to examine the factors which influence the selection of direct versus indirect channels, the use of manufacturers' agents, and cost and revenue considerations.

CHANNELS OF DISTRIBUTION DEFINED

A channel of distribution is *a combination of institutions through which a seller markets his products to the user or ultimate consumer.* Some of the institutions in different channels of distribution may be shown as follows:

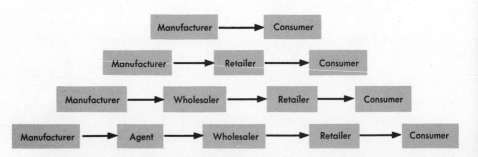

The important thing to remember is that each of the institutions in the channel represents a composite of activities, the performance of which is essential to the efficient distribution of goods. The institutions selected to represent the channel must perform all of the activities that are required to move goods from points of production to points of consumption. We have previously described a number of the institutional alternatives, and these institutions might be considered as available for hire to the manufacturer for the performance of activities deemed necessary.

CRITERIA FOR THE SELECTION
OF CHANNELS OF DISTRIBUTION

To select a channel of distribution requires extensive knowledge of the different middlemen available and their capacity to perform the needed activities. Decisions must be made on: (1) the market coverage needed and (2) the degree of market control desired. Of overriding importance is the aggressiveness of marketing effort achieved.

Market Coverage Needed

The question of market coverage has primarily two facets. The first is the type of outlet which should handle the product, and the second is the intensity of distribution needed.

Type of Outlet Required

What types of institutions should carry the product? Should hardware stores carry camping equipment, and should variety stores carry outboard motors? The increase in scrambled merchandising referred to in Chapter 18 represents a continuing problem to the manufacturer. The change in product assortments offered by different types of retailers is reflected in the assortments handled by different types of wholesalers.

Often the initiative for channel change comes from a retailer or wholesaler seeking to carry new lines—in a sense pursuing different product strategies by altering the usual assortments. Examples of this are the addition of building materials by hardware wholesalers, the handling of small appliances by drug and jewelry stores, and the inclusion of magazines, photographic equipment, ladies' hosiery, and housewares in the product assortments offered by food stores. In each case, the manufacturer must decide whether these outlets are appropriate for his products.

In other cases, the manufacturer may be seeking new ways to reach different markets and may take the initiative in attempting to alter traditional patterns. Such is the case with a large paper manufacturer placing stationery in a number of different kinds of outlets, or the manner in which book publishers have broadened their market for paperbacks by departing from the traditional book channels. More and more, the job of determining the proper type of outlet to handle a product is becoming a difficult one. As the character of retail stores changes, manufacturers must keep abreast, or find their products in the wrong channel.

In order for the manufacturer to determine the type of outlets best suited to sell his product, he must know the caliber of each of the potentially suitable outlets. If his product requires a substantial investment in inventory, the potential number of available outlets is immediately reduced. Where a particular environment for sale is needed, such as that required by expensive luxury items (for example, china and silverware), the number of outlets capable of providing this environment is limited. Other factors, such as need for consumer credit, availability of service facilities, or maintenance of repair parts inventories, may also restrict the number of available outlets.

Intensity of Distribution

The objectives of the company, the nature of the product, and the nature of the market determine the intensity of distribution required. The exposure to sale required by a manufacturer of toothpaste differs substantially from that required by a manufacturer of fine crystal. In general, more intense distribution calls for more indirect channels.[1] That is, more middlemen are used to fan out the distribution to make the product available to a large number of potential customers. Three degrees of intensity of distribution are discernible: (1) intensive distribution, (2) selective distribution, and (3) exclusive distribution.

Intensive distribution involves three different ideas. First, it can refer to the total marketing area over which distribution is desired. Using the term in this way makes a distinction between local or regional distribution and national distribution. Second, it can refer to the desire to gain exposure to sale in all outlets in which buyers are willing to purchase the product. That is, if drugstores are the proper type of outlet through which to offer the product, intensive distribution attempts to gain representation in every drugstore. Third, it may refer to the number of outlets, without regard to type. For example, chewing gum may be, and is, offered for sale in a number of different types of outlets. Distribution in this case is intensive because it is made available for sale in just about every kind of outlet that will handle it. Most low-unit-value high-frequency-of-purchase, staple products require intensive distribution. Representative of such products are foods, beverages, light hardware, and drug and sundries.

Selective distribution, as the name implies, involves a reduction in the number of outlets through which the product is made available. It is usually used in conjunction with products commonly referred to as "shopping goods." That is, the consumer rarely purchases the first product examined, but shops in many different outlets before coming to a final decision. By carefully selecting the outlets that handle the product, the manufacturer is assured that his product is represented as he desires. Restriction of the number of outlets handling a product, and selectivity within a type of outlet, are closely related problems. The number of outlets is restricted because the product requires an outlet that can provide specific services or environment in order to achieve desired sales volume. To place the product in just any outlet might damage the product's

---

[1] The terms *direct channel* and *indirect channel* are often used in marketing. The directness of the channel refers to the number of channel members involved. The most direct channel is from manufacturer to ultimate consumer. For consumer goods, manufacturer-to-retailer-to-consumer is usually considered a direct channel. Indirect channels include either full-service or agent wholesale establishments.

prestige. Such products as women's and men's clothing, ranges, and refrigerators and freezers, as well as many home furnishings, are selectively distributed.

Exclusive distribution may be considered a special type of selective distribution: a single outlet is given an exclusive franchise to handle the product in a prescribed territory. Products which have a high level of brand loyalty, which the customer will go out of his way to purchase, are distributed in this manner. If the product requires certain specialized efforts and heavy investment in facilities or inventories on the part of middlemen in the channel, they may be unwilling to handle it without assurance of exclusive representation. Wholesale paints, for instance, require a large investment in inventory and, consequently, paint distributors may insist upon exclusive representation for a given line. This, on the other hand, limits the manufacturer's market in the area. Consequently, multiple branding is sometimes used by the manufacturer to expand distribution through giving an "exclusive" on each brand to one dealer or distributor in the area.

Exclusive distribution at the wholesale level is more frequent than at the retail level. Wholesalers may insist upon exclusive representation in an area, but they, in turn, sell to retailers on an intensive or selective basis. The legal implications involved in the use of exclusive agencies will be discussed in Chapter 17. The decision of how intensive distribution is to be is most wisely made only after analyses of the market, the way in which the consumer buys, and the availability of channel members that can be induced to handle the product are complete.

The Degree of Market Control

For many reasons, the task of selecting the channel of distribution is the responsibility of the manufacturer. The widespread branding of merchandise forces responsibility upon him. The act of identifying the source through a brand name, together with promoting the brand to achieve some level of customer loyalty, is public notice that responsibility is assumed. Likewise, the use of warranties has a similar effect. The increase in technically complex products, with a need for before- and after-sale service, is another factor forcing the manufacturer to assume responsibility. Perhaps the most pervasive influence is the fact that unless goods move through the channel, repeat orders will be at a minimum. The act of promoting a product line directly to the ultimate consumer in an effort to pull goods through the channel is evidence of the manufacturer's desire to control the channel. Through control, the manufacturer attempts to insure that his product will receive the required sales aggressiveness as well as all the other essential elements necessary to produce results that meet the objectives of the enterprise.

Different products require different degrees of control. Where close control is necessary, one of the ways of achieving it is through using relatively *direct* channels. By reducing the number of middlemen, it is easier to insure that all requirements are met. The use of direct house-to-house selling by manufacturers represents the ultimate in control—although it is quite costly. When *indirect* channels must be used—that is, when more middlemen are involved—attempts at control are made through establishing efficient dealer-manufacturer systems (discussed in Chapter 17). As a rule of thumb, the degree of control achieved is directly proportionate to the directness of the channel.

There is a widespread belief that the more direct the channel, the less the cost of distribution; this belief is fostered by the familiar advertising slogan, "Direct from factory to you." In some cases, savings *are* achieved through direct sale. However, we have already seen (in Chapter 19) that direct house-to-house selling is one of the most costly forms of distribution. Savings are achieved only if the manufacturer is able to perform the necessary activities at less expense than that incurred were independent middlemen to perform some of them. In most cases, direct sale is *more* costly, but it is the price paid to insure that the product is properly presented in the market. In general, manufacturers desire the control provided by the more direct channels of distribution.

DIRECT VERSUS INDIRECT CHANNELS

The activities that must be performed by the channels of distribution are a function of the needs and desires of buyers and the objectives of the manufacturer. Since the needs and desires of buyers vary with every product, it is difficult to explain in detail *all* the marketing factors which may be considered in selecting a channel of distribution. However, practitioners of marketing have been able to mark out definite areas of inquiry.

As we have seen in Chapter 19, approximately 97 percent of all goods sold for personal or household consumption pass through a retail store. Therefore, in consumer goods the question is how to get the goods into the retail stores. Should the manufacturer use an indirect channel, relying on various types of middlemen to sell to retailers, or should he go direct and assume responsibility for getting his goods into the retail stores? Likewise, in industrial goods a decision must be made on what reliance to place on industrial distributors versus going direct to the buyers with his own sales force. The approach is to analyze the characteristics of the product, the market, and the manufacturer, keeping in mind the types of institutions which, when combined as a channel of distribution, can most effectively perform the various activities so vital to the successful marketing of the product.

Product Characteristics Which Influence the Choice of Channels

The purpose of analyzing the product is to identify its characteristics to detect: (1) financial requirements, (2) any special handling needs, (3) storage requirements, and (4) requirements in sale. A discussion of some of the product characteristics and their relevance to channel selection follows.

Unit Value of the Product

The unit value of the product provides a clue to the funds available for distribution. In the case of high-unit-value products, more funds are available per unit of product sold than there are for low-unit-value products. Although a number of other influencing characteristics are generally associated with high-unit-value products (such as the need for servicing technical products), the general tendency is toward more costly, direct channels. Where the unit value is low, there is a tendency toward intensive distribution; channels are usually indirect just because of the need for intensive coverage. Direct channels for more market control are not generally used because there is not sufficient margin to cover the cost. However, low-unit-value products purchased in large quantities generate a favorable financial picture. That is, the absolute margin created in any single sale is large, and there is a large margin to absorb the cost of marketing.

Bulk

An important consideration is the value of the product relative to its weight. If it has a high value per pound, the extent of the market is not limited. If it is low, the cost of movement frequently restricts the entire market to an area reasonably close to the point of production. This has been true in the past in the brewing industry, wherein local brands play a major role. Some brewers have extended their markets by decentralization of producing facilities, along with attempts to build brand loyalty and to penetrate a larger geographic market at a premium price. The principle of *postponement,* whereby product adjustments are postponed to a point as close to the consumer as possible, is another means of overcoming this product characteristic. Coca-Cola is an excellent example. Bottled Coca-Cola, if distributed from a single plant over a wide area, would be considerably more expensive than it is under present methods of distribution. The shipment of the concentrated syrup to the bottling plant, and restriction of the market for each bottling plant to an area reasonably close to it, help to keep the cost down.

Perishability

Perishability may refer to physical deterioration, fashion perishability, or technological perishability. In each case, an element of risk is introduced. This risk is offset by the members of the channel purchasing on a hand-to-mouth basis, forcing a storage problem on the manufacturer. In physically perishable goods, the manufacturers or processors must find middlemen with the proper storage facilities. In the case of fashion perishability, the risk in inventory is enormous, and one that cannot easily be passed on to channel members. With technologically perishable goods, such as extremely complex machinery, leasing has become a prevalent policy, with the manufacturer assuming responsibility for all distribution factors. In general, perishable products tend to be handled through the shorter channels of distribution; with them, speed of movement through the channel is essential.

Technicality of the Product

When the product is technical, several requirements must be met. First, it may require a highly skilled technician to represent it to potential purchasers. Second, it may require more than just personal solicitation of customers; perhaps actual demonstration. Third, if the product must be adjusted to the customer's needs, the skills must be available to provide this before-sale service. Fourth, if there is a constant need for adjustment, after-sale service facilities must be provided. In this connection, it is often necessary to make sure that inventories of repair parts are conveniently available.

The technical features of the product generally relate to the particular skills needed to sell and service it. You will recall that most capital goods discussed in Chapter 8 have these characteristics. Since a large measure of market control is needed to insure that the product is represented properly, the more direct channels are used.

Breadth of the Line

A group of products associated in use and purchase usually is sold to a single market. In this sense, the broader the line, the higher the average-size sale, providing funds to take care of other requirements. Contrary to previous statements about the influence of the unit value of the product on the channel of distribution, a broad product line of low-unit-value products can be intensively distributed by direct methods. This is true because the average-size sale is relatively large. Many companies, such as the H. J. Heinz Company and the Campbell Soup Company, distribute broad lines directly to retail outlets from their own distribution centers. Care, however, should be exercised in combining products and attempting to sell them in the same channel. In Chapter 11, much attention was given to building the product line, and it is emphasized here to underscore the necessity of making sure that no attempt is made to mix products in a single channel unless it is appropriate for the line.

Seasonality in Production or Consumption

Whenever production and consumption do not coincide, a storage problem is present. The middlemen within the channel are not usually willing to assume the out-of-season storage function, as it means an investment in inventory with no immediate return. Consequently, this activity is forced onto the manufacturer. Since storage is for many products an important activity, and since manufacturers have been forced to assume its responsibility, some have integrated vertically and assumed all of the activities that must be performed relative to it.

Degree of Market Acceptance

This characteristic is related to the aggressiveness needed to sell the product. Usually, for new products without a high degree of acceptance, very aggressive effort is required. Because many middlemen carry a wide range of competitive products, it often is not possible to achieve any special treatment for a given line. In these cases, the manufacturer must seek ways and means to control the channel of distribution. If the product is such that it lends itself to exclusive distribution, this may be the means used. When intensive exposure to sale is necessary, he may seek some more direct channel for distributing goods to a large number of outlets. If for any reason this is not possible, the use of independent middlemen, backed by the manufacturer's own salesmen (called "missionary salesmen" or "detail men") calling at various levels of distribution, may be used.

Missionary salesmen or detail men only incidentally take orders for merchandise. When they do, the order is turned over to the appropriate middleman servicing the account. Their purpose is to work with all middlemen to insure that the product is handled in the proper way. This may involve training wholesaler and retailer sales forces, building displays in retail outlets, and securing favorable shelf space in retail outlets, as well as seeking the proper use of advertising and promotional materials supplied by the manufacturer.

New products generally require a high level of aggressive selling, and to insure this the first channel used may be a more direct one. As a product achieves acceptance, a switch to more indirect channels may be possible.

Substitutability of Product

This is closely related to market acceptance. If there is little brand loyalty, and substitution is easy, maximum exposure to sale is essential. Not only must the product be conveniently available, but point-of-purchase communication is important. In many consumer goods, this means achieving favorable shelf space in self-service retail outlets, insuring effective display and aggressive personal selling at the retail level. These are not always easy to obtain. There is no particular reason why any of the middlemen carrying a wide range of products, including competing brands, should favor a given manufacturer. With exclusive or selective distribution, more than normal margins may be offered; or, to cite a more common occurrence, missionary salesmen, or detail men, may be used to gain the desired channel support.

Market Characteristics Which Affect the Choice of Channels

In part, analysis of a product identifies its users. However, precise analysis of the quantitative and qualitative aspects of the market is necessary to determine the size of the marketing job to be done and probable channel costs.

Users of the Product

The users must be identified, as the same product is often used by more than one type of consumer. For example, tractors are sold to farmers, manufacturing enterprises, county road commissions, municipal governments, and a number of other classes of customers. The activities necessary to sell to some classes differ from those necessary to sell to others; consequently, the channels used to reach these different classes vary. For example, the custom market is made up of a large number of individuals who purchase light tractors for commercial and residential landscaping and grading. They usually work part-time and use this as a source of extra income. The task of reaching these buyers and the method of selling to them differs substantially from reaching and selling to municipal governments. In the latter case, many buyers are large, buying in large quantities on a specification and bid basis. Frequently, demonstration is necessary, and technical service must be readily available.

Size of the Market

The size of the market gives an indication of the funds available for performing the activities needed. If the size of the market is large, even though the unit value of the product is small, the absolute dollar sales volume is large and provides considerable funds for allocation to the many activities which must be performed. Where the market is small, available funds are scarce, and the manufacturer might have to be content with a less elaborate program, relying more on the normal services that can be performed by middlemen without special incentives.

Geographic Concentration or Dispersion

When the market is geographically concentrated, ease of reaching all potential customers at low cost is greater. When it is thin and dispersed over a large area, the cost of solicitation is much higher. In the former case, there is reason to believe that direct channels will be feasible. In the latter, the product must be sold with others to increase the size of the average sale so that costs may be absorbed. This generally calls for indirect channels and the use of many middlemen.

Frequency of Purchase

When the consumer purchases frequently, this fact is reflected throughout each level of distribution, as each middleman will adjust to the rate of the flow of goods to the ultimate buyer. When purchase is frequent, the frequency of calls necessary is great. There is no sense in using a wholesaler who makes, on the average, four calls a year on an account, when proper service of the account requires eight calls a year. The selection of middlemen must take this into account. If the manufacturer deems it wise to go direct, the frequency of calls necessary gives some indication of the magnitude of the job. If twelve calls a year are necessary and there are 28,000 potential accounts, some 336,000 calls are required. If the salesman can make an average of 4,000 calls a year, approximately eighty-four salesmen are required. The cost of eighty-four salesmen can easily be determined, and some idea of expense arrived at.

Impulse Versus Deliberate Purchase

Some analysis must be made of buying behavior. This indicates the kind of product-image the manufacturer must provide. Since a part of this job is delegated to and performed by channel members, it is necessary to select only those members who will perform in the required way. If the product is purchased on impulse— that is, without preplanning—exposure to sale and effective point-of-purchase material are essential. If considerable deliberation is involved, then more reliance must be placed on personal representation. Some middlemen are able to provide this, but care must be exercised in the selection of the channel members to insure that the product is represented properly. The use of selective distribution serves this purpose.

Characteristics of the Manufacturer Which Affect the Choice of Channels

Financial Capacity

It has already been demonstrated that some channels are more costly than others. A manufacturer may have a real need and desire to use a more costly channel, but not be able to, because he does not have funds sufficient to absorb the cost of all the activities usually performed by middlemen. He may perform them, or have reason to believe he can perform them, more efficiently, but the capital investments necessary to absorb the wholesaling activities will prove too great for him to afford.

Reputation of the Manufacturer

As we stated earlier, there are a number of middlemen within the distributive network from which the manufacturer selects. Sometimes the middlemen most likely to do the most effective marketing job for a manufacturer are tied up with competitive manufacturers, making proper entry into the channel impossible. In this case, the manufacturer may have to be satisfied with something less than optimum in terms of the middlemen he uses and assume the job himself, or set out to build an effective organization among those middlemen available to him. The reputation of the manufacturer has a good deal to do with the ease of entry into the channel. The better his reputation, the easier it is to attract the desired type of outlet.

A related aspect of this problem is found in those situations in which there is no appropriate middleman to do the job. Two examples will illustrate this situation. In the automobile industry, middlemen are tied, on an exclusive basis, to a single manufacturer. When Kaiser-Fraser entered the market, there were no middlemen available. It was necessary to build a complete dealer organization. When mobile homes were introduced, there was no ready-made terminal institution to handle this product. Eventually a new class of retailer developed, known as the mobile-homes dealer, but this took both time and the persistent efforts of the manufacturers.

Policies of the Manufacturer

Policies with respect to sales, service, price, and advertising influence the channels of distribution used. The manufacturers of the Kirby vacuum cleaner believe that demonstration within the home under actual operating conditions is the best way to sell the product. Since this task cannot very well be delegated to another institution, they use a direct house-to-house channel. Although this is costly, they prefer to compete on a quality basis. The price of the product reflects both the method of distribution and the quality of the product. Electrolux follows a similar policy. Most other vacuum cleaner manufacturers rely heavily on middlemen to perform the selling task.

Many pharmaceutical manufacturers state that service is the most important aspect of their marketing effort. By service, they mean service to the medical profession. This service is performed primarily by the detail man, whose costs account for 50 percent of marketing expenditures for purposes of providing information to the medical profession on the literally hundreds of new products appearing each year. Doctors could not possibly be fully acquainted with each drug on their own.

The cosmetic industry provides an example of contrast. The typical channel employed is indirect, using wholesalers to secure intense distribution in a large number of retail outlets. The manufacturer spends as high as 30 percent of sales in advertising to consumers to *pull* the product through the channel of distribution. Frequently, manufacturer demonstrators are used at the retail level to give the product a push at this point. Contrast this typical channel of distribution with that used by Avon. This company relies almost totally on a direct house-to-house selling force. Again the difference is attributed to a difference in policy, based upon the company's judgment as to the role of different marketing techniques.

Pricing policies often influence the channel of distribution. If the company follows a high-price, limited-market policy, which skims off the top of the market, the margins available to support different kinds of selling effort may be large. Consequently, expensive channels can be used. Usually, either selective or exclusive distribution is used, involving a minimum of middlemen. In contrast, if the company follows a low-price, mass market policy and attempts to penetrate every market in depth, intensive distribution is essential. Since the low-price policy reduces margins, lower-cost channels must be used. This is usually accomplished by mixing the product with those of other manufacturers in the assortments carried by wholesalers. In doing so, the selling cost is spread over many products, and the unit cost of the channel is low.

After the product, the market, and the characteristics of the manufacturer have been analyzed, the activities that must be performed by the channel can be stated. The second step is to determine and analyze those institutions which can most efficiently perform the required activities. Rather than repeat much of the material presented in Chapters 18 and 20, suffice it to say that different middlemen must be evaluated in terms of their abilities to perform the necessary activities and the manufacturer's capacity to gain their support.

The Tendency Toward Direct Channels

Many manufacturers wish to circumvent wholesalers and sell directly to retailers, or in some cases directly to individual users and ultimate consumers. There are a number of reasons for this. Besides those associated with the characteristics of the product, such as technicality, perishability, and the need for aggressive sale, there are other forces at work contributing to this trend. Foremost is the desire of manufacturers to control the market. There has been a constant struggle between middlemen and manufacturers for market control. In general, wholesalers have been unwilling to give special attention to any particular manufacturer's product. When one considers the breadth of the line handled by the typical wholesaler, the manufacturer's expectation of special attention does not seem warranted. The lack of intensive cultivation of markets by wholesalers has caused manufacturers to establish brands wherever possible and promote their products directly to the consumer in an attempt to force middlemen to handle the product. This, in turn, has resulted in reductions in margins to wholesalers, which has only intensified the battle. Many middlemen have turned to their own private brands, coming into direct competition with the manufacturer's that were handled.

In the past, wholesalers, having experienced slight recessions in which large inventories were devaluated overnight, began buying on a hand-to-mouth basis. This, in turn, increased the warehousing burden on the manufacturer and, he having assumed this rather costly activity, found that the next logical step was to completely circumvent the wholesaler. Many manufacturers also found themselves under pressure from some large retailers who wished to buy direct at prices which reflected the performance of some wholesaling activities carried on by the retailer (purchase in large quantities). When the manufacturer did sell directly to retailers, charges of price discrimination were made by wholesalers handling the line.

The relationship between more direct channels and market control is clear. However, the ability to take advantage of it depends on a number of circumstances. Foremost is the financial capacity of the manufacturer. Can he afford to invest in the facilities necessary to assume the activities of the wholesaler? The ability to stand this cost depends upon the margins available and on the average-size sale. This means that it is possible only with high-unit-value products or a broad line of low-unit-value products. In the latter case, there must be some parallel between the line and the market in which the products in the line are sold. A broad line is of no value unless all products, or nearly all products, are sold to all customers. Also, the geographic dispersion of the market has a bearing on the economies of direct sale. Where the market is concentrated, direct sale is much more economical than where it is dispersed. The frequency of calls necessary, as well as the size of the account, also has a bearing. If a very high frequency of calls is needed with a large number of small accounts, the cost of direct sale may be prohibitive.

Because of these limiting factors, one of three combinations is used. First, manufacturers may sell directly to the larger accounts and use wholesalers for others. Second, they may use wholesalers completely and back up the wholesalers' selling effort with their own sales force, usually called missionary salesmen. Third, they may sell directly to retailers in the large cities, where there is a concentration of customers, but use wholesalers in the thinner parts of the market. Regardless of the desire to circumvent the wholesaler, the capacity to do so is still determined by the characteristics of the product, the market, and the manufacturer.

THE USE OF
MANUFACTURERS' AGENTS

The agent middlemen, such as brokers, commission merchants, selling agents, and manufacturers' agents, provide services for hire and are available for inclusion in the distribution mix. The manufacturers' agent has been selected for further discussion in this chapter for three reasons. First, manufacturers' agents are more numerous than any other type of agent middlemen. Second, the use of manufacturers' agents in the distribution mix poses more management problems than the use of other types of agent middlemen. This is so because the broker does not represent the principal on a continuing contractual basis, the commission merchant deals primarily in agricultural products on a non-continuing contractual basis, and the selling agent takes responsibility for the entire distribution of the principal's output. Third, the manufacturers' agent is a substitute for the manufacturer's own sales force. Management must decide whether to have its own sales force or use the services of a number of manufacturers' agents. The management considerations in making the decision are many.[2]

Some elaboration on the definition of a manufacturers' agent is helpful in better understanding his operations.

> The manufacturers' agent is an independent business establishment that sells on a continuous contractual basis in a limited or exclusive territory, a part of the output of two or more client manufacturers whose products are related but noncompeting. The agent does not take title to the goods in which he deals, but is paid a commission and has little or no control over prices, credit or other terms of sale.[3]

The major competition of the manufacturers' agent is limited to a few types of operation. As a marketing institution, the agent faces his greatest competition from manufacturers who choose to use their own sales force, decentralized perhaps by means of sales branches or offices. Sporadic or limited competition is provided by other types of wholesale establishments. Some evidence exists of competition from other types of agents and brokers, yet the manufacturer seldom appears to face the problem of choosing between manufacturers' agents and other types of agents. Auction companies, brokers, selling agents, commission merchants, and the like are generally used under somewhat different circumstances than the manufacturers' agent, a fact which tends to limit competitive overlapping among the various agents. For example, the selling agent is used when the manufacturer needs, or prefers, one institution to take over his entire marketing task. Brokers are most frequently used when only intermittent market representation is necessary, although food brokers are a major exception to this rule and are in fact identical to manufacturers' agents. When a manufacturers' agent operates in packaged foods, he is called a food broker—a confusing term from a technical definition point of view, but one desired in the trade.

The following material, set in extract form, indicates the characteristics of the market, product, and firm that favor the use of manufacturers' agents.[4]

> The manufacturers' agent is or can be effectively utilized when one or more of a number of characteristics are present.
>
> (1) *Characteristics of the individual firm*
>
> > (a) The manufacturer is relatively weak financially, possessing ample resources for production purposes but lacking additional pecuniary strength to organize and maintain his own sales force.
> >
> > (b) The manufacturer produces a single product or narrow line of products, such that revenue forthcoming from the sale of such products is inadequate to support a sales force.

[2] For a more detailed discussion of manufacturers' agents, from which the bulk of this material was taken, see the census monograph by Thomas A. Staudt, *The Manufacturer's Agent as a Marketing Institution* (Washington, D.C.: Government Printing Office, 1951).

[3] *Ibid.,* p. 135. There are many hybrid types of operations that do not exactly conform to the above definition. For instance, the agent may at times deal in some goods on his own account (take title), or in some cases he may have considerable control over prices, or extend credit. But these cases are not typical.

[4] Staudt, *The Manufacturer's Agent,* p. 132.

(c) The manufacturer, even though large and producing a wide line of products, diversifies his line to include an item going to an entirely different market from his major line. The regular sales organization may be unable to distribute such a product effectively, or the cost to maintain separate sales personnel may be prohibitive.

(d) The manufacturer has his own sales force which is operating profitably in concentrated territories but wishes to expand sales coverage to geographic areas where the expected sales volume does not warrant use of his own salesmen.

(e) The manufacturer finds the administrative problems of maintaining a year-round or continuous sales force to be troublesome and undesirable.

(f) The manufacturer desires to retain primary control of distribution policy while shifting some of the burden of selling to others.

(g) Rigid control of selling costs is necessary.

(h) Rapid nationwide distribution is desired.

(2) *Characteristics of the product*

(a) A product is being introduced by a new manufacturer. The manufacturers' agent, to the extent he is well known and respected in his territory, can lend his prestige to the product. In contrast, a substantial expenditure is usually necessary before a sales volume is attained which offsets the cost of a sales force. The manufacturer avoids much of this cost when agents are used in the introductory marketing program.

(b) Wholesale merchants may not handle the product satisfactorily. For example, the manufacturer may feel that training the sales forces of numerous distributors is impractical because distributor salesmen must be conversant with a multitude of products. Also, the commission which is paid to the agent is likely to be less than the margin which a wholesale merchant must have.

(c) Sales personnel with considerable technical knowledge is required to sell the product. Such salesmen may not be available; the training period may be too long or beyond the company's capacity; the cost of retaining such personnel may be prohibitive.

(d) Long periods of negotiation are involved in consummating sales. The manufacturer wishes to avoid large presale costs as well as the expense of salaried salesmen who would be essential if a company sales force were used.

(3) *Characteristics of the market*

(a) The market will not support the company's own sales force.

(b) The market is at a distance, making sales cultivation from the home office too expensive.

(c) The market is thin, the few customers and prospects being located at a distance from each other. Costs in time and travel tend to prohibit the manufacturer from selling by means of his own sales force.

(d) Sales to individual customers are relatively infrequent. Close contact with customers is desirable to avoid possible loss of orders, yet needless sales expense cannot be afforded. The manufacturers' agent meets this difficult problem by having multiple lines which permit periodic customer calls, even though sales of the individual product are infrequent.

(e) The manufacturer wishes to secure entrance to relatively inaccessible buyers. Manufacturers' agents of standing in such markets may provide an entree that would be difficult to develop with a company sales force.

(f) The market for the product is somewhat seasonal, but continuous representation in the market is promotive of sales.

(g) The manufacturer is vulnerable to wide cyclical fluctuations in demand. Under such conditions, a company may be forced to expand and contract the sales organization in a somewhat comparable manner. Since reducing the size of the sales department as rapidly as sales decline in a depression is difficult and undesirable, marketing costs as a percentage of sales may materially increase. If agents are used, however, selling expenses of the manufacturer are automatically curtailed while the sales representation is still preserved.

Since the agent's major competition is supplied largely by manufacturers who consider it advisable to use their own salesmen, let us consider the competitive advantages and limitations of the manufacturers' agent in relation to manufacturers' salesmen.

Competitive Advantages of the Manufacturers' Agent

The nature of the agent operation provides special advantages in competition with manufacturers' own salesmen. Some of these advantages are inherent in agent operation; others may relate to, or depend upon, the capabilities of the individual agent. The capability factor suggests that competitive advantage depends upon the ability of the manufacturer to obtain high-caliber representatives. This same limitation, however, appears when the manufacturer uses his own salesmen. The advantages of selling by means of representatives include the following:

Predetermined Selling Expenses

When an agent sales force is used, the manufacturer can maintain comparatively rigid control of selling costs. Personal selling expenses as a percentage of sales are fixed. Other sales costs, such as advertising, research, and related expenditures, can be controlled in dollar amounts, but their ratio to sales depends on the volume of sales. The major selling cost of cultivating customers by means of personal selling to customers, however, varies with sales volume. When manufacturers' agents are used, this cost automatically stabilizes, inasmuch as the compensation rate is absolute. Selling expense as a percentage of sales can thus be predetermined regardless of volume of trade. Control of costs may be of special importance to the manufacturer of small size or one whose sales are characteristically vulnerable to seasonal or cyclical fluctuations. As sales decline in periods of restricted business activity, commission compensation automatically curtails dollar costs. The ability to predetermine selling costs with some exactness facilitates better planning and control of the marketing program.

Little or No Cost Until Sales Are Forthcoming

When an agent sales force is used, direct selling costs may be minimized by the manufacturer until sales have been made. This factor is particularly advantageous to the new, small, or weakly financed manufacturer. Were such a manufacturer to use his own sales force, a substantial investment would be necessary prior to obtaining any volume of trade. Expenditures for recruiting, selecting, training, and maintaining salesmen would be necessary in advance of any income obtained from sales. For the type of manufacturer noted, these expenditures may be impossible. The avoidance of such advance expenses may be the dominant consideration in making the decision to sell through manufacturers' agents. When this advantage is considered in conjunction with the ability to predetermine sales costs, an agent sales force has some inherent advantages over company salesmen.

Economy

The use of an agent sales force may provide marked sales economies. Sales economies are most pronounced when the manufacturer produces a narrow line or sells in a market of limited sales potential. Revenue received from a limited volume of trade, as a result of such conditions, may not cover the cost of sustaining a company sales force. When the manufacturers' agent is used, costs are spread among several producers. Agents can thus provide the manufacturer with a low sales-expense ratio by virtue of their ability to spread costs over the merchandise of several producers.

Intensity of Territory Coverage

An agent sales force may provide more intensive coverage of the territory than manufacturers' salesmen. To obtain sufficient volume to offset the cost of the salesmen, the territory may need to be large, implying extensive sales coverage. Under these circumstances, company salesmen tend to "skim the cream" off the market by calling on only those accounts that can provide sizable sales. From necessity, the smaller and less profitable accounts tend to be overlooked or avoided by manufacturers' salesmen. On the other hand, the manufacturers' agent may be able to obtain a profitable volume from a more restricted territory because of his multiple lines. An adequate all-product volume from an individual account may justify regular customer calls on all sizes of customers. More intensive coverage of the territory may thus result from an agent sales force.

Accessibility to the Trade

The manufacturers' agent may have greater access to markets than a salesman. Greater accessibility may result from several factors. First, entree to otherwise difficult prospects may be aided because of the agent's multiple lines. For example, a plumbing supplies agent may be able to sell a new client's product to a particular customer because he is already doing a regular business with the buyer. Multiplicity of lines also increases trade accessibility because the agent usually can secure the audience of a regular customer to present adequately a new client's line. Certain groups of large customers are also sometimes relatively inaccessible to salesmen of new or small manufacturers. The agent who has been calling on this type of customer for a long period of years can more easily introduce products in such a market.

Ease of Sales Administration

The manufacturer who uses an agent sales force minimizes the problem of recruiting, selecting, and training salesmen. The management problems incident to maintaining a sales force are, in a large measure, shifted from the manufacturer to a more specialized marketing institution. Although the sales administration burden cannot be eliminated, the magnitude of the problem is substantially reduced. Once representation has been established in the various territories, the marketing program can be carried out with a minimum of management control. Responsibility for maintaining offices, employing capable personnel, keeping records, routing salesmen, and meeting payrolls is substantially curtailed. Such a shift of administrative responsibility may be most desirable for the manufacturer who lacks marketing experience or possesses a limited staff. By using agents, the manufacturer has the benefit of numerous "sales offices" maintained throughout the territories by his representatives. This advantage is inherent in the use of manufacturers' agents.

Quality of Sales Representation

The manufacturer can sometimes acquire more capable and experienced sales representation from agents than he can from his own sales force. The client may be able to obtain agents having long years of experience in a given trade and possessing a comprehensive knowledge of the market for a particular line. The manufacturer may have difficulty in recruiting this type of salesman for his own sales force. In industrial goods, the agent is often a professional sales engineer, who frequently earns a large annual income. By using such skilled agents, the manufacturer may be able to obtain capable representation which he could not otherwise afford to hire. To obtain a comparable salesman, the manufacturer might have to offer up to $50,000 per year; yet, because an agent has other lines, the client may be able to engage the agent's services for selling his product at a commission cost of perhaps $10,000 per year.

Aggressive Selling

Aggressive selling is not an inherent competitive advantage of the manufacturers' agent, nor is it impossible to obtain aggressive selling through other channels of distribution. Obviously the degree of aggressiveness depends upon the individual agent. The point to be made, however, is that the agent's remuneration is entirely dependent upon the productivity of his own efforts because of the inherent nature of commission compensation. This advantage is primarily contrasted to manufacturers' salaried salesmen. A commission plan can be used for manufacturers' salesmen, but such an arrangement does not eliminate the need to maintain offices and to carry the attendant administrative burden. The aggressive selling promoted by commission compensation can be obtained without facing these limitations by using agents.

Immediate Entry to the Market

Sales may be forthcoming almost immediately when the manufacturers' agents are appointed. By electing to sell through representatives, a new manufacturer or an old one entering a new field taps experienced and established sales organizations with a definite clientele of relatively permanent customers. Were the manufacturer to organize his own sales force, a substantial lapse of time might pass between the initiation of action and the receiving of any significant volume of orders. Management that is impatient for sales results may thus find an agent sales force attractive.

Rapidity with which Regional or National Distribution Can Be Obtained

Closely related to immediate market entry is the opportunity for rapid nationwide distribution. One manufacturer, for example, obtained national market coverage by means of an agent-type sales force in five weeks. Several years may be saved in attaining complete market coverage by the manufacturer who elects to distribute through agents rather than his own salesmen.

Limitations to the Use of the Manufacturers' Agent

From the manufacturers' point of view, an agent sales force involves some limitations. Several are as follows:

Cost

Although the suggestion has been made that the use of an agent sales force may be less expensive than the use of a company sales force, the comparative economy of the types of sales representation depends upon the volume of business that can be obtained from a given trading area. Manufacturers with a wide line of established products which are in an advanced stage of sales development may find the cost of manufacturers' agents excessive. After a given volume of trade has been attained, manufacturers' salaried salesmen may be employed at less cost as a percentage of sales. Particularly in times of strong markets, company salesmen appear more economical in expense per dollar of sales.

Lack of Control

The manufacturer does not have the same control over an agent sales force that he has over his own salesmen. The manufacturer can control the major policies and procedures of the agent, but has trouble in controlling the agent's detailed activities. This lack of control is an inherent limitation. The agent is in business for himself, and thus is responsible for guiding the daily operations of his establishment. As a result, the client manufacturer cannot route salesmen, control sales demonstrations, the length of the work day and work week, the frequency of salesmen's calls, the amount of services rendered, the selection of subagents, or similar matters.

Partial Representation

The manufacturer who uses an agent sales force obtains only a portion of the agent's time. Obviously, each client must share the selling efforts of the agent with other manufacturers. This limitation may prohibit maximum coverage of a given territory and the continuous promotion of the one line. The sales manager of one firm believed that his company received no more than fifteen minutes of active selling time per day from each agent. This company, in the process of transition from agents to its own salesmen, felt that the amount of time devoted to selling the company's product in each territory would be quadrupled merely by replacing agents with company salesmen. The manufacturer, in addition, cannot always control the number of lines his agents carry. If the manufacturer is interested in increasing the amount of selling effort on his company's product, then salesmen can better provide this result.

Obtaining Maximum Market Potential

Opportunities to obtain maximum market potential may be jeopardized. Partly as a result of multiple lines previously noted, the manufacturer may be unable to obtain maximum sales from a given territory. But in addition the agent, fearing replacement by a manufacturer's own salesman if his commissions get too high from a large volume of trade, may deliberately limit his effort when this point of cost equilibrium is reached. (Agents' commissions are equal to salary plus field expense of salesmen.) Proper selection of agents, complete understanding, and explicitly stated objectives may minimize the likelihood of such a possibility. Yet, this risk must be faced when agent representation is used.

Less Market Stability

Should the agent choose to discontinue his relationship with the principal, the manufacturer may find that the agent is able to shift a substantial volume of the trade on his products to another manufacturer. While this may not always be a significant factor, the manufacturer is unlikely to retain the same volume of trade immediately after the loss of a competent agent. Such an issue is less significant with salesmen because they must, of necessity, primarily promote their company and its products. Sales volume gained by the manufacturers' agent, however, may have been inspired more by the agent's prestige and acceptance than by the manufacturer's acceptance.

Direct Contact with Buyers More Difficult

The manufacturer normally desires to be as closely associated with buyers as possible. As has been indicated, a sound marketing plan begins with a consumer or user and is based upon his needs and desires. When a manufacturer uses an agent sales force, he removes himself one more step from his customer. More difficulty is then experienced in closely observing marketing conditions, buying habits, and customer needs or preferences.

Thus, the manufacturer, as well as receiving special benefits, faces limitations in the use of an agent sales force. Proper utilization of agents depends upon the individual situation and conditions and requires a balancing of the various factors involved.

COST AND REVENUE CONSIDERATIONS

After qualitatively assessing the functional needs of the market for the products in question, it is necessary to predict the revenues anticipated and the costs of serving the market through alternative channels. An example will illustrate the effect of the costs of different channels on profits.

In Figure 21-1 the costs of the following three channels are shown: (1) manufacturer to retailers, (2) manufacturer to manufacturers' agents to

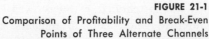

FIGURE 21-1

Comparison of Profitability and Break-Even
Points of Three Alternate Channels

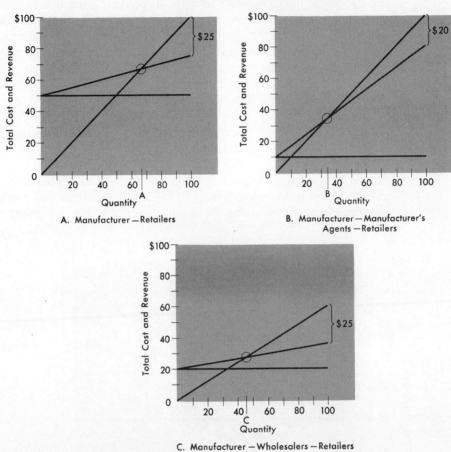

A. Manufacturer—Retailers

B. Manufacturer—Manufacturer's
Agents—Retailers

C. Manufacturer—Wholesalers—Retailers

retailers, and (3) manufacturer to wholesalers to retailers. In this hypothetical case the product is sold for $1.00. In the first case, direct from manufacturer to retailers, the revenues will be high because no trade discounts are given to middlemen for the performance of marketing functions. On the other hand, the fixed costs of maintaining a sales force to call upon thousands of retail outlets are high. The costs of selecting, training, and maintaining the sales force in the field are primarily fixed. The direct costs of shipping, order assembly, billing, etc. are substantial, as a large number of retailers must be serviced. In this alternative, profits are $25 at a capacity of 100 units. The break-even point with this cost structure is 65 units. In the second case, from manufacturer to manufacturers' agents to retailers, the revenues are the same as in the first case, since no trade discounts must be given. Fixed costs are materially smaller as the manufacturers' agents are a substitute for the firm's own sales force. Direct costs are somewhat higher than in the first case, as the agents' commissions must be paid. With this cost structure the profit is $20 at a capacity of 100 units, but notice how much less is required to break even—35 units. In the third case, from manufacturer to wholesalers to retailers, the revenues are sharply reduced because of the trade discounts, usually 40 percent, given to wholesalers. Fixed costs are less than in the first case, because not as many corporate salesmen are required to call upon the smaller number of wholesale establishments. They are higher than in the second case, however, as some salesmen are required. The direct costs, such as shipping, customer credit, order assembly, and billing costs, are less than in the other two cases because of the smaller number of customers. The profit in this case is $25 at a capacity of 100 units and the break-even point is 45 units.

In Figure 21-2 all three alternatives are superimposed on one break-even chart to demonstrate the variations in revenues, costs, profits, and break-even points.

With accurate cost and revenue information the decision as to which channel to use is dependent upon (1) the market coverage and market control requirements as perceived by the manufacturer, (2) the availability of a suffi-

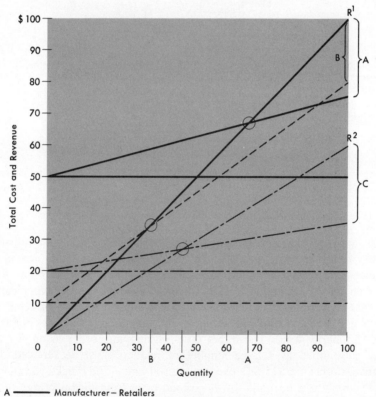

A ———— Manufacturer – Retailers
B — — — Manufacturer – Manufacturers' Agents – Retailers
C — · — · Manufacturer – Wholesalers – Retailers

FIGURE 21-2
Profitability of
Three Alternate
Channels

cient number of middlemen that will perform in the desired way, and (3) the risks inherent in using one channel versus another. Referring to Figure 21-2 it can be seen that if Channels B and C are equally effective, the volume at which the profitability of each channel is equal is between 60 and 65 units. If it is assumed that this volume can be reached easily, then the additional profits from higher volumes accrue much faster using Channel C than Channel B. This is so because the profit angle on Channel C is larger than the profit angle on Channel B. If the probability of reaching this volume is low, then Channel B, with the lower break-even point may be the preferred choice. Or the analysis of potential revenues may be conducted on a market-by-market basis, demonstrating the need for different channels in different markets. If market control is perceived to be desirable and growth opportunities are present, it could be desirable to move toward Channel A as the profits accrue beyond the break-even point at an accelerated rate.

Once a channel is decided upon, effective implementation of the channel is crucial. Channel members must be selected with specific criteria in mind. These include "distributor sales strength (number of salesmen, their technical competence), distributor product lines already stocked (whether they are competitive, compatible, complementary, and of high quality vis-à-vis the products of the investigating manufacturer), distributor reputation, market coverage (geographic, industrial), sales performance, inventory and warehousing, and management ability." [5]

The task of motivating the distributors in the manufacturer's interest was discussed in Chapter 17. Evaluating performance of the channel members is an element of control and is discussed in Chapter 31.

Summary

A channel of distribution is *a combination of institutions through which a seller markets his products to the user or ultimate consumer.* The major criteria involved in selecting channels of distribution are: (1) the coverage needed, and (2) the degree of market control desired.

In selecting a channel of distribution it is necessary to consider the needs and desires of consumers, the objectives of the manufacturer, and the availability of competent middlemen to perform the required services. The first two considerations can best be determined by examining the characteristics of the product, the market, and the manufacturer.

In analyzing the product, such aspects as unit value, bulk, perishability, technicality, breadth of the line, seasonality of production or consumption, degree of market acceptance, and substitutability of product should be considered. In analyzing the market, users of the product, size of the market, geographic concentration or dispersion, frequency of purchase, and impulse versus deliberative purchase are fruitful areas of analysis. Financial capacity, reputation, and sales,

[5] *Selecting and Evaluating Distributors,* National Industrial Conference Board, Studies in Business Policy, No. 116, 1965, p. 1.

price, service, and advertising policies are characteristics of the manufacturer influencing the channel activities that must be performed.

An important trend is the tendency toward more direct channels. Of particular significance is the circumvention of wholesalers. A number of factors have contributed to this trend; of foremost importance is the desire on the part of manufacturers for market control.

After qualitatively assessing the functional needs of the market, consideration must be given to the cost and revenue results of alternative channels. Based upon both qualitative and quantitative assessments, a particular channel will be selected. Matching needs with competent middlemen depends upon a comprehensive knowledge of the characteristics and operating methods of the various middlemen available. The selection of specific channel members should be based on specific performance criteria.

Questions and Problems

1. Define what is meant by the term *channel of distribution*.
2. Do physical movements of goods parallel the channel of distribution?
3. What criteria for channel selection should the marketing manager employ?
4. How do selective distribution and exclusive distribution differ?
5. Is the marketing manager who employs an exclusive distribution policy also generally selective?
6. What kinds of goods lend themselves well to a direct-to-user channel?
7. Since there are fewer middlemen involved, how do you account for the fact that direct distribution is often more costly than indirect distribution?
8. What are the principal product characteristics which influence or control the selection of the channel of distribution?
9. Name a well-known consumer product and, using the criteria discussed in Question 8, show how the theory of channel selection applies to the distribution of this particular good.
10. Would you expect a product that had high repetitive repurchase by consumers (high flow characteristics) to have direct, indirect, or split-channel characteristics? Why?
11. Would a firm always choose the lowest-cost channel of distribution?
12. Why do high-fashion goods tend to have such direct channels of distribution?
13. Why should manufacturers periodically audit their marketing channels?
14. Does the consumer have any influence on marketing channels? How?
15. Conceptually speaking, how many gas stations would be too many? What different criteria could be used in making this judgment?

Bibliography

Alt, Richard M., "Competition among Types of Retailers in Selling the Same Commodity," *Journal of Marketing,* XIV (1949), 441.

Barger, Harold, *Distribution's Place in the American Economy since 1869* (Princeton, N.J.: Princeton University Press, 1956).

Bartels, Robert, ed., *Comparative Marketing: Wholesaling in Fifteen Countries* (Homewood, Ill.: Richard D. Irwin, Inc., 1963).

Bowersox, Donald J., Edward W. Smykay, and Bernard J. LaLonde, *Physical Distribution Management,* rev. ed. (New York: The Macmillan Company, 1968).

Brown, Robert G., *Statistical Forecasting for Inventory Control* (New York: McGraw-Hill Book Company, 1959).

Clewett, Richard M., ed., *Marketing Channels* (Homewood, Ill.: Richard D. Irwin, Inc., 1954).

——, "Checking Your Marketing Channels," *Management Aids for Small Manufacturers* (Washington, D.C.: Small Business Administration, January 1961).

Cox, Eli P., and Leo G. Erickson, *Retail Decentralization* (East Lansing, Mich.: Bureau of Business and Economic Research, Michigan State University, 1967).

Davidson, William R., *Retailing Management,* 3rd ed. (New York: The Ronald Press Company, 1966).

Duncan, Delbert J., and Charles F. Phillips, *Retailing: Principles and Methods* (Homewood, Ill.: Richard D. Irwin, Inc., 1967).

Hill, Richard M., *Wholesaling Management* (Homewood, Ill.: Richard D. Irwin, Inc., 1963).

Holdren, Bob R., *The Structure of a Retail Market and the Market Behavior of Retail Units* (Englewood Cliffs, N.J.: Prentice-Hall, Inc., 1960).

Hollander, Stanley C., ed., *Explorations in Retailing* (East Lansing, Mich.: Bureau of Business and Economic Research, Michigan State University, 1959).

Lazer, William, and Eugene J. Kelley, "The Retailing Mix: Planning and Management," *Journal of Retailing* (Spring 1961).

Lewis, E. H., "Comeback of the Wholesaler," *Harvard Business Review* (November-December 1955), pp. 115–25.

Magee, John F., *Physical-Distribution Systems* (New York: McGraw-Hill Book Company, 1967).

Management of the Physical-Distribution Function, Management Report No. 49 (New York: American Management Assn., 1960).

McVey, Phillip, "Are Channels of Distribution What the Textbooks Say?" *Journal of Marketing,* XXIV, No. 3 (January 1960), 61–65.

Nelson, Richard L., *The Selection of Retail Locations* (New York: F. W. Dodge Corp., 1958).

Revzan, David A., *Wholesaling in Marketing Organization* (New York: John Wiley & Sons, Inc., 1961).

Ridgeway, Valentine P., "Administration of Manufacturer-Dealer Systems," *Administrative Science Quarterly,* I, No. 4 (March 1957).

Smith, Paul E., and Eugene J. Kelley, "Competing Retail Systems: The Shopping Center and the Central Business District," *Journal of Retailing* (Spring 1960).

Staudt, Thomas A., *The Manufacturers' Agent as a Marketing Institution* (Washington, D.C.: Government Printing Office, 1952).

Programming the Elements of Market Cultivation

We have emphasized that the firm seeks differential advantage—or competitive superiority—in markets, to the end that corporate objectives may be achieved. The enterprise must seek a total market posture that builds impact at the point of ultimate sale. Market action may then be precipitated to permit the fulfillment of the firm's objectives. We have emphasized the need for the perceptive and comprehensive investigation of market forces and market opportunities as the foundation for various strategies directed toward impact. We must understand both the overt and subtle forces that underlie market impact. Likewise, we have considered the way in which products are matched with market forces in the product strategy of the firm. And finally, we have analyzed the distribution network as it constitutes the link between the marketing enterprise and consumer purchase and use. Now we turn our attention to the communications function which energizes or activates the process of exchange.

Since market cultivation is to a great extent a matter of communication with potential customers, we shall examine some of the interesting developments in communications theory. Next, we shall consider the complicated analytical problem of determining expenditures to be allocated to the various parts of the communications mix. Then, we shall turn our attention to the individual components in the communications mix, such as advertising and personal selling, and treat the principal managerial considerations in each of these areas. Finally, we shall cover an important element related to market cultivation—pricing. While this area could have been treated in Part 3, because of its relation to product strategy we have chosen to examine pricing policies here. Its placement here reflects the following important considerations: (1) pricing is an important tool of market cultivation, as are advertising, sales promotion, and personal selling; (2) price adjustment is to some extent an alternative to communications expenditures; and, (3) pricing should serve to integrate and bring into focus all aspects of markets, products, the distribution network, and expenditures in other forms of market cultivation.

Communications Theory and Marketing

22

Marketing effectiveness depends significantly upon communications effectiveness. The market, in reality, is energized (or activated) through information flows. The way a buyer perceives the market offering of the seller is influenced by the amount and kind of information he has about the offering and his reaction to that information. Indeed, it is difficult for the buyer to distinguish in his perceptual field the market offering itself from his cumulative interpretation of information concerning the offering. Since communications effectiveness so pervades the exchange process, and in view of the fact that the bulk of market cultivation effort involves communication, some basic understanding of the theory of communication itself will serve as a useful preliminary consideration to the analysis of advertising, personal selling, and other forms of market cultivation.

This chapter first sets forth a simple communications model; then, the various elements in the communications process are discussed in considerable detail, with emphasis on the problem of attitude change. The marketing implications of these elements are treated as the chapter progresses.

A COMMUNICATIONS MODEL

The word *communication* is derived from the Latin *communis,* "common." Communication may be regarded as a process by which a verbal or nonverbal effort is made by a source to send a message through a channel to establish a "commonness" with a receiver. All human communication has a source—a person, group, or institution—and a purpose—usually to arouse, inform, or elicit some sort of response. Given a source with ideas, needs, intentions, information, and a purpose, an encoding process must take place which translates these ideas into a systematic set of symbols—into a language, expressing the source's purpose. The function

379

of encoding is thus the provision of a form in which ideas can be expressed as a coded message. Next, a channel, medium, or carrier of messages is required. The appropriate choice of medium is a critical variable in effective communication.

Obviously a transmitted message is intended to reach some receiver. If a receiver is lacking, no communication has taken place. Before a receiver can respond to a message, it must be decoded in terms of relevance to the receiver. In person-to-person communication, encoding and decoding are performed by the source and receiver via their motor skills and sensory capacities. In more complex communications situations, the source is often separated from the encoder, as often are the decoder and receiver. For example, the advertising manager may be the source, and a copywriter, the encoder. These five elements are inherent in the communications process and are diagrammed as follows: [1]

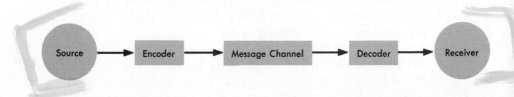

A breakdown, an interference, a distortion, or a *noise* can occur anywhere within the communications process. *Noise* is used in this context not only as representing an audible sound, but as anything which will interfere with the communications process—a distraction, a misinterpretation, different meanings assigned to the same words by different people, mind wandering, etc. All these factors serve to distort a message or reduce fidelity, and can be termed noise. Because message fidelity is rarely, if ever, 100 percent perfect, provision for feedback in the communications process is desirable. Feedback provides a channel for audience or receiver response; it permits the source to determine whether the message has been received and has produced the intended response. Feedback of information may be carried through the same channel as the original message or through an entirely different channel. With the addition of the elements of noise and feedback, our model can now be diagrammed as follows:

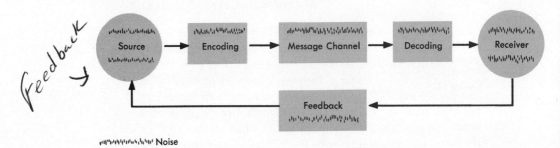

[1] David K. Berlo, *The Process of Communication* (New York: Holt, Rinehart & Winston, Inc., 1960), pp. 30–32.

The system as a whole has great interdependency and is no stronger than its weakest component. Distortion can come about through malfunction in any of the parts. If the source does not have adequate or valid information or his purpose is unclear; if the message is not encoded accurately, fully, and in transmittable signs of relevance to the receiver; if the message is not transmitted fast enough or accurately enough despite interference; if the message is not decoded in precisely the way it was encoded; or if the receiver is unable to accept the decoded message in such a way as to produce the desired response—then the communications process lacks perfection.

One hundred percent efficiency, however, is an unattainable goal. For example, the efficiency rating of an electric motor measures the ratio of output to input. It must always be below 100 percent because of the slight loss which must occur in the conversion of one form of energy to another. So it is in communications; the conversion of abstractions through encoding into messages and the conversion back through decoding into precisely the same abstractions is unattainable. The objective of the communicator is to attain as closely as possible perfect fidelity in producing the desired response. Conversion losses will be discussed further as we examine more thoroughly the various elements in the communications process.

THE COMMUNICATIONS SOURCE

Purpose

Purpose is one of the most important of all the essentials in communication. If communication does not have purpose, it is meaningless. Stated positively, every conscious and deliberate communicative act has a purpose. Purpose influences all other considerations in the communicative process—the structuring of the message, choice of symbols, language, selection of medium, even the choice of the intended receiver. Therefore, the clearer one is about his purpose, the more likely he is to succeed in communication. This is one of the first reasons for the failure of many marketing communications—the objectives or goals of advertising and other communicative acts are not clearly, explicitly, and specifically stated. Only the generalized hope is held that eventually such efforts will lead to greater product sales.

The broad notion of purpose can be broken down into the more technical classifications of purpose—namely *consummatory purpose* and *instrumental purpose*. These two types of communicative purpose refer to the extent to which the purpose of a message is accomplished at the moment of its consumption or in a deferred period. If the purpose of a message is satisfied by consumption of the message when it is received, we call this consummatory purpose. When consumption of a message produces behavior only in a deferred period, we call this instrumental purpose. Any given message can have many purposes, some highly consummatory, others highly instrumental. In marketing, instrumental purposes are very important because attitudes must often be changed to pave the way for later action (purchase of the product). Emphasis in marketing communications has been on the instrumental purpose with less attention on the explicit consummatory purposes.

Some writers have chosen to classify purpose as *immediate purpose* and *ulterior motive*.

> As a first step in analyzing purpose, we will find it useful to distinguish between the immediate purpose of a communication and any ulterior motives that the source may have in preparing it. The immediate purpose is always to stimulate ideas or feelings in the receiver—to get some response from him. Thus the immediate purpose is stated in terms of the desired audience response. On the other hand, the ulterior motive of the source is what he hopes to get as a result of his communication.[2]

Perhaps it is more correct to say that marketers have been more generally aware of their ulterior motives than clear concerning their immediate purposes in communications.

Receivers, on the other hand, sometimes are influenced subconsciously by their *own* ulterior motives.

> They (receivers) may believe that they are searching for unbiased information on a given subject, but actually they may be seeking support for, and agreement with, opinions they have already formed. They may have made up their minds and their ulterior motive is now to find support for their decisions. If so, they tend to reject anything they read or hear that does not support the preconceived idea and to accept anything that does.[3]

Some studies have been conducted on after-purchase dissonance among consumers. Dissonance develops whenever a decision has been made. The decision maker can never be sure he made the right decision, and anxiety over the choice develops. It was hypothesized that many people are much more inclined to read communications of a producer after they have purchased his product. This is done to convince themselves that they made the right choice. Earlier studies showed that recent automobile purchasers read car advertisements that supported their purchases significantly more often than nonpurchasers read such ads.[4] More recent studies show the same general tendency, but variation in individuals depended upon personality traits and also on differences in the quality of service recent purchasers have enjoyed.[5]

The key point here is that the communicator needs to clearly define his purpose—both immediate and deferred—and the more he comprehends receiver purpose, the more effective his message will be. This point relates to earlier parts of the book, where objectives were emphasized in all programming attempts and in referring to consumer problem solving.

[2] Howard H. Dean, *Effective Communication* (Englewood Cliffs, N.J.: Prentice-Hall, Inc., 1954), p. 10.

[3] *Ibid.*, p. 11.

[4] See D. Ehrlich, I. Guttman, P. Schonbach, and J. Mills, "Post-Decision Exposure to Relevant Information," *Journal of Abnormal and Social Psychology,* LIV (1957), 98–102.

[5] See Gerald D. Bell, "The Automobile Buyer After the Purchase," *Journal of Marketing,* XXXI (July 1967), 12–16.

Purpose and audience are not separable; that is, all communication has as its purpose the stimulating of a specific response or the influencing of the behavior of an intended receiver in a particular way. The classes of response desired, or effects intended, require that the "who-ness" of purpose be specified. The source needs to understand who is likely to decode messages, who is likely to be influenced, who is likely to take action upon receipt of the message. These "whos" can be a single person, or several individuals.

The first requisite, then, of effective communications is: know the audience. This is why we have stressed market knowledge throughout this book. Marketing communication, to be effective, must proceed from a comprehensive knowledge of audiences. In this sense, the sequential elements in the communications model are partially discontinuous, as well as continuous. That is, the source does not take mental pictures and proceed to encode these abstractions into messages without regard to intended receivers or an understanding of the decoding skills of intended receivers. Actually, the source jumps from his purpose to consideration of the receivers *before* he constructs messages. His knowledge of the receivers influences the content and structure of his message, the signs and symbols chosen, the media used, and, perhaps, even his purpose.

Communication purpose should be stated with some precision and in such a way that:

1. It is not logically contradictory or inconsistent within itself. When a message conveys argumentation that is contradictory within itself, it tends to be self-defeating.

2. It is specific enough to relate to the behavior patterns of intended receivers.

Goals or purposes are not the property of the message itself: they relate to the source or the receivers of messages. The purpose must be such that intended receivers can do something about the message, otherwise the communications media simply become cluttered with competing messages that seem to lack relevancy for receivers, who are perhaps even unspecified.

An example of marketing communications that lacks these qualities will perhaps help to clarify the point. A major chemical company was advertising a highly specialized product that was sold to less than ten customers, normally in tank-car quantities. The demand for the product was inelastic and was derived from the end demand for the products produced by this handful of customers. Moreover, on close analysis, it appeared that purchasers from the two competing producers of the product reflected a significant element of reciprocity on the part of buyers. Under these circumstances, it is doubtful that advertising could contribute to the sale of any additional volume whatsoever; and conversely, it is doubtful that no advertising at all would result in any appreciable decline in sales. When the advertising manager was asked the reasons for the advertising campaign on this product, he replied, "I don't know, the product accounts for 4 percent of our sales and I thought it should have its fair share of the promotional expenditures (4 percent)." The wastefulness of these market communications can be seen because the source's purpose was not behaviorally centered. Purpose and specified audience are therefore critical elements in communications effectiveness.

Among those companies that do state specific communication objectives, there is a tendency to separate them from overall marketing objectives.[6] This is done because marketing objectives describe the overall aim of the total marketing effort. They are of limited value in establishing a communications plan as a part of the total effort. Since communications should be designed to create a different state in the mind of the receiver after the message is received, it is important to specifically set forth as an objective what kind of states are desired. After a thorough review of obstacles to attaining the marketing objectives, it is possible to identify those obstacles that may be overcome by appropriate communications.

The Quaker Oats Company at one time established its communication objectives with respect to advertising as follows:[7]

1. Increase consumer recognition of a product as a source of protein.
2. Create consumer awareness of a pet food as nutritious for both dogs and cats (rather than dogs alone).
3. Register in the public mind the fact that a certain food product is non-fattening.
4. Create new usage or serving suggestions in order to increase home consumption of a product that is already widely purchased.
5. Convince the consumer that the costlier ingredients used in the product justify its higher price.

Source Attributes That Influence Communications Effectiveness

There are several factors related to the source that influence communications effectiveness:

Thought and Language Competence

The major units of thought seem to be language units. Recently, it has been hypothesized that man's language affects his perception and thinking.[8] Whorf postulates that a person's language will, in part, determine what he sees, what he thinks about, and the methods used to think and arrive at decisions. While scientific evidence on this point is somewhat lacking, it does appear that we have difficulty thinking completely outside our experience and the names we have for that experience. Linguistic ability is vital, if the source is to achieve a given purpose. Also, if thought is tied to linguistic competence, then inadequacy here limits the ideas available and the capacity to manipulate ideas, which is important in message construction.

[6] See *Setting Advertising Objectives,* Studies in Business Policy, No. 118 (New York: National Industrial Conference Board, 1966).

[7] *Ibid.,* p. 23.

[8] Benjamin L. Whorf, "The Relation of Habitual Thought and Behavior to Language," in *Language, Thought and Reality* (Cambridge, Mass.: The M. I. T. Press, 1956), pp. 134–59.

Attitudes

The source's attitude toward his receivers will affect communications behavior. If the receiver perceives that the source respects his competence or
capacity to understand, message fidelity is likely to be enhanced. If, on the other
hand, the receiver denotes an attitude (real or imagined) of contempt, then the
commonness between sender and receiver will be diminished. Advertisers that
continually talk down to their audiences, that presume a mentality of a five-year-
old when they are attempting to reach adult receivers, seem increasingly to have
difficulty achieving their purposes.

Knowledge Levels

Knowledge of communications processes within the source itself affects
communications behavior and effectiveness. The more one knows about the
various treatments of messages, their form and content, the way receivers decode,
the kinds of analysis required of receivers, and the values of alternative media,
the more effective his communications are likely to be. The source's knowledge
of the specific subject matter involved in the communication also has a bearing
on effectiveness. When a salesman is selling a product in direct person-to-person
communication, he needs to know his subject in depth—all its characteristics,
its qualities, production methods, applications to customer problems, the buyer's
situation, and the many other dimensions of product-market communications
elements—to maximize his prospects of achieving his intended purpose.

Cultural Class

Who the source is, the reference group he belongs to, the context he is
perceived in, the roles he is expected to play, the validity that can be attached
to what he has to say, the group and individual pressures he is reflecting, the
values he holds, the experience he represents, and the cultural level he portrays
all condition receivers and affect their decoding of messages. This is why the
source needs to ask, "Who am I, in the receiver's eyes?" This requires the source
to figuratively place himself in the receiver's shoes for the purpose of antic-
ipating how his messages are likely to be received. Messages should be receiver
oriented, rather than source oriented, and it is useless for the source to perceive
of himself as outside the perspective of the decoding that is likely to take place.
"Who's talking" makes a great deal of difference to the attention you pay to any
messages reaching you, but only you can really perceive who actually *is* talking.
You will receive the same message very differently, depending on the source.
For instance, you are likely to reflect quite different communications behavior
in connection with the same message about the causes of lung cancer, depending
upon whether the source is a layman or a research physician.

The following suggests very clearly the importance of the receiver's image
of the source.[9]

[9] B. Berelson and G. A. Steiner, *Human Behavior: An Inventory of Scientific Findings*
(New York: Harcourt, Brace & World, Inc., 1964), p. 537.

The more trustworthy, credible, or prestigious the communicator is perceived to be, the less manipulative his intent is considered to be, and the greater the immediate tendency to accept his conclusions.

Three factors may be combined to improve the receiver's image of the source. Endorsement by prominent individuals in advertising copy placed in prestigious media brings the prestige of all three elements—the advertiser, the endorser, and the media—to bear on the image perceived by the receiver. The initial advertisement can be capitalized on by reproducing a tear sheet from a prestigious media, such as *Life,* on point-of-purchase display material.

Past Communications

Frequently a receiver is not decoding a message from a source for the first time. The receiver may well have been a destination for many messages in the past. All previous communications condition the response to any new message. Attention-getting capacity in the present may partially depend upon what has been said in the past and how much redundancy there appears to be in messages. The relevancy of this point can be judged by your own past experience of having discussions with various acquaintances. The communications of some have led you to consider them bores.

The advertiser, as a market communicator, should attempt to comprehend how his messages are conditioning receivers in the market. This is one of the reasons for the current interest in "corporate image" research. What attitudes are being reflected about the company and its statements among various publics? The advertiser faces the problem of the most appropriate frequency and timing of his messages, and must choose between repeating the same messages and transmitting new messages. Our discussion of learning theory later on will clarify this point.

ENCODING AND DECODING

Perhaps the most important factor that breaks down the desired "commonness" in communications between the source and the receiver, and therefore the overall effectiveness of the whole process, is the variation that takes place in encoding and decoding. Some of the most effective communication, in this respect, takes place among a neighborhood gang of youngsters of similar age. Chances are they have all come from a common environment—the same neighborhood, school, drugstore, playground, and type of living quarters. They have all shared a majority of common experiences and, frequently, they will have a large number of common interests. They may speak in a slang language (that exists without anyone ever carefully defining terms) that seems incomprehensible to adults. The encoding and decoding, however, are almost precisely identical —they communicate most effectively even with a limited vocabulary. But over a period of time the homogeneous nature of these conditions tends to break down. Environments, experience, vocabulary, knowledge, interests, attitudes, values, personalities, and goals vary increasingly with age; that is, they grow farther apart. Norbert Weiner refers to this condition as "entropy," or the inherent nature of human processes to break down rather than come closer together as a civilization advances.[10] The result is that great barriers to effective communications are erected, which reflect themselves in inexact encoding and decoding. Schramm diagrams the nature of this problem as follows: [11]

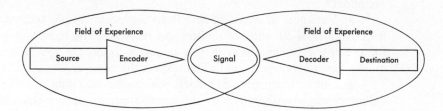

The circles represent the accumulated experience of the two participants in the communication process. If the circles have a large area in common, then communication is facilitated. If the circles do not meet—if there has been no common experience—then communication is impossible. Let us look at some of the more specific factors that are involved in dealing with the encoding-decoding process.

Frames of Reference

We structure our experience so as to make it meaningful to us. Our accumulation of observations, impressions, interpretation, knowledge, experience, contacts with past environments, and all other factors that have ever affected our conscious and subconscious awareness go together to influence the way we perceive any new event or stimulus. Psychologists broadly call this our *frame of reference*. The frame of reference which serves as a backdrop to our perception of new stimuli tends to be functionally centered; that is, we structure experience in such a way as to make it work for us. In any given circumstance we almost automatically select a part of our past experience that relates to current experiences and is useful to us in forming judgments. There is a good deal of research evidence to indicate that this is so—that experience is perceived in such a way as to work for the perceiver, so as to match his needs, values, and expectations.[12]

The practical implications of this phenomenon for communications effectiveness are several.

1. There are no impartial "facts." Data do not have a logic of their own that results in the same perception and meaning for everyone. Data are perceived and interpreted in terms of the individual perceiver's own needs, emotions, personality, and previously formed frame of reference.

[10] Norbert Weiner, *Cybernetics, or Control and Communication in the Animal and the Machine* (New York: John Wiley & Sons, Inc., 1948).

[11] Wilbur Schramm, "How Communications Work," in *The Process and Effects of Mass Communication,* ed. W. Schramm (Urbana, Ill.: University of Illinois Press, 1954), p. 6.

[12] See David Krech and Richard Crutchfield, *Theory and Problems of Social Psychology* (New York: McGraw-Hill Book Company, 1948), p. 94.

2. When we talk about information transfer in succeeding chapters we must recognize that even the most specific objective information involves subjective perceptions. We cannot consider alone what "information" is required by buyers to facilitate purchase in a particular market. The way this information is likely to be perceived is important. What frames of reference will color interpretations?

3. Variances in encoding and decoding occur mostly because of the different frames of reference of senders and receivers. The burden of responsibility for effective communication in this respect falls on the source or sender. He must adjust to receivers, rather than expect the reverse.

4. Simple language alone does not resolve encoding and decoding difficulties. Many advertisers rely on the use of short words and uncomplicated sentences in copy to reduce message distortion. But even the simplicity of copy is perceived with certain connotative meanings by receivers. Inferences are drawn from this simplicity that may not be in accordance with the desired purposes of the advertiser.

5. The frame of reference is directly related to the matter of congruity in attitude change. As you will see in the chapters on advertising, the market communicator frequently desires to change attitudes.

Frames of reference are particularly important in tailoring messages to the youth market. Youth, as pointed out in Chapter 7, have established a set of values and a language which are unique to this group. Unless the source is familiar with this language, serious mistakes can be made. For example, the selection of the brand name *Score* for a hair cream for young males is indicative of an understanding of teen-age lingo.[13]

Congruity in Attitude Change

Judgmental frames of reference tend toward maximum simplicity. Polarized judgments of good or bad are much easier than finely discriminated judgments. Absolute polarized judgments are characteristic of less intelligent, less mature, less well-educated, and less emotionally stable individuals, but there is a latent polarizing potential within all of us. Over time, there is a tendency toward elimination of differences, so that we seek final judgments of good or bad rather than maintain finely held discriminations of values. That is, even the most mature and sophisticated individual is likely to press toward a polar conclusion as to whether, for example, foreign aid is good or bad. Changes in evaluation tend in the direction of increased congruity with the existing frame of reference.

The issue of congruity arises whenever a message is received which relates two or more objects by way of assertion. For instance, we have a positive attitude toward America, and a negative attitude toward communism and China. We have some relatively neutral attitudes toward certain concepts, such as disarmament, which we would have a tendency to polarize over time. Now if two positive attitudes are associated through a message assertion, then there would tend to be congruity. Likewise, if two negative attitudes were associated by assertion,

---

[13] Cited in James H. Meyers and William R. Reynolds, *Consumer Behavior and Marketing Management* (Boston: Houghton Mifflin Company, 1967), p. 252.

there would be congruity. An assertion linking a positive attitude with a neutral one would tend in the direction of changing the neutral one in the direction of positiveness and, of course, vice versa. For example, if the American government ($+$) were to sponsor a campaign of freedom of the press ($+$), this would be congruent. If the Communist bloc ($-$) were to sponsor such a campaign ($+$), this would be incongruent. If the Communists ($-$) sponsored limited controlled nuclear inspections, ($\pm$), the effect would be to make attitudes toward this notion less favorable, because this puts together a relatively neutral attitude— disarmament—with a relatively negative attitude—communism.

Since the marketer is continually attempting to structure attitudes toward his market offerings, the matter of congruity is especially relevant. He needs always to be sensitive to establishing congruity and to recognizing the means at his disposal to shift attitudes. To enhance the prospect of changing attitudes, he must: (1) understand the frames of reference of his receivers, (2) determine the variations in frames of reference between various segments of his receivers (varying market segments by education, social class, etc.), (3) determine prevailing attitudes toward any two entities he wishes to associate, (4) recognize that he is dealing with dynamic perceptions which in time tend toward polarization, and (5) assess whether the balance is more emotional or rational. (Contrast the difference in purchasing habits and attitudes, for instance, between the industrial purchasing agent and the consumer housewife.)

While these matters arise in all market communications, they are especially relevant in new-product introduction (often met initially by neutral consumer attitudes), the use of testimonials (associations), and campaigns to rejuvenate old products. For instance, is it congruent to use Zsa Zsa Gabor for a commercial on dishwashing detergent? Is it congruent to show an attractively dressed woman painting a wall at one end of a room, while the rest of the room is in perfect order? Decoding effectiveness will be related to the degree of perceived congruence in the message.

Balance of Arguments

In communications, the receiver rarely decodes just one message; most often it is a series. It is at the end of the series of decoding acts that he makes a balanced judgment of the overall exchange. This is especially true in personal selling, when the salesman presents a series of points in the hope of persuading the prospective purchaser to buy. In marketing communications the usual practice has been to present only one set of arguments—those favorable to the marketer's offering. This policy is reflected in the slogan "Put your best foot forward," meaning, leave out any unfavorable factors, and don't say anything about competitors at all. Recently, we can observe some change in this typical marketing practice, and it would seem to be consistent with some of the later communications research. Some of this research, done by Hovland and others, can be summarized as follows: [14]

[14] Carl I. Hovland, Arthur A. Lumsdaine, and Fred D. Sheffield, "The Effect of Presenting 'One Side' versus 'Both Sides' in Changing Opinions on a Controversial Subject," in *The Process and Effects of Mass Communication*, W. Schramm, ed., p. 274.

1. Presenting both sides of an issue was found to be more effective than giving only one side among individuals who were initially opposed to the point of view presented.
2. Better-educated people are more favorably affected by presentation of both sides; the poorly educated are more favorably affected by communication that gives only supporting arguments.
3. For those already convinced of the point of view presented, the presentation of both sides is less effective than a presentation featuring only those items favoring the general position being advanced.
4. Presentation of both sides is least effective among the poorly educated already convinced of the position advocated.
5. Leaving out a relevant argument is more noticeable and detracts more from effectiveness when both sides are presented than when only the side favorable to the proposition is being advanced.

These findings are relevant to a number of marketing communications, and in some cases verify the validity of existing practices. In other cases they seem to be counter to a good deal of observable behavior. In the introduction of new pharmaceuticals to the medical profession, the data would seem to indicate that the doctor ought to be given all information surrounding the use of the drug, not just the points in its favor. Unexpected side effects, for instance, have been known to badly impair the future use of some drugs. The doctor is a highly educated receiver, and can be expected to be more favorably affected by being informed "on both sides" rather than by only supportive arguments. Putting one's best foot forward in this case would seem to indicate putting both feet forward. Also, this procedure has an effect over time of structuring the frame of reference within which the doctor judges the source, and conditions his expectations of it. (The author's own unpublished research into the medical market seems to confirm this viewpoint.)

A second application can be drawn from advertising in the automobile market. Perhaps Cadillac's advertising need not reflect arguments other than the simplicity of its own case. If people are already convinced of its position, introducing any actual or implied comparisons, or notions related to competitive makes, would seem unwise—it would detract from communications effectiveness.

A third illustration can be drawn from the same market. For other automobile producers, perhaps the reverse procedure might be more appropriate. The tendency in some parts of the market has been for a maker to communicate only the features of his make which give it some sort of relative advantage. This could lead many receivers, not convinced by this argument, or possibly initially opposed to it, to presume (as indeed they do) that competitors have a number of different relative advantages not mentioned in the first maker's advertisements or other communications. If the first maker is somewhat of an underdog and attempting to change attitudes, presenting both sides should be more effective. We have seen this very kind of total comparison used; it should be especially effective among the more intelligent segments of the market.

Receivers usually decode several marketing and advertising messages, not just one, and their perception of the totality is what is of concern to the source.

As a consequence, consideration of the balance of messages to be used is important, as is the way messages structure the receiver's perception of the source and his expectation of it. This all leads to the matter of credibility of the source, and its effect on decoding.

Influence of Credence

The effects of credibility of the source on acquisition and retention of messages have been studied.[15] Apparently, there is little difference in the amount of factual information learned from "high credibility" sources and "low credibility" sources, and very little in the amount of information retained. Consequently, initiators of market communications need not be concerned as to how their communications are viewed from the standpoint of credibility, insofar as having receivers learn and retain information is concerned. However, opinions change, in the direction advocated by the communicator, to a greater degree when the material is presented by a trustworthy source than when presented by an untrustworthy source.[16] Since marketing communications are directed so frequently to influencing opinions, this factor is of particular relevance. When the source of a message is an advertiser, he can expect receivers to have a certain skepticism as to the trustworthiness of the source. That is, the advertiser is regarded as prejudiced to begin with, and naturally biased in favor of his own product.

This condition, other things being equal, would lead in the direction of considering the advertiser as a source of relatively low trustworthiness. Research indicates that "no advertisement is likely to be completely 'believable' when its purpose is to change people's minds. Moreover, an advertisement need not be believed completely to be effective." [17] By the very fact that the purpose of much advertising is to change attitudes, it will of necessity be in conflict with prevailing beliefs of the receivers. Receivers will decode the message within the context of existing frames of reference. If the receiver is already in accord with the message, it simply maintains the congruency. The most that can be expected from the message is that it will "nudge" the receiver along a path of acceptance if reinforced with other messages and experiences. Of course, care must be exercised not to overdo attention-getting devices such as overuse of superlatives, false or misleading statements, or exaggerated claims. These only add to the receivers' distrust and make an already difficult job that much more difficult.

If dramatic claims are used to gain attention, it is best to go all the way. That is, use fantasy. The famous "I dreamed I —— in my Maidenform" series gets attention without implying that the source expects the receiver to believe the message.

[15] See, for example, Hovland, Lumsdaine, and Sheffield, *Experiments in Mass Communication* (Princeton, N.J.: Princeton University Press, 1949), pp. 101 ff.

[16] Carl I. Hovland and Walter Weiss, "The Influence of Source Credibility on Communication Effectiveness," in *The Process and Effects of Mass Communication*, W. Schramm, ed., p. 280.

[17] Research conducted by Leo Burnett Company reported in John C. Maloney, "Is Advertising Believability Really Important?" *Journal of Marketing*, XXVII (October 1963), p. 1–8.

⌈THE MESSAGE⌋

Schramm has indicated the conditions that must be fulfilled if the message is to arouse its intended response: [18]

1. The message must be so designed and delivered as to gain the attention of the intended destination.
2. The message must employ signs which refer to experience common to source and destination, so as to "get the meaning across."
3. The message must arouse personality needs in the destination and suggest some ways to meet those needs.
4. The message must suggest a way to meet those needs, which is appropriate to the group situation in which the receiver finds himself at the time when he is moved to make the desired response, and we can add:
5. The message must be so constructed as to meet the conditions of congruity and credence.
6. The elements of the message must be so ordered that maximum learning and opinion influence take place.
7. The message must be suitable in form for the channel or medium being used to reach intended receivers.

Let us now look in greater detail at some of the various elements in message effectiveness.

Attention

Obviously a message must be made available before it can be decoded, but even if it is available, it may not be selected. There are far more communication attempts made than anyone can possibly accept or decode. A person therefore tends to scan his environment (in much the same way that we scan newspaper headlines), choosing messages according to the way they fit his needs and interests. Usually this selection is made on the basis of an impression gained from a "cue" in the message. A cue could be a headline, an illustration, a splash of color, a sound—any individual impression that arouses the senses. The surrounding environment influences the capacity of these cues to be effective. That is, if they are transmitted at a time when the receiver is extremely busy or tired, or when his attention is held by other matters, or if there are many messages competing for attention, the cues may pass unnoticed, whereas under different circumstances they might have been effective. The designing of a message for attention, then, involves timing and placement, and the equipping of it with the kind of cues that will appeal to the receiver's interests, needs, and personality. A great deal of effort is spent in the design and layout of advertising for this very purpose. Knowing the receivers intimately helps, but still a good deal of success in this area reflects the artistic ability of the communicator.

[18] Schramm, "How Communications Work," in *The Process and Effects of Mass Communication,* p. 13. Much of the material presented in this section is taken from Schramm.

Common Experiences of Source and Receivers

Since this subject has already been treated, only a footnote is offered here. The source must adapt to the cues, sign language, symbols, and perceptions of the receiver. *Commonness* in this sense means pursuing a receiver orientation if one would structure a message for maximal effectiveness. There may be the rare occasion when the opposite can be useful for its attention-getting qualities, or the longer chance of developing interest; however, this is a rather risky procedure, because of the prospect of the message's being lost as a result of the selective scanning that takes place. (In Chapter 25, techniques are discussed for measuring both the level of message complexity and the capacity of the receiver to decode messages of varying complexity.)

Arousal of Personality Needs

We react to various stimuli on the basis of our needs, drives, and goals. Usually, we choose actions out of an assortment of alternatives that lead us along a path to our goals. Therefore, a prime requisite of an effective message is that it relate itself to personality needs or desires—desire for security, approval within a group, expression of a certain station in life. The message should propose a way in which these requirements can be fulfilled. They must be motivationally and behaviorally oriented. The suggested action may or may not be regarded by the receiver as the best of his alternatives, and it is not likely to take place at all unless it raises his threshold of expectation to the necessary level. What is being communicated, therefore, goes beyond words, pictures, and sounds—images are being transmitted that must stimulate the imagination and the initiative of the receiver to venture beyond the threshold of the subconscious and beyond mere contemplation. The problem is the large number of personality types with which the source must deal. What will work for one will not work for another.

It has been suggested that Riesman's typology of social character may be a meaningful variable for communication processes. Riesman suggested that the majority of Americans are either inner-directed or other-directed.[19] Inner-directed people turn inward for their values and standards of guidance for their behavior. Other-directed people depend on other people for guiding their behavior and establishing their norms and values. In a study to test the hypothesis that these two types respond differently, a sample of 200 was tested for inner-other-direction and then shown a series of twenty-seven pairs of advertisements selected for their inner-directed and other-directed appeals. The respondents then rated the ads in terms of which they thought would tend to influence them most and which they thought would influence other people most. The results showed that inner-directed people tended to prefer ads with inner-directed appeals and other-directed people preferred other-directed appeals. Both groups, however, thought that people in general would prefer other-directed appeals.[20]

[19] David Riesman, Nathan Glazer, and Reuel Denney, *The Lonely Crowd* (New Haven: Yale University Press, Abridged Edition, 1961).

[20] Harold J. Kassarjian, "Social Character and Differential Preference for Mass Communication," *Journal of Marketing Research*, II (1965), 146–53.

Reference Groups

Any individual lives as a member of various groups, and develops his stand-ards and values from them. Berlo estimates that in a complex society like that in the United States, an individual may have roles in from twenty-five to fifty groups.[21] (A more detailed discussion of reference group theory was made in Chapter 7.) For purposes of this discussion, a key question then becomes: Related to any particular message, what group or groups is an individual using as a reference for his behavior? Evidence is continuing to pile up concerning the importance of groups to attitude change. Stated differently: A receiver's reference groups must be kept in mind when designing a message intended to change attitudes. As a consumer moves up the income ladder, he tends to take the spending pattern of each new group, just as students coming into new reference groups have been found to shift their attitudes in the direction of group norms. When majority opinion has been made known, group members' attitudes have tended to move toward it. Reference group influence has resulted in the concept of the *two-step flow of communication*.[22] This concept recognizes that the source may send messages to several receivers but only a few respond directly. Others respond indirectly after influencers or opinion leaders communicate the message to others not exposed to it or endorse the message to those already exposed. Marketing analysts have spent considerable time trying to identify "influence centers" (individuals) within groups, on grounds that if they could attract such individuals to their products, the group attitude toward the marketer's products would become more favorable. On the other hand, some advocate ignoring the opinion leaders and short-circuiting the two-step flow. Particularly is this feasible when there is little risk for the purchaser in making a choice on his own, such as in the sale of low-unit-value, high-frequency-of-purchase items.[23]

Change in Related Factors

Messages that are accompanied by changes in other (for instance, environ-mental) factors underlying attitudes have a better chance of acceptance. The more advantage that can be taken of a favorable change in environment, the better. For instance, a high-protein breakfast food was introduced almost twenty-five years ago with little success. Kellogg's "Special K," likewise a high-protein breakfast food, on the other hand, was an outstanding success when introduced only a few years back. A great deal of general emphasis had been placed, since the original product offering, on diet in general, amount of calories in foods, and the importance of protein. Kellogg's advertising capitalized on these points and was extremely successful.

[21] Berlo, *The Process of Communication,* p. 158.

[22] See E. Katz, "The Two-Step Flow of Communication: An Up-to-Date Report on an Hypothesis," *Public Opinion Quarterly* (Spring 1957), pp. 61–78.

[23] See Maloney, "Is Advertising Believability Really Important?" p. 8.

Primacy "Ordering" Element

Should a message begin with its strongest point or build up to it? This problem of ordering or sequencing the various points is inherent in all communications, but it is particularly relevant in such market communications as advertising and personal selling. Carl Hovland offers two guides from communications research findings.[24] Where the audience is familiar with the subject, and particularly if it has a known interest in the subject, there seems to be a good reason for "climax" order, that is, leading up to the main point at the end. If the audience is unfamiliar with the subject or uninterested, it appears to be more desirable to introduce the main point first. This procedure enhances the prospect of gaining attention and interest, and would seem to apply to much new product communication and promotion. The opposite approach might better apply to older products in the technical field.

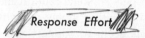 Response Effort

Other things being equal, receivers tend to make responses which require little effort, and avoid responses which seem to require much effort. Direct-mail advertising, for example, often includes a self-addressed, stamped envelope. Advertisers (the source) have found that if the receiver can respond without having to find an envelope, address it properly, and put a stamp on it, more returns are received. The reduction of effort increases the chances of getting the desired response—the major purpose of communication. The same basic consideration is involved in the frequent use of "Call Operator 25," "Send no money," "Free home trial," and "Just phone and we will deliver a new television set to your door within the hour." Where the response involves some difficulty, the communicator needs to minimize the factor. For example, making a mail questionnaire even *appear* shorter improves returns.

Time Lags

The message needs to reflect the time period in which a favorable response by the receiver can be gratified. If immediate action is desired by the source, then a stronger emotional appeal would be used than might be if time lags were allowable. If a long-range or continuing response is the purpose of the source, then a milder appeal seems warranted. Schramm has said that recent research indicates that, when a strong appeal is used, the audience is more likely to remember the "threat." When a milder one is used, the audience is more likely to remember the *source* and *explanation* of the "threat." This point will have particular relevance in Chapter 24, where direct action and indirect action advertising are discussed.

[24] Hovland and others in *The Process and Effects of Mass Communication*, p. 213.

Message Repetition

Learning theory indicates that learning increases and is strengthened with repetition and practice, or when the same subject is covered from a number of different directions or points of view. Research on learning from mass communication leaves the implication that more examples make for more learning as long as the repetition is not so similar or unvaried as to be boresome. Also, there is some indication that there is a saturation point beyond which the amount of learning no longer increases. Market communicators, particularly advertisers, have come to recognize these points, but have a difficult time measuring the threshold of saturation.

Reinforcing Media and Messages

A suggestion carried by a mass medium plus personal reinforcement is more apt to be accepted than a suggestion carried by either alone, other things being equal. Both research and advertising practice seem to support this conclusion. It seems to make some difference, however, as to how the two media or channels are used. Greater learning takes place if different stimuli are used rather than merely repeating the same ones, only through different media. The two channels should be combined so that the receiver has a different learning experience. In the next chapter we indicate that advertising and personal selling should be used for transmitting different kinds of communications, that one is more suitable for particular purposes than the other, and that they need to be integrated. The consideration we have just mentioned is a major reason for that proposal. Also, this consideration has a bearing on determining the composition of the promotional mix discussed in the same chapter.

Summary

Communication may be regarded as a process by which a verbal or nonverbal effort is made by a source to send a message through a channel to establish a "commonness" with a receiver. In human communication, the source has a purpose for engaging in communication; his objective is to elicit a response.

A simple communications model includes a source; the process of encoding the abstract ideas of the source into a message or signal, which is transmitted through a channel; and message decoding at the destination by receivers.

Difficulties which reduce message fidelity can arise at any stage in the communications process, distort its intent, or preclude its being received. A good deal of the difficulty can arise because of the lack of clearly defined purpose on the part of the source, or his lack of understanding of receivers. Perhaps the most important factor that accounts for ineffective communications is the variation in the encoding and decoding processes. These variations primarily reflect the differing frames of reference and fields of experience of source and receivers. Emphasis was placed upon the need for credence, congruity, and balance of argument in attitude change.

Among the principal elements of message effectiveness are: the message must be so designed and delivered as to gain the receiver's attention (it needs the appropriate "scanning clues"); it must employ signs and language common to source and receiver; it must arouse personality needs in the receiver and suggest a way of meeting these needs; it must be ordered for maximum learning, and suited to the channel.

The related matters of reference groups, changing environments, response effort, time lags, message repetition and variation, and the use of reinforcing media are recognized as having relevance for market communications, which is a large part of market cultivation. The discussion presented was designed to serve as a backdrop to the whole problem of determining the communications mix.

Questions and Problems

1. How is communications related to market affairs?
2. Diagram and explain a simple communications model.
3. In the communications process, what is meant by "noise"?
4. What is the difference between consummatory purpose and instrumental purpose? Which of these have marketers tended to emphasize in advertising?
5. What are the attributes of the source of messages that seem to have a significant bearing on communications effectiveness?
6. Why is it important to "know thy audience" as a prerequisite to effective communications? What should be known about the audience? What is the marketing analogy here?
7. Explain why the slang language of neighborhood boys seems to be such an effective means of communication.
8. What basic communications issue is raised by a streetcar ad devoted to the sale of mink coats? *incongruent*
9. Comment on the use of the term *facts* as related to the communications process.
10. Discuss the role of congruity in attitude change. One of the major automobile companies rejected the idea of using a famous movie star in commercials for its lowest-price car on the grounds that it would have destroyed the "credence" of the advertising. How would you explain this position?
11. Should the marketer present the full story of his product in direct comparison with his competitors? Explain.
12. What do reference groups have to do with the effectiveness of market communications?
13. What is the "climax order" in arranging sales points for a product? When should a salesman use this order in place of alternatives? Under what conditions might he use a different arrangement?
14. What do you think of advertisers who place the same ad in different media over and over? What principles of learning are at issue in this practice?
15. "If a message is believed, it is therefore likely to be effective for marketing purposes." Comment and elaborate.

Determination of the Optimum Communications Mix

23

Market action is precipitated through the communications function. The exchange process is energized (or activated) only on the basis of information flows which bring buyer and seller together. The marketer seeks to close the gap between the information potential buyers have, and what they should have if impact requirements that trigger the desired purchase decisions are to be met. Market impact is, of course, a much broader complex of forces than merely information flow. It is the result of a total market posture—the collective offering of product, services, information, and intangibles such as company reputation—which registers in the potential buyer's mind as one collective package of utilities. In achieving the desired level of market impact, the proper composition of the communications mix and the level of expenditures to be allocated to the various components will have a major bearing on market results, but presents an extremely complex analytical problem. The problem and the decisions related to it, however, cannot be escaped. Every company will have made decisions by the end of the year as to the manner in which its resources will have to be allocated for marketing purposes. Collectively, these decisions will account normally for well over half of all marketing expenses incurred. Although these decisions are pervasive, inescapable, and difficult, rich opportunities exist for the development of more penetrating theory and improved practices.

In this chapter we will examine some of the complications of the communications mix problem in a broader decision spectrum—namely, the choice of product to devote significant resources of market cultivation to; the theoretical solution to communications mix expenditures and the practical limitations to reaching the ideal solution; and finally, changes in the composition of the mix through time for products at various stages of market development.

399

Determina-
tion of the
Optimum
Communica-
tions Mix

THE COMMUNICATIONS MIX:
PART OF A BROADER
PROBLEM SPECTRUM

The communications mix problem for individual products is actually part of a broader problem. It includes decisions as to which products to devote significant resources to in the hopes of winning a position in the market place, as well as decisions as to the character of adjustments in total appropriations, and composition of the mix as the product proceeds through the various stages of market development.

The choice of products to devote significant communications resources to is complicated by the rate of product failure, the rate of product displacement, and the conglomerate sales results achieved by products that do survive market competition. This is immediately relevant to the communications mix question of the variations that are made for products of expected limited longevity in the market, those of considerable uncertainty of survival, and those expected to be highly successful.

Rate of Product Failure

Few consumer goods products have any definite assurance of a future share of the market. While satisfactory data in this area are conspicuously lacking, we indicated in Chapter 11 that some 80 percent of all packaged consumer products put on the market fail. Interestingly enough, exactly the same situation prevails in the widely unrelated field of ethical pharmaceuticals. Data in this field indicate that for every 100 products introduced, only 8 will be among the best prescription sellers and high profit makers; another 10 to 12 will merely pay their own way, and the other 80 percent will fail.[1] This poses a major problem in the allocation of marketing effort to new products in terms of both quantity of effort and choice of instrument.

The choice of products to devote sizable market expenditure to, including communications expenditures, can come only through the results of market and technical research. There is obviously no easy means for measuring the potential acceptance of new products. The magnitude of the problem, however, in terms of the number of new products and the few that will be successful, makes it a very important one. To determine communications expenditures intelligently requires having some estimate of the potential returns that can be expected or at least a measure of the level of market opportunity.

Rate of Product Displacement

While the rate of product failure is high, so also is the rate of product displacement. This is particularly true of the newer and more dynamic areas of

---

[1] Thomas A. Staudt, "Determining and Evaluating the Promotional Mix," *Modern Medicine Topics*, XVIII, No. 7 (July 1957).

technology. Product displacement in such fields as electronics, chemicals, and pharmaceuticals, for instance, is particularly dramatic and rapid. In the pharmaceutical industry especially, there are about 500 new products introduced each year. In a given two-year period, 73 new products were added to the best-seller list (400,000 prescription sales a year, or more), and 78 were dropped.[2] This means that an extended period of time is not available for experimentation in the communications mix. Years ago more time could be taken for experimentation and trial and error in arriving at an optimum mix. Presently, a great need exists for better decisions at a product's introduction. Also, quick adjustments are called for after the product is launched.

Figure 23-1 shows the conglomerate sales results for all products produced by just one manufacturer. Obviously, great variations are required in the mix for each of these products. Variations are required in total appropriations for each product, and in the composition of the mix of a given product through time, as well as adjustments in aggregate appropriations for the firm as a whole as its cumulative market opportunity changes.

FIGURE 23-1
Typical Sales Curves for All Products
Marketed by One Manufacturer

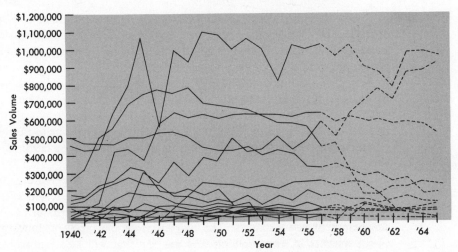

DETERMINING COMMUNICATIONS
MIX EXPENDITURES

The Model Solution

We must recognize in considering a model solution to the mix problem that the various instruments of communications, such as personal selling, advertising, and sales promotion, allow for a certain substitution among themselves. It is possible that a number of different combinations of these instruments could produce

---

[2] Staudt, "Determining and Evaluating the Promotional Mix."

401

Determina-
tion of the
Optimum
Communica-
tions Mix

the same net profit. Notice the great differences in expenditures in Table 23-1—undoubtedly with similar profit results in a number of cases. On the other hand, there may be a considerable difference in the net profits obtained between one combination of personal selling, magazine advertising, television advertising, dealer promotion, etc., and another. The fact that there are substitution possibilities leads to the belief that large expenditures in any one instrument such as advertising, when coupled with neglect of others, is likely not to lead to an optimum mix. It must be conceded, however, that some extremely successful marketing campaigns have been predominantly oriented toward only one communications instrument. The huge market success Listerine antiseptic enjoyed a few years ago was achieved almost exclusively with heavy advertising outlays that were continuously increased.

Although substitution of communications instruments is possible, there is evidence that some consensus exists concerning the proper allocation, depending upon the product. In a study designed to determine how communication strategies differ for different classes of products, 486 general managers or vice-presidents were questioned.[3] They were asked to allocate 100 points among five communications instruments according to their perceived importance in the success of industrial goods, consumer durables, and consumer nondurables. The results are shown in Table 23-2.

Let us pause here to reflect on how a scientist might handle a similar kind of problem. Suppose the chemist wanted to determine the combination of ingredients that gave the greatest rust resistance to paint. He would conduct a series of experiments under controlled conditions in which he would hold all but one variable constant, observing the effects of different quantities of the particular ingredient being studied. After a series of such observations, he could determine the combination of quantities that produced the best result in terms of his objective—maximum resistance to rust.

The problem we face in marketing, and other social sciences for that matter, is that we cannot hold the variables constant for a series of controlled observations. We cannot keep competitors' actions, and market conditions and all the myriad of variables influencing communications effectiveness, constant. Moreover, as a practical business matter, we may not want to go too far in running experiments on products that are an important source of revenue. In the case of some products, for example, millions of dollars of sales volume are at stake, and management may well be reluctant to experiment on these products with already proven methods of communication merely to come a bit closer to a theoretically optimum solution. The penalties of failure result in a risk not worth incurring if "good" profitability is being achieved.

Marketers, therefore, frequently must work backward from results already achieved. An attempt is made to duplicate the experiment, as it would likely have been run under controlled conditions, using historical data. This is done by taking territories of equal potential (or by making precise adjustment for differences in potential) and selecting a previous year in which the kinds of differ-

[3] Jon G. Udell, "The Perceived Importance of the Elements of Strategy," *Journal of Marketing*, XXXII (January 1968), 34–40.

TABLE 23-1

Distribution of the Market Cultivation Budget
of 23 Pharmaceutical Firms (in percentage, by size of firm)

	UNDER $500,000		$500,000–$1,000,000		$1,000,000–$5,000,000		$5,000,000–$10,000,000		OVER $10,000,000	
	Majority of Firms Allocate Between	*Adjusted Average*	*Majority of Firms Allocate Between*	*Adjusted Average*	*Majority of Firms Allocate Between*	*Adjusted Average*	*Majority of Firms Allocate Between*	*Adjusted Average*	*Majority of Firms Allocate Between*	*Adjusted Average*
Detail representatives	9.5–71.4	26.4	3.0–76.2	54.0	8.0–74.5	40.9	8.0–68.0	45.7	42.3–89.4	70.6
Direct mail	12.0–27.8	16.7	1.0–65.0	19.7	7.9–31.0	17.0	5.8–18.9	12.2	0.9–29.4	9.1
Medical journals	16.7–62.4	33.8	4.3–18.5	12.2	9.4–55.0	21.0	7.7–17.3	12.3	0.8–4.3	2.8
Drug magazines	1.9–21.0	4.6	0.4–2.0	1.0	1.0–6.0	2.1	1.0–17.3	4.6	0.5–1.0	0.8
Hospital and industrial magazines	0	0	0	0	0	0	17.4–17.4	4.4	0.1–0.3	0.2
Other magazines	0	0	0	0	0	0	0	0	0.1–0.3	0.2
House organs	0	0	1.2–1.2	0.3	1.0–1.0	0.2			1.5–9.6	2.4
Window displays	0	0	0	0	0	0	0.5–0.5	0.1	1.2–1.5	0.7
Moving pictures	9.0–9.0	1.8	0	0	0	0	0	0	0.1–0.1	0.1
Samples	1.0–40.0	12.4	4.8–11.8	5.9	6.1–23.1	11.3	2.5–20.0	14.2	2.1–7.9	4.4
Literature	1.8–2.1	0.8	1.0–5.9	2.9	1.0–10.0	4.0	2.0–5.8	2.7	1.1–3.2	2.3
Conventions	3.7–4.8	2.6	1.2–3.0	2.3	1.1–5.1	1.9	1.0–10.0	3.7	0.4–0.9	0.7
Gifts; souvenirs	0	0	0	0	0.5–0.5	0.1	0.5–0.5	0.1	0.1–0.9	0.4
Reserve	0	0	0	0	3.0–3.0	0.5	0	0	4.8–4.8	1.2
Miscellaneous	1.0–3.7	0.9	2.0–2.9	1.7	0.3–9.0	1.5			0.9–9.9	4.3
		100.0		100.0		100.0		100.0		100.0

Source: Thomas A. Staudt, "Determining and Evaluating the Promotional Mix," Modern Medicine Topics, XVIII, No. 7 (July 1957).

403

Determina-
tion of the
Optimum
Communica-
tions Mix

TABLE 23-2
Relative Importance of the Elements
of Marketing Communications *

Sales Effort Activity	PRODUCERS OF:		
	Industrial Goods	Consumer Durables	Consumer Nondurables
Sales management and personal selling	69.2	47.6	38.1
Broadcast media Advertising	.9	10.7	20.9
Printed media Advertising	12.5	16.1	14.8
Special promotional activities	9.6	15.5	15.5
Branding and promotional packaging	4.5	9.5	9.8
Other	3.3	.6	.9
Total	100.0	100.0	100.0

* The data are the average point allocations of 336 industrial, 52 consumer durable, and 88 consumer nondurable goods producers. Nine responses are excluded because of point allocations which did not equal 100.
Source: Jon G. Udell, "The Perceived Importance of the Elements of Strategy," Journal of Marketing, *XXXII (January 1968), 38.*

ences or variations in the communications mix exist in different territories in much the same way they would have if an experiment had been structured. The differing effects produced by variations in the quantity of advertising, selling effort, and the like are then observed in the various territories through a series of time periods. In this way it is possible to duplicate (within limits) an experiment by using historical data. With proper statistical analysis and a perceptive understanding of marketing operations in the different territories, it is possible to draw sound inferences as to the return on a given product from specific variations in the communications mix. It is possible to test the validity of the conclusions, to a degree, by observing their predictive value in other territories, again using historical data, or in the same territories from which the analysis is made, using other years than those to which the data apply.

One of the major industrial goods producers, employing several hundred salesmen, once undertook such a study for developing a sound sales compensation plan. The proper incentive compensation plan cannot be precisely determined until the most effective use of the salesmen's effort is known. This depends upon the productivity from using their effort in alternative ways. The proper quantity of effort can then be determined, and the compensation plan should provide the proper incentive to do those things affording the greatest return to the firm. Studies such as these are for the purpose of developing the data for approximating a model solution, which involves two maximization rules.

Maximization Rules

The model communications mix involves two problem areas requiring solution: (1) how much in total appropriations should be spent on all forms of communication, and (2) what the relative relationship should be between each of the communications instruments in the mix. The theoretical solution to each of these problems involves a similar maximization rule: continue increasing expenditures until marginal cost equals marginal revenue.

How much in total should be spent on all forms of market cultivation? The objective here is to match total effort with market opportunity. Again this requires as clear a definition of market potential as can be secured and some indication of the returns that can be expected from the communications effort. Knowing these two factors would enable one to approximate the model solution, which would be to increase the total expenditure to the point where the last dollar spent on communications just pays for itself in additional revenues—which would be the point where marginal cost and marginal revenue are equal.

The rule for any single communications instrument is to increase expenditures until the marginal revenue equals the marginal cost of the expenditure. The communications mix is optimum when the marginal revenue per dollar of cost is equal for each of the instruments used. This simply means that if there are differences in marginal revenues, expenditures should be increased or decreased until equal marginal revenues exist for all. Because of the tendency in business practice to think in terms of profit contributions resulting from additional expenditures, rather than marginal revenue or marginal cost, the optimum expenditure level is reached when the marginal net profit from an expenditure is equal to zero. This is the point at which marginal cost equals marginal revenue.

The practical problem, of course, is one of measurement, or knowing when expenditures are close to the point where marginal revenues are equal. Research can provide fairly good answers in many cases, as we shall shortly see. In many cases management decisions are not so much oriented to perfection as to improvement; for example, Can advertising be profitably increased? Is it desirable to add more salesmen? What results could we expect from a 20 percent increase in the sales promotion budget? Before dealing with the practical problem, however, let us consider some of the relevant factors precluding the model solution, aside from the measurement problem.

Practical Limitations to Model Solutions

First, present assets, which are fixed in the short run, must be used as efficiently as possible. If 200 salesmen are already employed, whether or not this is the ideal number, these men must be used as efficiently as possible. Obviously we could not say to the sales force, "You men just go home and take the week off. We won't pay you because we are now past the point of greatest profit from your efforts."

Second, not all forms of communication are such that small adjustments can be made.[4] A page of space for advertising in many of the major magazines must go nationwide. It is not possible to decrease journal advertising in California

---

[4] Also, government regulation provides some limitations to development of communications resources. According to the Court's interpretation of the Robinson-Patman Act, for example, you cannot place cosmetics demonstrators in only the large department stores. You must make proportional allowances available to all competing dealers. This limitation is discussed in more detail in Chapter 29.

405

Determina-
tion of the
Optimum
Communica-
tions Mix

and increase it in New York, and one cannot say to the publisher, "Please leave out the Rocky Mountain states because we have no distribution there." There have been, however, some recent attempts by publishers to make more of this flexibility possible.

Third, certain costs really ought to be considered investments rather than as current expenditures in a given operating period. Advertising is of this character. Some portion of advertising impact is assumed to be cumulative in its effect. We have presumed that there is some carry-over, momentum, inertia, or longer-run institutional value in advertising. Just how much such value is involved is difficult to quantify.

Fourth, there is a partial degree of interdependency among some of the forms of communication. The effectiveness of a direct-mail campaign, for example, may depend on having salesmen follow up promptly on the interest that may have been aroused in potential purchasers. In a related, but not exactly comparable way, the effectiveness of price reductions may depend upon making the knowledge of such reductions widespread through the use of advertising. From the analytical viewpoint, this interrelationship is a most unwelcome complicating factor.

Fifth, in real life, one means of communication may need to be somewhat overextended because of poor performance in another area. That is, it is difficult to separate quantity of effort from quality of effort. If personal selling is poorly organized, with inadequately trained and supervised personnel, advertising—or some other communications form, beyond what would normally be justified— may be necessary to reach marketing objectives.

Approaching the Theoretical Solution in Practice

Even though these factors, plus the extremely difficult one of measurement, tend to preclude exact solutions, the model can often be used in conjunction with research analysis to obtain solutions of sufficient precision for management purposes. Let us examine the problem of expenditures for personal selling, or how many salesmen a firm can profitably employ in its communications mix.[5]

According to the marginal model, the solution to this problem is simple, provided we can obtain the necessary data, and the conditions prevailing at the time of analysis remain relatively constant. The marginal formula indicates that we can increase the number of salesmen profitably if the sales volume obtained by additional salesmen, times the expected gross profit margin of these sales, minus the cost of maintaining the salesmen, is greater than zero. It is expressed algebraically as follows:

$$S(P) - C > 0$$

Where:

S = sales volume that each additional salesman will be expected to produce.
P = the expected profit margin on his sales volume.
C = the total cost of maintaining him in the field.

[5] For detailed analyses, see Walter J. Semlow, "How Many Salesmen Do You Need?" *Harvard Business Review*, XXXVII, No. 3 (May–June 1959), 126.

In other words, when the total cost of maintaining an additional salesman just balances the additional gross profit on the sales volume he is expected to produce, it is no longer desirable to increase the sales force. Fairly close estimates of two of the three parts of the data required can usually be obtained from an analysis of accounting information, at least over levels of *output* that our experience applies to—namely, the profit margins pertaining to various volumes and the total cost of maintaining salesmen. The real problem is to determine the incremental sales that additional salesmen could be expected to generate. In order to make this determination it is necessary to know what happens to volume when the typical salesman spreads his effort over territories of varying potential. It can usually be expected that an increase in total sales volume results whenever another salesman is added. Usually, but not always, a substantial increase in the number of salesmen does not produce a *proportional* increase in sales. If the firm is operating above the break-even point, thereby already covering all fixed costs, but below plant capacity, an increase in sales can be very profitable. In order to know just how profitable, and how much volume can be anticipated, we must have estimates of market potentials.

TABLE 23-3

Basic Factual Data Pertaining to 25 Salesmen's
Territories (in thousands of dollars)

Territory Designation	Size of Territory (Percentage of Total Potential)	Total Sales per Territory	Sales per 1% of Potential
1	11.89%	$351	$ 29
2	9.53	300	31
3	7.68	244	32
4	6.36	179	28
5	6.07	393	65
6	4.78	200	42
7	4.75	192	40
8	4.64	312	67
9	4.58	169	37
10	4.10	187	45
11	3.75	218	58
12	3.42	210	61
13	3.33	151	45
14	3.08	186	60
15	2.65	234	89
16	2.61	235	90
17	2.56	194	76
18	2.50	398	160
19	2.16	208	97
20	1.86	344	185
21	1.83	288	158
22	1.80	140	78
23	1.43	252	177
24	1.39	346	250
25	1.25	257	206
	100.00%		

Source: Walter J. Semlow, "How Many Salesmen Do You Need?" in Harvard Business Review, *XXXVII, No. 3 (May–June 1959), 128.*

407

Determina-
tion of the
Optimum
Communica-
tions Mix

In some instances market potentials are relatively easy to compute; in other cases complex analytical and statistical analysis must be employed. In the appliance industry, for instance, regular data are available on industry-wide sales by products for various geographic areas, making reasonably good indicators of market potentials of various territories readily available. If a particular firm has or can develop these kinds of data, and has a sufficient number of salesmen for reasonably reliable statistical analysis, the next task is to observe the volume of sales derived in the various territories in relation to the available potential. Table 23-3 shows such analysis. When these data are plotted on a graph (Figure 23-2) it is easy to see that sales are proportionately much higher in territories of small potential, which immediately suggests that additional salesmen would be profitable. That is, more intensive coverage of markets is shown to produce sales above average levels for all territories. Sales (per 1 percent of market potential) increase as the size of territory in terms of market potential decreases. By graphing these data we can quickly compute the sales volume that could be expected from various numbers of salesmen, assuming the new salesmen would do relatively no better or no worse than the existing sales force. For example, we can see in the graph that if we had fifty salesmen, allocated to territories of even potentials of 2 percent, we could expect an average yield from each man of approximately

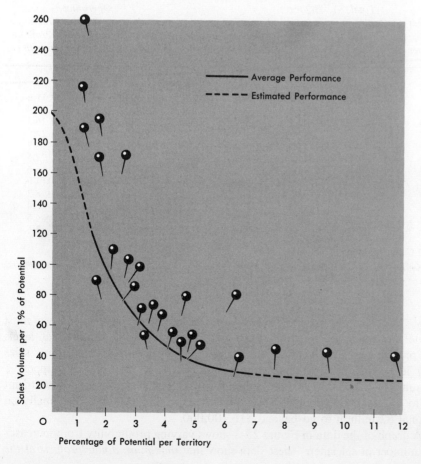

FIGURE 23-2
Relationship
Between Sales
Potential per
Territory and Sales
Volume per One
Percent of Potential

$200,000 ($100,000 per 1 percent of potential) or a total sales revenue of $10 million, from the fifty men.

We must now develop data related to profit margins, so as to be able to determine the value of additional sales volume. This can be done by taking the average profit margin obtained by present salesmen on an average mix of products to obtain rough estimates, or we can derive more precise data by break-even analysis. Break-even analysis enables us to show fixed costs of production, direct and semidirect costs of production at various levels, "fixed" or "fully committed" costs of marketing, and finally, direct marketing costs. The difference between these totals and gross revenues at various levels would be the amount available to cover the additional costs of selling and profits. Costs of maintaining a salesman in the field are calculated to be $20,000 per year. A computation of operating profits before cost of salesmen is shown in Table 23.4.

TABLE 23-4

Determination of Operating Profit with Varying
Numbers of Salesmen (in thousands of dollars)

Number of Salesmen	Estimated Total Company Sales Volume	Operating Profit Before Variable Selling Cost	Variable Selling Cost	Operating Profit*	Total Investment	Operating Profit on Sales Volume	Operating Profit on Investment
200	$19,000	$5,350	$4,000	$1,350	$17,600	7.1%	7.7%
150	18,000	5,000	3,000	2,000	17,200	11.1	11.6
100	16,000	4,500	2,000	2,500	14,400	15.6	17.4
80	14,100	3,835	1,600	2,235	13,640	15.8	16.3
65	12,200	3,470	1,300	2,170	9,880	17.8	22.0
50	10,000	2,700	1,000	1,700	9,000	17.0	18.9
40	8,000	2,200	800	1,400	6,200	17.5	22.5
30	6,000	1,500	600	900	5,400	15.0	16.6
25	5,000	1,150	500	650	5,000	13.0	13.0
20	4,000	800	400	400	4,600	10.0	8.7
16	3,300	555	320	235	4,320	7.1	5.4
13	3,000	450	260	190	4,200	6.3	4.5
10	2,700	345	200	145	4,080	5.4	3.6

* Column 3 minus Column 4.

Source: Walter J. Semlow, "How Many Salesmen Do You Need?" in Harvard Business Review, XXXVII, No. 3 (May–June 1959), 130.

Finally, to determine profitability in terms of return on investment, we must estimate any new investment in plant and working capital required at levels above present capacity. Assume that working capital is 40 percent of gross sales at any level, and that present plant investment of $3 million will support a maximum of $8,100,000 of sales volume, with $2 million additional investment to go to $12,300,000, another $3 million to go to $16,100,000, and finally an additional $2 million to go beyond $16,100,000.

A graph of the data in Figure 23-3 shows varying profitability from increases in the number of salesmen. These data show that *maximum dollar profit is at the level of 100 salesmen, maximum return on invested capital at 40 salesmen, and maximum profits to sales at 65 salesmen.* Here we see the relevance of profit standards indicated in Chapter 4. Different actions, based upon different objectives, can be taken by management. Since 65 salesmen produce almost as much operating profit as 100, and almost as good a return on investment as 40, and provide the maximum profit to sales, a compromise of the ideal number of men may be considered by many managements as 65. But since the firm might not be able to assimilate so many additional salesmen in any given year, it may decide to add 5 to 10 each year over a period of several years. This change can be undertaken with full confidence that the expenditure will be productive.

If funds are limited, which is the usual case, management must weigh the additional commitment of $100,000 (five salesmen) in personal selling against the potential returns of the same commitment in another instrument—advertising, for example. Here the maximization rule applies in the selection of the alternative instruments. This requires some measure of marginal net returns. However, even if we have been able to develop these data, which is no easy matter, we still have some difficult choices and judgments to make. Using the applicable data from the previous illustration, let us assume that from historical data ("experiments" using data from previous years, mentioned earlier in the chapter) we have been

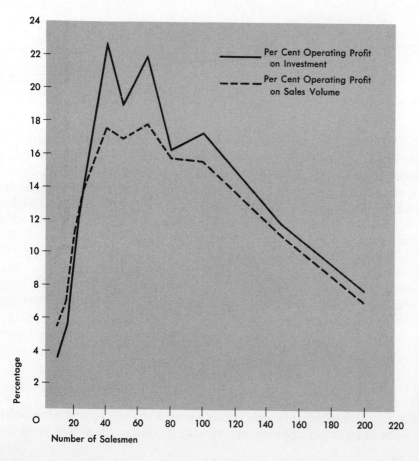

FIGURE 23-3
Relationship Between Number of Salesmen and Percentage of Operating Profit to Sales Volume and Investment

able to graph the relationship between advertising expenditures and sales volume as shown in Figure 23-4. If the firm is currently spending $250,000 on advertising, an additional expenditure of $100,000 would not be as well spent as the same amount would be on increasing the sales force. The marginal profitability from the advertising expenditure would be $75,000 from generating a sales volume of $5,500,000. This compares with an expected $6 million in sales from 30 salesmen producing a marginal profitability of $250,000. On the basis of these two alternatives, the optimum decision is clear—add the salesmen.

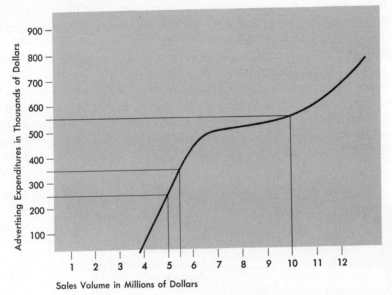

FIGURE 23-4
Relationship
Between
Advertising
Expenditures and
Sales Volume

Look at what happens, however, when the next increase in expenditures is considered. Adding 10 more salesmen (40 total) produces an expected profit increment of $500,000 from increasing sales to $8,000,000. Had the firm elected to increase advertising initially instead of the sales force, and then spent the equivalent monies in the second round of decisions on advertising, the $200,000 increase (plus the first $100,000) would produce sales of $10 million, and a profit increment of $1,175,000, compared with $500,000. Spending all the increase in both rounds on the sales force produces a total expected profit increment of $750,000, while spending it on advertising produces $1,250,000. This situation dramatizes the problem of long- and short-term moves, the judgment that must be exercised by executives in making these decisions, and the way objectives influence decisions.

CHANGING THE COMPOSITION
OF THE COMMUNICATIONS MIX
THROUGH TIME

Because the multiproduct firm is characteristic of the structure of industry today, we must focus our attention on individual product needs as well as on the line as a whole. It is apparent that various products reaching different markets of special characteristics have individual communications needs. Also, the same product has different communications requirements as it passes through the various stages of market development. An increasingly common practice in companies today is to build communications budgets product by product or by broad product lines.

Whereas up to now we have considered the communications mix for the product mix as a whole, let us now turn our attention to particular products. The basic models and decision rules are exactly the same for an individual product as for the total line. Several additional complications set in when we attempt the same determination of communications mix expenditures for particular products. The same difficulties exist in forecasting revenues from varying expenditures as existed before, but greater complications develop in cost and profit determination. The principal reason for this is that cost records are frequently inadequate for measuring the profitability of specific products; yet it is apparent that the communications mix problem cannot be solved satisfactorily except on the basis of cost-versus-revenue relationships.

By way of illustration, let us consider the case of a company that had an average marketing expense ratio of 17 percent of sales. Without distribution cost analysis, product X, having a gross margin of 12 percent, showed a loss, and product Y, with a gross margin of 22 percent, showed a profit. However, when expenditures in the communications mix were allocated to individual products, it was found that the item with 12 percent gross margin actually showed a profit, and the item with 22 percent gross margin showed a loss. This is illustrative of the kind of misconceptions which can occur without adequate cost information. Unfortunately, this condition prevails in a great many firms. The role of cost and profit analysis is explored in Chapter 31.

A further matter that complicates the problem of mix decisions for individual products is the larger judgmental factors implicit in trying to develop cost data. For instance, in a specific case, a company does not allocate any of the time of salesmen to the promotion of old products, and therefore does not charge any of the costs of personal selling to these products. On the other hand, a part of the reason for the extensive use of personal selling is simply to develop a favorable relationship with the customer, to create a responsive environment for doing business with the account. If this is true, then a part of the cost of selling should be allocated to these older products even though the salesman does not mention them. But how much should be charged? What is the true "institutional value" of these calls that should be shared by all products? This is why this area is replete with "value judgments" as compared with exact data. The complexity of these problems and the inexactness of the data make careful analysis and judgment imperative. The basic objective in these assignments is to produce workable and effective results, as the performance of the executive is evaluated along these lines rather than on an "optimum standard." Therefore, it is necessary to develop the most adequate data possible and then apply the rules of decision outlined earlier.

Let us turn our attention now to the character of the changes in the communications mix that takes place between old and new products. In new-product introductions the total cost of marketing is exceptionally high. In the case of cold cereals the ratio of "marketing expenditures (of which advertising is about two-thirds) to sales during a product's first year is more than 3½ times as great as the corresponding ratio for cereal companies' total operations; in the second year, marketing expenditures are typically twice as high as the normal 'level'; and in the third year, about 1½ times normal." [6] The weighted average ratio of marketing costs to total sales of new cereals, cake mixes, dog foods, frozen dinners and specialties, and margarine, as well as a number of other product categories was 57 percent during the first year and 37 percent during the second. [7] Table 23-5 lists the changes in the mix employed by one pharmaceutical company for products in various categories.

TABLE 23-5

The Communications Mix for Products of Various
Types as Used by a Pharmaceutical Company

Means of Market Cultivation	New Products of Good Potential and Life Expectancy	Products of Uncertain Potential or Limited Life Expectancy	Old Products
Personal selling	50%	25%	none
Journal advertising	10	20	15%
Direct mail	15	30	70
Sales promotion	10	10	10
Exhibits and conventions	10	10	none
Other	5	5	5
Total equals	100%	100%	100%

Source: Thomas A. Staudt, "Determining and Evaluating the Promotional Mix," in Modern Medicine Topics, XVIII, No. 7 (July 1957).

The categories shown are new products of good expected potential, those which have an uncertain or limited life expectancy, and well-established older products. In this case, the largest total communications budget is given to new products of high potential, with the lowest total budget going to established older products. The following observations seem pertinent with regard to the composition of the mix.

New Products of Good Potential and Life Expectancy

It is apparent that personal selling is heavily relied upon to win a place in the market for this product type. The salesman in this case must influence the doctor who prescribes for the patient—the customer. For all practical purposes the doctor is the customer from a selling point of view. Face-to-face communication is perhaps the most powerful medium for breaking down established

[6] Robert D. Buzzell and Robert E. Nourse, *Product Innovation, the Product Life Cycle and Competitive Behavior in Selected Food Processing Industries, 1947–1964* (Cambridge, Mass.: Arthur D. Little, Inc., 1966), p. 48.
[7] *Ibid.*, p. 98.

413

Determina-
tion of the
Optimum
Communica-
tions Mix

habit patterns in purchasing and for overcoming resistance to change in markets. In some cases there is no adequate substitute for personal contact. The salesman performs a vital role in carrying strategic information (as compared with routine information such as terms of sales, quantities, etc.); he can pinpoint his message, and in many cases adjust information to the particular needs of the individual customer; he provides a channel for two-way communication—for answering questions—thereby obtaining feedback for the marketer; and finally, the salesman is likely to obtain a responsive audience when the purchaser is accustomed to receiving new information from salesmen's calls. For instance, the customer may see the salesman as a valuable source of early information concerning new products.

On the other hand, personal selling is an expensive medium—perhaps three to five times as expensive as advertising, on a "per call" basis. Consequently, *how* the salesman is used is important. If he is used to provide all potential buyers with identical and basic information, an expensive instrument is being used in perhaps an inefficient way in performing a function that could be better served by advertising.

Journal advertising is an efficient way of providing scattered customers with the same basic information. The message can be carefully controlled: it reaches the buyer without the distortion which can occur when twenty-five different salesmen attempt to tell an identical story; it reaches buyers sometimes inaccessible to salesmen, or too expensive to contact; it reaches the buyer in a leisurely environment; and it cannot be screened by secretaries or front-office personnel, as can direct mail or salesmen. Finally, through advertising, all buyers get the same information at the same time; the time lags required for salesmen to cover their entire territory prevent simultaneous dissemination of information.

Table 23-5 seems to indicate that in this case the basic relationship between media can be characterized as, "reinforce personal selling through advertising." A good case could be made for, "pave the way for personal selling through advertising." Actually, both approaches have their place and are frequently used. The remainder of the mix is rather evenly spread among sales promotion devices such as free samples, exhibits at professional conventions, and direct mailing pieces to individual potential buyers.

Products of Uncertain Potential and Limited Life Expectancy

Products of expected short life or uncertain market potential receive a more balanced communications mix. They also receive a complete mix, as marketers employ a wide variety of devices to probe the market for either pockets of response or quick exploitation of latent demand. Notice that personal selling is curtailed while publication advertising is increased, as is direct mail. The same proportional emphasis is given sales promotion and exposure at exhibits and conventions in the mix for these products. In uncertainty, marketers are usually wise to rely on advertising and other devices that are relatively inexpensive and provide quick feedback of results. Exhibits, publication advertising, and direct mail can all be used as a form of research to test out the market. Personal selling may prove vital to the success of such products but, because of its cost, it cannot be emphasized—particularly in the early and uncertain stages.

While the total communications expenditure will be lower for products in these categories, it is likely that proportionately heavy outlays will be made at the time the product is launched, in order to get some early estimate of results. In the case of the uncertain market, the executive does not wish to lose a potentially good-selling product through failure to give it sufficient communications coverage. In the case of expected short-life products, he wants to capitalize on demand quickly, knowing that the product is likely to be soon displaced. The result is that a large proportion of expenditures is pushed into the early part of the budget period.

Old Products with Established Market Positions

In observing the mix in this case, we see three particularly striking changes. One is the complete absence of personal selling. This policy presumes that there is little, if any, gap between the strategic product information that the market holds and that which the manufacturer wishes to make known concerning his product. As a consequence, personal selling, which on a per call basis is the most expensive of all methods but is particularly well suited to the function of strategic information flows, is withdrawn. This policy (not as widely followed by narrow-line producers) is most pronounced when producers market extremely broad lines of perhaps several hundred individual products.

A second striking change is the great reliance placed on direct mail for doing almost the entire market cultivation task. Perhaps this is one reason for the growing antagonism toward direct mail. In the particular case of pharmaceuticals, for example, one study has shown that half the doctors believe that this is the least worthwhile of all media; one-third have direct resentment; over half the doctors spend only 15 minutes per week reading it; one-fourth do not read it at all; and only six out of ten doctors even sort it themselves. A bombardment of direct mail having to do with old products conditions the market over a period of time not to expect much of significance from this medium. Therefore, when needed refresher information or new information about the product is transmitted, it is often repulsed by or lost among the resistance barriers that this conditioning has developed.

The third change of note is that these products are dropped from exposure at exhibits and conventions. They are not regarded as "traffic stoppers," the type of drawing-card article for which eye-catching exhibit booths and displays are designed. The new and different are what attracts attention and interest, so new products are featured. Journal advertising, however, is sustained on these products.

Lest one be tempted to generalize that the mix discussed here is the desirable approach for all types of products, or even pharmaceuticals for that matter, let it be recognized that no such intent was meant. It is believed, however, that the case serves to indicate the types of changes that take place in the communications mix as products pass through a cycle of growth and decline. Many variations will exist among particular companies and differing markets.

415

Determina-
tion of the
Optimum
Communica-
tions Mix

Summary

The purpose of communications is to aid in the development of impact at the point of ultimate decision or sale. Decisions concerning the communications mix must be viewed in a decision spectrum over time. They are part of a broader total problem which includes decisions as to what product candidates to devote sizable resources to, as well as decisions on the composition of the mix, and the allocation of expenditures to different communications instruments. The high rate of product displacement calls for frequent reevaluation of product candidates.

The model solution for determining communications mix expenditures involves what may be called a maximization rule. The total appropriation is optimum when the last dollar spent on communications just pays for itself in additional profit. The allocation of expenditures to different communications instruments is optimum when the marginal revenue per dollar of expenditure is equal for each instrument used. Helpful as these rules may be conceptually, they are of little practical value, for the following reasons: (1) sufficient flexibility is not available, since expenditures on many communications instruments are fixed in the short run and are not divisible; (2) there is a degree of interdependence among communications instruments, which makes it difficult to equalize marginal returns; (3) some expenditures should be recognized as having investment characteristics and are not solely period costs; and (4) since not all instruments are executed with perfection, it may be necessary to compensate for a poorly executed instrument with a greater expenditure in another.

The practical solution is approached through analysis of historical data on the costs of different communications instruments, the sales volume additional increments of expenditure can be expected to produce, and the profitability of incremental sales volume. If reasonably accurate estimates can be made for each instrument, it is possible to assess outcomes from combining instruments in different ways.

The multiproduct firm with products at different stages of development must adjust the communications mix according to market conditions for particular products.

Three classes of products were described: (1) new products of high potential and life expectancy; (2) products of uncertain potential and limited life expectancy; and (3) old products with established market position. Each of these requires a substantially different communications mix.

Questions and Problems

1. What is meant by the term *communications mix?*
2. Is market impact largely a matter of information flows?
3. Why is the problem of determining the optimum communications mix such a difficult analytical problem?
4. What does the high rate of new-product failure have to do with the communications mix problem?
5. Is it possible that the same market results could be obtained from different combinations of communications instruments? Why?

6. What are the two decision areas in the model communications mix solution?
7. What are the theoretical decision rules for dealing with these problems?
8. What tends to limit the precision that can be achieved in practice in reaching these model solutions?
9. How can the marketer "simulate experiments" in striving for the most effective communications mix?
10. How are market potentials used in analyzing the effectiveness of particular communications instruments?
11. How are time periods and time lags a complicating factor in solving this problem? Give examples.
12. What guidelines might you propose with respect to communications instruments for new products of uncertain sales potential or of a short life expectancy?
13. What differences do you see in communications needs between new and old products.
14. Can the communications mix problem be solved effectively for the firm as a whole, or must it be handled on a product-by-product basis?
15. "Although the communications mix problem is extremely complex, it is inherent, pervasive, and inescapable." Comment on this statement. Is it essentially valid? Why?

Advertising Management and Evaluation I: Purpose and Scope

24

Thus far in our discussion of programming the various elements of market cultivation, we have tried to establish a proper setting for dealing with the individual components of a total program. Most importantly, a communications orientation has been established, for all market cultivation in one way or another involves information transfer with the market. The exchange process is actuated essentially through communications. That is, demand is triggered, or purchase precipitated, through information flows of all kinds between buyer and seller. Some understanding of the essential elements of the communications process is regarded as a prerequisite to programming considerations in the individual components of market cultivation. Because the various means of market cultivation are partially substitutes for one another (that is, each to some extent can be considered as an alternative communications system for the transmittal of market information), we have considered the complicated analytical problem of determining the optimum communications mix.

In this chapter we turn our attention to that part of the communication process which is usually the first stage of market cultivation. Advertising is that part of the communication process which has as its purpose the persuasion of others to act favorably upon an idea, product, or service which has commercial significance to the vendor.

The successful management of the nonpersonal selling function (advertising) is built upon an adequate comprehension of the communication function. In order to achieve effective communication, the source (communicator) must present a favorable total image of the company, product, or service to an audience (receiver) in order to elicit a favorable response (purchase) by the receiver. In advertising, unlike in personal selling, one cannot observe the reaction of the receiver and tailor the message to the reaction. The advertiser must, in advance of sending the communication, anticipate the reaction and attempt to develop and transmit his message in such a way that the receiver's reaction will be favorable.

The word *advertising* has its root in a word that means to turn. This suggests the purpose of advertising—*to turn* people to or toward the idea being advertised. The marketing manager knows that advertising and selling are not synonymous, and that to sell successfully one must ordinarily have an adequate mix of personal selling and advertising. The purpose of this chapter is to examine the informational background of advertising which permits the marketing manager to effectively employ advertising in his marketing mix. The objectives of advertising must be clearly understood before proceeding to the complicated task of managing advertising effort. From a managerial point of view, those charged with marketing responsibility must determine those circumstances under which advertising can be used productively, and have some basis for judging the returns that can be expected from it.

We will begin with a definition of advertising and then classify some of the many different types used.

THE TERMINOLOGY OF ADVERTISING

Advertising is any paid form of nonpersonal presentation and promotion of ideas, goods, or services by an identified sponsor.[1] Two characteristics are important in this definition: first is the requirement of payment, and second is the need for authorship. Many times, a company is successful in communicating messages about itself or its products through the usual advertising media such as newspapers or magazines but does not pay for the message. This comes about through editorial comment by newspapers on new products or new policies of the company. This information reaching the market is generally referred to as publicity and is not therefore advertising. One of the reasons for excluding publicity from advertising is that the frequency of such messages cannot be planned and managed, as is the case with the normal advertising message. The phenomenal success of some companies in achieving publicity, which undoubtedly has influenced sales, has led many advertisers to seek publicity statements. When a highly reputable medium carries a true editorial comment on a product, it imparts an element of impartiality, authenticity, and believability to the statement. When publishers on occasion accept payment for printing such "news," what appears to be publicity is in reality a paid advertising message without identification of authorship by the advertiser.

The question arises, What activities are included under *nonpersonal presentation and promotion of ideas, goods, or services?* A distinction is made between advertising and sales promotion. Messages conveyed through the usual communications media, such as newspapers, magazines, radio, television, outdoor signs, car cards, and direct mail, are considered advertising. Messages conveyed

[1] R. S. Alexander and others, *Marketing Definitions* (Chicago: American Marketing Assn., 1960), p. 9.

419

Advertising
Management
and
Evaluation I:
Purpose
and Scope

through labels, tags, store signs, point-of-purchase display material, calendars, blotters, catalogs, and circulars are technically advertising but are more often called sales promotion. Other activities, such as the use of demonstrations, displays, and exhibits at fairs and conventions, and the giving of premiums to consumers, are also considered sales promotion. The distinction between advertising and sales promotion is made because of the differences in objectives sought and skills needed to manage these two types of activities. Often the sales promotion activities are found to be run by a separate department in the organization of the firm. In the remainder of this chapter we will consider the management of advertising communicated through independent communications agencies.

Types of Advertising

The following illustration has been constructed to show the many different types of advertising used today. An explanation of each follows.

Types of Advertising

THE ADVERTISER

Manufacturer
Middlemen
Service Establishments

TARGET	PURPOSE	THEME	COPY	PAYMENT
Consumer	Primary demand	Indirect action	Product	Individual
Trade	Selective demand	Direct action	Institutional	Cooperative
Producers				

Advertiser

Advertising is both planned and paid for by the manufacturer, the middlemen, and service establishments such as banks and insurance companies. A glance at any newspaper reveals the huge amount of advertising placed by retailers. In fact, the greatest share of the advertising dollar—approximately 23 percent—is spent on newspaper advertising.[2] Some of this is of course placed by manufacturers and service establishments, but the bulk is by retailers. Wholesalers also advertise to their customers—retailers, manufacturers, and other wholesalers.

Targets

All advertising is directed to either (1) consumers, who purchase for ultimate household consumption; (2) middlemen, who purchase for resale; or (3) producers (industrial users), who purchase for further processing or fabrication. The advertising directed to producers or middlemen is known as trade advertising. Advertising directed to consumers—the kind with which we are all familiar—is called consumer advertising.

[2] See *Advertising Age,* January 2, 1967, p. 46.

Advertising either emphasizes the products or services of the advertiser or attempts to convey a favorable impression of the advertiser as a business firm in general. The latter is called institutional advertising; the former, product advertising. A glance through any magazine will reveal examples of institutional advertising. Most of the advertising of the ethical pharmaceutical houses is institutional; they are trying to convey an image of a competent research-oriented institution with the skills and technology necessary to bring the latest findings of science to the medical profession. Confidence in medical preparations by the consuming public is essential in building sales patronage. The size of some of our largest corporations has resulted in their using institutional advertising to combat some of the unfavorable images and concepts the general public has of them.

Theme

Advertising themes may seek either indirect action or direct action. Indirect action is for the purpose of building broad recognition and acceptance. It tries to create a favorable attitude toward a brand in the hope that, when a purchase is about to be made, the brand will at least be considered. Indirect-action advertising also features appeals, such as service policies, that will indirectly influence the sale of the product, and emphasizes the advantages of a full merchandise line to dealers. A good example of indirect-action advertising is Boeing Aircraft's announcing the names of all airlines using Boeing jetliners.

Direct-action advertising, in addition to developing brand recognition and acceptance, tries to stimulate the recipient of the message to immediate action. It attempts to motivate him to purchase the product immediately, to request further information, or to undertake some other direct action desired by the advertiser, such as requesting a salesman to call. Most retailer-sponsored newspaper, radio, or television advertising is of the direct-action type. The purpose of placing an advertisement in the Thursday food section of a newspaper is to stimulate weekend purchases.

Both types of action can be combined in the same advertisement. When a department store advertises specific merchandise and at the same time stresses some of its policies, such as credit or adjustments, or some of its store characteristics, such as air-conditioning and courteous employees, it is combining these two types.

Purpose

Another dichotomy in advertising types is primary and selective demand stimulation. The stimulation of primary demand, you will recall, attempts to increase the demand for a product type rather than for the specific brand of any particular manufacturer. In the early days of television, much advertising was directed toward the enjoyment to be received from television itself; the value of the particular advertiser's brand was of secondary importance.

Primary-demand advertising is particularly important in new products which are truly innovations. It is also widely used where one firm dominates an

421

Advertising
Management
and
Evaluation I:
Purpose
and Scope

industry; that is, wherein market share is a high proportion of total industry sales. For instance, Kodak, by promoting home photography on a primary-demand basis, seeks to expand the film market, recognizing that it will receive by far the greatest share of any expansion in the sale of film that the advertising produces.

Selective-demand advertising emphasizes the advertiser's own brands. Rather than primarily trying to expand existing demand for the class of product, it attempts to redivide existing demand in favor of the advertiser. There is always an element of primary-demand stimulation in selective-demand advertising; however, the emphasis favors either one or the other. There is little sense in emphasizing primary-demand stimulation in the advertising of salt. The only expansibility of demand comes from an increase in the size of the population. Consequently, most salt advertising is highly selective.

Payment

Payment may be made by the individual manufacturer or middleman, or it may be on a cooperative basis. There are two types of cooperative arrangements for the payment of advertising. One we shall call *horizontal cooperative advertising.* In this, payment is shared by a group of firms on the same plane of manufacturing or distribution. The largest campaigns of this sort are by manufacturers or producers. Some of the more common campaigns are those sponsored by the American Meat Institute, the National Hat Foundation, the American Trucking Association, and the brewing industry. A number of regional campaigns have been conducted by producers' cooperatives in the agricultural field. Most horizontal cooperative advertising is an attempt at primary-demand stimulation, the exception being that some growers' cooperatives may emphasize their own brand name in competition with rival producing units. An example is the California orange growers' promotion of Sunkist against the competition of the various brands proffered by the Florida orange producers' cooperatives.

The other cooperative form, which is much the more important in terms of advertising expenditures, is *vertical cooperative advertising.* The cost of advertising in this setup is shared by firms on different levels of manufacturing or distribution, most often by manufacturers and retailers of consumer goods. You will recall, in Chapter 21, the use of selective and exclusive distribution to achieve aggressive selling throughout the channel. When selective distribution is used and care is given to choosing the middlemen allowed to handle the product, a number of cooperative services usually are included in the arrangement. Vertical cooperative advertising is one. It spreads the cost of advertising and can result in a wholly integrated advertising campaign, from the manufacturer throughout the entire channel to the ultimate consumer. The manufacturer may provide the dealer with ads to run locally over the dealer's name; the manufacturer will pay for these either in whole or in part, or he may pay for advertisements of the dealer's own choice that emphasize the manufacturer's product.

It is not uncommon for cooperative advertising arrangements to exist between wholesalers and retailers. The voluntary wholesale chains discussed in Chapter 18 engage in it. The initiative is taken by the wholesaler and the cost shared by each retailer participating.

By now it should be clear that any number of combinations of advertising types can exist. For example, it is possible to have manufacturer-product, indirect-action, primary-demand, horizontal cooperative advertising directed to all consumers. Some combinations, however, are unlikely. In terms of the explanations given, a combination of direct-action, institutional advertising would be highly unlikely.

The Advertising Agency

The advertising agency plays an extremely important role in such a large part of advertising media that an understanding of its function is necessary. Advertising is a highly technical field, and almost all the large advertisers work through an advertising agency. The first advertising agencies in the United States were organized in the early part of the nineteenth century. Their principal function was to act as agents in buying space from publishers and selling it to advertisers. In fact, the agencies were called "space merchants" at that time. Today, the advertising agency aids the advertiser in planning the advertising program, and may even provide counsel on the total marketing program.

The major function of the advertising department of the manufacturer or producer is to provide a broad policy framework that the company wishes to follow, and to make all final decisions. In some of the largest corporations, the advertising departments perform many of the activities available through an agency. Many companies prefer to conduct their own market research, evaluation of advertising, and independent analysis of media. There are innumerable arrangements in the division of tasks between the agency and the advertiser. The role of the agency is determined by the advertiser's desire to control certain aspects of the program. But in almost all cases an agency is retained, because the method of payment rarely raises the overall advertising cost to the client.

Compensation to the agency is on a commission basis. The media cost of any advertisement placed by an agency is billed to the agency by the media at a 15 percent discount from its published prices. The agency in turn bills the client for the total amount (if the advertiser were to buy the space directly from the media, he would also be charged the total amount). The 15 percent usually covers the agency functions of planning, creating the advertising campaign, producing the particular advertisements to run, and analyzing and buying the desired media time or space. And if the advertiser's campaign is a large one, the 15 percent media discount may be a large enough fee to cover the cost of market research done by the agency to provide the basis for planning the campaign. Charges for special services performed by the agency are billed separately to the client.

The 15 percent commission, which has long been trade practice, was questioned by the Justice Department in 1955. The department charged the American Association of Advertising Agencies with fixing the amount of agency commission. In 1956, the association entered a consent decree to refrain from any overt efforts to maintain the 15 percent rate. Nevertheless, the rate has continued as the standard fee.

The real danger inherent in the commission method of payment is related

423

Advertising
Management
and
Evaluation I:
Purpose
and Scope

to the three-party arrangement which exists. The advertiser, the agency, and the media are all attempting to look after their own self-interests. The agency's revenue is provided by the media and depends on the amount of advertising done; this structure could cause the agency to favor certain media and advertising expenditures, the use of which would be contrary to the best interests of the advertiser. The need to protect the professional reputation of the agency (the agency's principal source of attraction of new clients), and the watchful eye of the advertiser in making all final decisions, has probably prevented widespread manipulation between agency and media. There is little evidence that the commission method of remuneration is on the way out, although this method has been a subject of widespread controversy for many years.

THE OBJECTIVES OF ADVERTISING

The overall objective of advertising is to increase the profits of the advertiser or to prevent their reduction by influencing the level of product sales. Many times, a firm is forced to advertise because of the actions of competitors. Under such circumstances, there may be little chance to increase profits, but failure to advertise could result in sales and profit losses. The ability to increase profits or to prevent loss depends on how successfully this communications instrument achieves three other objectives. At the risk of oversimplification, the specific objectives of advertising are: (1) to expand demand, (2) to create inelasticity of price demand, and (3) to aid the salesman in the performance of his duties.

Demand Expansion

In a technical sense demand is expanded if the demand curve is shifted to the right, as shown in Figure 24-1. Demand expansion may be viewed from the standpoint of the industry and of the firm. Since the total demand is the

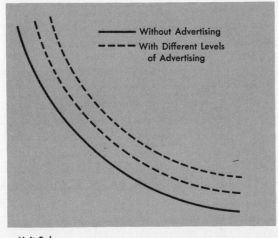

Price

Unit Sales

FIGURE 24-1
Demand with and
without Advertising

total of the demand curves facing all firms in the industry, it is possible for a single firm to shift its demand curves without any expansibility of demand for the industry. This is a redivision of existing demand.

In quantity sold, a distinction must be made between increases resulting from a shift in demand, and those resulting from moving along or down through a demand curve. The firm always has the alternative of increasing the quantity it can sell by sliding down the demand curve by price adjustments. The decision to favor price changes depends on how profitable the increased volume is at the same price with advertising versus the increased volume at a lower price without advertising. This depends on: (1) the amount of the increase and (2) the relative costs of production and marketing at the different volume levels.

Figure 24-2 is a highly simplified explanation of the use of price adjustments versus advertising. In Chart A, point O_1 on the price line P_1 represents the quantity sold at P_1, and O_1A_1 is the profit. Point O_2 on price line P_2 repre-

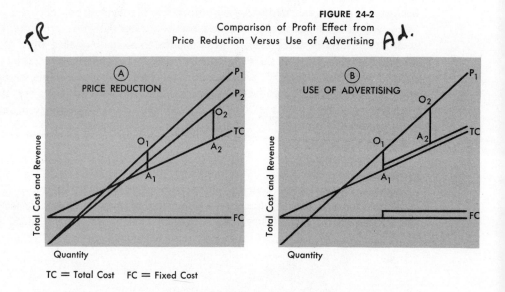

FIGURE 24-2

Comparison of Profit Effect from
Price Reduction Versus Use of Advertising

TC = Total Cost   FC = Fixed Cost

sents the quantity that may be sold with the lower price P_2. Profit is O_2A_2, and the difference between this and O_1A_1 is the increase in profit.

In Chart B, point O_1 on the price line P_1 represents the quantity that will be taken, and O_1A_1 is the profit. Through making an expenditure for advertising at quantity O_1, an increase in the fixed-cost curve results, and the total-cost curve is no longer a continuous function. If the quantity sold is increased to O_2, the new profit is O_2A_2, representing an increase over the previous quantity level. If the profit is greater than that achieved through the price reduction in Chart A, advertising should be favored. If not, price reductions should be favored. It is quite possible that neither procedure will leave the firm better off in its profit returns. Conceivably, neither the price reduction nor the advertising expenditure would have an effect on the quantity sold.

425

Advertising
Management
and
Evaluation I:
Purpose
and Scope

The above analysis applies to any form of demand cultivation effort. Price reduction is always an alternative to promotional expenditures, and expenditures to expand demand must be compared with the possible effect of price adjustment. This analysis is greatly simplified and omits four complicating factors.

First, to carry out such an analysis requires a determination of quantities that will be sold at different prices and at different expenditures for advertising. This is a measurement problem which almost defies analysis. Nevertheless, such attempts are made.

Second, the increased quantities cannot be moved without increases in cost. The straight-line cost function is used, and the break-even charts are not wholly realistic. Determination of the decreases and increases in cost which result from increased volume is necessary.

Third, the firm may be in a very competitive situation, and it is not known what reductions in volume take place without advertising or with failure to increase advertising. It is quite possible that the end result of an advertising expenditure is no change in profit from previous periods. However, if this expenditure were not made, it certainly could result in losses from the level of previous period.

Fourth, the firm very rarely has the simple choice of electing one alternative or the other. Usually, a combination of price, advertising, sales promotion, and personal selling is used. To determine the effect of the total communications mix beforehand is a multivariable problem, which, as was recognized in the preceding chapter, is extremely difficult to solve.

Inelasticity of Price Demand

If demand becomes more inelastic through advertising, the firm can sell the same quantity at higher prices. And if successful at demand expansion too, it may even increase the quantity. In direct-price competition, it may maintain the same quantity at the same price if it has achieved inelasticity of price demand. How does this come about? The effect is generated through selective-demand advertising. If the firm can develop a loyalty among consumers through establishing brand preference, a distinction is made in the consumer's mind between that firm's products and competitors' products. By so doing, a firm is removed from direct-price competition. Of course, this is not a complete isolation, and counterefforts by competitors may become so great that buyers' preferences will weaken. But, in general, advertising attempts to achieve this objective. A firm with a highly differentiated product may even extract a price premium because of the customer loyalty it enjoys. In doing so, it may reduce volume slightly but still enjoy greater profits than if it sought an expansion of demand through price reduction.

A curious reaction sometimes takes place when a firm has been very successful in creating inelasticity of price demand. In time its product demand might become quite elastic once this condition is achieved. If, for many years, a firm has advertised and sold its product at a given price and has suffered no adverse consequences from price competition, a cut in the price of that product will result in a large increase in the quantity sold. The market has become accustomed to a given price, and a lower price is recognized as a bargain. It will bring in customers. This is why price-cutting middlemen favor national brands. To cut the price of an unknown product is not recognized as a price cut by customers, since they do not know its prevailing price beforehand.

These two objectives, demand expansion and inelasticity of demand, may be sought independently of each other or together. Most primary-demand advertising, as well as horizontal cooperative advertising, reflects the desire to expand demand and rarely seeks inelasticity of demand. Much advertising by middlemen, especially to consumers, seeks to expand demand and may even, at the same time, use price as the major competitive weapon. Most manufacturer advertising seeks a combination of each. It first tries to build brand preference and achieve inelasticity of demand, and, in so doing, expand the demand curve it faces.

Aids to the Salesman

Advertising is rarely used alone to communicate the firm's offer to the market. Almost always, some form of personal selling is used, and the advertising may be used to pave the way for the salesman or even to develop leads of interested prospects. In paving the way for the salesman, the advertising is of an institutional or indirect-action nature. It maintains the name of the company in the market, making the task of the salesman somewhat easier when he approaches potential customers. Or, it may seek inquiries from potential users of the product, thus providing a prospect list for the sales force. This objective is particularly relevant in the industrial goods market, where actual sale of the product depends on some form of personal solicitation. Advertising is used also to increase the effectiveness of other promotional activities. When displays are used at fairs or exhibits, the traffic visiting the display can be increased through advance advertising of the fact that the firm is an exhibitor.

Consumer advertising may be used for merchandising the advertising to the trade. This usually results in a limited amount of manufacturer advertising in prestige media. The manufacturer relies primarily on personal selling, but the salesman has an excellent talking point in the efforts of the manufacturer to create demand for the dealer. The dealer, in turn, may utilize this advertising by displaying tear sheets, in his displays, announcing that the product "As advertised in *Life*" is available. Advertising by manufacturers to the trade, particularly retailers and wholesalers, has some special objectives. It may be used to make announcements to dealer organizations, such as announcements of new products, new policies, and price changes. It also may be designed to stimulate dealers to advertise and to tie in their advertising with that of the manufacturer.

COST OF ADVERTISING
TO THE CUSTOMER

Much controversy has taken place over the cost of advertising to the customer. Some advertising is wasteful from the customer's point of view, some is not. The issue is directly related to the previous discussion—namely, advertising's

427

Advertising
Management
and
Evaluation I:
Purpose
and Scope

effect on demand and the cost of production and distribution at various levels of output, both for the industry as a whole and for the individual firm.

A simplified explanation and conclusion related to this issue are that if advertising expands demand over what it otherwise would be, and if there are economies of scale in production and marketing such that the lower costs on the greater volume meet or exceed the cost of advertising, then such advertising is in the customer's interest. If, on the other hand, expenditures for advertising do not expand demand, but merely result in the shifting of competitors' shares of market in an existing demand, then the case is much more doubtful as to its customer value. It is this kind of situation that raises the question about wasteful advertising from a customer welfare point of view. There is some evidence that advertising does have an effect on demand. For example, three products with very high advertising expenses are toilet preparations (14.7 percent of sales), cleaning and polishing preparations (12.6 percent of sales), and drugs (9.4 percent of sales). Between 1947 and 1966 the consumption of these products as a percent of total personal consumption, after making adjustments for price changes, increased from 0.68 percent to 1.12 percent for toilet articles and preparations, from 0.87 percent to 1.05 percent for cleaning and polishing preparations, and from 0.82 percent to 1.24 percent for drugs.[3] To what extent these industries have experienced decreasing costs is not known. It is probably true, however, that the bulk of our major industries are decreasing-cost industries and will become more so in the future as automation increases. Advertising in most cases does influence the level of demand and, therefore, does not adversely affect customer value. The bulk of our mass production industries rests upon mass consumption, and advertising is usually a major means of high-level demand cultivation.

The case is complicated by the fact that some amount of market information is essential to consumers.[4] This information has to be communicated in some way or another—possibly through salesmen, or expensive training meetings of personnel in distributive organizations in order for them to pass the necessary product and market information through the various channels. It may be in such cases that advertising is a more economic means of transmitting this information than any other device. In this instance, then, advertising would not be a wasteful expenditure from the customer's viewpoint. When the level of advertising, however, is substantially above the level of "necessary information," it may be wasteful. The controversy is over the issue of when this point is reached.

From the individual firm's standpoint, several factors bear on the cost of advertising to the customer. Charges are frequently made among the lay public that the customer pays for a great deal of advertising in heavily promoted brands as contrasted to less heavily advertised brands, and that therefore superior value may be offered to the customer in the latter case, particularly when price differentials exist between the two. This issue is related to other categories of cost in

[3] Jules Backman, "Is Advertising Wasteful?" *Journal of Marketing,* XXXII (January 1968), 6.

[4] For a more complete discussion of the information role of advertising, see *ibid.,* pp. 5–6.

market cultivation and needs careful consideration by would-be customers. Frequently, the heaviest-advertised brand has a lower per unit advertising cost than less heavily promoted rival brands. Chevrolet does the greatest amount of advertising among car makers, yet its cost of advertising per vehicle is among the lowest. If brand "X" has advertising expenditures of $1 million and sells one million units, then its per unit cost is less than that of brand "Y," which sells only 500,000 units but has an advertising expenditure of $700,000.

This point is often confused. Consumers hear a great deal about the "savings" that can be made by buying clothing from "low-overhead stores out of the high-rent district." If a store in a prime downtown location sells 1,000 suits of men's clothing per month from a location costing $1,000 per month in rent, the cost of rent in a suit of clothes is less than that from a store in an outlying location out of the "high-rent district" that sells 300 suits per month from a $500 per month location. Customers need to be wary of all such promotional claims, and managements need to be prepared to deal with this issue in their customer relations.

There is no reason to believe that a decrease in cost equal to advertising expenditures would be reflected in a price decline. The amount of advertising cost is a very small proportion of total sales price. The percent relationship of advertising to total compiled receipts for the period July 1962–June 1963 was 1.09 for all industrial groups.[5] It is only in a very few categories, such as toilet articles and preparations and cleaning and polishing preparations, that the ratio is over 10 percent. These, on the other hand, amount to less than 1.25 percent of total personal consumption expenditures. Price is determined by many factors other than advertising costs.

Finally, customers normally should be more interested in which competitor can provide them a superior value than with what part of the price they pay is accounted for by research, engineering, material, administrative, or advertising expense, and the like. Manufacturers in all cases are trying to adjust their cost centers in an optimum way from a profitability standpoint.

Summary

Advertising is defined as *any paid form of nonpersonal presentation and promotion of ideas, goods, or services by an identified sponsor.*[6] The distinction between advertising and publicity is that advertising is paid for by the advertiser, and he is identified as the sponsor, whereas the advertiser does not pay for publicity, nor does he identify himself as the sponsor. Advertising includes all types of messages, including those usually considered as sales promotion, such as point-of-purchase display material, labels, tags, store signs, calendars, blotters, and circulars. Because of the difference in managing these types of advertising,

[5] U.S. Treasury Department, Internal Revenue Service, *Statistics of Income—1962 Corporation Income Tax Returns* (Washington, D.C.: Government Printing Office, 1966), pp. 58–125, cited in Jules Backman, *Advertising and Competition* (New York: New York University Press, 1967), pp. 226–29.

[6] Alexander and others, *Marketing Definitions*, p. 9.

429

Advertising
Management
and
Evaluation I:
Purpose
and Scope

we have considered these as sales promotion, along with such usual sales promotion activities as demonstrations, displays and exhibits at fairs, and consumer premiums and contests.

There are many different types of advertising, and they are divided into manufacturer, middleman, or service establishment advertising; advertising directed to consumers, the trade, or industrial users; and advertising stressing the product or the institution for the purpose of stimulating direct action or indirect action by the receiver. Advertising seeks to stimulate either primary demand or selective demand. Payment may be made by the individual advertiser or on a cooperative basis.

The cost to the consumer of advertising depends upon its ability to expand demand, and the nature of economies of scale in production and marketing it produces. Customers need to be wary of making overall value judgments on the basis of individual cost components in price, and advertisers and their management need to be prepared to deal with this issue in the market place.

The objective of advertising is to increase the profits of the advertiser or prevent their reduction. This is achieved if the advertising is successful in expanding demand and/or creating some degree of inelasticity of price demand. Since price may be used as an alternative to advertising for demand stimulation, estimates should be made of profits accruing from a price reduction versus those accruing from an advertising expenditure.

Questions and Problems

1. Give a technical definition of advertising.
2. Distinguish between advertising, personal selling, publicity, and sales promotion.
3. Of the various advertising media, which one accounts for the greatest proportion of advertising expenditures? What features of the medium do you think account for this position?
4. What is institutional advertising? What are some of the reasons for widespread use of this type of advertising?
5. What is trade advertising?
6. Define horizontal cooperative advertising. Give examples. Under what kinds of conditions is this type of advertising used? How is it different from vertical cooperative advertising?
7. For the usual kinds of service provided by an advertising agency, what fees would be charged the advertiser? Do you agree with this form of payment? Why?
8. What are the principal functions of an advertising agency?
9. Technically distinguish how advertising and price adjustments can be substitutes for each other.
10. "Advertising is a business expense and is therefore a cost that is paid for by the consumer." Comment.
11. "A major difference between the price of heavily advertised and nonadvertised brands is simply the cost of the advertising." Take a position and defend your answer.
12. There are cases in which advertising hardly redounds to the customer's benefit. Under what conditions might this be the case?

13. Price-cutting middlemen or retailers often prefer heavily advertised national brands for their merchandise. Why?

14. Can advertising ever be profitable when it does not lead to an increase in sales? Explain.

15. From the customer's point of view, does it make a difference whether a company spends a particular sum of money on advertising, executive salaries, or employee benefits? Develop your thoughts on this subject.

Advertising Management and Evaluation II: Planning and Control

25

The management of advertising may be divided into five areas: (1) Determination of the role advertising should play in the total communications mix. (This requires an analysis of those factors which contribute to the successful use of advertising.) (2) Determination of the size of the advertising appropriation. (3) Selection of the advertising media. (4) Integration into a coordinated communications system. (5) Evaluation of results.

FACTORS AFFECTING THE SUCCESSFUL USE OF ADVERTISING

Most companies allocate a part of their total communications budget to advertising. Although the value is not completely measurable, it perhaps is a safe assumption that funds spent in this way will have a desirable effect. The problem, however, is to spend money in a manner which will produce the *most* desirable effect. Fortunately, there are identifiable circumstances which indicate that advertising, more than other instruments of communication, will be effective. Similarly, there are circumstances which act as a deterrent to its successful use and which indicate the need for other means of market cultivation. Since the factors affecting the use of advertising differ somewhat according to whether it is used for primary-demand stimulation or selective-demand stimulation, we will deal with each of these areas independently. Since the primary purpose of advertising is to expand demand and/or create some degree of inelasticity of price demand for the advertised product, our discussion will deal with these objectives.

Primary-demand Stimulation

As stated earlier, primary demand is demand for a particular product class and not for the product of a single

431

supplier. The use of advertising for this purpose is necessitated by several conditions. First, new products require an introduction to the market and an explanation of their value. Second, advertising may be necessary when the consumption of old products declines. Third, advertising may be used when one firm strongly dominates a market and stands to gain from its overall expansion. Before any expenditures are made to expand primary demand through advertising, the following aspects should be investigated.

Extent of Use

An investigation of potential users and the way their needs are being met reveals both the market opportunity available for many new products, and the product that must be displaced. For old products which have enjoyed widespread use, an investigation of current usage is necessary. Comparing existing markets with those of previous periods shows the substitutions which have taken place, and the changes necessary to regain previous position.

Demand Trends

What social forces are at work affecting demand? Many new products have come on the market which have run counter to deep-seated social forces. Some examples will illustrate. Attempts by manufacturers to promote the use of self-service dry cleaning establishments were made at least fifteen years ago. The venture was unsuccessful. It appears that present efforts in the same area are more successful. The reasons for failure are unknown, but outdoor living, suburbia, self-service, and drive-in establishments in general had not yet reached their present levels, and the social environment prevented the public's acceptance of this service. In another case a manufacturer of teaching machines was until recent years faced with considerable resistance, rooted in years of tradition.

The covering of entire fields of crops with paper or polyethylene for mulching purposes has been advocated for over thirty years without success. High-protein foods were introduced twenty-five years ago without success. The strikingly streamlined automobile was introduced in the 1930's and was not accepted. The point is that change is relative. Consumers seem willing to accept rather sizable amounts of absolute change as long as relative change is limited. Relative change most frequently relates to the surrounding social environment. The acceptance of contemporary furniture had to await many changes in peoples' tastes for functional design, architectural advances, suburban developments, living styles, and other social changes.

In the case of old products which have suffered reduced consumption, the cause of the reduction must be determined. If the decline reflects changes in fundamental economic or social forces, the use of advertising to reverse the trend is risky. When per capita consumption of meat declined during the 1930's, extensive primary-demand advertising tried to reverse the trend, and met with only limited success. The cause was found in consumers' dietary beliefs that too much meat was not healthy. It was not until the medical profession reversed this belief that consumption increased.

Sometimes consumers' failure to use a certain product is simply based on habit or prejudice. Instant coffee and margarine battled with whole-bean or

433

Advertising
Management
and
Evaluation II:
Planning
and Control

ground coffee and butter for acceptance; primary-demand advertising on the older products is aimed at convincing consumers that there is no substitute for "the real thing"—"the same as Mom used to buy." Under proper circumstances, primary-demand advertising may change habits. The forces underlying demand must be carefully analyzed to assess the ability of advertising to overcome or change them.

Price-income Relationships

Often the consumption of old products declines because of the failure of manufacturers to adjust prices to new income levels. This is particularly true in recession periods. The composition of products that the family purchases changes throughout the economic cycle. This is a reflection of the consumer's desire to adjust to new price-income relationships. If the price of a product is not in accord with the new income levels, advertising can do little to reverse the demand trend. Frequently, the situation calls for product adjustments to make it possible to bring the price of the product more in line with economic conditions.

The price of a new product must be related to the income and to the price of current means used to meet the need. Market acceptance may not be gained, even if the new product is superior, if the price is much higher than that of currently available products that perform the same basic function. Often this situation prevails, and it is not until the price of the product is reduced that mass markets can be developed. Television sets and the automatic washing machine are examples. The automatic washing machine was introduced at a considerable price differential over the wring washer. The mass market did not develop until the price was more in line with the incomes of a large group of potential buyers.

This problem, as related to the stages of market development noted earlier, creates a dilemma for the manufacturer. A mass market cannot be developed until the price is reduced, and the price may not be reduced until the economies of mass production are achieved—a most difficult task in timing and pricing strategy. (The alternative pricing strategies for dealing with this matter are taken up in Chapter 28, dealing with pricing new products.) In part, this problem is responsible for the long time period necessary to achieve profitable volume on many new products.

Extent of the Market

Through analysis of use, social trends, and price-income relationships, the advertiser should be able to make some judgment on the potential size of the market. Most primary-demand advertising failures result from overoptimism in this area. The qualitative side of market investigation is not given sufficient attention, and all consuming units are regarded as potential customers. Generally, primary-demand advertising will affect some consumers, but not all, and the number it will affect is crucial. The advertiser must calculate market size, the cost of reaching the market, the number of potential buyers that will be influenced, and potential profitability if successful. If the market is small, it may be impossible for advertising to generate a profitable sales volume. If the market is large, the risks and dollar value of the investment must be projected.

Funds Available

The extent of the market, along with the price of the product, the frequency of purchase, and the other costs of marketing, gives some idea of the margin available and the size of the revenue pool for advertising. If the product is of high unit value and can look forward to a large potential market, there may be substantial funds available. If it is of low unit value and high frequency of sale, the total number of units sold will produce considerable funds for advertising. If, however, the market is small, the unit value low, and the purchase infrequent, funds available are not large. The advertiser should be familiar with some of the costs of reaching different markets and should determine the amount of advertising he can purchase with the funds available. It generally is not wise to spend only token sums in advertising. A certain level of expenditure is needed to achieve impact, and unless enough funds can be allocated to reach this minimum point, probably the money can be spent in more productive alternative ways.

Appeals

Conditions may seem to favor the use of primary advertising, but unless a satisfactory appeal can be made, little return can be expected. What can the advertiser say about his product? Among new products, the innovation that makes possible substantial product differentiation usually provides a wealth of material for advertising appeals. The problem of course is to be sure the most effective ones are used and that they will, in fact, have customer impact. In trying to recapture market position for old products, the question of appeal poses more problems. Unless an appeal can be made which will be effective against products currently used to fill the need, advertising can be of little help. As a rule, this condition will become apparent early in the analysis.

Some form of horizontal cooperative advertising is usually the first idea that members of an industry turn to when demand declines. Sometimes it proves useful, but at other times it does not. Experience indicates certain factors which, unless overcome, prevent its success. First is the reason for reduction in demand. If it reflects deep-rooted social trends, it is not likely that this form of advertising can do much about the adverse conditions. Second, if the number and size of cooperating advertisers is small, or if there are a large number of small cooperators, there are generally not enough funds for advertising expenditure to create any significant impact in the market place. Third, if there are any dominant brands among the cooperators, the benefit of the program will accrue to the best-known brand. (Usually, this is the largest company, and brand jealousies develop.) Fourth, the inability to demonstrate immediate results causes the cooperators to lose interest and give up on the program before sufficient time has elapsed for it to succeed. Horizontal cooperative advertising has been used by a large number of trade associations in trying to reverse a declining primary demand, but the number of actual successes is relatively small.

Selective-demand Stimulation

This type of advertising, which emphasizes the advertiser's own products in an attempt to redivide existing demand in his favor, may or may not seek

435

Advertising
Management
and
Evaluation II:
Planning
and Control

to create inelasticity of price demand. As with primary-demand stimulation, a number of factors determine the feasibility of using advertising for this purpose. There are differences in the ways in which certain factors affect the use of advertising by manufacturers and by the trade. Whenever these differences are significant, their relevance is indicated. There are certain similarities between selective-demand and primary-demand advertising in the area of market factors, but these will not be repeated here.

Ability to Brand

Identification of a manufacturer's products is necessary before selective demand may be stimulated. Without identification, the benefits of advertising do not necessarily accrue to the advertiser. Although there are many objectives sought through branding, its promotional value is one of the more important. Since there is considerable confusion in terminology in this area, a brief discussion of the different terms used is necessary.

The term *brand* is a broad term, used to refer to a company name, trade name, trademark, or brand name. A brand is *any letter, word, name, symbol, or device, or any combination thereof which is adopted and used by a manufacturer or merchant to identify his goods and services and to distinguish them from those manufactured and sold by others.*[1] The term *brand name* simply refers to the oral expression of the brand. A trademark is the legal term for a brand name. Since there are certain restrictions on the registration of brands, all brands are not trademarks, but it is a safe assumption that all trademarks are brands. A brand name may be a company name, if the name of the company is used to identify its products. Such is the case with Cannon towels. To avoid becoming entangled in legal implications, we shall use the term *brand*.

Both historically and legally, the purpose of a brand is to identify the source and to connote a uniformity of quality. The first purpose has lost some of its original significance. A brand does not always identify the source. This can easily be demonstrated by asking people to identify the manufacturer of some of the more famous brand names, such as All, Alpine, and Maxwell House. It does, however, identify a given product, and this is essential to the use of advertisers in stimulating selective demand. Although it may appear that no particular problem is present in identifying the product, this is not always true; some very difficult branding problems have occurred. One of the most striking examples is that of branding meat. Those who first attempted to brand this product stamped the brand on the outer carcass. The outer carcass, however, was the first thing cut off by the butcher before the meat was sold to the customer. While the branding of coal (sold in bulk) has never been successfully solved, stamping names like "Sunkist" on oranges, and "Diamond" on walnuts has proved a costly, yet successful, means of product identification.

Packaging, in addition to its functional purposes, has provided a means for identification and subsequent advertising of the brand. For many agricultural products these benefits would be impossible without packaging.

Although it is difficult enough to establish identity of source through a brand

[1]Public Law 489 (Lanham Act, H.R. 154), U.S. Statutes, 1946 (79th Congress, 2nd Session). (Washington, D.C.: Government Printing Office), p. 19.

name, to signify a tradition of uniformity of quality through a brand name is often far more difficult. The purpose of advertising brands is to build customer loyalty to the point where the purchaser will buy by brand rather than by inspection. Brand preference by customers can be achieved only if they feel that every time they purchase the brand, they will receive similar merchandise. If wide ranges in quality are experienced by a customer, he will no longer insist upon the brand.

In manufactured goods, manufacturing processes and quality-control systems tend to insure uniformity of quality from one period to another. In agricultural goods, however, quality is not always under the control of the brand owner, and the decision to spend large sums on advertising is more risky. The degree of quality uniformity does not have to be absolute to brand and advertise. However, the amounts expended on advertising brands of limited uniformity are less than in those cases in which quality uniformity can be insured. The reason is simply that the likelihood of building brand preference for these products is not as great. Most agricultural products fall in the limited-uniformity class.

Middlemen are not concerned with this problem unless they are advertising their own brands. The only problem even remotely connected is the need of multiunit retailers to identify their locations and to provide some uniformity in product assortments handled, price lines, and other store policies.

The Product

A differentiated product favors the use of advertising to stimulate selective demand. Creating customer loyalty through the development of brand preference is much easier to accomplish if substitution of brands by the customer is difficult. If the product has hidden qualities which are not readily apparent, the complexities of developing brand preferences are greatly increased. The customer must rely on the advertiser's message regarding the characteristics of the product. Such is the case with watches, paints, and proprietary medicines. It is no accident that the advertising of nonprescription medicines receives a larger share of the sales dollar than any other product. In addition to the appeal to better health that can be made, qualities of the product beyond the buyer's observation can be extolled, and the buyer must rely on the reputation of the advertiser and on the veracity of the claims made.

Physical differentiation can be achieved through skillful packaging. In fact, this is a primary basis for differentiation in the advertising of cosmetics. Differentiation need not rest on physical differences, and a number of other bases have proved useful. First, an image of differentiation may be achieved through the means used to communicate to the buyer. All the skill and ingenuity of the advertising copywriter may be called upon to create differentiation in the buyer's mind. An example is the unique copy used to advertise the dry goods of Indianhead Mills. In this case, the central theme was Indian folklore, with amusing and interesting copy. This became a famous campaign.

Differentiation can be achieved through concentrating on assurance of satisfaction in use. The advertising of warranties and service policies is a basis for differentiation in the consumer's mind. For many complex technical products,

437

Advertising
Management
and
Evaluation II:
Planning
and Control

this characteristic is equally as important as the product itself. Sometimes the environment in which the purchase can be made is an important basis for differentiation. This differentiation is frequently used by middlemen in their advertising, but manufacturers also have used it.

There are also those cases in which the major theme emphasized in advertising is not the product but some premium given with the product. Much advertising of household detergents, as well as breakfast cereals, has followed this course.

Another product characteristic which must be analyzed is the number of design variations available. Multivariable designs in products can cause certain difficulties in advertising. Products of this type include silverware, ties, and jewelry. Design is an important product characteristic in purchase. You can well imagine the difficulty a buyer might experience if he were to respond to a tie manufacturer's advertisement showing four different designs. Even if he could find a store that handled the manufacturer's ties, could he find the particular design in the assortment offered? This does not mean that ties cannot be advertised —only that some characteristics other than design must constitute the appeal. However, the advertising then is not aimed at the most important product characteristics operative in the purchase decision.

Although product differentiation usually contributes to the successful use of advertising to stimulate demand, there are exceptions. When the advertiser is attempting to develop the gift market, he can be successful without a high degree of differentiation from competitors' products. Through very extensive advertising, the product name may become well known and the general price level established. Often, when the value of the product is known, the giver of a gift will prefer to give well-known merchandise, to assure that the recipient is familiar with its value. Another exception is found in the way in which the customer purchases the product. A discussion of this follows.

The Customer

The prospective advertiser must analyze the way in which the customer purchases. The major forces operative in the purchase decision must be analyzed and the capacity of advertising to stimulate these forces assessed. Purchase decisions have been classified in a number of ways; one classification was presented in Chapter 7. Another simple classification divides purchases into habitual, routine purchases and purchases calling for more skill in decision making.

Habitual, routine purchases are generally limited to goods with little visual product differentiation; yet, they are heavily advertised. Such products as cigarettes, razor blades, soft drinks, and many food products fall into this category. Since the unit value of these products is low and the frequency of purchase high, once a satisfactory brand is found, the buyer will continue to purchase without the exercise of care in the purchase decision. Under these circumstances, "reminder advertising," which constantly keeps the brand name in the market, can be successful in diverting demand to the advertiser.

Another variation is the use of trial and error in purchasing such products. Since it matters little to the buyer if an unwise selection is made on any one occasion in view of the frequency of purchase, there is a very good chance that those brands which are most heavily advertised will be foremost in his mind and will be favored in trial-and-error purchasing.

The second class of purchase taxes a buyer's ingenuity much more. Purchases calling for more skill in decision making usually involve higher-unit-value products, purchased less frequently and, on the whole, more complex technically. Here, the buyer must have considerably more information, and some basis for comparing the value of the various brands available.

Advertising can emphasize the differentiated characteristics of the brand and stimulate selective demand for the advertiser. The major problem in advertising products purchased in this way is the funds available. The case of industrial goods best illustrates the problem.

Many industrial goods are differentiated from competitors' products, and the buyer does require information. On the other hand, as pointed out in Chapter 8, these goods require personal solicitation. Advertising cannot do the job alone, and since so much is required in other means of market cultivation, there is little left for advertising. Advertising is not the major communications instrument used. A less extreme case is in the sale of refrigerators. Advertising is made use of, but it is by no means the only communications instrument. The costs of maintaining an efficient dealer system may be more than the advertising appropriation. The advertiser must determine the way in which the consumer buys, assess the capacity of different instruments of communication to influence purchase, and allocate funds to advertising accordingly. Often advertising can help, but other things must be done first.

The Market

Analysis of the market is an extension of customer analysis but emphasizes the quantitative aspects of the market. One of the first characteristics to be analyzed is the location of potential customers. Can they be reached by the available media without considerable waste in circulation? If buyers cannot be identified and a broadcast form of advertising through many media is used, this can be very costly. An example will illustrate.

The makers of do-it-yourself kits for radios, high-fidelity systems, and tape-recording instruments have sought to expand their market. The earlier market was made up of people with special interest and skill and was reached through a number of technical and semitechnical magazines. Manufacturers today believe that assembly methods and instructions have been perfected to the point where just about anyone can assemble these kits. However, the task of determining the media to use to reach the broader market has been hampered by their inability to clearly identify the most likely potential buyers.

Size of market, frequency of purchase, and probability of repeat sales are, of course, important to the determination of funds available for advertising. The channel of distribution used also has a bearing on the ability to advertise.

When goods are distributed on a selective or exclusive basis, advertising becomes rather costly. For example, manufacturers of furniture find it difficult to advertise, since their products are available to consumers only in selected outlets. This means that identification of the outlet for the consumer must be

439

Advertising
Management
and
Evaluation II:
Planning
and Control

provided in some way. Advertising over the retailer's name by the manufacturer, or some form of vertical cooperative advertising, is used to accomplish this. On the other hand, selective or exclusive distribution is used when the product requires aggressive effort. The very use of this form of distribution means that advertising is not relied upon as the major communications instrument. That is, its role is secondary to other instruments of demand cultivation, such as store prestige, product availability, display, and personal selling.

Vertical Cooperative Advertising

As we have already seen, the channel of distribution used may require that the manufacturer use some form of vertical cooperative advertising. Other factors favor its use. Where dealer interest is important in the sale of the product, using cooperative advertising forces an investment on the part of the dealer. With money invested, the attention given to the product by the dealer is thought to be greater. Sometimes this is useful to the manufacturer, as it enables him to trade on the prestige of the dealer. This is true when large, well-known department stores cooperate.

There are a number of factors which must be taken into consideration before embarking upon a cooperative campaign. First, some means must be found to insure participation by the trade. If it is purely on a voluntary basis, limited participation is the result. Incentives in the form of tie-ins with manufacturer advertising can be useful; or, the supplying of mats for newspaper advertising and of examples of advertising copy, along with follow-up by the personal sales force, can do much to stimulate participation. Many manufacturers publicize their cooperative campaigns to local newspaper-space salesmen, hoping that space salesmen will persuade local retailers to take advantage of the manufacturer's cooperative arrangements.

Second, administration of the program is difficult. Evidence of funds spent for advertising by the trade is essential to the manufacturer in his effort to maintain control of the program. Also, if the manufacturer pays for advertising which was not placed, the payment is a price reduction and can, under the Robinson-Patman Act, result in prosecution for illegal price discrimination.[2]

Third, the Robinson-Patman Act requires that if a cooperative advertising allowance is offered to the trade, it must be made available to all buyers on proportionately equal terms. Obviously, it may be more useful to make the offer to large dealers and exclude small ones. That is, there are many cases where the manufacturer would prefer to concentrate his funds on a few large, prestigious dealers, rather than dissipate them in small amounts over many different accounts. The manufacturer is legally precluded from following this policy.

Fourth, a conflict in objectives frequently arises. The manufacturer is more interested in indirect-action, selective-demand advertising. The trade is more interested in direct-action advertising. That is, the dealer is concerned about bringing traffic to the store and selling merchandise, rather than selling a *specific brand* of merchandise. The manufacturer, on the other hand, is not nearly so concerned about the dealer's level of sale of general merchandise as he is with

[2] A more complete discussion of the Robinson-Patman Act is presented in Chapter 29.

the sale of his brand. This conflict is usually at the root of dealers' refusals to use manufacturers' advertising suggestions.

Fifth, the budgeting of expenditures for cooperative programs is difficult for manufacturers. The advertiser never knows what level of participation will be forthcoming.

In spite of all these difficulties, however, vertical cooperative advertising is widely used today. One of the greatest stimuli to its use is financial. The retailer purchases space at local rates, which are lower than those offered to the manufacturer, who must pay the higher national rate for the same space and advertising. For a given sum of money, therefore, more space can be purchased through vertical cooperative advertising than if the entire campaign is undertaken by the manufacturer.

Conclusion

The decision to use advertising in the total communications mix is not an easy one. The extreme cases can generally be determined, that is, those products which are highly advertisable versus those which are not. For the many products which lie between the extremes, there is always a question of whether funds allocated to advertising would be more productive if spent in other ways. Here, the advertiser must rely on experience and the more sophisticated means of evaluation discussed at the end of this chapter. Nevertheless, the factors we have discussed, affecting the successful use of advertising to stimulate either primary or selective demand, must be investigated. Their analysis will identify the problems which must be overcome and will minimize the indiscriminate allocation of money to this communications instrument.

DETERMINATION OF THE
ADVERTISING APPROPRIATION

A discussion of the advertising appropriation is presented at this point because it is the next logical step in the management of advertising. However, it is unwise to consider the sums to be allocated to advertising as a separate and distinct problem. Advertising is only one of many activities which may be used in the communications mix. The amount that should be allocated cannot be determined without reference to the other means, such as personal selling, and sales promotion, which may be used. Rarely is advertising used alone, and its success as a part of the communications mix is dependent on the amounts allocated to the other parts and how well they are executed. Depending upon the sums allocated for other purposes, the amounts allocated to advertising can vary. The objective is to find the optimum allocation of each means used (this was the subject of Chapter 23).

THE SELECTION OF MEDIA

Although the management of media is only one phase of advertising, it is a complex business in itself. In 1967, $17.3 billion was spent in the media avail-

441

Advertising
Management
and
Evaluation II:
Planning
and Control

able to advertisers.[3] Table 25-1 shows the allocation of these funds to different classes of media. Once the decision is made to use advertising in the communications mix, it is necessary to select the media types and the specific media companies that will carry messages to the market. Depending upon the purpose of the advertising, the media selected must meet certain specifications. Since media vary in their capacity to meet these specifications, a matching of advertiser needs with media capacity is prerequisite to the development of an effective program that contributes the greatest return on dollars invested.

TABLE 25-1

How Advertising Expenditures Were Divided
Among Media, 1967 (in millions of dollars)

Media	Amount in Dollars	Percentage of Share
Newspapers	$ 3,941	22.8
Magazines	991	5.7
Radio	876	3.4
Television	2,271	13.1
Direct mail	2,144	5.0
Business papers	590	12.4
Outdoor signs	241	1.4
Point-of-purchase display	639	3.6
Agency income	1,227	7.1
Other	4,410	25.5
Total	$17,330	100.0

Source: Advertising Age, *April 8, 1968, p. 56.*

At this point, a number of additional terms which refer primarily to media requirements must be introduced.

Media Requirements

Selective or Mass Coverage

What is the purpose of the advertising? Is it the desire of the advertiser to rifle the message directly to a well-delineated market? Or is it to convey a message to a mass market at low cost? Some media, such as radio or television, are known as mass media. Direct mail, on the other hand, is a more selective medium. The term *impact* refers to the capacity of the medium to transmit a real selling message to the market. For example, reminder advertising may not be high-impact advertising. On the other hand, most direct-mail advertising concentrates on impact in the selling message.

Audio or Visual

All of the printed media can convey only a visual message, whereas radio conveys an audio message and television both audio and visual messages. Con-

[3] Reprinted with permission from the April 8, 1968 issue of *Advertising Age,* p. 56. Copyright 1968 by Advertising Publications, Inc.

sider the case of selecting a medium to advertise combination storm windows. In an audio medium, such as radio, it would be difficult to convey a clear explanation of the way these windows work. Radio may be useful for a selling message that simply states that windows are available at a given location, but it is not very useful for explanation purposes. Newspapers may illustrate the window, but it is difficult in printed copy to convey the window's mechanical operation. Television, with its combination of audio and visual messages, is ideal—the major limiting factor being its relatively high cost compared with other media.

Package identification is another aspect in the choice of audio versus visual media. Since packaging has become such an important selling device, package identification is an important element in the advertising message. Obviously, a visual medium is necessary. If package identification is not important and product recognition is the important element, either an audio or a visual medium may be used.

Frequency of Insertion

Some types of advertising require very frequent insertion if they are to be successful. For example, reminder advertising, or advertising aimed primarily at brand recognition, requires a medium which can communicate the message a great number of times. Newspapers, radio, television "spots" (brief commercial announcements), and direct mail are all media which offer opportunity for frequent insertion. Weekly or monthly magazines are less acceptable for this purpose.

Type Selectivity

The type selectivity of a medium refers to its ability to reach a specific type of person. If the medium reaches a large number of different types, it must offer the advertiser some means to assure that the specific market is reached without excessive waste in circulation. For example, professional trade journals reach specific types of individuals. To try to reach these people through a national household magazine would result in too much waste circulation. Direct mail is highly selective in this respect, if adequate mailing lists are available. Newspapers, radio, and television offer little type selectivity. An attempt is made in these media, however, to achieve type selectivity in the following ways: (1) Position in newspapers affords some type selectivity; an advertisement in the sports section will be exposed to a different type of reader than an advertisement on the social pages. (2) Radio and television attempt the same thing by varying the time at which the advertising is broadcast and the programming in connection with which it is used.

Geographic Selectivity

This refers to the capacity of the medium to reach only certain geographic areas and not others. There are three major reasons why the advertiser prefers geographic selectivity. First, if he does not market the product nationally, there is little value in using a national medium. Second, competitive conditions may vary, and the advertiser may wish to allocate more advertising to some areas

443

Advertising
Management
and
Evaluation II:
Planning
and Control

than to others. Third, because of ethnic variations or different habit patterns in different parts of the country, different appeals may be necessary.

Some national magazines vary their content for different parts of the country, and thus provide geographic selectivity. Local newspapers inherently provide geographic selectivity; many provide quite precise selectivity through the practice of publishing both a home edition and a rural edition. In the large cities, such as New York, some of the newspapers even vary the content going to different sections of the city.

An advertiser may have several specific objectives in mind and have to use a combination of media to do the job. The important thing to remember is that some media are better than others for doing certain things.

Media Characteristics

Table 25-2 has been developed to rate the various media on the basis of the characteristics discussed. A rating of 1 means that the media offers the maximum in that characteristic, 2 means it is average, and 3 means it is poor or does not offer the characteristic at all.

Magazines, radio, and television have been subdivided for this comparison, since there are variations in these media, depending upon the specific type of magazine used or on the way radio or television is used. Trade magazines are specialized magazines, read by specialized people. There are a large number of these going to just about every occupational and professional class. Household magazines are more general in content and, as the name implies, are aimed at a broader group of readers. Three trade magazines are *Chain Store Age, Engineering News,* and *Chemical Week.*

Spot (or *local*) radio and television stations, concentrating on advertising, broadcast many one- or two-minutes advertisements of certain products or services of only local importance. *Network* radio and television, on the other hand, emanate from the network studios and concentrate on programming, giving advertisers the opportunity to be part- or full-sponsor of entire half-hour or hour-long programs, which are usually broadcast to the entire network area.

Direct mail is perhaps the most versatile of all media. It receives a rating of 1 on every characteristic except audio and coverage. But even coverage can be achieved if the advertiser is willing to absorb the cost. Generally, it does not seek wide coverage but relies on type selectivity to reach a specific market. Outdoor signs and car cards are very low in impact. The time period of exposure is so short that they are used primarily for reminder advertising.

The selection of media is not solely a matter of the user's matching his requirements with media characteristics. There is still the question of the relative cost of each medium. Cost may be a deterrent to the media type desired and is of course a critical variable.

Selection of the Specific Medium

Since most media within a type have many common characteristics, the selection of the specific medium to carry the advertising is importantly related

TABLE 25-2

Ranking of Advertising Media on Specific Characteristics

Characteristic	NEWS-PAPERS	MAGAZINES		RADIO		TELEVISION		OUTDOOR SIGNS	CAR CARDS	DIRECT MAIL
		Trade	*House-hold*	*Spot*	*Network*	*Spot*	*Network*			
Impact	2	1	1	2	1	1	1	3	3	1
Coverage	1	2	1	1	1	1	1	2	2	2
Audio	3	3	3	1	1	1	1	3	3	3
Visual	1	1	1	3	3	1	1	2	2	1
Frequency of insertion	1	3	3	1	3	1	3	3	3	1
Type selectivity	2	1	2	2	2	2	2	3	3	1
Geographic selectivity	1	2	3	1	3	1	3	1	1	1

445

Advertising
Management
and
Evaluation II:
Planning
and Control

to cost. Cost, however, has little meaning unless it is related to circulation. The *milline rate* has been developed to make cost-related-to-circulation comparisons among newspapers. It is computed as follows:

$$\text{Milline Rate} = \frac{\text{Line Rate} \times 1,000,000}{\text{Circulation}}$$

Examination of the formula indicates that it converts the cost line to a ratio of the cost per line per million of circulation to the actual circulation of the newspaper. In this way, the milline rate takes into consideration the differences in circulation among newspapers.

Magazine space is usually sold on a page or fraction-of-page basis. A measurement similar to the milline rate, called the *cost per thousand,* has been developed to make comparisons among magazines with different circulations. The calculation is as follows:

$$\text{Cost Per Thousand} = \frac{\text{Page Rate} \times 1,000}{\text{Circulation}}$$

Comparison of radio or television stations is based upon measurements of the listening or viewing audience. There are a number of syndicated data organizations supplying this information. Some of the largest raters of radio and television audiences are the A. C. Nielsen Company, *Trendex,* The American Research Bureau, *Pulse,* and Television Impact Service. Many methods are used for measuring radio and television audiences, and consequently, the results are not always consistent. The advertiser should be familiar with these techniques.[4]

The audiences of outdoor advertising are measured by the number of cars passing the billboards. The Traffic Audit Bureau supplies this information by stationing observers at outdoor advertising locations to observe the number of people and vehicles passing the point at different times of the day.

The Advertising Research Foundation has been conducting studies of transportation car-card advertising. These studies measure the number of persons who read car cards in the different transportation systems in which they are used.

Although the number of potential consumers reached is an important criterion in selecting a specific medium, the quality of the audience must not be overlooked. Practically all media do market research on those exposed to the medium to try to provide for advertisers a detailed profile of their audience. Many magazines and radio and television stations can supply detailed information, such as age groups, occupational classes, and income groups. This information is also important in selecting a specific medium, because it does little good to reach a large audience that is not particularly suited to the purchase of the product. For this reason, advertisers have attempted to develop more accu-

[4] For a more detailed discussion of broadcast media research, see D. J. Luck, H. G. Wales, and D. A. Taylor, *Marketing Research,* 3rd ed. (Englewood Cliffs, N.J.: Prentice-Hall, Inc., 1970), Chap. 18.

rate measurement of media effectiveness—especially media related to their own markets.

The cost per reader, listener, or viewer reached has been indicated as a starting point in media evaluation and selection. A second, more precise, measure figures the cost per potential customer reached, which requires that a knowledge of the composition of the medium's audience be matched with the company's own market definition. Next, measures of effectiveness may be related to the effectiveness of the media in serving the advertiser's purpose and desire for impact. For instance, he may wish to compute the cost of inquiries received from two different media in the past in making current choices of expenditures. Or even more significantly, the advertiser may try to develop by various purchase-tracing procedures the cost-of-customer-generated by alternative media. For instance, a retail store will run an advertisement on men's shirts of a particular make at a specific sales price in one newspaper. The next week it will run the same advertisement in another paper and attempt to determine the cost of the space on a per-customer-generated basis. National advertisers make similar kinds of evaluations by offering merchandise, or free home trials, or by including redeemable coupons of various sorts in the advertisement. The point is that one medium could have a lower cost per reader, while another has a higher cost per reader but a lower cost-per-inquiry-generated; the latter could thereby be a more economical purchase of space by the advertiser. The problem is thus essentially one of matching *effective audience* with *potential purchasers* on a cost basis.

It should be clear that the task of selecting a specific medium cannot be done on a completely scientific basis. The data available to the advertiser may be sketchy, and there is frequently conflicting evidence as to the circulation of any given medium. Nevertheless, cost comparisons, along with more qualitative appraisals which take account of the composition of the audience, should enable the advertiser to select the medium which most likely will meet his requirements.

COORDINATION WITH
OTHER MARKETING EFFORT

Rarely is advertising used alone. It is but one activity in the total communications mix, and it is imperative that it be coordinated with whatever other means of market cultivation are used. There are three activities with which advertising must be coordinated. Experience indicates that it is in these three areas that most difficulty occurs.

1. Proper timing of advertising with the physical distribution of the product is essential. Advertising expenditures can be wasted if the advertising is placed before adequate product distribution is achieved. If the advertising is successful in getting the consumer to seek out the product, failure to make it available means a sizable waste of the advertising dollar. Furthermore, failure on the part of the consumer to find the product makes it much more difficult to stimulate him to the same level of desire in the future. This difficulty may appear as a simple scheduling problem. In many instances, however, the problem goes

447

Advertising
Management
and
Evaluation II:
Planning
and Control

well beyond scheduling difficulties. For manufacturers without substantial reputations selling a new product, the problem of obtaining an adequate number of distribution outlets is present. Wholesalers and retailers alike often refuse to stock the product on the basis that there has been no demand stimulated for it. Evidence of an attempt to stimulate demand by the manufacturer is present in the amount of advertising allocated to the product. Under such circumstances, the manufacturer frequently must advertise to gain distribution. It is essential that the product be made available immediately after the advertising is placed if the advertising is to be useful.

2. Advertising should dovetail with personal selling effort. The sales department should be made aware of every aspect of the advertising campaign, including the media used, the appeals made, and any special offers included. The salesman should be trained to capitalize on appeals made in the advertising. The company should present a unified posture to its purchasing public. When campaigns are seasonal, they should be timed to precede, by a short period, the sales force's coverage of territories. This is particularly true where there is a marked seasonal pattern in sales, such as in school materials and sporting goods.

3. Advertising should be coordinated with sales promotion activities in a number of ways. Of primary importance is the need to coordinate point-of-purchase display materials. In one sense, media advertising tries to build a favorable impression about the product, whereas point-of-purchase display material attempts to deliver impact at the point the buying decision is made. Most product advertising has an indirect-action effect. Point-of-purchase display material tries to convert this into a purchase through stressing direct-action appeals. There should, however, be comparability in the appeals and in the buying motives emphasized if the media together are to produce maximum effectiveness. When other forms of sales promotion are used, such as fairs or exhibits, the advertising can be used to communicate this fact to those interested. It has been demonstrated that the use of advertising to publicize the fact that the advertiser is exhibiting at a certain fair increases the sales effectiveness of the exhibit.[5] When dealer sales-training programs are used, the advertising schedule and objectives should be emphasized to the dealer's salesmen, to give them the opportunity to tie into the advertising program in their own sales efforts.

It may appear that the need for coordination is self-evident. However, there have been numerous cases of advertising programs which have been unsuccessful because of failure to coordinate the campaign with other communications and marketing effort. In part, this is a problem of organization. When the total communications function is divided into autonomous departments, such as sales, advertising, and sales promotion, extra care must be exerted to prevent each from following its own separate program to perhaps even the reduced effectiveness of the others. Through visualizing all of these activities under a single communications function, there is a much better chance that all three will be coordinated into a well-balanced program.

[5] See "How Much Promotion Backs Exhibits," *Sales Management* (May 19, 1961), p. 116.

EVALUATION OF
ADVERTISING EFFECTIVENESS

Reasons for Evaluating Advertising

The effectiveness of advertising must be evaluated for a number of reasons:

1. It is necessary to have some measure of the effect of advertising on sales to intelligently determine the size of succeeding advertising appropriations.

2. When one considers the alternatives in media and copy available, some measure of the effectiveness of different copy, different media, and frequency and seasonality of insertion is necessary for efficient management of this phase of advertising.

3. The market to which advertising is directed is in a steady state of change. The dynamic nature of the market is such that price reduction may produce a greater sales response in one period and advertising in another.

4. There is a saturation point in advertising beyond which sales response is negligible. It is necessary to know when this point has been reached.

Those charged with responsibility for all marketing effort will rarely engage directly in research studies designed to evaluate the effectiveness of advertising. Nevertheless, they will be exposed to those studies which have been conducted to ascertain effectiveness. For this reason, it is essential that they have some familiarity with the methods and, most important, that they understand precisely what these various methods measure. With this purpose in mind, the methods currently used to evaluate advertising effectiveness are presented.

METHODS OF EVALUATION

With few exceptions, the overall objective of advertising research is to determine whether or not advertising is producing additional sales revenue that more than justifies its cost.[6] On the other hand, for most companies sales are generated by a number of activities, of which advertising is only one. The multivariable character of the problem makes it almost impossible to measure those sales which can be attributed to advertising, those to personal selling, and those to sales promotional activities. Because of this, most advertising research concentrates on those characteristics of the advertisement which must be present if it is to be successful. That is, an advertisement cannot be successful if it is not seen or heard. Furthermore, it must be understood, believed, and remembered. If the advertiser can demonstrate exposure, comprehension, retention, and believability, it is inferred that the advertisement will produce more sales than one for which these characteristics cannot be demonstrated. Consequently, research

---

[6] For a more detailed discussion of this topic, see Luck, Wales, and Taylor, *Marketing Research,* 3rd ed., Chap. 18.

449

Advertising
Management
and
Evaluation II:
Planning
and Control

done to evaluate advertising falls into four categories: (1) media research to determine exposure; (2) copy research to determine such characteristics as the ability of the consumer to comprehend, retain, and believe the message; (3) "image" studies to determine whether the customer's perception of the product and company has changed along desired lines; and (4) sales-results tests to determine the sales effectiveness of advertising.

Media Research

As mentioned in the section on the selection of media, circulation figures are necessary to determine the economy of the various printed media. All printed media provide circulation data, and these, because of the objective of the media— selling space to the advertiser—are verified by such companies as the Audit Bureau of Circulation and Business Publications Audit of Circulations, Inc. The advertiser, however, is forced to rely on the medium's claims for detailed analysis of the composition of its circulation. In broadcast media, such as radio or television, the measurement of audience size is more difficult. The problem is to determine how many radio and television sets are in use at any given time and to what program they are tuned. Current methods do not measure the number of *people* reached: audience size is expressed in terms of the number of *households* reached.

Two major methods are used in radio and television audience measurement: (1) coincidental and (2) postbroadcast. The *coincidental* method checks the number of households tuned in, either by making phone calls at the time of the broadcast or by using machines which record the time the set was turned on and the station tuned in. In both cases, probability samples are used, which are later projected to determine total audience size. A more recent development is an electronic device called the "Arbitron," used by the American Research Bureau. A controlled sample of approximately 500 homes is electronically linked with a scoreboard which records each set as it is tuned in to any station. The primary value of the coincidental method is that it does not rely upon recall by the respondent. On the other hand, it measures only the number of households tuned in. It does not measure whether anyone was listening or how many were viewing the message.

Most *postbroadcast* methods, in addition to measuring audience size, seek additional information about the respondent's attitude toward the advertising message. They are conducted with a probability sample and use either personal interviews with aided recall or a diary method. When aided recall is used, the respondent is shown a list of programs broadcast the previous day and asked to identify those heard. He may also be asked to identify the sponsor and indicate knowledge about the product advertised. In addition, information regarding the composition of the household, such as the size of the family, economic level, and education and occupation, is also acquired. The diary method provides an inexpensive means of getting information. A probability sample of families is provided by means of a diary, in which they record all programs listened to. The postbroadcast methods get more information, but they must rely on the respondent's ability to recall those programs viewed or listened to. In neither the coincidental nor the postbroadcast means of measurement is there any indication of sales effectiveness.

Copy Research

Copy research measures the effectiveness of different elements in an advertisement—that is, differences in theme, size, layout, illustration, and color that may be used in printed media. Almost as many variables are present in the preparation of both radio and television advertising messages. Research may try to measure the effectiveness of each element or of different elements in combination. Copy research is divided into prepublication and postpublication research. Among the prepublication tests which may be applied are the consumer-jury test, the arousal test, the eye-camera test, readability studies, the program analyzer, and the Schwerin test. A brief description of each follows.

The *consumer-jury test* is designed to test the preference of a group of representative customers for one advertisement over another or for several advertisements from a group. Advertisements are mocked up and shown to a representative group of customers, who are asked to select the preferred advertisement. If a group of advertisements is used, it is necessary to restrict the range of choice to enable the respondents to make a comparison easily. If eight advertisements are being tested, they are divided into fifty-six groups of two each in the number of combinations possible. This is known as a *paired-comparison test*. Another method often used is a *ranking scale,* on which the respondent lists in order his preferences of advertisements. The major limitations to this method are four: (1) The respondent may select his preference for an advertisement from the group, but none of the advertisements in the group may be desirable. (2) The respondent may react differently than would be the case if he were exposed to the advertisement under actual conditions of publication. (3) It is difficult to insure that the jury is representative of the potential customers for the product. (4) There is no indication of the sales power of the advertisement. At best, it may separate the stronger from the weaker advertisements.

Arousal tests use equipment similar to a lie detector to measure a respondent's emotional response when shown the advertisement. The subjects must represent typical potential customers. This method does not indicate whether the response is favorable or unfavorable to the advertiser. However, by questioning after the test, it may be useful in indicating the attention-getting power of different advertisements.

The *eye-camera test* mechanically records the movement of the eye across the advertisement, and the time spent on each element. The test does not indicate what the person thinks about the advertisement, nor can it determine whether a sustained look at a certain part of the advertisement is caused by difficulty in reading or in comprehending the copy or by the attention-getting power of the copy. There is a belief, however, that the most-read advertisements hold the eye the longest.

451

Advertising
Management
and
Evaluation II:
Planning
and Control

Readability studies test advertisements to determine if they are readable by people in different educational levels. Formulas have been developed which state the number of words per sentence, the number of affixes per hundred words, and the number of references to people per hundred words. Variations in these elements make the copy readable to people in different educational levels—which should match the educational levels of potential purchasers in the advertiser's market.

The *program analyzer* is used in broadcast media and is similar to a consumer-jury test. It is based on the premise that the program with which the advertisement is used determines, in part, the reviewer's response to the advertising. The jury member views the program and indicates those parts he likes or dislikes by pressing different colored buttons. These answers are recorded and cross-tabulated with characteristics of the jury, such as age, sex, economic level, and educational level.

The *Schwerin test* uses a survey method to gather information about a large group of potential listeners or viewers. They are given lists of brand names and asked to select those brands they would choose if offered as a prize. Later, they are exposed to a program and commercials, usually in a theater, and afterward are asked to select those brands they would choose as a prize. Any shifting in preference is attributed to the effect of the commercial to which they have been exposed. This method still does not test the sales effectiveness of the advertisement, and a number of random variables are difficult to isolate.

The major postpublication tests are known as penetration or progress tests. *Penetration tests* measure such things as recognition and recall. There are many companies providing this service. Although there are differences in the methods used, many common characteristics exist. Practically all use a personal-interview technique in which the respondent is asked about an advertisement. His answer reveals the depth of his impressions. The major difference is the aid given to the respondent in recalling the advertisement. Some services use unaided recall, in which the respondent is asked, "What advertisements have you seen recently that impressed you most?" Aided recall can be of varying degrees. The respondent may be asked, "What brand of coffee do you remember seeing advertised lately?" The answer given indicates that the advertisements for the brand made a positive impression. It does not indicate any particular advertisement or medium and is, therefore, only a general test of brand dominance.

Another form of aided recall is to show the respondent a publication and ask if he has read any of the advertisements on each page. Then a series of questions are asked to determine the degree of penetration the advertisement has had. Wide differences in readership claims by different rating agencies result from differences in methods used. The Advertising Research Foundation, in comparing the different methods, found that one overstimulates the respondent to recall and results in a much larger number of presumed readers. Other methods greatly understimulate the reader and result in a much smaller number of readers being indicated than is actually the case.

Progress tests measure different stages in buyer awareness, preference, and intention to buy. Surveys are used which compare the proportion of those preferring a brand but who have not been exposed to advertising with those preferring a brand who have been exposed. If the two groups are identically matched, the difference in preference is attributed to the advertising. This can also be carried to the purchase level; a comparison of exposed purchasers and unexposed purchasers gives some measure of the sales-getting power of the advertisement.

Inquiry tests are those in which an invitation is made in the advertisement to write in to the sponsor for additional information. The number of inquiries resulting from one advertisement is compared with those resulting from another. There is an implication that the inquiry pulling power of the advertising is correlated with its selling power. This correlation may not always be valid. The inquiry pulling power of the advertisement is influenced by the offers made in the inquiry, and if these vary or the circumstances surrounding the offer vary, it is difficult to isolate net effects. Furthermore, the task of converting inquiries into prospects usually requires additional marketing effort of a different kind, such as personal selling. Nevertheless, the method has much validity, and is useful for comparing advertisements for this purpose.

Image Studies

A new area of investigation for determining advertising effectiveness is called *image studies*. Presumably, if advertising is effective, it should change the attitude of the relevant public toward the product and sponsor in the desired way from the point of view of the advertiser. Before- and after-advertising studies are made using motivational research techniques to gain these customer perceptions. For example, an appliance manufacturer was having difficulty in his trade relations, in that distributors and dealers were not giving his products the aggressive marketing effort desired. The manufacturer, using motivational techniques, had a study made of the company image among the trade. The study showed that dealers believed the manufacturer was offering different prices to different accounts, that his merchandise had substantial servicing difficulties, and that his merchandise was not selling well—that there was a substantial carry-over of last year's goods still in the distribution channels. The appliance manufacturer then developed a trade advertising campaign to help alter this image. At the end of the program a similar image study was conducted which did not identify the client, and a noticeable improvement could be perceived. This procedure holds some promise for the future because it gives advertising and advertising research a specific problem-solving orientation.

Sales-results Tests

As stated earlier, the multivariable nature of the influences affecting sales makes it difficult to measure the sales effectiveness of advertising alone. However, methods have been used to determine the effects of advertising when none has been used before or when there has been a change in campaigns, or a change in major media. The technique involves setting up an experiment by selecting test areas and control areas. These should be as near alike as possible; the factor tested is tried in the test area and sales results observed in each. The difference in results is attributed to the factor under test. Since the maintenance of complete

453

Advertising
Management
and
Valuation II:
Planning
and Control

uniformity between the test area and the control area is difficult, several areas are selected and the experiment rotated among them, in hopes that the differences in the areas will compensate for each other. The method does measure the sales effectiveness of major parts of the advertising, but it is of no value for measuring the sales effectiveness of minor variations in copy, layout, etc.

Methods of evaluating advertising are far from utopian. There is still no satisfactory means for measuring sales effectiveness of advertising. At most, historical analysis gives some clues, but the dynamic nature of markets and competition makes it excessively risky to rely solely on historical, as compared with current or projected, conditions.

Summary

The management of advertising involves five areas: (1) determining those factors affecting the successful use of advertising, (2) determining the size of the advertising appropriation, (3) the selection of media, (4) the coordination of advertising with other activities, and (5) evaluating effectiveness. The factors affecting the use of advertising for purposes of stimulating primary demand are the extent of use of the product, demand trends, price-income relationships, extent of the market, funds available, and appeals. The factors affecting the use of advertising to stimulate selective demand are grouped into ability to brand, the characteristics of the product, the customer, and the market.

The task of determining the advertising appropriation must include consideration of the other forms of communication used. (For this reason, a discussion of this subject was presented in Chapter 23.)

The selection of media involves two problems: (1) determining the media type, and (2) selecting the specific medium within a type. The first problem may be solved by matching such media requirements as impact, coverage, audio or visual, frequency of insertion, and geographic and type selectivity, with the capacity of different media to meet these requirements. The selection of a specific medium within a type primarily reflects selective cost comparisons.

Coordination of advertising with physical distribution, personal selling, and sales promotional activities is essential if each activity individually and collectively is to deliver maximum effect.

Evaluation of advertising is divided into media research, copy research, and sales-results research. The multivariable forces influencing sales makes it almost impossible to measure with high precision the sales effect of advertising. Consequently, most advertising research measures characteristics of an advertisement, such as exposure and ability of the receiver to comprehend, retain, and believe the advertisement. If all of these are present, it is inferred that the advertisement will be effective in producing sales. The problem of measuring advertising effectiveness is still a frontier area for the application of complex scientific methods to market cultivation effort.

Questions and Problems

1. Under what kinds of conditions would primary-demand advertising be used?

2. "The forces underlying demand must be carefully analyzed to assess the ability of advertising to overcome or change these forces." Comment.

3. Describe and give some examples of the kinds of markets in which advertising would tend to do relatively little good.

4. What advice or words of caution would you give to an executive of a trade association of an industry that has had a serious decline in demand if one of the association members proposes a horizontal cooperative advertising program?

5. Distinguish between brands and trademarks. What is the relationship between branding and advertising?

6. What are the various purposes of branding? Does a brand always identify the source of the product? Give examples of the kinds of products that are difficult to brand.

7. Discuss the advertising influences of hidden (not readily apparent upon inspection) product qualities. What are the various ways in which these kinds of products can be differentiated?

8. "Advertising copy has a close relationship to the market delineation and purchase motivation functions." Explain.

9. What kinds of factors favor the use of vertical cooperative advertising? What problems are involved in this kind of advertising that should be considered prior to embarking upon such a campaign?

10. What are the various factors that the advertiser should consider in choosing media?

11. What is the term *milline rate,* and what is it used for? Does the lowest milline rate represent "best buy" for the advertiser?

12. What are the various methods used for evaluating advertising effectiveness?

13. What are the various *planning* uses of carefully evaluating advertising effectiveness?

14. What are the limitations of the consumer-jury test used in copy research?

15. If it can be proved that the consumer believes the advertising message, can it then be presumed that the advertising is effective?

Management of Corporate and Agent Sales Forces

26

The management of personal selling activities falls into two broad categories as follows: (1) the development of a personal selling strategy and (2) the establishment of a sales force development program. Just as in the case of advertising, decisions must be made on the specific role personal selling is to have in the total marketing mix. Once decisions are made on the objectives of personal selling, manpower requirements may be specified, and the task of molding the sales force into an efficient managerial unit commenced.

Modern business enterprise has reached a point where market requirements preclude using inept selling efforts. Rapid product diversification, expanded markets, changing channels of distribution, and more exacting purchase requirements all demand in today's market place a salesman keenly sensitive to customers' needs and equipped with the technical knowledge and skill necessary for effective communication to the mutual advantage and profit of both parties. The following objectives are the broad goals of a sales force development program:

1. To obtain personnel with the proper qualifications to meet the requirements of job performance.

2. To develop in each individual, through training, a proper personal adjustment to his job and essential market and product knowledge and sales skills in order to accomplish maximum job performance.

3. To provide the proper environment which develops a sense of loyalty to the company and encourages each person to fit himself for responsibility to the limit of his capacity.

4. To assure an adequate supply of trained personnel to fill job openings created by promotion, expansion, retirement, transfer, resignation, or termination.

Our approach in this chapter is to examine some considerations in establishing a personal selling strategy and to outline an approach to sales force development, through examining techniques used and highlighting the most important factors to be considered in using these techniques. Since management usually has the option of employing its own sales force or using the services of a manufacturers' agent, we shall examine any differences which exist in managing one or the other.

PERSONAL SELLING STRATEGY

As we have seen in Chapter 23 the use of personal selling varies among product types and over time. Each change in the amounts allocated to personal selling involves a change in personal selling strategy. How does management decide upon the role of this communications medium?

Figure 26-1 suggests the steps to be taken in establishing an overall per-

FIGURE 26-1
The Selling Strategy Decision Process

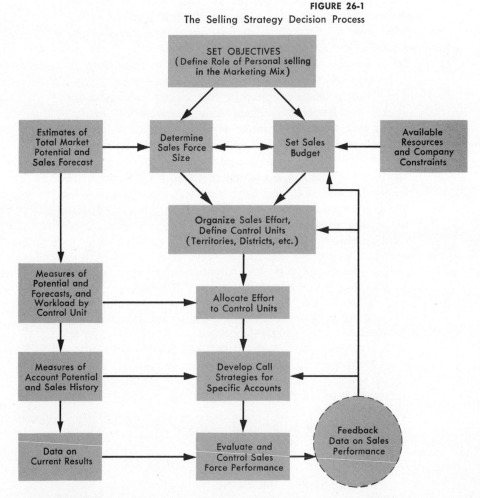

Source: David B. Montgomery and Frederick E. Webster, Jr., "Application of Operations Research to Personal Selling Strategy," Journal of Marketing, *XXXII (January 1968), 54.*

sonal selling strategy.[1] It begins with the objectives of personal selling in the marketing mix. It was suggested in Chapter 22 that communication objectives be stated for advertising; they can also be stated for personal selling. If the obstacles to achieving the marketing objectives are identified, a decision may be made as to which may be overcome by advertising and which by personal selling. In effect, the objectives of personal selling represent a statement of the salesman's responsibility to the company. For an example of this, see the job description in the next section of this chapter, "Sales Force Development." Parts I and II indicate the *first order goals* of personal selling in the Farm Supply Division of Farm Bureau Services, Inc. These goals specify the salesman's responsibility for gaining distribution and disseminating information about the company's products. In conjunction with estimates of the total market opportunity for the products of the company, the statement of objectives may be used as a basis for determining the approximate sales force size and the approximate sales budget to support such a force. (See Figure 26-1.) The actual size of the sales force will depend upon the financial capacity of the company and the specific sales task to be performed. Of course, optimization of revenues and cost is desirable in deciding the size of the sales force, and one approach to this was suggested in Chapter 23.

The next step is to decide upon the control units to be used in assigning and controlling personal selling effort. Usually these are geographic units, but they can be product groupings, channels of distribution, or classes of customers, as well. This is a problem in organization and is discussed in Chapter 30. Before the number of control units is decided upon and the assignment of manpower made, the workload of each man must be specified. More specific statements, or *second order* goals must be established, which detail the precise activities the salesman is to engage in to meet the *first order* goals. Part III of the job description for a Feed Field Representative is a statement of *second order* goals. With these tasks in mind, it is possible to establish an average workload for a salesman. Using this measure in conjunction with measures of market opportunity, the size of a control unit (size of geographic area or number of customers) can be determined, or if the control units are already established, the number of men that have to be assigned for maximum cultivation of the unit can be determined. At this point a more precise statement can be made about the number of salesmen needed and the sales budget necessary.

The determination of sales assignments usually involves assigning responsibility for a geographic area or territory to the salesman. There are a number of reasons for making each salesman responsible for the company's sales activities in a specific area. First, it establishes the salesman's task and clearly defines his area of responsibility. When the extent and limits of the job are known, it is possible for the man to program his own activities to accomplish the goals set forth. Second, it insures effective market coverage of the designated area or customer group. Without definite territories there is a tendency for the salesman to skim off the cream and sell only the easier accounts over a larger area. Third, more intensive market coverage may give a competitive advantage, as it will

---

[1] See: David B. Montgomery and Frederick E. Webster, Jr., "Application of Operations Research to Personal Selling Strategy," *Journal of Marketing,* XXXII (January 1968), 50–57.

become more difficult for competitors to make inroads into the company's total marketing area. Fourth, the territory is a managerial unit. The total marketing effort may be evaluated territory by territory, and appropriate remedies taken to correct poor situations. Fifth, territorial responsibility by the salesman prevents crisscrossing of salesmen which inevitably results in high cost of solicitation. Sixth, it minimizes disputes over commission payments on sales made where joint effort was involved.

The determination of territories is an extension of quantitative market delineation. The objective is to determine areas of equal sales opportunity. This can never be completely realized, since the size of customers, the frequency of calls necessary, and the accessibility of customers varies geographically. The steps in approaching the ideal follow: (1) divide the total market area into areas of approximately equal sales opportunity; (2) identify the accounts; (3) calculate the length of time for an average call, including travel time, waiting time, and interview time; (4) determine the number of calls that can be made per day; (5) calculate the frequency of calls for various accounts; (6) determine how many accounts a man can service in a month; and (7) put together areas with a number of customers the man can be expected to service. This kind of analysis provides a beginning for the establishment of sales territories.

A number of other factors must be considered. For example, the volume of business necessary to operate the territory profitably must be taken into consideration. There might be some areas where the accessibility of customers is such that the number of accounts that could be adequately serviced by one man would not produce profitable sales volume. It may be necessary to give parts of this area to adjacent territories. The state of sales development may be a consideration. A territory may be smaller than usual simply because the company is trying to enter the area and much development work must be done. Ability of the salesman may also be a variable which has to be taken into consideration. As not all men have the same capacity, some men may have to be given smaller territories. Geographic variations in economic conditions may call for frequent realignment of territories. Also, the basis upon which market information is available from published sources must be taken into account for purposes of evaluating territorial performance. The determination of territories and the assignment of responsibility to salesmen for territory management is necessary for effective use of personal selling in the total communications mix.

A continuing function is constant solicitation of each account for which the salesman is responsible. Based upon market information about each account in the control unit, call strategies should be developed for each. As competitive and market conditions are constantly changing, careful planning of the strategy to be used on each call is important if personal selling is to produce maximum results. A final step is monitoring sales force performance so that adjustments can be made when results depart from expectations. This is an element of control and is discussed in Chapter 31.

The decision areas suggested above are not significantly different if an agent sales force is used to carry out the personal selling task. As pointed out in Chapter 21, such a force may be used at the same time as the manufacturer's own sales personnel. The determination of personal selling objectives is the same in either case, but the number of agents needed differs from the number of salesmen needed. The control units or areas selected by the firm will probably have to parallel those currently covered by the agent. The agent may not handle all lines offered by the firm, a possibility that does not arise when using a corporate sales force. In this event, two or more agents may be required in a control unit, whereas one corporate salesman would suffice. Since the agent is not an employee of the company, it may be more difficult to insist on careful planning of call strategies for maximum effectiveness in cultivation of the accounts assigned. This can only be assured through careful selection of the agents in the beginning. Analyses which attempt to optimize costs and revenues are easier in the case of agents. Agent sales force costs are a known percent of sales as represented by the commission payment agreed upon. Corporate sales force costs include fixed costs, such as training costs and salaries, when paid. The exact cost per dollar of revenue produced depends upon the total revenues generated and is not known ahead of time. In spite of these differences the procedures suggested above can be used, with only minor modifications, when an agent sales force is employed.

SALES FORCE DEVELOPMENT

The tasks to be accomplished have been identified through the establishment of a personal selling strategy. Accomplishment depends upon careful selection of manpower, continuous attention to training for the job, and provision for motivating the salesmen to perform in the desired manner. These areas are usually referred to as the major aspects of sales management.

The same job description useful in establishing a personal selling strategy is absolutely essential in selecting, training, and motivating the sales force. In the example of the agricultural feed salesmen every aspect of the job is stated. Unless this is done it is impossible to determine the kind of individual capable of performing the job. After potential salesmen are selected, the areas in which they need specific training cannot be identified without comparing the characteristics of each man with the job requirements.

JOB DESCRIPTION
FEED FIELD REPRESENTATIVE, FARM SUPPLY DIVISION
FARM BUREAU SERVICES, INC.

I. *Objective*

    A. To promote and expand the distribution of Farm Bureau and Unico products and supplies distributed by the above-mentioned department.

    B. To disseminate in the assigned territory the practical and technical knowledge related to these products and their uses.

II. *Scope of Activities*

    To plan and operate in such a manner that will best fulfill the above objectives. This should be done in accordance with the responsibilities listed below throughout the specific territory assigned.

III. *Responsibilities*

    A. To know his products thoroughly by studying all available product information and attending special schools, lectures, and tours.

    B. To keep dealers and their employees properly informed about all the Farm Bureau products they distribute.

    C. To assist dealers in improving sales and merchandising techniques on Farm Bureau products.

    D. To be ready and willing to work with dealers in:

        1. Calling on feeders to explain Farm Bureau's feeding programs.

        2. Setting up contracts on feeder financing.

        3. Supervising all feeder financing within respective district and making biweekly inspection reports on all poultry financing, and monthly reports on hog and beef financing.

        4. Checking flocks and herds for illness.

        5. Holding district commodity meetings for dealers.

        6. Seeking desirable new dealer outlets and following the recommended procedures for setting them up.

        7. Making periodical analyses of territory and dealer accounts.

        8. Selling the complete line of Farm Bureau feeds.

        9. Meeting sales quotas given the territory.

      10. Conducting local employee commodity training programs.

      11. Training local employees in resale work in the field.

      12. Assisting in the planning of dealer advertising programs.

      13. Keeping dealer accounts with F.B.S. on a current basis.

    E. To plan and manage the territory by:

        1. Arranging a routine for most effective coverage of the district.

        2. Maintaining a "frequency of call" on dealers according to account desirability and need for personal calls.

        3. Balancing time spent with each dealer against potential volume.

        4. Preparing special reports on unusual local conditions.

        5. Conducting studies and surveys to make improvements on our distribution and service programs.

        6. Serving as two-way channel of communication between Farm Bureau Services and local dealer outlets.

        7. Coordinating activities between commodity department heads and warehouse managers.

        8. Meeting with local co-op. boards of directors or dealer advisory committees when requested or deemed desirable.

        9. Maintaining a harmonious relationship with affiliated company field representatives and keeping them informed of general activities.

      10. Submitting a weekly work plan and routing statement.

      11. Making daily written reports to department manager on work operations.

      12. Promoting the sale of Farm Bureau stocks and debentures whenever it is deemed necessary by Management.

IV. *Authority*

    A. To carry out above responsibilities in accordance with the policies set forth by management.

    B. To recommend levels of inventory at warehouses consistent with demands of territory.

    C. To recommend to department head and warehouse managers the allocation of commodities not in sufficient supply to meet demand.

    D. No direct authority over personnel, but consists mainly of consultation, cooperation, and recommendation.

E. No direct authority over facilities other than supply recommendations or suggestions when requested.

V. *Relationships*

A. Report to and responsible to Feed Department manager.
B. Work with Farm Bureau Services dealer outlets and managers of Farm Bureau Services Branch Stores and Management Contracts.
C. Maintain a harmonious working relationship with the other fieldmen and personnel of Farm Bureau Services and affiliated companies to the fullest benefit of all people concerned.
D. Work with the representatives of our suppliers to become better versed in the products we get from them.

VI. *Personal Qualifications for this Job*

A. Education
   1. Should have at least a high school education—college training desirable but not essential.
   2. Should be able to do an average job of public speaking.
   3. Should understand, believe in, and be able to explain the corporate philosophy.
   4. Completion of special schools or correspondence courses on animal nutrition and feeds would be helpful.
   5. An understanding of the manufacturing processes of the products handled is desirable.
B. Experience
   1. Should have a farm background, including the care and feeding of farm animals and poultry.
   2. Retail sales experience with farm supplies is desirable.
   3. Experience as a contact man for elevator or warehouse would be very helpful.
   4. Must have a general knowledge of our products and their uses.

VII. *Personal Characteristics*

A. Must be aggressive, resourceful, and ambitious.
B. Must be capable of sound reasoning and good judgment.
C. Must have ability to plan and accept responsibility.
D. Must have emotional stability and be resilient to discouraging conditions.
E. Must have a pleasing personality and ability to get along with others.
F. Must be willing to admit mistakes and accept criticism.
G. Must be neat in personal appearance and have personal mannerisms that are appropriate and pleasing.

Courtesy of Farm Bureau Services, Inc.

How should the job description be formulated? A basic understanding of the nature and scope of markets and of the forces influencing these markets is, of course, the foundation for the formulation. Management will have some ideas about the activities that must be performed as a result of having determined the role of personal selling in the communications mix. However, to achieve unanimity of opinion about the job between management and the field sales force is most difficult. The development of a job description requires extended discussion between management, the sales supervisors, and the salesmen. The purpose of these discussions is to establish the views of the groups concerning what the duties of the salesman are, and to resolve differences in points of view.

Likewise, discussions with customers and prospects should be used to determine the buyers' opinions of what activities the salesman should engage in to be of maximum service and influence in the purchase decision. These discussions should serve as a basis for developing precise job descriptions, which take into consideration the problems the salesman faces in the field and the objectives of management in using personal selling as a part of the total communications mix.

A more analytical approach to the development of job descriptions uses time-and-duty analysis. Time-and-duty analysis of salesmen is analogous to time-and-motion study of production employees. Its purpose is basically the same. Time-and-duty analysis involves stating precisely what the salesman does every minute of his working day. The information is collected either by having the salesman keep a detailed diary of his day's activities or by having skilled analysts observe the salesman over a period of several days. Both methods run the risk of incurring the ill will of the field sales force unless the salesman is apprised of the purpose and can be made to recognize the value to him of such studies. After the activities of the entire sales force or a large sample have been recorded, the salesmen are divided into most productive and least productive groups. This division is usually based on such standards as sales volume, gross margin, and profitability. The activity data are then analyzed to determine if there are differences in the activities of good salesmen and poor salesmen. Those activities performed by the good salesmen, and not by the poor salesmen, are determined to be essential in the job description. Of course, activities common to both groups are also included. In this way job descriptions which have some relationship to success are developed.

When precise job descriptions are available it is possible to proceed to the major aspects of a sales force development program: selection, training, assignment, and motivation of the sales personnel.

SELECTING SALESMEN

The Man Specification

With an understanding of the tasks to be performed by the salesman, specifications are developed, which state the characteristics needed in the salesman to perform on the job. By studying the job description carefully, it is possible to establish deductively a reasonably accurate man specification. This is particularly true if the person developing it has had experience on the job. In the job description previously given, sections VI and VII indicate the personal qualifications thought to be necessary in a potential agricultural feed salesman.

There is much controversy over which characteristics of temperament and aptitude are necessary for selling success. One approach is to recognize that the characteristics needed for any job may be grouped under a number of categories. One such grouping includes: (1) previous experience, (2) sociability, (3) maturity, (4) leadership capacity, (5) manner and appearance, and (6) training. The problem then is to determine what is needed in each category for a particular selling job.

Not all selling jobs require the same requirements in each category. Some decisions must be made regarding the kind of previous experience a man should have to perform well on the job. Variations in previous experience requirements exist from industry to industry. For example, the selling requirements for many industrial goods require familiarity with buyers' needs, and with technical terminology in their business. In the case of house-to-house direct selling of household items, previous experience may not be necessary. There are also variations between companies in the same industry. Some companies have elaborate training programs and are not concerned with the previous experience of the applicant. Others, to minimize the sales training job, seek only those with experience in the same industry.

It is fair to assume that all salesmen must be socially acceptable. Different types of selling, however, require that salesmen possess this trait in different degrees. The salesman selling agricultural chemicals to farm supply houses, and sometimes direct to farmers, generally needs different personality traits to achieve social acceptability than the salesman representing pharmaceutical companies to the medical profession.

Likewise, maturity requirements vary. The investment banking house representative is usually an older, dignified individual, in whom the client can place confidence. In fact, in this business, younger men are given extensive training in the head office until they acquire the maturity necessary for this kind of selling. On the other hand, salesmen representing food processors, calling on the retail trade, do not need the same level of maturity.

Leadership capacity is important in different types of selling jobs. Some companies give the salesman considerable latitude in negotiating terms of sale, adjusting complaints, and adjusting the product to the buyer's needs. Other selling jobs are more routine, and the salesman is not called upon to exercise judgment beyond a minimum amount spelled out in company operating procedures. In the former case, the traits required are initiative and ability to make decisions. These are leadership qualities. In the latter case, leadership is not so important. But, as it is almost universal practice to use field selling experience as a steppingstone to managerial positions, leadership is looked for in all salesmen. The sales force is viewed by many companies as a pool of managerial talent.

Acceptable manner and appearance are essential for salesmen in general. Beyond the basic requirements, such as cleanliness and capacity for expression, these traits must be tailored to the buying group. The manner and appearance needed in the investment banking house representative differ greatly from these requirements in the agricultural chemical salesman.

Training requirements of salesmen also vary. Different levels of formal education are required for different types of selling. For example, whereas the salesman of chemicals in the industrial market generally must have an engineering or chemistry degree, or at least substantial specialized education, the formal educational requirements of salesmen representing most consumer goods manufacturers can be set at a lower level.

Although the main requirements can be grouped under the six categories mentioned above, some decisions must be made about the requirements needed in each category to perform satisfactorily on the job. This may be done deductively by those having had experience on the job, or a search may be made to demonstrate empirically the relationship between objective identifying characteristics of the salesmen and success on the job. To develop salesmen profiles for a specific job, a number of objective characteristics of all salesmen are recorded. Such illustrative items as age at time of employment, home ownership, marital status, amount of insurance carried, and formal education are used. The good and poor salesmen are determined by some standard of performance, such as sales volume, gross margin, or profitability. The characteristics of good salesmen are compared with those of poor salesmen. In this way profiles of good salesmen and poor salesmen, based on these characteristics, are available, against which new applicants may be measured.

These various means may be used to establish the main specifications necessary to perform the activities detailed in the job description. The next step is to determine whether the applicant possesses the characteristics in the desired degrees and combination.

Some writers have suggested that more attention should be given to the emotional and interactional demands of the sales job. That is, job descriptions and man specifications should reflect a recognition of the many roles the salesman plays, such as persuader, serviceman, and information gatherer; each has slightly different emotional demands. The numerous personality types with which the salesman must interact require flexibility in adaptive behavior. Selection procedures should seek to specify these demands and identify capacity to deal with them in potential candidates.[2]

The four methods most widely used for determining whether the applicant has the characteristics stated in the man specification are: (1) application blanks, (2) references, (3) interviews, and (4) tests. All four methods can be used successfully only if the preceding step of preparing a detailed man specification has been carefully executed. All methods must be used in combination before a composite picture of the applicant can be assembled.

The *application blank* serves as a means for gathering factual information about the candidate. It can be as extensive and detailed as is necessary to acquire the desired information. The important requirement is that the information that is acquired be used. Unless the information asked for has some relevance to the man specification and will be used to assess the applicant's potential ability to perform well, it should not be sought.

The application blank also aids in identifying obviously unqualified candidates. If formal educational background is not sufficient or age and previous experience is unsatisfactory, there is no need to pursue the selection procedure further. If ability to write legibly is a requirement of the job, the application blank is a ready test of this quality. Lastly, it provides cues from the applicant which can be used in planning the interview.

References are an evaluation technique which has been subject to much controversy. There are those who believe that they have little or no value. Perhaps the greatest value of references is to help identify very risky applicants

[2] James A. Belasco, "The Salesman's Role Revisited," *Journal of Marketing*, XXX (April 1966), 6–8.

who have not performed well on past jobs. It is rather rare, however, for a previous employer to adversely affect an applicant's employment opportunity in writing. As a rule, statements are generalized and vague. This tendency, along with the fact that replies are often slow in coming, has caused many employers to put little confidence in this technique. Some have found that telephone discussions have some advantages over the written reference. Form letters with evaluation scales have been used to overcome the vagueness of reply, but even here it is difficult to check an evaluation scale with accuracy. Often references are of the verification type and ask for verification of statements made in the application blank about the applicant's work history. When they are used in conjunction with the other methods, they may aid in developing a total picture of the applicant.

The *interview* is the most widely used selection technique. Often it is the only means used. A variety of interviewing techniques, such as the patterned employment interview, or interview guide and rating sheet, as well as multiple interviews and interview reports, are utilized in selection today. All of these have proved to be valuable variations in interview procedures. Regardless of the particular kind of interview used, certain requirements should be met.

It is desirable for the interviewer to get as much information as possible about the candidate ahead of time (the application blank serves a useful purpose in this respect). By so doing, the interviewer is able to plan the course of the interview and guide it along the lines necessary to evaluate the man in terms of the man specification. Too frequently interviews are conducted without plan. A pleasant exchange of viewpoints is the result, but little is gained from the point of view of evaluation of the applicant. Without a plan, the interviewer often talks too much and the applicant learns a great deal about him, but the objectives of the interview are not achieved. The interviewer must draw out the applicant and get him to talk along the lines that are useful in the evaluation process, at the same time remaining sufficiently flexible to go down potentially useful avenues of investigation not called for in the plan. Without a plan, many topics which should be covered are overlooked, and in the final analysis of the applicant this serious deficiency becomes apparent. A plan, along with providing sufficient time to cover all topics, enhances the prospect of an effective interview.

It is difficult for the participants of an interview to establish rapport if privacy is not provided. Lack of privacy not only keeps the applicant from speaking freely, but also produces a certain tension which will not allow him to be at ease. An employment interview is a tense situation under any circumstance, and there is no need to contribute to it by providing an improper environment.

A recording of the interviewer's impressions after the interview is desirable if the information acquired is to be useful in making the final selection. It is difficult for the interviewer to differentiate between each applicant interviewed unless some written statement is made immediately following the interview. If conducted with the man specification in mind and the proper environment provided, the interview may serve as the cornerstone of the entire evaluation.

Tests are used to acquire information on those facets of the applicant's total personality which are not revealed through the other methods. Using tests has been stimulated by a desire to reduce the task of selection to a numerical process. Although employing tests in this manner is not desirable, they do permit an apparently objective evaluation and lend a scientific "halo" to the selection process when they are used. It may be argued that numerical rating through the use of tests is no more conclusive than subjective rating without their use, since subjectivity must be introduced in developing any numerical standard evaluation. On the other hand, if those administering the tests are fully aware of their limitations, they can be a valuable technique when used with the other means.

For the most part, tests for salesman selection measure mental ability, aptitude, and personality. One source of difficulty with tests is the way in which they are interpreted. Most companies rely on standard tests, which may be purchased from companies which provide testing services. Results must be interpreted in the light of the job for which the applicant is to be selected. To effectively use tests of any kind, standards of test performance must be established. This can be done only by administering the test to both good and poor salesmen alike. Once a significant variation in test results between good and poor salesmen is demonstrated, the test may be used to evaluate the presence or absence of certain characteristics detailed in the man specifications. This is called *validation of the test*.

Validation of tests for a specific purpose complicates their use, but unless this is done they may do more harm than good. They become a means of shifting responsibility for the selection of capable personnel. Responsibility is shifted to the test, and it becomes a substitute for the exercise of sound judgment by management.

When the time comes to make a final decision on an applicant, the person or persons responsible for making the decision ordinarily have at their disposal a wealth of information about the applicant. If the selection program has been soundly conceived, they also have a detailed statement of the requirements necessary to perform on the job in the man specification. Through the exercise of careful judgment, the characteristics of the applicant and the man specification must be matched and a final decision made. There is no way of evading the exercise of judgment in this procedure.

Selecting Manufacturers' Agents

Selecting manufacturers' agents is very similar to selecting any distributor that will represent the manufacturer in the market place. Agent selection will be improved when attention is directed to the following practices:

1. Comprehensive knowledge of the agent and his lines and operations should be obtained. Inquiries should be made of some of the manufacturers the agent is already representing and some of the customers the agent is selling to, or should be selling to. Personal interviews should be conducted with the prospective agent in all cases.

2. The agent should select his lines with the objectives of: each line being closely related to the others; each customer called on as a potential buyer of all

lines handled; the price and quality of each line is compatible; lines limited to the extent that aggressive representation may be afforded all.

3. Similar or identical territories should exist for all products sold by the agent so that maximum trade cultivation and continuous representation of all client-manufacturers is possible.

4. The agent-principal relationship should be surrounded with an environment of mutual confidence, cooperation, and integrity. The manufacturer should sincerely declare his intentions of permanent agent representation and thus alleviate the agent's fear of loss of the line. The representative should accept the line only if he intends to devote sufficient time and effort so that gratifying sales will be forthcoming.

5. The rate of commission should be carefully determined. Adequate commissions should be established to entice high-caliber agents as well as to promote aggressive representation. In other words, compensation should be lucrative enough to command the quality of representation capable of supplying gratifying sales volume.

6. The manufacturers' agent should be supplied with adequate tools to operate effectively in the field. Promotional aids and engineering and sales assistance should be made available to the representative. Agent suggestions should be freely solicited. By the same token, the representative should make a sincere effort to honor his principal's reasonable requests for information, records, and other pertinent data related to the territory and to his operation.

7. A comprehensive contractual agreement should be formulated in writing. Such contracts normally have termination clauses, but many techniques can be applied to free either party from such an agreement. The purpose of the contract is not primarily to supply legal protection. Rather, its major benefit is that the agent and his principal are forced to consider and come to a definite understanding about numerous policies and procedures at the outset of the relationship. Even in good faith, misunderstandings may develop without such an explicit agreement. For example, the division of split commissions may cause friction unless the division of the shares is clear in advance.

SALES TRAINING

With the sales force selected, the next task is to provide the kind of training necessary to insure performance on the job. It is not often that a company can escape the need to provide some training for the sales force. Even if in the selection process it sets its standards high, there will always be some aspects of the job description that require knowledge that a new employee is not likely to have. If some training is necessary, the major questions are: How much? and How should it be conducted?

Many factors influence the amount of training necessary. First is the experience of the new salesmen. If they have had considerable selling experience, this may be one aspect of training that can be minimized. However, some training must be given because of variations in company practice. If they are "green," so to speak, considerable training in salesmanship may be necessary. The second factor is the product lines they are to sell. If the products are complex, technical familiarity with them might require extensive training. The ease with which familiarity with the product may be accomplished will depend on the levels of knowledge required in the man specification. Third is the customer group upon which the salesmen are to call. A salesman selling processed foods to a divisional food chain-store buyer needs an altogether different kind of understanding of the buyer's problems than one selling to the small independent retail store. Both customers talk an entirely different language.

The task of determining how much training is needed cannot be separated from the knowledge and skills in which training is needed. The job description again provides the basis for establishing the content of the training program. In the job description all of the duties of the salesman are described. Experienced personnel must then determine what kinds of knowledge and skills are necessary to perform these duties. As soon as a list of knowledge and skills and levels of accomplishment in each is established, these can be compared with the characteristics of the salesman. The man specification used for selection purposes dealt with requirements that would *potentially* enable the man to perform the job. There may be wide differences between the knowledge and skills necessary to perform on the job and those necessary for selection. Matching the list of knowledge and skills needed with the characteristics of the man will give some indication of the content and extent of the training program. By approaching training in this way there is some assurance that the sales force will be provided with the skills and knowledge necessary for effective performance on the job.

Although variations in training programs are found between different companies, the National Society of Sales Training Executives has found that the content of most sales training programs covers: (1) company organization, (2) sales policies and procedures, (3) selling techniques, (4) technical knowledge or information, and (5) production practices. The specific content in each of these areas will vary by need; however, some generalizations may be made.

Company Organization

Two purposes are served by providing the new salesman with information about the company. First, it may serve as convenient subject matter for indoctrination. By going over the history of the company and its present organization and competitive position, it is possible to develop in the new employee an enthusiastic attitude toward the company and the job he has undertaken. Second, some understanding of the history of the organization is needed to provide a rationale for the present policies of the firm. The general policies which guide the operations of a firm evolve for the most part over a period of time. Familiarity with its history provides a logic for current attitudes within the company. Familiarity with the lines of authority and responsibility is essential in the work situation. When the employee is familiar with the organization of the company, waste of time can be reduced in the search for solutions to exceptional problems.

Training in this area is needed by all employees, and it is not related to the caliber of the employee, the product, or the customer groups to which they are selling.

Sales Policies and Procedures

Since the policies and the operating procedures used to implement policy are the guidelines within which the salesman works, he must know and understand them. Policies relating to customers, such as adjustments, service, credit, delivery, and discounts, as well as the operating procedures used to carry out these policies, must be known to each salesman. Policies relating to the salesman, such as compensation, reports, vacation, and working hours, should be fully understood if the salesman is to perform his duties in the desired way. An understanding of policies relating to activities in support of personal selling, such as advertising, sales promotion, price, and physical distribution, should also be known to the salesman. Without a complete understanding of company policies, the salesman will appear unsure of himself to the customer, and a breakdown in confidence by both the customer and the salesman is likely to result. Policies and procedures, like company organization, are unique to the company providing the training, and must be understood by all salesmen.

Selling Techniques

After the indoctrination material is covered, attention may be turned to the development of other skills needed to perform the selling job. Training in salesmanship must be provided in varying degrees, depending on the previous experience of the salesman. If many of the men have had considerable sales experience in the same industry or in selling similar products, the amount of training in selling techniques may be minimal. If they have had little previous sales experience, this area may well constitute the bulk of the program. Regardless of experience, some training must be given to insure that the salesman incorporates the personality of the company in his selling efforts. It is common to find different selling techniques being used by two competitors in the same industry.

Technical Knowledge or Information

Technical knowledge may be grouped into three types. The first is knowledge of the customer's operation. The salesman selling industrial equipment needs to be familiar with the customers' production processes and the way in which the equipment he is selling may be used in those processes. The pharmaceutical detail man must be familiar with the drugs he is handling and the clinical results of their use in order to talk intelligently with the physician. The second type of technical knowledge is of the markets in which the salesman is selling— the kinds of users, the number of potential buyers, and their location. As much qualitative information as possible about the forces operating in the purchase decision must be passed on to the salesman. Any research information on the effectiveness of advertising and other supporting activities should be made available.

The third type of technical knowledge concerns the production practices of the company. A working knowledge of the materials used and the production processes employed in the manufacture of the goods the salesman is selling is desirable. Many customer questions can be answered and many customer objections overcome with this kind of information. It is also desirable for the salesman to be familiar with the production practices of competitors. Many a sale can hinge upon convincing the customer that what he sells offers advantages in materials and processes over competitors' products.

Once the subject matter to be included in each of the general categories suggested has been decided upon, decisions must be made on how, where, and by whom the material should be presented. The most logical approach is to examine the subject matter to be covered in the training program. Methods of imparting information are limited to books, charts, slide films, motion pictures, models, or lectures. A review of the subject matter will indicate the best methods for imparting certain types of subject matter. In all likelihood the organization and history of the company can be imparted by a combination of lectures, charts, and written materials or, if available, by motion pictures. It is doubtful whether the same methods can be used to impart information about selling techniques. Unfortunately, imparting information is not training; the material imparted must be used in some way to enhance the learning process.

When a means of imparting the information is selected and a method of training decided upon, individuals from the management team should be selected to fit the method of training to be used. It is obvious that some of these people will be top management personnel located in the head office and others will be line management in the field. This gives a partial answer as to where the training should be carried out. Generally, the indoctrination sessions dealing with company organization, policies and procedures, and production practices can be given best at the head office. The lack of physical facilities, the number of salesmen to be trained, and the cost of keeping all salesmen at the head office for a period may shift the training location to the field, where training in selling is usually conducted.

Training is not only concerned with the preparation of new salesmen. Because of the constant introduction of new products, expansion into new markets, and changes in policies and procedures, training is continuous. It must be provided in some form for experienced salesmen. As we approach the problem of continuous *development* of experienced salesmen, the objectives change. Training and development programs must be designed to meet specific objectives and problems.

If manufacturers' agents are used, arrangements should be made to have the agent spend a sufficient amount of time at the manufacturer's plant to gain an intimate knowledge of the products, manufacturing processes, company policies, and the marketing program. Inasmuch as the training period must, of necessity, be brief, it should be well planned and executed.

Without some attention to sales training requirements a company cannot expect to use personal selling as an effective communications instrument. But even with sales training, much care must be exercised if the field sales force is to be able to deliver the maximum impact at the point of sale.

MOTIVATION

With the sales force selected, trained, and assigned to their respective territories, the remainder of the task of sales management is to insure that performance is as planned. If one could be certain that salesmen properly selected and adequately trained would perform as expected, the only task left would be that of providing a system of rewards for effort expended. Unfortunately such utopian performance cannot be expected, and a number of activities must be undertaken to prevent deviations from expected performance.

The word *motivation,* as used here, is not meant to convey only the development of enthusiasm. It is used in a broader sense to connote the direction of salesmen's activities in conformance with plans. A number of different elements such as personal supervision, salesmen's reporting systems, sales meetings, sales contests, sales correspondence, job rotation, promotion, salary administration, and compensation all influence the motivation of the salesman. We shall examine only two of these: supervision and compensation.

Supervision

The salesman in the field is somewhat removed from personal contact with his superiors. He works alone most of the time, representing the company to prospective and actual customers. He needs direction when dealing with particularly unusual problems, and he needs his enthusiasm stimulated from time to time. This is the job of supervision.

Personal supervision means the use of sales supervisors or managers who are periodically in touch with the salesman. Their job is to insure that the man is performing in accordance with the job description. They identify weak spots in the salesman's management of the territory, and take the necessary steps to get the man to remedy the situation. Salesmen's reports are frequently an integral part of the supervision process. Reports are used principally for two reasons. First, they are an evaluation device, and through analysis of them management is able to determine those situations calling for corrective action. Second, they force the salesman to engage in certain activities deemed desirable by the company simply because these activities must be reported.

In supervision systems there is a problem of balancing the positive benefits to be derived against the possibility of negative results. All forms of supervision run the risk of negative results in the form of high cost and a loss of initiative on the part of the salesman. There is always the irate salesman who believes management does not understand the problems in the territory. Personal supervision which aims at excessive control of the salesman's activities can stifle initiative.

The important question to answer is, How much supervision—and what kind—is needed? This will vary from company to company. Although no specific answer can be given, the type of product, capacity of the salesmen, and size of the organization are influencing factors. If the products are such that there is little variation in the sales task from customer to customer, there is a tendency to standardize the selling operation, use a minimum level of sales personnel, and obtain effective effort by close personal supervision. The sale of tobacco products and of many branded food items falls into this category. Contrast the sale of these goods with the sale of capital goods in the industrial market, where there is frequent adaptation of the product and variation in conditions of sale from customer to customer. This type of sales task cannot be routinized; a high quality of individual is required, and close personal supervision would be very costly and, perhaps, ineffective. In those cases where inexperienced, lower-level field salesmen are used, personal supervision must compensate for the lack of initiative on the part of the salesmen. In smaller companies, informal supervision comes about through constant contact with management. When the company is large and there is little opportunity to confer with management, various levels of personal supervision must be inserted to compensate for the gap.

Complete inbound reporting systems in some cases have been used as a partial substitution for close personal supervision. Analysis of the reports by management may take the place of the personal supervisor's evaluation of conditions in the territory. However, the identification of problems does not solve them, and a reporting system should be accompanied with some form of personal supervision in order to bring about solutions to problems, as well as to serve other motivational purposes.

Compensation

The plan for sales compensation should accomplish two objectives: (1) reward the salesman for his effort, and (2) direct the salesman along certain lines of endeavor. When developing a plan of sales compensation, the developer is faced with two questions: How much should the man receive? and How should this amount be given to him? The answer to the first question achieves the first objective—to reward the salesman for his efforts. The way in which the man earns this amount achieves the second objective—to direct the salesman along certain lines of endeavor.[3]

The company must decide how much the salesman should receive. This will be dependent upon the caliber of man wanted and the state of the labor market, as well as specific policies of the company regarding its own wage structure. Once the level or range of income is established, a return to the job description is necessary to identify those things that must be done to earn the income. The next step is to select a means of payment which will induce the salesman to do the things specified in the job description, and avoid doing those things which are contrary to company policy.

There are available three methods of payment: *salary, commission,* and *bonus.* They may be used singly or in any combination. The point to remember

[3] For a more detailed account of this approach, see Frederick E. Webster, Jr., "Rationalizing Salesmen's Compensation Plans," *Journal of Marketing,* XXX (January 1966), 55–58.

is that these methods direct the salesman along certain lines. For example, the *salary* method offers greatest opportunity for control, in that control may be exercised through other means, such as personal supervision. Also, since the salesman receives income regardless of his productivity, he is more willing to follow directions given to him by management. *Commission* reduces the opportunity for close control of the salesman and even encourages him to promote the easiest products in the line, neglect new accounts, and generally skim the territory. Since the salesman's income is based solely on his own results, it is difficult to control his activities by supervision if he happens to be in disagreement with company policy. These malpractices can be overcome to some extent by separate commission rates on different products, payments for opening new accounts, and bonuses for achieving sales quotas in the territory. However, the plan then becomes excessively complex and costly to administer. *Bonuses* can be used with both salary and commission payments to induce the salesman to engage in certain activities.

Once a method of payment is selected which, it is thought, will direct the salesman's actions properly, the rate of payment must be established. If salary alone is used, there is no problem. If commissions are used, the rate of pay must be adjusted to the sales opportunity in the territory to insure that the man receives the amount deemed desirable.

Prevailing practice is to use a combination of salary and commission and/or bonus. The salary provides the major part of the income, and commissions and bonuses are used to provide incentives up to approximately 20 percent of the base figure established as the income level. A polling of members of the Detroit Sales Executive Club revealed that, of the members present, 20.3 percent used straight salary and 65.6 percent used salary plus bonus or commission.

The *compensation plan* should be viewed as a part of a broader program of incentives and motivation. It must be integrated into all the other activities designed to insure proper direction of the field sales force, and not work at cross-purposes with other activities used to direct the salesman.

If all phases of selecting, training, and motivating the sales force are conceived in an integrated program, the probability of developing a hard-hitting, aggressive sales force is enhanced.

Summary

In almost all markets, an aggressive, well-trained sales force is a necessary condition to surviving competition. Failure to establish a personal selling strategy and to make the necessary investment in the proper development of the sales force is to turn one's back on market opportunity.

Establishment of a personal selling strategy involves the following decision areas: (1) determine objectives of personal selling as they relate to overall marketing objectives; (2) in conjunction with measures of market opportunity, establish preliminary estimates of sales force size and sales budget needs; (3) decide upon control units to be used in assigning manpower and controlling sales effort; (4) in conjunction with workload measures and measures of sales opportunity, determine number of control units and size of sales force needed;

(5) calculate final sales budget to support sales force needs, (6) based upon market information, develop call strategies; and (7) make provision for monitoring sales force performance.

The specific objectives of a sales force development program are as follows: (1) to insure maximum job performance, (2) to develop men to the limit of their capacity, (3) to develop loyalty to the company and reduce turnover in sales personnel, and (4) to assure an adequate supply of trained personnel. Implementation of the program is concerned with selection, training, assignment, and motivation of the sales force. The beginning point in all of these activities is the job description—a detailed statement of what the salesman is expected to do. In the selection program, the main characteristics necessary to potentially perform in the field are derived from the job description. Once the main specifications are known, such tools as the application blank, references, interviews, and tests can be used to evaluate the presence or absence of the necessary characteristics. In training, the job description, along with the characteristics of the sales force, provides the basis for determining what the content of the training program should be. The content of the program is used to determine how information is to be imparted, which training methods shall be used, and by whom, and where training shall be conducted.

Since none of the previously mentioned sales activities can be carried out to perfection, personal supervision and inbound reporting systems are used to insure a minimum of deviations from planned objectives. Various devices are used to generate enthusiasm for the kind of performance desired.

Sales compensation rewards the salesman for productivity and induces him to perform certain activities. The amount the salesman is to receive accomplishes the first purpose, and the method of payment the second.

When all activities are integrated into a total program of sales force development, personal selling as a communications instrument can be a powerful contributor to the total communications mix.

Questions and Problems

1. Why is development of a personal selling strategy important?
2. What decision area is the most difficult in establishing a personal selling strategy? Why?
3. What are the reasons for assigning a salesman a specifically delineated geographic area for which he is responsible?
4. What are the elements involved in determining territories? Should territories ideally be of equal sales opportunity or geographic size? Why?
5. Why should management be especially concerned about the effective development of the sales force?
6. In particular, what should such a program seek to accomplish?
7. What are the uses that can be made of a salesman's job description? How should the job description be formulated?
8. What advantages does the use of time-and-duty study have in job description analysis? How often should job descriptions be reviewed?
9. What are the various devices that can be used to determine whether a particular candidate or sales applicant meets the desired man specifications? What is the particular purpose or special feature of each?

10. What do the tests commonly used in the selection of salesmen measure? What are the advantages of using tests? Are there any dangers?

11. What differences exist between the selection of manufacturers' agents and corporate salesmen?

12. What factors will influence how much training a salesman will need?

13. "Salesmen, properly selected and trained, do not need any special incentives or supervision to obtain desired results. Such practices are only necessary when the men are not fully competent." Comment on this proposition.

14. What are the major compensation plans that tend to be used with salesmen? What are the principal advantages and limitations of each?

15. "The salesman's performance face-to-face with his customer is practically the culmination of the whole marketing process. Virtually all that has gone before is simply preparatory to making a sale. As a result, it is only natural that the best salesmen often earn as much or more than some members of management." Comment.

Models for Price   **27**
Determination

There are no more important decisions in market affairs than those connected with pricing. No matter how intelligently the product, distribution, and communications mixes are conceived, improper pricing of a product may nullify the effect of all other actions. But in spite of the importance of pricing decisions, the skills and analyses which are often used in practice do not approach the professional orientation used in the management of advertising, sales promotion, or personal selling. Perhaps one of the reasons is that price decisions cut across all areas of business operation, and are not centered in any of the functional divisions of the firm's organization. Nevertheless, there are some fundamental theories and principles underlying pricing decisions, and it is the purpose of this chapter to examine them.

In this chapter much reliance is placed on economic theory in developing concepts useful in the determination of price. The role of price as a means of relating the firm to the market is examined first. The role of the price system, the aggregate of all prices, is then explored, with special attention given to interpretation of price behavior within an industry. Theoretical models relating to price determination are developed and applications of the fundamental concepts are made.

THE ROLE OF PRICES

It would be presumptuous to attempt to develop the comprehensive role of prices in a free enterprise economy in a part of one chapter. In a limited way, however, we can present some concepts which will aid in our understanding of prices and how they operate (and influence operations) in the market place.

A natural consequence of freedom is specialization in productive effort. The point is developed in Chapter 15 that whenever specialization exists, exchanges are essential to enable the members of society to satisfy their wants in varying degrees. It is within the process of exchange that value is created. Value is the result of the capacity of the participants in the exchange to resolve conflicts through a process of negotiation. Price is a monetary expression of value and is the focal point of the entire exchange process. The customer's evaluation of the compatibility of the product-image with the self-image, discussed in Chapter 5, is expressed in the price he is willing to pay. Price quantitatively expresses a large number of subjective evaluations made by the consumer and by the supplier concerning the value of the money exchanged for goods sold. Any change in these evaluations will result in a change in the quantity exchanged or a change in price.

The price system, the aggregate of all prices, is a very delicate mechanism which conveys to those concerned the present state of evaluations of buyers and sellers. Another characteristic of the price system is the way in which it operates to keep the conflicts between the participants in an exchange in balance. The equilibrium concept describes a condition in which the conflicts between exchange participants are kept in balance through the adjustment of price. The price will adjust until the quantities demanded and the quantities supplied are equal and a state of equilibrium is achieved. An *equilibrium price* is one that prevails when the quantity of product that suppliers are willing to offer and that consumers are willing to purchase is equal. Consequently, one of the roles of price is to allocate scarce resources in a manner most satisfactory to both consumer and supplier. How does this theory work today?

In Chapter 1 the idea of competition for differential advantage was developed. The objective of competition on this basis is to isolate the competitor from the price of his rival. One of the objectives of advertising as expressed in Chapter 24 was to achieve some degree of inelasticity of demand for purposes of removing the competitor from direct price competition. It is true that much competition today is implemented through marketing action and prevents the price system from allocating resources according to the theoretical model. In fact, firms are faced with the problem of determining price precisely because they have differentiated their product sufficiently to remove them from total reliance on prevailing market prices for similar goods. On the other hand, the effect has not been to nullify completely the role of price in allocating resources. Rather, it has been to slow up the rate of adjustment to new evaluations of consumers and suppliers. Price movements are more sticky, but prices in the long run still exert an influence in the allocation of resources. The discount battles of the fifties are one indication that price is a potent competitive weapon.

Rarely is it necessary for the price system also to direct the allocation of scarce resources. The rapid rate of technological development and the commercial implementation of these developments have not waited for the price system to force efforts in other directions. The initiative has been seized by the manufacturer and intermediaries. Developments are taking place at such a rapid rate that the function of the price system is in large measure relegated to providing a means whereby the consumer can register his evaluation of the new goods that are offered to him. If products and the price at which they are offered are not to his liking, he refuses to purchase until either product or price is changed.

To summarize current affairs: the price system still performs its traditional role of resource allocations. Furthermore, the motivating forces influencing new directions of economic activity do not wait for price movements to telegraph the need and thus stimulate action. The effect of price is after the fact, and in many cases signals the need for continuation or modification of a resource allocation.

From the manager's point of view, it is important to recognize that price functions to some extent in its theoretical role. The prices set by the firm must reflect its best judgment of consumers' evaluations of the offer. They must also reflect the firm's judgment of its capacity to achieve its objectives within the prices established. Since both are in a state of flux, prices do change or, more technically, are volatile. The alert competitor will assess what these price changes mean and adjust his own prices accordingly.

Much concern has been manifested over the pricing practices of entire industries; the prevalence of uniformity of prices among suppliers and little variation in price through time is sometimes interpreted as evidence of undesirable competitive practices. In some cases, this might be a valid interpretation; however, recognizing the role of prices in the economy, such price behavior may be the result of economic forces.

In older industries, where there is less opportunity for any single supplier to gain production economies from scale or more efficient methods, it is logical that there would be some uniformity of price between suppliers. This is particularly true in the case of standardized or homogeneous products in which no supplier has much opportunity to gain a differential product advantage. In fact, there is little reason for any competitor to compete on a price basis, since all would follow, and existing demand is redivided at lower prices and lower revenues to each supplier. Consequently, there is a tendency for all suppliers to move prices upwards together, and little tendency for suppliers to move prices downward, particularly if demand is relatively inelastic.

The relative stability of prices through time may well reflect these basic economic forces. Wide variations in price through time may simply be an indication of changing conditions of supply, such as in the case of agriculture. Excess supply, with no change in demand, can be moved only through price reductions.

For the most part, the arguments concerning the relationship of price behavior to desirable competitive practices are not concerned with the price itself. Rather, they are concerned with the profits which the maintenance of certain prices generates. The moral and ethical considerations here do not rest entirely on economic matters. The question of a "fair" or "just" price cannot be easily resolved. As long as we maintained convictions about the essential value or worth of a free enterprise economy, we are relying on a price system to allocate resources in the most efficient manner. If prices are not freely determined or if there are barriers to entry into a particular industry, price behavior may reflect these rigidities. It is equally possible, however, that in the absence of restrictions on price movement or barriers to entry, profits may still be high or low, with identical price behavior. Care must be exercised in making judgments concerning price behavior and the degree of competition existing.

THEORETICAL CONCEPTS
OF PRICE DETERMINATION

A point of primary importance is to recognize that management is not confronted with just a single pricing problem, but with many. Since the forces which determine the efficacy of pricing decisions vary depending on the problem faced, it is important to realize the kind of pricing problems confronting management. A major distinction divides pricing problems into those dealing with: (1) the determination of price and (2) the administration of price. As these two areas of pricing differ so greatly, this chapter and the next deal with price determination and Chapter 29 with price administration.[1]

The specific problem in price determination is to establish the price for a specific product. A part of this problem is to determine relative prices for variations in a product type as well as relative prices of different products in a line which are associated in purchase and in use. For example, a manufacturer of fishing equipment may be faced with the need to determine a price for a fishing rod, then a price for different rods, and a price for fishing reels and other equipment within the line. Since the subsidiary problems of determining relative prices of products within the line are secondary to determining the price of a specific product, this chapter deals basically with the primary problem.

There are differences in the problems associated with determining prices for new products and products with which the market is familiar. For this reason, Chapter 28 explores some of the unique problems connected with determining prices for new products.

The Role of Prices in the Firm

Pricing may be considered by management as just another element in the mix of market cultivation. Just as advertising, sales promotion, and personal selling are forms of market cultivation, so is price. It is possible, as discussed in Chapter 24, to vary price and other forms of cultivation to achieve that combination which best meets the firm's objectives. On the other hand, price is something more than just another cultivation device. Price is a reflection of all of the actions of the firm. It is symbolic of the kind of product strategy followed, of the system of intermediaries used to make the product available, and of the communications instruments used to persuade the market to purchase. Price is related to product strategy in that interpretations of markets and the development of products to cultivate these markets are expressed in the price placed on the products. In Chapter 12, "Product-Market Integration," the need to

---

[1] For a more detailed classification of pricing problems, see D. M. Phelps and J. H. Westing, *Marketing Management,* rev. ed. (Homewood, Ill.: Richard D. Irwin, Inc., 1960), pp. 271–72.

segment products either physically or psychologically was developed. To place a core price on a product designed for the broader market, including its fringe, would constitute a gross error in management judgment and price analysis.

Price is related to the system of intermediaries used. In Chapter 17 the need for the performance of a number of activities in a manner which meets the objectives of all concerned was emphasized. To price a product at any stage of distribution without giving consideration to the needs of the manufacturer, channel members, and the consumer, materially increases the prospects of market failure. Prices are also related to the entire communications mix, in that the price selected reflects the reliance placed on other communications instruments. Rarely can large sums be spent on various communications instruments concurrent with low prices. Usually, if a company's pricing policy is one of using low prices to increase quantities sold, some sacrifice in other means of demand cultivation must be made.

In the final analysis, price is a major determiner of profits or losses. The conventional accounting identity of price-cost-revenue relationships gives price a significant role to play in determining profit. The size of revenues from which costs are deducted is dependent on price in two ways: (1) revenues are a function of *unit prices* times *quantity* and (2) price as a means of market cultivation is a determinant of quantity. Since quantity has a major bearing on the level of production costs and marketing costs, price again influences the profit equation. This series of relationships must be evaluated by those charged with responsibility for determining prices. Although the basic relationships are shown in accounting statements, a more refined discussion of these relationships is found in economic theory.

Contributions of Economic Theory

Frequently the allegation is made that economic theory has little relevance to the real world and is of little value to the practitioner. However, there is value in theoretical economic models if they are accepted for what they are. The theoretical model describes the way in which competitive forces interact to create profits or losses. It is well to have some technical comprehension of these forces, although they are explained in simpler managerial terms later.

Economists have established four market structures to explain how prices are determined in a free economy. Each is examined separately.

Pure Competition

In this structure the number of sellers is so large and the output of each so small that no single firm can influence the price. The product is completely homogeneous, and each buyer and seller has complete knowledge of conditions in the market place. In such a structure the demand curve is a horizontal straight line; it is perfectly elastic. That is, if a firm raised its price over the market price, it would sell nothing; and as it can sell all it makes at the market price, there is no tendency to lower price. Under these circumstances the firm has no pricing problem. It simply makes a quantity adjustment to the market price in a manner that maximizes profits. Prices in this kind of structure are often called market prices.

Cases of pure competition are rare, with the agricultural commodity markets coming closest. But even here there is so much governmental interference in both supply and demand that these markets are not purely competitive markets.

Pure Monopoly

This market structure is the reverse of pure competition and is characterized by the dominance of one firm. Since there are no substitutes, the demand curve is the same as the industry curve and slopes to the right. Any increase in price, decreases the volume that will be purchased, and any decrease in price may increase the volume a little. The pricing problem in this kind of market structure is to determine the best combination of price and quantity to achieve the goals of the company. These prices are often called business-controlled prices because the firm does control the price it will ask. Sometimes, as in the case of public utilities, the price is set by a governmental agency and is called a government-controlled price. It is doubtful whether there is such a thing as a pure monopoly, as the firm must still compete for a share of the consumers' disposable income. From a theoretical point of view, it does, however, represent a polar extreme.

Monopolistic Competition

In this market structure there are a large number of buyers and sellers, but each seller differentiates his product slightly. In effect each firm becomes a small monopolist. On the other hand, the offerings of rivals are substitutes, and the demand curve slopes to the right but is not nearly so steep as in the case of the pure monopoly. This is so because of the number of close substitutes.

Since this is the most typical market structure in which corporate enterprise functions today, we shall examine it in more detail. The most common geometric description of the way a firm will price in this kind of market structure is shown in Figure 27-1. Let us examine it and determine what relationships are implied. Figure 27-1A describes the relationship between input and output and is sometimes referred to as *the production function*. The total output curve is divided into four stages. In Stage I, output is increasing at an accelerating rate until the rate of increase reaches a maximum at point A. In Stage II, output increases at a slower rate until the rate of increase is equal to average output at point B. In Stage III, output continues to increase at a slower rate until maximum output is reached at point C, at which point output begins to decline in Stage IV. Marginal output and average output are derived from the total output curve.

Marginal output—the increase in total output resulting from an additional unit of input—reaches a maximum when the rate of increase in total output is at a maximum, and will decline to zero when the total output is at a maximum. Average output—the number of units of output per unit of input—reaches a maximum when the rate of increase in total output is equal to average output, and declines thereafter. Another relationship of interest is that marginal output equals average output when the latter is at a maximum.

In Figure 27-1B, the costs connected with the output characteristics described in 27-1A are portrayed. The behavior of both fixed and variable costs are shown. *Fixed costs* are those costs which do not vary with output. They are fixed in total and vary per unit and, consequently, influence the average total cost curve. Fixed costs do not influence the marginal cost curve because by definition *marginal cost* is the increase in total cost necessary to produce an additional unit of output. *Variable costs* are those which vary with output. These costs are fixed per unit of output but vary in total cost. The average fixed-cost curve declines over the entire output range. Marginal cost is at a minimum where marginal output is at a maximum. Average variable cost is at a minimum where average output is at a maximum. Marginal cost is equal to average cost

FIGURE 27-1
Output, Cost, and Demand Curves

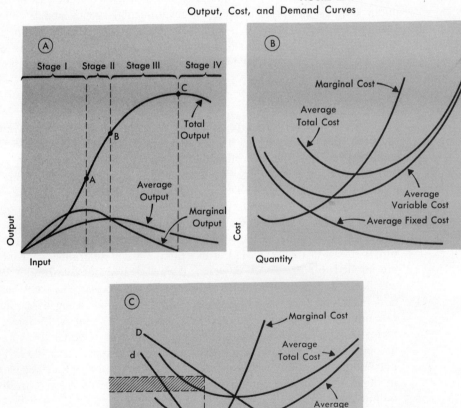

where average cost is at a minimum. Average total cost, the combination of average fixed cost and average variable cost, is at a minimum to the right of the point where the average variable-cost curve is at a minimum, as it must reflect the constantly decreasing influence of the average fixed cost.

In Figure 27-1C the demand curve is added to the cost curve. The curve DD represents the average revenues associated with each unit sold. The average revenue is simply the price charged. As price declines, the quantity which will be demanded increases. The curve dd is the marginal revenue curve and depicts the increases in total revenue from the sale of the last unit sold. Marginal revenue must fall faster than the average-revenue curve as output increases. Any increase in units sold can only come about at a lower price, and consequently the decrease in average revenue is equal to the reduction of selling price, but the decrease in marginal revenue is affected by the lower selling price averaged over all units sold.

In simpler managerial terms, under the conditions set forth in Figure 27-1, the firm will make a price and quantity adjustment which will maximize profits. It will sell that quantity at which marginal cost equals marginal revenue and set the price at the average revenue for that quantity. To offer less than this amount would be foregoing the opportunity to reap additional profits on additional units sold. To offer a greater quantity would incur loss on each unit sold beyond the point at which marginal cost equals marginal revenues. Conceptually, this matter shows that two sets of forces have a bearing on the determination of profitable prices. The first set of forces is costs. They are internal to the firm and, for the most part, are controllable. The second set of forces are those included in the demand schedule. They are external to the firm and, although not controllable, are subject to influence by different marketing actions.

Circularity between the two sets of forces exists in the following way. The costs of the firm are not totally production costs. Marketing costs are also included. Since some of these are incurred as a result of activities designed to persuade potential customers to buy the product, they have an influence on the quantity that will be demanded. Likewise, price itself influences the quantity demanded. Quantity, on the other hand, influences the unit costs at different levels of output, as shown in Figure 27-1. The general objective of the firm in determining prices is to combine these internal and external forces in such a way that objectives are achieved. A satisfactory level of long-run profit is an absolute essential to the maintenance of a healthy enterprise. Once the relationship is established between both sets of forces, final pricing decisions can be made with full recognition of the outcome, if precision in measurement can be presumed. The prices in this market structure are called business-controlled prices because the individual firm has some control over the price it will charge.

Practitioners often complain that costs do not behave as depicted by the theoretical model. To be sure, current accounting systems do not allow the measurement of cost with the precision assumed, nor do they isolate decision costs. It matters little whether costs do behave as assumed, since some cost structure is prevalent in every combination of the factors of production. Regardless of the nature of cost behavior, it does influence the profit outcome of different prices in some way.

The difficulty of determining the demand schedule presents serious problems. The demand schedule assumes rational, economic behavior. The "diminishing marginal utility" explanation of demand does imply a highly simplified mechanism of the way in which consumers satisfy their wants. On the other hand, a demand schedule is a combination of monetary, real, and psychic forces. It is psychic in that it really depicts a balancing of the utility expected against the disutility required to earn the income necessary to purchase the product. This disutility is expressed in terms of price, a monetary expression. The utility is expressed in terms of the quantity that will be taken at a series of prices, a real expression. The important thing to keep in mind is that utility represents a host of psychological forces bearing upon the individual's desire for goods and his assessment of the value of different quantities of goods to him. The explanation for purchase behavior developed in Chapter 7 is treated here in this simplified way for the purpose of geometric description. Obviously, we cannot draw a highly precise demand curve for a given product, but since we know that price does influence the quantities that will be demanded, we must make some approximation of the demand schedule in making price decisions.

Although the theory of the firm does present some difficult measurement problems, it is a valid point of departure in price determination. Its most valuable contribution is to depict the way cost, demand, and price interact to create profits or losses. The most significant lesson of all to be learned from the model is that a profitable price cannot be determined from demand alone or cost alone, but only from a combination of both. While the practical measurement problem is a severe one, we must deal with it as best we can with currently available tools of sales-cost-profit forecasting.

Oligopoly

A few large sellers characterizes the oligopolistic market structure. Because of the fewness of sellers the actions of any one has an effect on the others, and so in pricing each will carefully consider retaliatory actions. If the product is homogeneous, there will be a tendency for price uniformity. If the products are differentiated, there may be different prices with the degree of difference dependent upon the extent of differentiation in product. The demand curve in this kind of market structure is depicted in Figure 27-2, and is known as a "kinked" demand curve. In this case the prevailing price is OB. There is little tendency to decrease price below OB, as all sellers would follow suit and they might end up sharing the market as before, but at lower total revenues. If a firm were to increase price to OE, the other firms will not likely do so, and the firm increasing its price will lose a considerable share of the market. Consequently, the demand curve faced by the individual firm is much more elastic above the prevailing price OB than below it. In oligopolistic industries the price does change over time. All firms increase the price together, establishing a new price from which there is not likely to be any departure for some time.

APPLICATION OF
PRICING FUNDAMENTALS

Recognizing the relationship between cost and demand, let us look more closely at the central problem of price determination—that of *prediction*. If no

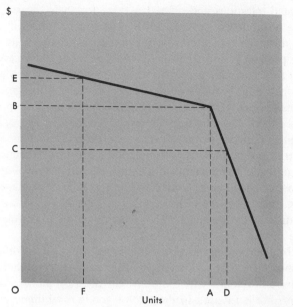

FIGURE 27-2
Demand Curve
under Conditions
of Oligopoly

uncertainties were present, the task of determining prices to meet any objective would be comparatively simple.

The types of predictions that must be made may be divided into three groups: (1) determine the effect of different combinations of distribution mix, communications mix, and price on quantity; (2) determine the effect of quantities on production costs; and (3) determine the effect of quantities on marketing costs.

Quantity Effects of the Marketing Mix

Some decision must be made regarding which distribution mix to use and the preferred combination of advertising, sales promotion, and personal selling. The kinds of analyses necessary to do this have been developed in the chapters dealing with these activities. In the initial stages of price determination these must be held constant, and an attempt must be made to determine the quantities that may be expected at different prices, utilizing a fixed combination of distribution and communications mixes. This is a forecasting problem. All of the techniques developed in Chapters 6 and 7 must be used to gain some estimate of quantities that will be demanded at different prices. This task is most difficult when dealing with new products, and some of the techniques used are treated in Chapter 28.

With old products, experience can give some clues. *Historical approaches* to quantitative market investigations may be useful. *Experimental pricing* can be used in test markets to assess quantity responses to different prices. *Surveys* have been used to gain consumers' opinions and attitudes about the value of products to them and the price they may be willing to pay. Barter experiments have been used to estimate the quantities that may be taken at various prices. A situation is created in which a group of potential customers is asked a series of unrelated questions and offered a prize for their cooperation. They are given a choice of products, and it is assumed that the choice will reveal the product they value most. They then may be asked a series of questions about their evaluations. If the product is too expensive to give as a gift, they may be offered the opportunity to participate in a raffle, in which the item is the prize. Sometimes a sum of money may be offered as a prize as well. Willingness to select the money rather than any of the merchandise may indicate the upper limit for any of the goods offered (barring present ownership). *Customer analysis* may indicate the quantities that can be achieved at various prices. This is particularly useful in industrial goods markets in which there are trade practices concerning the percentage cost of components in the finished item. For example, in the shoe industry the cost of shoe soles rarely exceeds a certain percentage of the manufacturer's selling price. The size of the market for varying price levels of shoes gives some indication of the range of prices which would successfully include each segment of the demand for soles.

In determining the amounts that will be taken at different prices, consideration should be given to psychological reactions of potential buyers. Three practices have developed which do have an effect on the quantities that will be taken. *Odd pricing* is favored in the sale of goods to ultimate consumers. Although its origin relates to the control of sales personnel in retail establishments, it is thought that more can be sold at a price of $5.99 than at $6.00. In Figure 27-3A, it can be seen that at prices O_1 and O_2 more is sold than at prices E_1 and E_2 respectively. Likewise, it is thought that there are natural break points in prices. *Psychological pricing* attempts to determine these points. Over a range, price decreases will increase volume sold until a critical point is reached. Further reductions in price will not affect the quantity sold until the next critical point is reached. This situation is depicted in Figure 27-3B. Prices P_1, P_2, P_3, and P_4 are critical points. *Prestige pricing* is another pricing practice usually found in high-priced luxury goods. The principle followed here is that at low prices a low quality interpretation is made by the consumer, and the quantity sold will be less than at a higher price. Figure 27-3C shows a larger quantity sold at P_2 than at P_3. Of course there is a higher price at which less will be sold, P_1. The practice is not solely confined to high-priced goods and is very prevalent in the cosmetics industry.

In all cases, an attempt is made to measure the size of the market at various prices for a given product type. The share of that market which can be expected at these prices by the firm trying to establish a price must be taken into consideration. Competitive conditions must be analyzed. It is a purely judgmental decision which can be made only on the basis of experience—experience concerning the relative merits of products offered, past penetration of markets, and the reputation of the seller. Often a total market estimate is made and relatively small shares of the market at different prices are assumed. The analysis is continued and the resulting position of the firm is determined, assuming these quantities. If a price can be selected which meets objectives at a very small quantity, the assumption is made that surely that quantity threshold can be achieved. This may be considered a case of eternal pessimism. If a price can be established which requires only one half of one percent of the total market to meet ob-

FIGURE 27-3
Odd, Psychological, and Prestige Pricing

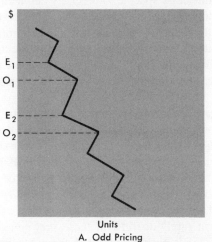

A. Odd Pricing

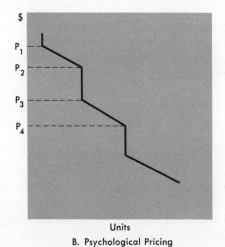

B. Psychological Pricing

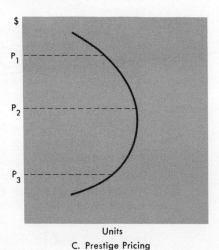

C. Prestige Pricing

Source: Adapted from Edward R. Hawkins, "Price Policies and Theory," Journal of Marketing, XVIII (January 1954), 233–40.

jectives, surely the firm can capture this share, and if this share proves to be conservative, operating results will be just that much better.

Quantity Effect on Production Costs

Quantity, as established in the theoretical model, does affect unit production costs. It is assumed that any combination of the factors of production results in a successive condition of decreasing cost, constant cost, and increasing cost. All of these are related to the returns to scale demonstrated in the output curve in Figure 27-1A. If cost does not behave in this manner, accounting procedures are not sufficiently specific to precisely delineate these stages. This does not mean that accountants are not capable of tracing cost more closely than they currently do, only that the cost of such systems has not been considered by management as warranted. Such systems would be particularly difficult and costly in multi-product firms. The need to allocate joint costs to each product can only be done arbitrarily, and there is no assurance the result actually describes the true cost function.

Regardless of the accountant's ability to isolate the true cost function, the assumptions in the theoretical model have been challenged.[2] It is argued that the average variable cost curve is a saucer-shaped line which indicates some increases in unit costs at very small quantities and at the outer limit of capacity, and constant unit costs in between. When fixed costs are added to variable costs, the total average cost curve declines over the entire range of output until capacity is reached. Fortunately, there is some empirical evidence to support this belief.[3] Since a firm rarely operates at those very small volumes where average costs are high, and avoids pushing output to the outer limit of capacity, it is a fair assumption that a constant variable cost approach is both conservative and acceptable.

Another approach views production as an integration and aggregation of a series of operating stages. The number of stages to be used can be varied depending upon output. Since each stage has certain fixed proportions, discontinuities in the fixed-cost curve are much more marked, and it must be represented as a step function over the entire output range.

It is impossible to relate these fixed inputs to specific outputs, and it is assumed that fixed costs have no value in estimating the short-run cost function. Thus, variable costs are the only costs which need to be considered in making price and quantity adjustments. This approach, called *direct costing,* is gaining rather widespread current use, and we can expect more company managements to pay major attention to variable cost components in making pricing decisions.

Translated into accounting terminology, fixed costs are "period costs," or costs which produce results only through the passage of time. Since nothing can be done about fixed costs in the short run, all price-quantity adjustments should be carried out in terms of variable costs, or *product costs,* as they are called by the accountant. Attention is directed toward maximizing net revenue contributions to period costs.

Since variable costs are assumed to be constant over a wide output range, the prediction of the effect of different quantities on production cost is not difficult.

[2] T. Scitovsky, *Welfare and Competition* (Homewood, Ill.: Richard D. Irwin, Inc., 1951), pp. 308–11.

[3] Joel Dean, *Managerial Economics* (Englewood Cliffs, N.J.: Prentice-Hall, Inc., 1951), pp. 292–96.

Quantity Effect on Marketing Cost

The classification of all costs into fixed and variable is a function of the time period covered. All costs are variable in the long run, and all are fixed in the short run. Within the usual planning period of a year, the classification has merit. However, the classification of marketing costs into fixed and variable is not so simple as in the case of production costs.

Marketing costs are of three types: (1) sales-getting costs, (2) order-filling costs, and (3) sales-maintenance costs. Sales-getting costs, such as advertising, sales promotion, and personal selling costs, with the exception of salesmen's commissions, cannot be related to any specific result. Simple dividing of past sales volume into historical cost data does not make the resulting unit cost variable. In fact, the dynamic nature of markets makes this procedure dangerous. Even if it were possible to impute sales revenues to specific marketing costs, there is no assurance that a similar expenditure a year later would produce a similar result.

Sales-getting costs are not variable. Once an expenditure is made or contracted for, such as salesmen's employment agreements or advertising contracts awarded, it is most difficult to reverse the procedure if the expected sales volume is not forthcoming. Further, these costs are not present over the entire sales volume range, as is the case with those fixed costs associated with plant and production equipment. Sales-getting costs are made at different points in time over the entire sales volume range. A new cost situation exists each time additional sales-getting costs are incurred. They are fixed in nature and are analogous to the integration and aggregation of operating stages in production and must be represented as a step function.

Can they be disregarded, as in the case of fixed production costs? This would be a faulty approach, for two reasons. First, the sales-getting costs represent the greatest share of total marketing costs. Since marketing costs may represent almost 50 percent of selling price, to disregard them is to disregard a large proportion of cost. Second, it denies the opportunity to manage sales-getting costs in the short run.

Order-filling costs, such as packing, shipping, and transportation and delivery costs, are necessary because the sales-getting costs have been successful. In this case the cause-and-effect relationship between input and output is reversed. With order-filling costs the output, sales revenue, makes necessary the input, the order-filling costs. In most cases it is possible to relate these costs to specific sales. They are variable costs and can be assumed to be constant over a wide sales volume range.

Sales-maintenance costs are those which must be made to maintain a sales volume level. If sales-getting costs are successful in generating sales, it may be necessary to add additional sales personnel or new storage facilities or transportation equipment. These costs are closer to fixed rather than variable, as are the sales-getting costs, and must be represented in a fixed-cost step function.

The greatest proportion of marketing costs are fixed for short periods of time. They are similar to the "period costs" of production. Since they are a substantial portion of total costs, they must be taken into consideration through a discontinuous fixed-cost function. From a prediction point of view it is necessary to: (1) determine at what points over the sales volume range marketing costs will be incurred and (2) determine what order-filling and sales-maintenance costs will be necessary at different volume levels.

Combining Quantity and Cost Measurements

In Figure 27-4 the relationships between cost, quantity, and price are manipulated. This is a modified break-even analysis. It assumes a constant variable cost both for production and the order-filling cost of marketing. It also assumes a step function for the other marketing costs. Fixed production costs are treated as "period costs" and disregarded. The vertical axis represents total revenues or total costs. The horizontal axis is a range of quantities. The price lines are plotted by assuming a price and multiplying it by different quantities to determine total revenues.

In this hypothetical case a manufacturer is selling 3,000 units without any

FIGURE 27-4
Combining Cost, Quantity, and Price Relationships

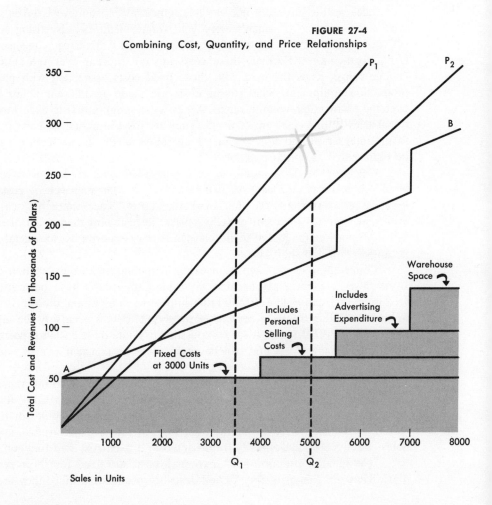

changes in the cost structure. The manager plans to increase sales volume, and plans additional marketing effort in the form of more intense cultivation of the market. At 4,000 units the plans call for two new salesmen on a salary basis. Advertising expenditures are held constant until the spring campaign, and at 5,500 units, additional expenditures are made. At 7,000 units new warehouse space must be added.

With these assumptions as to marketing expenditures for the year, the total cost function is represented in the line AB. In reality the method of treating costs approaches a marginal cost calculation. Instead of dealing with the marginal cost associated with the last unit sold, attention is directed toward increases in marketing cost associated with additional chunks of sales volume.

With the marketing mix represented by the line AB, the quantity assumptions at different prices may now be taken into consideration. If with P_1, a quantity of Q_1 is forecast, certain profits result. If with P_2, Q_2 is forecast, another profit situation results. It is possible to speculate on the outcome of any price.

Of particular importance is the effect of the total cost step function. It creates pockets of profitability. Unless an additional cost input moves the volume beyond a cost peak on the total cost line, it may be more profitable to forego the additional volume.

Determining Price Differentials

At the beginning of this section it was stated that price determination involves setting the price for a specific product as well as establishing price differentials between variations of a single product type and between different products in the line. At the outset it should be recognized that there is little need to consider relationships in prices of products that are not related in purchase and use. When products are related there is some merit in maintaining relationships between the prices of the products within the line.

The problem is always present when there are variations in quality and size. The usual procedure is to determine the base price for the high-volume item, and establish differentials on the basis of cost differences. This appears to be a one-sided approach to the problem and denies the very reasons for the existence of product variety. In Chapter 12, product variety was shown as a major means of penetrating different segments of the market. To fail to include the demand elements in the pricing computation is impractical. A return to the basic reason for variety will indicate the types of price differentials which provide the maximum possibilities of achieving objectives.

When the problem is one of pricing different products within a line, the initial step is to price a specific product. Each product must be priced separately. Once the bench-mark prices are established, a blending of prices is attempted. For example, in the case of fishing equipment, fishing rods may be priced in the medium price range. If, in the establishment of the base price on reels, the price is drifting toward the top of the price range for reels, it may be necessary to scale downward to approach the medium price range. Judgment must be exercised in establishing price differentials of this sort.

PRICING TO ACHIEVE
CORPORATE OBJECTIVES

The objectives of the price established should parallel the objectives of the firm. The objectives of the firm, however, are not always internally consistent, and close inspection may show them to be very much in conflict. For example, there may be a conflict between the desire for short-run profitability and a desire to gain prestige by being the biggest firm in the industry. It is through a review of corporate objectives that specific pricing policies are developed. To state that the only objective of price determination is to maximize profits is to oversimplify the problem. Obviously, profits are a measure of success and are important for survival. The refinements introduced by stating long-run profitability as a goal may be a very logical and meritorious objective, but it is of limited value in guiding the determiner of prices. Pricing policies must be more specific and give direction to decision making.

Some of the most common policies related to price determination are: (1) return-on-investment pricing; (2) penetration pricing; (3) skimming pricing; (4) ethical pricing; (5) full-line pricing; and (6) minimization-of-loss pricing. *Return-on-investment pricing* requires that the price determiner calculate the returns available at the different prices and quantities assumed in the analysis of the preceding section. He will select that price which most nearly approximates the return desired. *Penetration pricing* is closely related to the overall corporate objective of growth. Under such a policy the price which maximizes profits would not be selected. Rather, a price which maximizes quantity at a satisfactory profit level would be chosen. It is selected on the assumption that it would enable the company to penetrate certain markets, win customer loyalty, limit new firm entrants, and generate long-run profitability for the firm. A penetration policy is generally analogous to a low-price policy.

Skimming pricing, on the other hand, involves pricing in such a way as to "skim off the cream" of a market. Those potential customers that are not adversely influenced by high price are the target of this pricing policy. It is generally followed where no entrants are expected to follow, and to enable a recoupment of investment as fast as possible. It results in a price at which profits are maximized and contributes to short-run profitability. *Ethical pricing* involves concern over questions of public welfare, as in the case of immunization drugs. In these cases the firm is faced with a responsibility to the public. In such cases, the price which produces satisfactory profits may be unacceptable to the market. It is unacceptable in the sense that only a small number can take advantage of the product, or that the price would bring a deluge of public criticism. Under such circumstances, a price much lower than that necessary to maximize profits or satisfactory return on investment may be used. The multiproduct firm is in a much better position to follow such practices than a single-product firm, as it can cover small losses on (spread their cost over) some products in the remainder of the line.

Full-line pricing is also similar to ethical pricing, but for a different reason. The offering of a full line may be predicated on the assumption that one product aids the sale of others. Because of cost-quantity relationships, it may be necessary to price some products at very high prices to satisfactorily insure a profit. The price in itself may defeat the purpose of the full line. Consequently, products may even be sold at below profitable price levels, with the result that the loss is absorbed by other products in the line. *Minimization-of-loss pricing* is another case of pricing below cost. In high-fixed-cost industries, idle plants are excessively costly. If by reducing prices the plant can be utilized, any contribution to fixed cost reduces losses. The firm may set prices which are below total cost but not below average variable costs.

Regardless of the pricing policy pursued, it is important to make the decision with some knowledge of the possible outcome. Only through measurement of the quantities expected at different prices and the effect of different quantities on production and marketing costs can intelligent price decisions be made.

LEGAL IMPLICATIONS
OF PRICE DETERMINATION

In addition to consideration of the relationship between cost and demand, the price maker is confronted with another external variable, the legal framework. The legal influences are of two types: (1) statutory law and (2) governmental intervention.

With respect to statutory law, there is only one law which is of concern, and it does not apply to the price determination practices of manufacturers. Rather, it governs the pricing practices of intermediaries. Unfair Sales Acts or Unfair Practices Acts have been passed in thirty states, and twenty-five of the acts are still in existence. These acts are designed to prevent predatory price cutting. Price cutting at any level of distribution cannot be prevented if it is based upon low-cost merchandise and efficient operating methods. It is the major means of passing on improvements and marketing efficiency to the consumer. However, the sale of merchandise below cost is considered predatory and it is prohibited in those states with unfair sales statutes.

The general effect of such laws has been negligible because of poor enforcement. Most laws require that a wholesaler add 2 percent at least and a retailer about 6 percent to the merchandise cost to cover the cost of doing business. In a retail or wholesale establishment the broad line of products carried does not permit the calculation of the cost of selling any single product. Consequently, the statutes usually state a percentage-above-invoice cost, which sets the floor below which prices cannot be set except under special conditions such as with damaged merchandise.

The effect of governmental intervention, although not so formal, is perhaps a much more difficult variable to deal with. In the last few years a number of governmental investigating committees have been inquiring into the pricing practices of certain industries. Their concern is not totally to establish unfair trade practices or collusive pricing arrangements, but rather to assess the fairness of pricing policies in a given industry. There is a tinge of exploitation of the public when high prices at large profits are demonstrated. It is a basic principle of law that the seller has the right to set his price as he pleases (except in regulated industries). As yet no laws have been passed regulating the levels at which prices may be set, but this is not an impossibility for the future.

Summary

Pricing is one of the most important decision areas in the market affairs of the firm. Price is the focal point of all other actions the firm has taken. In this chapter some concepts regarding the role of prices in the economy and in the firm have been developed.

Price is a monetary expression of value and quantitatively expresses the subjective evaluation of consumers and suppliers regarding potential benefits from exchange. The price system, the aggregate of all prices, may be viewed as a system which communicates the present state of evaluations of buyers and sellers. Whenever these evaluations change, either the price or the quantity exchanged will change. In this way the price system theoretically directs the allocation of resources. Although prices do not direct resources with the rapidity theoretically assumed, they still are influential in this respect. Prices do change, and the alert competitor must assess the reasons for change, and adjust accordingly.

Although price behavior within an industry may be indicative of unfair competitive practices, caution must be exercised in making such assumptions. Uniformity of price among all suppliers in an industry, as well as stability of price over time, may be the result of the interaction of economic forces.

From the point of view of the firm, the price established is a reflection of all other actions taken by the firm. Theoretically, the firm should price at that point at which marginal revenue is equal to marginal cost. Although the economic model depicting cost and demand is useful for portraying the internal and external forces which interact to create profits or losses, it is only of limited value to the marketing practitioner. The task of measuring cost and demand makes the model's use extremely difficult.

The difficult problem in price determination is one of prediction. Predictions must be made about (1) the effect of different combinations of distribution mix, communications mix, and price on quantity, (2) the effect of various quantities on production costs, and (3) the effect of different quantities on marketing costs.

In making cost predictions it is justifiable to assume a constant variable production cost and to represent most marketing costs in a fixed-cost step function. This materially minimizes the prediction problem. Once the cost functions are established, the quantities estimated at different prices may be introduced and reasonable assumptions made as to outcomes.

The exact prices selected depend on the objectives of the firm. A number of pricing policies have been used, such as: (1) return-on-investment pricing, (2) ethical pricing, (3) penetration pricing, (4) skimming pricing, (5) full-line pricing, and (6) minimization-of-loss pricing. In each case different objectives are sought.

The legal restrictions in price determination are of two types. The Unfair Sales Acts govern pricing practices of intermediaries, and are an attempt to prevent predatory price cutting, or sale below cost. The second type is less formal and involves governmental investigations into the pricing practices of certain industries. To date, no laws have been passed which in any way would set an upper limit on prices in nonregulated industries.

Questions and Problems

1. What is the role of prices in a free enterprise economy?
2. What is the relationship between price and value?
3. What is an equilibrium price?
4. Under what kind of conditions might price uniformity among rivals be evidence of competition or economic forces rather than of undesirable business practices?
5. "Care must be exercised in making judgments concerning price behavior and the degree of competition existing." Elaborate on this statement.
6. "Price is a reflection of all the actions of the firm." Elaborate.
7. What is the firm's objective in price determination? Explain in technical terms how it goes about this.
8. Explain the interdependence of costs and demand insofar as a particular firm is concerned.
9. It has been said that determining the demand schedule with some precision presents serious problems. What are some of these problems?
10. What are some of the different approaches used in attempts to measure demand or to construct demand schedules?
11. What is the effect of quantity on the major categories of marketing costs?
12. What is the nature of the problem in establishing price differentials between different products in a line? Do you know of any technical approaches to the solution of this problem?
13. Describe return-on-investment pricing.
14. What is penetration pricing? How does it differ from a skimming-price policy?
15. What kinds of legal constraints affect price determination? Should there be a law against excessively high prices? Defend your position.

Decision-Making Aspects
of Pricing New Products

In the previous chapter the theoretical economic model for the determination of price was explained. Its value as a conceptual model to identify the interaction of forces which create profits or losses was recognized. In the pricing of new products it is less tenable as a point of departure. For this reason, this chapter is devoted to a discussion of the problems faced by businessmen in pricing new products, and some of the ways they try to solve them.

Prior to any discussion of the new-product pricing problem itself, it is important to recall that every new product goes through a cycle of perishable distinctiveness. Successive stages of pioneering, market acceptance, turbulence, saturation, and obsolescence were identified and the problems of pricing and product strategy in each of these different competitive situations were characterized in Chapter 10. Price makers, therefore, must be prepared to deal with the pricing problem through time. This discussion, however, is concerned solely with the problems of stage one, namely, pioneering. First the business procedures employed in pricing new products are considered; then the limitations of these procedures are noted and the variations explained. Finally, new-product pricing is viewed from a decision-making perspective for the guidance that it may provide price makers.[1]

BUSINESS PROCEDURES
FOR PRICING NEW PRODUCTS

Formula Pricing from Cost Buildups

Extensive study of a number of companies shows that most companies initially develop a pioneering price from cost

[1] All of the cases cited and observations made in this chapter are derived from research conducted by one of the authors under a grant from the Alfred P. Sloan Research Fund and reported here for the first time.

497

Decision-
Making
Aspects of
Pricing
New Products

buildups. Often the formula price is modified slightly to adjust to competitive realities in the market place. The strength of the marketing department within the organization of the company is also influential in determining the amount of variance existing between the formula price and the market price actually charged. Where the firm is market oriented, more deviation occurs between the formula price developed initially and the actual price established in the market place. Nevertheless, the formula price is the starting point, and the different formulas used are explained first.

Table 28-1 illustrates the types of formulas used by companies in the initial stages of price determination. On the surface, these formulas appear to be quite simple, and one might easily conclude that they reflect unusually haphazard price determination. However, these formulas are the result of a more

TABLE 28-1
Formulas for Pricing New Products

EXAMPLE I		EXAMPLE II	
Direct labor	$ × 5.	Materials	$ × 1.75
Subassemblies from outside suppliers	$ × 3.	Subassemblies from outside suppliers	$ × 1.75
Materials	$ × 2.	Direct labor	$ × 6.
Royalty payments	$ × 1.	Total (+ 10% for	
Total = Price		development) = Price	

EXAMPLE III		EXAMPLE IV	
Direct labor	$ × 8.	Materials	$ × 1.
Materials	$ × 2.	Direct labor	$ × 1.
Total = Price		Factory overhead at 185% of direct labor	$ × 1.
		Total × 2 = Price	

penetrating analysis than at first appears. The formula shown in Example IV was derived from an historical analysis of operating statements. This company had as its dominant goal a profit of 10 to 15 percent on sales before taxes. Selling expenses were known to have averaged, over a period of years, approximately 17 percent; general and administrative expenses, 15 percent; amortization of development expense, 5 percent. With an expected profit of 10 percent, cost of goods sold averaged 53 percent of sales revenue. When manufacturing costs were analyzed, it was found that factory overhead expenses approximated 185 percent of direct labor costs. Consequently, the cost of direct labor plus material plus overhead at 185 percent of direct labor should equal the cost of goods sold and be approximately 50 percent of sales revenue. Doubling this figure should then give a price which would provide sufficient gross margin for the other expenditures as well as a profit of 10 percent on sales revenue. The limitations of this kind of cost buildup pricing are reviewed later.

The more detailed illustration of pricing from cost buildups shown in Table 28-2 is taken from a well-known company. This company is an integrated manufacturing-marketing concern in that it owns its own retail outlets. Management is decentralized, and an attempt is made to isolate operating profits

TABLE 28-2
Pricing Procedure for a New Product by a Major Integrated
Consumer Goods Producer (factories and retail stores)

Materials (62 parts, at actual purchase price)	$18.99
Labor charges (7 depts.—no. hrs. × avge. hrly. wage rate)	4.35
Factory burden (at 201 percent of direct labor)	8.74
Total	32.08
Variations contingency (at 2 percent)	.64
Administrative expenses (at 6.5 percent)	2.08
Subtotal—Manufacturing cost (less tools)	34.80
Factory profit (at 10 percent of manufacturing cost)	3.48
Total	38.28
Tools and tool tryout	4.00*
Freight factor	1.55**
Price to retail store	43.83
Retail markup (at 38 percent)	26.86
Awkward retail price	70.69
Psychologically adjusted price	69.95

* Based on expected production over a two-year period or computed by cost of special tools and fixtures divided by number of units forecast in first two years of production.
** Average expectancy.

in every segment of the company's business, primarily for the purposes of evaluating managerial personnel and profit-sharing participation. It should be noted that each manager of the company-owned retail stores is free to price the product at the level he pleases. Normally, however, the store manager follows the judgment of merchandise managers in these matters, for he relies on the judgment and analysis of the headquarters planning staff with respect to the suggested price that is expected to best meet merchandising needs at the retail level.

In this example all factory costs except tools are totaled and 10 percent added to cover manufacturing profit. The cost of tools and outbound freight are added to determine the cost to the company-owned retail stores. The markup of 38 percent on selling price is added on to the cost to the retail store, and the price is adjusted to one which is psychologically acceptable to the market.

Limitations to Formula Pricing

The limitations to formula pricing vary, depending on the extent to which the prices are adjusted for competitive factors. In Table 28-2 the limitations are not as pronounced as they might be. This company made an analysis of the demand factors which enabled it to set a target price. That is, the merchandise manager proposed a product development program that would lead to a product that would sell at a retail price of $75. However, when formula pricing from cost buildups is relied upon without concern for market forces, the procedure suffers from the following limitations.

499

Decision-
Making
Aspects of
Pricing
New Products

1. Demand analysis is cursory. Adequate attention is not given to buyers' needs and willingness to pay. Possible cross-elasticities of demand between products are ignored. The relationships of price among products sometimes acts as a stimulus or deterrent to sales. If two products are substitutes for one another, an increase in the price of one may increase the sales of the other. No projection is made of the number of buyers that can be expected to purchase at various price levels. No possibility exists, then, except by accident, for profit maximization to be reached.

2. Competition is not reflected adequately. Not only does immediate competition tend to be ignored but also potential competitors' reactions to the initial price are not adequately reflected in this kind of procedure. Consideration of whether market entry is invited by the price or whether it acts as a barrier to market entry is pertinent. Firms have a strategy choice here.

3. In general, formulas do not serve marketing strategy adequately. Price should be recognized as but one part of a total marketing mix designed to precipitate purchase of the product. It must be considered in the context of communications expenditures to be made, type of consumer to be reached, purchase motivation factors, consumers' habits in purchasing the product to be displaced, and the like. Also, the strategy choice exists as to whether price is to reflect current costs or is to be set at a level which will generate sufficient volume to produce a future cost structure justifying the price.

4. Formulas tend to overplay the precision with which costs are allocated. The most common basis for allocating overhead costs is to prorate them to products according to direct labor hours. At best, these procedures are arbitrary, and should be recognized as such. Many executives have unwarranted faith in the precision of their cost buildups. Other accepted accounting treatments could be used that would produce quite different results, yet the executive tends to accept the *cost* as an exact or precise measure.

5. Rigid application of formulas may result in uneconomic procedures. Managers may undertake uneconomic courses of action, depending upon the particular formula used. Product managers may find, for example, that they are better off to subcontract a large number of parts so as to reduce direct labor hours, because overhead is usually allocated as a percentage of direct labor cost. By so doing, the total cost may be reduced for pricing purposes. This was found to exist in one case even when the factory had unused plant capacity.

6. The procedure involves (to some extent) circular reasoning. This is true because price will in part determine the quantity of sales, which determines output, which influences cost, which in turn is used for determining price.

Since companies are often familiar with the limitations to formula pricing from cost buildups or variations thereof, why then do they prefer to follow it none the less? This can be explained in part by the great uncertainty that tends to pervade pioneering pricing when a product is new to the market. Such factors as resistance to change on the part of potential buyers, limited data with respect to the potential size of the market, and the uncertainty of future competition and business conditions, lead firms to seek procedures which are relatively simple and which will provide reasonably gratifying results if all goes well. Therefore, a trial price is used which, if accepted by the market, will provide a desirable ratio of profits to sales or investment with full allocation of overhead costs. While this may not be the price that is most profitable, it is considered by management to be a fair price, one characterized as producing profitable business. Moreover, prices are presumed to be more easily lowered than raised. If it is learned later that market conditions preclude a high price which may result from full-cost-plus formulas, downward adjustments can be accomplished with relative ease. In a sense, then, this is a trial-and-error approach to price determination in the market place, and selective trial and error is an experimental method which does have some commendable attributes.

Variations from Formula Pricing

While most firms profess cost-plus formula pricing in the pioneering period of market development, closer scrutiny shows that such is not strictly the case. A number of procedures are employed that in one way or another either directly or indirectly affect the introductory price. Most of these take the form of making some adjustment for the competitive conditions which exist, or providing built-in flexibility for a rapid retreat from formula prices if initial market reaction is not completely satisfactory. Some of the more important variations follow.

1. Initial selection of target prices. In the example of the integrated producer-marketer cited earlier, the company was seeking a product in the design stage that could be sold profitably at retail in the vicinity of $75. Initial market considerations convinced management that this was the vicinity of greatest competitive opportunity. However, once this target area was established and the design frozen, final pricing followed the cost buildups as demonstrated.

2. Introductory offers. Introductory offers can be made in such a way as to make possible any needed subsequent adjustments to the formula price, depending upon the market response received. This sort of initial demand probing provides an opportunity to measure the potential response of the market to the formula price level without placing psychological market barriers in the way of a price adjustment. This procedure is often used in the pricing of consumer goods innovations.

3. Adjustments for psychological barriers. Often adjustments are made from the formula price to better adapt the product to its competitive environment. In a case involving a piece of medical diagnostic equipment, a price of $1,985 was placed on the product, instead of the formula figure of just under $2,100, when it was recognized that many institutions that were potential buyers had purchasing policies requiring approval from the hospital board of directors for any expenditure in excess of $2,000. In another instance in the same industry, application of the formula produced a price that appeared to be high in relation to other equipment previously sold. The new product involved considerable miniaturization and did not look as expensive as other equipment sold by the firm. This obstacle was overcome by placing the equipment in a larger case (or housing) than was required and restyling the outside shell to give it a more expensive-looking appearance. This is a type of allowance, for competitive

501

Decision-
Making
Aspects of
Pricing
New Products

facets of the price problem, that is not immediately apparent in a firm professing formula pricing.

4. Adjustments for meeting payout policies of purchasers. In the industrial market, purchasers frequently have policies regarding the length of time allowed for a machine to pay for itself out of cost savings. These policies vary, but a usual range appears to be from one to four years, with twenty-four or thirty-six months common. Several detailed case studies were made by one company to determine the cost reductions possible to the buyer in the utilization of a new piece of textile-making machinery. Analysis of these data resulted in a downward price adjustment from the preliminary level to bring it within a three-year payout for the average user. This is a type of "demand analysis" that is somewhat different from the conventional form envisaged for price determination. Nevertheless, it reflects adjustment to demand forces within a competitive market.

5. Trial prices and cost modifications. A popular time for introducing new industrial equipment is during trade shows and exhibits. The immense national machine-tool show is an occasion for the announcement of new equipment by many producers. It also provides an opportunity to probe users' reactions to anticipated prices. Several companies introduced products at one show, with exhibit personnel instructed to inform prospects that the price for the equipment had not been set, and to announce the formula price as the approximate price. In two instances, one involving an automatic boring machine and the other an electronic data processing machine, this trial-balloon approach resulted in a post-show general management conference in which an all-out attempt was made to cut costs of the equipment because of market resistance. For both products, cost-reduction programs took the form of a reevaluation of material costs, tooling expenses, production layouts, time study of labor, design changes, and burden or overhead rates, to achieve costs which would permit a considerably lower price within the formula framework. This forcing of the formula tends to conceal important aspects of the total price-making process.

6. Research and development cost write-offs and amortization. Cost-plus pricing from a formula base can be illusory unless care is taken to inspect the costs included in the formula. Several procedures can be used which have the effect of lowering costs and, therefore, prices. One area for management manipulation has to do with government research and development contracts where commercial applications are feasible. Business firms holding sizable contracts of this type frequently maintain large engineering and development staffs for this primary purpose, but their work, either on a planned or unplanned basis, often leads to commercially useful products. Questions are then in order as to how the costs of these departments and common production facilities are to be allocated. In one case, commercial products were withheld until research and facilities costs had been largely covered with governmental charges. Even though government practices involve the prorating of costs, new commercial products can sometimes get a sizable cost advantage in the formula-pricing procedure under these circumstances.

7. "Scooping out the demand curve" prior to the application of formula pricing. Formula pricing can be an integral part of the pricing procedure, but

it may be withheld until initial advantage has been taken of the innovation. This variation may take the form of selecting for initial cultivation those potential buyers who are not especially cost conscious and covering sizable fixed or sunk costs from initially high prices to these customers prior to an attempt at a major market penetration with a formula or "adjusted formula" price. In the case of a wholly new type of blood-fractionating equipment, for example, initial sales effort was to be directed at military or government hospitals, principal Red Cross centers, and foundation-supported experimental facilities where large quantities of blood are separated and where equipment costs, in the light of these quantities, are relatively unimportant. After these purchases were accounted for (with the recapture of sizable fixed costs), a broader market-cultivation program could be launched on a formula-price basis to reach such buyers as the average- to larger-sized hospitals. This approach then might be called "scooping out the demand curve," but without the demand schedule being recognized as a curved line. Only two points in the curve are recognized and, within this framework, the cost-plus formula is an integral part of the price-making process.

8. Tooling amortization. Tooling decisions affect price levels in several ways. The first important way in which tooling decisions affect costs, and therefore prices, of manufactured product innovations, is the extent of tooling to be used in the production process. If extensive tooling is employed to make possible 'line" or "mass" production for the new item, it oftentimes reduces the direct labor costs in manufacturing and assembly. This is in contrast to employing "job-shop" procedures in the initial production process. If factory overhead charges are allocated to products on the basis of direct labor costs, then extensive tooling can have the effect of lowering these overhead burdens in absolute dollar amounts. Limited tooling resulting from job-shop procedures has the effect of increasing direct labor costs.

A second way in which tooling policy affects prices is the procedure used for charging tooling costs to products. Two predominant policies are observed. One approach is to carry tooling costs as a part of general overhead expense, as in the case of a large machine-tool manufacturer. Tooling is thus carried in the same way as management salaries. This, incidentally, results in buyers of products in the line with the most tooling involved paying the least proportionate share of this expense (because direct labor hours are reduced from what they would be with less tooling, and a smaller allocation of overhead is made). The second approach is to charge special tooling costs directly to the product; this has a pronounced effect on "costs" and, thereby, prices.

A third way in which tooling costs can affect prices has to do with the length of time or quantity of production over which tooling costs charged directly to the product are amortized. There are cases where tooling has been amortized over the first year's production, two years' production, the first twenty units, and the first production order. The effect on prices is obvious, particularly if tooling costs are large. In one case, to get a cost reduction, tooling costs were arbitrarily spread over two years of output instead of the normal first year's output, principally because of the competitive facets of the price problem. In another case, having to do with the pricing of a new piece of agricultural equipment, management decided to absorb all tooling costs into overhead (normally

503

Decision-
Making
Aspects of
Pricing
New Products

it was charged directly to the product) to give the product a better break in the introductory marketing program. This adjustment was made quickly after initial market response was sluggish when the price included tooling cost.

9. Safety costing through subcontracting. In introducing new products, some firms prefer to minimize risk by relying heavily on subcontractors for a large portion of the initial production of the product. Where opportunities exist for procuring subassemblies and fabricated parts on this basis, some managements feel there are important advantages to doing so. Needed capital is not committed on an unproven product in advance of a measure of potential market acceptance. Also, job-shop production methods may be bypassed by moving directly into line production when the firm decides to make the entire product with its own facilities. Costs are more definite at the initial stage of production as a result of fixed-price quotations on subassemblies, and profitability during introductory marketing is therefore easier to measure.

Moreover, there is believed to be a safety factor in this cost picture, in that managements often feel costs can be reduced when they assume manufacturing operations and absorb suppliers' profit margins. This is believed to provide a cushion for formula cost pricing until the exact nature of competition is more certain and the ultimate success of the new product is easier to judge.

10. Choice of alternate production lines. One very vivid case may show how the use of alternative production lines could have a pronounced effect on formula prices. The particular firm involved had three separate production lines, which to a large degree were interchangeable in terms of products. Line A was a low-speed line, principally because of older equipment and the necessity for more hand operations. Line C was a new high-speed line with modern, efficient equipment and many more automated operations. Line B was between the two in terms of efficiency and cost. In making a new product apparently headed for rather severe price resistance, management wanted the lowest price that costs would justify. The product was produced on line C. This produced a lower formula price because the costs were less on this line. This procedure, of course, raises the whole question of costs to a firm in such instances. Production of items originally on line C was moved to another line to make the facilities available for the new product. From a profitability point of view for the firm as a whole, was this move really necessary? At any rate, this choice of production lines is a facet of competitive flexibility that is not readily apparent in firms professing formula-pricing procedures.

11. Multiple-formula comparisons. Another approach to modifying prices derived from cost formulas was uncovered in the scientific instrument field. The formulas used by several competitors were compared by one firm which anticipated that competitors' models would be introduced shortly after the appearance of its product. In this instance, the price chosen was the lowest yielded by a comparison of three formulas. Management presumed that the price selected was unlikely to be too far out of line with what competition might be expected to charge. Here again is an allowance for the competitive aspects of pioneering pricing that is somewhat clouded by the umbrella of cost-plus formula pricing.

In view of all these factors, we may conclude that while studies have shown the predominance of cost formulas for pricing new products, many of the practices used actually take some account of demand and competitive factors, even though the firm may rely in general on a formula approach to price determination.

APPLICATION OF
DECISION-MAKING CONSIDERATIONS
TO PRICING PROBLEMS

In the past, economists have provided the principal theoretical foundation for dealing with pricing problems. The major contributions of economic theory, however, have been directed toward an explanation of prices for a class of product in the market as a whole. Economic theory seems not to have had a major impact in influencing the nature of business behavior, insofar as new-product price strategy is concerned. Since pricing involves an action decision, it may be that a decision-making orientation can broaden the perspective for dealing with this kind of problem and thereby make a contribution to improved pricing performance. This part of the discussion is directed to a consideration of pricing from this point of view.

Problem Definition

Action decisions take place through time. One makes a decision, action is taken on the basis of that decision, and some outcome is achieved which, hopefully, serves the purposes of the decision maker. A strategic decision is always made within the setting of a problem. A problem exists when there is uncertainty as to the wisest course of action to follow out of two or more alternatives. Decision making begins with a consideration of the problem itself—defining the problem and stating its dimensions. Decision makers should be aware of problems in time to allow optimum use of decision-making resources. Awareness of the problem should not wait until variables become rigid or there are fixed dimensions to the problem.

For example, when should the pricing problem emerge? Is it just before the introduction of the product after all other plans have been laid, or is it before the product has even been designed? These two extremes are common viewpoints, although the former is apparently a much more general procedure. In some cases the price decision is the very last one made in introducing a product to the market. In fewer cases the entire thinking and marketing strategy stems from an analysis of the price which provides the best competitive opportunity. Decision theory would suggest that the pricing problem be considered while many of the variables are still within the control of the price maker, namely, well before all other strategies are decided.

Objectives and Alternative Courses of Action

For action to be effective, certain goals or objectives must be established for it. In a broad sense these objectives may be a vision of the outcomes which the decision maker would regard as satisfactory. Therefore, the wisdom of any

505

Decision-
Making
Aspects of
Pricing
New Products

action, if evaluated in terms of its outcome, can be judged only in terms of the ends the decision maker sought to accomplish. Objectives are also important in that they provide the basis for determining the alternative courses of action open to the decision maker. For example, in a pricing decision several objectives may be present—a certain return on investment, a given share of the market, recoupment of development costs in two years, and profitable volume during introductory stages. This means that the decision maker must select from many alternative prices, as each objective probably cannot be achieved with a single price. Presumably he will select that price which comes closest to achieving all of his objectives. In some instances, decisions must be made even when all possible alternatives cannot be clarified. In other kinds of problem situations, there is a finite list of alternatives.

In a number of cases studied, at whatever time the price problem was considered, price makers generally proceeded from cost analysis of production rather than from market considerations. According to the decision model, this is not the starting point in decision making. Analysis of objectives should have precedence. Moreover, this procedure violates our basic managerial view, in which the administrative action of the firm is looked upon as a goal-directed effort in which market forces determine the way production and marketing factors will be combined to best meet profit opportunities.

Pricing seldom seems to be considered as an integral part of a total strategy designed to precipitate purchase action favorable to the seller. In fact, pricing seldom seems to be considered an alternative to other distribution or communications mix alternatives. When pricing is not dovetailed as an integral part of marketing strategy but is viewed as a wholly separate consideration, it is not in the proper context for decision-making purposes.

Lack of precision in operating goals helps to compound the difficulties inherent where price is looked upon as a mere adjunct to marketing strategy. Marketing strategy should be a major weapon used by management in achieving operating goals. When such generalized targets as greater sales and more profits are the principal framework for decision, the decision-making process in pricing can hardly have a sharp focus in a problem-solving sense. The price structure is an instrument which can be used to advantage in helping to control seasonal sales fluctuations, inventory levels in the distribution pipeline, full-line promotion by dealers, and rendering of particular services by dealers and distributors, and as the basis for shifting marketing risks among different sellers in the channel of distribution. Pricing difficulties arise, from a decision-making point of view, in direct relationship to the lack of precision by management in its operating goals.

Not only do operating goals often lack clarity from a price-decision point of view, but also the principal criterion—profitability—appears to be a rather loose concept among price makers. A relevant question is, What profit standard is to be used in judging the desirability of alternative choices? For example, is the profit standard based on incremental profits, marginal profits, dollar profits on full costs, a return on tangible net worth, etc.? Moreover, is the firm trying to maximize "future" earnings or the "present value" of future earnings, and over what time period? These issues make a difference in pricing decisions.

Decision Objectives vs. Decision Maker's Objectives

Objectives of individual decision makers should be as harmonious as possible with institutional decision objectives. Decisions are not likely to be optimum if the goals of the individuals making the decision are in conflict with the goals appropriate to the decision itself. For example, executives who are evaluated primarily on the basis of their *short-term* productivity are not placed in an ideal setting for making *long-run* corporate decisions.

In a study of the pricing behavior of a scientific instruments company, it seemed that the institutional objectives (as expressed by the chief executive officer of the company) were significantly different from the person-centered objectives of the participants in the decision. Extended discussions with the sales manager indicated that his actions and point of view reflected influencing factors not fully harmonious with pricing objectives. Management evaluation of the sales manager's performance and that of his department were unrelated to profits. Whether the company made a profit was regarded as depending upon many things outside the province of the sales department. Sales effectiveness was appraised almost entirely on the basis of reaching previously established volume goals. If sales were above the previous year by the targeted figure, the sales department was considered to have done its assigned task regardless of profit outcomes. In auditing price committee meetings, it was evident that the sales manager (a most important participant in all pricing decisions) argued eloquently for low prices. Such behavior would not appear inconsistent with his departmental objectives, for it increased the prospect of obtaining volume goals by benefiting from low prices, but it demonstrates the conflict of decision makers' objectives with the decision objectives.

This orientation in price decisions is the basis for the rather commonly expressed viewpoint of nonmarketing executives that "the sales department would like to give the product away." On the other hand, the production manager's natural bias may have an influence in the opposite direction. In the case just cited, the production manager was charged with estimating the amount of labor time required for assembly of the new product. If later on his estimate proved to be too low, he might presumably be called upon by management to explain the difficulty. Was tooling adequate? Did jigs and fixtures operate properly? Was adequate training given shop personnel? Were difficulties experienced with the product itself? These might be among the questions raised in trying to account for the actual assembly hours being greater than the forecast.

By the same token, if actual performance later proves to be below the forecast, this would seem to convey the image that production layouts, tooling, labor productivity, and supervision had been effectively mixed to achieve such gratifying results. The production manager's natural tendency, as a consequence, is to make a rather generous cost estimate. A high price which results from the use of an inflated cost formula is not necessarily contrary to the best short-term objectives of the production department or its officials. This notation raises the related issue of long- and short-term objectives on decisions and decision makers.

507

Decision-
Making
Aspects of
Pricing
New Products

The environment of modern corporate life seems to have resulted in an increased priority being given to short-run objectives by decision makers. Executive performance is frequently analyzed on the basis of a continuous evaluation of short-run results, as in the yearly evaluation of the sales manager in the company just cited. Where this method is used, it has a pronounced effect on decision making. One sales executive in a major industrial enterprise characterized this influence somewhat whimsically by saying, "Every time you get promoted in this company, you get closer to the street," (the executive offices were toward the front of the building with an outside view) "and, at this level, there is no way back, only out. I hold this office and position only so long as I produce results. Necessarily, I am far more concerned about sales in this model year than I honestly can be in any five- to ten-year forecast of corporate opportunities. If long-range marketing plans meant sacrificing short-run achievements, I would have to emphasize the short-run considerations; otherwise, I might not be around to have the opportunity of demonstrating the wisdom and judgment that went into the long-range plan." While one could place too much credence in this statement, it illustrates a friction point in decision making: often objectives of decision makers are not in harmony with decision objectives—especially in price determination.

Data for Prediction

A decision can be no better than the quality of data used in reaching it. A decision maker cannot choose the best of alternative courses of action open to him without making judgments about the possible outcomes of each action. Predictions about possible outcomes of each alternate course depend for their accuracy on the timeliness, completeness, and precision of data.

Data used for predicting should cover the same time period as the consequences of the action. This is extremely important, and one of the major reasons for decision-making misfortune. Too often data of limited historical relevance are used in making decisions, rather than data pertaining to the future decision environment. For example, price makers quite frequently show grave concern for recapturing sunk costs—particularly research and development expenditures. It is true that, in the long run, sales revenues must more than cover all the costs of doing business. However, this truism seems to confuse the point that cost and revenue expectations in the future are the relevant considerations for decision-making purposes. Insisting that the price of the product must be so high as to cover all historical costs related to that product may burden it in such a way as to forego opportunities for improving the profitability of the enterprise. Such use of historical data for making decisions involving future circumstances and events violates decision rules. This emotional attachment to retrieving research and development expenditures is analogous to a grocer refusing to cut prices on lettuce that will not sell at his price of twenty-five cents per head, on the grounds that he had paid that much for the lettuce and, by cutting the price, he would be losing money on every head sold.

With respect to completeness of data, decision rules prescribe that all data pertaining to the decision should be fed to the predicting system simultaneously to preclude partial judgments with limited data from becoming the basis for the fixed judgment. Pricing difficulties in this connection seem to center around the fact that tentative decisions or viewpoints are often expressed by important individuals in the decision process. Every company has a power structure made up of important executives who are a part of the decision structure. Instances have been observed where the dominant individual in the power structure made early statements and judgments based upon partial data, and tended to get emotionally attached or associated with this position. As later evidence became available (from trade shows or test marketing operations), earlier judgments should have been modified, but important psychological barriers were in the way of these modifications. Opinion fixation seems to have a significant effect in company pricing where organizational informality is pronounced and where little exists in the way of a formal and conscious decision-making process.

The relevancy of precise data in price determination is particularly pronounced in the "preciseness" of production costing versus "loose" distribution costing. In by far the majority of observations, rather detailed estimates of production costs were prepared. These estimates, in some cases, were calculated to the fraction of a cent. On the other hand, the most general kind of distribution cost analysis seems typical. Usually, the existing ratio of selling expense to total sales is used for costing purposes. In most instances, no attempt was made to forecast the amount of promotional effort that would be needed, the degree of personal selling activity required, the amount of time that the new product would require of various personnel in the distribution process, and so on. Supplemental appropriations to existing marketing budgets often were not given. In such cases, it was presumed that the new product would be handled within the existing marketing cost framework—and yet minute increments of production cost were calculated.

A second finding relating to the precision of data is found in management's faith in production inventiveness to lower costs after production has started and, particularly, as greater volume develops. It is true that there is a learning curve associated with the production of new products. Experience in military procurement indicates that costs do decline with production experience and that these decreases are reasonably predictable. However, such cost reductions do not just happen. A dramatic illustration of this concerned the pricing of a new engine component. Staff analysts recommended, on the basis of break-even analysis, that a division manager of a large corporation not set a price below eighty-five cents per unit. This figure was determined to be the minimum out-of-pocket cost with "full costs" being substantially above this point.

Research observers had the opportunity to record the division manager's reactions and to interpret the reasoning involved in his prior decision to quote a price of seventy-five cents to the customer. The division manager felt certain that after production personnel had gained experience with the making of the part they would find better means of manufacture that had not yet been uncovered. Secondly, as volume on the part increased, he felt equally (or even more) certain that lower costs automatically would be forthcoming, even though no significant cost reductions were forecast. We should mention here that econ-

509

Decision-
Making
Aspects of
Pricing
New Products

omies of scale are not always automatic—rather, greater volume merely provides the opportunity to adopt different methods which produce lower costs. The manager's action in this case amounts to throwing overboard any pretense of scientific methodology and is a reversion to mere intelligent artistry in price determination.

Flexibility for Later Actions

If data used for prediction are sufficiently limited or inexact, then flexibility should be preserved for later action and decision. A rational man, when confronted with uncertainty, acts in such a way as to preserve the power to act: namely, he considers his alternatives in terms of the opportunity each affords for constructive later action, and gives preference to those which allow flexibility. In some ways, this may be thought of as hedging one's bet.

This consideration in new-product pricing is involved in what might be regarded as incremental costing and subsidy pricing. Competitive opportunities for potential rivals sometimes develop because of subsidy pricing relationships which can result from the introduction of a line of new products of different models or sizes. For example, a company introduced a new kind of home appliance. The first model was priced at $169.95. The company recognized that a substantial market existed for a lower-priced model which could be sold to speculative home builders and price-conscious consumers. A smaller, stripped-down model was introduced, which had basically the same parts and components. Recognizing that many of its costs were already covered in the production of the larger unit, and on the basis of an incremental cost analysis, the company priced the smaller unit at $119.95. A substantial volume of sales on the smaller unit was achieved at this price.

A rival firm recognized a competitive opportunity here for two reasons. First, it found that many purchasers of the smaller unit actually preferred the larger size, but were attracted by the lower price. Second, in analyzing the production costs of the two units, only a small difference could be found in parts, materials, and labor. Therefore, the conclusion was reached that the buyers of the larger unit were actually subsidizing the purchasers of the smaller unit. The rival firm then introduced a product of the size of the original unit with limited trim and features at $139.95 and made a major inroad into the market by trading prospects both up and down from the lower- and higher-priced offerings of the innovator—who failed to foresee all the possible consequences of his price decision.

In conclusion, new-product pricing seems hardly recognizable as an orderly, conscious, decision-making process. Most firms market few basically new products during their existence, and therefore have very little experience, and few formal procedures or organizational arrangements for dealing with the problem of innovative pricing. It is interesting to note that every firm included in the study lacked confidence in itself in this area of pricing. In short, price making lacks the degree of professionalization found in production scheduling, quality control, advertising, personnel administration, public relations, legal counsel, and other such areas in which decisions are made. Much needs to be done to advance both the state of the art and the scientific tools available for dealing with the problem.

Summary

Because of the uncertainty that pervades pioneering pricing, executives seek procedures which are relatively simple. The resulting price may not be one that provides the greatest profit, but is considered by management to be a fair price and one characterized as producing profitable business. The formula-pricing practices employing cost buildups used by businessmen have the following limitations: (1) demand analysis is cursory, (2) competition is not reflected adequately, (3) in general, formulas do not serve marketing strategy adequately, (4) formulas tend to overplay the precision with which costs are allocated, (5) rigid application of the formula may result in uneconomic procedures, and (6) the practice involves circular reasoning. While most managers profess formula pricing from cost buildups for new products, this is not strictly the case. The following practices may actually take account of competitive conditions: (1) initial selection of target prices, (2) introductory offers, (3) adjustments for psychological barriers, (4) adjustments for meeting payout policies of purchasers, (5) trial prices and cost modifications, (6) research and development cost write-offs and amortization, (7) "scooping out the demand curve" prior to the application of formula pricing, (8) tooling amortization, (9) safety costing through subcontracting, (10) choice of alternate production lines, and (11) multiple-formula comparisons.

A decision-making perspective is believed to hold some promise in providing a partial reorientation to price determination. Through looking at pricing as an action decision and following the steps in decision making, many of the difficulties and imperfections of present methods are brought into sharper focus. The steps suggested for approaching pricing from a decision-making perspective include: problem definition; determination of alternative courses of action for achieving objectives; and the selection of accurate, timely, precise, and complete data for predicting the outcomes from alternative courses of action.

Much needs to be done in the way of basic research before new-product pricing can be materially advanced. For example, how can resistance to change in the market place be quantified? What is the propensity for assuming risk in new products by potential purchasers? How can potential purchasers who act as "circuits of influence in markets" in new-product adoption be identified? What thought processes are involved in the acceptance or rejection of new products by consumers? Some advances in cost forecasting are requisite to improved pricing performance, as are some changes in accounting practice.

Questions and Problems

1. What seems to be the basic approach used by firms in pricing products new to the market?
2. What is meant by formula pricing? How would it differ from theoretical price determination as discussed in the preceding chapter?

511

Decision-
Making
Aspects of
Pricing
New Products

3. What are the principal limitations to formula pricing?

4. "Cost of producing a product can vary substantially from competitor to competitor under identical conditions; it depends upon company policy in treating costs." Could this statement be true? Explain.

5. Since many companies are aware of the limitations to formula pricing, why is its use so prevalent?

6. Explain the ways that companies might actually make adjustments from formula prices in order to overcome psychological barriers.

7. Is "scooping out the demand curve" prior to applying formula pricing the same as a "skimming" policy, as explained in the preceding chapter?

8. How do variations in company policy with respect to the treatment of research and development expenses have a pronounced effect on costs, and therefore on formula prices?

9. What are the various ways in which tooling-cost policy can affect prices?

10. A company has three different production lines of varying efficiency. Since prices should in part reflect costs, should costs be determined on the basis of the particular line actually used, or should an average cost be used or some other method?

11. "Pricing is the final step in planning a marketing program for a new product. Since they serve to integrate cost and demand, price decisions should be delayed until advertising programs and all other expenditure categories are determined." Comment.

12. How can the variation between decision objectives and decision makers' objectives influence price?

13. What is the difference between "full costs" and "decision-making costs"? Is the usual accounting practice suitable for pricing? Explain.

14. Explain the potential danger of so-called subsidy pricing. Use an example to make your points clear.

15. New-product pricing in many firms may lack professionalism when compared with other decision areas. If this is true, explain why. Use some comparative examples in your answer.

Price Administration 29

Price administration as distinct from price determination is concerned with the way in which base prices are administered throughout the channel of distribution and the market area. It deals with price adjustments for sales made under different conditions, such as: (1) sales made in different quantities, (2) sales made to different classes of intermediaries performing different functions, and (3) sales made to purchasers in different locations. Another related problem has to do with the amount of control that should be exercised over the prices at which goods are sold at various levels of distribution. The legal framework for these variations and controls is quite important and must be clarified. Thus, this chapter is divided into three parts: (1) an examination of price administration practices used to recognize variation in conditions of sale, (2) means used to control price throughout the channel, and (3) legal implications resulting from the granting of discriminating prices.

METHODS OF PRICE ADMINISTRATION

Variations in price to reflect transactions made under different market or firm conditions are achieved in a number of ways. Reasons for the use of varying prices will be discussed as each of several such conditions is developed.

Negotiations

The strength of the buyer's position often results in his ability to negotiate a variation from the base price. His ability to do so may come from the alternative sources of supply available. The intensity of price competition among sources of supply is another factor influencing the negotiating ability of the buyer. The buyer's bargaining ability may also be strengthened by the fact that the seller may wish to expand his market. If the buyer is a new class of purchaser or in a new market area the seller is developing, the motivation to give special consideration is great.

Marketing enterprises that are willing to negotiate are said to be following a *variable-price policy,* or one in which prices may be varied on the basis of the bargaining strength of the participants. This practice can hardly be called a system of price administration; however, it is prevalent and should be identified.

To avoid the negotiating demands of purchasers, many companies follow what is known as a *nonvariable-price policy.* This does not mean that prices to different buyers do not vary, but they vary only under certain conditions, such as different prices for different quantities, different kinds of intermediaries, or variations in location of the purchasers. Although a firm may follow a non-variable policy and administer it well, there are instances in which variations will occur which are, to some extent, beyond the firm's control. Whenever advertising allowances are made or payments for special services, these amount to a variation in price, if in fact they are not used specifically for the purpose stated.

A related policy is that of the *single-price policy.* This means that the seller deals only in a single-price line, such as shoes at $9.95. Such a policy is even more restrictive than a nonvariable-price policy. No variations in price are made regardless of the circumstances under which the sale is made. This policy is not, however, a satisfactory one for large buyers whose negotiating strength could extract lower prices which reflect economies in larger order sizes.

Quantity Discounts

These are discounts given theoretically to reflect differences in costs in selling different quantities. Cost is reduced when buyers can be induced to order in large quantities. Personal selling costs are reduced, as are costs of credit investigation, order filling, packing, and transportation. When the discount is determined on the quantity purchased at a given time, it is known as a *non-cumulative quantity discount. Cumulative quantity discounts* are calculated on the total orders placed during a time period, and are not restricted to a single purchase. Except on continuity of buyer-seller relations, they are difficult to justify on the basis of reduced costs of selling, because the buyer may still place many orders. Cumulative discounts are promotional in nature, and have several purposes: (1) to tie a purchaser to a single supplier. There is a tendency for buyers to place succeeding orders with a seller because of the larger discount involved on his total purchase; (2) to increase sales in slow periods; and (3) in the case of perishable items, to encourage the buyer to purchase in large total quantities by placing frequent small orders without risking physical deterioration of the product. Cumulative quantity discounts have a tendency to increase peaks and valleys in the production schedule. At the end of a discount period, buyers frequently place large orders so as to qualify for the larger discount. These customers subsequently place smaller orders at the beginning of the next discount period.

Trade Discounts

These discounts are reductions in price given to different classes of buyers to compensate them for the performance of certain activities in the movement of goods to ultimate consumers. For example, wholesalers perform certain activities for manufacturers, which in their absence might have to be assumed by the manufacturer if he sold directly to consumers. It is common practice to give wholesalers a larger discount off the base price than that given to retailers. The justification for the discount is payment for the activities performed. The blending of wholesale and retail activities through the operation of retailer cooperative chains and the operation of retail stores by wholesalers and manufacturers make this justification somewhat weak. Some large retailers also operate their own wholesale establishments. They purchase directly from the manufacturer and perform all wholesaling activities.

If not justifiable on a "payment for services rendered" basis, trade discounts are sometimes justified as a means of maintaining distribution. If, because of variations in efficiency among different classes of intermediaries, one is able to undersell the other, the abolition of trade discounts would seriously hamper some, perhaps to the extent that they could not continue to distribute the product for the manufacturer. This defense hardly seems justifiable, for it frequently subsidizes the less efficient outlets.

Leasing Arrangements

Leasing is more than a variation from a base price; it really amounts to another form of payment. When a buyer purchases a product outright he is prepaying for the services to be rendered by the product over its life. In a leasing arrangement the buyer pays a predetermined rental fee for the services rendered by the product for a specified period of time or output.

There are many reasons for the use of leasing rather than outright sale.[1] This pricing arrangement is perhaps most frequently used as a means of expanding the market that would prevail under outright sale. The product may be useful to all size classes in the customer group; however, it may be so expensive that smaller companies cannot afford to purchase it outright. Leasing is also a useful means for increasing the total revenue from each buyer. For example, the savings from the use of some industrial products are dependent upon the output of the user. The greater the usage the greater the savings. Consequently, the larger buyer is willing to pay more than is the smaller buyer. To capture both markets by means of outright sale would involve setting a price much lower than the one the larger buyer would be willing to pay. By leasing and establishing a fee on the basis of unit output, total revenues are greatly increased.

Another reason for leasing on the part of the lessor is that equipment frequently is highly technical, and unless the lessor is able to completely control maintenance and service, it may not perform as intended. In using leased equipment, the user can be absolved of all responsibility for maintenance and service, and thus be relatively certain of its almost continuous operation.

Leasing also allows the user to avoid most risks present in the ownership of equipment. In products for which there is a rapid rate of technological advancement, such as electronic computers, buyers are hesitant to purchase outright

---

[1] For a detailed discussion of leasing, see W. J. Eiteman and C. N. Davisson, *The Lease as a Financing and Selling Device*, Report No. 20, Bureau of Business Research (Ann Arbor, Mich.: University of Michigan Press).

because the equipment is likely to become technically obsolete in a reasonably short period of time. Through leasing, users are able to maintain the most up-to-date equipment without running the risk of obsolescence. The major advantage to the lessee is the maintenance of capital which can be used for other purposes, since the capital burden is assumed by the lessor. In addition to the savings in capital to the lessee, a tax advantage may be available. The lease rental, which is fully tax deductible as an operating expense, often is greater than the allowable depreciation rate if equipment is purchased outright. Consequently, the actual total cost of leasing equipment is sometimes less than the cost of outright purchase.

Leasing was formerly a devise used primarily by manufacturers of highly technical, expensive industrial equipment. For years, the International Business Machines Corporation leased most of its equipment. Today the lease has spread to a large number of products. A number of leasing companies have developed which lease to industrial buyers just about every product imaginable.

Uniform Delivered Prices

Uniform delivered prices are those in which the same prices are charged to buyers irrespective of location. The opposite of uniform delivered prices is F.O.B. (free on board) factory prices. Buyers pay the same price to the seller, but the actual cost of merchandise to them must include the cost of transportation. Uniform delivered prices are a form of price variation, since the buyer located some distance from the supplier is not penalized in price. There are three types of uniform delivered prices: (1) freight absorption, (2) basing-point pricing, and (3) zone pricing.

Freight Absorption

This is a method whereby the seller is able to offer all buyers a uniform price, regardless of location, by absorbing freight charges for those located some distance from him. In Figure 29-1, A and B represent two producing points.

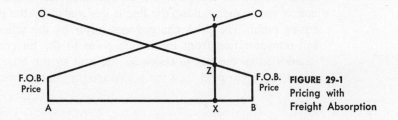

FIGURE 29-1
Pricing with
Freight Absorption

The price is set at A and at B. The lines OA and OB represent the cost of merchandise to any buyer located between A and B. These lines represent the cost to the purchaser if he were to buy from either A or B on an F.O.B. factory price basis. The total market is divided between A and B where lines OA and OB cross. Neither A nor B will cut the price to extend the market area, since retaliation by the other is almost certain. With a price cut, the two sellers would share the market in the same way at the higher price, but at lower revenues to each. However, a customer located at X could be induced to purchase from A, if A would charge the same price as B, and absorb the freight cost represented by the line YZ. By absorbing the freight costs both seek to expand their markets, and competition on some basis other than price is used in the respective market cultivation by the rival firms.

Basing-point Pricing

This pricing system is an outgrowth of nonsystematic schemes of freight absorption. Freight absorption reduces the net price to the buyer; and originally, basing-point systems were a means whereby freight absorption was wholly or partially offset by charging "phantom freight" to those located close to the buyer. Buyers paid the mill price plus rail freight from the nearest basing point, whether the actual freight was subject to more than or less than this charge. When actual freight costs were less than that charged, the differential was termed "phantom freight."

In Figure 29-2, a simplified basing-point pricing system is diagrammed. Points $B_{1,2,3}$ are buyers' locations, and $S_{1,2}$ are sellers' locations. The lines be-

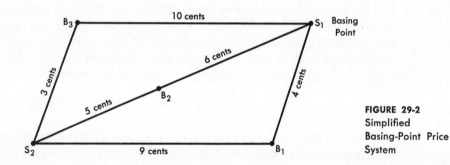

FIGURE 29-2
Simplified
Basing-Point Price
System

tween the points represent the distance between them. The cost of moving a unit of merchandise along the line is designated by the price on the line. S_1 is a basing point. The price charged any buyer by the seller is the base price plus rail transportation from the basing point to the buyer's location. Under these circumstances the net to seller S_2, the cost to the buyer, the freight absorbed, phantom freight paid, and the actual freight charges are as follows:

Buyer	Cost to Buyer	Freight Absorbed	Phantom Freight	Actual Freight	Net to Seller
B_1	$1.04	$ .05	$ —	$ .09	$ .95
B_2	1.06	—	.01	.05	1.01
B_3	1.10	—	.07	.03	1.07

This is an example of a single basing point. If it were followed by all members in an industry, the price quoted to the buyer would be the same, regardless of from what point the shipment was made.

Multiple basing-point pricing results in some variation in prices quoted, depending on location. Basing points are established for various districts. A seller could sell outside of his own district but would quote the base price of the basing point in the district of the buyer, plus transportation from that point to the buyer. For many years all steel and concrete was sold on a basing-point system regardless of the source of supply. Prices quoted in the original steel single basing-point system were Pittsburgh mill prices plus transportation from Pittsburgh to the buyer. After court action, the system was changed to multiple basing points as just described. This system finally came under court disfavor in 1948, in the Cement Institute case. Since that time, the tendency has been to make every mill site a basing point, with buyers having the option of specifying F.O.B. terms and choosing their own mode of transport. This alteration results in a system which permits sellers to absorb freight where necessary to compete in a particular market, but removes any element of phantom freight.

Both freight-absorption pricing and basing-point pricing are means used to expand the market for goods for which transportation costs are an important element in the final price to the buyer. Usually these price systems are found in goods which are standardized and in which price is an important factor in determining patronage. Participating producers are usually located some distance from their markets and are in high-fixed-costs industries, in which effective plant utilization is a major factor in maintaining profitable operations.

Zone Pricing

This form of pricing differs from the previous two in that the seller simply quotes prices F.O.B. buyer's location. He charges a uniform price in a single zone, and consequently penalizes some purchasers located close to the source of supply and subsidizes those distant. This policy expands market area and makes it possible to compete with rival sellers located closer to the buyer. Zone pricing also has the added benefit of permitting the seller to advertise a single price over the entire zone, making the quoting of prices much simpler.

Managerially speaking, the methods of varying prices to different buyers are used to achieve certain objectives. It is important for the price administrator to keep objectives clearly in mind and to select those methods which will achieve these objectives within legal constraints.

RESALE PRICE MAINTENANCE

Resale price maintenance is not a variation of price from a base price, but is a means of controlling prices at which goods are resold at the retail level. Some of the principal reasons why manufacturers are interested in controlling prices at this level follow.

Advantages to Manufacturers

Prevent Spotty Distribution

If the product is such that intensive distribution is necessary, volatile prices at the retail level may place a limit on the number of outlets willing to stock the item. If a low-operating-cost retailer offers the product at especially low prices, the high-operating-cost retailer will find it difficult to compete. The higher-cost outlet under these conditions is likely to seek a price reduction from the manufacturer, or refuse to handle the item and seek a different source of supply providing a comparable item. Neither is satisfactory to the manufacturer that needs intensive distribution.

Maintain Brand Prestige

Manufacturers spend large sums of money over a period of time to establish brand preference and some measure of consumer loyalty. This objective can be achieved only if the product develops significant prestige in the eyes of the consumer. When the product is offered at a number of different prices in the same market, it is thought that its prestige is weakened. This is a valid justification for maintained prices, in that the trademark to which all prestige attaches is a property right recognized in law. If the actions of some retailers are such that the property right is damaged, restrictive measures seem legally justified. The problem, however, is to prove damage to prestige.

Obtain More Profitable Unit Volume

Throughout this text, emphasis has been given to the desire of the manufacturer to compete on a basis of differential advantage. By so doing, the seller removes himself from direct price competition and makes it possible to achieve a more profitable price for his goods. The ability to support a price premium is not necessarily assured simply by using resale price maintenance, but the act of trying to maintain the price at which goods are sold at the retail level is a means to this end.

Minimize Dealer Conflicts

A sound dealer organization is essential in the distribution of most products. When some dealers in the system compete with others on a price basis, the system may be weakened. Often the selling of merchandise at excessively low prices requires a reduction in other services thought appropriate for the effective distribution of the product. The harmed dealers insist that the manufacturer exert the control necessary to prevent this form of competition or else that he remove the price competition from the system.

Advantages to Retailers and Wholesalers

From the retailer's point of view, devices used to maintain resale prices protect some retailers from low prices and more efficient retail operators. In general, the low-price operators are the large chain organizations. To the extent that they gain large shares of the total market for certain kinds of goods, they weaken the competitive and profit position of the smaller independent retailers. Since the large chains usually perform their own wholesaling activities, the weakening of the small independent retailers means a substantial loss in the markets of the wholesaler. Some wholesalers, therefore, vigorously support resale price maintenance.

These reasons for resale price maintenance all have a certain degree of validity. Most manufacturers and retailers seek the enviable position of being totally removed from price competition. The controversial question is whether or not they should receive the benefit of law to achieve and maintain this position.

Legal Background

The initial fair trade acts were passed in the early 1930's, with California passing the first in 1931. All states except Alaska, Missouri, Texas, Vermont, and the District of Columbia passed fair trade laws. These laws permit manufacturers to enter into contractual agreements with retailers handling their trademarked merchandise, to maintain the prices at which their goods are sold. Because of the difficulty in entering into an independent agreement with each retailer, practically all state fair trade laws have a "nonsigners" clause. This means that when the manufacturer enters into an agreement with one retailer in the state, this agreement, with proper notification, binds all other retailers handling the product in the state.

Since these state laws legalized intrastate vertical price-fixing agreements, they were legally valid as long as the goods did not enter interstate trade. If the goods were involved in interstate trade, such laws were a violation of the Sherman Act. In 1937, Congress passed the Miller-Tydings Act, which in effect removed such practices from violation of the Sherman Act.

In a celebrated case, the Calvert Distillers Corporation charged Schwegmann Brothers, a large retailer, with breach of contract when the latter sold at less than the maintained price.[2] The case was tried on the basis of the constitutionality of the "nonsigners" clause. In 1950, the Supreme Court held that it was not the intent of the Congress in passing the Miller-Tydings Act to also legalize the "nonsigners" clause. In 1952, the McGuire amendment to the Federal Trade Commission Act was passed, making the "nonsigners" clause legal in interstate trade.

Since 1952, a number of cases have been tried in state courts, testing the constitutionality of the state laws. The number of states now having fair trade laws has been reduced to thirty-one. Regardless of the legal status of fair trade acts, use of them by manufacturers is purely voluntary. The rash of discounting experienced during the decade of the 1950's is evidence that, economically speaking, they are breaking down. A manufacturer cannot afford to refuse to sell to some of the large retailers who compete primarily on a price basis. Enforcement is costly and difficult for the manufacturer, and during periods of intense price competition, enforcement is only token.

---

[2] *Schwegmann Brothers, et al., v. Calvert Distillers Corp.,* 341 U.S. 384.

Present Scope of Resale Price Maintenance

As we have pointed out, although legally supported in thirty-one states, the economic force of competition has diminished the use of fair trade laws by manufacturers. Although these laws are operative in such fields as drugs and cosmetics, appliances, sporting goods, liquor, and photographic equipment, it is not likely that more than 5 to 10 percent of all goods sold at retail is subject to them.

In summary, there are undoubtedly sound managerial reasons for the maintenance of resale prices. It is, however, doubtful whether a manufacturer should receive the benefit of law to achieve this position. To do so deprives the customer of the right to purchase at lower prices if he wishes to forego certain services. Further, forced maintenance all too frequently subsidizes the inefficient retailers. Therefore, these laws raise controversial issues of public policy and involve questionable elements of economic welfare. While their present status provides a materially weakened position for effective control, they could be reinstated at any time with more effective legislation. There are recurring attempts to bring this about, and the prevailing legislation and court interpretations could change at any time.[3]

LEGAL RESTRAINTS IN NONCOLLUSIVE
PRICE ADMINISTRATION

This section deals with the legal restraints placed on price administration practices employed in the absence of any collusive actions on the part of competitors in a single industry. The purpose of this section is to identify the legal problems for the marketing manager. The discussion is in no way intended to enable the manager to competently interpret the law. This task requires competent legal counsel. However, some general familiarity with the laws concerning certain price administration practices is essential. To that end, we shall now discuss the two major acts governing price administration: the Robinson-Patman Act and the Federal Trade Commission Act.

The Robinson-Patman Act

The Robinson-Patman Act, passed in 1936, was an amendment to the Clayton Act. The general purpose of the act was and is . . . "to prevent large buyers from using their economic power to extract favorable prices which are not granted to others less powerful and are not justified by savings to the seller resulting from differences in cost of manufacture, sale, or delivery." [4] In essence,

[3] See Jerome C. Darnell, "The Impact of Quality Stabilization," *Journal of Marketing Research* (August 1965), pp. 274–82.

[4] From an unpublished address entitled "Self Regulation Through Business Education: A Key to the Preservation of Our Competitive System," by Earl W. Kintner, former Chief of the Federal Trade Commission, delivered at Michigan State University, East Lansing, Mich., March 31, 1961, p. 5.

the law is designed to preserve competition by curbing the ability of buyers to extract discriminating prices and the willingness of sellers to offer them.

Section 2 details the kinds of action which are likely to result in illegal discriminations in price. The pricing practices prohibited by the act are reproduced here in summary form.

Section 2(a) makes unlawful any discrimination in price which lessens competition or tends to create a monopoly. It is aimed at such discriminations in price which may be prevalent in the use of variable price policies of manufacturers or those present in the offering of quantity and trade discounts. Even uniform delivered pricing practices may be declared illegal, since there may be a lessening of competition among buyers as those buyers close to the source of supply are not given the benefit of their proximity.

Section 2(c) is designed to prevent discrimination in price through the payment of brokerage fees to large buyers who perform their own brokerage services, or payment of brokerage fees to agents under the direct control of the buyer. Brokerage fees may not be paid to the buyer, except for services rendered, or to any agent of the buyer who is under the control of the buyer.

Sections 2(d) and (e) are designed to prevent indirect discrimination in price through the use of advertising allowances and the provision of certain services such as window displays, demonstrations, and the like. The only way in which these devices may be used is through offering to provide them to all buyers on equally proportionate terms.

Upon proof that a discrimination in price has been made, the burden of rebutting the case falls upon the giver of the discriminatory price. The bases for rebuttal are found in the defenses written into the act. These are as follows:

1. Goods are not of "like grade and quality."

2. No injury to competition.

3. Price differentials based on savings in cost associated with different quantities purchased.

4. Differences in price made in good faith to meet the equally low price of a competitor.

5. Differentials in price to reflect changing market conditions or the marketability of goods concerned.

Illegal price discrimination is confined to differences in price given to competing buyers purchasing "like grade and quality." The commission and the courts have not always been consistent in their interpretation of "like grade and quality." In *Federal Trade Commission* v. *The Borden Company,* the commission ruled that the private label brand of condensed milk sold to a large food chain at a lower price was equal in grade and quality to Borden's national brand sold to other retailers at a higher price. The products were chemically identical, but the national brand was highly advertised and sold under a different brand name. The Court of Appeals reversed the commission, upholding that the consumer preference for the advertised national brand makes the national brand different in grade, although chemically identical with the private label. The United States

Supreme Court reversed the Court of Appeals and upheld the commission's ruling.[5]

No injury to competition is, for all practical purposes, only a theoretical defense. In 1948 the United States Supreme Court ruled that it was not necessary for the commission to prove any injury to competition, but only to show that there is a "reasonable possibility" that this may be the effect. In *Federal Trade Commission* v. *Morton Salt Company,* the Court ruled that although the quantity discount structure was offered to all buyers by Morton, only a few were large enough to take advantage of it. The result was a "possible" injury to competition among buyers.[6] If the giver of discriminatory prices is charged with illegal price discrimination, he can be sure that injury to competition is involved in a prima facie way.

The cost defense is the most widely used defense but perhaps one of the least effective. A major source of differences in prices to buyers is the quantity discount structure used. To the extent the differences in prices can be justified on the basis of differences in costs, they are legal discriminations. The commission has not been willing in most cases to accept cost accounting designed to justify cost differences. Prior to 1962 there were only ten cases in which cost justification was a valid defense.[7] A part of the difficulty stems from the problem of allocating joint marketing costs to individual buyers. Computerized accounting may make this task somewhat easier in the future.[8]

The good faith defense has been subject to only a few special-fact cases. Two decisions are significant. In *Standard Oil Company* v. *Federal Trade Commission,* the commission had charged illegal price discrimination when Standard gave lower prices to four jobbers in the Detroit area than it gave to smaller service station customers in the same area. The Court of Appeals supported the commission, but the United States Supreme Court reversed the commission ruling. The Supreme Court reasoned that failure to allow Standard to meet the lower price offered to the jobbers by a competitor could result in a higher unit cost and a higher selling price to Standard's other customers if the jobbers did take a substantial portion of Standard's output.[9]

In 1963 the United States Supreme Court ruled against the Sun Oil Company. In *Federal Trade Commission* v. *Sun Oil Company,* the Court ruled that Sun could not give a lower price to one of its service station customers to allow that service station to compete with an adjacent service station selling another brand. It held that the equally low price being met by Sun was the price of a customer's competitor and not its own competitor. The defense can only be used among competitors at the same level of competition.[10]

Although the Robinson-Patman Act has existed for more than twenty-five years, it is still undergoing interpretation by the courts. The major issues in interpretation center around the language used—what is meant by such phrases

[5] *Federal Trade Commission* v. *The Borden Company,* 86 S. CT 1092 (March 1966).
[6] 334 U.S. 37, 68 S. CT 882, 92 L. Ed. 1196.
[7] Frederick M. Rowe, *Price Discrimination under the Robinson-Patman Act* (Boston: Little Brown and Company, 1962), p. 296.
[8] See Charles C. Slater and Frank H. Mossman, "Positive Robinson-Patman Pricing," *Journal of Marketing,* XXXI (April 1967), 8–14.
[9] *Standard Oil Company* v. *Federal Trade Commission,* 340 U.S. 849.
[10] *Federal Trade Commission* v. *Sun Oil Company,* 371 U.S. 505 (1963).

as "made available," "proportionally equal," "substantially to lessen," "tend to create a monopoly," "like grade," "services rendered," "competing buyers," and finally, and perhaps most important, what is legally meant by "competition" itself.

The effects of the law, however, have been to simplify discount structures in many firms; to diminish the use of cumulative quantity discounts; to do away with brokerage houses wholly owned by retailers; to change materially some prices placed on private brands by supplying manufacturers, by requiring similar cost treatment between their own brands and the private labels; and most important, to greatly increase the use of distribution cost analysis, since manufacturers must justify prices on the basis of provable cost savings.

The Federal Trade Commission Act

This act was passed back in 1914. It proclaimed: ". . . unfair methods in commerce are hereby declared unlawful." In 1938, the act was amended to include unfair or deceptive acts or practices as illegal. The determination of when an act is unfair or deceptive is left to the Federal Trade Commission, an agency established at the same time as the passage of the Act.

With respect to price administration, the Federal Trade Commission Act has been used in connection with uniform delivered pricing systems. The rigid adherence to a uniform delivered pricing system is considered to be an indication of price fixing among the members of an industry. Collusion need not be proved. The presence of price fixing is sufficient to constitute a lessening of competition among sellers and a violation of Section 5 of the Federal Trade Commission Act. There is no question concerning the legality of uniform delivered pricing systems under the Federal Trade Commission Act, if practiced only by a single seller. They, however, possibly may be unlawful under the Robinson-Patman Act.

The Federal Trade Commission has broad control over the almost boundary-defying area of trade practices. It is charged with the responsibility of preventing unfair methods of competition, without any attempt by the Congress in passing the legislation to spell out what is to be included under "unfair practices." The commission continuously undertakes a large number of investigations in an attempt to insure the preservation of "fair" competition. It has important jurisdiction over a number of areas beyond pricing, including: false and misleading advertising practices, promotional devices, packages, labeling, franchise agreements, and virtually every other means of market cultivation used by marketers in attempts to gain competitive advantage. Almost all observers would agree that the legislation creating the commission was desirable, and that the commission has performed an important and necessary function in the regulation of competition. Fewer would agree on the propriety of the commission's procedures, and, as would be expected, many of the commission's rulings have been the subject of great controversy.

Summary

Price administration is concerned with the way in which base prices are administered throughout the channel of distribution and the market area.

Variations from base prices are necessary because of sales made in different quantities and sales made to different kinds of intermediaries and to purchasers in different locations. Another facet of the price administration problem is the control exercised by manufacturers over the price at which goods are resold at distributive levels.

Variations in price made to reflect differences in conditions of sales result from variations in strategy, as well as quantity and trade discounts. A variable price policy is one in which the seller gives variations in price, depending upon the negotiating strength of the buyer. To avoid pressure from buyers to negotiate on price, some sellers follow a nonvariable price policy. Whenever there are variations in quantity sold, there may be a reduction in cost of selling to buyers of larger quantities. Quantity discounts are used to reflect these differences in cost. They are either cumulative and based on total purchases over a period of time or noncumulative, and apply to a single purchase. Cumulative quantity discounts do not provide the same savings in cost as from purchasing larger quantities. Trade discounts are given to different classes of intermediaries to reflect the differences in activities performed by the buyer for the sellers.

Leasing arrangements constitute an entirely different means of price administration. The buyer pays a rental fee for the services of the product for a specified period of time or output. The major reason for leasing, on the part of the seller, is to expand the market for his products over what it would be with a policy of outright sale. Leasing also has many advantages from the buyer's point of view, and is a market cultivation device that must be carefully considered in certain special lines of trade.

Uniform delivered prices are used to overcome geographic limitations in markets that would exist if F.O.B. factory prices were charged. Through a system of uniform delivered prices, a seller distant from the buyer can compete with a seller close to the buyer by absorbing all or a portion of the cost of freight to the customer. There are three types of delivered-price systems: (1) freight absorption, (2) basing-point pricing, and (3) zone pricing.

Resale price maintenance is a means used to control the price at which goods are sold at retail. The manufacturer is interested in controlling resale prices for the following reasons: (1) to prevent spotty distribution, (2) to maintain brand prestige, (3) to obtain higher prices, and (4) to minimize dealer conflicts. Retailers and wholesalers are also interested in resale price maintenance. The less efficient retailer views it as a way of preserving the *status quo* by preventing the more efficient lower-cost retailer from reflecting his economies in his prices. It also limits the advantage of some outlets in competing on the basis of reduced services. Wholesalers often favor it because they wish to preserve their markets, since the low-price retailers generally purchase directly from the manufacturer. Resale price maintenance is legalized through state fair trade acts and the Miller-Tydings Act, which ratifies the state acts. The fair trade acts today, although existing in a number of states, have limited effectiveness. Many manufacturers have given up trying to enforce their contracts, but legislation could reinstate these possibilities for price control at any time because of recurring pressure on legislative bodies for these laws.

Any variations in prices to different buyers of like merchandise is a discriminating price. Some discriminatory prices are legal, and some are illegal. They are illegal if they are in violation of the Robinson-Patman Act, that is, if their effect is substantially to lessen competition or to tend to create a monopoly or to injure, destroy, or prevent competition. The Robinson-Patman Act, passed in 1936, is designed to prevent large buyers from negotiating favorable prices not granted to other competing buyers and not justified by savings resulting from differences in cost of manufacture, sale, or delivery. A number of specific practices are detailed in the act, as well as the defenses available to those charged with illegal discriminatory prices.

The Federal Trade Commission Act, passed in 1914, declares illegal all unfair methods of competition in commerce. The commission has a broad responsibility for maintaining competition and for surveillance over the market cultivation practices of rival enterprises.

Questions and Problems

1. What is the difference between price administration and price determination?
2. "A nonvariable-price policy means that prices do not vary to different buyers." Comment.
3. What is the difference between a nonvariable-price policy and a single-price policy?
4. What is a trade discount? What is the justification for giving trade discounts?
5. What are the major reasons for the use of leasing rather than outright sale?
6. From the supplier's point of view, what are the disadvantages in leasing compared to outright sale?
7. What are the various types of uniform delivered prices?
8. Explain a simple single-point basing-point price system. Why do you suppose the courts frowned on this system?
9. Why might a manufacturer wish to use zone pricing? Are there special conditions that must prevail for this price policy to be used? If so, what are the conditions?
10. How might the use of resale price maintenance help a manufacturer to maintain brand prestige?
11. What are the advantages and disadvantages to retailers in resale price maintenance laws? What kinds of dealers would be most likely to support these laws?
12. What was the general purpose of the Robinson-Patman Act? In laymen's language, what are the major provisions of the act?
13. How is the Robinson-Patman Act different from all other laws with respect to prosecution and defense? What are the bases for rebuttal or defense in a proceeding under this act?
14. What are the specific unfair methods of competition declared illegal under the Federal Trade Commission Act? Should the FTC have the power of policing cigarette advertising to insist on having the nicotine content printed on packages?
15. State which of the following statements you most subscribe to, and why: (A) The marketing manager should be *thoroughly* familiar with legislation and court interpretations concerning pricing if he is to discharge his responsibilities knowledgeably. (B) The marketing manager can adequately meet his responsibilities if he is *generally* familiar with the major legislation affecting pricing, so as to know when legal counsel is required. (C) The marketing manager needs to know *little* or *nothing* about price legislation. This is an area where he shouldn't make a move without professional legal counsel.

Bibliography

Backman, Jules, ed., *Price Practices and Price Policies* (New York: The Ronald Press Company, 1953).

————, *Advertising & Competition* (New York: New York University Press, 1967).

Beckman, Theodore N., *Credits and Collections: Management and Theory,* 7th ed. (New York: McGraw-Hill Book Company, 1962).

Berlo, David K., *The Process of Communication* (New York: Holt, Rinehart & Winston, Inc., 1960).

Blood, J. W., ed., *Pricing: The Critical Decision,* Management Report No. 66 (New York: American Management Assn., 1961).

Borden, Neil H., *The Economic Effects of Advertising* (Homewood, Ill.: Richard D. Irwin, Inc., 1942).

Brink, E. L., and W. T. Kelley, *The Management of Promotion* (Englewood Cliffs, N.J.: Prentice-Hall, Inc., 1963).

Davis, Robert T., *Performance of Field Sales Managers* (Boston: Harvard Graduate School of Business Administration, 1957).

Evaluating Media, Studies in Business Policy, No. 121 (New York: National Industrial Conference Board, 1966).

Frey, Albert W., *Advertising,* 3rd ed. (New York: The Ronald Press Company, 1961).

————, *How Many Dollars for Advertising?* (New York: The Ronald Press Company, 1955).

Harper, Donald V., *Price Policy and Procedure* (New York: Harcourt, Brace & World, Inc., 1966).

Hovland, Carl I., *The Order of Presentation in Communication* (New Haven, Conn.: Yale University Press, 1957).

Hummel, F. E., *Market and Sales Potentials,* Part V (New York: The Ronald Press Company, 1961).

Kaplan, A. D. A., Joel B. Dirlam, and Robert F. Lanzillotti, *Competitive Pricing,* Management Report No. 17 (New York: American Management Assn., 1958).

————, *Pricing in Big Business* (Washington, D.C.: The Brookings Institution, 1958).

Katz, Elihu, and Paul F. Lazarsfeld, *Personal Influence: The Part Played by People in the Flow of Mass Communications* (New York: The Free Press, 1957).

Lucas, Darrell Blaine, and Steuart H. Britt, *Measuring Advertising Effectiveness* (New York: McGraw-Hill Book Company, 1963).

Lynn, Robert A., *Price Policies and Marketing Management* (Homewood, Ill.: Richard D. Irwin, Inc., 1967).

Mandell, Milton M., *Company Guide to the Selection of Salesmen,* Research Report No. 24 (New York: American Management Assn., 1955).

————, *The Field Sales Manager,* Management Report No. 48 (New York: American Management Assn.).

Martineau, Pierre, *Motivation in Advertising* (New York: McGraw-Hill Book Company, 1957).

Maynard, Harold H., and James H. Davis, *Sales Management,* 3rd ed. (New York: The Ronald Press Company, 1957).

Meyers, James H., and William H. Reynolds, *Consumer Behavior and Marketing Management* (Boston: Houghton Mifflin Company, 1967), Chap. 9.

Newgarden, Albert, ed., *The Field Sales Manager* (New York: American Management Assn., 1960).

Oxenfeldt, Alfred R., "Multi-stage Approach to Pricing," *Harvard Business Review* (July-August 1960).

Phelps, D. Maynard, and J. Howard Westing, *Marketing Management,* Part VII (Homewood, Ill.: Richard D. Irwin, Inc., 1960).

Schramm, Wilbur, ed., *The Process and Effects of Mass Communication* (Urbana: University of Illinois Press, 1960).

Setting Advertising Objectives, Studies in Business Policy, No. 118 (New York: National Industrial Conference Board, 1966).

Shannon, C. E., and W. Weaver, *The Mathematical Theory of Communication* (Urbana: University of Illinois Press, 1949).

Tosdal, Harry R., and Waller Carson, *Salesmen's Compensation* (in 2 vols.) (Boston: Division of Research, Harvard University, 1953).

Udell, Jon G., "How Important Is Pricing in Competitive Strategy?" *Journal of Marketing,* XXVIII, No. 1 (January 1964), 44.

Wolfe, Harry D., James K. Brown, and G. Clark Thompson, "Measuring Advertising Results," *Business Policy Study 102* (New York: National Industrial Conference Board, 1962).

Organization and Control of Marketing Resources

Early in the text we viewed the enterprise as a production-marketing system seeking its goals in an environment characterized as competition for differential advantage. We stressed the need for identification of goals. The starting point for programming marketing effort is the quantitative and behavioral investigation of markets. The need to establish targets as a means of achieving the broader goals of the enterprise was emphasized. Based upon precise market targets, the marketing mix—the product mix, the distribution mix, and the communications mix—are developed. The product strategies of the firm should reflect the internal requirements of the firm and the subtleties of the market place. The need for frequent adjustment of product strategy to resolve the conflicts of internal efficiency with market change underscores the dynamic qualities of this aspect of the marketing mix.

Next, the distribution network—the complex of intermediaries which provide the link between production and consumption—was examined. The activities necessary to efficiently make goods available to consumers are matched with the intermediaries who offer services for hire, in establishing a distribution mix. Recognizing that, along with availability of goods, communication is needed to energize or precipitate the process of exchange, the communications mix was considered. The various elements of market cultivation—advertising, sales promotion, personal selling, and price—should be combined in such a way as to create a maximum impact at point of ultimate sale, within cost-revenue constraints.

With the marketing mix established, we now examine the way the resources of the enterprise are organized to meet the requirements of effective competition. The need to develop organizational designs which accommodate a market orientation is especially important. Because the enterprise functions in a dynamic, competitive environment, the need for almost continuous change requires information flows to determine if the enterprise is maintaining a proper state of adjustment to its market. Information and control systems are an appropriate terminal consideration in the overall functioning of a business enterprise.

Market Orientation and Organizational Design

30

In order for the concept of market orientation to be an effective way of life for an enterprise, it must be translated into an organizational structure which is consistent with, gives meaning to, and provides an operating mechanism for that concept. The purpose of organizational design is to link people, facilities, and functions in the necessary concurrent and sequential relationships within the meaning of market orientation. Market orientation focuses on the needs of the enterprise for growth and survival in competitive markets. It recognizes that corporate objectives are achieved through instrumental action in the market place—action that is purposeful and precise for the ends sought. As an orientation to organizational design, market orientation involves the structuring of planning, decision, and control points to insure that those responsible for the achievement of market results have the requisite tools and resources to fulfill that responsibility.

This chapter explores the various ramifications of organizational design, first by reviewing certain trends that have precipitated organizational modifications for many companies; then by considering certain conceptual notions of organizational character; next by establishing criteria of organizational efficiency and applying these criteria to a detailed reorganization of a large consumer goods enterprise embracing the marketing concept; and finally by outlining certain organizational directions for the future.

MAJOR INFLUENCES LEADING TO ORGANIZATIONAL MODIFICATION

Evolution of Marketing Orientation

The evaluation of a managerial marketing philosophy as a way of corporate life has, in itself, called for organizational modification. The transition of an enterprise from production orientation to the intermediate stages of sales, then to promotion and, finally, to marketing orientation is accompanied by significant organizational change. When finally market forces and market opportunities become the basis for designing whole systems and subsystems of action, the organization must be capable of accommodating the new structure.

Marketing: A Profit Center in the Enterprise

A change that is developing slowly, but nonetheless perceptibly, is the growing desire to make marketing a profit center in the enterprise. In general, marketing personnel have been preoccupied with sales volume rather than profitability. This is primarily because their performance has been evaluated almost totally on sales volume. Other factors such as production costs and financial operations are recognized as influencing profitability and have tended to work *against* the idea of making marketing a profit center. These factors, along with the belief that "marketing profits" could not be fairly isolated, have led to excessive concern by marketing groups for structuring conditions favorable to volume attainment, sometimes at the expense of the welfare of the enterprise—as, for instance, pressure for low prices and big advertising budgets. More responsible administration may be achieved by making marketing a profit center through a system of intrafirm transfer prices. This has the effect of the factory selling to the marketing group and the marketing group having correspondingly greater freedom of action but more accountability for those actions. Organizational modifications and accompanying procedural changes are called for when such a system is introduced.

Centralization of Marketing Responsibilities at the Corporate Level

A tendency to centralize some responsibilities for marketing at the corporate level is evident. In the multiproduct or multidivisional firm, many decentralized marketing groups tend to come about as corporate growth takes place. This often reflects the widely divergent markets cultivated and the need for specialized sales forces and sales groups. As marketing divisions proliferate, a need is recognized for some degree of consistency in basic policy. Economies are recognized from having some centralized staff assistance available to all groups—as, for instance, economic forecasting and market research. Some areas require corporate-level decisions, such as the amount of money to be spent on institutional advertising. In order to accommodate these changes, a trend toward some degree of centralized marketing responsibility has taken place in the interest of tightening the administration and control of divergent marketing operations.

Delegation of More Decision-making Responsibility to Field Management

At the same time that there has been a trend toward centralization of responsibility at the corporate level, a countering trend has occurred in the form of an increasing pressure to delegate more decision-making responsibility to field management. At first glance, these two trends might appear to be in conflict. This isn't actually the case. The desire in the latter case is to push more decisions

533

Market
Orientation
and
Organiza-
onal Design

toward the scene of action and allow those who have adequate information to make decisions which they are capable of making. This is in contrast to holding *all* decisions for unnecessarily high-level consideration. The desire to get the right decisions made at the right point in the organization can accommodate both trends. It has been recognized that those responsible for individual territorial management must have some degree of decision latitude in order to adjust to local competitive conditions quickly and decisively.

Emergence of Long-range Planning

Long-range planning has emerged in many companies as a formal procedure. Increasingly, recognition is given to the view that operating executives burdened with day-to-day work requirements may have neither the time nor the inclination for the development of comprehensive, long-term, strategic plans. When allocation of scarce decision-making resources requires a choice between attention to immediate problems and long-range considerations, the tendency is for the immediate issues to receive priority. The consequence is that long-range planning may never be done. For these reasons, companies are increasingly giving long-range planning separate organizational status and personnel.

New and/or Increasingly Specialized Staff Groups in Marketing

Related to the previously mentioned trend is the growth of increasingly specialized staff groups in marketing and, at the same time, the evolution of new groups in the organization. Examples of the former include such staff services as sales training, sales promotion, parts and service, and forecasting and research. Examples of the latter include marketing comptrollers and managers of physical distribution. The emergence of these numerous staff groups has occasioned shifts in organizational alignments and, for that matter, organizational climate. In moving from largely a line organization to one comprised of both line and staff, with a large number of staff groups, profound changes occur in the environment for decision. Most organizations undergo a rather extended "learning period" before understanding how to work effectively with staff groups.

Corporate Growth

One of the principal factors that leads to reorganization is the expanded size and growth patterns of many firms. Organizational structure must be related to the scale of operations. What works well for a company of 500 employees will not work as effectively when growth to 5,000 employees occurs. To presume that ten times the same kind of effort will accommodate the growth is unrealistic.

It should be recognized that several, or conceivably all, of these factors and trends can be affecting a company simultaneously. It is when this happens that the greatest stress is placed on the organization and the most drastic reorganizations come about, which can change the whole fabric of an enterprise. One of the prices of such dramatic changes is often a substantial amount of tension and anxiety on the part of the many people affected in the organization.

CONCEPTS OF
ORGANIZATIONAL ORIENTATION

It is helpful in understanding organizational arrangements and relationships to recognize differences in organizational orientation that exist between different companies. Two principal orientations are examined in this section: (1) orientations which relate to formal and informal organization and (2) orientations which relate to centralization or decentralization.

Formal and Informal Organization

Every enterprise has two organizations, the formal and the informal, and the differences in orientation seem to relate more to the informal organization than to the formal. The formal organization is the one delineated by organization charts, job titles and descriptions, prescribed procedures, and the formal flow of information through the enterprise. It is the prescribed network of decision, power, and responsibility. The informal organization is what actually exists rather than what is intended. It is recognized by the operational pattern of power, decision, communication, and action. When persistent and fundamental variations exist between the formal and informal organizations, it usually signals the need for organizational realignment.

Concepts of leadership, authority, power, and decision are related to organizational structure. The informal organization is the structure within which these roles are played by participating personnel. We can distinguish at least three types of organizations with differences in their overall orientation. These are the *autocratically, bureaucratically,* and *democratically* oriented organizations. Within each, executives who are oriented to autocratic, bureaucratic, or democratic leadership can also be observed.[1]

Autocracy, Bureaucracy, and Democracy

The Autocratic Type of Organization

The autocratic organization is one in which compelling leadership and power are exercised from the top. Decision making is held within a small cluster of personnel or by, perhaps, even only one man. All but the most trival decisions are made within this very powerful group dominated by one man. Such decisions as are made at lower levels are made on the basis of subordinates' interpretations of what the authoritarian leader would want or do himself. The image of the leader is continuously present in any subordinate consideration. Under these circumstances, formal organization is relatively less important as a basis for the focus of decision, authority, and responsibility. All significant actions will be taken by the authoritarian leader or, if taken by others, reviewed prior to their promulgation and permitted to take effect only when they are completely consistent with his wishes.

[1] For a detailed discussion of these leadership forms, see Eugene E. Jennings, *The Executive* (New York: Harper & Row, Publishers, 1962).

535

Market
Orientation
and
Organiza-
ional Design

While an organization that is predominately oriented to authoritarianism may sound sinister, evil, and inefficient, the reverse is often the case. Objectives, values, and policies are frequently clear-cut and consistent. Understandable direction is provided for subordinates. Endless debate in policy formulation is eliminated or drastically curtailed. Implementation of programs tends to be very much according to plan because of the pressures toward conformity.

When the authoritarian system is headed by an intelligent, keenly perceptive person with good insights, sound intuitive judgment, and the ability to inspire confidence and loyalty, the end result can be exceptionally good. Some of the famous early industrial complexes were built this way.

This organizational orientation is hard to sustain, however, as an organization becomes large and invades complex areas of operations. The lack of system, the delays caused by extreme centralization, the complexity of decisions, and the morale problems among competent people who feel the lack of participation in decisions, all cause this form of organizational orientation to be self-defeating.

The Bureaucratic Type of Organization

The bureaucratic organization is most easily recognized by the extreme role of systems and procedures. Standard operating procedures exist for almost any action, even the most routine. Policies are established as normative rules of behavior at all levels of the organization. Formal communications characterize the operation of the system. Standardization is desired, as is uniform treatment of personnel. Very complete records usually are required. Controls are established in almost every facet of operations, and policing is practiced when necessary to insure compliance with established procedures.

One usually associates government with bureaucracy. Moreover, it is common to associate bureaucracy directly with inefficiency, red tape, endless delay, excessive personnel, and a great deal of paper shuffling. This is hardly a fair characterization. Some of the model forms of organization are characterized by considerable bureaucracy—the Roman Catholic Church, our military forces, and the court system of the United States. In any large and complex organization, great reliance must be placed on system. A continuous array of *ad hoc* decisions would lead to chaos—operations would ultimately break down completely. Men cannot realistically dominate the system, as is feasible in small organizations. To do so would lead to inconsistency, conflicting values, discordant methods, great overlapping of responsibility, hopelessly tangled communications lines, and little coordination of a series of actions in a total program. A modern, large, complex organization must submit to orderly systems, policy formulation, and organized communications and coordination devices, hopefully, with able, motivated people to operate the system and make it work effectively.

The Democratic Type of Organization

In recent years, a trend toward the democratic model as an organization form has taken place. Much has been made of the participative roles of personnel in the organization. Recognition has been given to the view that it is no longer feasible to publish policy directives and expect compliance—people respond with conviction only to that which they have had a part in determining. Respect for authority is not regarded as a right associated with organizational position; it is something that must be earned by the man. In its most persuasive form, it is argued that a pooling of the best brains available should precede the making of complex decisions—two heads are better than one, so to speak. Consequently, the most conspicuous manifestation of this organizational orientation is the large number of committees which it tends to foster. A very prevalent procedure in the contemporary enterprise is for the executive to assemble all subordinates who would be affected by any decision, to carefully solicit their views, then to discuss all aspects of each of the alternatives proposed, and, on the basis of collective judgment, reach a joint decision—presumably one that all will carry out earnestly and enthusiastically.

The advantages of this organizational form are that strong motivation is aroused; the best resources within the firm are brought to bear on any particular decision; the heads of subordinate units all have an opportunity to participate; communication is increased through direct access and participation by the larger number of people involved in policy formulation; less control is required when subordinates carry out programs they themselves have participated in planning; and, finally, executive development is nurtured by the very nature of the participative roles played at all levels in the organization. For many companies, this "management by committees" has worked well. Executives often prefer to work in such an enterprise, both for its genuine merits and perhaps because of the collective security it provides them.

Offsetting considerations are several. The most important of these is the inability to pin down responsibility for decisions—to appropriately place blame for failures or to gain credit for success. "We decided" or "they decided" is a common retort when things go wrong. Other considerations are the inefficiencies from the point of view of the time involved in reaching a decision that such an approach entails: it presumes a large number of competent personnel participating—collective ignorance or incompetence can be disastrous; it can generate a severe pressure for group conformity and stifle creative solutions; it can foster dissipation of energies in politics through the subtleties of vote gathering.

The "Multicratic" Organization

Some organizations try to embrace all three of the forms we have discussed, and for this reason are called *multicratic* organizations. The multicratic form has its own particular personality as well as elements of the other three, and is increasingly the sought-after model of modern corporate enterprise. It is characterized by bold, aggressive, imaginative leadership that is particularly evident in times of stress and provides a strong sense of direction for the enterprise. It expresses itself in the form of rather clear-cut objectives, flowing from the top down. It relies on systems to economize decision making in the complex enterprise and seeks order and reasonable amounts of formal procedure to insure that work gets done according to program requirements, with adequate information provided for decision making. It encourages decentralized decision making for its participative value, motivation, and efficiency. It uses committees with restraint, where their coordinative and judgmental value is evident without diluting responsibility. Job descriptions are specific in order to formalize work responsibility. It encourages individual enterprise, but within a prescribed frame of reference. High

537

Market
Orientation
and
Organiza-
ional Design

morale is sought through the harmony of individual objectives and values and group objectives and values. It produces organizational unity through the formal organization's being very much in line with the informal organization.

Centralized vs. Decentralized Administration

A second area of conceptual importance in organizational understanding and design involves centralized and decentralized management. A tension exists between these extremes, which must be reconciled or embraced in any operating organization. For our purposes, we need only discern the major differences between the two in terms of administrative consequences, and then relate them to market orientation.

Systems vs. Results

In centralization, emphasis is placed on system and internal procedures. Operating personnel are expected to follow carefully formulated procedures, with higher levels of authority accepting proportionally greater responsibility for the effect of the procedures. In the decentralized enterprise the emphasis is on external considerations and results. The individual manager's performance is thus gauged on the results he accomplishes, in contrast with his implementation skills.

Single vs. Multiple Methods

The centralized enterprise seeks the optimum or one best way of performing all operations. If careful analysis has gone into evaluating the promotional effectiveness of various layouts of toiletries in a food chain, for example, the optimum choice is extended to all units in the chain under centralized administrative concepts. In the decentralized organization, however, we find diverse and sometimes discordant methods being used. This is associated with the greater freedom of managers and the orientation to results rather than methods.

Relaxed vs. Close Control

Decisions tend to be made at the scene of action under decentralization and are not always coordinated throughout the company. Spontaneity of decision is more prevalent—controls are relaxed insofar as all but performance yardsticks are involved. In the centralized organization, more effective controls are exercised over the type of action taken, and prerogatives of individual managers are restricted. Coordination of effort is expected—through policing, if necessary.

Narrow vs. Broad Span of Control

The span of control refers to the number of subordinates reporting to a superior executive. A broader span of control is associated with decentralized administration. The number of subordinates an executive can have reporting to him effectively increases as the freedom of those subordinates increases. A district manager may have twenty-five store managers reporting to him if those store managers are held only for results and have great autonomy of decision. Or, a director of merchandising may have a large number of merchandise managers reporting to him if they have independence and need little coordination. Conversely, the centralized system has a narrow control span—a consistent feature in view of the system, control, and coordinative requirements of the individual manager's job.

Layers of Supervision

As a broader span of control exists in decentralized management, there are also fewer layers of supervision from the bottom to the top of the organization. While the manager at any level feels closer identity with top management, there are also fewer promotion opportunities. The opposite situation prevails in the centralized system.

Specialization

Centralization requires a large number of highly specialized personnel. More diverse staff groups tend to exist. Specialists can, with rather carefully defined fields of inquiry, be found in many areas. In decentralized organizations, more overlapping of job responsibilities occurs. It is common to find things never quite in order, as it might be somewhat unclear as to specifically what prerogatives are associated with various jobs. Individuals tend to "grow" in jobs for a period as compared with finding relatively comprehensive systems and job specifications. Informality is considerably more apparent. The system seems to breed more generalists than specialists.

Functions vs. Men

The organization is characteristically built on functions to be performed in centralized enterprises, whereas greater weight is placed on men in decentralized enterprises. The large enterprise is often considered to be more vulnerable when it fails to build the enterprise on a strong functional base which dominates individual executives. Many of the largest enterprises, such as government, the military, and the church, are built on a functional base rather than on individual personalities of the leaders involved. Critics of the functional view take the position that the quality of management resources is always of paramount consideration, and systems which foster the development of managerial personnel clearly enhance the long-run welfare of the enterprise.

There is no *pure* form of either centralized or decentralized administration. Companies tend toward one or the other form, and each presents mixed blessings and limitations. Perhaps this accounts for the heated debate over the years on the desirability of the two alternatives. It has been argued that decentralization is more compatible with market orientation and, in fact, is a natural outgrowth of market orientation.[2] This view postulates that centralization is more oriented toward the internal aspects of managerial concern, while decentralization has a focus of external considerations and results.

Actually, such a forced choice of polar positions is hardly the relevant consideration. The really pertinent issues are, *what decisions can appropriately be decentralized* and *what decision areas must be taken to a higher level of*

---

[2] See David G. Moore, "Marketing Orientation and Emerging Patterns of Management and Organization," in *Managerial Marketing: Perspectives and Viewpoints,* Eugene J. Kelley and William Lazer, eds. (Homewood, Ill.: Richard D. Irwin, Inc., 1958), pp. 243–48.

539

Market
Orientation
and
Organiza-
ional Design

centralized concern for efficient and effective administration. This is especially true of marketing organizations. The vigorous debate over recent years of the merits of the two systems has hardly been a productive argument, for it has involved the shooting down of straw men. Every organization has, and needs, some degree of centralized *and* decentralized administration—the critical problem is to be sure that decision points are at appropriate levels throughout the organization.

EVOLUTION OF AN ORGANIZATION EMBRACING A CONCEPT OF MARKET ORIENTATION

Before interpreting the criteria of organizational efficiency, it is useful to observe various organizational stages of an enterprise which went through three distinct stages before it evolved into an organization embracing a concept of market orientation.[3]

Figure 30-1 conveys the arrangement of activities some years back when the enterprise had a heavy production orientation, reinforced with good technical research and engineering skills. The sales department was responsible solely for the activities of the sales force. Responsibilities of pricing, advertising, sales

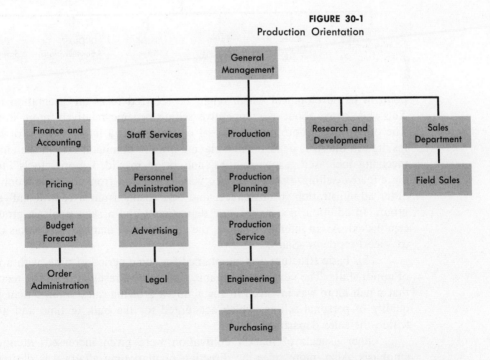

FIGURE 30-1
Production Orientation

[3] The illustrations are not precise—they are drawn, however, from an actual situation in a major American corporation and reflect quite sharply the character of change. The first three exhibits are not organization charts—they are intended to convey the general arrangement of activities.

forecasting, order handling, product planning, product service, and sales personnel functions were located in other than the sales department. The sales department was, in effect, an order-obtaining group operating in the consumer durable goods field.

After several intermediate shifts, in Figure 30-2 the organization is at a

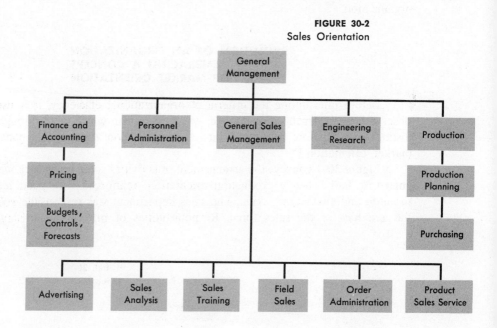

FIGURE 30-2
Sales Orientation

point in its development which might be referred to as an orientation to sales. This shift came about as competitive selling became relatively more important. The pressure for more rapid disposal of goods and a larger volume of business resulted in the sales department's playing a more dominant role in the enterprise, receiving increased responsibilities, and being provided more "tools" to carry out effective selling. Product service was transferred from the production group, order administration from finance, and advertising from a central-staff services group. In addition, a sales training department and a sales analysis group were established. As an interesting aside, the general sales manager's title was changed to Vice-President—Sales.

This basic structure was maintained for some period of time, with a number of minor shifts. The next major organization change resulted from the recognition that much more was involved in sustaining a growing sales volume than just the quality of personal selling, which accounted for the bulk of time and attention within the sales department.

Other aspects of market cultivation were given increased attention and emphasis. Also, more scientific direction of marketing affairs was desired. This led to the creation of several new staff groups and the realignment of others as shown in Figure 30-3. The principal change, however, was the creation of separate but equal groups responsible for the conduct of market affairs. The one

541

Market
Orientation
and
Organiza-
tional Design

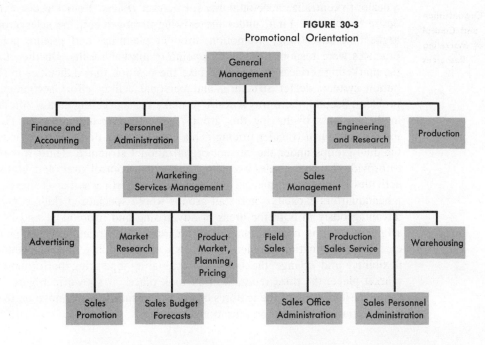

FIGURE 30-3
Promotional Orientation

is composed of the line field-selling organization and closely related *operating* groups. The other is responsible for the creation of promotional programs to be *executed* by the sales organization, where the programs involve distributors and dealers or any part of the distribution system; the research, forecasting, and budgeting functions; and the conduct of advertising campaigns. These two major groupings report independently to the top level of corporate management.

The purpose of this arrangement was to prevent one group from dominating the other and to prevent the bulk of expenditures for marketing effort from being allocated to the traditional area of personal selling activity. To provide a better integration of activities logically connected with the market place, several functions were transferred from elsewhere in the company or given formal participative roles in either of the two distribution groups. Forecasting was transferred from finance, and provision for product planning was made in the marketing services group, whereas it was previously the province of the production organization. Marketing and sales budgets were shifted from accounting and finance, and pricing recommendations were formally made a part of the responsibility of marketing services. Warehousing was shifted to the sales management group and the sales training function was broadened to include all aspects of sales personnel administration (recruiting, selection, etc.). This activity had formerly been part of the corporate personnel function.

This organizational structure is, in fact, a modern design, characteristic of many large corporate enterprises today. It can work effectively when manned by proper personnel. Several aspects of the organizational structure regarded as serious defects, however, led to the most recent dramatic reorganization.

After a period of time with the divided marketing responsibility, there was a desire to centralize accountability for market results. Four reasons explain this desire for change. First, under the existing arrangement, the sales group could argue that advertising, promotion, product planning, and pricing policies and practices were responsible for disappointing market results. On the other hand, the marketing services group could take the position that difficulties in the distribution system, dealer structure, and personal selling effort accounted for the problem. Second, there was a desire to make the marketing area a "profit center" in the business by having this group "buy" its merchandise from the factory through intrafirm transfer pricing. This could not be done with the existence of the dual groups under the current organizational structure. Third was the desire to provide the senior sales executive with direct control over staff groups whose activities immediately affected his operations. Fourth was the desire to place in a headquarters capacity some staff groups whose specialized skills could be used advantageously in both the areas of advertising and promotion, and in personal selling operations, namely, marketing research. So to streamline information flows, ease the coordination problem, pin down accountability, provide better budget flexibility, and change the basis for evaluating operating performance in the market place, the third reorganization took place, as shown in Figure 30-4. We shall consider some of the features of this organization as we move on to consider the criteria for effective organizational design.

CRITERIA FOR EFFECTIVE ORGANIZATIONAL DESIGN

In this section we are seeking specific tests that can be applied to an organization to determine whether it needs modification and, if so, in what way. In auditing an existing organization for this purpose, careful consideration should be given to the criteria of effective organizational structure in the following areas.

Organizational Orientation

Often the organizational design for a particular company begins with the president's office and works down through successive layers of management and supervision until finally consideration is given to field-selling operations. This is not the appropriate design starting point, since the purpose is to structure the organization in such a way as to put it in the best possible position to compete effectively in the market place. Hence, we ought not to organize the factories, research, engineering, and product-development groups until we have established the basic approach to be taken to the market. Therefore, *we should start with the market and work back,* instead of from the president's office out. We want to mobilize, at each point behind the market, the necessary resources and appropriate authority for the effective conduct of operations.

In Figure 30-4 the product representatives and service-and-parts representatives were formed into two competing teams to make up a district. This clustering of products and specialization of selling effort was regarded as essential to effective market competition. Also decided at this time was the choice that all

FIGURE 30-4
Market Orientation

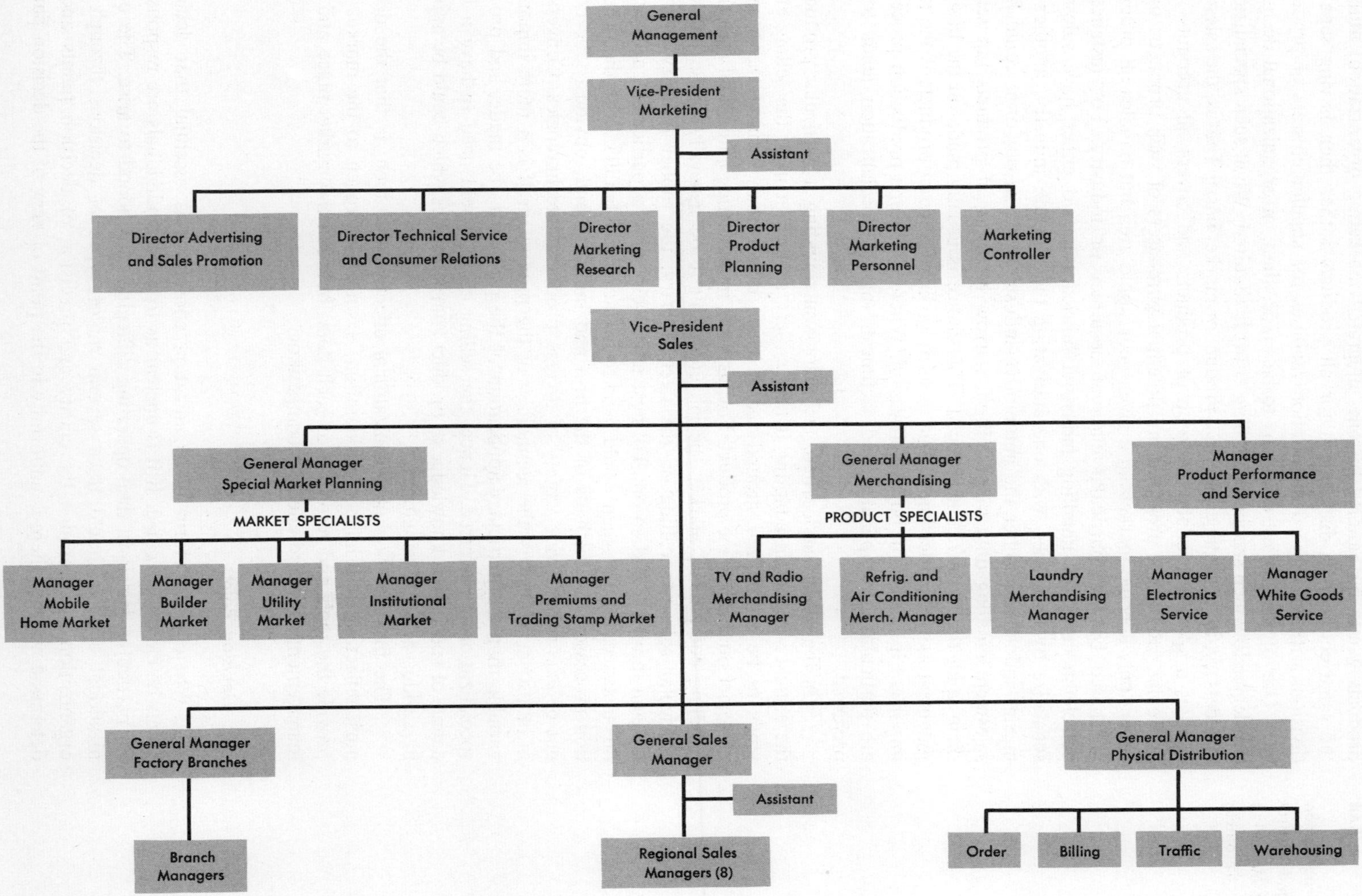

General Management

Vice-President Marketing

Assistant

Director Advertising and Sales Promotion

Director Technical Service and Consumer Relations

Director Marketing Research

Director Product Planning

Director Marketing Personnel

Marketing Controller

Vice-President Sales

Assistant

Manager Product Performance and Service

Manager Electronics Service

Manager White Goods Service

General Manager Merchandising

TV and Radio Merchandising Manager

Refrig. and Air Conditioning Merch. Manager

Laundry Merchandising Manager

PRODUCT SPECIALISTS

General Manager Special Market Planning

Manager Mobile Home Market

Manager Builder Market

Manager Utility Market

Manager Institutional Market

Manager Premiums and Trading Stamp Market

MARKET SPECIALISTS

General Manager Physical Distribution

Order

Billing

Traffic

Warehousing

General Sales Manager

Assistant

Regional Sales Managers (8)

General Manager Factory Branches

Branch Managers

products would be handled by one integrated marketing organization, utilizing the same channel of distribution for all products rather than having separate divisions with specialized distribution facilities for smaller clusters of products.

One of the earliest decisions to be made, then, in organizational design is the degree to which specialized selling effort is required. When such specialization is necessary, it is usually either on a product or market basis. That is, the salesman handles a specific product or group of products and covers all accounts in a particular geographic area that are potential purchasers of such products, or he covers only specific markets in a given geographic area but handles all products purchased by that particular class of customer or industry. For instance, a petroleum company handling industrial lubricants could either have salesmen specialize by industries, with one cultivating the aviation industry, another the marine industry, another the automotive industry, and so on; or it could have salesmen handling only a specialized, narrow grouping of products but selling them in all the industries mentioned. This choice is usually made on the basis of judgment as to whether knowledge of users or knowledge of products is the most important in successful buyer cultivation. Where the user's production processes are particularly complicated and technical, market specialization tends to be preferred.

On the other hand, where technology surrounding a particular product is the critical variable in adapting it to a variety of market uses, the selling effort tends to be specialized around the product rather than around the type of customer purchasing the product. For instance, in marketing automated materials-handling equipment, market specialization might be generally preferred, with particular salesmen calling on the steel industry, the rubber industry, the petroleum industry, and so on. To most effectively serve a particular customer in this instance, the salesman would need to be intimately familiar with the production processes and methods of the firm and industry; and, obviously, he could not be expert in a wide variety of diverse production technologies. Conversely, in industrial adhesives, the technology of the product itself is a more important variable than the particular application of the product to be made, and product specialization is preferred. Hence, the selling effort would need to have a high degree of specialized knowledge of product characteristics which could be applied in a wide variety of situations.

The first criterion of organizational effectiveness, then, is that the design must reflect, as a primary consideration, a sound approach to the market and provide the tools and resources at each point between the market place and top management to insure effective competition.

Decision Points

Whatever the form of organization chosen, it is essential that decision points be clearly specified. If it is unclear as to which individuals are responsible for particular decisions, then operating difficulties are bound to arise. The organizational analyst should trace several major types of decisions through the organization to determine the clarity and precision of decision points and to determine whether there is uniformity in the point of view of the decision partic-

545

Market
Orientation
and
Organiza-
ional Design

ipants as to particular roles and final jurisdiction. The second criterion, then, is that decision points in the organization must be clearly specified and that the power to act must not be impaired.

Line and Staff Relationships

The third criterion is that line and staff responsibilities for operations should be clearly distinct and separate. This criterion raises the issue of the primacy and sovereignty of the line organization. Staff personnel must not be in a position to usurp line management prerogatives, that is, the prerogatives of decision and implementation of programs. Notice in the organization chart shown in Figure 30-4 that the line organization is specified by double lines. Individuals in this chain of command are responsible for program decisions and implementation. Prior to reorganization, as many as twelve different people could give a field salesman or a district manager directions and operating orders. In the bulk of the cases, these were staff personnel, such as merchandising managers, product managers, the market research manager, and director of sales training. This condition is untenable, for it simply does not provide for orderly management. This is one reason why job descriptions are so important; they specify the duties and responsibilities of the particular position and help to eliminate confusion of this kind. The organizational design should specifically limit the possibility of multiple direction and control at various levels in the organization.

Adequacy of Staff

The fourth design criterion is the adequacy of staff groups for long-term planning and specialized evaluation. A noticeable and limiting deficiency in many organizations is the lack of good long-range planning. This condition often exists because line executives are excessively burdened with day-to-day operations and do not have the time (and sometimes the inclination) to formulate longer-term plans and programs. It is a natural human tendency, when faced with the choice between dealing with immediate matters and dealing with longer-range considerations, to choose that which cannot be delayed or put off to a later date. Consequently, the organization must be structured to insure provision for adequate planning and evaluation.

One way to handle this problem is to maintain a sufficiently narrow span of control or number of subordinates reporting to one person, making time available for the manager to personally handle the planning function. A more current tendency is to provide executives carrying important responsibilities with sufficient staff resources for this purpose. The number and diversity of staff units is partially dependent on the size of the organization, its sales volume, the complexity of its markets, the nature of its products, the technology surrounding the production and application of the product in the market, and the degree to which the organization follows centralized versus decentralized organizational patterns. No specific rules of thumb can be applied to determine the adequacy of staff groups. Rather, this is a matter of judgment. A good organizational design, however, has this feature.

Information Flows

Two considerations are important in planning information flows. First, does information moving both up and down the organization consistently skip a level without undergoing some change in form? If this happens regularly, then it raises questions as to whether that level of supervision is essential and necessary in the organization. If, for instance, the information required from the various districts by a general sales manager is precisely the same as that needed by the regional managers, it raises a question as to whether the regional manager is an essential supervision intermediary between the general sales manager and the district managers.

The converse of this situation is equally valid. That is, if the district sales manager needs the same information from the general sales manager as that received by the regional managers, doubts would be raised as to the design effectiveness of the organizational structure. There are occasions when it is desirable for information to flow from the very bottom to the top (and vice versa) without undergoing any change in form whatsoever, but these should be exceptions rather than the rule. Presumably, as information flows upward, it becomes more general and less detailed or specific. As information flows downward, at each step or level of supervision it should become more specific, tailored to the particular needs of that level in the organization.

The second consideration in information flows is related to the clarity of decision points mentioned earlier. Decision points should be specified at the lowest level in organization at which the individual holding the position has all the relevant information to make an intelligent judgment as to the course of action to be followed. In other words, decisions should be made at the first level reached in the organization, beginning with the market place, where all relevant information pertaining to that decision has been assembled. If decisions are made either above or below this point, we have a situation where either an individual is forced into a position of making judgments without adequate information and data, or the individual is burdened with a number of decisions that he should not have to make and which could more appropriately be made at a lower level. This criterion of organizational efficiency, then, deals with the matter of whether decision patterns are compatible with information patterns, and whether responsibility flows are matched with appropriate information flows.

Coordination Levels

Activities requiring close coordination ideally should be on the same level of organization, or if this is not possible, as close to similar levels of organization as possible. This can be noticed in Figure 30-4, which shows market-planning managers and merchandising managers directly opposite each other on exactly the same organizational level. They are positioned thus because advertising and promotional programs for a particular product line, and the planning for variations in that particular product assortment, must be coordinated and integrated with the plans to develop a particular market. If one manager is subordinate to

547

Market
Orientation
and
Organiza-
onal Design

the other, a tendency will exist for the proposals of the higher-ranking manager to prevail.

We should not confuse this point with the situation wherein top-level, general plans are made and specific actions at lower levels necessarily must be coordinated with the broader plan or strategy. *This* coordination criterion refers to the situation wherein *simultaneous lateral* actions, rather than *vertically integrated* actions, are taking place. When responsibility for lateral activities is on widely different levels in the organization, the higher-ranking manager might not be particularly prone to report his ideas and actions to a substantially lower-ranked executive whose programs should dovetail, or at least should not be in conflict. Notice that in Figure 30-4 the managers responsible for selling effort through distributors and those responsible for selling effort through manufacturers' branches are again on the same level of organization, in an attempt to insure consistency of action between the two channels of distribution.

Span of Control

Earlier reference was made to the span of control (number of subordinates reporting to one superior). No arbitrary number can be established that is universally applicable under all conditions. The number varies from as few as three to as many as fifty, depending on: the uniformity of the duties of subordinates (or the lack of it); the extent to which activities are routine or highly varied; the degree to which subordinates' activities must be coordinated; and the complexities and importance of decisions to be made. The Bible refers to units of ten in the organization of tax collectors and of the Roman army. A more current maximum seems to be seven at the upper levels of organization. This number may expand at the lower levels of supervision.

The problem of span of control is particularly difficult to deal with at the presidential level. Executives responsible for such areas as purchasing, personnel, labor relations, research, engineering, public relations, finance, comptrollership, legal counsel, manufacturing, international operations, and company acquisitions, all regard their functions as so important as to justify reporting to the company president. Inserting an executive vice-president hardly solves this problem—it merely transfers it from one level of responsibility to another. To a lesser degree, this same problem exists at lower levels of the organization. Notwithstanding the complexities involved, one of the criteria of good organizational design is that the appropriate span of control exist at all organizational levels.

Authority and Responsibility

One of the best known of the organizational design criteria is that authority and responsibility should be as closely matched as possible. This match can never be perfect, but there should not be great variances between the responsibilities of a position and the authority to act in such a way as to insure the proper discharge of that responsibility. This is a rather perplexing problem in marketing organization, because if the marketing manager is given responsibility for market results, then, according to the criterion, he should be given commensurate authority to control the variables that make for market results. However, it is not possible to delegate authority to administer all the factors that make for market achievement. For instance, pricing decisions, channels of distribution, and the nature of product lines are only illustrative of the kinds of variables that cannot necessarily be delegated to an individual market manager, for they may deal with broad matters of corporate and overall marketing policy.

Another example of the difficulty in applying this criterion in the marketing organization deals with the authority given regional and district sales managers in the recruiting, selecting, and training of salesmen. It may be uneconomical to have every district or regional sales manager perform these functions himself when they can be more efficiently handled at the central staff level. One sales training specialist or department can serve effectively the needs of a number of different district or regional offices. Similarly, college recruiting by a central staff may be more efficient than having six different regional managers all recruiting on the same campus. Yet, the criterion would indicate that if the district sales manager is to be held responsible for sales results in his area, then he should have authority over the hiring and training of people that account for his capacity to achieve the desired results.

This problem can be handled by giving the district or regional sales manager an approval or rejection prerogative. When a vacancy occurs in a field-selling position, the individual manager has the prerogative of accepting or rejecting a candidate supplied by the headquarters or central office staff unit. This means that the individual manager is hiring a new man from the headquarters unit and, consequently, does have jurisdiction over the men to be placed in his operating unit. This is a reasonable, but not exact, match of responsibility and authority. This same type of prerogative can be applied elsewhere to gain a realistic match of authority and responsibility.

Provision for Corporate Growth

Earlier in this chapter, corporate growth was mentioned as one of the principal factors accounting for the need for organizational modification. While the organization must be designed in such a way as to be consistent with the existing scale of operations, a good design provides some built-in flexibility for accommodating corporate growth. Growth within reasonable limits should not necessitate a basic change in the structure of the organization. Notice in Figure 30-4 the ease of adding district managers, regional managers, merchandising managers, branch managers, and market managers, as they are needed, and even new staff units. All of these positions can be added to the organization without changing its basic structure or operating procedures and systems. Substantial corporate growth can, therefore, be accommodated readily. If, however, corporate growth comes about through widely divergent patterns of product diversification, then it is likely that some change in the structure of the organization will be required to accommodate this type of growth. A good organization, however, provides some inherent versatility and flexibility. This criterion, then, is a test of whether additional corporate growth can be accommodated with ease.

549

Market
Orientation
and
Organiza-
ional Design

Formal-informal Organization Variances

The formal organization is the way in which the firm has been officially structured for operations. It is the organization as constituted by job descriptions, levels of authority, line and staff relationships, and the flow of information and decision. The informal organization describes the way the firm actually operates, not what is *supposed* to be but what in practice *is* the structure of decision and action. Because of flaws in organizational design, and variations in the abilities and personalities of executives, a separate power structure emerges as distinct from the organizational structure. The formal organization, as a result, is rarely an exact duplicate of the informal organization. One of the criteria of good organizational design, however, is that the formal and informal organizations be closely matched, if not exact duplicates. The organizational analyst should carefully observe the behavior of the organization to determine the degree of conformity between these two structures. If he observes substantial variation, then he must judge as to whether the structure of the organization needs modification or whether the behavior patterns of individuals within the organization need to be altered.

ORGANIZATIONAL DIRECTIONS
FOR THE FUTURE

While the discussion has stressed the criteria of good organizational design, certain directions for the future can be noted. Organizational evolution is continuous, and many firms find limitations implicit in any given structure; that is, there are certain advantages and limitations to each style of organizational arrangement. As firms grope for greater effectiveness in the future, directions for change might well lie along some of the following lines:

1. Organizations will be far more fluid than at present. Information will flow readily across organizational lines and up and down vertical levels, available to all in whatever form is most useful.

2. "Modular organizational units" will appear which can be readily recombined in novel ways to meet fluctuating needs as markets and products change.

3. Personnel will be deployed on the basis of more loosely clustered "task packages" rather than highly structured job descriptions. Job descriptions tend to be more activity oriented; task packages are more results focused.

4. Electronic data processing will make feasible a clustering of key decisions within a small core of highly competent executives. Yet, many firms are recognizing the critical need for decentralizing decisions. The cross-currents may lead to a new form of line and staff, with the high-talent corporate staff being given an official mandate to usurp operating line management prerogatives on the principle of the exception—that is, relatively infrequently when special strategic circumstances prevail.

5. Finally, organizational styles will shift far more readily than in the past.

The blend of autocracy, bureaucracy, and democracy will be varied depending on the stage of corporate development, professional differences between particular organizational entities, and the newness of missions, this without the accompanying supposition that personnel are being subjected to a kind of corporate schizophrenia.

Summary

Any enterprise is likely to prosper with three basic ingredients—vigorous, intelligent leadership; orderly systems; and capable, motivated personnel. But this obscures the complexities of organizational alignments which provide the structure for decision and action. Unfortunately, once designed, no matter how painstakingly and thoroughly done, organizational structure is subject to frequent modification and change. Business management is a continuous process of adaptive behavior to keep the firm in a good state of adjustment to its environment.

This chapter has traced some of the influences that make organizational modification necessary. The special features of what may be referred to as the autocratic, bureaucratic, and democratic types of organization were outlined, leading to the conclusion that the most effective organization incorporates some features of each and may be characterized as the multicratic type of organization. Next, the tensions between centralized and decentralized organization were considered; and finally, certain criteria of the effectiveness of organizational design were outlined in the context of some specific illustrations of marketing organization.

The relevant criteria for judging the effectiveness of an organization relate to: (1) organizational orientation, (2) decision points, (3) line and staff relationships, (4) adequacy of staff, (5) information flows, (6) coordination levels, (7) span of control, (8) authority and responsibility, (9) provision for corporate growth, and (10) formal-informal organizational variances. These criteria provide the basis for auditing an organization and for applying some specific tests of effectiveness against which to determine the suitability of the structure for the conduct of effective marketing operations.

Organizational design and style in the future might evolve along the following lines: more fluid organizational arrangements with units that can more easily be recombined to meet changing product and market needs; greater flows of information vertically and horizontally within the organization; design around more results-focused task packages rather than highly activity structured job descriptions; new line-staff relationships for handling key operating decisions; and more varied blends of autocracy, bureaucracy, and democracy to reflect varied stages of organizational growth and development.

Questions and Problems

1. Give a technical statement of the purpose of organizational design.
2. What are some of the factors in marketing affairs that have led to organizational modification in recent years?
3. Give an example of how centralizing some marketing responsibilities at the

551

Market
Orientation
and
Organiza-
tional Design

corporate level in a multiproduct, multidivisional company can be more economical; can be more effective.

4. How would you distinguish between the formal and the informal organization? What relevance does this have for organizational design?

5. Describe the essential features of an autocratic type of organization; the bureaucratic form; and the democratic model.

6. Which features of the above forms would be combined in an attempt at a kind of multicratic organization?

7. How would you compare and contrast the features of centralized and decentralized administration?

8. Is either form of administration just discussed better than the other?

9. Why does there tend to be a higher degree of specialization in the centralized organization? In which type of administration would you expect to find the greater number of staff personnel?

10. List the criteria that might be applied in judging organizational design effectiveness.

11. What are the alternative ways in which provision can be made for effective planning in an organization?

12. How can information analysis be used to judge organizational design effectiveness?

13. What are the limitations to dual marketing groups' (marketing services and the field sales organization) reporting independently to top management?

14. Why is it important to have the various areas of marketing that must be closely coordinated on as comparable a level of organization as possible?

15. Pick an actual or hypothetical company in a kind of business with which you are familiar and draw an organization chart for its marketing activity, assuming full-scale staffing.

Marketing Information Flows and Control Systems

31

After all marketing plans have been made and the operating procedures and organizational arrangements selected to execute these plans, it is necessary to find ways and means to determine whether the enterprise is on course. It is appropriate that this topic is discussed at this point, for it is through control that closure is made in the total system of business action. That is, market opportunities are assessed; appropriate product strategies are tailored to the opportunity; the distribution and communication mixes are selected; human and physical resources are organized to achieve the objectives; and the plans put into action. The system is then monitored for performance. Departures from objectives are highlighted and the next wave of programming begins. The foregoing point up a common interpretation of the word *control*. This use, however, ascribes to control a rather passive role in the management of the marketing program of a company. *Control must be considered throughout the development of the marketing system.* It is a part of the system itself, and, in this sense, may be considered an integral part of the programming process.

Because of the need to consider control in marketing, the first part of this chapter is devoted to a clarification of the meaning of control. Then we shall identify those tools necessary for effective control, the information we must have to make these tools work, and the necessity for and means of managing information flows to the firm.

THE MEANING OF CONTROL

Two views are held about the meaning of the word *control*. The subject is usually referred to as "management control," and the differences in viewpoint are more related

553

Marketing
Information
Flows
and Control
Systems

to the term *management* than to *control*. One view concentrates on the people who manage, and consequently, "management control" means "management of (by) the manager." In this sense, evaluation of the manager's activities is the major idea. Control of this sort is after the fact, as it cannot be exercised until the manager has done something or is supposed to have done something. In the other view, control is part of management. It is part of all of the activities necessary to enable the enterprise to achieve its objectives.

The latter view can be clarified by referring to our systems design approach developed in Chapter 3. In the systems discussed there no evaluation was necessary; the system worked automatically because the control mechanisms were built into it. In the simplest design a single thermostat automatically actuated the system and adjusted the system to a change in its environment. In the more complicated system a series of thermostats actuated the system in such a way that any number of preselected environments could be achieved. Let us examine again the way in which these systems work.

A disturbing element is introduced—a change in temperature. This triggers the thermostat, which in turn activates the system to either heat up or shut off, and the desired condition is restored. The thermostat is a control device that enables the system automatically to adjust itself to a change in the environment. The system can be controlled after the fact as well. If it is not functioning as desired or a change is required, the thermostats can all be manually reprogrammed to provide a new set of environments.

In designing managerial systems, the need is also present to introduce control into the system and, at the same time, to provide a means to reprogram the system when desired. It is doubtful, however, whether it is possible to design a managerial system that will operate as smoothly as a temperature control system. The reasons are as follows: (1) the multiplicity of objectives may call for several subsystems within the general system. Since there may be a conflict between objectives, there is conflict between the subsystems, which prevents a smooth functioning of the general system. (2) The forces which call for change are so varied and so dynamic that it is difficult to incorporate control devices which are sufficiently sensitive to react to all changes in the environment. In the case of the heating system, the only change to be monitored continually is a change in temperature, whereas in a managerial system a change in competitors' actions, a change in consumers' desires, or a change in technology or labor efficiency all may call for a change in the system if it is to meet its ultimate goals. (3) The need for a change is not immediately evident. If a change is needed and is not made, sooner or later its need will become evident. This, however, is not satisfactory for the managerial system, since it may be too late to take the necessary steps to recoup its position. In the heating system analogy, it is clear that if the temperature fluctuates too widely and the system does not respond, this fact is immediately known and some action will be taken. In the managerial system a decline in sales volume or a mounting expense ratio will not become evident soon enough, unless some means are incorporated to measure these consequences periodically. (4) Managerial systems function through individuals. It is unreasonable to expect a human being to possess the knowledge or even have the intuitive sensitivity to identify minute changes in the environment calling for a change in the system. Even in the simple case of the heating system, an individual is not nearly so sensitive to changes in temperature as is the thermostat.

That there are control problems in the managerial system does not mean that control is limited in any way. And in addition to trying to incorporate control devices within the system, we must also collect information to determine how well the system is functioning. Since the environment in which the system operates is so dynamic, continuous adjustment of the system is called for.

The viewpoint taken with respect to control is portrayed in the diagram in Figure 31-1. In this simplified portrayal of a marketing system, corporate

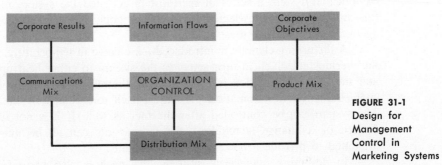

FIGURE 31-1
Design for
Management
Control in
Marketing Systems

objectives are achieved through appropriate product, distribution, and communication mixes. These mixes are designed to achieve the objectives and are control mechanisms. As such, they are inseparable from planning the entire system. Another major control device is the organization through which product, distribution, and communication mixes are executed. Once a marketing program is put into operation, information is necessary to measure actual results against anticipated results and to signal the need for change in the system. Control is anything that is done to insure attainment of the objectives of the firm.

CONTROL DEVICES
AND MARKETING INFORMATION

In reality, we have been dealing with control devices throughout the text. Reference to at least one aspect of control in each of the three mixes earlier discussed (product, distribution, and communication) will indicate the pervasiveness of control in the marketing system.

Some of the most striking examples of product strategy are found in Chapter 12, "Product-Market Integration." The care exercised in adjusting products to specific segments of the market is an attempt to establish a product line that will achieve objectives. A heating plant with a 30,000 Btu heating unit will not produce a 70-degree temperature in zero weather if 120,000 Btu are

555

Marketing
Information
Flows
and Control
Systems

needed. Similarly, if the firm is facing a saturated market and continues to attempt to achieve increased sales volume with the same product line it offered in an earlier period, it is not likely to achieve its objectives. By adjusting the product to specific segments of the market, however, management is introducing control in the development of the product line.

In the distribution mix, control is exercised at a number of points. One example is in the selection of a channel of distribution and the development of a manufacturer-dealer system. Through analysis of the product, the market, and the manufacturing firm, channels which have the greatest chance of achieving objectives may be selected. The wrong channel, no matter how well it is managed afterward, will probably not achieve satisfactory results. Even the right channel if improperly managed will fall short. The actual channels selected and the means used to resolve the conflicts among participants are attempts to insure attainment of the goals of the firm, and are essentially elements of control.

A number of control devices are introduced into the system in all forms of communication. The analysis of the situation to determine the role of advertising in the total communications mix is an element of control. Selecting and training personal salesmen are controls. It is hoped that if these functions are properly carried out, the men will perform in the desired manner. Recognizing that selection and training alone are not sufficient, management also uses supervision and compensation to make the salesmen perform in the desired way and sometimes imposes a penalty if they do not do so. These are all control devices.

No matter how carefully control has been introduced into the different points of the total system, improper delegation of authority and responsibility for execution will cause the system to malfunction. Organizational arrangement, therefore, is also a control device. This aspect of control is frequently overlooked, probably because it is too close to the activity we call programming or planning. But every management would like to plan its mixes with 100 percent certainty that they were the correct mixes for all time; just as the heating engineer can design a heating system with the proper number and type of thermostats and the required capacity furnace to achieve a predetermined objective. If this were possible, the company would have perfect control through establishing the proper mixes.

Because the firm is operating in a competitive environment, in which competitors' actions affect market shares, consumers' preferences are continually shifting, and channel members' objectives and modes of operation are changing, the managerial system must constantly adjust if objectives are to be met. The control built into the management system through product, distribution, and communication mixes is never fixed but must be changed frequently. An example will illustrate this situation.

A large paper manufacturer became concerned about its share of the cut-size bond paper market. The company was distributing its cut-size bond through full-service paper merchants, territorially protected by an exclusive franchise. An analysis of the cut-size market indicated that it had grown through the introduction and widespread use of business duplicating equipment—much of it by small firms. The paper merchants never called upon these small firms. However, through their service organizations, the business equipment manufacturers already had entry to the firms. By broadening their lines to include all accessories for use with their machines, the manufacturers could fill small orders at reasonable cost. By doing so, the business machine manufacturers had taken over about 50 percent of the cut-size bond market. This deviation from the paper manufacturer's expected results had its cause in a change in environment—the entry of another competitor. To its chagrin, the manufacturer learned that monitoring impending change is a most important aspect of control.

Even, however, if environmental changes were not present, management would rarely have sufficient information to make perfect decisions nor sufficient control to insure complete adherence to plans. For example, a regional insurance company was experiencing a higher than average lapse rate on new policies sold. Investigation showed that the sales force was using high pressure, misrepresentation, and near fraudulent means to sign up new policyholders. This deviation from expected policy retentions had its roots in poor selection and training of the field representatives—a malfunction in operations.

From a control point of view, the minimum the firm may settle for is a sufficient flow of information to signal deviations from expected results; for example, to indicate that the cut-size bond market is being taken over by the business equipment manufacturers or that the lapse rate experienced by the company is higher than industry average. Pinpointing the actual causes and effecting remedies are the result of another wave of programming effort designed to control such deviations. Unfortunately this kind of information often comes too late or after the damage is done. As a management tool, control involves managing the flow of information that will aid in determining when and where changes must be made in the managerial system. Once the need is identified, a new round of programming begins to develop better control devices within the system.

The Need for Orderly Information Flows

The marketing decision maker is engaged in a series of decisions whose efficacy depends upon the quantity and quality of information available to him. Unlike production or personnel executives the kinds of information needed are more often external to the firm. Normally he relies on the information he has from his experience and the judgment of others to pass critical information to him. This does not work, unfortunately. In an experiment conducted to determine the flow of information from customers through salesmen to decision-making executives, six pieces of market information were planted among customers who agreed to pass them on to the salesmen. Of the six, only two were passed on by the salesmen. One arrived at the executive level in three days, greatly distorted, and the other in ten days in accurate form.[1] Information of the right kind and quality simply is not available to the decision maker through the in-

[1] Gerald S. Albaum, "Horizontal Information Flow: An Exploratory Study," *Journal of the Academy of Management,* VII (March 1964), 21–33.

557

Marketing
Information
Flows
and Control
Systems

formal means relied upon for providing it. There is a great need to formalize information flows.

Some Difficulties in Information Flows

Marketing information for control purposes must flow vertically, that is, from the market (customers) through the channels to the sales force and through the sales force to the decision centers in the firm. It must flow in the reverse direction if management is to issue the kinds of instructions necessary to achieve the goals of the firm. It must also flow horizontally—between marketing, production, research and development, and finance and accounting executives. The free flow of market information is hampered by a number of special circumstances, some of which are peculiar to the market affairs of the firm.

As in the case of goods flow *time and space* too must be overcome. Almost always goods are produced far in advance of ultimate consumption in the market place. Actual results in the market place can only be ascertained after commitments of time, people, and money have taken place. It may be some time before any good reactions may be obtained regarding customer acceptance, and inventories will have piled up in the channel of distribution. By this time the second round of commitments will have been made, unless there have been special efforts to funnel information on inventory levels and customer acceptance to the decision centers almost continually. The space problem is also severe. Even with a reporting system for salesmen there is no assurance that pertinent information will be passed through space to the decision maker thousands of miles away in the head office. The salesman may not recognize the pertinence of a piece of information and thus fail to report it. Even if he does recognize its value, it only makes a longer report and he may elect to exclude it. Special efforts must be made to insure that the field sales force transmits information.

Organizational structures also are a hindrance to information flows. Because marketing systems are complex, there is usually some division of responsibility within the overall system. Responsibility and authority are allocated to particular units in the organization. Sometimes these units are called responsibility, or profit, centers. The organization may be structured on a product, geographic, customer, or channel of distribution base, or any combination of them. This division of responsibility is designed for efficiency and administrative ease. At the same time, it should not be forgotten that the firm is an integrated system, the various parts forming a complex whole. This organizational arrangement hampers the easy flow of information between the parts. The individual parts become so absorbed in their own activities that they are not concerned with the activities of other parts. For example, a product manager in a large soap company worked, as directed, to develop and commercialize a new product. The product met with success in the market place but was virtually stricken from the list of products earmarked for future support by top management. Unknown to the product manager the new item was gaining sales at the expense of other products that top management, for reasons unknown to the product manager, wished to maintain. Often the separate units become so autonomous that an aloofness from the remainder of the organization develops. Much internal information, for control purposes, must come from the accounting department. Sometimes this unit and market units are so far removed from each other, both in space and attitude, that it is almost impossible to get them together. And the kinds of information collected for financial and tax purposes are different from those needed for marketing control.

Another source of resistance to information flow is *executive fear*. Pertinent information is suppressed by administrative authority if the information is critical of past actions of individuals. This, of course, does not happen often, but it would be naive not to recognize that it exists. Closely allied to fear is jealousy. As individuals climb the management ladder, the positions to be filled begin to reduce in number; not all will occupy top positions. In the group dynamics of the process, frictions develop, and pertinent information is withheld to be used by individuals to enhance their own prestige at a later time.

We can recognize the importance of information flow for control purposes, and the difficulties in achieving adequate information flow are limited with informal arrangements. There is some justification for centralizing responsibility for it and systematizing routines for getting it.

Technological Developments in Information Processing

Along with the growing recognition of the need for orderly information flows in today's dynamic environment, there is the availability of the necessary hardware to process, manipulate, and store vast amounts of data. The computer has advanced the movement toward more orderly information flow more than any other single factor. Its value lies in its speed in processing, its computational capacity, and its tremendous storage capacity and ease in retrieval. With computerized hookups between plants and warehouses the decision maker in any location can get internal information, such as inventory levels, or how long it will take to fill an order, almost instantly. The development of simulation models on the basis of repeated observation of past occurrences allows the executive to change any variable he wishes and to have a measure of probable outcomes in a matter of minutes.

The computer provides a means of using information. It does this with rapidity, and if properly programmed, with little effort on the part of the decision maker. This does not mean that executive skill and judgment are no longer necessary. It does, however, provide a tool for the more efficient use of information.

MANAGING INFORMATION
FOR CONTROL PURPOSES

The firm needs three kinds of information to provide an adequate fund of knowledge for control purposes. These are: (1) information to measure performance against expectations; (2) information to determine the causes of deviations from expected results; and (3) information to signify impending changes in the environment. Each of these will be discussed separately.

559

Marketing
Information
Flows
and Control
Systems

Monitoring Past Actions

Standards of acceptable performance are established in relation to the specific objectives for achieving the overall goals of the organization. Some of the more common specific objectives are: (1) a designated share of the market, (2) profitability by product or product line, territories, and customer class, (3) a designated sales-expense ratio, (4) a given level of promotional activity in the channel, (5) stated standards of salesmen performance, and (6) competitive prices.

The kinds of analyses made to monitor past actions against the above standards are usually divided into the following: (1) sales analysis, (2) share of market analysis, (3) distribution analysis, (4) sales force analysis and (5) cost and profit analysis.[2]

Sales Analysis

Analysis of sales has been placed first because the making of a sale is one of the major purposes of a firm's marketing system (secondary only to profits), and because it is the most common type of analysis carried out. Four questions must be answered before an adequate sales analysis program can be established. They are: (1) What is a sale? (2) How will sales be classified? (3) How shall the information be expressed? and (4) What standards of comparison will be used?

A sale may be an order, a shipment, a cash receipt, a billing, or even a consumer purchase. The particular definition of a sale depends upon the way the company does business. If much time elapses between the time an order is taken and a shipment made, cancellations are frequent. In this case it would be a mistake to count orders as sales. If the company ships promptly out of stock, there is little difference between an order and a shipment. If the company sells an open book credit, sets up an account receivable, and bills the customer the moment goods are shipped, the billing may be considered a sale. If a long channel of distribution is used and inventories pile up in the channel, the actual rate of ultimate consumption may be important. In this case, consumer purchase may be the indicator of a sale.

Rarely is each individual transaction analyzed. Rather sales of similar type are grouped and the aggregate of that group analyzed. The particular grouping used depends on the kinds of analysis the company wishes to make. Some of the more common groupings are by product, territory, channel of distribution, and customer type. The actual categories selected are generally not available in accounting records, so it is necessary to work out a cooperative arrangement with the accounting department to get these data with the desired frequency.

Generally, sales data are expressed in monetary or physical units. However,

[2] This same classification is used by D. J. Luck, H. Wales, and D. A. Taylor in *Marketing Research,* 3rd. ed. (Englewood Cliffs, N.J.: Prentice-Hall, Inc., 1970), Chap. 15. Much of the material relating to the different types of analyses is taken from this book.

the way they are expressed depends somewhat on other kinds of analyses that will be made. If cost and profit analysis is to be performed, then sales data will be expressed in terms of profit contribution. If sales force analysis is made, it can be expressed relative to selling expenses, sales per call, sales to new customers, and so on.

Sales data alone, no matter how finely categorized, are of little value without standards of comparison. Past sales are often used as a basis. Their major weakness is that poor performance in the past makes it difficult to evaluate current performance. More current information is needed, and data on sales opportunity, derived from quantitative market investigation (discussed in Chapter 6) for specific products in specific areas and for certain sizes or classes of customers, should be collected.

Although the amount of data needed seems endless, most of it is available in the records of the average company. Figure 31-2 shows the sources of information in most companies. With the advances made in electronic data processing it is relatively easy to make this data available.

Market Share Analysis

Pure sales analysis does not give information as to the share of the market the firm is getting. It is possible to experience an increasing sales volume and a declining market share. Whenever there is expansibility of demand for a product, each supplier generally seeks to participate in the expansion. Even though there is no expansion in demand, knowledge of market share is necessary to plan marketing strategy. The firm may be doing well overall but may have varied strengths and weaknesses in different geographic locations, different product lines, or different classes of customers.

The data necessary to assess the standing of different brands at the level of ultimate consumption are external to the organization and sometimes difficult to obtain. In those consumer goods industries in which there is high product turnover at the retail level, syndicated data services gather and sell brand-position data. The A. C. Nielsen Company conducts store audits in the grocery and drug fields and some others. These are conducted in a panel of stores presumed to be representative of all stores in the country. Table 31-1 shows the kind of information available to subscribers to the A. C. Nielsen service. The Market Research Corporation of America, through a panel of consuming units, gathers information on consumer expenditures, and in this way is able to make brand-position information available. An intermediate step in measuring product flow is the data available from Speedata, Inc. This company measures the flow of products, by brand, through 100 major warehouses, servicing 31,404 retail outlets in 22 market areas. The data cover 259 product categories covering 18,000 grocery items.

Some newspapers and magazines also conduct studies in the markets they serve and periodically report the position of a number of brands in these markets. They usually do not disclose actual unit or dollar volume of different brands. These studies are conducted by the media to aid in selling space to prospective advertisers; they are available free of charge.

Trade associations often act as clearinghouses for industry-wide informa-

TABLE 31-1

Complete List of Data Secured Every 60 Days in Food Stores *

1. Sales to customers
2. Purchases by retailers
3. Retail inventories
4. Days' supply
5. Store count distribution
6. All-commodity distribution
7. Out-of-stock
8. Prices (wholesale and retail)
9. Special factory packs
10. Dealer support (displays, local advertising, coupon redemption)
11. Special observations (order size, reorder, directs vs. wholesale)
12. Total food store sales (all commodities)
13. Major media advertising (from other sources)

BROKEN DOWN BY:

Brands	Territories	Your Own Territory	Counties Pop. Range	Stores	Package Size	Product Type
Yours	New England	1	10 Metro. New York			
A	Metro. New York	2	11 Metro. Chicago	Chain	Small	X
B	Mid-Atlantic	3	12 Other Metro.	Independent:		
			19 next largest mkts.			
C	East Central	4	13 B counties	Super	Medium	
				Large		
D	Metro. Chicago	5	14 Metro. areas over 100,000			Y
	West Central	6	15 C counties 30,000–100,000	Medium	Large	
	Southwest	7	16	Small		
All others	Pacific	8	17 Rural		Giant	Z
	Southeast	9	18 Others Under 30,000			
Total	Los Angeles					

(Competitors)

* Substantially the same kinds of data are collected in all types of stores audited. Retail Audit Data. The indicated types and breakdowns are provided to clients of the Nielsen services in food, drug, variety, and several other merchandise lines. *Courtesy of A. C. Nielsen Co.*

FIGURE 31-2
Sources of Sales Information

The source of most information about company sales is the order form and invoice, but various other documents, records, and reports also serve as raw material for sales reports, as the tabulation below indicates. Of course a single company is likely to draw on only two or three of these sources of sales information.

Document	Source Information Provided	Document	Source Information Provided
1. Order forms and invoices	Customer name, number, and location	4. Salesmen's call reports (continued)	Products discussed
	Product(s) or service(s) sold		Orders obtained
	Volume and dollar amount of the transaction		Customers' product needs and usage
	Salesman (or agent) responsible for the sale		Other significant information about customers
	End use of product sold		Distribution of salesmen's time among customer calls, travel, and office work
	Location of customer facility where product is to be shipped		Sales related activities: meetings, conventions, etc.
	Location of customer facility where product is to be used	5. Salesmen's expense accounts	Expenses by day by item, hotel, meals, travel, etc.
	Customer's industry, class of trade and/or channel of distribution	6. Individual customer (and prospect) records	Name and location and customer number
	Terms of sales and applicable discount		Number of calls by company salesmen (agents)
	Freight paid and/or to be collected		Sales by company (in dollars and/or units by product or service by location of customer facility)
	Shipment point for the order		Customer's industry, class of trade, and/or trade channel
	Transportation used in shipment		Estimated total annual usage of each product or service sold by the company
2. Cash register receipts	Type (cash or credit) and dollar amount of transaction by department by sales person		Estimated annual purchases from the company of each such product or service
3. Salesmen's call reports	Customers and prospects called on (company and individual seen; planned or unplanned calls)		

FIGURE 31-2

Sources of Sales Information—Continued

Document	Source Information Provided
	Location (in terms of company sales territory)
7. Financial records	Sales revenue (by products, geographical markets, customers, class or trade, unit of sales organization, etc.)
	Direct sales expenses (similarly classified)
	Overhead sales costs (similarly classified)
	Profits (similarly classified)
8. Credit memos	Returns and allowances
9. Warranty cards	Indirect measures of dealer sales
	Customer service
10. Summary reports from distributors and dealers	Sales by product, geographic area, class of customer, etc.
11. Store audits	Unit and dollar volume and market share of consumer purchases of the company's brands in selected retail outlets
12. Consumer diaries (as a rule they cover only packaged foods and personal-care items)	Unit volume of purchases by package size of company's brand (and competing brands) made by selected families
	Details about prices, special deals, and types of outlets in which the purchases were made

Source: National Industrial Conference Board, "Sales Analysis," Studies in Business Policy, No. 113.

tion. Member firms periodically report sales to the association. These are analyzed on an industry basis, and the information is returned to the members. The association usually does not disclose the market share held by other members, but any single member can determine the share he is getting and identify trends in total sales volume.

In those product lines in which there is mandatory reporting of sales, such as insurance, liquor, and automobiles, it is possible to develop highly detailed information. One problem occasionally encountered in these areas is that the information is not made available rapidly enough to highlight growing problems in an early stage of development. When no data are available, the only recourse is to try to build estimates of sales opportunity through quantitative market investigation.

Distribution Analysis

If thorough sales and market share analyses show company weaknesses, distribution analyses is one area that may uncover possible causes. The most common type of distribution analysis is the number and quality of outlets in which the brand is distributed, relative to competition. This information may appear simple to obtain, but unless close control is exercised over the channels of distribution it frequently is not available. Where middlemen are used, some loss in control is imminent, and it is difficult to know what outlets are handling the product. Retailers or wholesalers may sell to unauthorized dealers even when selective or exclusive distribution is used. Salesmen's reports can be used to determine the outlets in which the products are sold. However, unless the salesmen call on every single outlet—and it is not often profitable to do so—only a partial picture is given. Salesmen can, however, be instructed to report the conditions of distribution in the markets in which they work.

The quality of performance throughout the channel is also important. A satisfactory level of product exposure is effective only if the middlemen handling the product perform in the desired way. Most performance evaluations of distributors are based upon three types of comparisons.[3]

1. Comparisons of the distributor's current sales with his sales attainments in prior periods (analyzing historical performance).
2. Comparisons of the performances of various distribution outlets (usually classified by outlet type or geographic region).
3. Comparisons of sales figures with predetermined quotas and other gauges of territorial potential.

The data needed for these kinds of comparisons are found in the company's records and are usually a part of its sales analysis program.

Overall performance in terms of stock conditions, number of facings (the front packages on a shelf), location of facings, pricing, and use of point-of-purchase display material all should be checked periodically. Some of this information is provided by syndicated data services. In Table 31-2, items 2 through 12 deal with distribution analysis. If no service is available, the firm will have

[3] *Selecting and Evaluating Distributors, Studies in Business Policy,* No. 116 (New York: National Industrial Conference Board, 1965), p. 109.

565

Marketing
Information
Flows
and Control
Systems

to find other ways to periodically assess performance. This usually involves establishing periodic research studies or developing some kind of reporting system utilizing the sales force.

Although much information may be collected about the conditions of distribution, without standards against which to judge results, little is achieved. It is in this area that distribution analysis is weakest. To establish standards of performance, some assessment must be made of what constitutes successful performance, both from the point of view of the middlemen and the manufacturer.

Sales Force Analysis

Since the field sales organization is the instrument through which sales are finally consummated, some evaluation of its activities is desirable. Whenever sales, brand-position, or distribution analyses are done on a territory basis, they are in part an evaluation of the efforts of the individual salesman, because the salesman is the territory manager. Sales by products in a given territory, when compared to opportunity in that territory, are a measure of the way in which the territory has been managed. There are, however, a number of other analyses that may be made which are equally important in assessing the way in which the sales force is performing. It is necessary to determine precisely the functions the salesman is to perform in the field. Then it is necessary to collect information which will identify whether or not the salesman has performed in the required way. Once the information is collected, care must be exercised in evaluating the findings through establishing fair standards of performance.

In Figure 31-3, the basic items measured and the ways of measuring them are shown. Most of the information needed for measuring sales results and sales-related nonselling activities is already available and has been described in the analyses already discussed. However, there are additional items of information not normally available. They are: (1) new account development, (2) investigation of complaints, (3) sales service and engineering, (4) sales promotion and engineering, (5) distribution assistance or training, (6) checks on distributors' stocks, and (7) price checks. The extent of the information collected depends on the kind of selling job being monitored.

This information may be obtained through establishing reporting systems for the sales force. These methods can usually be effective if any rewards are present in the compensation plan for performing these activities.

The determination of standards against which to compare results is important if this kind of information is going to permit effective control. All of the activities mentioned must be related to the opportunity to perform them. For example, the number of calls per day depends upon the length of call necessary and the number of outlets available to be called upon. Consequently, determination of standards may require original field studies to observe performance and relate it to opportunity.

Cost and Profit Analysis

This type of analysis was purposely left until last because it uses information from the areas of analysis already discussed. Further, sales, share of market,

FIGURE 31-3

How Companies Assess Their Salesmen's Performance

What Is Measured	*Common Ways of Measuring*
I. SALES RESULTS	I. Sales, expenses and/or profitability analyses:
A. Sales volume (total, or by product, account, etc.)	A. Sales analysis—Determination of absolute unit or dollar sales figures for the period; comparison with performance of other salesmen or salesman's own past performance
B. Quota attainment (unit or dollar sales—total, or by product, account, etc.; profitability of sales; new accounts; etc.)	B. Sales analysis—Comparison of actual achievement with predetermined quota(s) for the period; comparison of relative attainment of quota(s) with that of other salesmen
C. Selling expenses	C. Expense analysis—Determination of direct selling expenses for the period; computation of ratio of direct selling expenses to total dollar sales; comparison with predetermined standards or norms, with performance of other salesmen, or with past performance
D. Profitability of sales	D. Profitability analysis—Determination of profits on sales for the period; determination of relative profit contribution and assignment of profitability weights to product classes sold; comparison with predetermined standards or norms, with performance of other salesmen, or with salesman's own past performance
E. Product mix	E. Sales analysis—Determination of absolute unit or dollar sales figures by product for the period; determination of inclusion and/or relative importance of product classes in total sales; comparison with predetermined standards or norms, with performance of other salesmen, or with past performance

What Is Measured

Common Ways of Measuring

II. SALES-RELATED AND NONSELLING ACTIVITIES

A. New account development
B. Calls made (total, or by type customer, etc.)
C. Matters discussed or handled during calls
D. Investigation of complaints
E. Sales service and engineering
F. Sales promotion and merchandising
G. Distributor assistance or training
H. Check on distributor stocks
I. Price checks
J. Travel
K. Filing of reports
L. Time on job vs. time lost
M. Time selling vs. time spent on other activities

II. Sales and similar analysis—Determination of relevant numbers, time spent, or expense for given activity during the period; comparison with predetermined standards or norms, with performance of other salesmen, or with salesman's own past performance

III. PERSONAL QUALITIES, APTITUDES AND DEVELOPMENT

III. Personal observation by superior or other observer(s); self-evaluation; testing

Source: National Industrial Conference Board, "Measuring Salesmen's Performance," Studies in Business Policy, No. 114.

distribution, and sales force analysis may all indicate acceptable performance, but the company may not be making satisfactory profits. The revenue part of profit analysis has been dealt with in sales analysis, but the cost phase must be analyzed to complete the equation. The following types of cost analysis are possible: (1) natural expense analysis, (2) functional cost analysis, (3) responsibility cost analysis, and (4) gross profit and net profit analysis.

NATURAL EXPENSE ANALYSIS. This method uses the normal accounts of most accounting systems. The accounts identify the goods or services received, such as heat, light and power, rent, advertising, and freight. Hardly any diagnosis is possible with lump sum totals such as all freight charges during a period. From an analytical viewpoint, the major weakness with this form of analysis is that it is too aggregative and does not pinpoint those activities which are unprofitable to the company. At the same time, these aggregate figures must be compared against budgets to detect any items that are too far out of line.

FUNCTIONAL COST ANALYSIS. This method records cost in terms of the activity or task performed as a result of the expenditure, such as, direct selling, advertising and sales promotion, and physical distribution. Each cost outlay is charged to a natural expense. For example, a cash outlay is made for heat, light and power, and it is charged first to its "natural" purpose. But heat, light and power may be used by many parts of the total marketing function. Some of it must be charged to advertising and sales promotion, some to physical distribution, some to general marketing expense and some to nonmarketing activities. The difficulty with this kind of analysis is twofold. First a decision must be made on what functions are going to be used. They generally can be solved easily, but it will depend on the marketing operations of the particular firm.[4] Second, it is difficult to allocate natural expenses to the function benefiting from them. A logical basis for allocation may be found for some, but frequently the basis must be arbitrary.

RESPONSIBILITY COST ANALYSIS. For truly meaningful measures of profitability, costs must be assigned to those responsible for given functions in the organization. For management and control purposes the organization is divided into profit centers, with an individual responsible for the profitability of his domain. The normal profit centers used in business today are regions, branches or territories, products—single products or a group of products—sales to a given customer type or sales through a given channel of distribution. To determine profits for each of these managerial units, costs must be assigned to them; that is, the functional costs must be allocated to responsibility centers. Advertising and sales promotional expense must be allocated to territories if a territorial analysis is being made or to a product if a product profitability analysis is to be made.

Figures 31-4 through 31-7 are illustrative of the kinds of analyses that can

---

[4] For suggested functional cost classifications for marketing, see Charles H. Sevin, *Marketing Productivity Analysis* (New York: McGraw-Hill Book Company, 1965).

569

Marketing
Information
Flows
and Control
Systems

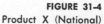

FIGURE 31-4
Product X (National)

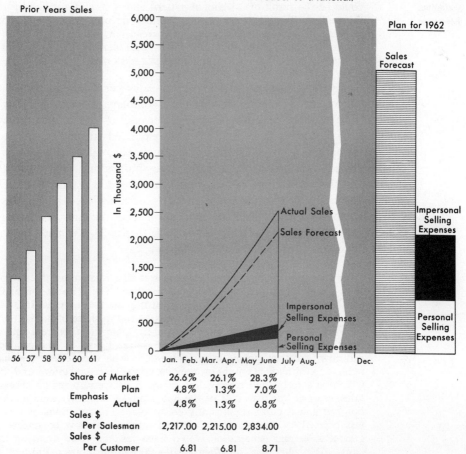

Share of Market	26.6%	26.1%	28.3%
Emphasis Plan	4.8%	1.3%	7.0%
Emphasis Actual	4.8%	1.3%	6.8%
Sales $ Per Salesman	2,217.00	2,215.00	2,834.00
Sales $ Per Customer	6.81	6.81	8.71

Source: Michael Schiff, "Reporting for More Profitable Product Management," The Journal of Accountancy *(May 1963), p. 67. Copyrighted 1963 by the American Institute of CPAS.*

be made.[5] These figures summarize the performance of a single product, Product X, both nationally and regionally. In Figure 31-4 the product manager is supplied with prior years' sales to indicate the product's stage in the life cycle; actual and forecasted sales; actual and budgeted impersonal selling expenses (advertising and sales promotion) and personal selling expenses (field-selling costs); share of national market (supplied by an outside service); comparison of salesmen's planned selling time on Product X versus actual selling time; and sales per salesman and sales per customer. At a glance several important bits of information are available.

[5] This example is taken from Michael Schiff, "Reporting for More Profitable Product Management," *The Journal of Accountancy* (May 1963), pp. 65-70. Copyrighted 1963 by the American Institute of CPAS.

The figure is interpreted as follows: [6]

> . . . it is apparent that sales exceeded forecast and that far less than one-half of the budgeted personal and impersonal expenses have been incurred. This could be the result of a seasonal pattern and is readily verified by reference to the budget. The field staff has apparently devoted time as planned, and the increase in sales is reflective of an increase in market penetration (share of market increased from 26.6 percent to 28.3 percent) accompanied by an increase in sales per salesman and sales per customer.

In Figure 31-5 share of market and sales per salesman and customer are recorded for the six regions in which the company sells through fifty sales districts. The number of salesmen varies because of the concentration in some regions of customers in urban areas and extended travel time needed in areas where customers are more scattered. Consequently, sales per customer and sales per salesman are important measures. The southeastern region had the highest sales per salesman and per customer and was second in market share. The poorest performance in all measures was in the western region. The reasons for these two extremes in performance are not known from this analysis. In Figures 31-6 and 31-7, an analysis similar to that made in Figure 31-4 is made for each region. These two charts are interpreted as follows: [7]

> The western region, despite its poor standing relative to other regions, shows sales above forecasted sales. Expenses incurred are at about the halfway point, and market penetration has increased in the last two months. It is well to note that in the second two months there was a drop in share of market, and this was followed by an increase in sales effort above plan (10.6 percent against 7.0 percent) with a sharp increase in sales and share of market. The product manager can now be rather specific in his discussions with the western regional manager relative to the shift in emphasis, the cost of the increased effort, and the products which as a result will receive less effort. Southwestern region shows increased sales, costs at less than half of the budgeted amount, increased market penetration but actual effort significantly below plan. The questions of why less effort was exerted by the sales force and its impact can now be reviewed. Perhaps greater sales and penetration would have resulted from applying the planned effort. Also what was the effect of the shift in effort from Product X to other products? Specific questions can be asked and the effects of alternative actions evaluated.

Gross Profit vs. Net Profit Analysis

An elementary form of profit analysis is obtained through reviewing periodic data on gross profit, the amount left from revenues after paying for the cost of goods sold. The resulting gross profit is considered to be a contribution to marketing and general expenses, and profits. Sometimes the gross profit is adjusted by deducting direct selling expenses to arrive at an adjusted gross profit. If the cost of goods sold had been included in the analysis described in Figures 31-4 through 31-7, the adjusted gross profit would have been readily ascertainable.

When gross profit is calculated for specific responsibility centers, such as a territory, a product, a class of customer, or any other meaningful unit, it can

---

[6] *Ibid.,* p. 68.
[7] Schiff, "Reporting for More Profitable Product Management," p. 69.

571

Marketing
Information
Flows
and Control
Systems

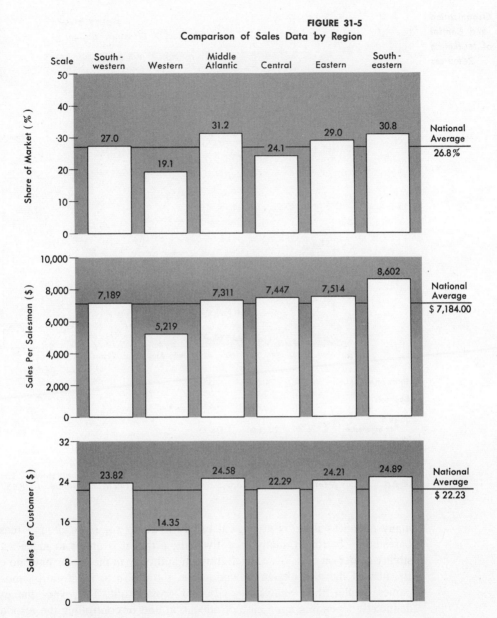

FIGURE 31-5
Comparison of Sales Data by Region

Source: Michael Schiff, "Reporting for More Profitable Product Management," The Journal of Accountancy (May 1963), p. 67. Copyrighted 1963 by the American Institute of CPAS.

be quite revealing. Often distinct differences between sales territories, products, or channels of distribution point toward the need for more complex research to determine causes.

Net profit for a responsibility center is the preferred measure. This, however, requires allocating every functional cost to every responsibility center. In

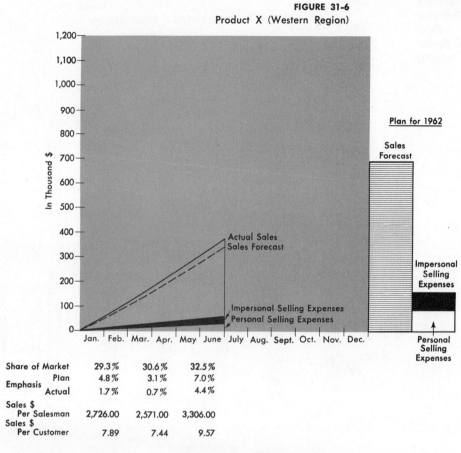

FIGURE 31-6
Product X (Western Region)

Share of Market	29.3%	30.6%	32.5%
Emphasis Plan	4.8%	3.1%	7.0%
Emphasis Actual	1.7%	0.7%	4.4%
Sales $ Per Salesman	2,726.00	2,571.00	3,306.00
Sales $ Per Customer	7.89	7.44	9.57

Source: Michael Schiff, "Reporting for More Profitable Product Management," The Journal of Accountancy (May 1963), p. 68. Copyrighted 1963 by the American Institute of CPAS.

many instances there is no logical basis for doing so. Even though reasonable bases could be found, many executives argue that it is unfair to judge a responsibility center on costs over which those in authority in the center have no control. Because of the difficulty in allocation and the desire to judge fairly, most companies confine their analysis to adjusted gross profit. They vary the expenses deducted, depending upon ease of allocation and of controlling the responsibility center manager.

Determining Causes

Little is gained if all control does is indicate departures from expectations. To be meaningful, it must identify causes, and before we can say that control

573

Marketing
Information
Flows
and Control
Systems

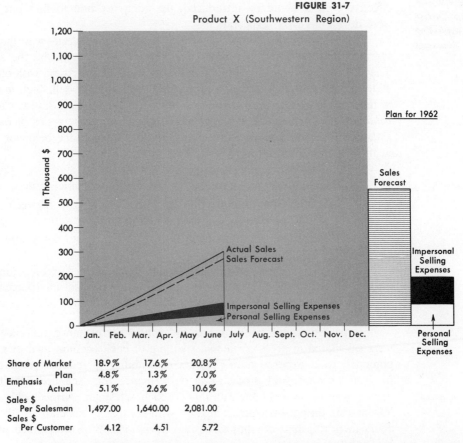

FIGURE 31-7
Product X (Southwestern Region)

Share of Market	18.9%	17.6%	20.8%
Emphasis — Plan	4.8%	1.3%	7.0%
Emphasis — Actual	5.1%	2.6%	10.6%
Sales $ Per Salesman	1,497.00	1,640.00	2,081.00
Sales $ Per Customer	4.12	4.51	5.72

Source: Michael Schiff, "Reporting for More Profitable Product Management," The Journal
of Accountancy *(May 1963), p. 69. Copyrighted 1963 by the American Institute of CPAS.*

has been restored, remedial action must be taken. The kinds of analyses discussed above sometimes do indicate the cause of a malfunction in the system;
more often, however, they only indicate the departure from expectations, and
specific studies must be made to get at the root causes. Most of these studies
are conducted by market research, a unit in the organization whose prime
responsibility is the gathering and analysis of information, generally to correct
problem situations. An example will illustrate this aspect of control.[8]

Oceanic Industries (name fictitious) experienced a declining sales volume
and deterioration of major accounts as measured against industry growths. The

[8] This example is taken from Jon R. Katzenbach and R. R. Champion, "Linking
Lo-Level Planning to Salesman Performance," *Business Horizons,* IX, No. 3 (Fall 1966),
Graduate School of Business Administration, Indiana University, 91–100.

usual methods were used to jack up the sales force, a round of sales meetings and a mass of written directives, with no appreciable improvement. Before effective control could be introduced, the company had to find out why there were deviations from expectations.

A review of the company's entire marketing program was made, and it revealed that the cause was poor planning and use of time by the sales force. They avoided systematic planning and spent most of their time with old accounts with whom they felt at home, and avoided the harder-to-sell, high-margin items in the line. It was decided that the solution to the problem lay in *changing the behavior of the salesman in the field*. At this point a new series of information-gathering forays was made and a plan devised to change the behavior. The steps in the plan were as follows:

1. Translate corporate goals into specific performance criteria.

2. Determine the "opportunity gap," that is, the gap between actual and gross profit opportunity for each major account.

3. Establish gross profit potentials for each account for purpose of measuring current performance.

4. Establish other performance targets, such as sales expense targets, small order reduction targets for each account, and product-mix percentage goals for each major product category and each account.

Expectations on performance and actual performance for each salesman were calculated in areas of: actual standing of each account against gross profit potential; sales expense ratio performance; ability to reduce orders below $20 for each account; and product-mix performance for each account. This information was made available monthly to each salesman. Armed with up-to-date information on performance compared with company expectations, the salesman could then plan his activities to correct deviations. With this added information it was relatively easy for the salesman, in consultation with his supervisor, to determine how much time each account warranted.

Just where control stops and a new phase of management planning begins in this case is difficult to determine. The remedy, however, is the establishment of a new system of control for monitoring past actions. It should be evident that control and information go hand in hand. Sometimes the information flow is on a continuous basis, such as that used to monitor past actions, and sometimes it results from specific studies designed to determine the causes of deviations from expectations.

Monitoring Impending Change

So far we have been discussing control in a passive sense. That is, provision has been made to monitor past actions on a continuous basis, and it was suggested that periodically specific information may be collected to remedy a malfunction in the system. In this sense control is passive and not anticipatory. Oftentimes indications of environmental change are present long before an actual change causes a deviation from expectations. Information on customers,

575

Marketing
Information
Flows
and Control
Systems

channel members, competitors, and government actions should be collected and disseminated to decision-making executives on a continuous basis. The kind of market information discussed in Chapters 6, 7, 8, and 9 should be carefully scrutinized for management use if it relates to an environmental change calling for a new direction in marketing effort. Information on channel members' actions, such as their sales volume, promotional activity, sales force quality, should be coming in continually, stored, and indexed for ready retrieval. Information on competitors' actions would seem to be essential. A carefully devised salesmen's reporting system can supply information on competitors' moves in new-product introductions, prices, and promotional activities. Last but not least provisions must be made to keep abreast of the numerous actions of government, that have an impact on markets and marketing activities. New laws, recent court decisions, government purchasing policies, and tax reforms are only a few of the many governmental actions which may affect the competitive environment.

Busy executives have little time to scan the thousands of bits of information that may be significant to them. Yet knowledge of the type suggested above would be helpful in many instances. Unless some means are found to provide this kind of information, the firm may find itself competitively displaced, even when the handwriting was on the wall years before deterioration set in in its market posture.

ORGANIZATION AND USE
OF INFORMATION
FOR CONTROL PURPOSES

The particular organization used for gathering information will depend upon the amount the particular firm wishes to collect. A complete information system covering all the possibilities suggested in this chapter would be very costly. Management practice today seems to favor monitoring past actions, as substantial sums are spent on sales, share of market, distribution, sales force, and cost and profit analyses. Once deviations from expected results are known, the amounts spent for additional information to determine causes vary widely. In only a few of the very large companies is any attempt made to monitor impending change. Expenditures in this area are a type of insurance, and the amount of information to be collected can best be determined by mature, experienced executives.[9]

Although there has been much talk about management information systems, they are not, with very few exceptions, reflected in organization structures, through the establishment of a special unit charged with this responsibility. Information-gathering activities are diffused throughout the company in the marketing, marketing services, advertising, marketing research, sales, and accounting departments. Unfortunately, the information often stays in these departments, and little is done to disseminate it to other parts of the organization. Every manager can make use of information, and some means must be found

---

[9] Bayesian statistics can be used to judge the feasibility of spending additional sums for information in specific cases but are not useful for determining how much should be spent on information in general.

to make all of the information available to all decision makers. Special skills are required to search for information, to judge its validity, and to synthesize it for control purpose. Perhaps the storage and retrieval capacity of the computer can be harnessed to make information available to all decision makers in an organization. With the advent of this equipment there undoubtedly will be a trend toward centralizing responsibility for collecting and disseminating marketing information.

Collection and dissemination of information, however, is not enough. The information must be used to guide the organization as it executes its marketing program. A mass of information must be collected, synthesized, and put into meaningful form so that executives may ascertain performance of any one of a number of activities. Whenever there are indications of malfunction, management action must be taken if control is to be complete. This action may vary from a flow of directives downward, designed to cause people to behave in a different manner, to conducting large-scale research studies to preplan various parts of the marketing mix or even to change corporate goals.

It may appear that we have come full circle and our discussion of control is reminiscent of some of the aspects of programming discussed in Chapter 4. But the question of where control stops and programming begins is somewhat academic if the procedures suggested here enable the corporation to achieve its goals year after year.

Summary

Control is defined as anything the company may do to insure attainment of its objectives. Control is built into the operating system through programming appropriate product, distribution, and communication mixes and through mobilizing human and physical resources to execute these mixes. Because of the impossibility of establishing control devices that are insensitive to human error in execution or sufficiently sensitive to changes in the environment, a continuous flow of information is needed to determine whether the system is functioning as desired.

Some of the difficulties in collecting information for control purposes, along with technological advancements in data processing, suggest the magnitude of the job if an efficient control system is to be developed. Three kinds of information are necessary if control is to be effective. The first is information to monitor past actions. This includes analyses of sales, share of market, distribution, sales force, and cost and profit. In each case the analysis should be made in such a way that it evaluates a responsibility or profit center. Although the firm functions as an integrated operating system, responsibility for activities is allocated to individuals. Control information must be assembled in such a way that performance of these responsibility centers is monitored. Second, information must be collected to determine the causes of malfunction so that the next round of reprogramming may begin. Generally this type of information is not collected on a continuous basis but rather in the form of separate studies. Third, information which will indicate impending change in the environment is needed.

The amount of information collected can only be judged by the needs of each company. Most companies collect some information to monitor past actions.

577

Marketing
Information
Flows
and Control
Systems

Yet all of the information suggested above is desirable. Perhaps the presence of the computer will enable many companies to increase their information flow and will require the centralizing of responsibility for this activity.

Questions and Problems

1. What is the meaning of control?
2. Why are control devices needed?
3. Do you think it is logical to place the discussion of control at the end of the book? Why?
4. Is control really an independent element in the programming process?
5. Is there an element of control present in the selection of salesmen?
6. Why are managerial controls unlikely to operate as smoothly as temperature controls on a furnace?
7. What is the relationship between objectives and controls?
8. Indicate as many different control devices for marketing systems as you can.
9. What is the significance of information in relationship to control?
10. What are some of the commonly used analyses for marketing control purposes?
11. Describe share of market analysis. What services are available to marketers for this type of analysis?
12. What are some of the standards of comparison that can be used in sales volume analysis?
13. What difficulties are present in collecting information and using it for control purposes?
14. Reflecting on your study of this book, why do you suppose it would be more difficult to precisely measure the marketing cost of a product than its production cost?
15. There is a current trend toward more emphasis on marketing profitability analysis as compared with marketing cost analysis. What difference do you see between the two? Which do you think would be more useful for the purposes of control devices? Why? What kinds of additional complexity are introduced by profitability analysis? Is one more suitable than the other for the emerging philosophy of this book? Why?

Bibliography

Alderson, Wroe, and Stanley J. Shapiro, eds., *Marketing and the Computer* (Englewood Cliffs, N.J.: Prentice-Hall, Inc., 1963).

Barnard, Chester I., *The Functions of the Executive* (Cambridge, Mass.: Harvard University Press, 1938).

Bass, Frank M., *et al.*, *Mathematical Models and Methods in Marketing* (Homewood, Ill.: Richard D. Irwin, Inc., 1961).

Clewett, Robert L., "Integrating Science, Technology, and Marketing: An Overview," *Science, Technology, & Marketing,* Raymond M. Haas, ed., Fall Conference Proceedings (New York: American Marketing Assn., 1966), pp. 11–20.

Cox, Reavis, and Wroe Alderson, eds., *Theory in Marketing* (Homewood, Ill.: Richard D. Irwin, Inc., 1950).

Crisp, Richard D., *Sales Planning and Control* (New York: McGraw-Hill Book Company, 1961).

Haire, Mason, *Modern Organization Theory* (New York: John Wiley & Sons, Inc., 1959).

Jennings, Eugene E., *The Executive* (New York: Harper & Row, Publishers, 1962).

Kelley, E. J., *Analyzing and Improving Marketing Performance,* Management Report No. 32 (New York: American Management Assn., 1959).

Koch, Edward G., "A Practical Approach to Management Planning and Control," *Advanced Management,* XXIV, No. 7 (July 1959), 10–14.

————, "New Organizational Patterns for Marketing," *Management Review,* LI, No. 2 (New York: American Management Assn., February 1962), 4–12.

Likert, Rensis, "Measuring Organization Performance," *Harvard Business Review,* XXXVI, No. 2 (March-April 1958), 41–50.

Longman, Donald R., and Michael Schiff, *Practical Distribution Cost Analysis* (Homewood, Ill.: Richard D. Irwin, Inc., 1955).

Magee, John F., "Operations Research in Making Marketing Decisions," *Journal of Marketing,* XXV, No. 2 (October 1960), 18–23.

Measuring Salesmen's Performance, Studies in Business Policy, No. 114 (New York: National Industrial Conference Board, 1965).

Moore, David G., "Marketing Orientation and Emerging Patterns of Management and Organization," in William Lazer and Eugene J. Kelley, eds., *Managerial Marketing: Perspectives and Viewpoints* (Homewood, Ill.: Richard D. Irwin, Inc., 1962).

"The Myth of the Organization Chart," *Dun's Review & Modern Industry,* LXXV, No. 2 (February 1960), 38–41.

Rubenstein, Albert H., and Chadwick J. Haberstroh, *Some Theories of Organization* (Homewood, Ill.: Richard D. Irwin, Inc., 1960).

Sales Analysis, Studies in Business Policy, No. 113 (New York: National Industrial Conference Board, 1965).

Schiff, Michael, and Martin Mellman, *Financial Management of the Marketing Function* (New York: Financial Executives Research Foundation, 1962).

Selecting and Evaluating Distributors, Studies in Business Policy, No. 116 (New York: National Industrial Conference Board, 1965).

Summary and Conclusions

As we have explored the role of marketing in the management of the enterprise, we have demonstrated its pervasive influence in all facets of enterprise existence. We have not specifically examined the contributions of marketing to economic processes, yet there is a suggestion that marketing is a prime influence in corporate progress and economic progress as well. In Chapter 1 the relationship between marketing and competition was explored. In this section we shall examine competition and its contribution to economic well-being via marketing influences.

In terminating our discussion of marketing, we summarize the many facets of marketing management, recognizing that they constitute a composite of activities contributing to the competitive vitality of the enterprise and the economic progress of the society which it serves.

Corporate, Market, and Economic Growth

32

In Chapter 1 we established the relationship between competition and the way the firm conducts its market affairs. In the remaining sections of the book the intricacies of corporate management in a competitive environment were cast in a marketing orientation. It is our contention that a third phenomenon, *growth*—corporate and economic—must be added to complete the triumvirate—marketing, competition, and growth. Economic growth is of concern domestically, and recently claims have been made that market orientation should be the central focus of economic development. We wish to concentrate on market orientation as a factor influencing our economic well-being. Not because it is the only factor but rather because we believe it to be an important one—and one which has not been studied as intensively as it might be—the subtleties of the relationship between marketing, competition, and growth should be explored.

In a competitive society the major unit responsible for economic progress is the business enterprise. Does this mean that growth of the enterprise is tantamount to economic growth? Unfortunately, the logic is not so direct. In this chapter we shall examine the role of marketing in corporate and economic growth and its relationship to economic development.

CORPORATE GROWTH

If you have understood our discussion to this point, it should be clear that the key to corporate growth is maintaining competitive superiority through a continuous process of matching market opportunities with total management effort. There are a number of ways of measuring corporate growth. Among these are change in profitability, return on investment, sales volume, share of market, or the company's share of the industry's share of gross national product. The particular measure used depends upon the purpose, and the crucial question is, Can we assume that companies aspire to grow?

Self-Renewal and Self-Destruction [1]

There are some interesting statistics which cast doubt on the proposition that the desire to grow is an intrinsic facet of corporate management. Of the 200 highest-growth companies during the 1940's, only 15 percent were in this category in the 1950's.[2] Of course, 170 new companies filled the slots. Did the 170 companies that dropped their rating just become sick and wither away? Were they competitively displaced? Or did the market just turn its back on their market offers?

We do know that not all companies have the desire, vitality, and aggressiveness to lead in the competitive race. Many family-owned and managed concerns reach a level of growth and then consciously try to maintain that size. Motivations vary; in some cases they are related to the age of the management and a reluctance to take on additional risks when life is very comfortable the way things are. Since competitively it is almost impossible to stand still, companies with such outlooks go into a decline.

Entrepreneurs have been classified as innovators, imitators, fabians, and drones.[3] True corporate growth is reserved for the innovators and, possibly with luck, the imitators, but the fabians and drones only act when forced to. Our concern is with the innovative and sometimes imitative firm. What is it that leads it to undertake the risks of growth?

Pressures for Growth

There are at least two major pressures acting upon the firm to stimulate its growth. One is the competitive environment and the other, the structure of ownership. The pressures exerted by competition on the market affairs of the firm have a profound influence on its aggressiveness in seeking differential advantage through innovation. The normal mentality of management would be to achieve a position of prominence in selected markets and then to hope that no moves were made by competitors to endanger their position or, at worst, dislodge them.

One of the major concerns of the structural economist is that in oligopolistic industries, conscious parallel action is tantamount to a cooperative arrangement that holds back innovation. The converse of this argument is that the uncertainty about retaliatory actions and the short lead times in innovation, cause such enterprises to continue to innovate even in the absence of a present threat. Judged on a performance basis, many firms in oligopolistic industries

---

[1] Joseph Schumpeter gave considerable attention to the desirability of *creative destruction* in the process of growth. See Joseph Schumpeter, *Capitalism, Socialism, and Democracy* (New York: Harper & Row, Publishers, 1942), Chap. VII.

[2] N. R. Maines, *Why Companies Grow* (Palo Alto, Calif.: Stanford Research Institute, 1957).

[3] Clarence Danhof, "Observations on Entrepreneurship in Agriculture," reported by R. Wohlin, *Change and the Entrepreneur* (Cambridge, Mass.: Harvard University Press, 1949).

583

Corporate,
Market,
and
Economic
Growth

have followed the latter course. The dynamic nature of competition forces many firms to continue to innovate and to establish market control through marketing effort in order to safeguard their positions. Growth goes hand in hand with this process of self-renewal.

It has been suggested by Baumol that it is the structure of ownership in the corporation that stimulates innovation and corporate growth.[4] Since ownership is held through stock certificates, management must continually pay out sufficient yields to keep the owners happy. It would be relatively easy to provide a satisfactory yield year after year; however, the fact that ownership is constantly changing complicates matters. Each time a share of stock is bought, the purchaser pays for past successes, since these are reflected in the purchase price of the stock. The new owner anticipates either a similar yield but on a larger value, or an appreciation in value, or both. To meet these demands, the company's growth is mandatory. Add to this pressure the pressures of competition, and it seems clear that the environment within which the firm functions acts to promote the growth of the enterprise. Why then is the composition of successful firms constantly changing?

The Possibility of Decay

Even the best-managed corporations sometimes lose their superior positions for a period of time—or forever. There are a number of cases of firms that after achieving unbelievable goals seem to go backwards. Coca-Cola, Singer Sewing Machine, American Motors, and Studebaker, are examples of companies that have at one time or another lost their momentum. The causes are many, and the road back is difficult. Perhaps success breeds complacency, which, in turn, produces a number of pathological disturbances within the organization.

At times the forces of competition are administratively neutralized by governmental action in the interests of national security. The U.S. aircraft industry, for example, probably would not be permitted to falter should it fail to compete effectively with foreign suppliers in the domestic market. Aside from such special cases, corporations—and even the giants are not immune—may pass from the business scene, an apparent economic waste. The economic waste, however, of a bankrupt company is minimal compared with the gains realizable by those innovators who have displaced it. And fortunately there is the process of self-renewal and self-destruction; as some firms drop from positions of leadership, others take their places. Who provides economic growth should be of little concern to society as a whole, so long as a sufficient number of firms are stimulated to grow.

ECONOMIC GROWTH

That the United States has experienced tremendous economic growth is not to be denied. There is no need to substantiate this fact by a mass of statistical

---

[4] William J. Baumol, *Business Behavior Value and Growth* (New York: The Macmillan Company, 1959), pp. 93–95.

data. Even those critics who describe the present-day U.S. economy as "pockets of poverty in the midst of plenty" would not question U.S. superiority on a relative basis. Why have we been so fortunate? One author suggests that education is a critical variable:

> The wealth of a nation does not seem to depend upon some of the more obvious or commonplace variables. For example, if natural resources were the sole criterion for wealth, Japan and Norway would be poor, which they are not.
>
> If, as some of the opponents of foreign investment allege, "colonial exploitation" were the stumbling block to progress, Siam and Abyssinia, which have never been colonized, would be rich, which they are not. Former colonies Canada and Australia would be poor, which they are not.
>
> If lack of heavy industry were the handicap, then Denmark and New Zealand would be poor, which they are not. If high population density drags down living standards, the Netherlands and Japan should be poor, which they are not. If capital for investment is the required ingredient, then Kuwait and Venezuela would be rich, which they are not.
>
> On the other hand, if a main factor in a nation's wealth is a high level of education spread widely over the population, the United States should be very rich, Western Europe should be fairly rich, Latin America should be fairly poor, and Africa should be very poor—which they all are.
>
> I would not want to conclude that education is the one and only prerequisite for an affluent society. But it is most certainly a prime one, for widespread ignorance and prosperity just are not found together.[5]

Certainly education is a major factor. However, we should like to add to the multiplicity of influences the system uses to accomplish economic well-being.

In the free world, growth seems to depend on the level of desire of the culture in question and the system used for accomplishing that level. It is a reasonable hypothesis that all societies strive for a higher level of material well-being. Although the composition of the output may vary, few are satisfied for any length of time with their economic lot. A reasonable explanation of growth may be found in the system used to accomplish it.

A prominent business leader expresses the proposition as follows:

> Few seriously doubt any longer our ability to avoid another depression of 1929 proportions.
>
> But it seems to me that while adroit fiscal and monetary policy can help to create a climate for progress, the needed economic growth rate can best be achieved by an intensified use of competition—among nations, among their institutions, and particularly among their various industries.
>
> If there is a distinguishing economic characteristic that sets the 20th century apart from all that has gone before, the intensity and creative breadth of modern competition is surely it.
>
> The real question is how to use both competition and the diversified corporation to best speed the economic growth of the entire world.[6]

[5] Monroe E. Spaght, Managing Director, Royal Dutch Shell, "Meeting Education Needs," *The General Electric Forum*, X (April–June 1967), 24.
[6] John B. McKitterick, "New Markets and National Needs," *The General Electric Forum*, X, No. 2 (April–June 1967), 8.

585

Corporate,
Market,
and
Economic
Growth

Through acceptance of the system of competition, society has set in motion some of the forces that call forth a level of innovation needed for economic progress. As we have observed in Chapter 1, a competition for differential advantage prevails, and it is the totality of market actions engaged in by the industrial and distribution complex that provides whatever growth pattern we have. Marketing is an integral part of competition and is a mandatory management function if the firm is to operate successfully in a competitive environment. As such, marketing is very closely tied to economic growth. One writer views the situation as follows:

> The very essence of our competitive system is the pressure placed on an individual business to produce better products at lower cost. . . . Businessmen therefore are constantly seeking new techniques, new products, and new ideas in all fields to give them competitive advantages. The market place today clearly is a place where a businessman innovates or fails.[7]

MARKETING AND TECHNOLOGY

The Need for Technology

It is inappropriate to examine the marketing effects of competitive behavior on economic growth without considering the function of technology. An intensely competitive state may exist without new technological developments, but it is not likely to be a growth economy in the sense that more and better products are made available for mass consumption. The new product, the improved quality, or the new way of doing business is far more enduring as a competitive weapon than engaging in a series of artificial and often superfluous differentiations. The latter may be tolerated if in the long run substantive improvements, as judged by the market place, are forthcoming. It is doubtful whether we could or would tolerate an automobile industry which offered nothing but changes in body styling year after year if it did not on occasion give us major functional improvements such as automatic transmission. In the ladies garment industry we perhaps do tolerate inconsequential differentiation from year to year, interspersed with substantive fabric changes from the textile industry. In an affluent society, however, the aesthetic values associated with changing styles can be very functional. We must provide for new technology, for without it the competitive posture of the economy is wasteful, and the desired end result, growth, is not attained.

The Source of Technology

Technology comes from two sources, private industry and the government. The research and development expenditures of the private sector have been increasing at an accelerating rate. In 1964 R & D expenditures of the private

---

[7] George A. Steiner, "Improving the Transfer of Government-Sponsored Technology," *Business Horizons,* IX, No. 3 (Fall 1966), Graduate School of Business, Indiana University, 60.

sector were approximately $5.7 billion, 2 percent of net sales.[8] In 1967 total R & D expenditures were estimated at about $24 billion, with $17+ billion contributed by the private sector, $13+ billion by government, and $3+ billion by educational institutions.[9] It should be understood that all that is labeled research and development is not necessarily research in the pure sense. Very few corporations engage in pure research. With few exceptions, the bulk of their R & D activities are developmental and are an attempt to analyze the commercial feasibility of innovations which come from other sources.

The federal government has spent roughly $100 billion on research, with the total research bill currently running at 15 percent of federal expenditures. These expenditures have produced approximately 40,000 patented inventions since 1945. It was estimated in 1965 that federally supported research efforts were well above 100,000 innovations per year.[10]

The large proportion of total research expenditures assumed by the federal government have led some observers to question the role of the American corporation in providing for our material progress. Although much of all research is government funded, much of it is conducted by private industry on a contractual basis. Of the $24 billion of R & D expenditures in 1967, 67 percent of the total funding was from government sources. Many firms have viewed government's interest in this area as a market opportunity and have geared themselves to capitalize on it. Some very large corporations, such as the Bendix Corporation, do a substantial share of their annual volume in federal contracts. It should also be remembered that R & D expenditures are a very small proportion of the total cost of a usable innovation. They are estimated to be only 5 to 10 percent of the total.[11] Further, the rapid rate at which patentable inventions are generated is not a very good measure of the rate at which they will be turned into commercially marketable products and find their way into the American standard of living. The role of the corporation in economic growth is, in part, to assume the risks inherent in making change palatable to the consuming public.

Commercialization and Technology

Among others, two conditions must be met to make effective use of technology for economic progress. First, some enterprising management must become aware of the new technology. Second, it must assess the market feasibility of the technology and be willing to incur the risks commercialization entails. Awareness of technology is not always easy. Although research activity is generating a large number of patentable inventions, what firm is organized to scan

[8] U.S. Department of Commerce, *Technological Innovation: Its Environment and Management* (Washington, D.C.: Government Printing Office, January 1967), p. 10.

[9] Unpublished address by Malcolm P. Ferguson, Retired Chairman of the Board, Bendix Corporation on WSMB Television, February 13, 1968.

[10] Richard L. Lester and George J. Howick, *Background, Guidelines and Recommendations for Use in Assessing Effective Means of Channeling New Technologies in Promising Directions* (Washington, D.C.: National Commission on Technology, Automation and Economic Progress, November 1965), p. 35.

[11] *Ibid.,* p. 9.

587

Corporate,
Market,
and
Economic
Growth

the thousands of technical journals in which new technology is reported? The time lapses between invention and first use are long. So great is the federal government's concern over the loss of technology that many agencies, such as the National Aeronautics and Space Administration, Department of Defense, National Science Foundation, and the Atomic Energy Commission, have established technology communication programs. The Technical Services Act of 1965 is specifically designed to make the output of the federal government's research activities available to small and medium-sized business.

Once a decision is made to explore a new technology further, the entire new-product development and market introduction process begins. Clewett makes a distinction between the R & D concept of integrating technology and marketing. He concludes that the latter focuses more on human want satisfaction, whereas the former focuses on transforming the technology into new products. The entrepreneurial concept, because of its difference in emphasis, is more productive of growth in the economy than the R & D approach.[12] It is in the commercialization attempt that we find a conjunction of marketing and technology. The management of opportunities and risks was discussed in Chapter 4 and there is no need to discuss them here. It should be made clear, however, that technology delivered to the market place is essential for economic progress. The incessant pressure of competition, which forces firms to seek differential advantage through continually capitalizing on market opportunity in their innovative actions, is a major factor in causing firms to grow, flourish, and perpetuate themselves, and at the same time, in giving society an economic system that provides it with a growing and improved stock of goods from which its members may satisfy their needs and desires.

NATIONAL MARKET INTEGRATION

That competition, technology, and marketing have had something to do with improving standards of living in the United States is established. Does it follow that they could start the developing nations on the way to a more abundant life? Walt W. Rostow, Counselor and Chairman of the Policy Planning Council, United States Department of State, came forward with the concept of national market integration in1965. In a speech before the American Marketing Association in Washington in September, 1965, he elaborated the notion as follows:

> In one developing country after another the perception is spreading that the next phase of marketing must be based on a systematic diffusion of the modern skills, now largely concentrated in urban areas, out into the countryside; on the making of efficient national markets; and from this widened basis, on the generation of new lines of diversified exports which alone promise to earn the foreign exchange which the developing countries will need in the years ahead. Only the pattern of widened domestic markets and diversified exports promises to provide

[12] See Robert L. Clewett, "Integrating Science, Technology, and Marketing: An Overview," *Science, Technology, and Marketing*, Raymond M. Haas, ed., 1966 Fall Conference Proceedings, American Marketing Association, pp. 11–20.

the foundation for that deepening of the industrial structure (from consumer goods down to capital goods and the heavy industry sectors) which a modern industrial society requires.[13]

The problem visualized is one of haves and have nots. In most developing countries more than half the labor force is engaged in agriculture at a very low level of subsistence. For all practical purposes they do not participate in the market economy. Notwithstanding the amount of effort devoted to agriculture most such economies suffer from food shortages. It is appropriate then that the economic revolution must start in the agricultural sector. The role of marketing in bringing about this revolution was suggested as follows:

> First, the farmer must receive a reliable and fair price for his product. Second, credit must be made available at reasonable rates for him to make the change in the character of his output or the shift in productivity desired. Third, there must be available, on the spot, technical assistance that is relevant to his soil, his weather conditions, and his change in either output or in productivity.

> Finally, there must be available at reasonable rates two types of industrial products: inputs such as chemical fertilizers, insecticides, and farm tools; and incentive goods—that is, the consumer goods of good quality he and his family would purchase in greater quantity or work harder to get if they were cheaper or if his income were higher.[14]

In this context marketing is involved in a two-way flow from the urban to the rural centers and vice versa. The concept is interesting and, when viewed in the perspective of our own economic history, appears to have merit. At the time it was announced, however, there was no theoretical accommodation of the idea, and the many difficulties present in inducing change were as yet not considered. Since then much attention has been devoted to the premise, and a body of empirical evidence is being collected to support it.[15]

The Typical Case

Developing nations typically have 50 to 60 percent of their labor force engaged in subsistence agriculture. Productivity levels are low and barely produce enough to feed the agrarian populace let alone the urban sectors. Low productivity levels are sometimes caused by a lack of fertile conditions but more generally by a failure to use the agricultural technology which is available. The structure of land holding is generally feudal. A change in production methods generally entails a substitution of capital for labor, and the oversupply of agricultural laborers makes this unattractive to the landowner.

In the urban sectors a very small proportion of the population, the wealthy,

---

[13] Walt W. Rostow, "The Concept of a National Market and its Economics Growth Implications," *Marketing and Economic Development,* Peter D. Bennett, ed. Proceedings of the Fiftieth Anniversary, International Symposium on Marketing, American Marketing Association, September 1965, pp. 11–20.

[14] Rostow, "Concept of a National Market," pp. 14–15.

[15] In 1965 the Latin American Market Planning Center was established at Michigan State University in cooperation with the United States Agency for International Development. This center has been engaged in a number of studies in Latin America in an effort to operationalize the premise espoused by Professor Rostow.

589

Corporate,
Market,
and
Economic
Growth

pay high prices for the trickle of foodstuffs that do reach the market on an uncertain supply basis. Manufactured goods are completely out of reach of the majority of the rural sector and a large portion of the urban sector as well. Incentives for increased investment and higher outputs in manufacturing are generally as dismal as in the agricultural sector. The inability to visualize a large market with effective money demand is a barrier to expansion in the nonfood sector as well.

A lack of availability of capital is usually not the reason for inaction. Of course, developing countries are short of capital, but many of the capital needs cited are for infrastructure buildup and not the kinds of investment inputs we are talking about here. If there is a demonstrated business opportunity within the marketing system, there is usually sufficient in-country capital to launch the venture.

The inability to visualize a market opportunity is a major retarder of economic growth. Mr. Rostow is absolutely correct in his assessment of what needs to be done, but what kind of rationale may be applied to cause people to do it?

A Rationale for National Market Integration

Our purpose is to devise a scheme in which we can predict an increase in both the food and nonfood sector and in which each pulls the other up by its own bootstraps. Let us assume that by some miracle there is an increase in productivity in the agricultural sector and a reduction in prices of food going to the urban sector. The immediate result is a reduction in the 97 percent of disposable income that the vast majority of urbanites now spend on food. This releases discretionary income for nonfood goods by the urbanites and at the same time provides some income to the rural sector. The increase in effective money demand in the urban sector provides a market for increased output in the nonfood sector. With proper merchandising of products, the increased income in the rural sector also begins to emerge as a market opportunity. This round of increases can theoretically spiral upward. Now the labor sector must be brought into the scheme. As the nonfood sector absorbs the excess labor pool present in the cities, it begins to draw upon the massive labor pool in agriculture, thus bidding up the wages of labor in that sector. As these wages are increased, the feasibility of the agricultural producer applying more technology is improved. As he does so, there is an increase in output and a reduction in prices, and the process continues to feed on itself. The concept known as Say's law, in which the very act of supply creates its own demand, is very much at work in this rationale. Our scheme is like two circles, one food and the other nonfood, moving in opposite directions but giving impetus to each other.

This is a very simplified explanation of the basic forces at work in development. Of course, such a sequence of events cannot correct all ills in a short period of time nor can the process go on without friction and disturbances. Imbalance between agriculture and industry has been characteristic of our own economy and is likely to be so in any developing economy. The unanswered question in this explanation is, What miracle started the process in motion?

Studies conducted in developing countries indicate that perceptions of market risk are by far the greatest barriers to innovative action. Often these perceptions by some participants are not based on fact, but a sufficient number are to rule out increased market participation moves. In a study in northeast Brazil among food and nonfood producers and the corresponding middlemen, it was found that invariably a very narrow concept of potential market size existed. No thought was given to remerchandising products in the nonfoods sector or establishing better price-income ratios to cater to those at the bottom level of the socioeconomic scale. The potential payoff of such a market orientation had been urged for some time by the Brazilian Ministry of Planning, but it was not heeded in spite of very favorable fiscal incentives to participate.[16] A similar attitude prevailed among food producers, but the perceptions of market risk were more closely allied to structural problems within the channels of distribution. Instability of price because of poor communications, monopsony on the demand side, poor transportation and the risk of spoilage, and inadequate middlemen to handle a greatly increased output were common explanations. Middlemen's concepts of market risk were closely tied to perceptions of limited market size plus all of the market structure difficulties perceived by food producers. A number of other more personal perceptions, such as "live and let live," and "trust in God," and extended family considerations were also prevalent. But these were not strong among the high performers as measured by local standards of performance.

Selected market reforms must then be implemented to remove a series of interrelated barriers if the process of national market integration is ever to be set in motion in these economies. The absence of an efficient distribution structure and a limited market concept are responsible to a great extent for the state these economies are in. Governmental skill in executing reforms without disturbing the private sector has not yet been put to the test. It is, however, evident that isolated reforms to take care of multidimensional interrelated problems will not correct these shortcomings. Each problem is related to another, and unless each is dealt with in an integrated way, the participants in the system, the people, will not react in a way which will change the *status quo*.

Summary

Marketing, competition, and growth are three intricately related phenomena. We have suggested that marketing, the direct concern of this book, provides a bridge between the other two. Corporate growth is a desirable state in our economy, but although we in the United States have experienced hitherto unprecedented levels of such growth, there does not seem to be an intrinsic desire for it on the part of all corporate managements. Through a process of

[16] Unpublished speech delivered by Brazilian Minister of Planning, Roberto Campos, in São Paulo, Brazil, April 27, 1965.

591

Corporate,
Market,
and
Economic
Growth

self-renewal and self-destruction, corporations come and go, but corporate growth in the absolute has been characteristic of the economy. Two pressures, the competitive environment and the structure of ownership, are major factors responsible for the fact that some corporations are always seeking to grow.

Economic growth of the total economy cannot be attributed solely to an abundance of natural resources, energetic citizenry, education, low intensity of population, or sophisticated fiscal management in the public sector. There are too many examples of societies that have achieved substantial economic growth in the absence of these circumstances or that have not achieved economic growth in their presence.

In attempting to explain economic growth, we have placed more reliance upon the system used to attain it. Marketing's role in this system is the part it plays in transferring technology, through creating differential advantage for the risk taken, to the standard of living of the consuming public. It is in the commercialization of the technological advances that the greatest costs are incurred, that marketing plays its greatest role, and that economic growth becomes a reality. The private and public sectors are the sources of technology, but the competitive environment provides the stimulus for innovation and commercialization of inventions.

That competition, marketing, and technology have had something to do with economic growth in the United States is evident. Their role in promoting economic development abroad is now being explored. The concept of national market integration, integrating economically the rural and urban sectors, will be speeded in developing countries if a marketing mentality can be created among the risk takers in these societies. Market opportunity for both the agricultural producer and the manufacturer must be visible, and all structural and cultural barriers must be removed. Historically, little attention has been given to establishing more favorable price-income ratios through remerchandising products in an attempt to broaden the market. Nor has there been much attempt to rationalize the process by which the food and nonfood sectors or urban and rural sectors nourish each other. The achievement of national market integration requires an integrated systems approach to reforms, which will rectify the many interrelated facets of a national market system.

Questions and Problems

1. Explain the major pressures on the corporation to grow.
2. Do all companies have a desire to grow? Explain.
3. "Our economic system contributes to the possibility of corporate failure and great economic waste. Protective legislation for the corporation is desirable." Discuss.
4. To what factors might the economic growth of a society be attributed?
5. Why must a society provide for a high level of innovation?
6. What role does the U.S. government play in technology?
7. Is it desirable to have the federal government so much involved in technology?
8. How is marketing related to technology?
9. What is the difference between an R & D approach to technology and an entrepreneurial approach?
10. What is the relationship of marketing to population growth?

11. Is market infrastructure more important in economic development than the market concept held by businessmen?
12. Do you believe the rate of innovation will increase, decrease, or stay about the same?
13. Explain the concept of national market integration.
14. What are some of the major barriers to economic growth in underdeveloped countries?
15. How might a marketing systems approach to national market integration work?

The Firm as a Market Entity

33

Throughout this book you have been exposed to a philosophy of enterprise administration which conceives of the firm as a market entity in which market forces and opportunities provide the orientation for the design of whole systems and subsystems of competitive action. This concept is the true meaning of market orientation for the firm, the focal point around which it organizes all its resources to serve markets productively and efficiently for the achievement of corporate objectives.

Our concern has been with the growth and survival of firms in competitive markets. As an organizing concept, marketing goes beyond the functionalism of distributing goods. It has elements of functionalism, but it goes beyond these boundaries to become virtually a way of life for the enterprise itself. A free enterprise system sanctions only those firms whose market offerings are judged by the market itself to constitute a useful rendering of economic services. This establishes the rivalry of firms as the fundamental basis for the allocation of resources throughout the economy. It is through this rivalry that we are confronted with a bewildering complex of competition and competitive strategies. It is in meeting the requirements of effective competition that a firm obtains the justification for its existence and derives its corporate vitality.

In embracing competition through market affairs, we do not deny the relevancy of all other operating entities in the firm. In fact, competition is so embracing that it pervades every facet of a business organization—research and development, purchasing, production, finance, labor, location, and even intangibles such as distinctive competence. Competition is a process of adjustment in which purchasing units adjust to supplying firms and supplying firms to purchasing units. Competition, as an ecological system, has the capacity to admit new parts or eject old ones. The level of uncertainty prevailing within the system results in continuous fluctuations from an equilibrium state and leads to power-seeking behavior by a firm over its rivals by attempting to establish a loyalty among purchasing units for its product through a complex process of negotiation. Thus, the firm always seeks differential advantage—a form of competitive distinctiveness which separates it from its rivals and constitutes the basis for enduring economic strength. Therefore, for managerial purposes, there is no other appropriate way to conceive of a firm, except as a market entity, for the market place is where the vigor of an enterprise manifests itself.

It is in this light, then, that we recognize the firm as a means-end system. It has resources and it seeks market ends. In fact, we can think of the firm as a target-seeking mechanism, continuously striving to adapt and adjust itself to the attainment of its end purposes. And if this be true, then it is immediately clear that the capacity to achieve its end purposes through the ability to adjust must be carefully considered. This is why the nature of corporate objectives was given early consideration. Objectives or ends sought will determine the way in which resources will be combined in the form of operating systems to produce the competitive distinctiveness that leads to the desired end result. In large measure these strategic objectives can be attained only through instrumental action, purposeful for the ends sought, in the market place. *That* will, in the end, judge the efficacy of managerial choices.

Because the market is the crucial point of action, we have dealt at some length with investigation of market forces and the measurement of market opportunity. The firm seeks a harmonious totality in its market offering, a market offering that blends all of its competency in an optimum way with the complexity of market variables in an affluent, highly industrialized, and advanced economy. Markets have equally important quantitative and qualitative dimensions. Each has its subtleties and obscure elements. The tools of measurement for the analysis of both components have advanced over the years, and we have attempted to show some of the scientific methodology that can currently be brought to bear in this area. Yet, for all these efforts, we are still far short of the requisite precision needed. However, whatever the future holds in more advanced market analysis, it will never displace the need for entrepreneurial instincts. Business itself is entrepreneurship, and entrepreneurship in market affairs involves both adjusting to markets and influencing them by entrepreneurial behavior.

The market offering, no matter how conceived, will be received only when it is in alignment with the complex of market forces operating at a particular time and place. This consideration provides the foundation for the formulation of product strategy, for products are a large part, although not the total composition, of the market offering. Products and product diversity are the principal linkage of the firm with its markets. They are the most important of all means of market adjustment. It is for this reason that we have devoted considerable attention to ways by which this integration can be achieved—the way a firm can develop a pattern of product diversity that suits its business purpose and competitive resources. Moreover, we have recognized products as proceeding through a life cycle of perishable distinctiveness—that is, through various stages of market development. We have seen that as this progression takes place, the nature of competition is altered, and that as competition is altered, the nature of marketing effort must be adjusted. This is why product strategies must be varied from time to time. But we have also seen that the need for diverse product assortments to more sharply mesh with market forces must always be reconciled with the economic penalties of excessive assortment throughout the entire production-marketing system. The firm must seek an optimum combination of cost centers throughout the system, a combination compatible with its revenue-generating capabilities. We have conveyed some of the means by which this need for integration, adjustment through stages of growth and decline, and variations in strategy can be achieved.

The product mix is only one part of the broader marketing mix which links the firm with the market place. It has a distribution mix that serves the purpose of moving products through time and space into purchase and use. Consequently, the distribution network to be employed has a logistical or supply element, as well as a market cultivation element. It is through reconciling the cost-revenue capabilities of varying institutional arrangements that the ultimate channel of distribution is selected. The various institutional intermediaries are recognized as performing a series of activities for hire. The functional needs of the marketer—those which blend his markets, products, and firm characteristics—are the bases for channel-of-distribution choices. These choices are of increasing complexity because of the conglomerate nature of competition which has emerged—the competition of a wide variety of institutions and types of intermediaries in selling the same class of commodity.

Because management chooses among these alternative institutional types in arriving at a final distribution mix, it needs a clear understanding of the types of establishments, the trends influencing these institutions, and the operational changes taking place within them. This is the reason for our coverage of institutional alternatives. Once these choices have been made, total effectiveness of the distribution mix will depend on the quality of the particular outlets selected, the reconciliations of conflicting claims within the network, and the management of the total network in terms of its collective objectives. We have recognized that entire production-marketing systems are in competition with other whole systems: one particular blend of manufacturer-distributor-dealer organizations competes with another. This sets up the conditions of both conflict and cooperation within the network itself.

Partially, then, a power structure emerges in which each participant would prefer to gain principal control of the system. More specifically, retailers would prefer to subordinate manufacturers to them, and manufacturers would prefer to maintain principal control over the system all the way to ultimate purchase and product use. For this reason, constant power alterations are taking place within the distribution mix, while simultaneous efforts at cooperation are being made. These volatile conditions precipitated treatment of the management of manufacturer-dealer or -agent systems to indicate the means whereby the system might function effectively. But this objective involves complex instrumentation that possibly precludes perfection in operating results. This is so not only for the reasons previously mentioned, but because end locational decisions, intermediate holding and dispersion points, transport modes, inventory levels in each of the stages, economic lot size of production, production scheduling, and information must somehow be brought into a compatible system-wide totality.

If the product offering, with its accompanying services, has been structured properly, the market or exchange process will be actuated through information flows. The offering must be communicated in a way that builds impact at the point of ultimate purchase. The market, at any given time, holds an inventory of information related to the solution of its own problems, which are solved through its procurement of goods and services. The marketer is most effective when he moves the potential purchaser along a path to his desired end purpose or self-image. The marketer needs therefore to close the gap between the information held in various parts of the market and the information it should hold if purchase action favorable to the seller is to be precipitated. But there is a great deal of "noise" in the market at all times, and in the channels of communication. *Noise* is distractions, misinterpretations, varying meanings attached to bits of information, and competing messages, which distort a particular message or reduce its fidelity.

Because communications of all kinds are not really *received,* but *perceived,* we have chosen to consider some elements of formal communications theory as they are relevant to market communication. Some knowledge of the form, structure, and content of messages has seemed an essential prerequisite to considering the various means of achieving these desired information exchanges. Since we conceive advertising, sales promotion, and personal selling to be partially alternative systems for communicating with a market, they offer a degree of substitutability among themselves. This condition leads to a part of the complexity in determining the optimum mix of the communications instruments to be used in market cultivation attempts. Determining appropriations for these various forms constitutes a most difficult, multivariable, analytical problem. But it is one a firm cannot escape, because by the end of the operating period, each enterprise will in some way or another have expended its funds in a distinctive communications mix.

We have considered the problem on both theoretical and practical levels. Marginalism was used to set up model solutions, and we have attempted to demonstrate how these decision rules can be practically applied to solve problems within reasonable levels of precision. Such problems as size of sales force required, level of advertising expenditure to be made, and other appropriations for market cultivation were examined. Moreover, we have recognized this as not only a general problem, but a specific one—these allocations must be directed toward particular products of varying need and profit potentiality. Further, adjustments must be made over time as product introduction and displacement take place. This point derives from a fundamental tenet that pervades the book: *The firm is engaged in a continuous process of adaptive behavior.*

The right quantities of effort in these market cultivation areas are not in themselves enough to sustain a firm in its competitive rivalry. The quality or artistic configuration of these forms of communication and cultivation also determine the level of effectiveness. It is for this reason that we examined in some detail the purposes of advertising, the conditions under which it could be used most effectively, the way in which content derives from assessment of motivational forces, the placement of it into various media, and the way in which its productivity could be judged. But if we provided a reasonable assessment of the current state of the art, our intention was to look more to the future, for no area covered leaves more opportunity for advancement in theory, measurement, or practice, than determining thresholds of advertising impact and identifying redundancy levels.

If advertising received considerable attention, hardly less could be said about the management of the sales force. The selection, supervision, assignment, and motivation of the field selling organization is often one of the largest of all cost centers. Its skillful administration is a strategic variable in the market affairs of the firm. Its effectiveness, however, is usually no more or no less than the quality of analytical effort that precedes its operations—analysis that determines the job to be done, the human qualities required, the number of men needed, the basis for their deployment, the level of remuneration required to attract the desired level of competence, and the information and evaluation criteria by which the success of their actions will be judged.

The fact that we have treated pricing last has not been by accident; neither does it necessarily reflect the significance of pricing. Price is a monetary expression of value and is the focal point of the entire exchange process. The customer can perceive the attractiveness of the market offering only through the price mechanism. In so doing he reflects a large number of objective and subjective evaluations in his perception of the compatibility of the value represented with his own desired goals.

On the other hand, price is a reflection of all the actions of the firm. It should reflect the kind of product strategy followed, the system of intermediaries used to make the product available, the communications instruments used to translate potential purchasing power into effective demand, and the objectives of the enterprise itself. Price indeed serves to integrate supply with demand, and for this reason its theoretical, legal, and managerial aspects have been explored. Determination of price levels, price systems and quotations, differentials between items in a line, associated items, the alternatives to be followed in price strategies on both new and old products, and the administration of prices all constitute managerial decisions that have ramifications throughout the market and the enterprise. Finally, price as a competitive instrument is an alternative to the use of *other* means of market cultivation that seek to insulate the firm from direct competitive forces.

Finally, for all these interlocking elements of the market affairs of the firm to be combined and integrated into a forceful totality, organizational alignments must be made which will provide the structure for decision and action. Action necessitates control devices that can signal appropriate modifications and corrections in the functioning of the system as it operates within a continuously changing internal and external environment. Organizational design has as its purpose the linking of people, facilities, and functions into the desired concurrent and sequential relationships. Market orientation, as the design focal point, involves the structuring of planning, decision, and control points to insure that those responsible for the achievement of market results have the requisite tools and resources to fulfill that responsibility. While marketing personnel in the past have been largely preoccupied with sales volume, we can expect them increasingly in the future to bear a profit accountability.

We have tried to indicate the evolution of organizational design in market affairs and to indicate the directions along which it might develop in the future, as well as to provide some of the criteria by which organizational effectiveness can be judged. For if it is all it should be, it will enable the firm to reflect a market orientation, and present a posture for meeting the requirements of effective competition. The firm will in fact be a market entity—an entity that draws its vigor from meeting the challenges of the market place and survives and grows through the achievement of its objectives there.

If you now have some integrated philosophy of the managerial implications of conceiving of the firm as a market entity, then we have done our job well. This understanding, however, is merely prologue. Meeting the requirements of effective competition in the future will demand better solutions to present problems and will present wholly new problems not currently foreseen. The search for better solutions to problems in the market affairs of the firm will continue. Among them will be attempts to: measure resistance to change in markets; quantify habit patterns in markets; understand more precisely the motivations of purchasers and the ways they express them; simulate mathematically the competition interaction in markets; develop new models for calculating inventory and logistical requirements; find a superior means of measuring the returns from a variety of communications instruments; retrieve easily from masses of data pertinent information for on-going decision purposes; and develop a more penetrating administrative science related to large-scale, complex, human organizations.

Marketing, in its fullest conception, will make significant contributions to economic growth for individual firms, particular industries, and market systems as a whole. Through a process of self-renewal and self-destruction corporations will continue to enter and leave markets as viable competitors, but corporate growth as a collective phenomenon is central to an advanced open economy. The marketing role in aggregate economic growth relates to the system used to sustain it—the transfer of technology through market processes. Both the private and public sectors are sources of technology, but the competitive environment provides the stimulus for innovation and commercialization of invention. The intense quest for fuller achievement of national market integration in the developing nations will be speeded if market orientation on an integrated systems basis can be created among risk takers in those societies.

This is but a brief glimpse of directions ahead. Advancements will be made in many other areas of marketing concern. With them all will be the continuing quest for more responsible marketing behavior and a larger measure of public conscience. These advancements will not only lead to more successful management performance in the administration of the enterprise, in the broader sense they will contribute to the capacity of a competitive economy to provide its people with abundance while preserving individual sovereignty and freedom.

Index